Encyclopedia of
EASTER,
Carnival,
and Lent

Encyclopedia of
EASTER,
Carnival,
and Lent

A Guide to This Season's Joyous Celebration and Solemn Worship, Including Folk Customs, Religious Observances, History, Legends, Folklore, Symbols, and Related Days from Europe, the Americas, and Around the World. Supplemented by a Bibliography, List of Web Sites, and Index

Tanya Gulevich

Illustrated by Mary Ann Stavros-Lanning

615 Griswold Street • Detroit, Michigan 48226 • 313-961-1340
2002

Helene Henderson, *Copy Editor*
Joan Margeson and Barry Puckett, *Research Associates*

Kevin Hayes, *Production Coordinator*
Jane Steele, *Marketing Coordinator*

Omnigraphics, Inc.

* * *

Peter E. Ruffner, *Executive Vice President*
Matthew P. Barbour, *Senior Vice President*
Kay Gill, *Vice President — Directories*
Laurie Lanzen Harris, *Vice President, Editorial*
Thomas J. Murphy, *Vice President, Finance*

* * *

Frederick G. Ruffner, Jr., Publisher

Library of Congress Cataloging-in-Publication Data

Gulevich, Tanya.
    Encyclopedia of Easter, Carnival, and Lent / Tanya Gulevich ; illustrated by Mary Ann Stavros-Lanning.
      p. cm.
    "A guide to this season's joyous celebration and solemn worship, including folk
customs, religious observances, history, legends, folklore, symbols, and related days
from Europe, the Americas, and around the world. Supplemented by a bibliography, list
of web sites, and index."
    Includes bibliographical references and index.
    ISBN 0-7808-0432-5 (alk. paper)
    1. Easter--Encyclopedias. 2. Lent--Encyclopedias. 3. Carnival--Encyclopedias. I. Title.

GT4935 .G85 2001
394.2667'03--dc21

                              2001054877

Printed in the United States

Contents

For my father, George D. Gulevich, who instilled
in me a great love and respect for books

Introduction

The Easter festival celebrates the resurrection of Jesus Christ and the corresponding assertion that new life blooms from the soil of death. The radical transformation honored by the holiday finds echo in its customs and observances, which move the faithful from fasting to feasting, from mourning to rejoicing, and from darkness to dawn. In the Easter-inspired ritual of the Eucharist, wine becomes blood, bread becomes flesh, and those who partake of these changed substances experience renewal and transformation through the connection to Christ that they impart. Finally, the egg—that well-known folk symbol of the holiday—itself undergoes a mysterious metamorphosis which ends with new life bursting forth from what appears to be a lifeless, stony enclosure.

Scope

The *Encyclopedia of Easter, Carnival, and Lent* addresses this marvelous holiday, its history, customs, observances, symbols, lore, and legends. It also treats the holidays and observances that Easter gave birth to, most notably the six-week period of preparation for Easter called Lent, and the festival preceding Lent, known as Carnival, or, in the southern part of the United States, as Mardi Gras. Though these observances receive substantial consideration, coverage also extends to other Easter-related days, such Ash Wednesday, Pentecost, and

Good Friday. Jewish holidays related to Easter, for example, Passover and Shavuot, are also included. Other non-Christian holidays — such as the ancient Roman festival of Hilaria, the Middle Eastern new year celebration called No Ruz, and the folk holiday known as May Day — appear as well, since they fall in the spring season and share customs and symbols with Easter and its related days.

The *Encyclopedia* provides information on religious observances, history, customs, symbols, legends, folklore, and folk celebrations associated with this period of the church year. Given the vast scope of this subject, the *Encyclopedia* does not attempt to furnish exhaustive coverage but rather to supply a solid introduction to the subject. Moreover, it attempts to represent the diversity of the world's Easter celebrations by including material from a variety of religious denominations and nations. For example, the *Encyclopedia* treats observances, symbols, and customs from the three main branches of the Christian faith — Roman Catholicism, Protestantism, and Orthodoxy — thereby offering the reader a broad perspective on the religious observance of Easter. In addition, the *Encyclopedia* furnishes descriptions of Easter and Carnival celebrations from twenty different countries. The majority of these countries are European, reflecting the history of Christianity as the dominant religion of that continent for over a millennia as well as the availability of reliable published materials on Easter celebrations in other countries. However, entries on holiday celebrations in countries outside western Europe, such as Russia, the Ukraine, the Philippines, Egypt, Mexico, Guatemala, Trinidad, Brazil, and Colombia, also appear in the book, rounding out the picture of Easter and Carnival celebrations in foreign lands.

Easter is a holiday rooted in the accounts of Jesus' death and resurrection related in the Christian Bible. Detailed, scholarly analysis of the biblical accounts of the first Easter is beyond the scope of this book. Nevertheless, some basic treatment is given to theological concepts associated with the holiday, such as repentance and redemption, as well as important figures in the biblical story of Easter. These subjects were chosen for inclusion because they shed significant light on the meaning of Easter-related observances, customs, legends, and symbols, and because this information may be especially handy to users less familiar with the Christian religion. Readers seeking more information on these subjects and on other religious matters related to Easter are invited to consult the many excellent church and Bible dictionaries, encyclopedias, commentaries, and analyses listed in the bibliography and in the suggestions for further reading following each entry.

The *Encyclopedia of Easter, Carnival, and Lent* does not reprint the four lengthy accounts of the first Easter found in the Christian Bible. This was deemed unnecessary as nearly all public libraries have multiple copies of the Bible. An entry titled *Gospel Accounts of Easter* lists the relevant Bible passages for the reader to look up at his or her convenience.

Organization

The *Encyclopedia* contains 154 entries listed in alphabetical order. Many entries contain information on more than one subject. For example, the entry titled "Fasting" not only discusses a number of Lenten fasting regimens, but also offers information on the cuisine that developed in various European countries as a result of these practices. Therefore, the reader is urged to consult the index in order to glean all materials that the book has to offer on any given subject.

Entries and References

Entries range in length from a single paragraph to several pages. Each entry concludes with a further reading list, and many also furnish the addresses to relevant web sites. All Bible quotes come from the Revised Standard Version. A general bibliography of all sources used in the writing of the *Encyclopedia* appears at the end of the book. Though not included in the bibliography or further reading lists, *Encyclopedia Britannica*, 15th edition (1997), *Colliers Encyclopedia* (1996), and *Microsoft Encarta Encyclopedia 2000* were also consulted.

Appendices

Two appendices supplement the *Encyclopedia*:

Appendix 1: Bibliography—Contains a complete listing of books and articles consulted.

Appendix 2: Web Sites—Furnishes addresses for more than eighty web sites offering information on a wide variety of Easter-, Lent-, and Carnival-related topics. These addresses were checked just prior to press time and found to be valid.

Index

The index provides the reader with an important tool for getting the most out of this book. It covers customs, symbols, legends, historical and mythological figures, ethnic groups, musical and literary works, foods, religious groups and denominations, geographical locations, keywords, and other subjects mentioned in the entries.

Audience

The *Encyclopedia of Easter, Carnival, and Lent* is intended for readers with an eighth-grade or higher reading level. Little to no familiarity with the Christian religion is assumed, and when religious vocabulary and concepts appear, they are glossed in the text. Entries are written simply enough to be understood by younger readers, but offer enough information to be of interest to adult users as well.

Acknowledgments

I would like to thank my editor, Helene Henderson, for her unwavering belief in this project and this writer. She also deserves the credit for honing the manuscript to a finished state and compiling a first-rate index. My gratitude also extends to the supportive editorial and production staff at Omnigraphics, especially Laurie Harris, Matt Barbour, Barry Puckett, and Kevin Hayes, and to graphic artist Mary Ann Stavros-Lanning, whose original illustrations grace the pages of this book. I would also like to thank publisher Frederick G. Ruffner for entrusting this project to me and to honor him for his fairness to writers and his love of books. I am grateful to Breen Mullins for taking the time to read sections of the manuscript at an early stage in its development, and for providing kind and useful feedback. Thanks also go to Joseph A. Lane and Katherine Lehman for offering their advice on certain portions of the manuscript.

The illustrations appearing in the *Encyclopedia* are all original watercolors. Some of the compositions were derived from paintings by the great masters. You may copy the designs and illustrations for classroom and library use free of charge and without special permissions. Electronic or mechanical reproduction, including photography, recording, or any other information storage and retrieval system for the purpose of resale is strictly prohibited without permission in writing from the publisher.

Advisors

This project was reviewed by an Advisory Board comprised of librarians who assisted the editorial staff in assessing its usefulness and accessibility. Any errors, however, should be attributed to the author and editor. The Omnigraphics editorial staff would like to list the Advisory Board members and thank them for their efforts.

Gail Beaver
University of Michigan School of Information
Ann Arbor, Michigan

Linda Carpino
Detroit Public Library
Detroit, Michigan

Helen Gregory
Grosse Pointe Public Library
Grosse Pointe, Michigan

Rosemary Orlando
St. Clair Shores Public Library
St. Clair Shores, Michigan

Alleluia
Hallelujah

Alleluia, also spelled "hallelujah," means "praise ye the Lord," or more simply, "praise the Lord!" The word comes from the Hebrew phrase of the same meaning, *hallelû* (praise ye) *Jah* (the Lord). It is one of the few untranslated Hebrew words or phrases that the first Christians adopted into their worship. It has remained in the vocabulary of the church until present times.

In the first centuries of the Western Christian tradition, the word "alleluia" appeared most often in **Easter season** worship services. Pope Gregory I, also known as St. Gregory the Great (540-604), ordered the word used throughout the church year, except during **Lent** and **pre-Lent**, the three-week period preceding Lent. The purpose of this prohibition was to emphasize the austere, solemn mood of this part of the church year.

1

In medieval western Europe, this period of abstinence from the word "alleluia" began on Septuagesima Sunday, the third **Sunday** before the beginning of Lent. In some places people performed rituals that bade a formal farewell to the word "alleluia." For example, in fifteenth-century France choir boys participated in a mock burial of this shout of praise. Carrying a coffin representing the alleluia, they filed out of the church in a formal procession, complete with **cross**, candles, holy **water**, and incense.

Similar folk religious customs still exist today. The Roman Catholic Church abandoned the observance of the three-week pre-Lenten period in 1969, so these customs shifted themselves to the day before **Ash Wednesday**, which is the first day of Lent according to the Roman Catholic Church calendar. In some Roman Catholic and Episcopal parishes, the word "alleluia," written on a scroll, is solemnly carried out of the church on the day before Ash Wednesday. Then the scroll is hidden or buried throughout Lent. During the **Easter Vigil**, the late-night service that takes place on **Holy Saturday**, the scroll is formally carried back into the church and the joyous word "alleluia" reinstated into worship.

In both the Anglican and Roman Catholic traditions, use of the word "alleluia" is still discontinued during Lent. It is first heard again at the late-night Easter Vigil service on Holy Saturday. For this reason Holy Saturday is sometimes referred to "Alleluia Saturday." The Orthodox churches of eastern Europe, north Africa and the Middle East never adopted this custom. They retain the use of alleluia throughout Lent and throughout the rest of the church year as well.

Further Reading

"Alleluia." In E. A. Livingstone, ed. *The Oxford Dictionary of the Christian Church*. Third edition. Oxford, England: Oxford University Press, 1997.

McBrien, Richard P. "Alleluia." In his *The HarperCollins Encyclopedia of Catholicism*. New York: HarperSanFrancisco, 1995.

Niemann, Paul J. *The Lent, Triduum, and Easter Answer Book*. San Jose, CA: Resource Publications, 1998.

Weakland, R. M. "Alleluia." In *New Catholic Encyclopedia*. Volume 1. New York: McGraw-Hill, 1967.

Weiser, Francis X. *The Easter Book*. New York: Harcourt, Brace and Company, 1954.

Annunciation
Annunciation of the Lord, Annunciation of the Mother of God, Annunciation of the Virgin Mary, Lady Day

The feast of the Annunciation often falls during **Lent**, bringing a little bit of Christmas joy into that otherwise austere season. The word annunciation means "announcement." When spelled with a capital "A" it refers to the announcement made by the angel Gabriel to the Blessed Virgin Mary, telling her that she would bear a son by the Holy Spirit whom she should name **Jesus** (*see also* **Mary, Blessed Virgin**). Christians commemorate this event with a festival that falls on March 25. The formal names given to this observance differ by denomination. Some Christians, including Roman Catholics, know the feast as the "Annunciation of the Lord," the Orthodox call it the "Annunciation of the Mother of God," and some Anglicans refer to it as the "Annunciation of the Virgin Mary."

Selecting the Date

Christian officials most likely derived the date of the Annunciation from the date of Christmas. Church leaders fixed the date of Christmas in the fourth century, selecting December 25 as the day on which to honor the birth of Christ. Once this date had been determined it then followed that Jesus must have been conceived nine months earlier, on March 25.

In the ancient Roman world both December 25 and March 25 marked important events in the sun's yearly cycle. According to the Julian calendar system which the Romans adopted in 45 B.C., the winter solstice, the shortest day of the year, fell on December 25. What's more,

the **spring equinox**, the spring date on which day and night are of equal length, occurred on March 25. Due to an error in the Julian calendar system, however, the events of the solar year slowly fell behind the dates on the calendar. For example, when the Council of Nicaea, an important gathering of the early Christian leaders, met in 325 A.D., the winter solstice was falling on December 21 and the spring equinox on March 21.

Although the events of the solar year were slipping behind the calendar, the Romans continued to recognize December 25 as the official date of the winter solstice. Some scholars suspect that early Christian leaders selected December 25 as the date on which to celebrate the Nativity of Christ because the Romans already celebrated the birth of the sun god on that date. Nevertheless, certain early Christian thinkers proposed other, more complicated explanations for the selection of December 25. They based these explanations both on their interpretation of Christian scripture and on then-popular beliefs in the significance of round numbers. According to one scholar, early Church leaders figured out the date of Jesus' birth from the date early Christian tradition assigned to his death: March 25. These leaders wanted to come up with a round number for Jesus' age at death, so they assumed he had also been conceived on March 25. Therefore, he must have been born nine months later on December 25. Some scholars believe that this line of thinking lies behind the selection of December 25 as Christmas day.

Other early Christians thinkers emphasized the idea that Jesus is a kind of new creation. The Bible tells that God's first act of creation was to bring forth light, an act which separated light from darkness. These early Christian leaders reasoned, therefore, that God must have created the world at the time of the spring equinox, when the world is separated into two equal halves of light and darkness. Jesus, as a kind of new creation, must also have come into being at the time of the spring equinox. Therefore he must have been conceived on March 25 and born on December 25. The idea that Jesus had been born on the winter solstice made sense to them because of several important Bible passages describing the Messiah as "the sun of righteousness" (Malachi 4:2) and Jesus as "the light of the world" (John 8:12). These passages led them to see the sun as a symbol for Jesus. Since the winter solstice may be thought of as the sun's birthday, it seemed an especially appropriate date for Jesus' birth.

Some writers assert that Eastern Christians, those Christians living in the Middle East, eastern Europe and north Africa, began observing a festival in honor of the Annunciation as early as the fifth century. By the eighth century this festival, celebrated on March 25, had established itself as an important observance throughout western Europe.

The Annunciation as New Year's Day

According to Christian doctrine the Annunciation honors the conception of Christ and therefore the dawn of a new era. Mindful of this connection between the Annunciation and new beginnings, a number of medieval European kingdoms began their new year on March 25. The idea that the new year begins in March also harks back to the ancient Roman tradition of starting the new year on March 1. Julius Caesar's (100-44 B.C.) reform of the Roman calendar, resulting in the introduction of the Julian calendar, derailed this old tradition by declaring January 1 to be New Year's Day. In the year 1582 Pope Gregory XIII ordered Christians to adopt the Gregorian calendar, which, among other things, proclaimed January 1 to be New Year's Day (*for more on the Gregorian calendar, see* **Easter, Date of**). Roman Catholic countries promptly switched to the new and more accurate calendar. Protestant and Orthodox countries delayed, for fear of seeming to accept the Pope's authority.

Great Britain adopted the Gregorian calendar several hundred years later, in 1752. This decision effectively installed the Gregorian calendar in her American colonies as well. Before that time the English recognized March 25 as their official New Year's Day, a custom adopted sometime around the twelfth century in honor of the Annunciation. The English also invented an informal and affectionate name for the festival, dubbing it "Lady Day." In past times the holiday not only served as New Year's Day, but also as one of the quarter days of the year, days on which rents came due and employers hired and dismissed help.

Prophecies

Because the date of Easter and its related festivals shift about on the calendar, they may occasionally coincide with the Annunciation. In past times some people found these coincidences ominous. In the Middle Ages a prophecy surfaced warning that the world would end in the year 970, when the Annunciation occurred on **Good Friday**. Needless to say, that disaster did not occur. Neither did it in the years 981 and 992, when the Annunciation again fell on Good Friday. Several hundred years later an Irish prophecy predicted that the end of the world would occur in the year in which the Annunciation fell on **Easter Sunday**. Records dating as far back as the early seventeenth century reveal that a variation of this prophecy was known in England in the form of a rhymed couplet:

> When Our Lord lights in Our Lady's lap,
> Then let England look for a clap.
> (Blackburn and Holford-Strevens, 134)

In this instance "clap" means ill fortune. King Charles I did experience serious political defeats in 1627 and was executed as an enemy of the nation in 1649, years in which Easter Sunday and the Annunciation coincided. Nevertheless, other years in which the two festivals fell on the same date—1722, 1733, 1744, 1883, 1894, and 1951—proved relatively disaster-free for England. The prophecy can again be tested in 2035 and 2046, when Easter will fall on March 25. When this occurs, however, both the Church of England and the Roman Catholic Church will transfer the celebration of the Annunciation to a different day.

Lore and Customs

According to the Gregorian calendar system now used throughout the world, the spring equinox falls around March 21. Thus the Annunciation still occurs near the time of the spring equinox. As a result many European folk traditions associate the Annunciation with natural events occurring at that time of year. For example, the old saying, "When Gabriel to Mary flies, this is the end of snow and ice," reminded farmers to begin sowing their summer crops on the day after the Annunciation. In addition, folk tradition named the Annunciation the "Feast of the Swallows." Around this time of year swallows return to Europe from their yearly migrations to Asia and Africa. An old Austrian saying explicitly linked this event with the Annunciation:

> When Gabriel does the message bring,
> Return the swallows, comes the spring." (Slim, 90)

This perceived linkage led many people to call swallows "Mary's birds" and sometimes even "God's birds." Folklore followed suit, declaring it bad luck to kill a swallow or to interfere with swallows' nests. As it turns out, swallows have more than just a folkloric connection with the Virgin Mary. When European Crusaders reached the Holy Land in the Middle Ages, they found Nazareth, the town where the Annunciation took place (Luke 1:26), to be a favorite haunt of swallows.

While many Europeans associate the Annunciation with the return of a favorite bird, Swedes associate it with a special food. In Swedish the formal name for the festival is *Varfrudagen*, "Our Lady's Day." Over time casual pronunciation of this phrase turned it into *Vaffeldagen*, or "Waffle Day." Swedish tradition therefore proclaimed waffles the specialty of the day. Swedes use special heart-shaped irons to make these waffles, which symbolize the loving heart of the Virgin Mary.

Oftentimes the Annunciation falls during Lent. When it does so, Orthodox Christians relax the rules of their strict Lenten **fast** in celebration of the day. Fish may be eaten and Orthodox churches celebrate the Divine Liturgy, normally forbidden during the weekdays of Lent (*for more on the Divine Liturgy, see also* **Eucharist**). When the Annunciation falls during the last week of Lent, that is, during **Holy Week** and the **Triduum**, the Roman Catholic Church shifts its observance of the festival to the second Monday after Easter Sunday.

Further Reading

Blackburn, Bonnie, and Leofranc Holford-Strevens. *The Oxford Companion to the Year*. Oxford, England: Oxford University Press, 1999.

Bradshaw, Paul F. *The Search for the Origins of Christian Worship*. New York: Oxford University Press, 1992.

Griffin, Robert H., and Ann H. Shurgin, eds. *The Folklore of World Holidays*. Second edition. Detroit, MI: Gale Research, 1999.

Gulevich, Tanya. *Encyclopedia of Christmas*. Detroit, MI: Omnigraphics, 2000.

Niemann, Paul J. *The Lent, Triduum, and Easter Answer Book*. San Jose, CA: Resource Publications, 1998.

Slim, Hugo. *A Feast of Festivals*. London, England: Marshall Pickering, 1996.

April Fools' Day
All Fools' Day, April Noddy Day, Gowkie Day, Huntigowk Day, St. All-Fools' Morn

April Fools' Day falls on the first of April. On this day people play practical jokes on friends, family members, and even strangers. Pranks often pulled on this day include putting sugar in the salt shaker and salt in the sugar bowl, gluing a coin to the sidewalk and watching to see who stoops to pick it up, and giving someone a false bit of news or information in order to enjoy their reaction. Sending someone on a fool's errand, especially one in which several friends conspire to send the person from one place to another in order to prolong his or her fruitless quest, is another old custom associated with the day.

Where did this observance come from? Perhaps the most plausible explanation for the holiday traces it back to the Gregorian calendar reform of 1582 (*for more on the Gregorian calendar, see* **Easter, Date of**). The Gregorian calendar set the beginning of each new year on January 1. Prior to that time, many European nations observed New Year's Day on March 25 (*see also* **Annunciation**). Some people celebrated the arrival of the new year with an entire week of fun and festivity. Begun on March 25, this week ended on April 1. When Pope Gregory XIII introduced the new calendar system, many Catholic nations adopted it immediately. Those individuals who forgot that New Year's Day had been moved, or those who resisted the change might still celebrate on April 1, however. They became the "April fools" whose forgetfulness or eccentricity aroused amusement in others.

Another explanation traces the holiday back to ancient Rome. On March 25 Romans observed **Hilaria**, a festival honoring the goddess Cybele and celebrated with **laughter** and rejoicing. Some writers suggest that traces of this observance remained after Roman civilization declined and floated a few days further ahead in the calendar, attaching themselves to April 1. This time of year also coincides with the **spring equinox**. Some commentators speculate that April Fools' Day pranks grew out of the high spirits associated with this happy time of the year when the daylight hours finally overtake the darkness.

Perhaps because April Fools' Day often falls close to Easter a legend sprang up attempting to forge a connection between the two observances. It claimed that sending people on fool's errands on April 1 memorialized the chain of events whereby the Jewish religious authorities sent **Jesus** to be judged by **Pilate**, Pilate sent him on to King Herod, and Herod sent him back to Pilate (Luke 22:66-23:12). Another religious legend about the holiday asserts that it commemorates the raven and the dove from Noah's ark, whom Noah sent in search of dry land during the great flood (Genesis 8:6-9).

The earliest historical reference to this observance dates back to the year 1656 and comes from France. Although the holiday had established itself in France by that time, it was not well known in Germany until the 1680s. It appeared in England, where it was sometimes called "All Fool's Day," at the tail end of the seventeenth century. By the nineteenth century people all over Europe observed April Fools' Day.

In France a person who falls for an April Fools' joke is called a *poisson d'avril*, or an "April fish." Indeed, in France one old April Fools' Day joke consisted of pinning a cardboard fish to someone's back without them knowing it. In Scotland the April Fool was called a "gowk" or "cuckoo." Playing an April Fools' Day joke on someone was known as "hunting the gowk." The holiday itself might be called Gowkie Day or Huntigowk Day. Other names for the observance include April Noddy Day and St. All-Fools' Morn. In Germany newspapers may attempt to hoax the public on April Fool's Day by printing false stories called *Zeitungsente*, or "newspaper ducks." According to German folklore **Judas** was born on April Fool's Day and Lucifer (the devil) was thrown out of heaven. Hence German folklore deems the day unlucky. Swedes also enjoy playing practical jokes on April 1. A Swedish folk verse declares,

> April, April, you silly fish,
> I can trick you however I wish.

Further Reading

Blackburn, Bonnie, and Leofranc Holford-Strevens. *The Oxford Companion to the Year*. Oxford, England: Oxford University Press, 1999.

Cooper, J. C. *The Dictionary of Festivals*. London, England: Thorsons, 1990.

Festivals and Holidays. New York: Macmillan, 1999.

Griffin, Robert H., and Ann H. Shurgin, eds. *The Folklore of World Holidays*. Second edition. Detroit, MI: Gale, 1998.

Henderson, Helene, and Sue Ellen Thompson, eds. *Holidays, Festivals, and Celebrations of the World Dictionary*. Second edition. Detroit, MI: Omnigraphics, 1997.

Hutton, Ronald. *Stations of the Sun*. Oxford, England: Oxford University Press, 1996.

Primiano, Leonard Norman. "All Fools' Day." In Mircea Eliade, ed. *The Encyclopedia of Religion*. Volume 1. New York: Macmillan, 1987.

Ascension Day
Holy Thursday

According to a well-known passage from Christian scripture, **Jesus** ascended to heaven on the fortieth day following the **Resurrection** (Acts 1:3-11). After this time Jesus no longer appeared to his disciples on earth in human form. The Gospels of Mark, Matthew, Luke, and John also record versions of Jesus' final departure, though they furnish fewer and sometimes conflicting details. Among the early Christians the version of Jesus' leave-taking recorded in the Book of Acts became the basis for a Christian festival known as Ascension Day. Falling forty days after **Easter Sunday**, which places it always on a Thursday, this observance commemorates Jesus' glorious ascent into the skies and the beginning of his heavenly reign. In the Western Church calendar, observed by Roman Catholics and Protestants, Ascension Day can fall anywhere between April 30 and June 3.

In England people sometimes call this festival Holy Thursday. This designation sows some confusion, since many Christians refer to the Thursday of **Holy Week** by the same name.

History

Early Christian leaders scattered references to the Ascension throughout their writings. One tradition claims that Christians began to commemorate the Ascension very early in their history, in the year 68 A.D. Nevertheless, historical records reveal that Church leaders disagreed as to when the ascension of Jesus Christ had actually taken place. Some argued that the event occurred exactly forty days after the Resurrection, as told in the Book of Acts. Other authorities believed that the phrase "forty days" was merely a figure of speech, meaning "a long time." Some researchers propose that early commemorations of the Ascension may have taken place on Easter Sunday, and point out that the Gospel according to Luke implies that the Resurrection and the Ascension took place on the same day (Luke 24:50-53).

One of the earliest mentions of the feast in any historical document comes from the diary of Egeria, a Christian woman who made a pilgrimage to Palestine in the late fourth century. She described her participation in a joint celebration of **Pentecost** and the Ascension that took place forty days after Easter. During this era Christians in Jerusalem celebrated the Ascension with a procession to Mount Olivet, the site from which Jesus is supposed to have ascended to heaven. According to Christian tradition, Jesus left footprints in the solid rock that crowns this hill. Early Christian pilgrims journeyed to see these stony footprints. A Christian noblewoman built the Ibomon church at this site sometime in the fourth century.

Historical evidence from the late fourth century confirms that by that time many Christian communities were celebrating the Ascension. Indeed, St. John Chrysostom (c. 347-407) called the feast "ancient" and "universal." In the year 400, the First Council of Toledo agreed that Christ had indeed ascended to heaven on the fortieth day after the Resurrection. This decision helped to anchor observances of the feast to the fortieth day after Easter, or Thursday of the sixth week of the **Easter season**.

Ascension Plays

In the Middle Ages Ascension plays, religious dramas representing Christ's miraculous disappearance into the clouds, often accompanied Ascension Day church services. According to one writer, this custom began in Rome with religious processions, led by the pope, in honor of Ascension Day. As Ascension Day processions spread throughout Western Christianity, people began to add dramatic details. This process of embellishment flourished in the eleventh through fourteenth centuries. During that era many congregations concluded their processions by reenacting Christ's ascension. Worshipers sometimes accomplished this feat by tying ropes around a statue of Jesus and hoisting it through a hole in the church roof.

A document describing one such fourteenth-century ceremony that took place in a monastery in Bavaria, Germany, furnishes some dramatic details. The writer marvels that as the statue of Jesus ascended towards the roof of the church angels descended to escort the rising Christ into heaven. These angels, played by costumed choir boys suspended from the ceiling by means of ropes, met Christ as he neared the clouds, which were represented by draperies of silk around the opening in the roof. After the statue of Jesus disappeared into the clouds a sudden shower of **lilies**, roses, other flowers, and communion wafers dropped from the roof to the disciples waiting below (*see also* **Eucharist**).

In the Austrian state of Tyrol similar Ascension plays survived until the twentieth century. Many Christian communities still practice related customs. For example, some congregations raise a crucifix to the top of a church steeple on Ascension Day.

Folk Customs

English folklore records a number of unusual Ascension Day customs and superstitions. At Tissington, in Derbyshire, people decorate a local well with flowers, buds, leaves, and other natural materials. They also participate in a well-blessing ceremony. The exact history of the custom is unknown. Some believe it dates back to pagan practices of ancient times, while others claim it began in the mid-fourteenth century as a means of giving thanks to God for sparing the town from the plague. In any case, the annual Ascension Day well dressing at Tissington attracts about 50,000 visitors a year.

Other English Ascension Day customs and superstitions regarding **water** include the belief that water taken from holy wells on Ascension Day has special healing powers. Ascensiontide rain, which according to folk belief fell straight from heaven, was said to cure sore eyes. According to another old English superstition, the figure of a **lamb** appears momentarily in the sunrise on Ascension Day. In the north country girls ran smock races on Ascension Day. The girls competed with one another in their smocks, an undergarment similar to a slip.

The winner of the race received a new smock. Another old folk custom, the beating of the bounds, occurred on Ascension Day as well as during the **Rogation Days** (*for more on this custom, see* Rogation Days).

In Florence, Italy, people collected grasshoppers on Ascension Day and took them home in cages. If the grasshopper sang in the first three days of its captivity the family was assured of good luck, and they let the insect go free. If the grasshopper died their fate was less certain. Hundreds of years ago in the sea-faring city of Venice, Italy, the city's ruler, called the doge, wed the sea on Ascension Day. Each year the doge renewed his, and by extension his city's, wedding vow by throwing a ring into the surf, accompanied by holy water. Today the city of Venice still hosts an impressive Ascension Day festival, during which contemporary Venetians reenact the traditional wedding with the sea (*see also* **Italy, Carnival in**).

In a few places in Europe people burn, chase, or dunk the devil in effigy on Ascension Day. This custom represents the defeat that the devil suffered when Christ entered heaven in glory. In Germany Ascension Day is sometimes called "Father's Day" since Protestant men participate in group outings into the countryside on this day. In rural Portugal people gather medicinal plants and herbs on Ascension Day. They also make symbolic bouquets of olive branches, wheat stalks, poppies, and daisies. These bouquets represent their hopes for peace and prosperity. The olive and wheat stand for a bountiful harvest, the poppy symbolizes peace, and the daisy represents money.

Common Ascension Day customs in many European countries include processions into the countryside to eat, drink, and admire nature. Often these processions lead to the tops of hills for picnics or religious services. This practice recalls the account of the Ascension given in chapter one of the Book of Acts, which implies that Jesus led his followers to the top of Mount Olivet before ascending into heaven (Acts 1:12). Another European folk custom that echoes the theme of rising into the skies calls for eating some kind of bird on Ascension Day. Thus European Ascension Day menus may feature pheasants, pigeons, partridges, and even crows. In western Germany bakers prepare bird-shaped pastries in honor of the day.

In the United States the Pennsylvania Dutch, whose ancestors immigrated to the United States from Germany and Switzerland, considered Ascension Day and **Good Friday** to be the holiest days of the year. Accordingly, they attached many superstitions to Ascension Day activities. One such folk belief declared it a fine day on which to cull herbs, teas, and wild flowers. Gathered on this day these leaves and flowers possessed special healing properties. In past times women warned each other not to sew on Ascension Day. Tales of those who had broken this superstition and met dire fates often accompanied these warnings. By contrast, men and boys spoke of Ascension Day as the luckiest day of the year on which to go fishing. This superstition probably evolved from the assumption that the fish, like Jesus Christ, would be sure to rise on this day.

Religious Customs

Before 1970 Roman Catholic clergy removed the Easter candle, or **paschal candle**, from the sanctuary on Ascension Day. The extinguishing of the paschal candle on this day symbolized the fact that after the Ascension the resurrected Jesus would no longer appear to his disciples on earth clothed in human flesh. The Roman Catholic Church currently specifies that the paschal candle should remain in use through the Feast of Pentecost each year. In 1969 Roman Catholic authorities permitted the transfer of Ascension Thursday services to the following Sunday, that is, to the seventh **Sunday** of the Easter season.

Ascension Day religious services frequently explore the meaning of Christ's bodily ascent into heaven, its effect on his original disciples, and its significance to today's Christians. They may also focus on Jesus' final instructions and his last pledge to his disciples. In the Gospel according to Matthew Jesus commands them to:

> Go therefore and make disciples of all nations, baptizing them in the name of the Father and of the Son and of the Holy Spirit, teaching them to observe all that I have commanded you; and lo, I am with you always, to the close of the age (Matthew 28:19-20).

17

Further Reading

"Ascension of Christ." In E. A. Livingstone, ed. *The Oxford Dictionary of the Christian Church*. Third edition. Oxford, England: Oxford University Press, 1997.

Griffin, Robert H., and Ann H. Shurgin, eds. *The Folklore of World Holidays*. Second edition. Detroit, MI: Gale Research, 1999.

Harper, Howard. *Days and Customs of All Faiths*. 1957. Reprint. Detroit, MI: Omnigraphics, 1990.

Henderson, Helene, and Sue Ellen Thompson, eds. *Holidays, Festivals, and Celebrations of the World Dictionary*. Second edition. Detroit, MI: Omnigraphics, 1997.

Hole, Christina. *Easter and Its Customs*. New York: M. Barrows and Company, 1961.

James, E. O. *Seasonal Feasts and Festivals*. 1961. Reprint. Detroit, MI: Omnigraphics, 1993.

McBrien, Richard P. "Ascension, Feast of." In his *The HarperCollins Encyclopedia of Catholicism*. New York: HarperSanFrancisco, 1995.

Metford, J. C. J. *The Christian Year*. London, England: Thames and Hudson, 1991.

Munoa, Phillip. "Ascension." In David Noel Freedman, ed. *Eerdmans Dictionary of the Bible*. Grand Rapids, MI: William B. Eerdmans Publishing, 2000.

National Conference of Catholic Bishops. *Holy Days in the United States*. Washington, D.C.: United States Catholic Conference, 1984.

Neyrey, Jerome H. "Ascension." In Richard McBrien, ed. *The HarperCollins Encyclopedia of Catholicism*. New York: HarperSanFrancisco, 1995.

Niemann, Paul J. *The Lent, Triduum, and Easter Answer Book*. San Jose, CA: Resource Publications, 1998.

Quinn, J. D. "Ascension of Jesus Christ." In *New Catholic Encyclopedia*. Volume 1. New York: McGraw-Hill, 1967.

Shoemaker, Alfred L. *Eastertide in Pennsylvania*. Kutztown, PA: Pennsylvania Folklife Society, 1960.

Slim, Hugo. *A Feast of Festivals*. London, England: Marshall Pickering, 1996.

Urlin, Ethel L. *Festivals, Holy Days, and Saints' Days*. 1915. Reprint. Detroit, MI: Omnigraphics, 1992.

Weiser, Francis X. *The Easter Book*. New York: Harcourt, Brace and Company, 1954.

Web Site

The web site maintained by Tissington Hall, in Tissington, England, describes various aspects of the local well-dressing ceremony at: http://www.tissington hall.com/well_dressing.htm

Ash Wednesday

Ash Wednesday marks the beginning of **Lent** for Western Christians. It falls on the Wednesday following the seventh **Sunday** before Easter — sometime between February 4 and March 10. Western Christians, that is, Roman Catholics and Protestants, follow a different church calendar than that adhered to by Orthodox and other Eastern Christians (*see also* **Easter, Date of**). Orthodox Christians begin Lent on the evening of the seventh Sunday before Easter, which they call **Forgiveness Sunday**. The first full day of Lent falls on the following day, **Clean Monday**.

The Date

Until the seventh or eighth century western European Christians began Lent on Quadragesima Sunday, the sixth Sunday before Easter. Begun on this date, Lent lasted forty-two days. The length of this season, approximately forty days, was modeled on the forty days of hardship endured by a number of important biblical figures before experiencing God's deliverance (*see also* **Salvation**). **Jesus** himself fasted in the desert for forty days before beginning his ministry (Matthew 4:1-11, Mark 1:12-13, Luke 4:1-13).

Some Christian thinkers argued, however, that Sundays could not be included in the Lenten **fast**, since all Sundays celebrate the **resurrection** of Christ and therefore should not be observed as days of penance (*for more on penance, see also* **Repentance**). This argument eventually prevailed. During the seventh or eighth century Christian authorities in western Europe gradually began to add four more days to Lent, making the total number of days forty-six. Subtracting the six Sundays that occur during Lent from the total number of forty-six days left the season with exactly forty days. This adjustment meant that instead of beginning on Quadragesima Sunday, Lent began on the previous Wednesday, a day which came to be known as Ash Wednesday.

Ash Customs and Symbolism

Ash Wednesday takes its name from a religious custom unique to the day. At special Ash Wednesday services clergy members dip their thumbs in ashes and paint a **cross** on the forehead of each worshiper. As they do so, they say, "Remember that you are dust, and that to dust you shall return." These words recall the warning God gave to Adam and Eve before banishing them from the Garden of Eden (Genesis 3:19). Alternatively, the officiant may declare, "Repent, and believe in the Gospel," thereby echoing Jesus' proclamation as he began his ministry in Galilee (Mark 1:15). This ritual reminds worshipers of their own mortality and therefore of the need to improve their relationship with God and their relationships with fellow human beings (*see also* **Sin** and **Redemption**). It introduces the theme of repentance, which will characterize the rest of the Lenten season. Repentance may be thought of as a change of heart and mind that inspires a return to God.

Palm fronds from the previous **Palm Sunday** are saved throughout the year and burned to provide the ashes needed for this ceremony. The imposition of ashes on Ash Wednesday is practiced in Roman Catholic churches as well as some Protestant ones. For example, some Episcopalian and Lutheran congregations observe this ritual. In addition, observant Roman Catholics fast on Ash Wednesday.

The imposition of ashes was inspired by the symbolic role of ashes in the Bible. In the Bible ashes accompany or represent grief, destruction, mortality, and repentance. When Job repents his questioning of God's judgment, he declares, "I . . . repent in dust and ashes" (Job

42:6). In biblical times rampaging armies often burned the towns they conquered, reducing them to ashes. Thus ashes stand for death and destruction in some biblical imagery. Other potent images connect ashes with mourning, as when the grief-stricken put on a rough kind of cloth known as sackcloth and covered themselves in ashes (2 Samuel 13:19, Esther 4:1, Isaiah 61:3).

History

By the Middle Ages Christians had adopted ashes into their religious devotions. Many writers believe that the use of ashes on Ash Wednesday grew out of customs surrounding the public confession of sins practiced during early Christian and early medieval times. According to these writers, Christians whose sins, or errors, were deemed especially great were expected to arrive barefoot at church on the first day of Lent. They declared their sins in the presence of the congregation and expressed grief for their transgressions. Afterwards the priest sprinkled ashes on their heads and gave them a sackcloth garment covered in ashes to wear. Thus attired they departed to complete the penance that had been assigned to them by the priest (*see also* Repentance; **Shrovetide**).

A penance is an act of religious devotion designed to nurture a change of heart and mind and inspire a return to God. In medieval days these penances might include prayer, charitable works, manual labor and physical hardships, such as sleeping on the ground and going barefoot. In addition, many Lenten penitents were forbidden to bathe, cut their hair, or talk to others during the six-week period. They returned to church again on **Maundy Thursday** to participate in a rite of reconciliation and to receive the **Eucharist** again for the first time since the start of Lent. Because a person's spiritual errors were often thought to stain his or her relatives, entire families might undergo this process of atonement together (*for more on atonement, see* Redemption).

Between the eighth and tenth centuries this kind of public confession declined in popularity. Instead, people began to confess their sins to a priest privately. The practice of ashing sinners at the start of Lent lingered in some places. Nevertheless the nature of the ceremony began to change. By the eleventh century congregations in both England and Rome had adopted the practice of ashing all parishioners at the start of Lent. In 1091 the Council of Benevento made the imposition of ashes universal among Western Christians, ordering that every member of a Christian congregation, including the clergy, should receive ashes on Ash Wednesday. In 1099 Pope Urban II officially adopted the name Ash Wednesday for this, the first day of Lent.

Further Reading

"Ashes." In Leland Ryken, James C. Wilhoit, and Tremper Longman III, eds. *Dictionary of Biblical Imagery*. Downers Grove, IL: InterVarsity Press, 1998.

"Ash Wednesday." In E. A. Livingstone, ed. *The Oxford Dictionary of the Christian Church*. Third edition. Oxford, England: Oxford University Press, 1997.

Metford, J. C. J. *The Christian Year*. London, England: Thames and Hudson, 1991.

Myers, Robert J. *Celebrations: The Complete Book of American Holidays*. Garden City, NY: Doubleday and Company, 1972.

Thurston, Herbert. "Ash Wednesday." In Charles G. Herbermann et al., eds. *The Catholic Encyclopedia*. New York: Appleton, 1913. Available online at: http://www.newadvent.org/cathen/01775b.htm

Weiser, Francis X. *The Easter Book*. New York: Harcourt, Brace and Company, 1954.

———. *Handbook of Christian Feasts and Customs*. New York: Harcourt, Brace and World, 1952.

Baptism

Christians initiate new members into their faith tradition through the ritual of baptism. According to Christian scripture **Jesus** himself commanded that his followers observe this custom. Several centuries after Christ's death Christian leaders encouraged newcomers to prepare for this initiation during the period we now call **Lent** and receive baptism at Easter. Thus their new lives as Christians were symbolically linked to the death and **resurrection** of Jesus commemorated during the Easter festival. Today Easter still serves as a traditional time for baptisms in a number of Christian denominations. In addition, many congregations jointly renew their baptismal vows on **Easter Sunday** morning or during the **Easter Vigil**.

Baptism, Purification, and Initiation in the Ancient World

The English word "baptism" comes from the ancient Greek word *baptein* or *baptizein*, meaning to plunge, dip, wash, drench, bathe or immerse. Throughout the ancient world peoples of many different religious traditions incorporated washing or immersion in **water** into their religious rites. In these contexts, water usually acted as a purifying force. Some of the mystery religions of ancient Greece and Egypt — pagan religious cults which promised secret spiritual knowledge to a select group of members — began their initiation rituals with water baths. Certain Greek cults also linked baptismal rites with the acquisition of immortality. A few Middle Eastern cults, including that of the god Mithras and the goddess Cybele, advocated a baptism in **blood**, which was thought to confer spiritual vitality or spiritual rebirth (*see also* **Hilaria**).

Around the time of Christ the ancient Hebrews practiced a number of bathing rites. They took ritual baths to cleanse themselves of impurities before taking part in certain religious activities. In addition they adopted the practice of baptizing converts to Judaism. This ceremony, which required that candidates immerse themselves nude in a body of flowing water, was thought to remove impurities and seal the convert's membership in the house of Israel. John the Baptist, a Jewish prophet whose ministry preceded that of Jesus, immersed his followers in the flowing waters of the Jordan river as a sign of their **repentance**, or desire to return to God, and the forgiveness of their **sins**. Jesus himself was baptized by John, an event which signaled the beginning of his career as a teacher and healer (Matthew 3:13-17, Mark 1:9-11, Luke 3:21-22). Jewish baptismal customs laid the foundation for the Christian sacrament of baptism.

Early Christian Baptism

The Bible relates that after his death on the **cross** the resurrected Jesus appeared to the original disciples commanding them to go forth and baptize new converts in the name of the Father, Son, and Holy Spirit (Matthew 28:19-20). This event, along with Jesus' own baptism, convinced early Christian leaders to make baptism a fundamental element of the Christian faith.

The New Testament gives few clues as to the nature of the very first Christian baptisms, but seems to suggest that as soon as interested newcomers accepted the gospel of Christ they were baptized (Acts

8:35-39, 16:30-33). By the second century, however, documents produced by Christian writers tell of a period of preparation for baptism which included prayer, **fasting**, and religious instruction. This process could last as long as three years.

By the third century a number of different baptismal ceremonies had taken shape. Easter had emerged as the preferred date for baptisms in several areas, although in some places **Pentecost** served as an acceptable alternative date. In the fourth century, especially after the Council of Nicaea, an important meeting of early Christian leaders that took place in 325 A.D., Easter became the standard date for baptisms. The baptismal ceremony usually took place during the Easter Vigil, which began late at night on **Holy Saturday**.

The following composite of early Christian baptismal customs offers a glimpse into these ancient ceremonies. The officiant began by asking the Holy Spirit to descend upon the water in the baptistery, a large tub or small pool used for baptisms (*see also* **Eight**). The baptismal candidate disrobed, faced west, and formally rejected the Devil and his works. (Since the officiants were men, women did not disrobe. Some scholars affirm that women completed this part of the ceremony under the supervision of a female deacon). The officiant then anointed the candidate with the oil of exorcism as a means of expelling evil spirits. After entering the water the candidate turned to face the east and expressed his or her faith in each person of the Holy Trinity, God the father, Jesus the son, and the Holy Spirit (*for more on the Christian significance of the direction east, see* **Easter, Origin of the Word**). After each one of these three confessions of faith, the officiant dipped the candidate in the water. The candidate then emerged from the water, was anointed, and dressed. There followed another anointing combined with the laying on of hands, signifying the coming of the Holy Spirit.

Afterwards the newly baptized Christians were given a cup of water and a cup of milk and honey, which represented the joys of heaven. Then they took part for the first time in the celebration of the **Eucharist**. During **Easter Week** they received instructions concerning Christian religious services and took part in special celebrations.

Preparation for Baptism

Just as the baptismal ceremony expanded over the centuries, so, too, did the required preparation for baptism. Some early Christian writings suggest that catechumens, or candidates for baptism, were expected to fast and pray for one or two days before the ceremony. Other Christian leaders thought a longer period of penance was in order (*for more on the concept of penance, see* Repentance). By the fourth century, the period of preparation had shifted from about forty hours to forty days. A number of important figures from the Bible endured forty-day periods of hardships after which they experienced spiritual aid (*see also* **Salvation**). Jesus himself fasted for forty days before beginning his ministry (Matthew 4:1-11, Mark 1:12-13, Luke 4:1-13). Influenced by these stories, third- and fourth-century Christians began to concentrate preparations for baptism into the forty days preceding Easter. Scholars believe that Lent, the forty-day period during which all Christians prepare to celebrate the great events commemorated at Easter, was in part modeled on the period of preparation that catechumens underwent before their Easter baptisms.

As time went on these preparations became increasingly elaborate. For example, not only did married candidates fast, but also they refrained from bathing and from conjugal relations during this forty-day period. They stood barefoot at church services, during which they received special instructions and admonitions. Separated from the baptized throughout the service, they were expected to leave before the celebration of the Eucharist. After their baptisms they put on new, white robes (*see also* **New Clothes**). They appeared in these robes at church until the following **Sunday**, later dubbed **Low Sunday**.

The Meaning of Baptism

For the early Christians baptism signified more than entry into a community of faith. It also conferred the forgiveness of sins and the companionship of the Holy Spirit. Certain scripture passages suggest that the early Christians viewed the central ritual act of baptism — the three total immersions in water — as symbolic of burial and resurrection (Romans 6:1-11, Colossians 2:12). Thus the ceremony was also thought to represent the candidate's spiritual death and resurrection, that is, the end of his or her old life and the beginning of a new, Christian life.

Infant and Child Baptisms

Among the early Christians adult baptism was the norm, although infant and child baptisms were not unheard of. As the new faith spread, these early baptisms became more frequent. By the fifth century Christians viewed them as unremarkable. In the sixth century the emperor Justinian I passed a law making infant baptism mandatory. The sheer number of baptisms wore away at the custom of the Easter or Pentecost baptismal ceremony presided over by the bishop. Moreover, the formal period of preparation for adult baptism, tied to the emerging Lenten season, fell into disuse as fewer adults and more children underwent the ritual. Together these trends weakened the once-strong preference for Easter baptisms.

Further Reading

Bradshaw, Paul F. *The Search for the Origins of Christian Worship*. New York: Oxford University Press, 1992.

Ferguson, Everett. "Baptism" and "Baptistery." In his *Encyclopedia of Early Christianity*. Volume 1. New York: Garland, 1997.

Johnson, Maxwell E. "Preparation for Pascha? Lent in Christian Antiquity." In Paul F. Bradshaw and Lawrence A. Hoffman, eds. *Passover and Easter: The Symbolic Structuring of Sacred Seasons*. Two Liturgical Traditions series, volume 6. Notre Dame, IN: University of Notre Dame Press, 1999.

Meslin, Michael. "Baptism." In Mircea Eliade, ed. *The Encyclopedia of Religion*. Volume 2. New York: Macmillan, 1987.

Metford, J. C. J. *The Christian Year*. London, England: Thames and Hudson, 1991.

Rees, Elizabeth. *Christian Symbols, Ancient Roots*. London, England: Jessica Kingsley, 1992.

Talley, Thomas J. *The Origins of the Liturgical Year*. Collegeville, MN: Liturgical Press, 1986.

Weiser, Francis X. *The Easter Book*. New York: Harcourt, Brace and Company, 1954.

Barabbas

The Christian Bible gives four separate accounts of **Jesus'** trial before Pontius **Pilate**. In each of these stories the assembled crowd clamors for the release of a prisoner named Barabbas. When Pilate presents them with a choice between Barabbas and Jesus, the mob chooses Barabbas.

The Bible reveals little else about this man whose escape from death by crucifixion came at Jesus' expense (*for more on crucifixion, see also* **Cross**). The four Gospels describe him as a robber (John 18:40), a man who had committed murder in a recent political uprising (Mark 15:7 and Luke 23:19), and simply as "notorious" (Matthew 27:16). Some scholars who have examined the meaning of the ancient Greek word used to describe him as a thief have argued that this word was more often used to describe political rebels than it was to describe ordinary thieves and criminals.

Another clue to Barabbas' identity lies in the meaning of his last name. In Aramaic Barabbas means "son of the father." Some scholars see in this name a potential reference to Barabbas' own father. They interpret this name as a possible indication that Barabbas' father was a rabbi. The Gospel according to Matthew records that Barabbas' first name was Jesus, the Greek version of the Hebrew name Joshua. Joshua was a fairly common name among first-century Jews.

What happened to Barabbas after Jesus' death? The Bible doesn't record this information. In 1950 Swedish novelist Pär Lagerkvist published *Barabbas*, a fictional account of Barabbas' life after the Crucifixion. In this story a lifelong fascination with Jesus and with Christianity takes root in Barabbas as a result of his momentary yet disturbing encounter with Christ. The English translation of this novel appeared one year later in 1951, the same year in which Lagerkvist won the Nobel Prize for literature. Some ten years Lagerkvist's novel inspired the production of the Hollywood film, *Barabbas* (1961), based on the book.

Further Reading

Crosson, D. M. "Barabbas." In *New Catholic Encyclopedia*. Volume 2. New York: McGraw-Hill, 1967.

Lagerkvist, Pär. *Barabbas*. New York: Vintage Books, 1951.

Perkins, Pheme. "Barabbas." In Paul J. Achtemeier, ed. *The HarperCollins Bible Dictionary*. New York: HarperCollins, 1996.

Trenchard, Warren C. "Barabbas." In David Noel Freedman, ed. *Eerdmans Dictionary of the Bible*. Grand Rapids, MI: William B. Eerdmans Publishing, 2000.

Bells

Before the advent of television, radio, wristwatches and loudspeakers, church bells served European towns and villages as a kind of public announcement system. From the Middle Ages onward, bells rang to announce births, deaths, weddings, funerals, communal work projects, and holidays. They also pealed to warn of fires, floods, and disease. Folk belief attributed special powers to the sound of tolling bells. Many thought, for example, that the sonorous tones could ward off witches, tame thunderstorms, and aid departed souls on their journey to heaven.

In addition to these civic uses religious officials developed their own schedule of church-related bell ringing. Small bells chimed at certain parts of the mass, the Roman Catholic religious service surrounding the celebration of the **Eucharist**. These bells announced the start of certain prayers, such as the Sanctus and the Angelus, so that parishioners who could not get to church could still join in these important devotions. A somewhat larger bell rang to announce daily prayer services, such as vespers and compline (evening prayer services). Two bells pealed to call parishioners to daily mass. A high mass warranted three bells. Four or five bells boomed in celebration of the church's holiest feast days, such as Easter and Christmas.

Lenten and Easter Bell-Ringing Customs

In medieval times church bells tolled on Shrove Tuesday reminding people of their duty to confess their **sins** to a priest before **Lent**, which began on the following day. In England, the Reformation, a sixteenth-century religious reform movement, reduced the importance of the **pre-Lenten** confession. The bell-ringing custom remained, however, although people reinterpreted its meaning. They began to hear the clanging bells as a reminder to use up all their butter, milk, and eggs before the start of Lent (*see also* **Fasting**). The English found that the quickest way to consume these foodstuffs was to make and eat pancakes. Hence they referred to the Shrove Tuesday bell as the "pancake bell" and to Shrove Tuesday as **"Pancake Day."** (*See also* **Shrovetide**.)

In some places bell ringers attempted to ring the bells in a subdued manner throughout Lent. This change in style reminded parishioners of the sober spirit of Lent (*see also* **Repentance**). As far back as the eighth century Roman Catholic custom called for the silencing or "stilling" of bells at the start of the Easter **Triduum**. Beginning on the evening of **Maundy Thursday**, the harsh cracks of wooden clappers replaced singing church bells. In some places clock tower bells, too, fell silent during these days. This unnatural stillness provoked many questions from curious children. In some Catholic countries of Europe, parents explained that the bells had flown off to Rome to visit the pope. In rural Germany and Austria the silencing of the bell towers inspired boys to bang sticks together as they raced through the streets calling out the time and singing Easter songs.

The English developed their own **Good Friday** bell-ringing customs. In some towns church bells remained silent on Good Friday. In others, only the bell possessing the lowest tone would be rung for church services, or the bells would be muffled in some way. In still others a single bell tolled at three in the afternoon, announcing the death of Christ. In Ayot St. Peter, in Hertfordshire, bell ringers sound a "death knell" at three p.m. on Good Friday. These traditional death announcements broadcast the age and sex of the deceased by ringing nine times for a man, six for a woman, and three for a child, followed by an additional number of rings representing the person's age. Thus, on Good Friday, the bells announce **Jesus'** death by tolling nine times, pausing, and then tolling thirty-three times.

All across Europe the sound of church bells glorifies the air on **Easter Sunday**. In France folk tradition identified the returning bells as Easter gift bringers, crediting them with delivery of the **Easter eggs** that all good children received on Easter morning.

Further Reading

Bigelow, A. L. "Bells." In *New Catholic Encyclopedia.* Volume 2. New York: McGraw-Hill, 1967.

Coleman, Satis N. *Bells, Their History, Legends, Making, and Uses.* 1928. Reprint. Detroit, MI: Tower Books/Gale, 1971.

Hole, Christina. *Easter and Its Customs.* New York: M. Barrows and Company, 1961.

Lord, Priscilla Sawyer, and Daniel J. Foley. *Easter Garland.* 1963. Reprint. Detroit, MI: Omnigraphics, 1999.

Tyack, George S. *A Book about Bells.* 1898. Reprint. Detroit, MI: Omnigraphics, 1991.

Beltane

Beltane was a Celtic or northwestern European holiday celebrated on the first of May. Although folklorists suspect that the roots of this observance stretch back to ancient times, most of the information we have about the holiday comes from folklore and folk customs recorded over the last several hundred years. With this evidence scholars have concluded that the festival marked the beginning of the summer season and the opening of the more remote pasture lands to grazing animals. In order to bless and protect their animals from harm, people held special fire ceremonies. They kindled fresh flames, built two bonfires, and passed between them. They also drove their herds and flocks between the bonfires. This ritual was thought to purify and protect all who participated in it.

Some snippets of folklore suggest that people also extinguished home fires on this day, which later were relit with freshly kindled flame. In Ireland people once thought it unlucky to lend fire to a neighbor on Beltane. Those who came asking for it were likely to be witches. Folklore also warns that fairies and witches were especially active on Beltane. Indeed, Beltane lies exactly six months apart from Halloween, another occasion associated with heightened contact between the natural and supernatural worlds. Some writers have concluded that the veil between these two worlds was thought to be especially thin at these turning points in the year.

One group of researchers thinks that the word "Beltane" came from an old Gaelic phrase meaning "Bel's fire." Many suppose Bel to be the name of a pagan god. Some commentators suspect that the god might be Baal, the pagan Middle Eastern deity denounced as an idol in the Bible. Others propose that the festival's name refers to the pagan god Belanus, popular in Austria and also known in France and Italy. This interpretation seems less likely, as few references to this god have been found in the ancient and medieval culture of the British Isles. Still another interpretation suggests that the "bel" of Beltane is the common Celtic prefix "bel," meaning bright, fortunate, or lucky. According to this interpretation, the name of the festival means "bright fires" or "lucky fires."

Some writers propose that the new fire ceremony which opens the **Easter Vigil** may have evolved at least in part from these ancient pagan fire customs (*see also* **Easter Fires**). Early Christian missionaries disapproved of these springtime fires, but were unable to convince people to abandon this old practice. According to legend St. Patrick, who set about converting Ireland to Christianity in the fifth century, provided a solution to this problem by adopting the flaming stacks as Easter bonfires. By the ninth century the Easter bonfire had been incorporated into the liturgy of the Western Church, where it is still used to light the **paschal candle**.

Some folklorists think that Beltane was an ancient Celtic observance. Others believe that the festival may have been observed throughout those regions of northwestern Europe in which people depended heavily on flocks and herds of animals that they moved seasonally from lowland to highland grazing grounds. Indeed traces of the fire ceremonies associated with Beltane have been found in English, Irish, Welsh, Scottish, Danish, Swedish, Norwegian, German, and Austrian folklore and folk customs connected with the day. In Germanic and Scandinavian lands, the festival survived in a transformed fashion into Christian times, when it became known as **Walpurgis Night**. People lit bonfires on this night to frighten away witches, who were presumed to be especially active on this evening (*see also* **Easter Witches**). Beltane also coincides with **May Day**, another old folk holiday honoring the arrival of spring.

In recent years contemporary pagans, also referred to as Neopagans or witches, have revived the ancient Beltane holiday. They celebrate it with bonfires, dances, the picking of wildflowers and ceremonies honoring the fertility brought about by the union of male and female principles in nature.

Further Reading

Cooper, J. C. *The Dictionary of Festivals*. London, England: Thorsons, 1990.

Frazer, James George. *The New Golden Bough*. Theodor H. Gaster, ed. New York: S. G. Phillips, 1959.

Hutton, Ronald. *Stations of the Sun*. Oxford, England: Oxford University Press, 1996.

Weiser, Francis X. *The Easter Book*. New York: Harcourt, Brace and Company, 1954.

Blood

Popular culture and folk tradition present us with gentle and pastel-colored Easter symbols, such as the **Easter Bunny**, baby chicks, and colored **Easter eggs**. Alongside these mild images there resides a lesser-known religious symbol that is both vivid and somewhat frightening. This symbol is blood. In addition to celebrating **Jesus' resurrection** each year on **Easter Sunday**, Christians also commemorate Jesus' death on the **cross** on **Good Friday**. What's more, many churches remember Jesus' willingness to sacrifice himself for his followers every week in a ceremony called the **Eucharist**. In this ceremony worshipers partake of **bread** and **wine**, presented to them as Jesus' body and blood. Although this blood imagery may strike some people as gruesome, it was originally intended as an emblem of spiritual liberation and renewal. An exploration of the religious significance of blood to the ancient Jews and first Christians illuminates the meaning of this symbol.

Blood Symbolism among the Ancient Jews

The Hebrew scriptures known to Christians as the Old Testament teach that a creature's life force is contained in its blood (Leviticus 17:11). This belief turned blood into both a powerful symbol and a source of potential physical and spiritual contamination. The association of blood with violence and death may have inspired belief in the power of blood to contaminate.

The power of blood could be turned to good purposes, however. Jewish scripture relates several important instances where blood was used to seal a covenant, or agreement, between God and his faithful people. For example, the Book of Exodus recounts how Jewish families enslaved in Egypt obeyed the Lord's command, relayed to them by the prophet Moses, to sacrifice a **lamb** to God and smear its blood over their doorways. God used this mark to identify which homes to pass over when wreaking vengeance on the Egyptians for their cruelty and disobedience. Jews still commemorate these events in the yearly **Passover** festival. After the Jews escaped from Egypt Moses informed them of God's new rules for them. Then Moses signified the Jews' agreement to this plan by scattering the blood of sacrificed bulls on the people and the altar (Exodus 24:3-8).

The ancient Jews also sacrificed animals to God on other occasions. They made these sacrifices for a number of reasons, including as a way of showing reverence, offering thanks, and asking for reconciliation with God. The Bible sometimes refers to this process of reconciliation as **redemption**. A passage from Hebrew scripture explains the role of blood offerings in gaining God's forgiveness. In the book of the Bible called Leviticus, God informs the Jews that ". . . the life of the flesh is in the blood, and I have given it for you upon the altar to make atonement for your souls: for it is the blood that makes atonement, by reason of the life" (Leviticus 17:11). Animal sacrifices entailed sprinkling the blood of the slain animals on the altar. This blood represented the life force of the animal, and so some scholars believe that in the context of the sacrifice it served as a symbolic substitute for the life force of the person or group making the sacrifice. Thus in offering the blood of slain animals to God, faithful Jews of this period were symbolically offering their own lives to God. Other researchers contend that the ancient Jews believed that their sins dirtied the temple and that sacrifices could restore the house of God to a state of purity.

Blood Symbolism among the First Christians

Although the Christian religion grew out of Judaism, it did not recreate the ancient Jewish custom of animal sacrifice. Instead Christians grew to understand Jesus' death as a one-time-only sacrifice on behalf of all his followers and the world. Nevertheless, Christians interpreted Jesus' sacrifice in terms of the blood symbolism already established in Jewish religious culture. Jesus himself instructed them to do so.

On the night before Jesus died he shared a meal with his twelve disciples (*see also* **Maundy Thursday**). During this meal he passed bread and wine to his followers, telling them that the wine represented his blood and the bread his body. In Matthew's version of the story Jesus not only identifies the wine as his blood, but also as "the blood of the covenant, which is poured out for many for the forgiveness of sins" (Matthew 26:28). Jesus, aware that he will soon die, is interpreting his own death for his followers. He describes it as a blood sacrifice which will establish a new covenant, or relationship, between God and humanity. Moreover, just as the blood of a sacrificial animal could confer the forgiveness of **sins**, Jesus' blood — freely offered on behalf of all his followers — will cleanse them of their sins. Jesus' blood thereby became the vehicle which reconciles his followers with God, that is to say, re-establishes good will and harmony between them.

Christian scripture records that Jesus indeed suffered a bloody death on the cross the following day. Christians commemorate this terrible event each year on Good Friday. They also honor Jesus' words and deeds at the Last Supper with the Eucharist, celebrated every **Sunday** in many churches. This rite offers worshipers the opportunity to share in the soul-sustaining consequences of Jesus' sacrificial death.

According to the Gospel of John, partaking of Jesus' body and blood imparts eternal life and a mystical connection to Christ (John 6:54-56). This doctrine builds on the ancient Hebrew belief that the life force of all creatures resides in their blood. Therefore, by consuming Jesus' blood, his followers absorb some part of Jesus' divine nature and his connection to God. Regular participation in this ceremony strengthens their spiritual bond with Christ. This ritual sheds additional light on the meaning of Jesus' death, implying that Jesus sacrificed his own life so that others could share in it (*see also* **Salvation**).

Further Reading

"Blood." In Leland Ryken, James C. Wilhoit, and Tremper Longman III, eds. *Dictionary of Biblical Imagery*. Downers Grove, IL: InterVarsity Press, 1998.

Mason, Steve A. "Sacrifices and Offerings." In David Noel Freedman, ed. *Eerdmans Dictionary of the Bible*. Grand Rapids, MI: William B. Eerdmans Publishing, 2000.

Potts, Donald R. "Blood." In David Noel Freedman, ed. *Eerdmans Dictionary of the Bible*. Grand Rapids, MI: William B. Eerdmans Publishing, 2000.

Roux, Jean-Paul. "Blood." In Mircea Elide, ed. *The Encyclopedia of Religion*. Volume 12. New York: Macmillan, 1987.

"Sacrifice." In Leland Ryken, James C. Wilhoit, and Tremper Longman III, eds. *Dictionary of Biblical Imagery*. Downers Grove, IL: InterVarsity Press, 1998.

Brazil, Carnival in

The people of Brazil celebrate **Carnival** with great enthusiasm. The most spectacular events take place in the city of Rio de Janeiro. Numerous neighborhood organizations called *escolas de samba*, or "samba schools," operate year-round planning the theme, music and costumes for their members' next Carnival parade. These parades feature marching bands pounding out catchy samba tunes and legions of gorgeously but scantily costumed dancers. Many Brazilians attend costume balls, while others prefer to party in the streets. In Rio de Janeiro the spirit of Carnival overtakes the city, urging people to stay out till all hours drinking, dancing, costume-watching and flirting. Although the inventive citizens of Rio de Janeiro hit the streets in a wide range of costumes, one favorite costume idea is for men to dress as women and women as men. In Brazil Carnival occurs in the middle of the summer, so many people take the heat into consideration when planning a costume. Indeed the long, hot days ensure that festivities generally begin in the late afternoon and continue on through the night.

History

When Portuguese colonists arrived in Brazil in the sixteenth century they brought Carnival with them. In Portugal people celebrated *Entrudo*, or Carnival, by wandering through the streets throwing oranges, lemons, eggs, flour, mud, straw, corncobs, beans, or lupines (a type of flower) at one another. They also staged mock battles with brooms and wooden spoons. People on balconies poured dirty **water**, glue, or other obnoxious substances on the crowds below. Indoors families and their guests feasted on rich foods. The wealthier homes might even toss cakes and pastries out the window to passersby.

The spirit of these rowdy Portuguese Entrudo celebrations crossed the Atlantic with the colonists and implanted itself on Brazilian soil. The Brazilian Entrudo lasted for about three centuries, even though official condemnations of the folk festival date back to the early 1600s. Brazilians especially enjoyed celebrating Entrudo by throwing water at one another. Rio de Janeiro newspapers frequently warned of the dangers this popular custom posed to the city's water supply. Another favorite sport consisted of tossing flour on top of sopping wet partygoers. Splattering passersby with vinegar-scented cologne or liquid dyes encased in balls of wax was another well-known Carnival prank. In time wax lemons became the favorite projectile of Brazilian Entrudo celebrations. People prepared for the festival by crafting dozens of these fake fruit.

The disorder unleashed by these spirited Entrudo customs often led to incidents of violence. As a result several mid-nineteenth century decrees attempted to do away with Entrudo, but they failed due to the festival's widespread popularity. In spite of these failures the holiday began to change shape during the second half of the nineteenth century as the well-to-do introduced elements of a more sophisticated European Carnival to Brazil. These included fancy costume balls and parades with elegant floats, including a "Float of Criticism," which ridiculed a recent political event. In addition, in 1900 the citizens of Rio de Janeiro introduced the custom of crowning a Carnival king to rule over the festivities. As cars became available to the wealthy, rich society members celebrated the festival by riding in automobile processions from which they threw confetti, streamers, and water.

In the early twentieth century Brazilian Carnival celebrations expanded again, this time to include elements of African culture introduced by the recently freed slave population. These elements included a custom called the "Congo," a kind of parade based loosely on the procession of a royal African court, and the *rancho de reis*, a parade whose participants attempted to tell a story through music, imagery, and dance. What's more, the numbers of people participating in *cordões*, small groupings of people wearing traditional Carnival costumes, also increased. These costumes included devils, Indians, bats, kings, queens, clowns, Death, and women from the Bahia region.

In the 1930s Carnival in Brazil took on a new twist with the introduction of *escolas de samba*, or samba schools. Samba is a particular style of music and dance that blends African and European musical influences to create jaunty tunes set to bouncy rhythms. Founded by members of the poorest segment of society and located primarily in Rio de Janeiro, the samba schools have set the tone of the modern Brazilian Carnival. Each year they organize thousands of their members into spectacular parades around a particular theme. At first, however, authorities persecuted the groups.

In 1935 Carnival became an official holiday. With legalization came government control, in the form of rules regarding permissible themes for the samba schools' presentations. In spite of their association with the lower classes, samba schools steadily gained in popularity. By the 1960s middle-class people and intellectuals became involved with them in significant numbers. Today the samba schools continue to present themes from Brazil's history and folklore, and people from various class and racial groups temporarily join together to participate in the school's parade. Poor people, however, may have to go into debt to pay for their extravagant costumes. Many choose to do so because of the very high value that Brazilians place on participating in Carnival.

Carnival in Rio de Janeiro

Rio de Janeiro's glamorous Carnival has gained worldwide fame. Each year millions of tourists descend upon the city to watch and participate in the sensuous spectacle. As the festival begins the mayor presents King Momo, the king of Carnival, with the keys to the city. This symbolic gesture formally ushers in the spirit of Carnival to Rio de Janeiro. The king is selected from among the city's well-known male citizens. In addition to social prominence the king must have a large waistline, thought to represent a jolly disposition, and good health, since he must attend an exhausting round of parties and parades.

For the four days of Carnival, which stretch from the Saturday before **Ash Wednesday** to the following Tuesday, King Momo rules the city. As the mascot of the holiday, King Momo rides on parade floats, attends parties, and makes other appearances. The king reigns alongside a Carnival princess. Various beauty queens make up the rest of the royal court. Carnival is such an important holiday in Rio de Janeiro that shops and offices close for a week or two so that everyone may prepare for and enjoy the festival.

Samba Schools

Rio de Janeiro's dozens of samba schools prepare for Carnival year-round. They begin by reviewing samba songs submitted by local folk musicians. After selecting a theme song, core members of the samba school proceed to organize a parade around it, designing costumes, constructing floats, choreographing dance moves, and coordinating

41

participants. Dues paid by the school's thousands of members fund these activities. While the samba schools' main purpose is to fund and organize Carnival parades, the groups also function as community clubs throughout the year.

The main Carnival parades take place on the Sunday and Monday before Ash Wednesday. They begin around seven p.m. and continue until dawn. Each samba school creates its own parade with six to eight floats and thousands of costumed participants. Each parade consists of a number of sections, called *alas*, or "wings," composed of hundreds of people wearing the same costume.

In the 1980s the citizens of Rio de Janeiro constructed a special cluster of buildings called the Sambadrome to provide comfortable seating for those who wished to watch the parades. Built along the main parade route, the Sambadrome is half a mile long and can seat 85,000 people. It also houses the main judging stand from which the presentations of each samba school will be evaluated and ranked against the others. Each parade may take as long as an hour to pass by the judges' stand.

Although the theme, song, and costumes of each parade differ from one another, they follow a similar format. First come the formally dressed members of the samba school's head committee. Then follows a float that summarizes the theme of the parade. After that enter standard bearers and pages, who hand song sheets to the crowd and urge them to sing along with the music. Behind them come the mistress and master of ceremonies. Dressed in powdered wigs and eighteenth-century clothing, their appearance contrasts greatly with the rest of the parade. They execute courtly dance steps as they make their way along the parade route. The enormous *bateria*, or drum section, then bursts onto the scene, pounding out the syncopated samba rhythms on small and large drums, tambourines, shakers, cowbells, triangles, and other percussion instruments. They are followed by ranks of sexy samba dancers. Other wings to watch for include the *baianas*, older women dressed in the traditional clothing of the Bahia region and dancing as nimbly as many who are years younger, and the *velha guarda*, men dressed in snappy white suits and Panama hats.

Street Parties

Rio de Janeiro also boasts an active street Carnival which includes many less formal parades. These informal parades, called *blocos* or *bandas*, feature an orchestra that marches along a set route, accompanied by a motley horde of dancers. Late in the afternoon people gather at local bars or plazas to socialize, drink, and listen to samba music. This gathering, called the concentration, energizes people for the parade. When the moment is right the group members spill out onto the streets and, propelled by tunes pounded out by the group's marching musicians, shimmy their way down the parade route. People attend these events dressed as they are, so some appear in costumes, others in street clothes, and still others in bathing suits. These parades often interrupt traffic and gather new participants as they wend their way through the city streets.

Carnival Balls

Carnival balls offer another opportunity for fun. They take place at various hotels and clubs throughout the city and feature live music, dancing, drinking, costumes, and flirtation. Some of these events cost quite a bit of money to attend and so attract members of high society. Others are more reasonably priced and thus pull in a wider variety of partygoers. Some, while open to the public, attempt to draw special audiences, such as men dressed as women.

Beach Parties

Beach parties present Carnival-goers with a less structured form of Carnival fun. The samba schools host massive beach parties in the Copacabana district, which are broadcast on television.

Kids' Carnival

The children of Rio de Janeiro step into the Carnival spotlight on the Saturday before Ash Wednesday. On this day children's samba schools hold parades complete with glittering costumes and elaborate floats. The miniature masqueraders march to the Sambadrome, where they are cheered on by family, friends, and fellow citizens.

43

Further Reading

Goldwasser, Maria Julia. "Carnival." In Mircea Eliade, ed. *The Encyclopedia of Religion.* Volume 3. New York: Macmillan, 1987.

Griffin, Robert H., and Ann H. Shurgin, eds. *Junior Worldmark Encyclopedia of World Holidays.* Volume 1. Detroit, MI: UXL, 2000.

Lau, Alfred. *Carneval International.* Bielefeld, Germany: Univers-Verlag, n.d.

Orloff, Alexander. *Carnival: Myth and Cult.* Wörgl, Austria: Perlinger, 1981.

Bread

Each Sunday millions of Christians around the world participate in a ceremony known as the **Eucharist**. In this ceremony worshipers partake of bread and **wine** identified as **Jesus'** body and **blood**. Since this ritual commemorates the events surrounding Jesus' death and **resurrection**, it may be thought of as an Easter symbol and custom that is celebrated throughout the year. In this ceremony, bread stands for the body of Christ. When the Eucharist is viewed in the context of the biblical spirituality from which it emerged, the full meaning of this bread symbolism comes into focus.

Bread in the Bible

Throughout the ancient Middle East people depended on bread as the mainstay of their diet. Hebrew scripture acknowledges the importance of this food source. A line from the book of Leviticus refers to bread as a "staff" (Leviticus 26:26), a poetic way of saying that bread supports life in the same way that a staff supports the body. In fact, bread was such an important food source to the ancient Jews that they sometimes used the word bread to stand for all food, as in the well-known saying "man does not live by bread alone" (Deuteronomy 8:3).

Biblical spirituality, both Jewish and Christian, again and again reminds us that we depend on God for our bread. The book of Exodus, for example, relates that after the Jews escaped from slavery in Egypt, they found themselves in a barren wilderness. They survived because God met their needs, feeding them with manna, or bread, that came down from heaven (Exodus 16). In Christian scripture Jesus teaches his followers what Christians now call the Lord's Prayer (Matthew 6:9-13, Luke 11:2-4). This prayer includes a request for "our daily bread." Indeed Christian scripture records a number of instances in which Jesus publicly gave thanks to God for food and drink.

The Bible not only reminds us of our dependence on God, but also assures us that God will provide for us. Christian scripture makes this point in a story that echoes the Exodus account of God's gift of manna in the wilderness. In a similar vein, Jesus supplied bread for those who had followed him far into the countryside to hear him speak. In this miracle, often called the Miracle of the Loaves and Fishes, or the Feeding of the Five Thousand, Jesus transforms a few loaves of bread and some fish into more than enough food to satisfy five thousand people (Matthew 14:13-21, Mark 6:30-44, Luke 9:10-16, John 6:1-13.). This story also recalls the way in which God helped the prophet Elisha to feed a large crowd with only twenty barley loaves and some grain (2 Kings 4:42-44). Stories such as these portray bread as a sign of God's hospitality to those on earth.

Jewish custom demanded that human beings offer bread back to God in various sacrifices and rituals. One such ritual required priests to keep twelve loaves of bread, called the "shewbread" or the "bread of the presence" on a golden table in the Temple at Jerusalem. Replaced weekly on the Sabbath, this bread served as a sign of the covenant, or special relationship, between God and the Jewish people (*for more on the Sabbath, see* **Sunday**).

Bread in Christian Scripture

Bread assumes a special place in Christian spirituality because of its role in the celebration of the Eucharist. This ritual can be traced back to the Last Supper (Matthew 26:26-29, Mark 14:22-25, Luke 22:16-19; *for more on the Last Supper, see* **Maundy Thursday**). Christian scripture recalls that at this meal Jesus gave thanks to God for bread and wine, and then identified the bread as his body and the wine as his blood. He passed them to his disciples asking them to eat and drink. Today Christians commemorate this event in the Eucharist, a ritual whereby worshipers take a sip of wine and a bite of bread identified by the clergy as Christ's body and blood.

The role of bread in the Last Supper and in the Eucharist echoes already established biblical themes. God's hospitality again expresses itself in a gift of bread. The old idea takes on a new twist this time, however. God not only gives bread, but gives himself in the form of bread. In the sixth chapter of John's Gospel, which contains a number of stories and teachings concerning bread, Jesus elaborates on this idea:

> Your fathers ate the manna in the wilderness, and they died. This is the bread which comes down from heaven, that a man may eat of it and not die. I am the living bread which came down from heaven; if anyone eats of this bread, he will live for ever; and the bread which I shall give for the life of the world is my own flesh (John 6:49-51).

Here Jesus contrasts a literal and a symbolic meaning of bread. Just as bread made from dough sustains life in the body, Jesus, "the bread that comes down from heaven," will sustain the spirit and impart eternal life. Jesus repeats another biblical theme here as well, when he describes his flesh as a sacrificial offering of bread, given on behalf of the world.

Bread Customs

The first Christians referred to their common meals simply as "breaking bread" (Acts 2:42). As time passed these informal meals became more ceremonious. Early Christians began to call these ceremonial meals *eucharistia* ("Eucharist" in English) which means "thanksgiving." Although only baptized Christians were permitted to partake of the bread prepared for the Eucharist, others could share in specially blessed bread decorated with Christian symbols. This blessed bread was eaten at communal meals, given to those preparing for **baptism**,

sent to the sick, shared at funerals, and made available at shrines and
on saints' days. Thus, for the early Christians bread served not only as
an abstract symbol but also as a concrete vehicle of God's hospitality
and blessing. Today's Orthodox Christians still maintain some of these
ancient customs surrounding blessed bread. They call the bread *anti-*

doron, which means "instead of the gift." This name distinguishes the blessed bread from the bread of the Eucharist, which they view as God's true gift to humanity.

Throughout the centuries Christians have experienced bread as an expression of God's hospitality and blessing in the ceremony of the Eucharist. Many Christians see the Eucharist as a ritual that represents the new relationship with God brought about through Christ. Viewed in this way, the bread of the Eucharist, like the ancient Jewish bread of the presence, symbolizes a covenant, or agreement, between God and human beings.

Bread Controversies

In the Middle Ages controversy simmered over the question of whether leavened or unleavened bread should be served at the Eucharist. The biblical accounts of Jesus' last meal with his followers found in the Gospels of Mark, Matthew, and Luke assume that the Last Supper was a **Passover** meal. This implies that Jesus and his followers ate unleavened bread that evening. For the most part, western European clergy, influenced by this interpretation of events, served unleavened bread at the Eucharist. The Gospel according to John, however, suggests that the Last Supper occurred the day before Passover. Eastern European and Middle Eastern Christians, influenced by this account of the Last Supper, tended to favor leavened bread for the Eucharist.

Even after the Eastern and Western churches split apart from one another in the twelfth century, bitter debate continued between them about the value of one another's eucharistic practices. In recent times debates over the validity of leavened versus unleavened bread for the Eucharist have receded as clergy from many denominations gained greater respect for one another's customs. Today the Roman Catholic Church still serves unleavened bread at its celebrations of the Eucharist. Orthodox churches continue to serve leavened bread. Most Lutheran and Anglican clergy favor unleavened over leavened bread for the ceremony. Other Protestants feel free to follow either form.

Further Reading

Ferguson, Everett. "Bread." In his *Encyclopedia of Early Christianity*. Volume 1. New York: Garland, 1997.

Latham, James E. "Bread." In Mircea Eliade, ed. *The Encyclopedia of Religion*. Volume 2. New York: Macmillan, 1987.

Myers, Allen C., ed. "Bread." In *The Eerdmans Bible Dictionary*. Grand Rapids, MI: William B. Eerdmans Publishing, 1987.

Noggin, J. F. "Bread, the Liturgical Use of." In Charles G. Herbermann et al., eds. *The Catholic Encyclopedia*. New York: Appleton, 1913. Available online at: http://www.newadvent.org/cathen/02749a.htm

Stein, Robert H. "Bread." In Paul J. Achtemeier, ed. *The HarperCollins Bible Dictionary*. New York: HarperCollins, 1996.

Butterfly

In Christian art the butterfly symbolizes the **resurrection** of **Jesus Christ**. It also represents the resurrection of all humanity. Butterflies sometimes appear in Christian art depicting the Virgin Mary and the child Jesus (*see also* **Mary, Blessed Virgin**). Often the butterfly rests in Jesus' hand.

The butterfly's own stages of growth require a dramatic transition from one form of life to another. This transition suggests the following symbolic formula. The caterpillar stage represents our earthly existence, the cocoon death, and the emerging butterfly eternal life. The ancient Greeks recognized a similar symbolism in the butterfly. They named the creature *psyche*, the same word they used for "soul." Although apparently not a popular symbol among the Greeks and Romans, butterflies flutter above the departed in a number of works of Greek art. Christians adopted the symbol sometime during the Middle Ages. In Christian art the butterfly usually stands for resurrection. Nevertheless, its beauty and short, meandering flights also led to its occasional use as a symbol of vanity and aimlessness.

Further Reading

Becker, Udo. "Butterfly." In his *The Continuum Encyclopedia of Symbols*. New York: Continuum, 1994.

Hogan, Julie. *Treasury of Easter Celebrations*. Nashville, TN: Ideals Publications, 1999.

Hulme, F. Edward. *The History, Principles and Practice of Symbolism in Christian Art*. 1891. Reprint. Detroit, MI: Gale Research, 1969.

Knapp, Justina. *Christian Symbols and How to Use Them*. 1935. Reprint. Detroit, MI: Gale Research, 1974.

Lord, Priscilla Sawyer, and Daniel J. Foley. *Easter Garland*. 1963. Reprint. Detroit, MI: Omnigraphics, 1999.

Webber, F. R. *Church Symbolism*. 1938. Second edition, revised. Reprint. Detroit, MI: Omnigraphics, 1992.

Carnival

Cheese Week, Mardi Gras, Maslenitsa, Packzi Day, Pancake Day, Shrovetide

Carnival is a holiday that developed in response to a religious observance, namely the six-week season of **Lent**. In the Middle Ages Christians endured many trying religious disciplines during Lent. As a result they celebrated the week before Lent began, enjoying one last fling before beginning these hardships.

Carnival celebrations last from several days to over a week and take place in early spring. Many festivals begin in earnest on the Saturday or **Sunday** before **Ash Wednesday**, the start of Lent. The Thursday before Ash Wednesday, sometimes called "Fat Thursday," also once served as a traditional starting date for Carnival. The date of Carnival changes from year to year, as its timing depends on that of Easter (*see also* **Easter, Date of**). The festival reaches its peak on the Tuesday before Ash Wednesday. In some countries people call this day "Fat Tuesday." Indeed Carnival began as a means of using up rich foods and indulging in lively behavior before the start of Lent with its accompanying **fast** and other religious disciplines.

Symbols and Customs

Although Carnival celebrations vary from country to country and region to region, they usually include some or all of the following customs and symbols. Most Carnivals offer participants various opportunities to take to the streets in costumes or masks. As people temporarily take on the identity represented by the costume or mask, they engage in a spontaneous kind of play-acting with other costumed participants and onlookers. The fool or clown plays an important role in many Carnival festivals and symbolizes the topsy-turvy nature of the holiday. Many celebrations also feature a mock king and queen, who rule over the kingdom of Carnival during the few days of its duration. Some festivals schedule a symbolic funeral at the end of the week's festivities. A dummy, or some insignificant item, such as a sardine, is "killed" and buried, and this burial represents the death and laying to rest of Carnival for another year. Often people throw things at one another during Carnival celebrations, whether it be **water**, flowers, candy, oranges, or party favors, such as confetti or beads. Finally, Carnival customs often encourage people to eat and drink heartily, and may also include some loosening of the usual rules of social conduct.

Origins of the Word "Carnival"

Researchers disagree about the roots of the word "Carnival." Some say it comes from the Latin phrase *caro levare*, which means to lift or remove meat. During the Middle Ages this phrase became *carne levare*, and eventually, *carne vale*. It passed into English as "Carnival." In some of the Romance languages that evolved from Latin, the word took on a similar form. In Spanish it's *carnaval*, in Italian *carnavale*, and in Portuguese *carnaval*. The French call it *Mardi Gras*, which

means "Fat Tuesday." Other researchers have drawn different conclusions about the origin of the word Carnival. They say it comes from *carrus navalis*, a boat-shaped cart drawn through the city streets during the ancient Roman winter festival of Saturnalia. Masked and costumed men and women rode in the cart, singing coarse songs.

Origins

Where did Carnival come from? Most researchers agree that it began as a celebration of the last few days before the beginning of Lent. During the Middle Ages, people observed Lent by fasting, refraining from marital relations, reflecting mournfully on their shortcomings, and in some cases performing penance for serious misdeeds (*for more on penance, see* **Repentance**; *see also* **Sin**). No marriages could be performed during this somber time. Therefore, people celebrated the week before they began this strict regimen by indulging in rich foods, gaiety, and outrageous behavior, in other words, by enjoying all that was soon to be forbidden.

While Carnival as we know it today began in Europe in the Middle Ages, some writers believe that its origins lie in various celebrations that took place in the ancient Mediterranean world. They point to a variety of festivals observed in ancient times which resemble Carnival in certain ways. For example, during Saturnalia people feasted, drank, and reveled in the streets, often in costume. Moreover, social rank temporarily disappeared, as those of high rank served those of low rank, slaves enjoyed a temporary holiday, and people engaged in madcap behavior of all kinds.

The Babylonian and Mesopotamian New Year festivals, rowdy celebrations that took place in mid-spring, also featured street masquerades (*for more on a related modern festival, see* **No Ruz**). In biblical times the Jewish people created a spring holiday called Purim. During this holiday, still celebrated today, people hid their identities behind masks, men and women wore each other's clothing, and people engaged in wild behavior normally considered inappropriate. Another Roman holiday, Lupercalia, which took place in early spring, offered certain young men an opportunity to dress in animal skins and run wild through the streets, flailing whips at young women who crossed their path. According to Roman folk belief, the strokes of these whips bestowed fertility. Finally, Roman devotees of the goddess Cybele observed a joyous spring festival called **Hilaria**.

Other writers disagree with the argument that Carnival evolved from these ancient celebrations. They point out that, with the exclusion of Purim, the last of these ancient festivals disappeared about five hundred years before 965 A.D., when the first mention of European Carnival celebrations appears in an historical document. This fact leads this group of researchers to conclude that, although Carnival shares some customs with ancient festivals, medieval Europeans invented the observance on their own as a means of letting off steam before beginning the hardships of Lent.

Medieval and Renaissance Carnivals

The earliest mentions of European Carnival celebrations in historical documents call it *carnelevare*, literally "lift up meat" or "take away meat." Indeed, judging by these documents, eating meat seems to be the primary custom connected with the season. Carnival rooted itself in the European folk calendar between the years 1000 and 1300 with celebrations focused around feasting in preparation for the fasting soon to come.

The full range of customs that came to characterize European Carnival celebrations developed in the fourteenth, fifteenth and sixteenth centuries. During these centuries, which coincided with a period of social and intellectual change that historians have dubbed the Renaissance, people adopted new ways of looking at the world. These new perspectives included humanism, a philosophy that emphasized the need to place human interests above other concerns, and naturalism, a doctrine that denied the existence of anything beyond the natural world. These philosophies influenced Carnival celebrations by increasing the value people placed on lighthearted foolishness as a means of counterbalancing the artificial social demands and seriousness required of people in everyday life.

During this era Carnival celebrations came to include a greater emphasis on clowns, fools, and social satire, that is, making fun of society and its rules. The famous Flemish artist Pieter Brueghel (c.1525-1530 to 1569) left us a visual description of the Carnival celebrations of this era in his 1559 painting entitled "The Battle of Carnival and Lent." By the fourteenth and fifteenth centuries those populations in which Carnival had taken root observed the festive season with masquerades, rich foods, drink, and rowdy revelry, especially antics that made fun of human folly or reversed social roles and ranks. Custom encouraged people to play pranks on one another, especially to throw water, flour, beans, dirt, or other substances at each other.

Criticism of Carnival

In the mid-fifteenth century Church authorities began to criticize Carnival celebrations for encouraging various kinds of excesses and creating public disorder. These criticisms often compared Carnival to pagan Roman festivals, suggesting that they indeed represented a survival of paganism and therefore should be suppressed. Active repression of Carnival celebrations began in the seventeenth and eighteenth centuries. In the year 1748 Pope Benedict XIV instituted a new custom in the Roman Catholic Church. This custom, called the "forty hours of Carnival," required Roman Catholic churches to hold special services on the evenings of the last three days of Carnival. Churches also left their doors open during these forty hours so that people could enter at any time to seek God's forgiveness for sins committed during the festival.

Carnival in the Modern Era

In the sixteenth century well-to-do Italians began to host costume balls in celebration of Carnival. This trend eventually spread to other parts of Europe, giving rise to a courtly Carnival. This same trend led to the introduction of elegant floats and magnificent parades, which encouraged a more civil and structured celebration.

In spite of official opposition and unease, Carnival celebrations proved impossible to stamp out in much of southern Europe. In northern

Europe, however, Carnival celebrations faded away in some regions where they had once been popular. During the eighteenth and nineteenth centuries people began to beautify the festival in response to new perspectives introduced by the Romantic movement, which tended to idealize old traditions and folkways. Over time many Europeans discarded some of the dirtier and more aggressive customs associated with the holiday, such as throwing water or oranges at one another, and replaced them with gentler gestures, like tossing confetti and flowers. It became fashionable in some cities to ride in flower-covered carriages, construct elaborate parade floats, and host elegant masked balls. As the parades grew in importance the nature of the festival changed. Previously everyone had participated in the masked hijinks. Now a division grew up between participants and spectators. In the past the spirit of Carnival swept over the entire town. Now it was concentrated along a specific parade route.

From Europe to the Americas

While some of these changes were felt in Spain and Portugal, their rural Carnival celebrations continued in the same rowdy spirit of ages past. People in the street threw oranges, lemons, eggs, flour, mud, straw, corncobs, beans or lupines (a type of flower) at one another, and people on balconies poured dirty water, glue or other obnoxious substances on the crowds below. Those in the streets battled one another with brooms or wooden spoons. Indoors people feasted on rich foods, to which they also treated guests. The wealthier homes might even toss cakes and pastries out windows to passersby. Colonists from these countries exported this version of Carnival, called *Entrudo* in Portuguese, and *Antroido* or *Entroido* in the Galician language of northwestern Spain, to Latin America.

Latin American Carnival celebrations blend European Carnival customs with African and Native American traditions of celebration. African-influenced music and dance, for example, play an especially important role in Carnival celebrations in Brazil and Trinidad (*see also* **Brazil, Carnival in; Trinidad, Carnival in**).

Meanwhile the French succeeded in transferring their Carnival celebrations to certain of their colonies in North America, namely those centered around the cities of New Orleans and Mobile. These celebrations, known as **Mardi Gras**, survive today, a regional American expression of an old European seasonal festival.

For more on Carnival, *see* Brazil, Carnival in; **Cheese Week**; **Germany, Carnival in**; **Italy, Carnival in**; Mardi Gras; **Maslenitsa**; **Paczki Day**; **Pancake Day**; **Shrovetide**; **Switzerland, Carnival in**; and Trinidad, Carnival in

Further Reading

Blackburn, Bonnie, and Leofranc Holford-Strevens. *The Oxford Companion to the Year*. Oxford, England: Oxford University Press, 1999.

Goldwasser, Maria Julia. "Carnival." In Mircea Eliade, ed. *The Encyclopedia of Religion*. Volume 3. New York: Macmillan, 1987.

Griffin, Robert H., and Ann H. Shurgin, eds. *Junior Worldmark Encyclopedia of World Holidays*. Volume 1. Detroit, MI: UXL, 2000.

Kinser, Samuel. *Carnival American Style*. Chicago: University of Chicago Press, 1990.

Lau, Alfred. *Carneval International*. Bielefeld, Germany: Univers-Verlag, n.d.

Orloff, Alexander. *Carnival: Myth and Cult*. Wörgl, Austria: Perlinger, 1981.

Cheese Week
Butter Week, Maslenitsa, Maslyanitsa

Orthodox Christians celebrate the week preceding **Lent** as Cheese Week. Although Lent has not yet arrived, the Lenten **fast** begins during Cheese Week with the elimination of meat from the diet. Instead people feast on cheese, eggs, butter, and other dairy products. Cheese Week ends with **Forgiveness Sunday**, the seventh **Sunday** before Orthodox Easter. Beginning on the evening of Forgiveness Sunday, observant Orthodox Christians remove eggs and dairy products from their diets for the remainder of Lent. The following day, **Clean Monday**, constitutes the first full day of Lent for Orthodox Christians.

Orthodoxy is one of the three main branches of the Christian faith. Orthodox Christianity developed in eastern Europe and the countries surrounding the eastern half of the Mediterranean Sea. The division between Western Christians — that is, Roman Catholics and Protestants — and Orthodox and other Eastern Christians began about 1,000 years ago. Therefore, Orthodox Christians follow a different church calendar than that commonly adhered to by Roman Catholics and Protestants (*see also* **Easter, Date of**).

In predominantly Orthodox countries people celebrate Cheese Week in much the same way that they celebrate **Carnival** in western Europe. The folk customs of Cheese Week and Forgiveness Sunday anticipate the upcoming fast and the solemnity of Lent by encouraging indulgence in what soon will be forbidden. For example, people feast on butter, egg and cheese dishes, and enjoy parties, masquerades, and other frolics.

Egg Customs

Some of the folk customs associated with Cheese Week and Forgiveness Sunday feature eggs, an Easter symbol and forbidden food during the Lenten season. Many follow an old Greek tradition which dictates that the last bit of food consumed before the beginning of the Lenten fast be a hard-boiled egg. Before eating the egg one declares, "With an egg I close my mouth, with an egg I shall open it again." After the late-night **Easter Vigil** service on **Holy Saturday**, those who observe this custom begin their Easter feast with a hard-boiled **Easter egg**. Thus the eating of an egg symbolizes both the beginning and the end of the seven-week Lenten fast.

In another egg custom popular in Macedonia and Bulgaria people suspend a boiled egg, piece of candy, or piece of cheese from the ceiling with a slender string. They circle round it and knock it with their foreheads to get it swinging. Then each member of the circle tries to catch it with their mouths. The egg may also be suspended from the end of a stick held aloft by one of the participants.

Cheese Week in Greece

In Greece Cheese Week ends a three-week-long Carnival season. This period coincides with the old **pre-Lenten** season once observed by Roman Catholics in western Europe. The first week of the Carnival season often goes by its folk name, "Announcing Week," since it begins the build-up towards Lent. Folk tradition has dubbed the second week "Meat Week," since it is the last week during which observant Orthodox Christians eat meat before Easter. The third week is known as Cheese Week. In Greece people attend masquerade parties, parades, folk plays, fireworks displays, and outdoor music and dance performances during these three weeks.

During Cheese Week Greeks enjoy such foods as *tiropita* (cheese pie), custard dishes, eggs, and macaroni prepared with cheese. These dishes are especially popular on Forgiveness Sunday, also called Cheese or Cheesefare Sunday, the last day of Cheese Week. Greek folk tradition associates a number of magical charms with this day. In some places people performed folk dances once thought to appease the North Wind, in others young people leapt through fires or used fortune-telling charms to find out the identity of their future spouses.

Butter Week in Russia

The Russians call the week preceding the start of Lent "Butter Week," **Maslenitsa** or *Maslyanitsa* in Russian. Indeed many traditional festival foods include large helpings of *masla*, or butter. *Blinis*, thin pancakes rolled up around a rich filling, head the list of these foods. Russian cooks may stuff the blini with sour cream, caviar, jam, salmon, mushrooms, salted herring, honey, or cheese. Any delicious, rich food will do, as long as it contains no meat, since Russian Orthodox Christians begin their long Lenten fast during this week by removing meat from their diets.

Further Reading

Blackburn, Bonnie, and Leofranc Holford-Strevens. *The Oxford Companion to the Year*. Oxford, England: Oxford University Press, 1999.

Henderson, Helene, and Sue Ellen Thompson, eds. *Holidays, Festivals, and Celebrations of the World Dictionary*. Second edition. Detroit, MI: Omnigraphics, 1997.

Rouvelas, Marilyn. *A Guide to Greek Traditions and Customs in America*. Bethesda, MD: Nea Attiki Press, 1993.

Spicer, Dorothy Gladys. *Book of Festivals*. 1937. Reprint. Detroit, MI: Omnigraphics, 1990.

Web Sites

See "Carnival in Greece," posted by the Greek National Tourism Organization at: http://www.gnto.gr/1/06/0604/ea0604000.html

Matloff, Judith. "Bingeing on Hot Buttered Blini in Frigid Moscow." *Christian Science Monitor* (February 3, 1999). Available for a fee online through Northern Light at http://www.northernlight.com. Document ID number: BM199 90203010020782.

"Russian Folk Holidays and Traditions," a page sponsored by the city government of Moscow, Russia: http://www.moscow-guide.ru/Culture/Folk.htm

Solovyova, Julia. "Holiday Mixes Paganism, Christianity." *The Moscow Times* (February 16, 1999). Available for a fee on the web through Northern Light at http://www.northernlight.com. Document ID number: EB19990216710000175.

Clean Monday
Kathari Deftera

Clean Monday constitutes the first full day of **Lent** for Orthodox Christians. It marks the beginning of Clean Week, the first week of Lent in the Orthodox faith tradition. Clean Monday falls on the Monday following the seventh **Sunday** before Orthodox Easter (*see also* **Easter, Date of**). This Sunday, called **Forgiveness Sunday**, is the last day on which observant Orthodox Christians may eat dairy products and other foods forbidden during the Lenten **fast**. Lent begins on the evening of Forgiveness Sunday, following the vespers, or evening, church service.

Orthodoxy is one of the three main branches of the Christian faith. Orthodox Christianity developed in eastern Europe and the countries surrounding the eastern half of the Mediterranean Sea. Orthodox Christians follow a different church calendar than that commonly followed by Western Christians. Clean Monday is an Orthodox observance not found among Western Christians, that is, among Roman Catholics and Protestants. Instead, they begin their observance of Lent on **Ash Wednesday**.

In Greece, a country in which the vast majority of the population are Orthodox Christians, Clean Monday, or *Kathari Deftera,* is a national holiday. Rather than treat it as a somber occasion, the Greeks celebrate the first day of Lent. In fact, most Greeks find the festivities of Clean Monday so enjoyable that they consider the day to be an extension of **Carnival**. Many Greek families pack picnic lunches and head out to city parks or picturesque sites in the country. These lunches usually include an assortment of foods permitted during the fast, including *lagana,* a special bread baked only on Clean Monday. Other Lenten foods that often find their way inside the picnic basket include *taramosalata,* a spread made with potatoes and fish eggs, shellfish, salad, pickled vegetables, green onions, fruit, and *halvah,* a sweet made of crushed sesame seeds and sugar. Kite flying is a customary pastime at these picnics.

Further Reading

Rouvelas, Marilyn. *A Guide to Greek Traditions and Customs in America.* Bethesda, MD: Nea Attiki Press, 1993.

Colombia, Holy Week in

Like many other Latin Americans, the people of Colombia celebrate **Holy Week** with prayer and processions. Although observances take place all over the country, the most famous Holy Week celebrations take place in the town of Popayán, located in southwestern Colombia, at the foot of the Cordillera Central mountain range.

History

Spanish settlers founded Popayán in the beginning of Colombia's colonial era. Holy Week processions themselves can be traced back to 1558. The people of Popayán credit their nighttime candlelit processions with saving the town early in its history. Although the Spanish colonists built and dominated the town of Popayán, the native peoples still occupied much of the surrounding area and remained hostile to Spanish rule. One night during Holy Week, the natives decided to attack the settlers. As they approached the town they saw a candlelit procession winding its way down through the streets of the city. Mistaking the glowing rope of flames for a mythical serpent of fire, they fled.

In the year 1983 the worst earthquake in the country's history struck the region on Thursday of Holy Week (*see also* **Maundy Thursday**). Several of Popayán's most beautiful churches were destroyed and three hundred people were killed, many of them while they were at prayer in the city's holy places. Maundy Thursday processions did not take place that day, but church **bells** normally silent on Holy Thursday and the rest of the **Triduum**, the last three days of Holy Week, rolled out funeral knells for those killed that day. The town's citizens vowed to return to their Maundy Thursday celebrations next year, and to rebuild the city's devastated churches in their original style. They have done so with such great success that few tourists visiting the town realize that a recent earthquake devastated the city.

Preparations

Today the citizens of Popayán prepare in advance for Holy Week, giving their homes a new coat of paint and preparing their gardens so that many beautiful flowers will be in bloom at Easter time (*see also* **Spring Cleaning**). Parish volunteers help to decorate the insides of churches and polish precious gold and silver devotional objects, many dating back to the days of the country's first Spanish colonists. Churches display these objects each year during Holy Week.

On the Saturday before **Palm Sunday**, two men designated as *cargueros*, those who carry sacred statues in religious processions, visit the Chapel of Bethlehem to decorate the statues of **Jesus** and his mother Mary that appear in the Palm Sunday processions (*see also* **Mary, Blessed Virgin**). Colombians view cargueros as men who have been given both a great honor and a great responsibility. This duty is passed from father to son.

Palm Sunday

The following morning, on Palm Sunday, people gather for the blessing of the **palms**. That afternoon the two images from the Chapel are carried down the hillside amidst waving palm branches. The army band, the police drum corps, and rows of schoolgirls in uniform take part in this palm procession. Thousands of people turn out to watch these processions, and many devout people are moved to kneel and pray in the street as they pass by.

Holy Tuesday

On Holy Tuesday the people of Popayán carry out an old custom known as the "Feast of the Prisoners." On this day a small battalion of politicians, priests, and schoolchildren, accompanied by the army band, march to the local jail bearing cartloads of food. When they arrive the prisoners assemble in the courtyard and are treated to an Easter feast. Those in authority select one prisoner, who has served most of his sentence, to receive an official **pardon**. He leaves the jail that afternoon, though he spends the rest of the day sitting on a street corner in town, under guard, where people offer him gifts of food and money to help him start his new life. The guards release him that evening. This custom recalls the biblical story of **Barabbas**, who was released from jail instead of Jesus.

The first nighttime religious processions begin on the evening of Holy Tuesday. The first person in the parade is the sweeper who carries a broom and brushes away all evil from the path of the procession. Church assistants called acolytes follow, bearing jingling bells and containers filled with burning incense. Next come the platforms on which rest the holy statues, borne on the shoulders of the cargueros. Townspeople carrying candles, referred to as *alumbrantes*, or light bearers, accompany the platforms. *Regidors*, whose task it is to set a solemn tone and keep everything in order, also walk in the processions, dressed in tuxedos and gloves. Finally, members of religious brotherhoods — such as the Knights of the Holy Sepulchre of Jerusalem, an organization that dates back to the Middle Ages — march, too, cloaked in their traditional garb.

Good Friday

The city's most impressive processions take place on **Good Friday**. **Penitentes** appear among the marchers on this day, dressed in brown robes and crowns of thorns. They express **repentance** for their own misdeeds or compassion for Christ's misery by bringing suffering on themselves. They do so by walking the procession barefoot or in chains, whipping themselves, or shouldering heavy wooden **crosses**. Similar processions of penitentes take place throughout the country. Other Good Friday religious parades feature the display of holy statues depicting the events associated with Good Friday, including the removal of Jesus' body from the cross and his burial. During these solemn processions the cargueros murmur the rosary, a Roman Catholic prayer addressed to the Blessed Virgin Mary.

Holy Saturday

Residents of the town of San Antero host a most unusual event on **Holy Saturday**. Local farmers compete to see who has the most beautiful burro. Both male and female burros vie for the crown in separate divisions of this beauty contest. Their human handlers costume the animals in dresses and hats, or suits and ties. Many consider the bathing suit contest to be the highlight of the show, along with the ceremony in which the most beautiful vet-certified virgin is awarded the queen's crown. Winners of the contest receive a prize designed to delight any burro: retirement to a life of leisure.

The people of San Juan hold boat races on Holy Saturday. Unlike the burro beauty contest, this event claims a vague tie to Holy Week celebrations, since the race is billed as a contest to see who will be the first to reach the Blessed Virgin Mary and tell her that her son has risen from the dead.

In many Colombian towns and villages people practice a folk custom known as the **burning of Judas** on Holy Saturday. A dummy, made of rags, straw or paper, is stuffed with firecrackers and then set on fire. Onlookers cheer the resulting blaze and attempt to beat or drown the bits of **Judas** that remain after the flames die down.

Further Reading

Clynes, Tom. *Wild Planet!* Detroit, MI: Gale Research, 1995.

Griffin, Robert H., and Ann H. Shurgin, eds. *Junior Worldmark Encyclopedia of World Holidays.* Volume 1. Detroit, MI: UXL, 2000.

Lord, Priscilla Sawyer, and Daniel J. Foley. *Easter the World Over*. Philadelphia, PA: Chilton Book Company, 1971.

Milne, Jean. *Fiesta Time in Latin America*. Los Angeles, CA: Ward Ritchie Press, 1965.

Cross

In every corner of the globe Christians and non-Christians alike recognize the cross as a symbol of Christianity. Christians adopted the cross as a symbol of their religion because **Jesus** Christ, the founder of their faith, died by crucifixion. Crucifixion was a form of punishment used by the ancient Romans which involved nailing a person's hands and feet to a large wooden cross planted in the ground. Christians commemorate Jesus' crucifixion on **Good Friday**. According to Christian scripture Jesus rose from the dead on the **Sunday** following his crucifixion. Christians refer to this event as the **Resurrection**. Easter, the most important holiday in the Christian year, celebrates the Resurrection. Both the Crucifixion and the Resurrection play central roles in Christian belief, worship, and symbolism.

In Christian symbolism the cross not only stands for the manner in which Jesus died, but also for the new life he bestows upon his followers. When used as a symbol of Jesus' death, the cross is an especially appropriate emblem for Good Friday. The crucifix, a variation of this symbol which depicts Jesus hanging on the cross, may also be used for this purpose. Christian thought teaches that Jesus willingly died for the sake of his followers and in so doing offered them a new relationship with God. Thus the cross also represents many Easter themes, including **redemption** and **salvation**. Because these themes and these events in the life of Christ are central to the Christian faith, the cross eventually became the most well known and frequently used symbol of Christianity (*for cross-related customs, see* **Flowering of the Cross; Sunday of the Veneration of the Holy Cross; Veiling; Veneration of the Cross**).

Crucifixion

Researchers believe that the ancient Persians invented crucifixion, which they used to torture and execute prisoners. The Greek general Alexander the Great (356-323 B.C.) adopted this form of punishment from the Persians. Though never practiced in Greece itself, it was sometimes employed in Greek colonies. The Romans learned of this cruel form of punishment from the Greeks. They used it more frequently than did the Greeks, finding it ideal to punish serious crimes, execute slaves, and terrorize the peoples that they conquered, including the people of Judea. Indeed, the Bible tells us that Jesus was crucified by Roman guards, carrying out an order given by Pontius **Pilate**, the Roman governor. Prior to crucifixion the Romans stripped their victims and beat them with metal-tipped whips. Roman guards then forced them to carry heavy wooden cross-beams to the place of their execution. When they arrived the guards nailed or tied the victim's feet to the supporting post and his arms to the cross-beam. The condemned man endured hours or days of pain before dying of exhaustion, as the sagging weight of his body finally prevented him from breathing.

The Romans recognized crucifixion as an extreme form of punishment, so extreme that they exempted Roman citizens from crucifixion, no matter what the crime. Instead they crucified non-Romans convicted of serious crimes, especially those suspected of rebelling against Rome. Thus crucifixion was not only a painful death, but also a shameful death, the fate of outlaws, slaves, and rebels.

Early Christian Symbols

The early Christians did not use the cross as a symbol of their faith very often. Instead they drew, carved and sculpted other, more peaceful images, such as the dove, the **lamb**, the fish, the shepherd, the ship sailing with the wind, and the anchor. They also used the Greek letters Chi and Rho, the first two letters in the word "Christ." In explaining the relative scarcity of the cross among early Christian symbols scholars remind us that during the first several centuries after Jesus' death, Christians were harassed and sometimes killed for their faith. The cryptic symbols mentioned above, used by pagans in both decorative and religious art, would not give away anyone's identity as a Christian and so expose him or her to danger. Moreover, some of these images, the anchor and the ship in particular, could

conceal a cross within them. Some scholars add that the stigma of crucifixion made some Christians reluctant to adopt the cross as a symbol, while those of other faiths found it difficult to understand how a divine man could have been crucified and thereby become a savior (*see also* Salvation). Nevertheless, in spite of their hesitation to depict the cross in material form, the early Christians often traced the sign of the cross over themselves in their private devotions.

The Cross Becomes the Leading Christian Symbol

The cross became an important Christian symbol in the fourth century with the conversion of the Roman emperor Constantine to Christianity. In the year 312, on the evening before an important battle the Emperor dreamed he saw a shining cross in the sky, on which were inscribed the words *in hoc signo vinces,* "in this sign conquer." Before going into battle Constantine had the cross inscribed on his banner and the shields of his soldiers. As predicted, the Emperor vanquished his enemy. Afterwards he granted Christians political rights, extended toleration toward the once-persecuted religion, outlawed crucifixion, and eventually converted to Christianity himself. Constantine decorated his palace, statues, and coins with the sign of the cross, as well as the Chi-Rho monogram. By the late fourth century Christianity had become the official religion of the Roman Empire. During the fourth and fifth centuries, as Christianity moved out into the open, the cross gained in popularity. By the fifth and sixth centuries it had became one of the most frequently depicted Christian symbols.

Although the crucifix can be traced back to early Christian times, it was not often used until the seventh century. After that time it was represented with increasing frequency, becoming an extremely popular form of the cross in the late Middle Ages. This change in imagery reflected a new emphasis on Jesus' suffering and death in the spiritual teachings of the time.

Over the centuries Christians have devised many variations on the basic design of the cross. For example, a Greek cross employs a horizontal and vertical bar of equal lengths. A cross in which the horizontal bar is shorter than the vertical bar is often referred to as a Latin

Left to right: Chi-Ro monogram, Greek cross, Latin cross, Russian cross, ankh, crux ansata, and swastika.

Cross. When the Russian people converted to Christianity they began to depict the cross with three horizontal bars. The highest bar, a short horizontal plank above the level of Jesus' head, represents the inscription, "King of the Jews," that Pontius Pilate ordered the Roman soldiers to nail to the cross (John 19:19). The second highest and longest horizontal cross bar stands for the plank to which Jesus' arms were nailed. The lowest, slanted cross bar represents the short plank which, according to Russian tradition, supported Jesus' feet.

Mystical Interpretations of the Christian Cross

Some Christian thinkers have expanded the meaning of the cross by adding more abstract interpretations to the literal ones mentioned above. Because the cross extends in all four directions some Christians have understood it to represent the totality of existence. Others have interpreted the vertical bar as a symbol of eternity while the cross bar represents time. Still others have viewed the vertical beam as representing heaven and the horizontal beam earth. Thus the cross joins time to eternity and weds heaven with earth. Many Christians thinkers believe that these abstract concepts found their best and highest expression in the life, teachings, and sacrificial death of Jesus Christ.

Non-Christian Crosses

The Christians were not the first people to use the cross as a spiritual symbol. It had been used before them by other ancient peoples, and has been found in many places throughout the world. For example, designs based on the shape of the cross can be found in the sacred

71

artwork of some American Indians. Here the cross appears to represent the four directions. These crosses may be thought of as a symbol of all that is, in other words, of the cosmos which stretches out in all four directions. Other peoples besides American Indians seem to have interpreted the cross in much the same way.

The ancient Egyptians used the cross as a symbol of life. Called an *ankh*, the ancient Egyptian cross looked like a capital "T" with a loop added on top of it. In Egyptian carvings and paintings a god often holds the ankh up to the nose of a dead person, offering him or her eternal life. The Christians later adopted this image into their repertoire of crosses, calling it a *crux ansata*, or "handled cross."

The swastika, a Greek cross with lines projecting at right angles from each of its arms, has been found in many parts of the world. It was used by the ancient peoples of Central and South America as a symbol of the rain god. Moreover, the symbol can be found throughout much of the ancient Middle East and India. Scholars suspect that to some of these peoples the swastika served as a symbol of the sun and solar power. In India it became a symbol of the cosmos spinning around on its central axis and also of the Hindu god Vishnu. The Buddhists adopted it as the sign of the Buddha, particularly his teaching regarding the wheel of law. Eventually the symbol migrated to China where it was adopted as an emblem of abundance, long life, prosperity, and the totality of all living things. In the twentieth century the German Nazis adopted the swastika as their symbol. Since that time many people have come to view the swastika as a threatening image, representing the kind of racism, violence, and totalitarianism that characterized Nazi rule.

Further Reading

Child, Heather, and Dorothy Colles. *Christian Symbols, Ancient and Modern.* New York: Charles Scribner's Sons, 1972.

Cooper, J. C. *An Illustrated Encyclopedia of Traditional Symbols.* London, England: Thames and Hudson, 1978.

"Cross." In Richard Cavendish ed. *Man, Myth and Magic.* Volume 4. New York: Marshall Cavendish, 1997.

Goldsmith, Elizabeth. *Ancient Pagan Symbols*. 1929. Reprint. Detroit, MI: Gale Research, 1976.

Horsley, Richard A., and Neil Asher Silberman. *The Message and the Kingdom*. New York: Grosset/Putnam, 1997.

Miller, J. H. "Cross." In *New Catholic Encyclopedia*. Volume 4. New York: McGraw-Hill, 1967.

Rees, Elizabeth. *Christian Symbols, Ancient Roots*. London, England: Jessica Kingsley, 1992.

Ries, Julien. "Cross." In Mircea Eliade, ed. *The Encyclopedia of Religion*. Volume 4. New York: Macmillan, 1987.

Schoenberg, M. W. "Crucifixion." In *New Catholic Encyclopedia*. Volume 4. New York: McGraw-Hill, 1967.

Web Site

For more on the history and practice of crucifixion in the ancient world, see "Crucifixion in Antiquity," an article by Joe Zias, a former curator for the state of Israel's Antiquities Authority. Posted on "The Jewish Roman World of Jesus" web site, compiled by University of North Carolina at Charlotte religious studies professor James D. Tabor at: http://www.uncc.edu/jdtabor/crucifixion.html

Czech Republic, Easter and Holy Week in

The Czech word for Easter is *Velikonoce*, which comes from the Czech phrase, "Great Night." This name refers to the night that falls between **Holy Saturday** and **Easter Sunday**, during which, according to Czech tradition, **Jesus** rose from the dead (*see also* **Resurrection**).

Black Sunday

Some writers believe that Czech Easter celebrations absorbed some of the pagan customs associated with spring in pre-Christian times. For example, on Black Sunday, the Czech folk name for the **Sunday** that falls two weeks before Easter, village girls band together and create a straw dummy called *Morena*, which serves as symbol of winter, want, and death (*for more on the second Sunday before Easter, see* **Passion Sunday**). After dressing her in some of their own clothes local youth parade the dummy to a nearby river or brook. Once there they undress her, beat her, and throw her into the **water** to drown. This act represents the death of winter and the arrival of spring and new life. Afterwards the youngsters parade back into town carrying small Easter **egg trees** in their hands. Sometimes they break into small bands to sing Easter carols door to door. In return householders give them ingredients to bake Easter cakes or other small treats. This custom has died out in many places, but is still carried on in a few rural areas.

Palm Sunday

A week later Czechs celebrate **Palm Sunday**, or as they often call it, Flower Sunday. This name comes from the old custom of bringing flowers and green branches to church on this morning to receive a blessing. The **palm** branch serves as the traditional symbol for this holiday, but because few palm trees grow in the Czech Republic people use pussy willow branches instead. Priests bless pussy willow branches, wood, and water at Palm Sunday services. An old folk tradition encouraged men to fashion **crosses** out of this wood which were then placed in fields as a means of blessing the crops.

Monday, Tuesday, and Wednesday of Holy Week

According to Czech custom, **spring cleaning** should be tackled during the Monday, Tuesday, and Wednesday of **Holy Week**. In the countryside tradition involves giving the home a new coat of whitewash, inside and out.

Maundy Thursday

The Czechs call **Maundy Thursday** "Green Thursday" (*for more on the origins of this name, see* Maundy Thursday). Indeed, tradition calls for a meal composed of herbs and green vegetables on this day.

Parents encourage children to rise early and bathe in streams or rivers on Maundy Thursday. Czech folklore interprets this practice as a cure for laziness. When the youngsters come inside to breakfast they are treated to *jidasky*, breakfast cakes twisted into the shape of a rope. The name and shape of these breakfast buns suggests the fate of **Judas** Iscariot, the disciple who betrayed Jesus and afterwards hung himself. In past times people practiced a custom called hunting for Judas on Maundy Thursday (*see also* **Judas, Burning of**).

Other old customs associated with the day include throwing honey-smeared rolls into wells to insure that they would be filled with water throughout the coming year and eating honey-smeared rolls as protection from snakebite. Czech folklore asserts that eating honey prevents misfortune. In some places women rose early and swept the house free of insects before sunrise.

In accordance with Roman Catholic custom, church **bells** stop ringing on Maundy Thursday. In Czech villages boys march through the street with wooden rattles, replacing the chime of church bells with the clamor of wood. This noisemaking continues until the time of the **Easter Vigil** on Holy Saturday, when the bells are returned to their normal function.

Good Friday

Old Czech folklore insists that the weather on **Good Friday** previews the weather for the coming year. In past times people rose early on Good Friday and went to wash in the cold water of a nearby brook. Crossing the brook with one's bare legs exposed to the water was said to confer good health. Women shook out their quilts on this day, which was believed to cleanse the house of sickness. Some believed the magic of this day to be so powerful that water sprites came out to live on dry land and the earth split open to reveal hidden treasures.

Holy Saturday

Czech folklore dubbed Holy Saturday "White Saturday." Some commentators believe that the name can be traced back to the white robes worn by candidates for **baptism**. This quiet and peaceful day ended in church services featuring the blessing of water and candles (*see also* Easter Vigil; **Paschal Candle**; **Easter Fires**). In past times people extinguished all household fires on this day and lit them again from the fire kindled at the Easter Vigil service. People also saved pieces of wood scorched by the newly lit fire of the vigil service, as these logs were believed to protect the household against fire and lightning. Another old custom encouraged people to shake fruit trees on this day to encourage them to bear. Holy Saturday was also considered a lucky day to sow seeds. The weather on Holy Saturday was thought to predict the weather for the coming year.

Easter Sunday

In some churches **Easter eggs** are blessed and distributed to the congregation on Easter Sunday. Upon returning from church services Czechs enjoy their own version of **hot cross buns** called *mazanec*. These sweet, round Easter loaves are flavored with raisins, nutmeg, and other spices. Before baking they are decorated with a cross and sprinkled with almond shavings. In the Czech Republic, a typical Easter dinner features roast **lamb** or goat. A folk tradition associated with this day reminds people to create willow wands, used in the days to come, by braiding the blessed willow twigs together and decorating them with ribbons.

Easter Monday and Tuesday

On **Easter Monday** tradition permitted men and boys to slap women and girls with pussy willow wands. Folklorists interpret this custom as the remains of an ancient rite thought to confer vitality and health. The men and boys sang Easter carols as they went about their work, after which the women and girls were expected to gift them with Easter eggs. A girl's family would entertain any boys who came calling to whip their daughter with mazanec and a drink. On Easter Tuesday the tables turned, and custom encouraged women and girls to pursue and slap men and boys with pussy willow wands.

Further Reading

Lord, Priscilla Sawyer, and Daniel J. Foley. *Easter the World Over*. Philadelphia, PA: Chilton Book Company, 1971.

Web Sites

A series of articles on various aspects of Lent, Holy Week, and Easter by Petr Chudoba, posted under the "Holidays and Traditions" section of Local Lingo's Czech Republic site: http://www.locallingo.com/countries/czech_ republic/culture

"Easter in the Czech Republic," a series of articles posted by Radio Prague, the international service of Czech Radio: http://voskovec.radio.cz/easter/

Descent into Hell
Harrowing of Hell

As the early Christians pondered the meaning of the Gospel accounts of the Crucifixion and **Resurrection**, some began to wonder about the time that elapsed between these two events (*for more on crucifixion, see* **Cross**). What had happened to **Jesus** during the time that he was dead? (*See also* **Holy Saturday**.) Christian scripture gives no definite answers, but hints that he "descended into the lower parts of the earth" (Ephesians 4:9). It also asks, "'who will descend into the abyss?' (to bring Christ up from the dead)" (Romans 10:7). Some commentators interpreted these texts to mean that during the time that he was dead, Christ descended to the abode of dead souls, deep under the earth. Belief in such a place was already widespread in the ancient world. The Jews called it Sheol, the Greeks called it Hades, and English speakers eventually came to call it Hell.

By the second or third century a document known as the Gospel according to Nicodemus circulated among Christians, offering a detailed account of Jesus' deeds among the departed. According to this document Jesus descended to the netherworld, where the dead were kept captive by Satan and a figure personifying death. As Jesus approached, the dead perceived a great light coming towards them. Biblical prophets like Isaiah and John the Baptist rejoiced and announced the coming of the Savior. Christ entered the underworld, defeated Satan, and lifted the dead up to paradise. This story not only provided an answer to the question of what Jesus did during the time that he was dead, but also answered the question of what became of the souls who had died before Christ entered the world with his offer of **salvation**.

This story, called the Harrowing of Hell, gained in popularity throughout the Middle Ages, reaching the height of its appeal in the last several centuries of that era. "Harrow" is an old-fashioned word meaning to agitate, to harass, or to plunder. It is associated with an old farm instrument known as a harrow, a kind of sturdy rake used to break up the ground. This sequence of events is also known as the Descent into Hell. The idea that Jesus descended into Hell before his resurrection became a firmly established teaching of the Church in the eighth century, when it was formally incorporated into the Apostles' Creed, a brief outline of the fundamental beliefs of the Christian faith. The Harrowing of Hell was depicted in many paintings and sculptures and dramatized in medieval mystery and morality plays, folk plays centered on religious themes. The image of Christ liberating the dead fills an especially important role in Orthodox Christianity, where it serves as the foremost representation of the Resurrection.

Further Reading

Every, George. *Christian Legends*. New York: Peter Bedrick Books, 1987.

MacCulloch, J. A. *The Harrowing of Hell*. Edinburgh, Scotland: T. and T. Clark, 1930.

Metford, J. C. J. "Descent of Christ into Hell." In his *Dictionary of Christian Lore and Legend*. London, England: Thames and Hudson, 1983.

Monti, James. *The Week of Salvation*. Huntington, IN: Our Sunday Visitor Publications, 1993.

Quinn, J. D., J. H. Rohling, and P. Verdier. "Descent of Christ into Hell." In *New Catholic Encyclopedia*. Volume 4. New York: McGraw-Hill, 1967.

Scott, Miriam Van. *Encyclopedia of Hell*. New York: St. Martin's Press, 1998.

Turner, Alice K. *The History of Hell*. New York: Harcourt Brace and Company, 1993.

Easter, Date of

Christians celebrate Easter on the **Sunday** following the first full **moon** that occurs on or after the **spring equinox**, which in the Northern Hemisphere occurs around March 21. Nevertheless, they generally don't celebrate it on the same day. Western Christians, that is, Roman Catholics and Protestants, follow the above rule in calculating the date of Easter, and use the same calendar system that they use in everyday life to determine the date of the spring equinox. Although the date of Easter changes from year to year, it always falls sometime between March 22 and April 25. Orthodox and other Eastern Christians—those Christians whose traditions of worship developed in north Africa, eastern Europe and the Middle East—rely on an older calendar system for the date of the spring equinox. Moreover, they also insist that Easter fall after the Jewish holiday of **Passover**. For these Christians Easter may fall anywhere between April 4 and May 8.

Historians believe that the earliest Easter celebrations took place around the middle of the second century. When Christians started to commemorate the yearly anniversary of **Jesus'** crucifixion and **resurrection**, they looked to Christian scripture for clues about the dates on which these events occurred (*for more on crucifixion, see* **Cross**). All four biblical accounts of the Resurrection agree that it happened on the Sunday following the start of the Passover festival. According to the Jewish calendar, Passover begins on the fifteenth day of the month of Nisan. Yet the Jewish calendar differs in important ways from the calendar systems used by many other ancient peoples. Trying to translate the date of Passover into these other calendar systems has created nearly two millennia of conflict and confusion among Christians as to the correct date of Easter.

The Challenge of the Calendar

It takes the earth 365.2422 days to complete its orbit around the sun. We call this period of time, based entirely on solar rhythms, a year. The moon runs through its cycle, from full to new to full again, in 29.5306 days. Calendar makers have named this unit of time a lunar month. These two units of time do not mesh well with each other. During the 365.2422 days of the solar year, the moon will complete twelve full cycles and will journey eleven days into the next lunar cycle. Moreover, the naturally occurring unit of time that we call a day doesn't divide evenly into either the solar year or the lunar month.

Throughout history calendar makers have proposed various formulas to reconcile these differences. Some calendar systems rely entirely on the yearly solar cycle and accept the fact that the stages of the moon will occur on different days from month to month. Extra days may be added from time to time to adjust for the additional 0.2422 day included in each solar year. Other calendar systems base their months on the lunar cycle and accept the fact that the months will drift from season to season as a result of the difference between the yearly solar and monthly lunar cycles. The history of calendar systems in the Western world reveals a long struggle to harmonize the solar year and the lunar month.

The Jewish Calendar

In addition to the solar and lunar cycles, the ancient Jews, who depended on agriculture and animal husbandry for their living, keenly observed another natural cycle, that is, the changing of the seasons. They developed a calendar system that tried to reconcile all three natural cycles. The Jewish calendar revolves around twelve lunar months, but also includes periodic readjustments to keep the solar and lunar cycles more or less in line. These readjustments take the form of an extra month added to some years which prevents the feast days from drifting forward in the seasons. Each month begins on the first day on which the new moon is visible in the sky. Thus Passover, which falls on the fifteenth of Nisan, always coincides with a full moon. Although this calendar system anchors Passover to the spring season, the holiday does float around a bit on the solar calendar. In our contemporary civil calendar, which is based on the solar year, Passover may fall anywhere between March 27 and April 24.

The ancient Jewish rule for determining the date of Passover stated that the festival was to begin at the close of the fourteenth day after the full moon that fell on or following the spring equinox. Since the Jews began each new day at sunset, the evening that followed the afternoon of the fourteenth was considered the start of the fifteenth day of Nisan. Preparations for Passover took place on the afternoon of the fourteenth, and the holiday itself began after sundown, which marked the beginning of the fifteenth of Nisan. Nevertheless, the Jews did not possess a very accurate astronomy, so they tended to base the timing of Passover more on seasonal changes, which directly affected their livelihood, than on astronomical observations.

The First Easter Celebrations

Christian scripture states that Jesus' crucifixion and resurrection took place around Passover. When Christians first began to commemorate these events this timing posed several problems for them. First, as Christianity spread to increasing numbers of non-Jews, its adherents found themselves less and less familiar with the Jewish calendar system. Some Christians may have felt embarrassed to ask their Jewish neighbors about the date of Passover in order to plan the most important festival in their own religious calendar. Others felt superior to the Jews and therefore thought that Christianity should not have to rely on the Jewish calendar. In addition, the diverse ethnic and religious groups that made up the ancient Mediterranean world employed a variety of different calendars. This made it even more difficult for Christian officials to set a standard date for Easter. So local Christian communities had to discover the date of Passover and translate it into their own calendar system in order to celebrate Easter.

In Asia Minor, now the modern nation of Turkey, Greek-speaking Christians relied on their own version of the official Roman calendar. When they began to commemorate the anniversary of the Crucifixion and Resurrection, some of these Christians simply timed their celebration to coincide with the Jewish holiday of Passover. Others did not want to rely on their Jewish neighbors to tell them when Passover would occur that year, and so assigned their Easter celebrations a specific date in their own calendar, namely, the fourteenth of Artemisios, the first month of spring. This translates to April 6 in our own calendar system. Amidst the welter of time-reckoning systems used by the subjects of the Roman Empire, the official Roman calendar — introduced by the Roman emperor Julius Caesar in 45 B.C. and known as the Julian calendar — furnished a potentially unifying factor. In the third century scattered Christian communities in northern Italy, Gaul, Spain, Syria, and Asia Minor began to celebrate Easter using a fixed date in the Julian calendar. They believed that the Crucifixion had taken place on the Julian calendar date of March 25, which was also the official date of the spring equinox in that calendar system. So, they scheduled their Easter celebrations on March 25.

Yet each of these methods of calculating the date of Easter fell short of completely reproducing the timing of Jesus' crucifixion and resurrection as recounted in Christian scripture. Since the Julian calendar date of Jesus' death and rising had not been recorded by witnesses, many Christians felt that assigning Easter a date in this calendar was inappropriate. Moreover, three of the four accounts of Jesus' death given in Christian scripture state that it took place on Passover, while the fourth implies that it took place on the afternoon before Passover, as the **lambs** were being sacrificed for the festival.

In spite of this slight discrepancy all four scriptural accounts of Jesus' resurrection agree that it took place on the first day of the Jewish week, a Sunday. Weekly Christian worship services were scheduled on Sunday in honor of this event. Therefore some Christian leaders believed that Easter should also be celebrated on a Sunday. Those who argued for a Sunday celebration felt that Easter should occur on the Sunday following Passover. They criticized those who celebrated on Passover itself for ignoring the importance of the Sunday Resurrection. In Rome the earliest celebration of Easter on the Sunday following the start of Passover took place around the year 165, though other communities may have begun the practice before that time. Christian authorities in Rome became strong advocates of this method of setting a date for Easter, and those communities that looked to Rome for leadership adopted this model.

Historians still debate when and where the first Easter celebrations took place (*see also* **Pascha**). Historical evidence uncovered to date suggests that they took place in Asia Minor around the middle of the second century and that they coincided with the Jewish festival of Passover. Nevertheless some scholars believe that earlier celebrations may have taken place in other Christian communities. The Asia Minor Christians who celebrated Easter on Passover became known as Quatrodecimans, or "fourteeners," to Latin-speaking Christians because their Easter observances began with a **fast** on the fourteenth of Nisan and coincided with the Jewish Passover. The Quatrodecimans and the Romans battled one another over the correct date on which to celebrate Easter. At one point Roman officials threatened to excommunicate — that is, to ban from full membership in the Christian Church — anyone who followed the quatrodeciman system.

Resolving Conflicts in Easter Dating Systems

In 325 A.D. Christian leaders from all corners of the globe converged on Nicaea, a small town near Constantinople, now Istanbul, Turkey. The Roman emperor Constantine convened this gathering, known as the Council of Nicaea, in order that Christian officials come to agreement on several important issues concerning Christian doctrine and worship. Constantine issued several pronouncements concerning the proper date of Easter based on the conclusions reached during this series of meetings. The Emperor decreed that henceforth all Christians should celebrate Easter on the same date. He also called for the complete separation of the timing of Easter from that of Passover. This decision further separated the Christian and Jewish faiths, and may have been motivated by rising feelings of anti-Semitism, that is, prejudice against Jews and other Middle Eastern peoples. Constantine also called for Christians to celebrate Easter after the spring equinox, saying that to schedule the festival beforehand was a grave error.

These decisions created new difficulties for Christians, since astronomy was not a very advanced science in those days and people weren't sure exactly when the spring equinox occurred. In 45 B.C., when the Julian calendar was first introduced, the spring equinox fell on March 25. The inventors of the Julian calendar, however, had calculated the solar year to be 365.25 days long. In fact, the solar year lasts 365.2422 days. While this difference only amounts to eleven minutes and fourteen seconds every year, each passing year compounds the error. As a result, the dates on the calendar slowly began to separate from the events of the solar year. By 325, the year that Christian leaders attended the Council of Nicaea, the spring equinox actually fell on March 21. Astronomers from the city of Alexandria, Egypt, realized this fact and publicized the correct date. Many Christian communities in the Middle East and north Africa accepted the Alexandrian date for the equinox. Roman Christians, and those who looked to Rome for leadership, tended to stick with the old Roman date for the equinox, March 25.

For several centuries Easter celebrations still took place on a variety of dates, in spite of Constantine's decrees. Many Christian communities attempted to celebrate Easter after the spring equinox, but disagreed on when the equinox occurred. Furthermore, in Ireland and the British Isles Christian authorities felt no obligation to accept the decrees of Nicaea, since no representative from their lands had taken part in that Council. When Christian missionaries under the jurisdiction of Rome showed up in the late sixth century, they found these Celtic Christians adhering to their own calendar. Tension came to a head around the mid-seventh century, when the Anglo-Saxon king Oswy, a Celtic Christian, found himself celebrating Easter a week earlier than his wife Eanfled, who followed the teachings of the Roman Church. Eventually Oswy called a council of Roman and Celtic church leaders throughout the British Isles, known to historians as the Synod of Whitby. Representatives from each side presented arguments for the adoption of their calendar system. In the end Oswy ruled in favor of the Roman system of dating Easter, decreeing that it be adopted throughout the land.

The Middle Ages

By the early Middle Ages a general agreement finally emerged among Christians that Easter should be scheduled for the first Sunday after the full moon falling on or after the spring equinox, which most Christians now agreed occurred on March 21. If the full moon were to fall on a Sunday, then Easter would be celebrated the following Sunday. This formula for setting the date of Easter is often attributed to the Council of Nicaea, and may well have originated there, although no records have survived to document that fact. It echoes Jewish regulations for setting the date of Passover, which in ancient times was supposed to begin on the first full moon after the equinox.

Church astronomers devised complicated tables for determining in advance the calendar date of Easter. These tables attempted to match up the solar cycle of the year with the lunar cycles of the months, and then mesh them with the seven-day cycle of the week so as to predict in advance the exact calendar date on which Easter would fall. This task proved difficult and the tables complex. As the Middle Ages slid by, these arrangements became more and more unsatisfactory. The original flaw in the Julian calendar once again took effect, driving a slow-moving wedge between the events of the solar year and the dates of the calendar.

The Gregorian Calendar Reform

Although Alexandrian astronomers had correctly identified the date of the spring equinox in the early fourth century, the inherent error in the Julian calendar system meant that the calendar was slowly falling behind the events of the solar year. Thus by the sixteenth century the calendar lagged ten days behind, with the result that the spring equinox fell on March 11 rather than March 21. Growing concern that the flaws in the Julian calendar might lead them to celebrate Easter on the wrong day prompted Roman Catholic officials to investigate the possibility of calendar reform. They reviewed several proposals for a new calendar system and finally settled on one of them, named the Gregorian calendar in honor of the reigning pope, Gregory XIII. In 1582 Pope Gregory XIII approved of the new calendar system and called for its immediate and universal adoption. In order to bring the spring equinox back to the traditional date of March 21, eleven days were dropped from the calendar. Thus in the year 1582 October fourth was followed by October 15 in all countries that accepted the new calendar.

Europe's Roman Catholic countries immediately took up the Gregorian calendar. Portugal, Spain, and Italy, for example, installed it in 1582, the same year of the Pope's proclamation. The unfortunate timing of the calendar reform, however, led to its initial rejection in much of northern Europe. The Roman Catholic Church introduced the Gregorian calendar in the same century that the Reformation, a western European religious reform movement, tore the religious fabric of the continent apart. Those countries that had embraced the religious reforms and were now primarily Protestant refused to accept the new calendar for fear of seeming to accept the authority of the pope. So they went on celebrating Easter according to the old calendar. Once again, Christians in different parts of the world and branches of the church celebrated Easter on different days.

In spite of the religious controversy that surrounded it, scientists across Europe recognized the new, Gregorian calendar to be far more accurate than the old Julian calendar. So, one by one, the nations that had initially refused the new calendar decided to accept it. Belgium instituted the Gregorian calendar in 1584. Most of the German Catholic states switched to the new calendar by the same year. Hungary followed suit in 1587. Denmark and Protestant Germany delayed until 1700, however. Great Britain finally made the change in 1752, along with her American colonies. Sweden followed close behind in 1753. As western European countries established military and economic dominance around the globe, they influenced others to adopt their calendar system. Japan started to use the Gregorian calendar in 1873. China finalized its adoption of the Gregorian calendar in 1949.

Continuing Orthodox Use of the Julian Calendar

Meanwhile, controversy concerning the merits of the Gregorian calendar still simmered in the Orthodox countries of eastern Europe. Religious authorities in these countries had rejected the Gregorian calendar at the time of its introduction in western Europe. They based their refusal on religious grounds, stating that such a major change could not be instituted by a single Christian official, but rather must be approved by a church-wide council similar to the one held in Nicaea. By the early twentieth century, the governments of these eastern European countries began to adopt the Gregorian calendar for civil use. The former Soviet Union adjusted to the new calendar in 1918. Greece began to use the Gregorian calendar in 1923. Nevertheless, religious officials in these predominantly Orthodox countries continued to rely on the Julian calendar to set the date of Easter.

Even today Orthodox Christians around the world maintain the ancient tradition of setting the date of Easter and its related festivals according to the Julian calendar, although many Orthodox Christians use the Gregorian calendar dates for other religious holidays. Orthodox Christians in Finland, who celebrate Easter according to the Gregorian calendar, provide the only exception to the rule. The Julian calendar currently trails thirteen days behind the Gregorian calendar. Thus, when the Julian calendar reaches March 21, the traditional date of the spring equinox, the Gregorian calendar counts the day as April 3. This means that Orthodox Easter tends to occur somewhat later in the spring than does Western Easter. Nevertheless, on occasion the

Western and Orthodox Easters coincide, uniting millions of Christians around the world in the common celebration of their most important holiday.

In Ethiopia the situation is even more complex. There a modified version of the Julian calendar still serves as the civil calendar used by all, as well as the religious calendar used by Ethiopian Orthodox Christians. This calendar is based on twelve months of thirty days each, as well as a thirteenth month of five or six days, depending on whether or not it is a leap year. In addition, the new year begins in September rather than January. Finally, the Ethiopian calendar lags about eight years behind both the standard Julian and Gregorian calendars. Long ago Roman Catholic and Ethiopian Orthodox religious officials disagreed over the date of the creation of the world. This difference in opinion is said to account for the fact that Ethiopia numbers the current year differently than does the rest of the world. For example, on January 1, 1999, calendars in Ethiopia read Tahisas (the fourth month) 23, 1991.

Proposals for a Unified Easter

In recent years some church leaders have advocated reuniting Christian Easter celebrations. The World Council of Churches has proposed the following three principles for fixing the date of Easter, which they hope will eventually be adopted by all Christians. First, Christians will maintain the rule set by the Council of Nicaea that Easter falls on the Sunday after the full moon occurring on or after the spring equinox. Second, they will set the date of the equinox with the use of modern astronomical and scientific measures. Third, they will base all reckoning that varies due to one's location on the earth on the meridian of Jerusalem, the city where Jesus' crucifixion and resurrection took place.

Further Reading

Achelis, Elisabeth. *The Calendar for Everybody*. 1943. Reprint. Detroit, MI: Omnigraphics, 1990.
Aveni, Anthony. *Empires of Time*. New York: Kodansha Books, 1995.

Bellenir, Karen. *Religious Holidays and Calendars*. Second edition. Detroit, MI: Omnigraphics, 1998.

Blackburn, Bonnie, and Leofranc Holford-Strevens. *The Oxford Companion to the Year*. Oxford, England: Oxford University Press, 1999.

Bradshaw, Paul F. *The Search for the Origins of Christian Worship*. New York: Oxford University Press, 1992.

Bradshaw, Paul F. "The Origins of Easter." In Paul F. Bradshaw and Lawrence A. Hoffman, eds. *Passover and Easter: Origin and History to Modern Times*. Two Liturgical Traditions series, volume 5. Notre Dame, IN: University of Notre Dame Press, 1999.

Duncan, David Ewing. *Calendar*. New York: Avon, 1998.

Eisenberg, Azriel. *The Story of the Jewish Calendar*. New York: Abelard-Schuman, 1958.

Talley, Thomas J. *The Origins of the Liturgical Year*. Collegeville, MN: Liturgical Press, 1986.

Web Sites

A summary of the events leading up to and including the Synod of Whitby, by Louise Elaine Burton, posted on *Christianity Today*'s web site: http://www.christianitytoday.com/ch/60h/60h038.html

"The Western and Ethiopian Calendars," an article by Y. M. W. Kirios published in the *Ethiopian Review* 6,1 (1996). Available online for a fee through Northern Light at: www.northernlight.com/ Document ID: GG1998042906 0015294

"The Calendar of the Orthodox Church," an article by Lewis Patsavos, Ph.D., posted on the Greek Orthodox Archdiocese of America in New York, NY, web site at: http://www.goarch.org/access/Companion_to_Orthodox_Church/calendar.html

Easter, Origin of the Word

Many European languages derive their word for Easter from *Pascha*, the ancient Greek term for the festival used by the early Christians. The word Pascha in turn came from *Pesach*, the Hebrew word for **Passover**. By contrast, English speakers call the festival "Easter," a word totally unrelated to the early Christian term for the observance. Where did this word come from?

Eostre and Other Explanations

Most writers assert that it came from the name of an Anglo-Saxon goddess, Eostre. They base this assertion on the writings of a scholarly monk known as St. Bede (672 or 673–735). Bede proposed that the Anglo-Saxons, the ancestors of the English people, named the month of April after a pagan goddess. According to Bede they called it *Eøsturmonath*, after the goddess Eostre, also spelled "Eastre." Bede explained that since the Easter festival fell in the month of the goddess, the people called the festival by the same name. What's more, the Anglo-Saxons also used the word *eastre* for the season of spring. English speakers eventually changed the word to "Easter," which came to refer solely to the holiday commemorating the **resurrection** of **Jesus** Christ.

German and English appear to share the same ancient root word for Easter. Modern German speakers call the festival *Ostern*. In the eighth and ninth centuries German speakers used a similar but longer word, *Ostarstruopha*, for the Easter festival.

While most writers support Bede's theory about the origins of the word Easter, a few researchers question his ideas. They point out that scholars have not found any other mention of Eostre in ancient or medieval documents. They believe that this lack of corroborating evidence may mean that Bede, who was raised and educated in a monastery and therefore may not have been conversant with folklore and pagan religious beliefs, was presenting his readers with an educated guess rather than solid facts. They offer several other theories to explain the origin of the word Easter. One proposal suggests that the word Easter comes from *Eostur*, an old Norse word for spring. Another asserts that it comes from an old Germanic and Anglo-Saxon word for "east." Early Germanic languages offered many variants of the word for east which appear to be related to the Anglo-Saxon term for east. These include *ôstana*, *ôsten*, and *austen*. Some researchers argue that the English term "Easter" has its roots in these old words.

Finally, other writers contend that the word Easter arrived in the English language via a mistaken interpretation of a Latin phrase. Early Latin-speaking Christians called the Easter festival *hebdomada alba*, or "the week of albs," a name that refers to the white robes worn by baptismal candidates during the **Easter Vigil** and the **eight** days following (*see also* **Baptism**; **Easter Week**; **Low Sunday**). Although in this context the word *alba* serves as the feminine form of *albus*, meaning white, some thought it was the word *alba* meaning "dawn." According to this theory, Old High German speakers called the festival *eostarun*, or "dawn" in their own language. The word *eostarun* evolved into the contemporary German *Ostern* and the English "Easter."

Some early scholars delved even further back into the history of the word Easter. For example, nineteenth-century folklorists discovered striking similarities between the Germanic root words for "dawn" and the name of the goddess Eostre. They noted, too, that the names for the ancient Roman, Greek, and Indian dawn goddesses, Aurora, Eos, and Ushas, evolved from the same root word. On the basis of these similarities nineteenth-century German folklorist Jacob Grimm, who accepted Bede's account of the word "Easter," declared that the goddess Eostre must represent the dawn. These linguistic similarities led Grimm further to claim that Bede's Anglo-Saxon goddess must also have been known to the Germanic peoples. He therefore assigned her a German name, Ostara. Grimm's interpretation stuck and many contemporary sources refer confidently to Eostre/Ostara as a dawn goddess in spite of the fact that Bede neither identified what she represented nor gave her a German name.

Early Christian and Biblical Connections

These associations with the names of pagan goddesses and natural phenomena make some Christians uncomfortable with the word Easter. Nevertheless, both the dawn and the direction east figure into the Easter story as recounted in the Bible and reflected in the devotional practices of the early church. For example, according to the Bible, **Mary Magdalene** and several other followers of Jesus, discovered his empty tomb at dawn on **Easter Sunday**. Many Protestant churches commemorate this dawn discovery by holding **sunrise services** on Easter morning.

The mystical significance accorded to the direction east by the early Christians also connects it to the Easter festival. The Resurrection occurred, or was discovered, at dawn, a time of day associated with the east. The early Christians believed east to be the direction of paradise. They also expected Jesus to return to them, an event described in the Bible's Book of Revelation and known as the Second Coming, from the east. Medieval Christians thought that the Second Coming would occur on the night before Easter, a belief that may have motivated participation in lengthy Easter Vigil services.

The early Christians incorporated the notion that east is the direction of the divine into their liturgy and architecture. In the ritual of baptism, newcomers to the Christian religion faced west to renounce the devil and east to declare their belief in God, Jesus, and the Holy Spirit. Early churches were built with doors along the western wall and the altars near the eastern wall so that worshipers faced east as they prayed.

Christians inherited this association between God and the east from their Jewish predecessors. Both Solomon's Temple and the Israelite tabernacle faced east. Hebrew scripture, which Christians call the Old Testament, furnishes many stories in which God sends blessings and relief from the east. Some scholars have suggested that in drawing an association between God and the east the ancient Hebrews echoed the spatial orientation of the sun-worshiping cultures that surrounded them. These people assumed that the home of the sun god lay in the east, in the direction of the dawn.

Scholars have also detected a biblical tendency to assign positive meaning to movement from east to west, the direction in which the sun itself appears to move. In the Old Testament in particular, people and groups who move towards the east, or against the direction of the sun, are out of alignment with God's purposes (*see also* **Sin**). For example, when Adam and Eve leave the Garden of Eden they journey to the East (Genesis 3:24). Conversely, characters who move towards the west, following the movement of the sun, have aligned themselves with God. In that portion of Christian scripture called the New Testament, the Magi, or Wise Men, associated with the story of Jesus' birth exemplify this principle (Matthew 2:1-2). They come from the East, the divine direction, and journey towards the west to find the Christ child. Similarly Jesus' star, which guides the Magi to his birthplace, rises in the east.

Conclusion

St. Bede's explanation of the word "Easter" remains the most widely recounted version of the word's origin. He asserts that the English word for this Christian festival came from the name of a pagan goddess. Some researchers believe, however, that the word is more likely to have evolved from ancient root words meaning dawn, east, or springtime. Most of these themes also play a role in the Easter story as recounted in the Bible. These concepts also find expression in the customs of the early Christians.

Further Reading

Baldovin, John F. "Easter." In Mircea Eliade, ed. *The Encyclopedia of Religion*. Volume 4. New York: Macmillan, 1987.

Billson, Chas. J. "The Easter Hare." *Folk-Lore* 3, 4 (1892): 441-66.

"East." In Leland Ryken, James C. Wilhoit, and Tremper Longman III, eds. *Dictionary of Biblical Imagery*. Downers Grove, IL: InterVarsity Press, 1998.

Hutton, Ronald. *Stations of the Sun*. Oxford, England: Oxford University Press, 1996.

Johnson, E. "Easter and Its Cycle." In *New Catholic Encyclopedia*. Volume 5. New York: McGraw-Hill, 1967.

Kselman, John S. "Easter." In Paul J. Achtemeier, ed. *The HarperCollins Bible Dictionary*. New York: HarperCollins, 1996.

Skeat, W. W. *An Etymological Dictionary of the English Language*. Fourth edition, revised, enlarged, and reset. Oxford, England: Clarendon Press, 1958.

Weiser, Francis X. *The Easter Book*. New York: Harcourt, Brace and Company, 1954.

Easter Bunny

Oschter Haws, Oster Haas

Every Easter millions of children look forward to the nighttime visit of a timid yet powerfully magical **rabbit** who scatters pretty colored eggs and baskets of Easter candy in homes and gardens across the United States. How did this delightful creature, known as the Easter Bunny, come to be associated with the holiday? Folklorists cannot give a precise answer to this question. Instead they point to a large and ancient body of European folklore in which the **hare** serves as a symbol of fertility, sexuality, springtime, the **moon**, and immortality. The people of central Europe somehow distilled the legend of the egg-laying Easter Hare from these strands of folk belief. German immigrants brought the notion of the Easter Hare to the United States. Americans adopted this long-eared legend into their own Easter celebrations in the late nineteenth century, changing its name into the Easter Rabbit or Easter Bunny.

German Origins

The earliest known reference to the Easter Hare in any known historical document comes from a German book printed in the year 1572. The author writes, "Do not worry if the bunny escapes you; should we miss his eggs, then we shall cook the nest" (Weiser, 189). A seventeenth-century German book describes the Easter Hare more thoroughly, portraying him as a shy creature that lays eggs in secluded spots in the garden (*see also* **Easter Eggs**). The German Easter Hare may date back even further than the seventeenth century, however, since the author of this book describes him as "an old fable" (Weiser, 189). Since at least the early nineteenth century German children have enjoyed special hare-shaped sweets at Easter time made out of pastry and sugar.

A German folk belief expands on the legend of the egg-bearing hare. It asserts that on **Maundy Thursday** the Easter Hare lays only red eggs. On the night before Easter the Hare lays eggs of various colors. Since real hares are mammals, however, they do not lay eggs, but rather bear live young. Nevertheless, eggs are an old Easter symbol (*see also* **Egg Lore**). Imagining an egg-laying Easter hare helps both to signal the magical qualities of this mythical creature and to link him firmly to the Easter holiday.

The Easter Hare Becomes the Easter Bunny

German immigrants brought legends and customs concerning the Easter Hare with them to the United States in the eighteenth century. In the nineteenth century, strengthened by new waves of German immigration, these legends and customs began to seep out into the wider American population. By the 1890s fashionable sweet shops in the big cities of the eastern United States featured Easter candy in the shape of rabbits. Since Americans in general tend to lump hares and rabbits together, Americans soon converted the German "Easter Hare" into the Easter Rabbit, and then the Easter Bunny.

Other changes accompanied this process of Americanization. These changes can best be seen by comparing the details of the Easter Rabbit's visit to children in the Pennsylvania Dutch country with the customs observed throughout the rest of the country. Pennsylvania Dutch country lies in the state of Pennsylvania, where many German immigrants settled and where their descendants have preserved many of the German folk beliefs and customs of their ancestors. In the Pennsylvania Dutch dialect of German, the Easter Hare is known as the *Oschter Haws.*

Among the Pennsylvania Dutch, the Easter Rabbit doesn't bring Easter eggs, but rather lays them. To facilitate this process children are encouraged to build nests for the hare's visit on Easter eve. Old customs encouraged children to use caps or hats for this purpose. Many children find a nice, secluded place for this nest outdoors, knowing that the bunny is somewhat shy of being seen. Others tuck the nest away in some nook or cranny of the house. Sometimes the bunny will dare to visit a nest left at a child's own spot at the table. Well-behaved children wake up on Easter morning to find the nest full of colored Easter eggs. Less obedient children might find an empty nest, or one filled with coal, rabbit droppings, or other disagreeable substances. Special **breads**, cakes, and candies shaped like rabbits also help to celebrate the visit of the magical hare. Pennsylvania Dutch bakers often place an egg underneath the rabbit's tail, symbolizing this magical creature's ability to lay eggs.

By contrast the American Easter Bunny brings eggs rather than lays them. Most American children are not taught to build nests for the Bunny. They are instead given the delightful task of searching for the eggs which the Bunny has scattered randomly throughout the house and garden. The Easter Bunny also drops off beautiful baskets filled with candy on his nighttime visits to American families. Mainstream American culture has dropped the notion that these baskets may contain unpleasant surprises for poorly behaved children. One American custom would seem to imply that the Germanic Easter Hare is a wilder and more independent animal than the American Easter Bunny. Unlike the Pennsylvania Dutch, who assume that the Hare can fend for itself, some American families encourage children to leave a suitable snack, such as carrots, for the Easter Bunny.

In an attempt to understand the role of the Easter Bunny in American culture, an American researcher, Cindy Dell Clark, has gone so far as to interview children regarding their belief in this flop-eared fable. She found out that American children perceive the Easter Bunny to have supernatural qualities, including immortality, eternal youth, the ability to understand all things, and the ability to disappear or to move so rapidly as to avoid detection. Clark concluded that children rather than adults keep the customs surrounding the Easter Bunny alive in this culture, and often take the initiative in making sure that these rites are observed in their families.

The Easter Hare in Europe

Legends and customs concerning the Easter Hare occur throughout central Europe. In Austria children search their gardens on Easter morning to find special nests harboring clutches of eggs, pastry, and candy deposited there by the Easter Hare. Danish children find similar nests on Easter morning, containing dyed eggs, chocolate eggs, and frosting roses. Toddlers in Luxembourg also enjoy an Easter morning egg hunt outdoors. They hope to catch a glimpse of the elusive Easter Hare who has left behind colored eggs, sugar eggs, and chocolate eggs. Swiss children find a similar bounty in their gardens. In addition, they receive chocolate and marzipan treats shaped like the Easter Hare.

In Germany, where the legend of the Easter Hare may very well have originated, children prepare nests for the visiting gift bringer, known as the *Oster Haas*. On Easter morning they find these nests full of colored eggs and candy. A German poem, translated into English for a book published in 1895, reveals that the legend of the Easter Hare has not changed too much over the last hundred years:

> What is that in the grass out there?
> Look, oh look, a hare, a hare!
> Peeping out, the long-eared puss,
> From his cozy nest at us.
> There he goes, away, away,
> Over earth and stones and clay.
> Quick, you children, come and see
> This glorious nest for you and me.
> The prettiest thing you ever saw,
> Grass and hay and moss and straw.
> Look inside, what have we found?
> Coloured eggs, so smooth and round.
> See them lie each by his fellow,
> Blue and green and red and yellow.
> Little hare in yonder wood,
> Thank you, thank you, kind and good (Lord and Foley, 106).

In addition to the legends and customs concerning Easter Hares that lay eggs and deliver candy, folklorists have recorded several European customs concerning the eating of hares at Easter time. In the region of Germany known as Pomerania, old traditions suggested that people hunt hares at Easter time, and make a communal meal out of their flesh.

The people of Leicester, England, once practiced a custom known as "Hunting the Easter Hare" on **Easter Monday**. In fact, rather than hunt an actual hare, the local people used a dead cat to entice the hounds to give chase. The hunt ended at the mayor's door, whereupon the populace presented the mock hare to him. This custom disappeared in the eighteenth century, however.

Another local English custom, the "Hallaton Hare-pie Scramble" continues till this day. This custom started at an unknown date in the past, when the local parish was granted a piece of land. The conditions placed on this grant maintained that each year on Easter Monday the rector must offer two hare pies, two dozen loaves of bread, and a quantity of ale to the people of the town. The pies were to be tossed to the assembled crowd and "scrambled for," much in the same way women and girls jostle one another to catch the bride's bouquet at a wedding. Today the people of Hallaton assemble in the parish rectory to partake of the feast beforehand. The remaining pieces of pie are then taken to "Hare-pie Bank," the traditional location for the scramble, and flung to whatever folk have gathered there.

The Easter Bunny in Europe

After the Easter Bunny achieved widespread popularity in the United States, the legends and customs associated with it began to travel back to Europe, establishing footholds in countries which had not recognized the original Germanic Easter Hare. For example, English children are now familiar with this four-footed Easter gift bringer and some may hope to receive treats from this new source of Easter bounty.

Further Reading

Billson, Chas. J. "The Easter Hare." *Folk-Lore* 3, 4 (1892): 441-66.

Clark, Cindy Dell. *Flights of Fancy, Leaps of Faith*. Chicago: University of Chicago Press, 1995.

Hole, Christina. *English Custom and Usage*. 1941-2. Reprint. Detroit, MI: Omnigraphics, 1990.

Hutton, Ronald. *Stations of the Sun*. Oxford, England: Oxford University Press, 1996.

Layard, John. *The Lady of the Hare*. 1944. Reprint. New York: AMS Press, 1977.

Lord, Priscilla Sawyer, and Daniel J. Foley. *Easter the World Over*. Philadelphia, PA: Chilton Book Company, 1971.

Schmidt, Leigh Eric. *Consumer Rites*. Princeton, NJ: Princeton University Press, 1995.

Shoemaker, Alfred L. *Eastertide in Pennsylvania*. Kutztown, PA: Pennsylvania Folklife Society, 1960.

Weiser, Francis X. *The Easter Book*. New York: Harcourt, Brace and Company, 1954.

Easter Cards

During the early part of the nineteenth century Easter was not widely celebrated in the United States. Many Protestants still harbored a deep suspicion of Christian holidays that dated back to the Reformation, the sixteenth-century religious reform movement that gave birth to Protestant Christianity. In general Roman Catholics, Episcopalians, Lutherans, and Moravians endorsed the holiday, while low-church Protestants — such as Methodists, Baptists, Congregationalists, and Quakers — tended to reject it. This state of affairs changed after the Civil War (1861-65), as many Protestant denominations previously hostile or indifferent to Easter warmed up to the holiday. The great surge in Easter merchandising that took place during the 1870s and 1880s helped to solidify this change. Many secular elements of American Easter celebrations, such as the **Easter parade**, the **Easter Bunny**, and Easter cards came to prominence during this era.

Easter cards became an established element of American Easter celebrations in the 1880s. Their production may have been inspired in part by the success that American card manufacturers enjoyed in the 1870s with Christmas cards. Flowers served as the most common decorative image on these early Easter cards. Religious sentiments and short quotations from Christian scripture also made frequent appearances. Oftentimes the cards blended religious motifs, such as angels and the **cross**, with folkloric emblems like frolicking children, eggs, and **hares** (*see also* **Easter Eggs**; **Egg Lore**).

Although today many people enjoy sending Easter cards, they have not achieved the same widespread popularity as Christmas cards. According to the Greeting Card Association in Washington, D.C., Christmas remains the single most popular holiday on which to send greeting cards. Christmas cards account for one quarter of all seasonal greeting cards sold in the United States. Other holidays on which

Americans exchange large numbers of greeting cards include, in order of popularity, Valentine's Day, Mother's Day, Easter, and Father's Day.

Further Reading

Gulevich, Tanya. *Encyclopedia of Christmas*. Detroit, MI: Omnigraphics, 2000.

Schmidt, Leigh Eric. *Consumer Rites*. Princeton, NJ: Princeton University Press, 1995.

Web Site

The Greeting Card Association, an organization composed of greeting card publishers and other industry members, offers a page of facts and figures concerning greeting card sales at: http://www.greetingcard.org

Easter Eggs
Pisanki, Pysanky

No one is sure exactly when the exchange of dyed eggs became part of the Easter festival. Nevertheless, folklorists believe they know why colored eggs became a symbol of the holiday. The egg has long served humanity as an emblem of new life (*see also* **Egg Lore**). All around the world Christians eat eggs at Easter. They also decorate them, using a variety of methods to dye them a single color or to cover them with elaborate designs. In some cultures these decorated Easter eggs are exchanged as gifts. In others people hang them on Easter **egg trees**. In still others they become part of Easter egg hunts and various other egg games, including **egg rolling, egg tapping,** and **pace egging** (*for more on Easter egg hunts, see* **Easter Bunny**).

Eggs as Currency

In late medieval Europe people paid their clergymen and made donations to their local church in the form of eggs. These "egg tithes" came due at Easter time. They might also pay their landlord in eggs. These customs can be traced back at least as far as the late thirteenth century in England. They also existed in the Netherlands, Estonia, and Germany during this era. Germans dubbed this unpopular levy of precious springtime eggs the *Osterrecht*, or "Easter Right."

In some countries people made these offerings on **Good Friday**, during the ceremony known as the **Veneration of the Cross**. As they approached the **cross** they left baskets of eggs, sometimes accompanied by other foodstuffs, such as bacon or grain. Documents reveal that this custom was practiced in England and Italy. It began to die out in the sixteenth century. Folklorists believe that traces of this old practice lingered for centuries in the common folk custom of making the local priest a small gift of eggs at Easter time. Researchers recorded evidence that this custom was still being practiced in parts of France, Hungary, and Italy well into the twentieth century. In some places families sent children to church with great baskets of Easter eggs. The priest blessed the eggs and the children gave some of them to him in return. Afterwards the children brought the eggs home and the family placed them on a beautifully decorated table, along with other elements of the Easter feast.

Easter Eggs as Gifts

The earliest historical records concerning decorated Easter eggs indicate that they were given as gifts. In 1290 King Edward I of England had his servants prepare 450 Easter eggs by boiling them and covering them with gold leaf. He presented them to members of his household on **Easter Sunday**. Historical documents reveal that Easter eggs were also known in Poland and Germany at this time. People gave Easter eggs as gifts in Tsarist Russia as well. The tsar and members of the nobility exchanged them at Easter time. In the late nineteenth century Tsar Alexander III commissioned famous jewelry designer Karl Fabergé to make an Easter egg-shaped trinket for his wife, which he presented to her on Easter morning. The gift so delighted the Tsarina that the Tsar decided to give her a new jeweled egg every year. Alexander III's son, Tsar Nicholas II, carried on this tradition. These eggs not only feature rare jewels and precious metals, but also exquisite craftsmanship. For example, Fabergé designed an egg for the Tsar measuring five inches in height which he covered with translucent lime-green enamel and a gold trellis of laurel leaves. At each intersection of the trellis he placed a doubleheaded eagle of black enamel with a rose diamond stud in its belly. The egg could be separated into two halves and indeed was made to house a miniature coach made from gold, a replica of the one that Tsar Nicholas II and his wife Alexandra rode in for their coronation. Eggs made by Fabergé have become valuable collectors' items.

Today people still enjoy giving and receiving decorated eggs at Easter time. In the United States, children participate in Easter egg hunts on Easter morning, searching for dyed eggs thoughtfully prepared for them by others, but often said to come from the Easter Bunny. This custom is also practiced in much of western Europe. In Germany, Switzerland, Hungary, Poland, Slovenia, Latvia, Lithuania, Portugal, Belgium, and the Czech Republic young women traditionally gave gifts of decorated Easter eggs to suitors or potential suitors. Ukrainians give Easter eggs to express their fondness for someone. In many European countries, families keep a bowl of dyed eggs on the table during **Easter Week**. Anyone who visits them during this time is presented with an Easter egg. In Poland, Russia and the Ukraine, families took their Easter feast, including their Easter eggs, to church on **Holy Saturday**, where the priest blessed the food. In return, each family gave him an Easter egg. On Easter Sunday the head of the family peeled one blessed egg for every member of the family. Then everyone ate the eggs, wishing each other long life and happiness. On Easter Sunday and the days following, an old Russian folk tradition encouraged people to greet one another with the gift of an Easter egg and the greeting, "Christ is risen!"

Dyes, Designs, and Techniques

Before the advent of modern dyes, people colored their Easter eggs with a variety of naturally occurring substances. Boiling eggs with onion skins, a common method of coloring eggs in many parts of Europe, turned out a golden, deep orange or reddish brown egg. Bulgarians, Ukrainians, Greeks, Russians, Slovenians, Serbians, Czechs, and Yugo-

slavians used a dye made from Brazil wood to impart a bright red color to their Easter eggs. Cochineal, a dye made from the bodies of female scale insects, was also used in some places. Inventive women in many lands found ways of transferring the color of local vegetables, flowers, moss, and leaves onto eggs.

While North Americans often dye their Easter eggs a single color, many central and eastern Europeans etch elaborate designs on their Easter eggs. Often these elaborate eggs are saved for display and other, plainer eggs are eaten. Over the years certain designs emerged as traditional favorites for the folk artists of various nationalities. In crafting their fancy display eggs Romanians favor flowers, the symbols of the evangelists, and even a serpent, as a reminder of the Garden of Eden. Russians and Armenians often paint icons of Christ or the saints on their eggs. An old Croatian design contrasts a crown of thorns with a garland of flowers. Other traditional Croatian designs include pine needles, ladders, wheat stalks, and roosters. Hungarian eggs often feature stylized flowers. Rakes and combs may appear on Czech, Slovak, Hungarian, Ukrainian, Hutzul, and Romanian eggs. Radiating spokes, which may be said to represent the sun, a star, or a daisy-like flower grace many eggs from Lithuania, the Czech Republic, the Ukraine, Poland, and other eastern European countries. Trees, crosses, and abstract geometric designs also appear on many eggs from Slavic lands.

In some parts of central and eastern Europe, folk artists preferred the scratch technique to create Easter designs. This technique produces eggs with a white design etched into a colored background. Folk artists working with the scratch technique first dye the eggs, then create white designs by scraping away a thin layer of eggshell. The scratch technique is popular in the Slavic countries, as well as Poland, Lithuania, Latvia, Slovenia, Slovakia, the Czech Republic, and parts of Germany.

In certain parts of Europe folk artists prefer the appliqué method, which involves attaching various material to the egg to create a design. Traditional egg designs in Portugal called for applying sea shells to eggs. In Austria people garnished their eggs with strips of dough, in Serbia metal coils, and in Poland paper cuts. In the early twentieth century Moravian and Bulgarian metalsmiths developed a technique that permitted them to attach metal ornaments to Easter eggs without breaking them. In parts of Poland and Germany, folk artists once decorated eggs with the pith of the rush plant and bits of wool or cloth. This method traveled to the United States with German immigrants and established itself in Pennsylvania Dutch country.

Many of the complicated designs found on eastern European eggs result from the careful application of a dye technique known as batik or wax-resist. This painstaking technique produces complicated, multi-colored designs.

Pysanky

Many experts and collectors believe that the most exquisitely designed and executed batik eggs come from Ukrainian and Polish folk artists. These artists create astonishingly intricate designs in bold colors such as red, yellow, black, and green. They call their creations *pisanki* or *pysanky*. This word comes from the Polish verb *pisac* or the Ukrainian verb *pysaty*, both of which mean "to write."

Traditional pysanky artists began by preparing their dyes. They made green dye from moss, a deep yellow-orange dye from crocus flowers, and black from alder bark and cones. Nowadays, however, most artisans use chemical dyes. They start by applying part of the design to the egg with hot wax funneled through the tip of a tiny metal tube, or dripped from the end of a needle. These miniature instruments permit them to inscribe delicate wax lines and shapes onto the surface of the egg. When they immerse the egg in the first dye bath, those areas covered with wax will not absorb the dye and so will remain white. After removing the egg from the first dye bath and letting it dry, the artist applies a second layer of design with wax. This second coating of wax preserves that part of the design which the artist wishes to remain the color of the first dye bath. Then the egg goes into its second vat of dye. The egg may be waxed and dyed a number of times, in order to build a multi-colored design. When the design is complete the artist holds the egg next to a candle flame in order to melt the wax. Then varnish is applied to protect the egg. The next day the artist completes the egg by piercing it on both ends and gently blowing out the white and yolk.

Ukrainian folklorists believe that pysanky date back to ancient times. Some of the symbols commonly painted on these eggs reflect this pre-Christian heritage. The most popular of these motifs is a stylized sun, often represented as a broken cross, triangle, **eight**-pointed star, or rosette. Other popular emblems include flowers, leaves, endless lines, birds, stags, and horses. Ukrainian folk artists also paint specifically Christian symbols on pysanky. These include crosses, fish, and churches. The colors used to paint these designs also have meaning. Red represents life, joy, and the sun. Yellow symbolizes fertility and wealth. Green stands for growing plants and the season of spring.

Polish folk custom calls for giving pysanky as gifts, especially to one's godparents and friends. Recipients treasure these gifts, both as symbols of their ethnic heritage and as beautiful pieces of art. In past times, however, people valued pysanky for practical as well as artistic reasons. Polish folklore asserted that pysanky planted in the vineyard could shelter the vines from storms, hail, and wind. Both Polish and Ukrainian folklore suggested that the decorated eggs could protect the home against evil forces and attract good luck. Ukrainian folklore added that in order to have these good effects, the artist making the pysanky must begin with prayer, and avoid arguments and ill will throughout the decorating process.

Green Eggs

In Germany and Austria people dye eggs green on **Maundy Thursday**. This custom springs from the folk name for the day in German-speaking countries, "Green Thursday." Researchers have come up with several explanations for this name. One theory traces it back to the reconciliation of penitents that used to take place on this day (*for more on the concept of penitence, see* **Repentance**). The penitents carried green branches as a sign of their joy. Indeed, *Dies viridium,* an old Latin name for the day which means "Day of the Green Ones," came from this custom. The green eggs match the green foods that are traditionally eaten on this day.

Red Eggs

Although red is not a popular color for Easter eggs in this country, many Europeans favor red eggs. This preference might come, in part, from old folk beliefs connecting the color red with magic, love, blessing, and renewal. In many places, however, especially those regions in which Orthodox Christianity has taken hold, red eggs represent the

blood of Christ. Indeed Orthodox Christians prefer red Easter eggs for this reason. Not only do they eat them, but they also bake them into braided Easter **breads** and use them in games (*see also* Egg Tapping). Orthodoxy is one of the three main branches of the Christian faith. It developed in north Africa, the Middle East, and eastern Europe, and most of its adherents still hail from these parts of the world. Orthodoxy and Western Christianity—that is, Roman Catholicism and, later, Protestantism—split apart from each other about 1,000 years ago. This split has resulted in the emergence of different folk customs and traditions between the two groups of Christians.

Many Orthodox Christians consume a boiled egg before beginning the long **Lenten fast**. Before eating the egg they announce, "With an egg I close my mouth, with an egg I shall open it again." This phrase signifies that the fast has begun. It also makes mention of the custom of ending one's fast by eating an egg. Accordingly, red Easter eggs are often distributed to parishioners after the **Resurrection** service, ending in the early morning hours of Easter Sunday (*see also* **Easter Vigil**). In some places people bring red eggs from home and crack them at that point in the service when the priest announces the Resurrection. Baskets of red eggs may also be brought to the church service to insure that they absorb the Easter blessing. The red eggs serve as a symbol of the Resurrection. The red shell represents Jesus' blood, the egg itself stands for his tomb, and the cracking of the egg recalls Jesus' emergence from the tomb.

Many Greeks and other Orthodox Christians dye their Easter eggs on Maundy Thursday. In reference to this custom Greeks have nicknamed the day "Red Thursday." In some lands the first Easter egg to emerge from the dye was thought to be blessed, especially with the ability to confer health and well-being. Often families keep a red Easter egg in the *ikonostasi*, a shelf or niche where the family keeps devotional materials such as icons (religious images used in prayer and worship), incense, blessed **palms** from **Palm Sunday**, a Bible, and a cross. The Easter egg and other seasonal items, such as palm crosses, remain throughout the year, until they are disposed of on the following Maundy Thursday.

Easter Egg Charms and Superstitions

Over the centuries many superstitions developed concerning Easter eggs. Folklore from many regions of Europe taught that they had mysterious powers, often to bless or to make fruitful. Accordingly, Easter eggs, or their shells, became important components in various magical charms.

In past times many people believed that Easter eggs stayed fresh for an unusually long time. Bulgarian and Tryolese folklore asserted that they might last as long as a year. Greek folklore taught that they might last indefinitely, but that after a few years the egg inside the shell would change into a pearl. In France, eggs laid on Green Thursday might yield an even greater prize. French lore presumed that the yolk of a Green Thursday egg, if preserved for one hundred years, would change into a diamond. In Alsace-Lorrain eggs laid on Maundy Thursday and tucked into cupboards and drawers were thought to protect wool and linen from moths and decay.

In Germany people hung Easter eggs from the ceiling with ribbon. The eggs were thought to act as good luck charms. In Russia one might find them dangling in front of icons, and in Catholic countries sitting at the bases of crucifixes. French folklore added that Good Friday eggs have the power to extinguish any fire that they are tossed into.

According to certain folk beliefs, one had to consume the egg to obtain a blessing. In parts of France and Germany people thought that eating an egg laid on Green Thursday insured the blessing of good health. The Pennsylvania Dutch believed that Good Friday eggs had medicinal properties, especially if consumed on Good Friday or Easter Sunday.

In some parts of eastern Europe Easter eggs were thought to increase the crop yield and protect plants from harm. In these zones Easter eggs might be planted alongside seeds and vines. Some Germans put them inside the first sheaf of wheat along with a loaf of bread to insure a smooth and bountiful harvest. Another cluster of folk beliefs centered around the power of Easter eggs to increase productivity and fertility in animals. Ukrainian beekeepers set an Easter egg under each of their hives to insure a plentiful supply of honey. French farmers placed a blessed Green Thursday egg into a clutch of newly laid eggs to help them hatch. Even the Easter egg shells were thought powerful in some places. In Slovakia people hung them on fruit trees in the belief that they would help the tree to become more fruitful. They also buried them in their gardens to support plant growth and scattered them between the garden rows to repel caterpillars. In France Easter eggs, especially those laid on Maundy Thursday, were thought to promote human sexuality and fertility. The Germans held similar beliefs, but placed more faith in Good Friday or Easter Sunday eggs.

Easter Egg Legends

Over the years numerous legends have sprung up concerning the origins of Easter eggs. Many of these imaginative tales propose an ancient and a Christian origin for these Easter symbols. One Polish tale claims that the first decorated eggs were created by the Virgin Mary as toys for the baby Jesus (*see also* **Mary, Blessed Virgin**). Searching about for something to amuse her child, she dyed a batch of eggs in various colors and gave them to him to play with. Another Polish story credits **Mary Magdalene** with the invention of Easter eggs. It says that on the morning of the Resurrection she took a basket of boiled eggs, her food for the day, with her to Jesus' tomb. When she arrived and found the stone sealing the entry to the tomb rolled away, the eggs suddenly took on bright, beautiful hues.

A Ukrainian tale says that Simon of Cyrene, the man who carried Jesus' cross for a while (Luke 23:26), spread the custom of coloring eggs for Easter. According to the folktale Simon was an egg peddler. After his encounter with Jesus, Simon found that his eggs always took on bright, cheerful hues. Another Ukrainian tale states that when Jesus hung on the cross, each drop of his blood that hit the ground became a red egg. As Jesus' mother Mary wept at the foot of the cross, her tears splashed onto some of the eggs, leaving behind intricate designs. Yet another Ukrainian story suggests that one winter the weather was so harsh that birds plummeted from the sky, overcome by the cold. Some peasants felt pity for the birds and took them into their homes until spring came. The birds returned to their foster homes several days after their release, each one bearing a beautifully decorated egg as a token of their gratitude.

A Romanian legend tells how Christ himself invented red Easter eggs. It states that the Blessed Virgin Mary brought a basket of eggs to the site of the Crucifixion, hoping that by presenting the soldiers with a gift of eggs she could influence them to spare her son (*for more on crucifixion, see* Cross). The soldiers, unmoved by this gesture, continued to mock Jesus, offering him vinegar and nettles. As Mary began to cry, blood poured down from Jesus' wounds, splashing some of the eggs and covering others completely. Jesus then instructed Mary that, in memory of this moment, all Easter eggs must be dyed red in whole or in part. The Blessed Virgin carried out this command, presenting those she encountered with a red egg and the greeting, "Christ is risen!"

A well-known legend among Orthodox Christians tells that after Jesus' **ascension** Mary Magdalene traveled about spreading word of Jesus' resurrection. When she arrived in Rome she visited the emperor Tiberius in order to lodge a complaint against Pontius **Pilate** and to bear witness to the Resurrection. During her audience with the Emperor she picked up an egg from a nearby table in order to illustrate the concept of resurrection. Tiberius scoffed at her, however, declaring that a man once dead couldn't rise again to new life any more than the egg in her hand could turn red. At once the egg flushed a deep, blood red. In Orthodox religious art Mary Magdalene is sometimes portrayed holding a red egg. Greeks and other Orthodox Christians tell this tale to explain the origin of the red eggs featured in their Easter celebrations.

Further Reading

Hogan, Julie. *Treasury of Easter Celebrations*. Nashville, TN: Ideals Publications, 1999.

Hole, Christina. *British Folk Customs*. London, England: Hutchinson and Company, 1976.

Krysa, Czeslaw M. "How to 'Write' and [sic] Easter Egg. Pisanki Comes from the Polish Word 'Pisac,' Meaning 'to Write'." *Polish-American Journal* 86, 3 (March 1, 1997): 9. Available online at: http://www.polamjournal.com/Library/Holidays/Easter/easter.html

Lord, Priscilla Sawyer, and Daniel J. Foley. *Easter Garland*. 1963. Reprint. Detroit, MI: Omnigraphics, 1999.

Lord, Priscilla Sawyer, and Daniel J. Foley. *Easter the World Over*. Philadelphia, PA: Chilton Book Company, 1971.

Luciow, Johanna, Ann Kmit, and Loretta Luciow. *Eggs Beautiful: How to Make Ukrainian Easter Eggs*. Minneapolis, MN: Ukrainian Gift Shop, n.d.

Newall, Venetia. *An Egg at Easter*. Bloomington, IN: Indiana University Press, 1971.

Thompson, Sue Ellen. *Holiday Symbols*. Second edition. Detroit, MI: Omnigraphics, 2000.

Weiser, Francis X. *The Easter Book.* New York: Harcourt, Brace and Company, 1954.

Zenon, Elyjiw. "Ukrainian Pysanky: Easter Eggs as Talismans." *Ukrainian Weekly* 13, 16 (April 16, 1995): 11.

Web Site

"Pysanky—Easter Eggs," a page sponsored by the Ukrainian Museum, New York City, New York: http://www.ukrainianmuseum.org/pysanky.html

Easter Fires

The world's spiritual belief systems make frequent reference to fire. Fire and sun gods can be found in many religions and fire itself often plays an important role in both magical and religious rituals (*see also* **No Ruz**). Often fire is seen as a purifying force. A number of religions attribute special significance to freshly kindled fire. In the ancient world, various ethnic groups, including the ancient Hebrews, kept sacred, ceremonial fires burning constantly, and saw in fire a symbol of the divine. Many of these beliefs and practices find faint echo in past and present Easter fire customs (*see also* **Easter Sun; Sunrise Service**).

Fire and Light in the Bible

Both the Hebrew Bible, or Old Testament, and the Christian scriptures, or New Testament, describe God in terms of light. Unlike other ancient religious teachings, however, biblical spirituality clearly states that God is not the same thing as light or the sun. Rather, God created light and the sun. In fact, the creation of light was one of the first things that God did in shaping the world (Genesis 1:3-4). Although God is something other or greater than light, God's presence is often accompanied by light, such as occurred at Solomon's dedication of the Temple (2 Chronicles 5:13-14) and at the conversion of Paul (Acts 9:3). The Bible also speaks of the gifts of God, such as life, goodness, truth, and wisdom, in terms of light. The Psalmist declares that "the unfolding of [God's] word gives light; it imparts truth to the simple" (Psalm 119:130). Godly behavior is also associated with light. Christian scripture demands of its adherents that they "cast off the works of darkness and put on the armor of light" (Romans 13:12).

In biblical times, fire was the only source of light beside the sun. Thus it is not surprising that the Bible likens the appearance of God to fire. The Bible's Book of Genesis describes God as a smoking fire pot and a burning torch (Genesis 15:17). In the Book of Exodus God takes the

115

form of a burning bush (Exodus 3:2). When the ancient Israelites fled from slavery in Egypt, God appeared to them by night as a pillar of fire leading them on through the wilderness (Exodus 13:21).

Early Christian Easter Fires

The early Christians celebrated Easter in the middle of the night with a ceremony now called the **Easter Vigil**. Perhaps in part because of the darkness of the hour, they quickly made the lighting of numerous lamps and torches an important feature of the festival. This custom led some to call the ceremony "the great service of light" and the evening itself "the night of illumination" or "the night of radiant splendor." An early Christian writer recorded the fact that the emperor Constantine (d. 337) "transformed the night of the sacred vigil into the brilliance of day, by lighting throughout the whole city . . . pillars of wax, while burning lamps illuminated every house, so that this nocturnal celebration was rendered brighter than the brightest day" (Weiser, 134). St. Gregory of Nyssa (c. 335-394) described **Holy Saturday** evening as the "glowing night which links the splendor of burning lamps to the morning rays of the sun, thus producing continuous daylight without any darkness" (Weiser, 134). This seeming contradiction, daylight shining at night, echoed the seeming contradiction celebrated in the Easter festival, that is, life emerging from death.

More specifically, the bright light in the darkness served as a symbol of Christ. This interpretation fits with Christian scripture, which describes **Jesus** as "the light of the world" (John 8:12). Another important passage that describes Christ in terms of light declares that "the light shines in the darkness and the darkness has not overcome it" (John 1:5). Indeed, in Orthodox churches this particular passage (John 1:1-17) is read out loud in several different languages, including Hebrew and Greek, at the **Resurrection** service held late at night on Holy Saturday.

The Paschal Candle

In Jerusalem the lighting of the lamps for the Easter feast had taken on a special, ceremonial quality by the end of the fourth century. This early, ceremonial lamp lighting gave birth to an Easter Vigil custom that survives today: the lighting of the **paschal candle** with newly kindled fire. The paschal candle is a very large candle used to shed light on the Bible passages read out loud during the Easter Vigil service. In explaining the origins of the paschal candle some researchers point to an ancient Christian service called the *Lucernarium,* a ceremonial lighting of the lamps in preparation for the evening prayer service. As time passed the Lucernarium became a service in its own right which included chanting, prayer, and psalms. Scholars believe that the early Christians based the Lucernarium on Jewish lamp-lighting rituals that preceded evening prayer. In time, however, the Christian observance disappeared. Some commentators think the ceremony that surrounds the lighting of the paschal candle on Easter eve is all that remains of this ancient observance.

Use of the paschal candle spread across western Europe during the Middle Ages. So too, however, did the tendency to schedule the Easter Vigil service at increasingly early hours. As the service crept towards the afternoon, then towards midday, and, by the late sixteenth century, into the morning hours, the earlier, lavish use of fire and light as a symbol of Christ lost its impact. In 1955, after a trial period of several years, Roman Catholic authorities ordered the restoration of the Easter Vigil service to Holy Saturday evening, renewing the power of these ancient symbols.

The kindling of new fire is an important part of the ceremony surrounding the paschal candle. The exact origins of the new fire ceremony are uncertain. Some writers believe, however, that Christians may have borrowed the ceremonial use of new fire from pagan sources. The kindling of fresh flame was an important aspect of the religious rites of the Romans, Greeks, Celts and other ancient peoples (*see also* **Beltane**).

Other Candle Ceremonies

The Orthodox Christians of eastern Europe, north Africa, and the Middle East did not adopt the paschal candle. Orthodoxy is one of the three main branches of the Christian faith. Orthodox Christianity split from Western Christianity, that is, Roman Catholicism and later Protestantism, about 1,000 years ago. Thus Orthodox traditions differ in some ways from those of Western Christians (*see also* **Easter, Date of**).

Instead of a single paschal candle, Orthodox Christians developed a candle-lighting ceremony in which worshipers carry their own individual candles. Clergy members begin the ceremony by lighting several parishioners' candles, after which worshipers pass the flame to one another until everyone's candle is lit. This ritual can be traced back to early fifth-century Jerusalem. By the tenth century Christians in Jerusalem had adopted a holy fire ceremony involving the kindling of new fire, which was then passed among the congregation. Records from that era describe the ritual that took place in Jerusalem's Church of the Holy Sepulchre, built over the supposed site of Jesus' crucifixion and burial (*for more on crucifixion, see* **Cross**). According to these records priests entered into the chamber over Jesus' tomb to kindle the new flame. Since the congregation could not see what was happening, many rumors spread about the source of this flame. Some said that the priests received the holy fire from angels who brought it down from heaven, while others whispered that the flame issued directly from the holy tomb. All over the city of Jerusalem Christians extinguished lamps and hearth fires on Holy Saturday in anticipation of relighting them with the blessed, holy fire. Those who attended the service transported the flames they received at church home to family, friends, and neighbors. Rumors concerning the heavenly origins of the Church of the Holy Sepulchre's holy fire survived into the twentieth century.

The Church of the Holy Sepulchre's holy fire ceremony still holds special significance for Orthodox Christians. In the early part of the twentieth century, Orthodox Christians from Palestinian towns and villages, and even from as far away as Russia, attended the ceremony in order to bring the flame that they received in the Church of the Holy Sepulchre back to their own countries, villages, and churches. Often they transferred the flame to a lantern so that it would be sure to survive the long journey home. Palestinian Christians carried the flame home to their village in triumph. The flame bearer, raised onto the shoulders of others so that the light would enter the town in honor, was carried first to the church. Then he visited homes, offering the holy fire to local Christian families. Today Orthodox Christians who attend this ceremony often save the candle with which they received the flames kindled in the holy fire ceremony, preserving it as a special devotional object. As attendance at this service may fulfill a lifelong religious goal, some attendees have a special tattoo inscribed on their right inner wrist, usually consisting of the date of the pilgrimage and a cross.

Roman Catholics as well as certain Protestants also observe an Easter Vigil ceremony whereby every member of the congregation lights a candle from the newly kindled flame. Roman Catholics, however, adopted this ceremony in the 1950s. The Roman Catholic ceremony involves the use of the paschal candle, which is lit first and then provides the flame with which to light the other candles.

Pre-Christian May Fires in Europe

Some writers believe that the Christian new fire ceremony, the lighting of the paschal candles, and related Easter fire folk customs have their roots in pagan as well as Christian beliefs. In northwestern Europe, pre-Christian religious rituals encouraged the lighting of ceremonial fires around Easter time. Some researchers believe that people in this region of Europe observed a festival on the first of May, known as Beltane in the British Isles, that celebrated the opening of the summer pasture lands to grazing animals (*see also* **May Day**). In observance of this festival they built a pair of bonfires and drove their cattle between them, in a ritual which they believed would purify the cattle and protect them from harmful forces. Traces of this seasonal observance have been found in English, Irish, Welsh, Scottish, Danish, Swedish, Norwegian, German, and Austrian folklore and customs. In Germanic and Scandinavian lands, the festival survived in a transformed fashion into Christian times, when it became known as **Walpurgis Night**. People lit bonfires on this night to frighten away witches, who were presumed to be especially active on this evening (*see also* **Easter Witch**).

119

The missionaries who labored to spread Christianity in this region of Europe disapproved of the local inhabitants' springtime fires, but were unable to convince people to abandon this old practice. According to legend St. Patrick, who set about converting Ireland to Christianity in the fifth century, provided a solution to this problem by adopting the flaming stacks as Easter bonfires. By the ninth century the Easter bonfire had been incorporated into the liturgy of the Western Church, where it was used to light the paschal candle. Roman Catholics continue to observe this old custom, although some parishes ignite the Easter fire in a brazier inside the church itself rather than build a bonfire out of doors.

Fire Folk Customs

In Germany, the Netherlands, and Austria old folk customs called for the burning of bonfires on Easter eve. These Easter bonfires continue in some places, including the town of Luegde, Germany, where inhabitants pull wheels of wood and straw, nearly six feet in diameter, to the top of a hill, set them aflame, and send them crashing downhill towards the river Emmer. Researchers investigating old, seasonal traditions in northwestern Europe have uncovered many folk customs involving these rolling wheels of fire, and believe that the custom dates back to ancient times. Some folklorists view the blazing wheels as symbolic of the sun. They suspect that unloosing these rolling torches may at one time have been thought to ensure the smooth progress of the solar year from the short, dark days of winter to the longer, brighter days of spring.

In many parts of western Europe old folk traditions reminded householders to extinguish all fires on Holy Saturday so that they might be replaced with flame kindled and blessed at the Easter Vigil service. In central Europe, many families living in and around the Alps extinguished all flames in their homes at three o'clock in the afternoon on **Good Friday**. The family endured the cold and dark until flames were brought home from the new fire ceremony on Holy Saturday. In the former Yugoslavia tradition assigned young boys the task of bringing the new fire home from the Easter Vigil. Armed with a slow-burning forest fungus, the boys waited until the priest blessed the new fire, then pressed forward to light their fungal torches. They dashed home with the new fire, where their parents would re-light the hearth and lamps with the holy flames.

Further Reading

Aivazian, Sirarpi Feredjian. "Pilgrimage: Eastern Christian Pilgrimage." In Mircea Eliade, ed. *The Encyclopedia of Religion*. Volume 11. New York: Macmillan, 1987.

Baldovin, John F. "Easter." In Mircea Eliade, ed. *The Encyclopedia of Religion*. Volume 4. New York: Macmillan, 1987.

Edsman, Carl-Martin. "Fire." In Mircea Eliade, ed. *The Encyclopedia of Religion*. Volume 5. New York: Macmillan, 1987.

"Fire." In Leland Ryken, James C. Wilhoit, and Tremper Longman III, eds. *Dictionary of Biblical Imagery*. Downers Grove, IL: InterVarsity Press, 1998.

Frazer, James George. *The New Golden Bough*. Theodor H. Gaster, ed. New York: S. G. Phillips, 1959.

Griffin, Robert H., and Ann H. Shurgin, eds. *The Folklore of World Holidays*. Second edition. Detroit, MI: Gale Research, 1999.

Henderson, Helene, and Sue Ellen Thompson, eds. *Holidays, Festivals, and Celebrations of the World Dictionary*. Second edition. Detroit, MI: Omnigraphics, 1997.

Hutton, Ronald. *Stations of the Sun*. Oxford, England: Oxford University Press, 1996.

"Light." In Leland Ryken, James C. Wilhoit, and Tremper Longman III, eds. *Dictionary of Biblical Imagery*. Downers Grove, IL: InterVarsity Press, 1998.

MacGregor, A. J. *Fire and Light in the Western Triduum*. Collegeville, MN: Liturgical Press, 1992.

Metford, J. C. J. *The Christian Year*. London, England: Thames and Hudson, 1991.

Monti, James. *The Week of Salvation*. Huntington, IN: Our Sunday Visitor Publications, 1993.

Niemann, Paul J. *The Lent, Triduum, and Easter Answer Book*. San Jose, CA: Resource Publications, 1998.

Weiser, Francis X. *The Easter Book*. New York: Harcourt, Brace and Company, 1954.

Wybrew, Hugh. *Orthodox Lent, Holy Week and Easter*. Crestwood, NY: St. Vladimir's Seminary Press, 1997.

Easter Monday

*Ball Monday, Dousing Day, Dyngus, Dyngus Day, Husvét
Hétfoge, Lany Poniedzialek (Wet Monday), Paasch
Maandag, Smigus, Swietego Lejka (St. Drencher's Day)*

People in more than eighty countries of the world celebrate the day
after Easter as a holiday. Easter celebrations continue, accompanied
in some cases by traditional folk practices. In much of central and
northern Europe these customs include walks in the countryside, egg
games, drenching people with **water**, and striking them with wands
made out of tree twigs.

History

Easter Monday stands as the last remnant of a once much longer season of post-Easter festivities. In the early Middle Ages people treated
the entire week following Easter as a holiday. In England King Alfred
the Great (849-899) decreed that none need to labor in the fourteen-
day period that surrounded Easter. This included **Holy Week**, the
week preceding the festival, and **Easter Week**, the week following.
People tended to their religious devotions in the week before Easter
and celebrated with feasts, parties, games, relaxation, and attendance
at religious services in the week after. By the thirteenth century this
two-week period had shortened and shifted to the latter half of Holy
Week and the ten days following Easter. These last two days, the second Monday and Tuesday after Easter somehow acquired the mysterious name of **Hocktide**. In 1552 Parliament passed a law restricting
post-Easter festivities to the Monday and Tuesday directly following
Easter. This state of affairs lasted until the nineteenth century, when
lawmakers further reduced rejoicing to the Monday following Easter,
known as Easter Monday.

Ball Games

In England ball games, such as stoolball, trapball, knurr-and-spell, ninepins, bowls, handball, and football, once enjoyed great popularity as **Easter season** diversions. In past times the inhabitants of Oxfordshire referred to Easter Monday as Ball Monday, because it kicked off a season of the year especially associated with these games. Some were played for the first time that year on Easter Monday.

Heaving and Related Customs

In England Easter Monday customs have evolved over time. In the Middle Ages folk tradition gave women the right to pull men out of bed on Easter Monday morning. Kings Edward I and II were both known to have submitted to this custom. In northern England folk tradition permitted men to catch any woman on Easter Monday, and, by grabbing hold of her arms and legs, heave her three times into the air. The next day women took the same liberty with men. In later centuries the more courtly lifters sat people of the opposite sex in a chair decorated with ribbons before hoisting them into the air. Others ignored this refinement. In England heaving, or lifting, died out in the nineteenth century. The custom seems to have survived in the Netherlands, however, where men are permitted to heave women into the air three times in a row between nine a.m. and noon on Easter Monday. According to tradition the women reward the men for their efforts with a kiss. The following day women lift men into the air.

Heaving or lifting customs are sometimes explained as symbolic of the rising motion associated with the **Resurrection**. Indeed, in England during the nineteenth century some Easter Monday lifters sang, "Jesus Christ is risen again!" as they approached candidates for heaving. It is also possible that this explanation was attached to the custom after the fact.

Egg Rolling, Pace Egging, and Other Egg Customs

Egg-rolling contests often take place in northern Britain on Easter Monday. Contestants choose what they hope to be prize-winning

Easter eggs and line up at the top of a hill. Egg-rolling rules vary from event to event. In some places the winner is the person whose egg rolls the farthest distance. In others victory attaches itself to the person whose egg survives the most rolls intact. In still others top honors go to the person whose egg rolls between two pegs. Some folklorists believe that egg-rolling may have originally symbolized the rolling away of the stone that sealed **Jesus'** tomb. In the United States a well-known egg rolling contest takes place each year on the White House lawn.

In past times children or young men in northern England and Scotland went **pace egging** on Easter Monday. The word pace comes from the original Greek word for Easter, *Pascha*. Gathering together in small groups, they would tour the neighborhood chanting folk verses or presenting a short folk play at each dwelling. In return for their efforts children asked for eggs, and young men for small change or something to drink. Pace egging was also once practiced in Belgium, Denmark, and the Netherlands, though on different days during the Easter season.

In the Netherlands children play egg games on *Paasch Maandag*, or Easter Monday. Younger children may continue to hunt for Easter eggs, a pastime called *eierrapen*. In another game, called *eierrikken*, children select hard-boiled, dyed Easter eggs of various colors and divide themselves into two teams. The teams form two lines that face each other, so that each child is paired with an opponent from the other team that carries an egg of the same color. By tapping one egg against the other, the paired opponents try to break each others' egg shells. The winner of each match keeps the loser's egg and goes on to face a new opponent. The child who gathers the most eggs wins (*see also* **Egg Tapping**). Both children and adults may participate in *eiergaren*, another Easter Monday egg game whose popularity can be traced back to the sixteenth and seventeenth centuries. Game organizers set a tub of water containing a large apple in the middle of a street. Then they place twenty-five eggs at twelve-foot intervals along the street. The game consists of a race between two contestants, one who must eat the apple with his or her hands tied behind his or her back, while the other must gather the eggs into a basket. Whoever finishes first wins.

Dousing and Switching

In many of the countries of northern and central Europe old folk customs encouraged people to douse one another with water or strike one another with wands of birch or willow twigs around Easter time (*see also* **Finland, Easter and Holy Week in; Sweden, Easter and Holy Week in**). Folklorists suspect that these switching customs evolved out of ancient beliefs that the gentle blows drive away bad influences and impart good health. Often tradition permitted the boys to vex the girls with these practices on Easter Monday, while the girls took revenge on the following day. Nowadays, in many places where these old practices have survived both boys and girls perform them on Easter Monday.

Old Czech Easter customs instructed boys to weave together willow branches and then decorate them with ribbons and flowers (*see also* **Czech Republic, Easter and Holy Week in**). Banding together on Easter Monday the boys went door to door, caroling for Easter eggs and switching the girls. Similar customs were also once practiced in Austria, southern Germany, Poland, and Slovakia.

In Hungary tradition invited boys to dunk girls in water on *Husvét Hétfoje*, or Easter Monday (*see also* **Hungary, Easter and Holy Week in**). For this reason the day is also known as "Dousing Day." Recent modifications to the old tradition encourage sprinkling rather than dunking. In return for the drenching girls traditionally presented boys with gifts of eggs, flowers, **bread**, cakes, and **wine**.

Polish lads also drenched girls with water on Easter Monday, a holiday known as *Smigus* or *Dyngus*, or as Dyngus Day to many Polish Americans. Throughout the centuries Polish boys have employed a variety of methods to wet the girls, from dunking them in a stream or water trough, to splashing them with water carried in a can, bucket, or other device. Some made a point of rising early in order to drench a girl as she laying drowsing in bed. In a more chivalrous version of this practice, some urban youth sprinkled girls with perfume rather than drench them with water. The girls sometimes attempted to buy off the more aggressive water-throwers with gifts of Easter eggs. Easter Monday is so closely associated with these customs that Poles often call the holiday *Lany Poniedzialek* (Wet Monday) or *Swietego Lejka* (St. Drencher's Day). The very next day tradition permitted girls free reign to drench the boys with water.

Polish youth continue to enjoy these dunking customs on Easter Monday, crying out, "Smigus!" as the water hits their mark. Nowadays, however, local girls are not the only targets. Passersby, people going to or from church, and tourists may be greeted with a bucketful of water on Dyngus Day. Polish police have threatened to fine those who make a public nuisance of themselves.

Visits and Walks

The Gospel reading traditionally associated with Easter Monday relates that the risen Jesus first appeared to his disciple **Peter** as he and a companion were walking from Jerusalem to the village of Emmaus (Luke 24:1-34). A number of old Easter Monday customs reflect this association, encouraging people to take small journeys on this day. In Austria Easter Monday customarily served as a day to visit the sick or the elderly. In central Europe Christians celebrated Easter Monday with an outing called an **Emmaus walk**. These group walks to a picturesque site in the countryside ended with a shared meal.

In Poland people once practiced *chodzenie* on Easter Monday. Young people gathered together in groups and went door to door singing songs and reciting bits of folk poetry. On Easter Monday some boisterous youths combined this custom with water throwing, threatening to drench householders who did not offer them anything in return for their efforts. Good-humored families usually presented the Easter carolers with a few treats, including Easter eggs, a taste of homemade liquor, small change, a piece of cake, or a bite of sausage. Polish folk tradition permitted chodzenie throughout the Easter season, a fifty-day period beginning on **Easter Sunday** and ending on **Pentecost**.

Further Reading

Blackburn, Bonnie, and Leofranc Holford-Strevens. *The Oxford Companion to the Year*. Oxford, England: Oxford University Press, 1999.

Griffin, Robert H., and Ann H. Shurgin, eds. *The Folklore of World Holidays*. Second edition. Detroit, MI: Gale Research, 1999.

Henderson, Helene, and Sue Ellen Thompson, eds. *Holidays, Festivals, and Celebrations of the World Dictionary*. Second edition. Detroit, MI: Omnigraphics, 1997.

Hole, Christina. *British Folk Customs*. London, England: Hutchinson and Company, 1976.

Howard, Alexander. *Endless Cavalcade*. London, England: Arthur Barker, 1964.

Hutton, Ronald. *Stations of the Sun*. Oxford, England: Oxford University Press, 1996.

Weaver, Robert S. *International Holidays*. Jefferson, NC: McFarland, 1995.

Weiser, Francis X. *The Easter Book*. New York: Harcourt, Brace and Company, 1954.

Web Site

"Dyngus and Lany Poneidzialek," an article by Robert Strybel published in the *Am-Pol Eagle,* a newspaper serving western New York's Polish-American population, posted at: http://www.dyngusday.com/

Easter Parade

The parade that takes place on **Easter Sunday** is not a parade in the traditional sense. Instead the Easter parade consists of ordinary people, dressed in their holiday finery, strolling to and from church or along the main streets of town. The citizens of New York City coined the term "Easter parade" near the end of the nineteenth century as a means of describing this informal fashion show. The 1948 movie, *Easter Parade*, starring Fred Astaire and Judy Garland, and featuring music by Irving Berlin, publicized this annual event.

Origins

Folklorists cannot pinpoint the exact origins of this custom. Nevertheless they point to old European folklore that promoted the idea of wearing **new clothes** on Easter day. In some places people not only wore the clothing to church, but also sauntered through town in their new gear. On **Easter Monday**, many central Europeans took part in **Emmaus walks** in which they donned their holiday clothing once more for a leisurely stroll and picnic in the countryside. The Easter parade, as we know it in this country, may have developed out of all these old European Easter traditions.

New York City's Easter Parade

The most famous American Easter parade takes place in New York City. It began in the mid-nineteenth century and achieved prominence during the 1870s and 1880s. By the mid-nineteenth century many fashionable churches had established themselves along Fifth Avenue, one of the city's main thoroughfares. On Easter Sunday hordes of people making their way to and from packed services in these churches created a surge in human traffic along Fifth Avenue's broad sidewalks. These churchgoers, decked out in beautiful new clothes in honor of the day, created something of a spectacle. The colorful crowds soon attracted more people, who showed up simply to marvel at the fashionable clothing. By the 1890s sightseers from as far away as Long Island and New Jersey elbowed their way onto Fifth Avenue to catch a glimpse of the fashionable and the wealthy in their Easter finery. In this era, well-dressed women never left home without a hat. A new hat put the finishing touch on the Easter outfit and quickly became an indispensable element of the Easter parade. These fancy head ornaments were also known as Easter bonnets.

Although the Easter parade may have its roots in old European folk customs, retailers and advertisers nurtured its development in the United States. Not long after it became an important event on New York's social calendar, manufacturers and retailers realized that promoting the custom could boost clothing and hat sales significantly. By the 1890s battalions of lavish store window displays and legions of persuasive newspaper advertisements urged the public to regard Easter as an occasion for full and formal regalia. The festival became the most important event of the year in the dry goods industry. Some retailers reported that their financial success or failure hinged on Easter sales.

Controversy

Shortly after the Easter parade claimed widespread public attention, some Christian leaders began to criticize it for distracting people from the religious celebration and significance of the holiday. Certain of them grumbled that the custom encouraged vanity, materialism, and self-absorbed competitiveness, exactly the opposite of the virtues taught by **Jesus** and demonstrated in the last days of his life. Others despaired over the fact that the surge in demand for fancy hats at Easter time worsened conditions in sweatshops, many of which employed children. Easter should not become an occasion to worsen the sufferings of others, they argued, especially when such sufferings served only to indulge the whims of the fashionable.

Other social critics used the parade itself to challenge the complacency of the well-to-do and lobby for social change. During the Depression, gangs of unemployed people sauntered up and down New

York's Fifth Avenue on Easter Sunday afternoon wearing worn trousers, lumberjack coats, ragged shoes, and tumble-down old top hats. Some even marched with signs that read "One Fifth Avenue Gown Equals a Year of Relief." During the 1960s young people opposed to the Vietnam war staged similar protests, handing out flyers and carrying placards that read "While you march down the avenue in your new clothes, the clothing is being burned off the backs of men, women and children in Vietnam."

Christian leaders' concern with the excesses of the Easter parade peaked in 1952, when the lure of free television coverage tempted celebrities and commercial promoters into staging a number of rather tasteless events on Fifth Avenue. Designers hired professional models to parade their clothes and hats in front of St. Patrick's Cathedral. A hair lotion company erected a platform in order that their model, dressed in black tights, could pirouette in full view of a crowd. Hired men wearing unusual, eye-catching costumes paraded with signs and placards advertising various products. Celebrities strolled up and down seeking a slice of camera time to promote their latest project. Church leaders felt that the situation, long troubling, had now gotten out of hand. Before the week was out the Protestant Council of New York City issued an official protest and called on citizens to restore dignity to the city's Easter celebrations. The following year police guarded churches and their immediate surroundings from the antics of publicity seekers. Upon the request of civic leaders and clergy, television networks covering the parade agreed to pay less attention to commercial gimmicks. These measures worked to reduce the more flagrant attempts of promoters and advertisers to take over the Easter parade. Nevertheless, many felt that an essential conflict remained between the values enshrined by the parade and those at the heart of the Easter festival.

Contests

Although New York City's Easter parade achieved nationwide fame, similar, lesser-known events also took place in towns and cities across the country. In some places these events evolved into structured contests in which a panel of judges awarded prizes to the best dressed man, woman, boy, and girl. These contests often bestowed a special award to the lady with the prettiest hat.

Decline

In the latter decades of the twentieth century, as Americans adopted increasingly informal attitudes towards church attire, and indeed, clothing in general, the New York City Easter parade lost some of its former luster. Nevertheless, curiosity continues to draw New Yorkers and tourists to Fifth Avenue on Easter Sunday afternoon to see the contemporary version of this American fashion show. The trend towards increasingly informal dress has also diminished the Easter parade in other parts of the country.

Further Reading

Myers, Robert J. *Celebrations: The Complete Book of American Holidays.* Garden City, NY: Doubleday and Company, 1972.

Schmidt, Leigh Eric. *Consumer Rites.* Princeton, NJ: Princeton University Press, 1995.

Weiser, Francis X. *The Easter Book.* New York: Harcourt, Brace and Company, 1954.

Easter Seals

Easter seals are small, decorative stamps issued by a charitable organization called the National Easter Seal Society. These stamps have no value as postage but may be used to ornament letters or packages. The Easter Seal Society offers these seals in exchange for donations to its various programs, which furnish a wide variety of services to the disabled.

Edgar Allen, a businessman from Elyria, Ohio, established the parent organization of today's Easter Seal Society. Allen's son died as the result of a streetcar accident which proved fatal due to a lack of adequate medical care. This tragedy spurred him to fight for the construction of a local hospital. After it had been built Allen found himself drawn to a boy brought in for orthopedic care. In following this boy's case Allen learned much about the special needs of children with disabilities. This newfound knowledge inspired Allen, in partnership with the Rotary Clubs, to found the Ohio Society for Crippled Children in 1919. In 1921, Allen started the National Society for Crippled Children in Elyria, Ohio. In 1922 the National Society expanded and formed the International Society for Crippled Children, while maintaining the National Society as a functioning body in the U.S.

The National Society for Crippled Children produced its first decorative stamps in 1934. The Society may have been inspired by the success of the National Tuberculosis Association (later the American Lung Association), which had been raising money with decorative stamps known as "Christmas seals" since 1919. These decorative stamps had no value as postage, but rather offered buyers a pleasing ornament for their letters in return for a small donation. The seals themselves, as they flew across the nation on letters and parcels, advertised the Association and its work. Paul H. King, who became head of the National Society for Crippled Children after Allen, advised that the Society promote their seals at Easter time. King reasoned that "Easter means, of course, **resurrection** and new life, and certainly the rehabilitation of crippled children means new life and activity—complete or partial—physically, mentally, and spiritually." In this way the decorative stamps became "Easter seals."

The Easter seals project succeeded beyond expectations. It brought in $47,000 in cash, attracted new members, and publicized the organization. The Society decided to continue the triumphant campaign by issuing new seals each year in the early spring. In 1944 the National Society for Crippled Children broadened its sphere of concern, becoming the National Society for Crippled Children and Adults. By the 1950s the Easter seals had become such an established symbol of the Society and its work that people had begun to refer to the organization as the "Easter Seals Society." In 1952 the Society acknowledged the popularity of the seals by adopting a stylized Easter **lily** as

132

its logo. In 1967, in recognition of the public's response to Easter seals, the Society adopted the words "Easter seal" into its official name, becoming the National Easter Seal Society for Crippled Children and Adults. This lasted until 1977 when the phrase "for crippled children and adults" was removed from the organization's title in response to growing awareness of the negative connotations of the word "crippled."

Today direct mail fund-raising campaigns which include the decorative stamps still provide the Society with an important source of revenue. In spite of the fact that the organization's name contains the word "Easter," the Society maintains no religious affiliation and serves people from all religious and ethnic backgrounds. Over one million clients each year benefit from the services provided by the National Easter Seal Society and its local affiliates. These individuals come from all age groups and suffer from all kinds of disabilities, both physical and mental. The Society welcomes clients whose conditions were diagnosed at birth or acquired as a result of accident, disease, or old age. Through its local affiliates the Easter Seal Society offers them medical rehabilitation, job training and employment services, inclusive child care, adult day services, and camping and recreation opportunities.

Further Reading

Lord, Priscilla Sawyer, and Daniel J. Foley. *Easter Garland*. 1963. Reprint. Detroit, MI: Omnigraphics, 1999.

Web Site

The National Easter Seal Society web site can be found at: http://www.easter-seals.org/

Easter Season

Eastertide

From ancient times Christians have honored the fifty days including and following **Easter Sunday** as a holy season. Today we call this period of time Eastertide, or the Easter season. In those days, however, this seven-week festival was known as *Pentekoste*, the Greek word for "fiftieth." The early Christians celebrated each of the fifty days as if it were a **Sunday**. This meant that they neither **fasted** nor knelt to pray, both of which activities carried penitential overtones (*for more on penance, see* **Repentance**). Instead they rejoiced over the **Resurrection**, **Ascension**, the coming of the Holy Spirit, the gift of **redemption**, and the hope of **salvation**.

Scholars believe that the early Christians patterned this festive season on a series of pre-existing Jewish observances. For example, Christians celebrated Easter Sunday on or near the date when Jews celebrated **Passover**. Christian scripture states that **Jesus'** crucifixion took place on Passover (or the day preceding Passover) and weaves Passover themes into accounts of his death and resurrection. After Passover Jews observed *Sefirat Haomer*, or "Counting the Omer." They dedicated this seven-week period to prayers for the spring harvest (*for more on Sefirat Haomer, see* **Shavuot**). After Sefirat Haomer came Shavuot, a spring harvest festival.

Sometime around the fourth century the long festive season attached to Easter Sunday dissolved into three separate festivals, each with its own themes. Easter Sunday, along with **Easter Week**, commemorated the Resurrection and the associated themes of redemption and salvation. The last of the fifty days of rejoicing became **Pentecost**, a holiday honoring the coming of the Holy Spirit. In addition, **Ascension Day**, a festival celebrating Jesus' ascent into heaven, attached itself to the fortieth day after Easter. The old fifty-day season that stretched seven weeks from Easter Sunday remained in place though its importance declined. The English dubbed this period of time "Eastertide." It is also known as the Easter season. Some call the first forty days of the Easter season "the forty glorious days," since they commemorate the time during which the risen Jesus still visited his disciples in bodily form.

Customs

Some churches observe the Easter season with special rituals and customs. The word **alleluia** or hallelujah, which comes from an old Hebrew phrase meaning "praise the Lord," rings out frequently in worship services. Among those churches that use the liturgical colors associated with the festivals and seasons of the Christian year, priests wear special white robes and church decorations feature the color white. In Christian symbolism white signifies joy. The **paschal candle**, a tall white candle decorated with emblems of Christ, stands near the altar during the fifty days. It reminds worshipers of the presence of the risen Jesus among his followers, the central theme of the Easter season.

Further Reading

Metford, J. C. J. *The Christian Year*. London, England: Thames and Hudson, 1991.

Slim, Hugo. *A Feast of Festivals*. London, England: Marshall Pickering, 1996.

Talley, Thomas J. *The Origins of the Liturgical Year*. Collegeville, MN: Liturgical Press, 1986.

Easter Sun

Old European folk beliefs teach that the sun dances for joy as it rises on Easter morning. In England this folk belief can be traced back at least as far as the seventeenth century, as demonstrated in this snippet of a poem called "Ballad upon a Wedding," written in 1641 by Sir John Suckling:

> Her feet beneath her petticoat
> Like little mice stole in and out,
>   As if they feared the light:
> But, oh, she dances in such a way
> No sun upon an Easter-day
>   Is half so fine a sight (Weiser 1954:158).

In the British Isles folk tradition advised that the best way to view the sun's elusive Easter morning movements was to place a pan of **water** in an east-facing window at sunrise. One then simply looked down into the water which captured and reflected the image of the dancing sun *(for more on the Christian significance of the direction east, see* **Easter, Origin of the Word***)*. Armenians used a mirror to reflect the sun's dancing rays.

A related legend suggested that if one looked at the sun just as it rose over the horizon on Easter morning one could see the figure of a **lamb** superimposed upon it. Local lore offered many suggestions as to the right spot and right angle from which to catch this marvelous sight.

Gathering to watch the sun rise on Easter morning is an old European folk tradition. Favorite spots for these informal celebrations included hilltops or flat, open plains. As the sun rose people cheered, sang or prayed, according to local custom. In some places **bells** rang or canons boomed to greet the Easter sunrise. In others bands and choirs caroled a salute to the sun. Today many churches schedule special **sunrise services** on Easter morning.

The sun and the sunrise have several symbolic connections to the Easter story. According to the Bible, Jesus' followers first discovered the **Resurrection** at daybreak (Matthew 28:1-7, Mark 16:1-7, Luke 23:1-9, John 20:1-18). Furthermore, the sun itself sometimes serves as a symbol of Christ. Finally, Easter falls shortly after the **spring equinox** *(see also* **Easter, Date of***)*. The spring equinox marks that turning point in the year after which the days are longer than the nights. Thus Easter comes at that time of year in which the sun and its light triumphs over night and darkness.

Further Reading

Cohen, Hennig, and Tristram Potter Coffin. *The Folklore of American Holidays*. Third edition. Detroit, MI: Gale, 1999.

Lord, Priscilla Sawyer, and Daniel J. Foley. *Easter Garland*. 1963. Reprint. Detroit, MI: Omnigraphics, 1999.

Weiser, Francis X. *The Easter Book*. New York: Harcourt, Brace and Company, 1954.

Easter Sunday

Al-'Id Al-Kabir, Husvét, Ostern, Paasch Zondag, Pääsiässunnuntai, Paaske, Pâques, Pascha, Paschen, Paschoa, Pascua, Pashka, Paskdagen, Påske, Pasqua, Velikonoce, Velykos, Vuzkresenie, Wielkanoc, Zadig

On Easter Sunday Christians celebrate the **resurrection** of **Jesus Christ**. Although American popular culture often pays more attention to Christmas, Christians believe Easter to be the most important festival in the church year. It represents the climax of **Holy Week**, as well as the end of the long **Lenten** season. Moreover the Easter festival, with its focus on Jesus' death and resurrection and their significance for his followers, embodies some of the most important teachings of the Christian religion (*see also* **Redemption**; **Salvation**).

According to the Bible, Jesus' followers returned to his tomb early in the morning on the first Easter Sunday. They found it empty. Then they received the glorious news that Jesus had risen from the dead. The four accounts of this event recorded in the Christian Bible vary somewhat. In three of the four versions, an angel or angels were the first to bring the joyous news to Jesus' followers (Matthew 28:1-8, Mark 16:1-8, Luke 24:1-12). The risen Jesus appeared soon afterwards. In the other account, Christ himself, in the company of two angels, delivered the news of the Resurrection to **Mary Magdalene**

137

as she stood outside his tomb and wept (John 20:1-18). (For more on the events of the first Easter, *see also* **Peter**.)

History

Some scholars believe that the earliest Easter celebrations took place in the mid-second century in Asia Minor, a region which now lies in the nation of Turkey. Christians in this area focused their Easter celebrations on the sacrificial death of Jesus Christ, a theme later assigned to **Good Friday**. They called the holiday *"Pascha,"* a Greek word inspired by the Aramaic pronunciation of the Hebrew word *Pesach*, which means **Passover**. Indeed, the Asia Minor Christians held Pascha on the same dates that their Jewish neighbors prepared for and celebrated Passover, that is, on the fourteenth and fifteenth days of the Jewish month of Nisan. The observances included **fasting**, prayer, and readings from scripture, including the writings of the Jewish prophets and the Passover story as recounted in the Book of Exodus.

Other scholars contend that the first Easter celebrations took place in Rome around the year 165. The Romans celebrated Pascha on the Sunday after Passover. Their celebrations, too, emphasized Jesus' sacrificial death on the **cross**.

By the third century Christians from Alexandria, Egypt, began to advance a new interpretation of the Easter festival. They understood it to honor Jesus' passage between death and new life. Therefore their celebrations focused on both the Crucifixion and the Resurrection (*for more on crucifixion, see* Cross).

By the early fourth century Church authorities sought to unify these diverse Easter worship services. In the year 325 the Council of Nicaea, an important meeting of early Church leaders, settled the issue of when to celebrate Pascha. The Council decreed that all Christians adopt the Roman date for the festival (*for more on this issue, see* **Easter, Date of**).

The fourth century also witnessed the blossoming of Holy Week. Christian communities began to assign the commemoration of various aspects of the story of Jesus' betrayal, arrest, and execution to different days in the week preceding Easter Sunday. This left the celebration of the Resurrection to Easter Sunday alone. Before this development the Pascha festival served as an occasion to ponder the entire mystery of Christ's incarnation, suffering, sacrificial death, resurrection, and **ascension**, as well as the coming of the Holy Spirit (*see also* **Pentecost**). Afterwards, Easter Sunday observances increasingly dedicated themselves to celebrating a single aspect of this mystery, that is, the Resurrection. In a certain sense Easter Sunday observances became less important, as various aspects of what had once been a unified festival were spread out over the days of Holy Week and the weeks that follow.

During the Middle Ages western European Christians began to focus their Holy Week devotions more and more on Good Friday. This emphasis made sense to medieval Christians because the spiritual teachings of the time linked human redemption and salvation more to Jesus' death, commemorated on Good Friday, than to his resurrection. Nevertheless this development tended to further diminish the attention given to Easter Sunday celebrations.

Until the early Middle Ages, the **Easter Vigil**, beginning late at night on **Holy Saturday** and lasting until the early morning hours of Easter Sunday, functioned as the primary church service commemorating the Resurrection. In the seventh century Roman Catholic officials introduced a Sunday morning Easter service. Over the centuries the Sunday service gained in popularity among western European Christians, even as the Easter Vigil service attracted fewer and fewer worshipers. By the dawn of the twentieth century the Easter Vigil service was one of the least attended services in Holy Week. Reforms made in the latter half of the twentieth century, including the restoration of the Easter Vigil from daylight to evening hours, have helped to reintegrate this once-vital service into the round of Holy Week observances.

Religious Customs

Many Christians attend church services on Easter Sunday morning. Those scheduled near dawn take their name, **sunrise service**, from

this early hour. In addition, some churches offer an Easter Vigil beginning late at night on Holy Saturday. Easter services often include special sights, sounds, and rituals — all designed to express the happiness inspired by the arrival of the long-awaited Easter festival. In Roman Catholic churches as well as those Protestant churches that observe liturgical colors, priests wear white robes. Easter Sunday services may also include special musical offerings and **bell** ringing. The word **alleluia** is reintroduced into worship in those churches which have abstained from using it during Lent. **Baptisms**, or the renewal of the congregation's baptismal vows, may also be added to the Easter service. In addition, some Protestant churches include a folk custom known as the **flowering of the cross** at some point during their Easter Sunday ceremonies.

Orthodox Easter

In Orthodox churches Easter Sunday celebrations take place both on Holy Saturday and on Easter Sunday. Orthodoxy is one of the three main branches of the Christian faith. This ancient division of the church took root in eastern Europe, the Middle East and north Africa. Roman Catholicism and Orthodoxy split apart from each other about 1,000 years ago, so some Orthodox customs differ from those observed by Western Christians, that is, Roman Catholics and Protestants.

The earliest Orthodox service associated with Easter Sunday takes place on the morning of Holy Saturday (*for more on this service, see* Easter Vigil). A second observance, known as the Resurrection service, begins late at night on Holy Saturday. This ceremony, too, belongs to Easter Sunday, and in past times began in the pre-dawn hours of **Sunday** morning. Those attending the service bring white candles from home, or pick them up as they enter the church. The church fills with worshipers as the hour nears midnight and the lights inside the church dim. Then at midnight, the priest emerges from behind the screens that enclose the altar holding a single lit candle. The flame represents the risen Christ. As he holds the candle before the congregation the priest declares, "Come ye and receive light from the unwavering Light; and glorify Christ, who has risen from the dead." Then he passes the flame to several worshipers, who in turn light their neighbors' candles until everyone in the church is carrying a glowing candle. Next, the priest leads the candle-bearing congregation in a procession around the church, which represents the arrival of the myrrh-bearing women at Jesus' tomb early on Sunday morning (*see also* Mary Magdalene). The priest proclaims the Resurrection outside the main doors of church, and the congregation reenters the building, now ablaze with lights.

In Greek Orthodox churches the Resurrection service is punctuated with the singing of a joyful hymn strongly associated with Easter, *"Christos Anesti"* (Christ Is Risen). Red **Easter eggs** may be distributed to the congregation as they leave the church. At the end of the service some people take their lighted candle home with them and use the flame to light the vigil lamp in front of their icons, religious images used in prayer and worship (*see also* **Easter Fires**). Among the Orthodox the Resurrection service is the most well-attended event of the year. Orthodox churches also offer a Sunday service, known as the Great Vespers of Agape, on Easter Sunday.

At the end of the late-night Resurrection service, many Orthodox Christians enjoy a large meal which marks the beginning of Easter and the end of the Lenten fast. This late-night Easter feast typically includes several items forbidden during Lent, such as cheese, meat soup, eggs, and **wine**. Many feel that the first food to pass their lips at this time should be a traditional, red Easter egg. The red color represents the **blood** of Christ, the egg itself new life, and the shell Jesus' tomb. The cracking of this egg represents Christ's emerging from the tomb. Slavic and other Orthodox families often bring a basket of Easter foods to church with them so that the priest may bless the Easter meal. On Easter Sunday and throughout **Easter Week** Greeks and other Orthodox Christians greet each other with the phrase "Christ is risen!" (*Christos Anesti* in Greek, *Khristos voskrese* in Church Slavonic). The correct reply is, "Indeed he has risen!" (*Alithos anesti* in Greek, *Voistinu voskrese* in Church Slavonic). Greeks may also respond *Alithos o Kirios*, "Truly the Lord." Some Orthodox Christians use this greeting throughout the **Easter season**.

Easter Foods

All over the world Christians feast in celebration of Easter. In many countries the Easter banquet features roast **lamb**. In others the feast centers around ham (*see also* **Pig**). Easter eggs not only serve as a traditional holiday food, but also provide a focal point for many Easter activities and games. In many countries special **breads**, often made with the rich dairy products forbidden during Lent, grace the Easter table. Greeks usually serve *tsoureki*, a sweet, braided loaf with red Easter eggs tucked into the dough. Portuguese Easter celebrations often feature *folar*, another sweet braided loaf studded with Easter eggs. Russians enjoy *kulich*, a sweet bread often baked in coffee cans to insure a tall majestic loaf, which is later topped with white icing. Many Italians bake an Easter bread called *columba pasquale* in a brown paper mold shaped to resemble a dove in flight. On Easter Sunday mornings Czech families often wake up to a breakfast of *bábovka*, a sweet, frosted bread filled with whipped cream. Many Austrians breakfast on a rich coffee cake known as *guglhupf.*

Folk Customs

Of all the old folklore associated with Easter, the tales and customs concerning the **Easter Bunny** have probably left the greatest mark on the popular observance of the holiday. Certainly children in many lands have come to view the candy and other sweet treats distributed by the Easter Bunny as traditional Easter foods. The Easter egg hunt, also popular with children, traces its roots back to legends concerning the Easter Bunny. Other Easter egg activities appear to have developed independently of the Easter Bunny legend, including **egg rolling, egg tapping,** and constructing **egg trees.** Easter customs less familiar to contemporary Americans include practices related to the special qualities of Easter **water** and Easter sunlight (*see also* **Easter Sun**). The custom of wearing **new clothes** at Easter grew out of ancient religious practices linking the festival with baptism. The **Easter parade** also evolved from an old religious custom known as an **Emmaus walk.** Although many contemporary Americans return to work on **Easter Monday**, the day following Easter, in past times the games, feasts and festivities associated with Easter continued through Easter

143

Week. In most predominantly Christian countries Easter Monday is a holiday.

Names for Easter

In numerous European languages, the word for Easter comes from the ancient Greek term for the festival, Pascha. For example, the Greeks still call the festival *Pascha*, while the Russians know it as *Pashka*. The Italian word for Easter is *Pasqua*, the Spanish *Pascua*, the Portuguese *Paschoa*, and the French *Pâques*. Belgians refer to the holiday as *Paschen*, the Danes as *Paaske*, the Dutch as *Paschen* or *Paasch Zondag*, the Norwegians as *Påske*, and the Swedes as *Paskdagen*. By contrast the English word "Easter" and the German *Ostern* evolved from a different root word (*for more on this issue, see* **Easter, Origin of the Word**). Other European words for Easter include the Bulgarian *Vuzkresenie*, the Czech *Velikonoce*, the Polish *Wielkanoc*, and the Lithuanian *Velykos*, as well as the Hungarian *Husvét* and the Finnish *Pääsiässunnuntai*. The Armenians call the holiday *Zadig*, while the Syrians know it as *Al-'Id Al-Kabir*.

Easter Symbols

Symbols of the holiday found in many churches at Easter time include the cross, the **lily**, the lamb, and the **paschal candle**. Fire, light, and sunrise also recollect the events of the first Easter and have been incorporated into many Christian Easter observances (*see also* Easter Fires; Easter Sun; Sunrise Service). Other Easter-related symbols include the **butterfly**, the **peacock**, the **phoenix**, and the number **eight**, which stand for the Easter themes of resurrection and eternal life. In churches where bells have been silent for the last several days of Holy Week, ringing bells denote Easter joy. Representations of the empty tomb found by Jesus' followers on Easter Sunday morning also serve as religious symbols of the holiday. Throughout the year weekly Christian worship services are scheduled on Sundays to recall the fact that Jesus rose from the dead on that day of the week.

The liturgical color for Easter is white or gold. White represents joy and purity, while gold stands for glory, exultation, and illumination.

Liturgical color schemes dictate the color of clerical robes and other church decorations in those churches that observe them.

The Easter egg is probably the most widely used folk symbol of the holiday. In the United States the Easter Bunny also serves as a popular Easter folk symbol. In past generations many people wore new clothes, especially new hats, on Easter Sunday, to represent the Easter themes of renewal and new beginnings (*see also* **Easter Parade**). This custom has fallen somewhat out of favor in the United States, however. In Sweden the **Easter witch** is a popular symbol of the holiday.

Further Reading

Bradshaw, Paul F. "Easter in Christian Tradition." In Paul F. Bradshaw and Lawrence A. Hoffman, eds. *Easter and Passover: Origin and History to Modern Times*. Two Liturgical Traditions series, volume 5. Notre Dame, IN: University of Notre Dame Press, 1999.

Bradshaw, Paul F. "The Origins of Easter." In Paul F. Bradshaw and Lawrence A. Hoffman, eds. *Passover and Easter: Origin and History to Modern Times*. Two Liturgical Traditions series, volume 5. Notre Dame, IN: University of Notre Dame Press, 1999.

Lord, Priscilla Sawyer, and Daniel J. Foley. *Easter the World Over*. Philadelphia, PA: Chilton Book Company, 1971.

Monti, James. *The Week of Salvation*. Huntington, IN: Our Sunday Visitor Publications, 1993.

Rouvelas, Marilyn. *A Guide to Greek Traditions and Customs in America*. Bethesda, MD: Nea Attiki Press, 1993.

Slim, Hugo. *A Feast of Festivals*. London, England: Marshall Pickering, 1996.

Spicer, Dorothy Gladys. *Book of Festivals*. 1937. Reprint. Detroit, MI: Omnigraphics, 1990.

Weiser, Francis X. *The Easter Book*. New York: Harcourt, Brace and Company, 1954.

Web Site

"Pascha — Sunday of the Resurrection. Christ Is Risen! Truly He Is Risen!" a brief article on the Resurrection service posted at the Greek Orthodox Archdiocese of Australia's web site at: http://cygnus.uwa.edu.au/~jgrapsas/pages/Pascha.htm

Easter Vigil

The Easter Vigil service is the oldest of all Easter observances. It takes place late at night on **Holy Saturday**, though it officially marks the beginning of **Easter Sunday** celebrations. During the Middle Ages, the Easter Vigil service fell into a long, slow decline. In the second half of the twentieth century both Roman Catholics and Protestants began to revive this ancient service.

Early Christian Vigils

The word "vigil" comes from the Latin word *vigilia*, a noun which refers to the act of staying awake and alert in order to protect, guard, or look after something. In English we refer to this activity as keeping watch. In the specialized language of the Church a vigil is a nighttime prayer service, usually ending with a celebration of the **Eucharist**. Some scholars think that the early Christians held frequent vigils. They suspect that these vigils were motivated by the widely held belief that the Second Coming of Christ would occur at midnight. The selection of midnight as the hour of Christ's return may have been inspired by the Parable of the Wise and Foolish Virgins, a story from Christian scripture in which the long-awaited bridegroom, interpreted by many as a veiled reference to Christ, arrives at midnight (Matthew 25:1-13).

Early Christian Easter Vigils

The earliest historical record of a Christian Easter service comes from the region of Asia Minor, which included most of what is now the modern nation of Turkey, and dates back to about the middle of the second century. The faithful held this service on the evening of **Passover** and described it as a watch or vigil. It began some time after dark, lasted past midnight, and finally ended before dawn, when the roosters began to crow. This service celebrated the **redemption** of humanity that was brought about by the life, suffering, death, **resurrection**, and glorification of **Jesus** Christ. It placed a special emphasis on Jesus' death on the **cross** as the moment of his greatest triumph. The end of the service was marked by an early form of the Eucharist. Historical records also indicate that the faithful fasted during the daylight hours preceding the service, breaking their **fast** with the eucharistic meal that closed the ceremony. Among the early Christians the Easter Vigil was one of the most well attended services of the year.

Historical records allow us to trace the celebration of Easter in Rome back to the year 165. The Roman Easter Vigil differed from that of Asia Minor, however, in that it was held on the Saturday evening following the start of Passover. This difference in timing gave rise to a long debate over the date on which to commemorate the death and resurrection of Jesus Christ. In the fourth century, the Council of Nicaea, an important meeting of early Christian leaders that gave birth to the Nicene Creed, decreed that all Christians adopt the Roman date for Easter (*see also* **Easter, Date of**).

Elements of the Easter Vigil Service

From early Christian times fires and lights served important functional and symbolic roles in the Easter Vigil (*see also* **Easter Fires**). Not only did lamps, candles, and torches light up the darkness, but they also served as symbols of Christ and the divine presence of God. This uncanny nighttime brightness led some to call the ceremony "the great service of light" and the evening itself "the night of illumination" or "the night of radiant splendor." An early Christian writer recorded the fact that Emperor Constantine (d. 337) "transformed the night of the sacred vigil into the brilliance of day, by lighting throughout the whole city . . . pillars of wax, while burning lamps illuminated every house, so that this nocturnal celebration was rendered brighter than the brightest day" (Weiser, 134). St. Gregory of Nyssa (335-394) described Holy Saturday evening as the "glowing night which links the splendor of burning lamps to the morning rays of the sun, thus producing continuous daylight without any darkness" (Weiser, 134).

147

In Jerusalem the lighting of the lamps for the Easter feast had taken on a special, ceremonial quality by the end of the fourth century. This early, ceremonial lamp lighting gave birth to an Easter Vigil custom that survives today: the lighting of the **paschal candle** with newly kindled fire. The paschal candle is a very large candle used to shed light on the Bible passages read out loud during the Easter Vigil service. In explaining the origins of the paschal candle some researchers point to an ancient Christian service called the *Lucernarium*, a ceremonial lighting of the lamps in preparation for the evening prayer service. As time passed the Lucernarium became a service in its own right which included chanting, prayers, and psalms. Scholars believe that the early Christians based the Lucernarium on Jewish lamp-lighting rituals that preceded evening prayer. In time, however, the Christian observance disappeared. Some commentators think that the ceremony that surrounds the lighting of the paschal candle on Easter eve is all that remains of this ancient observance.

By the fourth century, especially after the Council of Nicaea, the Easter Vigil had emerged as the preferred occasion for baptisms, although in some places **Pentecost** served as an acceptable alternative date. This development coincided with the formation of **Holy Week**. During the first few centuries after Jesus' death, the faithful commemorated the entire story of his life, suffering, crucifixion, and resurrection at the Easter Vigil. By the late fourth century Christian communities had begun to separate out various elements of the story and assign their commemoration to different days in Holy Week. Thus, they honored the Last Supper on **Maundy Thursday**, mourned Jesus' crucifixion on **Good Friday**, and rejoiced in his resurrection at the Easter Vigil. Certain passages in Christian scripture cast **baptism** as a kind of spiritual death and resurrection (Romans 6:1-11, Colossians 2:12). Therefore, Church leaders deemed it appropriate that baptisms be performed at the festival commemorating the resurrection of Jesus Christ.

Since early Christian times the Easter Vigil service has included numerous, lengthy readings from the Bible. The readings begin with God's creation of the earth as told in Genesis, the first book of the

Bible. They also include the story of ancient Israelites' escape from slavery in Egypt. Other stories from the Hebrew scriptures, or Old Testament, along with readings from the Hebrew prophets follow. The Bible readings close with a selection from Christian scripture concerning the resurrection of Jesus Christ. Christian authorities chose these passages because, presented together, they illustrate God's unfolding plan for humanity's redemption and **salvation**.

The Middle Ages and Beyond

During the early Middle Ages the timing and the character of the Easter Vigil began to change in western Europe. As the number of adult converts to the Christian religion decreased and the number of infant baptisms increased, the importance of the vigil service as an occasion for baptism diminished. In addition, by the eighth century many churches offered the Easter Vigil on the afternoon rather than the evening of Holy Saturday. In the twelfth century the service had shifted to midday. In 1570, Roman Catholic authorities advanced the hour of the vigil service yet again to the early morning of Holy Saturday. This change in timing undermined the powerful symbolic use of fire and light so prevalent in early Christian vigil services. In addition, the sixteenth and seventeenth centuries witnessed the flowering of the Reformation, a religious reform movement that gave birth to Protestant Christianity. Many of the new Protestant denominations abandoned the Easter Vigil, along with many other rituals and festivals observed by Roman Catholics. Finally, in the seventh century the Roman Catholic Church introduced the Easter Sunday service. Over the centuries this service grew in popularity as attendance at the Easter Vigil declined. By the early part of the twentieth century the Easter Vigil was one of the least well attended services of Holy Week.

In the second half of the twentieth century Western Christians, that is, Roman Catholics and Protestants, began to restore the Easter Vigil service to its former glory. In 1955, after a trial period of several years, Roman Catholic authorities ordered the Easter Vigil service to be moved back to Holy Saturday evening. This act revived the symbolic power of the fires and lights used in the vigil service. This same era witnessed a liturgical renewal movement among Western Christians which has influenced both Roman Catholic and Protestant attitudes towards the Easter Vigil service and its associated customs and ceremonies.

Contemporary Services among Western Christians

Contemporary Easter Vigil services among Western Christians feature many elements that have characterized the observance from ancient times. These include the kindling of new flame, the lighting of many candles, including the paschal candle, the baptism of new members and the congregation's renewal of their baptismal vows, lengthy Bible readings, and the celebration of the Eucharist.

The vigil service also marks the end of the many prohibitions that characterize **Lent**. Those who have fasted break their fasts, congregations that have refrained from using the word **alleluia** throughout Lent once more proclaim it, **bells** silenced on Maundy Thursday ring out again, and **veiled** images are revealed.

Orthodox Easter Vigil and Resurrection Services

Orthodox and other Eastern Christians also attend services on the evening of Holy Saturday. Orthodoxy is one of the three main branches of the Christian faith. Orthodoxy developed in eastern Europe, the Middle East, and north Africa. The Orthodox and Western Christian traditions split apart from one another around 1,000 years ago. Therefore, Orthodox Christians observe slightly different customs and ceremonies than do Western Christians (*see also* **Easter, Date of**).

Orthodox churches offer services on both the morning and the evening of Holy Saturday. The morning service addresses Jesus' **Descent into Hell** to liberate the dead and his observance of the Jewish Sabbath by resting in the grave (*for more on Sabbath, see* **Sunday**). The service begins in a somber tone but brightens as it turns to consider the Resurrection. In Greek Orthodox churches the priest scatters flower petals or bay leaves around the church while chanting, "Arise, O God, to the world." The leaves and petals represent Christ's triumph over death. Although celebrated on the morning of Holy Saturday, this observance technically serves as the vespers, or evening, service for Easter Sunday and thus as the Easter Vigil. Indeed, it resembles the Easter Vigil service observed by many Western Christians in its overall structure. A second service, known as the Resurrection service, is offered late at night on Holy Saturday. This service, too, belongs to Easter Sunday (*for more on this service and related customs, see* Easter Sunday).

At the end of this long service, the faithful enjoy a late meal which marks the end of the Lenten fast. This late-night Easter feast typically includes several items forbidden during Lent, such as cheese, meat soup, eggs, and **wine**. Many feel that the first food to pass their lips at this time should be a traditional Orthodox red **Easter egg**. The red color represents the **blood** of Christ, the egg itself new life, and the shell Jesus' tomb. The cracking of this egg represents Christ's emerging from the tomb.

Further Reading

Baldovin, John F. "Easter." In Mircea Eliade, ed. *The Encyclopedia of Religion*. Volume 4. New York: Macmillan, 1987.

Bradshaw, Paul F. "Easter in Christian Tradition." In Paul F. Bradshaw and Lawrence A. Hoffman, eds. *Easter and Passover: Origin and History to Modern Times*. Two Liturgical Traditions series, volume 5. Notre Dame, IN: University of Notre Dame Press, 1999.

Bradshaw, Paul F. "The Origins of Easter." In Paul F. Bradshaw and Lawrence A. Hoffman, eds. *Easter and Passover: Origin and History to Modern Times*. Two Liturgical Traditions series, volume 5. Notre Dame, IN: University of Notre Dame Press, 1999.

Hopko, Thomas. *The Orthodox Faith. Volume Two, Worship*. Syosset, NY: The Orthodox Church in America, 1972.

Monti, James. *The Week of Salvation*. Huntington, IN: Our Sunday Visitor Publications, 1993.

O'Shea, W. J. "Easter Vigil." In *New Catholic Encyclopedia*. Volume 5. New York: McGraw-Hill, 1967.

Rouvelas, Marilyn. *A Guide to Greek Traditions and Customs in America*. Bethesda, MD: Nea Attiki Press, 1993.

Talley, Thomas J. *The Origins of the Liturgical Year*. Collegeville, MN: Liturgical Press, 1986.

"Vigil." In E. A. Livingstone, ed. *The Oxford Dictionary of the Christian Church*. Third edition. Oxford, England: Oxford University Press, 1997.

Weiser, Francis X. *The Easter Book*. New York: Harcourt, Brace and Company, 1954.

Wybrew, Hugh. *Orthodox Lent, Holy Week and Easter*. Crestwood, NY: St. Vladimir's Seminary Press, 1997.

Easter Week

Bright Week, Renewal Week,
Week of New Garments, White Week

The seven days that follow Easter constitute Easter Week. In early Christian and early medieval times, Easter festivities and related religious services continued through this week. During Easter week the newly baptized attended church daily wearing the white robes given them at their **baptisms** during the **Easter Vigil** service. This custom gave rise to two folk names for Easter Week: "White Week," a name popular among western Europeans, and the "Week of New Garments," a name heard more frequently in eastern lands. Greeks often call the festival "Bright Week." This name comes from one of the titles associated with Easter itself, *Lambri*, meaning "bright." The word bright recalls the fires and lights associated with the Easter Vigil service, which in turn symbolize the spiritual light brought into the world by **Jesus** Christ (*see also* **Easter Fires**). The Orthodox also sometimes call Easter Week "Renewal Week." This name reflects the Christian teaching that by Jesus' **resurrection** all things are made new (2 Corinthians 5:17). In Greek Orthodox and other Orthodox churches the doors to the sanctuary remain open during this week in honor of the Resurrection.

The Easter Week holiday ends at the close of **Low Sunday**, the first Sunday after Easter. Low Sunday serves as the last day of the Easter octave. In the language of the church an octave is an **eight**-day period defined by a festival and the seven days that follow it. Among the Orthodox the Sunday after Easter is sometimes referred to as *Antipascha*, a name signifying that the day closes the *Pascha*, or Easter, festival. The Orthodox also call the day "St. Thomas Sunday," since church services on this day retell the story of St. Thomas the Apostle's encounter with the risen Christ.

History

Around the year 389 the Roman emperor made it easier for the newly baptized to attend church daily during this week by declaring the entire period a holiday. All Christians, however, not just the newly baptized, celebrated this week as a holiday and a holy time. Many refrained from working and attended church daily.

The religious obligations associated with Easter Week, or the octave of Easter, diminished over time. By the late eleventh century Church authorities expected the faithful to attend church only three times during this week. By the turn of the twentieth century only **Easter Monday** remained as a day of obligatory church attendance for Roman Catholics. In 1911 Roman Catholic authorities released the faithful from this last Easter Week obligation.

The feasting and revelry associated with Easter Week also declined over time. In England this slow decline eventually whittled a week of post-Easter festivities down to a single day. In the ninth century King Alfred the Great (849-899) ruled that none need to labor in the fourteen-day period that surrounded Easter. This included **Holy Week**, the week preceding **Easter Sunday**, and Easter Week, the week following. People tended to their religious devotions in the week preceding Easter and combined attendance at religious services with feasts, parties, games, and relaxation in the week following. By the thirteenth century this two-week period had shortened and shifted to the latter half of Holy Week and the ten days following Easter. These last two days, the second Monday and Tuesday after Easter, somehow acquired the mysterious name of **Hocktide**, and occasioned some of the most hilarious hijinks of the post-Easter celebrations. In 1552 Parliament passed a law restricting post-Easter festivities to the Monday and Tuesday directly following Easter. This state of affairs lasted until the nineteenth century, when lawmakers further reduced rejoicing to Easter Monday alone.

Today only the name, a faint spirit of festivity, and a few old customs remain as remnants of this once widely celebrated holiday. Modern work schedules have made it difficult to honor the old obligation to rejoice for a full week following Easter.

Further Reading

Hutton, Ronald. *Stations of the Sun*. Oxford, England: Oxford University Press, 1996.

Metford, J. C. J. *The Christian Year*. London, England: Thames and Hudson, 1991.

Rouvelas, Marilyn. *A Guide to Greek Traditions and Customs in America*. Bethesda, MD: Nea Attiki Press, 1993.

Weiser, Francis X. *The Easter Book*. New York: Harcourt, Brace and Company, 1954.

Easter Witch

One old Swedish Easter custom might remind many Americans more of Halloween than Easter. On **Maundy Thursday** or **Holy Saturday**, Swedish schoolgirls dress up as witches and go door to door begging for sweets or coins. These smiling Swedish Easter witches charm rather than frighten their neighbors, however. The traditional costume requires a shiny copper kettle, a broomstick, and a black cat, though nowadays not every child comes up with all the customary gear. Some end up carrying their parents' coffee pots in lieu of a copper kettle. Prospective Easter witches usually transform their mothers' skirts, shawls, aprons, and kerchiefs into a costume. Rosy red cheeks, dabbed on with makeup, complete the look. Some Easter witches slide a decorated Easter letter under the door of each house they visit with the understanding that this seasonal greeting may prompt the inhabitants to offer them an Easter treat. In Sweden the Easter witch has become such a symbol of the holiday that little Easter witch dolls are sometimes used as centerpieces for dining room tables at this time of year.

In Finland children also dress up as Easter witches and visit their neighbors. Although this custom can be traced back to the nineteenth century in Finland, it became more widespread during the 1980s, when schools, daycare centers, and the media began to publicize and promote it. Some Finns have reacted negatively to the concept of children begging from door to door. Finnish Easter witches do offer something in return for the sweets and coins they hope to receive. In addition to reciting good luck poems, many also carry willow switches with which to whisk householders. This old Finnish Easter custom was believed to confer good health and well being.

Easter falls at a time of year associated with witches and their activities in northern European folklore. Old German, Austrian, and Scandinavian folk beliefs warned that witches from this part of the world gathered in Germany's Harz Mountains for a wild celebration on the evening of April 30. An old Czech folk custom called for the burning of bonfires on this same evening in the hopes of frightening off witches. Folk tradition dubbed this occasion **Walpurgis Night**, as it falls the evening before St. Walpurga's Day.

Old Swedish folk beliefs taught that witches were active during **Holy Week**, too. One such belief taught that witches gathered at Blåkulla, a mysterious location somewhere in Sweden, for a celebration of their own on Maundy Thursday. People hid their broomsticks and billy-goats on this day, fearing that a witch in sudden need for transportation might steal them and, by means of a spell, fly away on them to Blåkulla.

Another old folk teaching, also found in Finland, warned that witches were especially active on **Good Friday** and Holy Saturday, the two days that **Jesus** Christ spent in the grave. People protected themselves from evil enchantments on these dangerous days by burning bonfires, painting **crosses** on their doors, hanging crossed pairs of scythes in their barns, shooting off firearms, and other activities thought to frighten away witches. Nowadays, neighborhood children, dressed up as Easter witches in their mothers' old clothes, are all that remains of these folk beliefs.

Further Reading

Downman, Lorna, Paul Britten Austin, and Anthony Baird. *Round the Swedish Year*. Stockholm, Sweden: Bokförlaget Fabel, 1961.

Griffin, Robert H., and Ann H. Shurgin, eds. *The Folklore of World Holidays*. Second edition. Detroit, MI: Gale Research, 1999.

Lee, Tan Chung. *Festivals of the World: Finland*. Milwaukee, WI: Gareth Stevens Publishing, 1998.

Web Site

"Finnish Easter Traditions," an article by Sirpa Karjalainen, Assistant, Department of Ethnology at the University of Helsinki, posted on the Virtual Finland website: http://www.finland.fi/finfo/english/paaseng.html

Egg Lore

Fresh green leaves, flowers and, in the countryside, baby animals surround us at springtime. Perhaps this seasonal emphasis on new life explains why the egg became an Easter symbol. In cultures from around the world, both past and present, the egg serves as a token of new life. This symbolism extends far beyond Christian lands, and in fact predates the existence of Christianity. Among some Christians, the egg has become an Easter symbol representing the concept of **resurrection** (*for more on the Christian symbolism of eggs, see also* **Easter Eggs**).

Creation

In some societies the egg came to represent much more than new life. It became an emblem of the mysterious source from which sprang the world, the universe, and life itself. An ancient Egyptian myth about the creation of the world states that in the beginning the earth god, Geb, joined with the sky goddess, Nut. Together they produced an egg, out of which hatched the entire universe. From this egg also sprang the **phoenix,** an immortal bird which later became a symbol of Christ. Another Egyptian myth asserts that the creator god, Khnum, took a lump of mud from the Nile river, put it on his potter's wheel, and spun it into an egg. The world emerged from this egg. Another old Egyptian legend recounts that the chief of all the gods, Ptah, sat down before a potter's wheel and created a golden egg out of which hatched the sun and the moon.

In ancient India early proponents of the Hindu religion claimed that the "world egg" took shape in the waters of chaos that existed before the creation of the world. The egg gave birth to Prajapati, the father of all the gods, human beings, and other creatures. Another version of the myth states that the egg itself gave birth to the world. One half of the shell became the earth, the other half the sky. In yet another variation of the tale Prajapati creates the world egg from his own sweat. The upper half of the egg encloses the sky and the lower half the earth.

The idea that the world emerged from an egg has also found expression in myths and tales from ancient Greece, Phoenicia, Iran, Indonesia, Latvia, Estonia, Finland, west Africa, Central America, and western South American.

Where did our world come from? How did living creatures come into being? The above legends attempt to answer these questions. Perhaps they represent this process as the hatching of an egg because the egg, which does not appear to be alive itself, eventually breaks open and brings forth new life.

Sacrifice, Fertility, and Magic

Many folk customs concerning eggs emphasize their association with life and with the creation of new life. For example, egg sacrifices have been found in many different cultures. Folklorists speculate that the close association made between eggs and life may have inspired these sacrificial customs, the eggs serving in some way as a substitute for other living creatures. Some European folk traditions taught that the spirits guarding homes, rivers, or other parts of the landscape demanded a sacrifice of eggs before they permitted humans to pass through or dwell there. If they didn't receive this sacrifice, they took revenge by causing accidents and other mishaps.

Fertility rituals often include eggs. In many European lands farmers once left them in fields and pastures to increase the harvest and the number of offspring borne by farm animals. In some parts of Germany, Holland, and Belgium villagers celebrated a festival called *Kirmis* or *Kerwe* during the summer. In many locations this festival featured the construction of a large crown of eggs hung over the town's main streets. This decoration remained in place until the summer crops were in. Many egg charms designed to increase human fertility have also been recorded by folklorists.

In European folklore eggs often serve as important ingredients in magical spells. All across the continent, including such diverse countries as France, Holland, Sweden, Portugal, the former Yugoslavia, and Russia, folk tradition teaches that witches use discarded eggshells to travel to their midnight gatherings. By means of a spell the eggshell is made to serve as some kind of vehicle, often a boat. Perhaps their association with the creation of life itself suggested to the superstitious that they could become potent elements in magical practices.

Soul Transfers and Mourning

Certain folk beliefs and customs surrounding grief and mourning as well as those concerning methods of magically evading death also reveal the powerful cultural connections made between eggs and life. Folklore from many corners of Europe taught that supernatural creatures could empty the source of their strength into an egg or even hide their soul there. After making this transfer they usually hid the egg in some unusual place, often inside the body of another animal. After that, the only way to diminish their powers or to kill them was to find the egg and break it. Folktales describing these kinds of soul transfers have been collected from Ireland, Iceland, and Italy, as well as Brittany in northern France, Bohemia in the Czech Republic, and Lapland, or Saamiland, which extends across the northernmost territories of Sweden, Norway, Finland, and Russia's Kola Peninsula.

Studies of traditional funeral practices in many different cultures reveals that rituals associated with burial and mourning often include eggs. Eggs are served at Jewish funerals as a reminder of the continuity of life. Real eggs, or marble facsimiles, have been found inside ancient English burial sites as well as ancient Greek and Roman tombs. In past times mourners in Russia and the Balkans placed eggs on top of graves. Russian folklore also recommended leaving a dish of fried eggs beside graves or underneath the birch trees said to be inhabited by the spirits of the dead. Venetia Newell, author of an extensive study of egg folklore, concludes that in these contexts eggs serve as symbols of resurrection, or life after death. These funeral eggs may represent the idea that although death appears to be final, the apparently lifeless body in fact gives birth to the immortal soul.

Further Reading

Eliade, Mircea. *Patterns in Comparative Religion*. Cleveland, OH: Meridian, 1963.

Leach, Maria, ed. *Funk and Wagnalls Standard Dictionary of Folklore, Mythology and Legend*. New York: Harper and Row, 1984.

Lord, Priscilla Sawyer, and Daniel J. Foley. *Easter Garland*. 1963. Reprint. Detroit, MI: Omnigraphics, 1999.

Newall, Venetia. *An Egg at Easter*. Bloomington, IN: Indiana University Press, 1971.

Watts, Alan W. *Easter*. New York: Henry Schuman, 1950.

Egg Rolling

Egg rolling is a traditional Easter game often played on **Easter Monday**. Participants choose dyed, hard-boiled **Easter eggs** and place them along a starting line on top of a hill or slight incline. Contestants release their eggs and cheer them on as they roll downhill. In some versions of the game players push the egg along rather than simply let it roll.

History, Legend, and Symbol

The earliest known egg-rolling games took place in Paris in 1587. Danish folklorists have also documented the existence of the custom in their country as far back as the sixteenth century. The earliest record of the game in England dates back to 1694. An old Ukrainian folktale proposes an ancient origin for the custom. It claims that the Blessed Virgin Mary obtained an audience with the Roman governor, Pontius **Pilate**, when she heard that her son, **Jesus**, had been arrested. Before setting off for the governor's palace Mary filled her apron with eggs. When she knelt before Pilate the eggs rolled out of the sides of her apron. The eggs kept going until they reached the ends of the earth inspiring the invention of egg-rolling games (*see also* **Mary, Blessed Virgin**). Folklore common to both Orthodox and Protestant Christians sees in egg rolling a symbol of the rolling away of the stone that sealed Jesus' tomb. Thus the custom serves as a reminder of the **Resurrection**.

Egg Rolling in Europe and the Middle East

Egg-rolling customs can be found all across Europe. Egg-rolling contests often take place in northern Britain on Easter Monday. Contestants choose what they hope to be prize-winning Easter eggs and line up at the top of a hill. Egg-rolling rules vary from event to event. In some places the winner is the person whose eggs roll the farthest distance. In others victory attaches itself to the person whose egg survives the most rolls intact. In still others top honors go to the person whose egg rolls between two pegs. In Denmark egg-rolling contests take place on **Easter Sunday**. There the winner succeeds by knocking their egg against another person's egg. Sometimes the winner must repeat this feat or execute it with such force that their opponent's egg cracks. Afterwards contestants eat their eggs with **bread** and butter. In Sweden children eat the eggs that crack as the contest proceeds. In Austria children sometimes compete with wooden eggs. Egg-rolling contests can also be found in Switzerland, northern Italy, the Netherlands, France, Slovakia, Slovenia, Bohemia, Germany, and Latvia. The custom also exists in some countries in the Middle East, such as Azerbaijan and Egypt.

Egg Rolling in Washington, D.C.

In the United States a well-known egg-rolling contest takes place each year on Easter Monday at the White House. This contest dates back to before the Civil War (1861-65). In those days the main event took place at the Capitol building, where an assortment of Washington's children launched their eggs down the terraced lawns of the building's west front. While the public enjoyed itself at the Capitol building, the president's family sometimes hosted small egg-rolling parties on the White House lawn. The children of Presidents Abraham Lincoln (1860-65) and Andrew Johnson (1865-69) were known to have enjoyed these parties.

The Civil War ended just before Easter in the year 1865. In spite of this joyous event sadness enveloped Washington's egg-rolling affairs and all other Easter festivities that year. Just two days before Easter, on **Good Friday**, an assassin shot and mortally wounded President Abraham Lincoln as he attended the theater. President Lincoln died the following day, and the nation plunged from shock into mourning.

The Washington egg-rolling event first attracted public attention in the years following the American Civil War. The festivities taking place at the Capitol building brought together children of every race and color and so came to the attention of reporters. Journalists praised the event for effortlessly achieving the integration that the War and social reform programs had failed to bring about.

In the 1870s senators and congressmen began to complain about litter left behind by the egg rollers and the destruction of the grass that resulted from the enthusiastic tread of many little feet. To be sure, the elected officials also began to take offense at cattle crossing the grounds of the Capitol building, feeling that the dignity of the nation —not to mention the landscaping—suffered from the intrusion of such rustic activities on the seat of government. In 1876 Congress passed a law which forbade anyone from using the gardens of the Capitol building as a playground. In 1877 the egg-rolling event was rained out. Those who returned to the Capitol building for egg games on Easter Monday 1878 were kept off the grounds by the Capitol Hill police.

Egg Rolling Moves to the White House

When it came to finding a new place to roll eggs the informality of Washington life in those days worked in the children's favor. The first official White House egg-rolling event took place in 1878 thanks to the initiative shown by one young lad. The boy spied President Rutherford B. Hayes (1877–81) walking down the street a few days before Easter and called out to him, "Say! Say! Are you going to let us roll eggs in your yard?" The President, disarmed by both the request and the breezy manner of its delivery, replied that he would look into the matter. After the White House staff explained the nature of the event to him President Hayes instructed them to let the children use the White House lawn for their egg games. The following year another boy approached President Hayes in the same casual manner. The president again agreed to host the Easter Monday egg-rolling party and a tradition was born.

The popularity of the White House egg-rolling affair grew as the years passed. In the early years the children set up their own games without much interference from the White House staff. An audience with the president, however, was one of the treats that children came to expect on this day of fun and games at the White House. Many presidents obliged them. A rule developed fairly early on that no adult would be admitted to the event unless accompanied by a child. Some cunning children cashed in on this regulation by escorting childless adults past the entry gates for a small fee. Then the enterprising youngsters snuck out the back way in search of another paying customer. In the mid-1930s White House officials got wind of these goings-on and broke up this miniature Easter Monday racket.

Cancellations

The Easter Monday White House egg-rolling event has suffered several setbacks in its history. White House officials cancelled it in 1917, the year the United States entered World War I, in the belief that the enormous waste of food involved would be inappropriate in a time of hardship. The event resumed in 1921. In 1942 the White House again cancelled the egg roll due to wartime difficulties. As a result the egg rollers temporarily reclaimed their old grounds at the Capitol building. After the war President Harry Truman (1945-53) dawdled in welcoming them back to the presidential gardens. Then extensive repairs made to the White House turned its lawns into a construction yard for a number of years, preventing the annual egg roll from taking place.

Renewal

The south lawn egg roll finally returned in 1953 under President Dwight D. Eisenhower (1953-61). In these later years of the event's history, however, it proved much more difficult for youngsters to catch a glimpse of, much less speak with, the president. From 1961 to 1975, Easter Monday found Presidents Kennedy, Johnson, Nixon, and Ford away on business. Finally, in 1976, President Gerald Ford once again attended the event being held in his own backyard.

In the late twentieth century the White House egg roll has become a more structured and a more polished event, as new elements have been added to the celebration by successive presidents and first ladies. In 1969 the **Easter Bunny**, in reality a White House staffer in a white rabbit costume, appeared at the event for the first time. In 1974 the first organized egg races took place. In the White House version of this game children line up eight abreast and, with the use of metal spoons, roll their eggs down lanes marked in the lawn. During the Carter administration (1976-80) party organizers added other attractions, such as dancers, lasso-twirling cowboys, and petting animals. The Reagans (1980-88) also expanded the variety of entertainments offered. The Clintons (1992-2000), who attended every Easter Monday party held in their backyard during their eight years in the White House, made egg-rolling history by cybercasting the event on the White House web site, www.whitehouse.gov.

A brigade of nearly 500 volunteers aided the White House staff in preparing the annual Easter Monday festivities for the year 2000. White House staffers cooked up the official equipment for this event: 7,200 hard-boiled Easter eggs. They estimated that 30,000 children and their families would attend the presidential Easter party. Therefore they ordered 20,000 souvenir wooden eggs, to be given away as parting gifts for the youngsters. As has become customary in order to regulate the crowds, attendees must obtain advance tickets for the event. These tickets, given free of charge to parties containing a child between the ages of three and six, assign partygoers a specific time during which they may enter the south lawn area in order to participate in the egg-roll contest.

Further Reading

Hole, Christina. *British Folk Customs*. London, England: Hutchinson and Company, 1976.

Newall, Venetia. *An Egg at Easter*. Bloomington, IN: Indiana University Press, 1971.

Web Sites

"White House Easter Egg Roll Scheduled for Monday, April 24," a White House press release available at: http://ofcn.org/cyber.serv/teledem/pb/2000/apr/msg00122.html

"With Easter Monday You Get Egg Roll at the White House," an article by C. L. Arbelhide, posted at the National Archives and Records Administration at: http://www.nara.gov/publications/prologue/eggroll1.html

Egg Tapping
Egg Dumping, Egg Fighting, Egg Knocking, Egg Picking, Egg Shackling

In Europe many people celebrate **Easter Sunday** by playing egg-tapping games. As a result of immigration from Europe and the Middle East, this game may also be found among pockets of the U.S. population. The custom goes by many names, including egg dumping, egg fighting, egg knocking, egg picking, and egg shackling. Players select hard-boiled, dyed **Easter eggs**, pair off, and face each other. One person grasps his or her egg tightly in hand, revealing only the tip, while the other knocks their own egg against it. Whoever emerges from this encounter with an unbroken eggshell wins. Then winners from each pair compete with each other until only one person with an intact eggshell remains. He or she is declared the winner. In some versions of the game players may compete with either end of the shell, and are not disqualified until both have cracked.

Egg Tapping among Orthodox Christians

In Greece egg tapping constitutes a popular **Easter Week** pastime. The bright red Easter eggs used by Greek and other Orthodox Christians have a special religious significance. The red color represents the **blood** of Christ, the egg itself **Jesus'** tomb, and the cracking of the egg Jesus' emergence from the tomb, or his **resurrection**. Greek families may place any egg that survives the egg-tapping contest intact in the home *ikonostasi*, a special shelf where the family keeps devotional objects, such as religious images, candles, incense, and the Bible. In Greece egg tapping is such a common Easter game that the image of two red eggs knocking against one another may be found on many Greek **Easter cards**. Winning the egg-tapping game is thought to bring good luck for the year. Some players make a wish before testing their egg against an opponent. Greek folklore teaches that the winner's wish will come true.

In Romania, another predominantly Orthodox country, families play an egg-tapping game that requires each family member to knock their egg against the one possessed by the head of the household. On Easter Sunday they use the small end of the eggs. On **Easter Monday** and Tuesday they may use either the narrow or the blunt end, or even the sides of the egg. According to Romanian folklore, the person whose egg remains whole will outlive the others.

In Albania the game has spread beyond the Orthodox Christian community, a minority in this predominantly Muslim country, and is played by Muslims and Christians alike.

Armenians also enjoy egg-tapping games on Easter Sunday. Armenian folk tradition encourages a pair of contestants to face each other with a clutch of hard-boiled Easter eggs. They line these up in two rows, pick up the first pair of eggs, and begin "egg fighting." The last to possess an intact egg wins, and may keep all the eggs.

Egg Tapping in Western Europe

In the Netherlands children play an egg-tapping game called *eierrikken*. They gather hard-boiled, dyed Easter eggs of various colors and divide themselves into two teams. The teams form two lines that face each other, so that each child is paired with an opponent from the other team who carries an egg of the same color. By tapping one egg against the other, the paired opponents try to break each others' shells. The winner of each match keeps the loser's egg and goes on to face a new opponent. The child who gathers the most eggs wins.

In Switzerland, too, traditional egg-tapping rules permitted the winner of each egg-tapping encounter to take the loser's egg. In past times egg tapping also enjoyed great popularity in the neighboring states of Austria and Germany. German-speaking immigrants brought the custom along when they settled in Pennsylvania. In the nineteenth century the Pennsylvania Dutch, as these immigrants and their descendants came to be known, called the game "egg picking." There, too, losers forfeited their egg.

In some places children play egg-tapping games by knocking the egg against their own forehead. This method of play is popular in Spain and Sweden.

In England the game is known as egg shackling or egg dumping. The winner of each match receives the loser's egg. English historians trace these egg games as far back as the late seventeenth century. In nineteenth-century Dorset people played the game at **Shrovetide**, or **Carnival**, rather than at Easter (*see also* **Pancake Day**). Indeed the Saturday before **Ash Wednesday** was once known as Egg Saturday in some parts of England. In the Dorset variation of the game players placed their eggs in a sieve which someone shook until only one egg was left uncracked. The owner of that egg was declared the winner.

Hard Eggs

The desire to win at egg tapping has motivated people to invent ways of coming up with an especially hard, champion egg. Some try to strengthen the shells of their eggs by boiling them, or by soaking them in alcohol or lime for a week. Others seek out guinea-fowl eggs, which are tougher than hen's eggs. Syrian children test their Easter eggs for hardness in advance, by tapping them against their teeth. Bulgarian folklore teaches that eggs laid on **Good Friday** are bound to be the hardest, as they gain strength from their birth on that holy day.

Further Reading

Griffin, Robert H., and Ann H. Shurgin, eds. *The Folklore of World Holidays*. Second edition. Detroit, MI: Gale Research, 1999.

Henderson, Helene, and Sue Ellen Thompson, eds. *Holidays, Festivals, and Celebrations of the World Dictionary*. Second edition. Detroit, MI: Omnigraphics, 1997.

Hole, Christina. *British Folk Customs*. London, England: Hutchinson and Company, 1976.

Newall, Venetia. *An Egg at Easter*. Bloomington, IN: Indiana University Press, 1971.

Rouvelas, Marilyn. *A Guide to Greek Traditions and Customs in America*. Bethesda, MD: Nea Attiki Press, 1993.

Shoemaker, Alfred L. *Eastertide in Pennsylvania*. Kutztown, PA: Pennsylvania Folklife Society, 1960.

Egg Tree

Some families celebrate Easter by hanging **Easter eggs** on a small tree, bush, or branch. Thus decorated it becomes an Easter egg tree. Easter egg trees serve as holiday decorations and as emblems of the new life associated with the spring season.

Folklorists believe that the Easter egg tree got its start in central Europe, possibly in Germany. In this region of Europe people often make indoor egg trees by placing cut branches in a vase and hanging eggs from them. In Germany Easter trees may also be called Easter pyramids or Easter wreaths, names perhaps borrowed from the pyramids and wreaths that Germans use as Christmas decorations. Swedes also enjoy making egg trees out of cut branches. They decorate them with dyed eggs and ornaments representing small birds and witches (*see also* **Easter Witch**).

German immigrants brought the notion of Easter egg trees with them to the United States. In the German-American communities that make up the Pennsylvania Dutch country, Easter egg trees can be traced back to the second half of the nineteenth century. The earliest form of the custom seems to have been the outdoor egg tree. According to historical documents from this era, when decorating outdoor Easter trees and branches the Pennsylvania Dutch used blown egg shells (pierced eggshells out of which the egg itself had been emptied). They jammed them onto the ends of twigs without dye or decoration. In the late nineteenth century indoor Easter egg trees constituted something of a novelty. In making these trees folk artists hung dyed and decorated eggs onto small trees or barren branches with thread. Early commentators speculated on the similarity between the Easter tree and the Christmas tree, suggesting that the popularity of the Christmas tree had inspired the new Easter custom.

In 1950 Katherine Milhouse published a children's book called *The Egg Tree*. In this book Milhouse described the Pennsylvania Dutch customs concerning egg trees and Easter egg designs. Folklorists credit this popular book with spreading the egg tree beyond German-American communities into the wider U.S. population.

Egg Trees on Other Holidays

In many European countries trees and branches decorated with eggs make appearances at festivals other than Easter. In parts of Germany people put them up for **Pentecost** and the summer solstice, or St. John's Day (June 24), as well as Easter. Traditional adornments for the St. John's Day tree include fresh flowers, candles, and chains of eggshells. In parts of France and Germany old folk customs called for egg trees at harvest time.

On **May Day** in the Czech Republic folk tradition encourages young men to give branches or small trees decorated with ribbons and dyed eggs to their sweethearts. Over the past two centuries folklorists have spotted May trees decked with eggs and other ornaments in parts of Ireland, England, Hungary, and Germany. Germans decorated their May trees with cakes and sausages as well as eggs. Following an old Polish folk tradition, young people decorated green branches with colored eggs and took them door to door on May Day. With these branches in hand they sang for their neighbors and received in return a gift of eggs. Traditional crafts appearing in Swedish markets around May Day included maypoles covered with colored paper and gilt eggshells in honor of the holiday.

Laetare Sunday is another day traditionally associated with green branches adorned with eggshells. In past times these were carried in processions as symbols of summer. In Germany this custom can be traced as far back as the seventeenth century. Although the carrying of these branches was forbidden in the late nineteenth century, the practice still survives in some places, often as a children's custom. It can still be found in parts of Germany, Moravia, and Bohemia. Often, ceremonies depicting the burial of winter precede the triumphant carrying of these branches (*see also* **Czech Republic, Easter and Holy Week in**).

Further Reading

Newall, Venetia. *An Egg at Easter.* Bloomington, IN: Indiana University Press, 1971.

Russ, Jennifer M. *German Festivals and Customs.* London, England: Oswald Wolff, 1982.

Shoemaker, Alfred L. *Eastertide in Pennsylvania.* Kutztown, PA: Pennsylvania Folklife Society, 1960.

Egypt, Easter in

Although the vast majority of Egyptians are Muslims, the nation's tiny Christian community (about seven percent of the population) celebrates Easter with great enthusiasm. The celebrations of these Coptic Christians hark back to the first several centuries after **Jesus'** death when the new, Christian religion established a stronghold in Egypt. The religious practices of Coptic Christians are more similar to those of other Eastern Christians than they are to those of Western Christians, that is, Roman Catholics and Protestants.

Palm Sunday

In early Christian times the biggest **Palm Sunday** celebrations took place in the city of Alexandria. Christians decorated churches with **palm** and olive branches and marched in religious processions carrying palm fronds.

In the seventh century Egypt was invaded by Arab Muslims. Although the new rulers did not outlaw Christianity, the religion entered a long, slow decline as Islam became the dominant faith in the region. Christians continued to celebrate Palm Sunday with religious processions led by priests and other officials who carried incense burners, **crosses**, and the Bible. The processions stopped at the houses of judges and other politicians, whether Christians or not, where Bible verses were read aloud. In the thirteenth through fifteenth centuries a new Palm Sunday custom developed. People went to bathe and be blessed at a well in Matariya, north of Cairo. According to legend Mary, Joseph, and the baby Jesus had stopped there on their journey into Egypt (*see also* **Mary, Blessed Virgin**). Even Muslims participated in this custom.

Nowadays many Coptic Christians attend midnight services during which palm branches are blessed by priests. The priests carry crosses decorated with palm fronds and walk around the inside of the church seven times. The procession stops in front of all the church's relics, items once owned by a saint, and icons, religious images used in prayer and worship. Outside the church people buy special loaves of **bread** stamped with religious symbols. They bring the loaves home along with the blessed palm branches. Coptic Christians prepare for morning services on Palm Sunday by weaving palm fronds into beautiful shapes. Shields, stars, triangles, anchors and, of course, crosses are among the most popular designs. Many people embellish these palm weavings with fresh flowers. The resulting ornaments may be finished by attaching a tassel to the top of the design or by mounting them on a stem or branch. Great numbers of children attend Palm Sunday church services carrying their woven palm fronds. After the story of Jesus' entry into Jerusalem is read aloud, the priests sprinkle holy **water** on the palm ornaments, sometimes tossing water out into the crowd to reach all the palms. Families then take the blessed ornaments home and hang them on their front doors that they might confer a blessing on the house.

Easter Sunday

Easter Sunday celebrations begin late at night on **Holy Saturday** with the **Easter Vigil** service. This long church service honors the **resurrection** of Jesus Christ and lasts until the early hours of **Sunday** morning. Afterwards Coptic Christians return home for the Easter feast which marks the end of the long **Lenten fast**. Many Egyptian families prepare a stuffed turkey or a leg of **lamb** for their Easter meal. Stuffed grape leaves are another popular Easter dish. Parents often give their children **new clothes** and small gifts of money to mark this festive occasion.

Egypt's Coptic Christians enjoy a long tradition of including their Muslim neighbors in their Easter celebrations. In the Fatimid period (tenth through twelfth centuries), Muslims and Christians alike celebrated Easter by setting up tents along the banks of the Nile and throwing a great party at which everyone shared food, drink, and entertainment. Police, palace representatives, and sometimes even the king himself appeared at this festival. After this period, however, official Easter celebrations ceased. When the Ottoman sultans ruled Egypt (1517-1915) they reinstated the official celebration of Easter, though they themselves were Muslims. Indeed in 1528 one sultan is reported to have given away 20,000 **Easter eggs**. Today a big Easter celebration takes place at St. Mark's Cathedral in Cairo. The Coptic pope heads up the affair, which is attended by important officials representing the presidency and other branches of the Egyptian government.

Further Reading

Abbas, Jailan. *Festivals of Egypt*. Cairo, Egypt: Hoopoe Books, 1995.
Millen, Nina. *Children's Festivals from Many Lands*. New York: Friendship Press, 1964.

Eight

To the early Christians the number eight represented several important religious concepts, including **resurrection**, **redemption**, and eternity. These associations also led to its linkage with the practice of **baptism**. The number eight acquired these meanings because **Jesus** rose from death on the day after the Jewish Sabbath, that is, on the eighth day of the week (*for more on the Sabbath, see* **Sunday**). Thus, the number eight functioned as a symbol of the Easter story and message in early Christian times.

Jewish Tradition and the Seven-Day Week

In the Jewish tradition in which Jesus was raised, people celebrated the Sabbath on Saturday. The Sabbath, a day of rest and worship, fell on the last day of a seven-day cycle which we today call a week. According to the Hebrew scriptures, God himself started this seven-day cycle at the beginning of time, creating the world in six days and resting on the seventh (Genesis 2:1-3).

Easter as the Christian Eighth Day

All four Gospel accounts of Jesus' resurrection from the dead agree that it occurred on the day after the Jewish Sabbath, that is, on the first day of the Jewish week. This remarkable event so astounded the first Christians, however, that it shattered their view of the endlessly repeating cycle of the seven-day week. They began to view the day of the Resurrection as the eighth day of the week, because on that day God had added something utterly new to his Creation by raising Jesus from the dead. This symbolic eighth day of the week in fact coincided with the first day of the Jewish week. The early Christians found this overlap between the Jewish first day and the Christian eighth day extremely meaningful. In their eyes the first day of the Jewish week represented the beginning of the world and the creation of light, as told in the first chapter of the book of Genesis. The eighth day of the Christian week represented the beginning of a new kind of light and a new kind of creation, namely, the new relationship between God and humanity made possible through the death and resurrection of Jesus Christ. The association between the Resurrection and the eighth day convinced the early Christians to schedule their weekly worship services on Sunday rather than Saturday.

Baptism and the Number Eight

Because of its association with the resurrection of Christ, the number eight came to represent the spiritual themes associated with Easter, especially resurrection. It also symbolized redemption, **salvation**, and eternity. These themes also played an important role in the Christian sacrament of baptism, which the early Christians practiced primarily at Easter time. Early Christian architects constructed many octagonal, or eight-sided, baptisteries. The shape of these sunken tubs or small pools used for baptisms presented worshipers with a physical symbol connecting the ritual of baptism with the resurrection of Christ. Circular and hexagonal baptisteries also found favor among the early Christians.

Early Christians in northern Italy exercised an especially strong preference for octagonal baptisteries. On the baptistery of St. John for the

Church of St. Thecla, in Milan, Italy, an inscription attributed to St. Ambrose (339-397) alludes to the sacred symbolism attached to the number eight:

> Eight-niched soars this church destined for sacred rites,
> eight corners has its font, which befits its gift.
> Meet it was thus to build this fair baptismal hall
> about this sacred eight:
> here is our race reborn (Ferguson, 164).

Newly baptized members of the Christian faith observed special customs for eight days following their baptism. They attended church daily for special religious instruction and wore white robes to signify their joy and their new status as Christians. At the end of this eight-day period they began their life as ordinary members of the congregation. By the fourth century, the eighth day after Easter was recognized as a feast day in its own right. Known today as **Low Sunday**, it marked the close of **Easter Week** and the end of eight days of Easter celebrations. This eight-day celebration sparked the invention of other eight-day periods of religious rejoicing following major Christian festivals. These eight-day periods are known as "octaves."

The Number Eight as a Christian Symbol

Although the Resurrection may have been the scriptural event that most influenced how Christians viewed the number eight, other Bible stories also colored their thinking. For example, Noah's ark saved eight people from drowning in the great flood (Genesis 7). This story furthered the connection between the number eight and the concept of salvation. It also linked the number eight with the image of **water**, an affinity which may also have influenced the preference for eight-sided baptisteries. Other events from Christian scripture further tie the number eight to Jesus' life and teachings. The Bible tells us that Jesus was circumcised and named on the eighth day after his birth, according to Jewish custom (Luke 2:21). Later in life, his famous sermon on the mount described eight beatitudes, or states of blessedness (Matthew 5:3-10).

Further Reading

Cabrol, Fernand. "Octave." In Charles G. Herbermann et al., eds. *The Catholic Encyclopedia*. New York: Appleton, 1913. Available online at: http://www.newadvent.org/cathen/11204a.htm

Ferguson, Everett. "Baptistery." In his *Encyclopedia of Early Christianity*. Volume 1. New York: Garland, 1997.

Hatchett, Marion J. *Commentary on the American Prayer Book*. New York: HarperSanFrancisco, 1995.

Metford, J. C. J. *The Christian Year*. London, England: Thames and Hudson, 1991.

———. *Dictionary of Christian Lore and Legend*. London, England: Thames and Hudson, 1983.

Emmaus Walk

In the Gospel according to Luke, the risen **Jesus** first appears to his disciple **Peter** as he and a companion were walking from Jerusalem to Emmaus. This account implies that the event took place on the **Sunday** of the **Resurrection** (Luke 24:1-34). In central Europe Christians honored this story with an **Easter Monday** outing called an Emmaus walk. These outings revolved around walks to a picturesque site in the countryside where everyone would share a meal together. Some writers believe that in past times these informal processions had a religious dimension to them, but that with the passing of time they became less religious and more social. In more recent times groups of friends or families dressed in their fine Easter clothes, packed a picnic lunch, and headed for some scenic spot. Once they reached their destination they spent the rest of the day enjoying their meal, playing games, dancing, and singing. German speakers sometimes called a meadow frequently used for this purpose an *Osteranger*, or an "Easter field." The Poles named these festive sites "Emmaus groves." This old European custom may have inspired the American **Easter parade**.

The biblical story of the disciples' walk from Jerusalem to Emmaus has intrigued scholars, who so far have not been able to agree upon the location of this village. The name Emmaus means "warm wells" in Hebrew. According to most Bible manuscripts, this town lay about seven miles (sixty stadia) from Jerusalem. Scholars following up on this clue have proposed that such modern towns as Abu-Ghosh, Qaloniyeh, Motsa, and el-Qubeibeh may be ancient Emmaus. None of these locations, however, were associated with the name "Emmaus" in ancient times. A few Bible manuscripts as well as an old Palestinian folk tradition provide an alternative solution. They locate Emmaus about twenty miles from Jerusalem. Therefore, some researchers believe that Emmaus may have been a town now called Amwas, which lies nineteen miles from Jerusalem. The Romans and Greeks knew the town as Nicopolis but the Israelites called it Emmaus. It was the site of an important Jewish military victory in ancient times (1 Maccabees 3:40, 57; 4:1-15). Indeed, early church tradition names this site as the Emmaus of the Easter story.

Further Reading

Barth, Edna. *Lilies, Rabbits, and Painted Eggs.* New York: Houghton Mifflin/ Clarion Books, 1970.

Carey, Greg. "Emmaus." In David Noel Freedman, ed. *Eerdmans Dictionary of the Bible.* Grand Rapids, MI: William B. Eerdmans Publishing, 2000.

Miller, Charles H. "Emmaus." In Paul J. Achtemeier, ed. *The HarperCollins Bible Dictionary.* New York: HarperCollins, 1996.

Weiser, Francis X. *The Easter Book.* New York: Harcourt, Brace and Company, 1954.

———. *Handbook of Christian Feasts and Customs.* New York: Harcourt, Brace and World, 1952.

England, Easter and Holy Week in

Over the centuries the people of England invented numerous Easter customs and accumulated a variety of Easter-related folk beliefs. Many of these customs and beliefs have fallen out of fashion, though some still exist, and at least one, the **hot cross bun** associated with **Good Friday**, has become an international Easter food.

Palm Sunday

Many English churches distribute **palm** crosses to their parishioners on **Palm Sunday** (*see also* **Cross**). In past centuries parish priests blessed greenery on Palm Sunday. In the eighteenth century walking out into the countryside to gather greenery was a popular Palm Sunday custom. People referred to these outings as "going a-palming" or "going a-palmsoning." When they returned home they hung the green fronds in their homes for good luck. This practice survived into the early twentieth century as a child's custom, then disappeared entirely.

Maundy Thursday

English royalty invented a special **Maundy Thursday** custom still practiced today, the distribution of Maundy money. This custom began as a **footwashing** ritual, in which English monarchs washed the feet of poor men on Maundy Thursday as a gesture of humility and a sign of their willingness to follow the example set by **Jesus**. In England historical records reveal that King John (1167-1216) was the first English monarch to perform this ritual. King John and his successors washed the feet of thirteen men. King Edward III (1312-1377) added a new twist to the ritual by tying the number of people whose feet he washed to his own age. He also gave them gifts of food, money, and clothing. After the time of King James II (1633-1701) the English monarchs discarded the custom of washing the feet of the poor, although they continued making gifts of food, clothing, and money. In time the customary gifts were replaced by money. Queen Victoria (1819-1901) limited her gift giving to specially minted coins called "Maundy money." The current English monarch, Queen Elizabeth II, carries on this version of the tradition. The number of recipients equals her age in years.

Good Friday

Hot cross buns are a traditional Good Friday treat in England. These buns consist of sweetened **bread** dough enhanced with spices, citrus peel, and currants or raisins. After baking the cooled buns are decorated with a cross made from sugar icing.

Among the English a preference for eating hot cross buns on Good Friday can be traced back at least as far as the eighteenth century. In 1733 *Poor Robin's Almanack* printed the following verse:

> Good Friday comes this month, the old woman runs
> With one or two a penny hot cross-buns
> Whose virtue is, if you believe what's said,
> They'll not grow mouldy like the common bread.
> (Weiser, 129)

In the nineteenth century researchers recorded many English folk beliefs concerning hot cross buns. According to these beliefs, these small loaves of bread would neither mold nor decay. Some assumed this to be true of all bread baked on Good Friday. Moreover, according to folk medical lore, hot cross buns had the power to cure disease, especially intestinal disease. Some people hung hot cross buns in their homes all year long as a means of protecting the household against illness, lightning, fire, and other misfortunes.

Other old superstitions connected with Good Friday include the belief that it is unlucky to wash clothes on this day. Those who did would find their laundry spotted with **blood**. Another superstition assured people that **water** dipped in silence before the rising of the sun would stay fresh and pure all year long. Folk belief also taught that Good Friday was a lucky day to plant seeds because Jesus had been put in the ground on this day. It was also considered an especially lucky day to sow parsley, beans, peas, and potatoes. Other actions destined to bring luck on Good Friday included eating salt fish, moving bees, pruning roses, jumping rope, and spinning tops. On the other hand, those who used a hammer and nails, set out to sea, went fishing, shod horses, and plowed fields on this day were certain to attract ill luck.

In medieval times English kings blessed gold or silver rings, known as "cramp rings," on Good Friday. The rings were then used to treat epilepsy and palsy. Rooted in ancient beliefs that the ability to heal accompanies royal blood, this practice began with Edward II (1284-1327). The ceremony resembled in part the **Veneration of the Cross**. The king knelt on a specially laid carpet and crept, on his hands and knees, towards the crucifix at the front of the church. A bowl, containing a number of rings, lay beside the crucifix. When the king reached the bowl, with his almoner (an official in charge of distributing alms) kneeling beside him, he said a prayer over the rings. By 1522 the monarch no longer crept to the cross but rather simply knelt before it. Queen Elizabeth I (1533-1603) discontinued the custom for unknown reasons.

In past times **Ash Wednesday** kicked off the English **marbles** season. Throughout **Lent** men and boys played competitive marble games with one another. The marbles season ended on Good Friday, which was known as Marble Day in Surrey and Sussex, regions where the game was particularly popular. After that time anyone caught playing marbles might be forced to forfeit them. Some researchers believe that the practice of playing marbles on Good Friday may have come from Holland or Belgium. At least one writer suspects that the game of dice that the Roman soldiers played at the foot of the cross (Mark 15:24, Luke 23:35, John 19:24) inspired the association between marbles and Good Friday.

The village of Tinsley Green, near Crawley in Sussex, hosts a marbles championship every year on Good Friday. The competition dates back to the year 1600, when, according to legend, a local girl convinced her suitors to compete for her favor by playing a game of marbles. Today the tournament winner is declared the "Champion of Great Britain" and receives a silver cup.

Easter Sunday

Easter egg hunts take place on **Easter Sunday**. Adults hide the eggs in the garden before the children arrive, and youngsters compete to see who can find the most eggs. The **Easter Bunny** is not the traditional bringer of eggs and candy in England, though today English children are aware of his existence. **Egg-tapping** games are also popular on Easter Sunday. According to an old English folk belief, the sun dances with joy as it rises on Easter morning (*see also* **Easter Sun**). In past times people would get up early to witness this miracle. Some would climb to the top of a hill to catch a clear view of the sunrise. Others would watch the rays of the rising sun reflected in a pond or bowl of water.

Easter Monday and Tuesday

Another egg game, **egg rolling**, is a traditional **Easter Monday** pastime. In this game children set their eggs rolling at the top of a hill and see whose egg will go the farthest. In the past some English children also went **pace egging** on Easter Monday. This old custom, in which youngsters went door to door in costumes begging for eggs, began as a means for poor people to enhance their Easter feast. It died out in the twentieth century but has been revived in a few places.

In the eighteenth century Easter Monday and Tuesday served as the occasion for fun and rivalry between the sexes in northern England and Scotland. One Easter Monday custom permitted men to "heave" or to "lift" any woman they came across. They did so by picking her up or putting her in a chair and lifting her up into the air. On Easter Tuesday women heaved the men. This custom died out by the late nineteenth century. Easter Monday is still a legal holiday in England, however.

Hocktide

During the late Middle Ages English Easter celebrations continued long after Easter Sunday (*see also* **Easter Week**). They ended on the Monday and Tuesday following **Low Sunday**, or the second Monday and Tuesday after Easter. These two days were known as **Hocktide**, Hobtide, the Hoke Days, or the Hock Days, and served as an occasion for various financial and legal transactions as well as boisterous fun and games pitting one sex against the other. Hocktide festivities disappeared long ago, except in the town of Hungerford, which continues to celebrate Hock Tuesday.

Further Reading

Chambers, Robert. *The Book of Days.* Volume 1. 1862-64. Reprint. Detroit, MI: Omnigraphics, 1990.

Griffin, Robert H., and Ann H. Shurgin, eds. *The Folklore of World Holidays.* Second edition. Detroit, MI: Gale Research, 1999.

Hutton, Ronald. *Stations of the Sun.* Oxford, England: Oxford University Press, 1996.

Lord, Priscilla Sawyer, and Daniel J. Foley. *Easter the World Over.* Philadelphia, PA: Chilton Book Company, 1971.

Weiser, Francis X. *The Easter Book.* New York: Harcourt, Brace and Company, 1954.

Web Site

Photos of Tutti Day in Hungerford on the Hungerford Chamber of Commerce web site: http://www.hungerford.co.uk/tutti_day.htm

Epitaphios

Plaschanitsa, Winding Sheet

On **Good Friday** Christians commemorate the death and burial of **Jesus** Christ. Just as Roman Catholics turn to the customs associated with the **holy sepulchre** to help them focus their devotions, the Orthodox turn to an object called the *epitaphios* or "winding sheet." This icon, or religious image, depicts Jesus' burial. Unlike most icons the image is painted or sewn onto a piece of cloth rather than something solid, like a piece of wood. Among the Orthodox the winding sheet is most commonly known by its Greek name, the epitaphios, or its Slavonic name, the *plaschanitsa*.

Orthodox Christianity constitutes one of the three main branches of the Christian faith. It developed in eastern Europe and the countries surrounding the eastern half of the Mediterranean Sea. Most members of this ancient faith tradition still hail from these eastern countries although nowadays Orthodox Christian communities can also be found in western Europe, the United States, and other western countries. Orthodox Christians follow a different church calendar than that commonly adhered to by Western Christians, that is, Roman Catholics and Protestants (*see also* **Easter, Date of**).

History

The ceremonies surrounding the epitaphios have evolved over time. From ancient times to the end of the Middle Ages, the city of Constantinople, now known as Istanbul, Turkey, served as the capital of the Orthodox Byzantine empire. Records from as far back as the seventh century indicate that, like their counterparts in western Europe, Christians in Constantinople practiced the **Veneration of the Cross** on Good Friday. Indeed Christian officials from that city claimed to possess the horizontal beam of the true **cross**, the actual cross on which Jesus had been crucified (*see also* **Tree of the Cross**). Over the next few centuries, however, Eastern Christians shifted this observance to the fourth **Sunday** in **Lent**. Today Orthodox churches still observe the fourth Sunday in Lent as the **Sunday of the Veneration of the Holy Cross**.

The shifting of the Veneration of the Cross to another date may have created a gap in Orthodox Good Friday observances. Nevertheless, it took the ceremonies surrounding the epitaphios another several hundred years to take shape. Some suggest that the epitaphios itself was inspired by the presence in Constantinople between the tenth and thirteenth centuries of a shroud believed to be the same one in which Jesus was buried (*see also* **Shroud of Turin**). Scattered historical records suggest that this revered religious relic was displayed for public veneration on Good Friday. Other scholars reason that the epitaphios evolved from a ceremonial cloth used to **veil** the chalice containing the **wine** and the platter holding the unconsecrated **bread** of the **Eucharist** as they were brought to the altar. One mystical tradition interpreted this ceremonial cloth, called an *aer*, as a symbol of the stone that closed the door of Jesus' tomb. It further saw the *eiliton*, a second ceremonial cloth on which the chalice of the Eucharist rested, as representing the burial shroud of Christ. By the fourteenth century the once-plain cloth used for the aer had been replaced by cloths embroidered with the image of Christ in death, thus reinforcing the old symbolic interpretation.

In the thirteenth and fourteenth centuries Orthodox authorities began to interpret one element of their Good Friday services — the clergy's procession throughout the church with the Gospel book — as representing Jesus' funeral procession. During the fourteenth century, influenced by this interpretation, Orthodox priests began to wrap the Gospel book in the aer for this procession. By the fifteenth century the aer used for this purpose had acquired a new name, the epitaphios. In the sixteenth century the clergy began to carry the epitaphios above the Gospel book during these processions, using it as a kind of canopy. It is still carried in the same manner at today's Good Friday services.

Current Ceremonies

Orthodox churches frequently schedule three services on Good Friday. Many parishes offer the **Royal Hours** during the morning, a service originally associated with **Maundy Thursday**. In Greek Orthodox churches parishioners who arrive at church during the morning may help to decorate the *kouvouklion*, an object that serves as Christ's funeral bier, with flowers. During the afternoon service, which commemorates Jesus' burial, the epitaphios and Gospel book lie side by side on the altar. At the end of the service the celebrant processes around the church carrying the Gospel book while others hold the epitaphios over it like a canopy. The procession ends at the kouvouklion. The priest lays the epitaphios down on the kouvouklion and then places the book on top of it. Clergy members and lay people approach the epitaphios one by one, bowing deeply before it and kissing both the cloth and the book. Clergy members offer each worshiper a flower from the kouvouklion. The bowing and kissing may be repeated up to three times. Parishioners take these flowers home with them and place them in the home *ikonostasi*, a special shelf or niche used to hold icons and other religious paraphernalia. The epitaphios remains on display in the church, inspiring worshipers to pray and to meditate on the death of Christ (*see also* **Sin; Redemption; Salvation**).

Religious services begin once again in the evening. Because Orthodox religious authorities follow the Jewish tradition of beginning each new day at sundown, these services are technically considered **Holy Saturday** rather than Good Friday observances. The high point of these evening services comes when clergy members pick up the funeral bier and lead the worshipers, each one carrying a lit candle, in a procession around the interior of the church. Some processions actually exit the church and circle the church grounds or go around an entire city block before returning to the church. In Greece and other predominately Orthodox countries these processions make even longer trips through village and city streets. In some towns the procession includes a tour through the local cemetery where the bearers guide the bier over gravestones. In the Greek capital city of Athens the head of state and other political leaders play important roles in this Good Friday procession.

Those carrying the bier halt just outside the door of the church, so that to gain readmittance everyone must duck under the epitaphios. This mode of reentering the church is thought to confer a blessing. Before passing under the epitaphios worshipers blow out their candles, a gesture that signifies the death of Christ, and clergy members sprinkle rosewater, representing tears, on the congregation.

Further Reading

Hopko, Thomas. *The Orthodox Faith. Volume Two, Worship.* Syosset, NY: The Orthodox Church in America, 1972.

Monti, James. *The Week of Salvation.* Huntington, IN: Our Sunday Visitor Publications, 1993.

Rouvelas, Marilyn. *A Guide to Greek Traditions and Customs in America*. Bethesda, MD: Nea Attiki Press, 1993.

Weiser, Francis X. *The Easter Book*. New York: Harcourt, Brace and Company, 1954.

Wybrew, Hugh. *Orthodox Lent, Holy Week and Easter*. Crestwood, NY: St. Vladimir's Seminary Press, 1997.

Eucharist

Holy Communion, Lord's Supper

Three of the four Gospel accounts of **Jesus'** death state that on the night before he died he shared a ceremonial meal with his followers. Christians call this meal the Last Supper and honor it with religious observances that take place on **Maundy Thursday**. This meal is also commemorated each **Sunday** in churches throughout the world in a ceremony called the Eucharist. The Eucharist serves as the central and most important ritual in Christian communal worship. As this ceremony recalls the events surrounding Jesus' death and **resurrection**, it may be thought of as an Easter symbol and custom which millions of Christians participate in every Sunday.

The Last Supper and Passover

Jesus himself founded the ceremony of the Eucharist at the Last Supper (*for more on the Last Supper, see* Maundy Thursday). Christian scripture asserts that at this meal Jesus gave thanks to God for **bread** and **wine**, identified them as his body and **blood**, and passed them to his disciples to eat and drink (Matthew 26:26-29, Mark 14:22-25, Luke 22:16-19). These words and actions form the basis of the contemporary celebration of the Eucharist. A closer examination of their historical and cultural context illuminates their significance to Jesus' followers and to the first Christians.

The Gospels of Mark, Matthew, and Luke assert that the Last Supper was a **Passover** meal. (The Gospel according to John implies that the

Passover supper would take place on the evening of the following day.) The yearly Passover festival originated in biblical times as a means for Jews to express their gratitude to God for leading their ancestors out of slavery in Egypt over a thousand years before Christ was born (*see also* **Salvation**). Through participation in the religious ceremonies associated with Passover, Jews also reaffirmed their relationship with God.

The Book of Exodus tells that the Jews enslaved in Egypt sacrificed a **lamb** to God and smeared its blood over their doorways as a sign of their faithfulness to the Lord. Afterwards they consumed the sanctified flesh of the lamb, waiting in readiness for God to deliver them.

In Jesus' time religious custom required those celebrating Passover to make a pilgrimage to Jerusalem. Once there they brought a lamb to the Temple, where the animal was killed as an offering to God. The sacrificial lamb recalled the original offering their ancestors made while slaves in Egypt. In Jesus' day worshipers took the lamb home after it had been offered to God by the Temple priests. Then it was roasted and eaten by a gathering of family and friends. This ceremonial meal also included unleavened bread and wine.

Scriptural accounts of the Last Supper describe a meal that resembles a traditional Passover supper in some ways and diverges from Jewish custom in others. As in a traditional Jewish Passover meal, Jesus gave thanks to God for the bread and wine before passing them to his disciples. But in a sharp break from Jewish religious teaching he proclaimed that the bread was his body and the wine his blood. In Matthew's account Jesus adds that his blood is "my blood of the covenant, which is poured out for many for the forgiveness of sins" (Matthew 26:28). Here Jesus is painting himself as a new kind of sacrificial lamb, one whose death will rescue his followers from the consequences of **sin**, and pave the way to a new relationship with God.

Origins of the Eucharist

The first Christians quickly interpreted Jesus' words and deeds at the Last Supper in terms of the Passover themes of sacrifice, **redemption**, and salvation. Jesus' death on the **cross** on **Good Friday** became the sacrifice which reunited a straying humanity with God. By accepting Jesus' body and blood as represented in bread and wine at the Last Supper, Jesus' original followers accepted both his act of sacrifice and the spiritual renewal that sprang from it. The early Christians developed a ceremony called the Eucharist in order that Jesus' growing numbers of followers could also share in this new relationship with God and one another through Christ. Just as religious Jews consumed the flesh of the Passover lamb, the new ceremony required Christians to consume the body and blood of the Savior who had died for their sakes. The body and blood were represented, as they had been at the Last Supper, by bread and wine.

The word "Eucharist" is an English pronunciation of the ancient Greek word *eucharistia*, which means "thanksgiving" or "gratitude." This name, given to the ceremony by the early Christians, reflects their attitude towards it. The ceremony and the prayers that accompanied it expressed their gratitude to Christ for rescuing them from sin, opening the door to a new relationship with the Divine, and promising them eternal life. At first, groups of Christians shared bread and wine together informally, as part of an everyday meal. As time went by this sharing of bread and wine grew increasingly ceremonial. By the fourth century Christians were celebrating the Eucharist in public buildings under the supervision of robed clergy, accompanied by Bible readings, prayers, chants, homilies, and the prayer of thanksgiving, which retold Jesus' words and deeds at the Last Supper.

Interpreting the Eucharist

Over the centuries many controversies have erupted over differing interpretations of the Eucharist. One of the most significant debates took place during the sixteenth-century western European Reformation. This period of religious strife gave birth to Protestant Christianity. Among other things, Protestants disagreed with the Roman Catholic doctrine concerning the Eucharist. This doctrine states that although neither the bread nor the wine of the Eucharist seems to change in appearance, they change in actual substance, becoming the real body and blood of Christ. Roman Catholic theologians explained the mechanics of this transformation in a doctrine known as transubstan-tiation. Protestant reformers disagreed with the idea that the bread and wine change into the actual body and blood of Christ. Today's many Protestant denominations attribute varying shades of meaning to the ceremony, but most tend to view the bread and wine as sym-bols that represent the body and blood of the Savior. They would also affirm, however, that Christ, through the power of the Holy Spirit, is indeed present with those who participate in the ceremony.

Other differences distinguish Protestant and Roman Catholic views of the Eucharist. Whereas Roman Catholic theology views the ceremony as an invitation to worshipers to partake of Jesus' sacrifice, many Prot-estant theologians instead see it as a memorial, or reminder, of Jesus' sacrifice.

The Orthodox Christians of eastern Europe, the Middle East, and north Africa offer yet another perspective on the ceremony. Like Ro-man Catholics they tend to view the ceremony as Jesus' renewed offering of himself to the assembled worshipers. They also agree that worshipers partake of the actual body and blood of Christ. Yet unlike Roman Catholic theologians, Orthodox theologians offer no definite explanation for how this miracle takes place. Instead they view Christ's presence in the bread and wine of the Eucharist as a mystery. By "mystery" they mean one of the hidden and unfathomable ways that God works in the world, sometimes perceived by those who look through the eyes of faith. Therefore the best way to "understand" the Eucharist is to participate in it with reverence, prayer, and meditation. In sum, Orthodox Christian authorities approach the ceremony as a spiritual experience to be savored rather than an intellectual problem to be solved.

Contemporary Ceremonies and Services

Today many different versions of the ceremony exist. Nevertheless, the heart of the ritual consists of the identification of bread and wine as Jesus' body and blood and the invitation to worshipers to partake of them. In doing so Christians remember Jesus' sacrificial death and resurrection and commit themselves again to the new covenant, or relationship with God, that these events brought about. They ask to draw nearer to God through Christ, and accept the spiritual healing, or salvation, that comes from this relationship. Participation in the ceremony helps to create a feeling of fellowship between worshipers as they together share in God's hospitality, expressed in spiritual food and drink. At some contemporary Protestant services grape juice substitutes for wine (*for more on this issue, see also* Wine).

In many churches, including those of the Roman Catholic, Orthodox, and Anglican traditions, the Eucharist stands at the heart of the Sunday worship service. Protestants, in general, celebrate the Eucharist less frequently. In some denominations the ceremony is known as the Eucharist, while in others it may be called the Lord's Supper or Holy Communion. Various Christian denominations have assigned different names to the worship service centered around the celebration of the Eucharist. Roman Catholics and some Anglicans call it a "Mass" and Orthodox Christians know it as the "Divine Liturgy." Protestants refer to the service by a variety of names, including the Eucharist, the Lord's Supper, or Holy Communion.

Further Reading

Ferguson, Everett, ed. "Eucharist." In his *Encyclopedia of Early Christianity*. Volume 1. New York: Garland, 1997.

Hellwig, Monica K. "Eucharist." In Mircea Eliade, ed. *The Encyclopedia of Religion*. Volume 5. New York: Macmillan, 1987.

"Hospitality." In Leland Ryken, James C. Wilhoit, and Tremper Longman III, eds. *Dictionary of Biblical Imagery*. Downers Grove, IL: InterVarsity Press, 1998.

McNicol, Allan J. "Lord's Supper." In David Noel Freedman, ed. *Eerdmans Dictionary of the Bible*. Grand Rapids, MI: William B. Eerdmans Publishing, 2000.

Peifer, C. J. "Passover Lamb" and "Passover Meal." In *New Catholic Encyclopedia*. Volume 10. New York: McGraw-Hill, 1967.

"Redemption." In Leland Ryken, James C. Wilhoit, and Tremper Longman III, eds. *Dictionary of Biblical Imagery*. Downers Grove, IL: InterVarsity Press, 1998.

Reumann, John. *The Supper of the Lord*. Philadelphia, PA: Fortress Press, 1985.

"Supper." In Leland Ryken, James C. Wilhoit, and Tremper Longman III, eds. *Dictionary of Biblical Imagery*. Downers Grove, IL: InterVarsity Press, 1998.

Williams, Sam K. "The Lord's Supper." In Paul J. Achtemeier, ed. *The Harper-Collins Bible Dictionary*. New York: HarperCollins, 1996.

Web Sites

An explanation of the Orthodox understanding of the Eucharist, posted by the Orthodox Church in America web site: http://www.oca.org/pages/orth_chri/Orthodox-Faith/Worship/Holy-Eucharist.html

An article entitled "The Holy Eucharist," by the Rev. Thomas Fitzgerald, posted at the Greek Orthodox Archdiocese of America in New York, NY, web site: http://www.goarch.org/access/orthodoxfaith/eucharist.html

Fasting

Fasting is the practice of purposely going without food or without certain kinds of food. Since ancient times many different cultural traditions throughout the world have encouraged people to fast, frequently for religious reasons. Often fasting occurs before initiation ceremonies, or as a means of opening oneself to communion with the Divine. In recent times fasting has also served as a form of political protest. In the ancient Mediterranean world into which **Jesus** was born, however, fasting was primarily religious in nature.

Christianity inherited the custom of fasting from Judaism. Nevertheless, early Christian leaders adapted the practice to suit the demands of the Christian religion. They identified appropriate occasions for fasting, creating a schedule of Christian fast days, and later modified the practice itself. By the fourth century many Christians had begun to observe an entire season devoted to fasting and prayer, known as **Lent**. These devotions prepared Christians to celebrate the Easter festival that followed. Today many Christians who fast at no other time of the year continue to fast during some or all of Lent.

From Judaism to Christianity

The ancient Hebrews fasted as a means of expressing grief, enhancing prayer, opening oneself to God, cultivating humility, and displaying **repentance**, that is, the desire to return to an upright way of life. These fasts required going without food and **water** for a specified period, often from sunrise to sunset. They might also involve going barefoot, sitting on the ground, wearing clothes made from a rough kind of material called sackcloth, and smudging one's head with ashes (*see also* **Ash Wednesday**). The ancient Jews also fasted on the afternoon preceding **Passover**, a religious holiday which begins at sundown on the fifteenth day of the Jewish month of Nisan. Some writers believe that the short fast that preceded early Christian Easter celebrations may have been modeled on this Jewish practice.

Christian scripture informs us that Jesus himself fasted. Nevertheless, he criticized those who made a public display of their fasting, identifying it as a form of bragging. Instead he recommended that those who fast act and dress as they would normally and direct their prayers privately to God (Matthew 6:16-17).

Early Christian Fasting

The early Christians fasted for a variety of religious purposes. Like the Jewish fasts which inspired them, these early Christian fasts involved going without food for all or part of the day. Christian scripture demonstrates that the devout fasted as a means of intensifying prayer (Acts 14:23). Fasting was also a common means of expressing repentance. Candidates for **baptism**, that is, initiation into the Christian faith, were expected to fast before undergoing the ritual. Other special religious occasions also called for fasting. Priests fasted before their ordination, the ritual whereby they were formally accepted as Christian ministers. By the fourth century many Christians had adopted the practice of fasting before receiving Holy Communion (*see also* **Eucharist**).

193

In addition to fasting on special occasions, the early Christians established regular, weekly fast days. Evidence from as early as the year 100 A.D. shows that Christians fasted on Fridays, in commemoration of Jesus' crucifixion, and Wednesdays, in commemoration of his betrayal (*see also* **Good Friday** and **Spy Wednesday**). By the fourth century these weekly fast days had become widespread. Around the year 400 A.D., however, Christians living in western Europe abandoned the Wednesday fast and instead began to fast on Fridays and Saturdays. These fasts were modified over time and eventually eliminated. Christians from eastern Europe, the Middle East and north Africa, however, kept both the Wednesday and Friday fasts, practices which they maintain to this day.

The early Christians fasted in order to bring about a desired state of mind, heart, and spirit. More specifically they fasted as a means of cultivating repentance, of deepening prayer, and of identifying with the sufferings and sacrifice of Christ. These spiritual activities eventually came to be seen as the proper way to prepare for the annual Easter festival. Thus fasting became an important component of Lent, the forty-day period of preparation for Easter.

The Origins of Lenten Fasting

Historical evidence shows that some early Christian communities observed **Holy Saturday**, or both Holy Saturday and Good Friday, by fasting. These devotions prepared them for the Easter feast to come. Nevertheless, community leaders disagreed as to exactly how long the fast should last. Writing about Easter preparations in the year 190 A.D. a Christian leader named Irenaeus declared that "some think they ought to fast for one day, others for two days, and others even for several, while others reckon forty hours both of day and night to their fast." In some communities these fasts coincided with the fasts undertaken by catechumens in preparation for baptism at Easter time. In other communities Christians carried out forty-day fasts in commemoration of Jesus' forty days in the desert (Matthew 4:1-11, Mark 1:12-13, Luke 4:1-13). These forty-day fasts were scheduled in January and February, however. By the fourth century all of these customs had merged together giving rise to Lent, an approximately forty-day season of fasting and prayer preceding Easter which we now call Lent.

At roughly the same time Christian leaders began to emphasize the parallels between the observance of Lent and Jesus' fast in the desert at the start of his ministry. This comparison tended to increase the importance of fasting as a Lenten custom. Moreover, it inspired some Christian authorities to argue that the Lenten fast should last exactly forty days to mirror Christ's ordeal in the desert. In early times Christian communities showed little concern for the exact number of fast days contained in the six-week Lenten season. As fasting became a more important component of Lenten devotions, however, critics began to charge that beginning the fast on Quadragesima Sunday short-changed the Lenten season. Quadragesima Sunday falls six **Sundays**, or forty-two days, before Easter. These critics also pointed out that Sundays couldn't count as true days of fast and penitence since they commemorate the **resurrection** of Christ. This left the season of Lent with only thirty-six days. Sometime during the seventh and eighth centuries Christian leaders across western Europe started to add four more days to the fast, expanding Lent from six to six and one-half weeks. This meant that Western Christians began Lent on the Wednesday following the seventh Sunday before Easter, a day which became known as Ash Wednesday. The Lenten fast ended with the late-night **Easter Vigil** service on Holy Saturday.

Lenten Fasting in Medieval Western Europe

During the Middle Ages a series of complex rules governed Lenten fasting in western Europe. Much later, in the eighteenth century, the Roman Catholic Church began to distinguish fasting from abstinence. Roman Catholic religious authorities defined fasting as going without food and abstinence as refraining from eating certain kinds of foods, such as meat. In everyday speech, however, people tend to refer to both of these practices as fasting.

In the early Middle Ages western European Christians observed Lent by going without food until after sundown or after vespers, the evening prayer service. Then they ate a meal that contained no meat or dairy products. This discipline proved too severe, however, since the fast lasted for forty days. Around the ninth century some communities began to eat their daily meal around 3:00 p.m., after the afternoon service called "nones." By the twelfth century the practice of eating one daily meal after nones had become commonplace. Yet those who engaged in physical labor, including monks and nuns, still found it difficult to wait until mid-afternoon to eat. So religious communities began offering the service of nones earlier and earlier in the day, until it followed the service called sext, scheduled for around 12:00 p.m. In fact, this practice explains the origins of the English word "noon." The word "nones" comes from the Latin word for nine, and refers to the fact that 3:00 p.m. was considered the ninth hour of the day. During Lent, when nones was moved to midday, people began to refer to that time of day as "noon." By the thirteenth century most Western Christians ate their one Lenten meal around noon.

In the late Middle Ages, people began to supplement the daily Lenten meal with snacks. This practice began in monasteries, whose inhabitants observed many more days of fasting throughout the year than did lay Christians. On monastic fast days, monks took a snack, called a collation, in the evening in addition to the daily meal. This snack consisted of a small amount of **wine** and a small portion of **bread**, fruit, or vegetables. Eventually the monks allowed themselves this privilege during Lent as well. Following their lead, lay Christians began to supplement their one daily meal with beverages at other times of the day. By the thirteenth century this practice had become commonplace. By the fourteenth century most Western Christians had begun to take an evening snack as well as a midday meal. In the sixteenth century Church authorities also approved a morning snack.

In western Europe the rules governing which foods could be eaten during Lent began to loosen around the ninth century. Some scholars believe that at the start of the Middle Ages Western Christians included fish in the list of foods forbidden during Lent. Others disagree. In any case it appears that fish was an acceptable Lenten food during the Middle Ages. By the ninth century dairy products were permitted in many locations as well, especially in areas where they were considered dietary staples. In other places people made a small donation to the church in return for the privilege of eating dairy foods during Lent. These donations were often used for building projects. This custom funded the construction of a magnificent cathedral in the city of Rouen, France. Even today one of its steeples is still called the "butter tower," since it was reportedly paid for by donations made by local people who wanted to eat butter and other dairy products during Lent.

Protestant Customs

During the sixteenth century a religious reform movement called the Reformation surged across western Europe, giving birth to the Protestant churches. The founder of this movement, Martin Luther, criticized Roman Catholic teachings on fasting, because he suspected that these teachings led people to think that they could cancel out their **sins** by depriving themselves of food. He also opposed indulgences, arrangements whereby certain sins were officially forgiven by the Church in exchange for a donation, such as those that funded the building of the Rouen Cathedral's butter tower. Nevertheless, Luther did not ban the Lenten fast.

In England civil laws as well as church law required citizens of the realm to fast during Lent. A 1570 Lenten law threatened those who broke the fast with three months in jail and a fine of sixty shillings. In the late seventeenth century, however, Londoners could obtain a license to eat meat from officials at St. Paul's Cathedral in exchange for a donation to the poor.

During the time of the Reformation people began to openly question the practice of Lenten fasting. In a poem entitled "To Keep a True Lent" English poet-priest Robert Herrick (1591-1674) expressed these sentiments concerning fasting and the observance of Lent:

> ...'tis a fast to dole
> Thy sheaf of wheat,
> And meat,
> Unto the hungry soul.

It is to fast from strife,
From old debate,
And hate;
To circumcize thy life.

To show a heart grief-rent;
To starve thy sin,
Not bin;
And that's to keep thy Lent. (Myers, 60-61)

Today Protestant Christians vary in their Lenten observances. Most denominations do not officially require that their members fast, but rather leave such practices up to the individual. In the United States Episcopalians and Lutherans tend to be among those Protestants more likely to observe the Lenten fast.

Roman Catholic Customs

Throughout the nineteenth and twentieth centuries Roman Catholics continued to relax the fasting rules they had inherited from medieval times. Until 1917 Roman Catholics were expected to fast throughout Lent, except on Sundays. This meant limiting food intake to one full meal per day. In practice, however, many faithful Catholics took an evening and morning snack in addition to the midday meal. Like the meal itself, however, these snacks must not contain meat, eggs, or milk products. Although meat was allowed on Sundays, it could not be combined with fish. What's more, observant Roman Catholics were expected to abstain from eating meat both on Fridays and Saturdays throughout the year. Finally, fasting and abstinence were practiced on the eve of many feast days, and other days as well. The new code of Canon Law, adopted in 1918, changed some of these fast rules for Roman Catholics. For example, dairy products were no longer included in the list of foods from which Roman Catholics must abstain on fast days or days of abstinence, and Saturdays were no longer observed as fast days. Other major changes in the rules governing fasting occurred in the 1960s.

Today Roman Catholic authorities maintain that the faithful must fast only on Ash Wednesday and Good Friday. They must also abstain from eating meat on these days, as well as on all Fridays during Lent. During the rest of the year, however, they are no longer required to forgo eating meat on Fridays. These changes encourage Roman Catholics to observe Lent by engaging in activities other than fasting and abstinence, especially charitable works, exercises of piety, and other activities likely to foster repentance and spiritual renewal. Still, many Roman Catholics, and some Protestants, choose to observe Lent by giving up a favorite food for the duration of the season.

Orthodox Customs

Orthodoxy is one of the three main branches of the Christian faith. Orthodox Christianity developed in eastern Europe and the countries surrounding the eastern half of the Mediterranean Sea. The Orthodox churches split apart from the Western Christian tradition about 1,000 years ago. They follow a different church calendar than that commonly followed by Western Christians, that is, Roman Catholics and Protestants. Since the Orthodox use a different set of rules to calculate the date of Easter, Western and Eastern Lent are out of synch with one another (*see also* **Easter, Date of**). In addition, Orthodox Christians developed their own distinctive Lenten fasting customs.

Sometime during the early Middle Ages Orthodox Christians expanded their Lenten fast from six to seven weeks. Many writers assert that in early medieval times, Eastern Christians fasted neither on Sundays nor on Saturdays, except on Holy Saturday. Thus Orthodox Christians decided to begin their fast somewhat earlier than did Western Christians, in order to fill the tally of forty days. Today Orthodox Lent begins on the evening of the seventh Sunday preceding Easter, called **Forgiveness Sunday**. The first full day of Lent falls on the following day, **Clean Monday**. Nevertheless, fasting begins a week before the start of Lent, with the removal of meat from the diet (*see also* **Pre-Lent**). Unlike Western Christians, Orthodox Christians have maintained the strict fasting rules they inherited from medieval times.

Contemporary Orthodox Christians fast by abstaining from eating certain foods rather than by going without food. Throughout Lent strictly observant Orthodox Christians will not consume meat, fish, eggs, dairy products, olive oil, and alcoholic beverages. The removal of meat products from the diet in the week before Lent gives Orthodox Christians an opportunity to ease into this regimen. Some Orthodox Church leaders assert that the faithful may relax the fast somewhat on Saturdays and Sundays, adding olive oil and alcoholic beverages to their diet on those days. The fast is also eased on the Feast of the **Annunciation** and sometimes also on **Palm Sunday**, when fish is permissible. In practice, however, not all Orthodox Christians follow this regimen throughout Lent. Many modify the fast in order to suit their own abilities and needs. For example, some shorten its duration by fasting only during the first week of Lent, all Wednesdays and Fridays during Lent, and **Holy Week**.

Creative Cuisine

Over the centuries creative cooks compiled a variety of recipes that satisfied the stomach as well as fulfilled the rules of the fast. Throughout southern Europe cooks depended on dried, salted cod to meet both of these requirements. Until the sixteenth century, when Europeans began to fish for cod in North America, fresh fish was difficult for many Europeans to obtain during winter. This made salt cod a real boon to Lenten cooks. The Portuguese developed more than 100 recipes for it and the French have more recipes for salt cod than they do for any other fish. Russian cooks invented mushroom pies to take the place of meat pies during Lent. To this day Russian cooks tend to view mushrooms as a meat substitute rather than a vegetable dish or garnish. Greek chefs served up vegetable pies, without the feta cheese that one finds in them during the rest of the year, as well as bean dishes. In addition they also invented *taramosalata*, a spread made with olive oil, fish eggs and garlic. Until the nineteenth century, **pretzels** were a favorite Lenten snack in Austria, Germany, and Poland. Italian bakers came up with a sweet, hard, almond cookie called *cantucci* as a substitute for pastries during Lent. Somewhere along the way the people of Tuscany discovered that these cookies taste even more delicious when dipped in wine. They are still enjoyed this way today. In Malta the Lenten cookie *kwarizemal*, made with honey and almonds, bears a name that comes from the local word for Lent. As the hardships imposed by the Lenten fast declined, many of these dishes lost their association with the season and became year-round favorites.

Purpose of Lenten Fasting

Although Christians may differ in their fasting methods, all agree that fasting should be practiced as a means of achieving a spiritual goal, rather than as an end unto itself. In general Christians view Lenten fasting as an aid to mindfulness, that is, as a tool that keeps one's attention from wandering. Many also view it as a means of disciplining the body, thereby freeing the soul to attend to matters of the spirit. Thus the mild discomfort endured while fasting serves to remind fasters of their own limitations and errors, their commitment to ethical behavior and service to others, the need for prayer and communion with God, or the sacrifice and sufferings of Christ.

Further Reading

Clancy, P. M. J. "Fast and Abstinence." In *New Catholic Encyclopedia*. Volume 5. New York: McGraw-Hill, 1967.

"Fasting." In Leland Ryken, James C. Wilhoit, and Tremper Longman III, eds. *Dictionary of Biblical Imagery*. Downers Grove, IL: InterVarsity Press, 1998.

"Fasts and Fasting." In E. A. Livingstone, ed. *The Oxford Dictionary of the Christian Church*. Third edition. Oxford, England: Oxford University Press, 1997.

Gammie, John G. "Fasting." In Paul J. Achtemeier, ed. *The HarperCollins Bible Dictionary*. New York: HarperCollins, 1996.

Hinson, E. Glenn. "Fasting." In Everett Ferguson, ed. *Encyclopedia of Early Christianity*. Volume 1. New York: Garland, 1997.

Hopko, Thomas. *The Orthodox Faith. Volume Two, Worship*. Syosset, NY: The Orthodox Church in America, 1997.

Hopley, Claire. "Lenten Delights." *The World and I* 16, 3 (March 2001): 112.

Lynch, J. E. "Fast and Abstinence." In *New Catholic Encyclopedia*. Volume 16. New York: McGraw-Hill, 1967.

Myers, Robert J. *Celebrations: The Complete Book of American Holidays*. Garden City, NY: Doubleday and Company, 1972.

Niemann, Paul J. *The Lent, Triduum, and Easter Answer Book*. San Jose, CA: Resource Publications, 1998.

Rader, Rosemary. "Fasting." In Mircea Eliade, ed. *The Encyclopedia of Religion*. Volume 5. New York: Macmillan, 1987.

Rogers, Eric N. *Fasting: The Phenomenon of Self-Denial*. New York: Thomas Nelson, 1976.

Roth, Cecil, ed. "Fast." In his *The Standard Jewish Encyclopedia*. Garden City, NY: Doubleday and Company, 1959.

Rouvelas, Marilyn. *A Guide to Greek Traditions and Customs in America*. Bethesda, MD: Nea Attiki Press, 1993.

Smith-Christopher, Daniel J. "Fasting." In David Noel Freedman, ed. *Eerdmans Dictionary of the Bible*. Grand Rapids, MI: William B. Eerdmans, 2000.

Talley, Thomas J. *The Origins of the Liturgical Year*. Collegeville, MN: Liturgical Press, 1986.

"Wednesday." In E. A. Livingstone, ed. *The Oxford Dictionary of the Christian Church*. Third edition. Oxford, England: Oxford University Press, 1997.

Weiser, Francis X. *The Easter Book*. New York: Harcourt, Brace and Company, 1954.

Wigoder, Geoffrey. "Fasting and Fast Days." In his *Encyclopedia of Judaism*. New York: Macmillan, 1989.

Web Sites

"Fasting," an essay by the Rev. George Mastrantonis describing Greek Orthodox fasting customs posted on the Greek Orthodox Archdiocese of America, New York, NY, web site at: http://www.goarch.org/access/orthodoxfaith/lent/fasting.html

"The Great Lent," an essay by the Rev. George Mastrantonis describing the history and customs of Lent in the Greek Orthodox Church, posted on the Greek Orthodox Archdiocese of America, New York, NY, web site at: http://www.goarch.org/access/orthodoxfaith/lent/great_lent.html

"Great Lent," a page describing the beliefs and practices of Orthodox Christians concerning Lent, sponsored by the Orthodox Church in America: http://www.oca.org/pages/orth_chri/orthodox-faith/worship/great-lent.html

Finland, Easter and Holy Week in

In Finland **Holy Week** is known as "Silent Week." This name comes from the time when Finland was a predominantly Roman Catholic country and followed an old Roman Catholic custom of silencing all church **bells** during this week. Folk custom added its own restraints, frowning on all forms of noise, including work-related noise and even **laughter** during these seven days.

Palm Sunday

Holy Week begins with **Palm Sunday**, called "Willowswitch Sunday" in eastern Finland. This name refers to the custom of whisking friends and neighbors with willow branches. In past times children used to go house to house on the Saturday before Palm Sunday carrying decorated willow switches and offering to whisk housewives. As they did they chanted, "Switching, switching, switches go, wishing freshness and health for the year." Indeed folklorists suspect that this custom originated in the belief that this whisking conferred health and well-being. The following day the children applied their switches to unmarried girls. On **Easter Sunday** the children returned to the homes they had previously visited to receive eggs, sweets, or a coin in return for their switching services. During the twentieth century this custom spread all over Finland.

Those who attend Orthodox churches on Palm Sunday may bring blessed willow branches home with them. An old folk tradition recommended using them to sprinkle **water** on one's cattle, so drawing good luck to the animals. In western Finland children once dug willow or birch twigs out of snowdrifts and stuck them in vases at home. Folklore taught that when these twigs sprouted the forest trees would begin to bud. Old formulas also taught how to use Palm Sunday weather to predict the size of the harvest. According to folk belief, when farmers saw good weather on Palm Sunday they could expect a fine barley harvest.

Maundy Thursday

Another clump of superstition and custom attached itself to **Maundy Thursday**. According to one belief, the weather on this day foretold the weather to come over the next forty days. In some places people once called Maundy Thursday "Tail Thursday," as farm lore advised that this was a good day to trim the cow's tail. People prepared "tail soup" on this day as well. In spite of its name, this soup is made from barley rather than a cow's tail. In Savo Province people called Maundy Thursday *"Kiira* Thursday," meaning "Evil Spirit Thursday." This name came from the old folk custom of driving evil spirits away from the homestead on this day. One method of scaring them off consisted of dragging or pulling a container of burning tar around the property while chanting a command that the Kiira depart. Some people walked about their land striking a birch basket with an alder switch, or swinging a cow bell rather than dragging a burning tar basket.

Good Friday

Finns call **Good Friday** "Long Friday." Good Friday superstitions once included the belief that the day was ruled by evil spirits. This made it an appropriate day to buy magical goods designed to ward off evil influences. Youngsters may have feared the day for another reason. In past times parents spanked children on Good Friday to remind them of **Jesus'** suffering. A host of old folk customs reflect the solemn honor past generations of Finns accorded to this day. For instance, these customs forbade sweeping floors, spinning thread, visiting, and lighting cooking fires. Therefore people made meals out of cold leftover food on this day, customarily eating only after sunset. Proper behavior consisted of staying home and reading the Bible, attending church services, and engaging in other sedate activities. Dark clothing was considered appropriate on this somber holy day. Especially religious people even frowned on laughter, which they felt was out of keeping with this holiday memorializing Jesus' agony on the **cross**. In more recent times laws and decrees concerning Good Friday have restricted the operation of business establishments that offer food and entertainment to the public. These laws were relaxed in the 1990s.

Witches and Trolls

According to old folk beliefs, witches and trolls were especially active between Good Friday and Easter Sunday, the days when Jesus Christ lay in the grave. Indeed the witch became such a common theme of the holiday that her image could be found on Finnish **Easter cards**. In past times people protected themselves from evil enchantments on these dangerous days by burning bonfires, painting crosses on their doors, hanging crossed pairs of scythes in their barns, shooting off firearms, and other activities thought to frighten away witches. Today all that remains of these beliefs are the **Easter witches**, neighborhood children dressed as witches who go door to door asking for Easter treats. In Finland this custom dates back to the nineteenth century, but media campaigns in the 1980s greatly boosted its popularity.

Holy Saturday

Holy Saturday once saw the blaze of many Easter eve bonfires in the plains of Osterbotten (*see also* **Easter Fires**). Presumably these fires frightened away lurking trolls, who otherwise would have taken advantage of the darkness to harm their neighbor's livestock or "steal" their prosperity (*for more on Easter season fires, see* **Walpurgis Night**).

Easter Sunday

Weeks before Easter Finnish children sow rye grass seeds in pots and place them along the windowsill. The sprouting grass serves as a sign of spring, and therefore, an appropriate Easter decoration. Finns also enjoy decorating with flowers, especially tulips, **lilies**, and daffodils. In past times, when slower modes of transportation did not permit fresh flowers to be flown in from the European continent, people often made floral decorations out of colored tissue paper and dyed feathers. Images of baby chicks, dyed eggs, and **rabbits** also appear in Finnish Easter decorations.

In past times Easter Sunday brought children welcome relief from the restrictions of Silent Week. Children played, visited friends, and walked about ringing cowbells or playing musical instruments. Parents set up swings and see-saws to further their enjoyment of the day. These activities continued on **Easter Monday**.

Easter egg hunts are a relatively new children's pastime. The Finns began celebrating Easter with dyed eggs in the nineteenth century, an era when increasing numbers of Finns began to raise poultry. They adopted the idea of Easter eggs from their Russian and central European neighbors. Although Easter eggs have established themselves in Finland, the **Easter Bunny** has achieved far less success and is known only in a few parts of fhe country.

Like many other Europeans, the Finns once cherished a folk belief that the sun dances for joy on Easter morning (*see also* **Easter Sun**). Devout Finns used to gather at lookout points before sunrise to catch a glimpse of the sun shimmering over the horizon (*see also* **Sunrise Service**).

In olden times food was scarce around Easter time, falling as it does in the early spring when snow is still on the ground in Finland. Only the well-to-do could be assured of an ample Easter feast. This state of affairs inspired two Easter-related sayings. One declared, "On All Saints' Day for all, on Christmas for most, but on Easter for the 'head-house'," meaning that food was plentiful around All Saints' Day in the autumn, still available at Christmas in the early winter, but running low at Easter time. Another saying, "He has cheeks like an Easter saint," was inspired by the pale skin and sunken cheeks resulting from the dwindling food supplies in early spring. One food that did appear on many Finns' tables during **Lent** was *mämmi*, a dark brown cereal dish made from sweetened rye malt and water. Mämmi cooks for a long time in a low-heat oven. In past times mämmi was considered a Lenten dish. These days, however, it appears in bakery windows shortly after Christmas. Moreover, today people enhance its flavor with cream and sugar.

Further Reading

Lee, Tan Chung. *Festivals of the World: Finland*. Milwaukee, WI: Gareth Stevens Publishing, 1998.

Lord, Priscilla Sawyer, and Daniel J. Foley. *Easter the World Over*. Philadelphia, PA: Chilton Book Company, 1971.

Web Site

"Finnish Easter Traditions," an article by Sirpa Karjalainen, Assistant, Department of Ethnology at the University of Helsinki, posted on the Virtual Finland web site: http://www.finland.fi/finfo/english/paaseng.html

Fire Sunday

Feast of the Torches, Spark Sunday

In past times many Germans called the first **Sunday** in **Lent** *Brandsonntag*, "Fire Sunday," or *Funkensonntag*, "Spark Sunday." The name refers to the customary lighting of bonfires on that day, a practice also known in some regions of Austria and Switzerland (*see also* **Germany, Carnival in**). In some areas people lit these fires around the base of a tree, in others on a hilltop. The contents of the blaze as well as its location varied from region to region. In some regions local custom called for the burning of a living tree, in others the bonfire featured a straw or wooden witch. In still other locales people set fire to a large wooden wheel and rolled it down a hill, or sent flaming wooden disks whizzing through the air. Some folklorists view these wheels of fire as symbolic of the sun. They suspect that these customs may at one time have been thought to ensure the smooth progress of the solar year from the short, dark days of winter to the longer, brighter days of spring. Local folk traditions often asserted that the fires protected against witches, predicted the size of the harvest, or foretold coming weather patterns.

In France the first Sunday in Lent was known as *Fête des brandons*, or "Feast of the Torches." In some areas not only did the local people light bonfires, but they also marched through field and village with flaming torches. French folklore attributed many powers to these flames. In some regions they were thought to protect against fire throughout the rest of the year, in others to ward off witches, and in still others to bring fruitfulness to fields and orchards. Indeed, in some places ashes from the fires were scattered across farmlands and may have served as a kind of fertilizer. In other regions young men paced through orchards and fields with firebrands in order to frighten away mice and other pests and to increase crop yields. Courting customs and love charms attached themselves to these bonfires in some places. According to one such folk tradition, a maiden who leaped over the bonfire without singeing herself was sure to find a good husband in the coming year.

In Belgium the first Sunday in Lent was known as the "Sunday of the Great Fires." People built bonfires on hilltops as evening fell. Young people leapt over the fire, making wishes for healthy crops, good marriages, and personal health. Old folk beliefs taught that those who had seen seven fires on this night were protected from witchcraft. Another old bit of folklore warned children that the number of fires they had seen on the first Sunday in Lent determined the number of eggs they would receive at Easter. Another more dire warning aimed at adults threatened that if anyone should neglect to kindle fire on this evening, God would see to it Himself, meaning that God would set fire to their home.

History

Some writers trace the origins of these customs back to the early Middle Ages, when Lent began on Fire Sunday, the sixth Sunday before Easter. Around the seventh or eighth centuries Christian authorities decided that Sundays, even if they fell during Lent, didn't count as true days of **fast** and penitence since they celebrate the **Resurrection**. With the Sundays removed, Lent now fell short of forty days. Therefore Christian authorities decided to begin the season four days earlier, on **Ash Wednesday**. Some communities, however, resisted the change. They continued to celebrate **Carnival** right up to the sixth Sunday before Lent. The bonfires, which in Germany can be traced back to the fifteenth century, marked the end of Carnival and the beginning of Lent.

Further Reading

Frazer, James George. *The New Golden Bough*. Theodor H. Gaster, ed. New York: S. G. Phillips, 1959.

Gelling, Peter, and Hilda Ellis Davidson. *The Chariot of the Sun*. New York: Frederick A. Praeger, 1969.

Lord, Priscilla Sawyer, and Daniel J. Foley. *Easter Garland*. 1963. Reprint. Detroit, MI: Omnigraphics, 1999.

Spicer, Dorothy Gladys. *Festivals of Western Europe*. 1958. Reprint. Detroit, MI: Omnigraphics, 1994.

Weiser, Francis X. *The Easter Book*. New York: Harcourt, Brace and Company, 1954.

Flowering of the Cross
Greening of the Cross

On **Easter Sunday** morning some Episcopal, Lutheran, and other Protestant churches incorporate a folk ceremony called the flowering of the **cross** into their worship service. Members of the congregation bring flowers or greenery to church. A bare wooden cross, dotted with pin holes, covered with chicken wire or strung with vines, stands in the church. At some point before, during, or after the service worshipers are invited to approach the barren cross and twine a flower around one of the wires or vines, or to place a blossom in one of the pinholes. The congregation continues to decorate the cross until flowers cover it completely.

Some churches link this ceremony to other events in the Christian year by making the cross out of the previous year's Christmas tree.

The barren cross may then be brought into the church on **Ash Wednesday** or on some other suitable occasion during **Lent**.

The flowering of the cross represents the transition from **Good Friday** to Easter, from meditation on **Jesus'** death to joyful celebration of his **resurrection**. The ceremony transforms a barren cross, a reminder of Jesus' death, into an Easter symbol. Covered with fresh, living flowers, the cross serves not only as an emblem of Jesus' resurrection but also of the continuing presence of Christ among today's Christians. In another variation of this ceremony worshipers cover the cross with homemade **butterflies**, another symbol of new life.

Further Reading

Greene, Debra Illingworth. "Easter: Promise of New Life." *The Lutheran* (April 1999). Available online at: http://www.thelutheran.org/9904/page35.html

Web Site

The Christian Resource Institute's page on Lenten observances and customs, written by Dennis Bratcher, a minister with a Ph.D. in biblical studies: http://www.cresourcei.org/cyeaster.html

Footwashing

On **Maundy Thursday** some churches and religious institutions practice an old ceremony associated with the day known as footwashing. In this ceremony a member of the clergy washes the feet of people in the community or congregation. In some churches, for example, the priest bathes the feet of twelve boys or men. Seated in a half circle around the priest, the boys and men represent **Jesus'** twelve apostles. In other Christian denominations clergy members wash the feet of all who wish to participate in the ceremony. This ritual developed sometime around the seventh century as a means of commemorating the example Jesus set for his disciples at the Last Supper (*for more on the Last Supper, see* Maundy Thursday).

Origins of the Ceremony

The Gospel according to John tells us that Jesus washed his disciples' feet at the Last Supper, the last meal that Jesus ate with his followers before his arrest, trial, and crucifixion (John 13:4-9; *for more on crucifixion, see* **Cross**). This gesture so surprised the disciple named **Peter** that he at first refused to let Jesus do it. The idea of having someone wash his feet was not new to Peter, since in those days it was customary for people to have their feet washed when they entered a home so as not to bring the dust and dirt of the street into the house with them. But this task was usually performed by someone of low status. In humble families the women of the house performed this task for guests. Slave-owning families assigned the task of washing family members' and guests' feet to a slave. Since footwashing was considered among the most menial of tasks it was given to the lowest-ranking servant, usually a female slave. So when Jesus approached Peter with the intention of washing his feet, Peter at first refused because he believed Jesus to be far greater, not lesser, than himself.

211

In washing his disciples' feet Jesus sought to teach them a final lesson about his relationship to them and their relationship to each other. After he had finished, he explained the meaning of his actions:

> Do you understand what I have done to you? You call me Teacher and Lord; and you are right, for so I am. If I then, your Lord and Teacher, have washed your feet, you also ought to wash one another's feet. For I have given you an example, that you also should do as I have to you. Truly, truly, I say to you, a servant is not greater than his master; nor is he who is sent greater than he who sent him. If you know these things, blessed are you if you do them (John 13:12-17).

According to some of the biblical accounts of the Last Supper the meal took place on the Thursday before the Crucifixion and **Resurrection**. Therefore the washing of the disciples' feet is commemorated on Thursday of **Holy Week**, otherwise known as Maundy Thursday.

Footwashing in the Middle Ages

By the early Middle Ages Christian religious authorities participated in ceremonial reenactments of the washing of the disciples' feet. In these ceremonies those in authority honored Jesus' teaching concerning love and humility by washing the feet of those below them. In the Roman Catholic Church this ritual became known as the *mandatum*, which means "commandment" in Latin. The name comes from another teaching given by Jesus at the Last Supper. In the Gospel according to John, Jesus tells his disciples:

> A new commandment I give to you, that you love one another; even as I have loved you, that you also love one another. By this all men will know that you are my disciples, if you have love for one another (John 13:34-35).

Ceremonial footwashing, instituted by Jesus himself, came to symbolize this commandment.

During the Middle Ages priests, abbots, bishops, and even the pope washed the feet of poor or humble people on Maundy Thursday. The

ceremony was practiced from a very early date in Spain. In 694 the seventeenth Synod of Toledo, an important meeting of Spanish clerics, warned that those religious authorities who did not perform it risked a two-month excommunication, or expulsion, from the Church. St. Bede, a scholarly English monk who lived in the eighth century, wrote that churchmen were practicing the custom in Lindisfarne, England, in the seventh century. Indeed the ritual was well known in medieval monasteries, where the monks customarily invited a group of poor men to have their feet washed on Maundy Thursday. After the poor men took their seats, the monks knelt before them, washed, dried, and kissed their feet. Then they touched their foreheads to the men's feet. Afterwards the monks provided the paupers with beverages, kissed their hands, and gave them two pence. Then the monks retired to their chapter-house to repeat the ceremony among themselves. This time the abbot and prior, the highest ranking people in the community, washed the feet of the other monks. Then the abbot and prior washed each others' feet.

Footwashing began to be practiced in Rome in the twelfth century, at a time when monastic traditions and ideas gained influence with the pope. Historical records from this era tell that the pope washed the feet of thirteen poor men on Maundy Thursday. Twelve of them represented the twelve original apostles. The additional thirteenth man may have represented St. Matthias, who replaced **Judas** after his desertion and death. He may also have stood for St. Paul, an angel, or even Christ himself. This ceremony quickly fell into disuse, although another ceremony in which the pope washed the feet of twelve sub-deacons survived for centuries.

In the Middle Ages European monarchs and noblemen also reenacted Christ's gesture of love and service by washing the feet of poor people on Maundy Thursday. In France the tradition dates back to the eleventh century. Saint Elizabeth, the thirteenth-century Hungarian princess, reportedly adopted the custom of washing the feet of twelve lepers on Maundy Thursday. In England historical records reveal that King John (1167-1216) was the first English monarch to perform this ritual. Like the pope, King John and his successors washed the feet of thirteen men. King Edward III (1312-1377) added a new twist to the ritual by tying the number of people whose feet he washed to his own age. He also gave them gifts of food, money, and clothing. Queen Elizabeth I (1533-1603) heaped these gifts into a basket known as a "maund." After the time of King James II (1633-1701) the English monarchs discarded the custom of washing the feet of the poor, although they continued making gifts of food, clothing, and money. In time the customary gifts were replaced by money. Queen Victoria (1819-1901) limited her gift giving to specially minted coins called "Maundy money." In Spain, however, both the king and queen continued to wash the feet of the poor well into the twentieth century. The current English monarch, Queen Elizabeth II, carries on the tradition of Maundy Thursday gift giving, bestowing Maundy money on one person for each year she has lived.

Current Observance

After the close of the Middle Ages footwashing ceremonies gradually began to fall into disuse, especially outside of the Church. They have experienced a revival of sorts in the twentieth century. In the Roman Catholic Church the restoration of the Holy Week liturgy in 1955 made the ceremony once again an integral part of Maundy Thursday religious services. Anglicans have also maintained this ancient custom as part of their Maundy Thursday observances. Footwashing is also practiced, though to a much lesser extent, by Orthodox Christians.

Further Reading

Blackburn, Bonnie, and Leofranc Holford-Strevens. *The Oxford Companion to the Year*. Oxford, England: Oxford University Press, 1999.

"Feet." In Leland Ryken, James C. Wilhoit, and Tremper Longman III, eds. *Dictionary of Biblical Imagery*. Downers Grove, IL: InterVarsity Press, 1998.

Ferguson, Everett. "Footwashing." In his *Encyclopedia of Early Christianity*. Volume 1. New York: Garland, 1997.

Metford, J. C. J. *The Christian Year*. London, England: Thames and Hudson, 1991.

Monti, James. *The Week of Salvation*. Huntington, IN: Our Sunday Visitor Publications, 1993.

Myers, Robert J. *Celebrations: The Complete Book of American Holidays*. Garden City, NY: Doubleday and Company, 1972.

Rouvelas, Marilyn. *A Guide to Greek Traditions and Customs in America*. Bethesda, MD: Nea Attiki Press, 1993.

Slim, Hugo. *A Feast of Festivals*. London, England: Marshall Pickering, 1996.

Weiser, Francis X. *The Easter Book*. New York: Harcourt, Brace and Company, 1954.

Forgiveness Sunday
Cheese Sunday, Cheesefare Sunday

For Roman Catholics and other Western Christians **Lent**, a period of spiritual preparation for Easter, begins with an observance called **Ash Wednesday** and lasts a little over six weeks. For Eastern, or Orthodox, Christians, Lent lasts a full seven weeks and begins on the evening of Forgiveness Sunday (*see also* **Pre-Lent**). Orthodoxy is one of the three main branches of the Christian faith. Orthodox Christianity developed in eastern Europe and the countries surrounding the eastern half of the Mediterranean Sea. Orthodox Christians follow a different church calendar than that commonly adhered to by Roman Catholics and Protestants (*see also* **Easter, Date of**).

Forgiveness Sunday falls on the seventh **Sunday** before Orthodox Easter. On this day church services recall the story of Adam and Eve's expulsion from Paradise. The Gospel reading (a selection from Christian scripture describing the life of Christ) presents **Jesus'** teaching on forgiveness and **fasting** (Matthew 6:14-18). The name "Forgiveness Sunday" comes from the Gospel reading and also from the custom of forgiving others and asking for others' forgiveness on this day. By practicing forgiveness with one another, Orthodox Christians hope to invite God's forgiveness and to begin Lent with the proper spirit of humility. Some Orthodox parishes, monasteries, and schools follow a formal ritual of forgiveness after the Sunday evening worship service. Members of the community bow to one another, ask forgiveness for their offenses, and offer forgiveness to each other.

Forgiveness Sunday is also called Cheese or Cheesefare Sunday since it is the last day on which strictly observant Orthodox Christians eat milk, cheese, and other dairy products before the beginning of the full-fledged Lenten fast. Cheesefare, or Forgiveness, Sunday marks the end of **Cheese Week**. This, the first week of the Lenten fast, is only partial. Meat products are forbidden during this week, but dairy products may still be eaten. The full Lenten fast begins on Forgiveness Sunday, after the evening, or vespers, service. Some Orthodox Christians exchange the greeting "May your fast be light" as a means of expressing well wishes at this holy time of year. For the next seven weeks strictly observant Orthodox Christians will consume no meat, eggs, dairy products, olive oil, fish, **wine**, or alcohol. The following day, known as **Clean Monday**, constitutes the first full day of Lent.

The folk customs of Cheese Week and Forgiveness Sunday anticipate the upcoming fast and the solemnity of Lent by encouraging indulgence in what soon will be forbidden. For example, folk tradition encourages people to feast on egg and cheese dishes. Also, since Forgiveness Sunday constitutes the last day of **Carnival** for Orthodox Christians, people enjoy dances, masquerades, and other frolics. In Greece, a predominately Orthodox country, people also treat the following day, Clean Monday, as a joyous occasion.

Some of the Orthodox folk customs concerning Cheese Week and Forgiveness Sunday feature eggs, an Easter symbol and forbidden food during the Lenten season. Many follow an old Greek tradition which dictates that the last bit of food consumed before the beginning of the fast be a hard-boiled egg. Before eating the egg one declares, "With an egg I close my mouth, with an egg I shall open it again." For those who observe this custom the eating of an egg symbolizes both the beginning and the end of the seven-week Lenten fast. After the late-night **Easter Vigil** service on **Holy Saturday**, they begin their Easter feast with a hard-boiled **Easter egg**.

217

In another egg custom popular in Macedonia and Bulgaria people use a string or thread to suspend a boiled egg from the ceiling. Sometimes a piece of cheese or candy is substituted for the egg. They circle round this treat and knock it with their foreheads to get it swinging. Then each member of the circle tries to catch it with their mouths. The egg may also be suspended from the end of a stick held aloft by one of the participants.

An old Russian folk tradition required people not only to ask forgiveness of family members, friends, and neighbors, but also to visit the cemetery in order to ask forgiveness from the dead. The living embraced one another as a sign of **pardon**; the dead were offered *blini*, a kind of thin Russian pancake eaten during Cheese Week (*for more on Cheese Week in Russia, see* **Maslenitsa**).

Further Reading

Griffin, Robert H., and Ann H. Shurgin, eds. *The Folklore of World Holidays*. Second edition. Detroit, MI: Gale Research, 1999.

Henderson, Helene, and Sue Ellen Thompson, eds. *Holidays, Festivals, and Celebrations of the World Dictionary*. Second edition. Detroit, MI: Omnigraphics, 1997.

Hopko, Thomas. *The Lenten Spring*. Crestwood, NY: St. Vladimir's Seminary Press, 1998.

Mathewes-Green, Frederica. *Facing East*. New York: HarperSanFrancisco, 1997.

Spicer, Dorothy Gladys. *Book of Festivals*. 1937. Reprint. Detroit, MI: Omnigraphics, 1990.

Wybrew, Hugh. *Orthodox Lent, Holy Week and Easter*. Crestwood, NY: St. Vladimir's Seminary Press, 1997.

Web Site

"Pre-Lent," a document describing the beliefs and practices of Orthodox Christians concerning pre-Lent, posted on the Orthodox Church in America web site: http://www.oca.org/pages/orth_chri/orthodox-faith/worship/pre-lent.html

Germany, Carnival in

In those regions of Germany inhabited primarily by Roman Catholics, people celebrate **Carnival** with zest. To enter into the fun at Carnival time is almost a requirement in these zones, as illustrated in the popular Rhineland saying, "Whoever is not foolish at Carnival is foolish during the rest of the year." In Germany Carnival goes by many names. Hessians know it as *Fassenacht*, Bavarians refer to it as *Fasching*, the people of the Black Forest region call it *Fasnet*, and in the Rhineland it is *Karneval*. The first three of these names mean "Fast Eve," and refer to the six-week **fast** of **Lent** that follows the close of the Carnival season. Germans may also refer to Carnival as the "Fifth Season," "Season of Fools," or the "Crazy Days." They celebrate this zany festival with masks, costumes, parties, parades, and other fun street activities. *Faschingskrapfen*, or Carnival doughnuts, are a popular festival treat. One of the most common costumes seen at Carnival time is that of the fool or clown. Many towns and cities feature parades of people dressed as Carnival fools. Other common customs include the staging of witty and mocking speeches criticizing those members of the community, celebrities, or politicians whose behavior during the past year has been outrageous. Special costume parades for children are often held on the Saturday or **Sunday** before **Ash Wednesday**.

Many Germans give November 11 at 11:11 a.m. as the traditional start of the Carnival season. No one can say exactly how this association between Carnival and the number eleven began. Some speculate that it came about because German folklore associated the number eleven with fools. Others have suggested that the number eleven stands for both unity and equality since it is represented by two "1s" standing side by side. Karneval societies, groups of citizens who meet to plan the celebrations, call their association the "Council of Eleven." Carnival preparations officially begin on November 11. The festivities themselves, however, usually begin after Epiphany on January 6 and end at midnight on Shrove Tuesday, the last day of Carnival (*see also* **Shrovetide**). In Cologne people begin celebrating Carnival on New Year's Day.

History

Historians believe that Germany's medieval Carnival celebrations were simple, loud, and rowdy affairs. Bands of men clothed in animal skins roved through villages and hamlets shouting nonsense and acting wildly. In the fifteenth century the hairy men became fools, or clowns, who entertained people with their witty criticism of society. Between the fifteenth and seventeenth centuries fools' societies sprang up in many German towns and cities. The members of these societies not only poked fun at individuals whose behavior was deemed unacceptable by the community, but also organized parades that made fun of vanity, pride, and other vices. In addition, they often staged folk plays whose plots gave the main character, the fool, an opportunity to make fun of human failings.

Around the year 1500 masked balls gained favor among the highest ranks of the nobility. They became increasingly popular throughout society in the centuries that followed until they reached the peak of their appeal, extravagance, and glamour in the seventeenth and eighteenth centuries.

Carnival in Southwest Germany

In the Black Forest and other zones of southwest Germany the festival still bears the stamp of medieval Carnival celebrations. In rural areas Carnival-goers may splash one another with **water** or toss soot at each other. The costumes favored by Germans from these regions include spirits, demons, animals and witches, frightening figures that hark back to the old hairy men and their wild antics. Another popular costume is that of the "wise fool." The wise fools wear smooth, wooden masks, many of which have been in the same family for generations. In Rottweil some fools cover their costumes with large **bells**. Others wear red fringes on their clothing, cover their hats with snail shells, and carry an inflated hog bladder which they use to beat anyone who comes across their path.

Old Fasnacht

In some parts of southern Germany Carnival continues until the Sunday after Ash Wednesday, called **Fire Sunday**. This period of time, from the Thursday after Ash Wedesday to Fire Sunday is known as *Alte Fasnacht*, or "Old Fasnacht." Some writers date it back to the early Middle Ages, when Lent began on Fire Sunday, the sixth Sunday before Easter. Around the seventh or eighth centuries Christian authorities decided that Sundays, even if they fell during Lent, didn't count as true days of fast and penitence since they celebrate the **Resurrection**. Yet with the Sundays removed Lent fell short of the required forty days. Therefore Christian authorities decided to begin the season four days earlier, on Ash Wednesday. Some communities, however, resisted the change. They continued to celebrate Carnival right up to the sixth Sunday before Easter. These late Carnival celebrations continue till this day in the towns and hamlets near Lake Constance.

Carnival in Saxony

In some parts of Saxony, located in northwest Germany, Carnival celebrations feature symbolic battles between spring and winter. When spring vanquishes winter, people celebrate with music and merrymaking. In Eisenach, "Dame Summer" vanquishes another folk figure representing winter, which is then burned in effigy. In other places in Germany similar battles between spring and winter take place on different dates (*see also* **Laetare Sunday**).

Women's Carnival

In past centuries men were allowed to participate in many Carnival activities off limits to women. In 1824 a group of washerwomen in a small town near the city of Bonn decided to do something about this. They took over city hall and declared the day a holiday for themselves. They elected a "washing princess" to lead their celebrations. The tradition caught on with women and eventually spread throughout Germany. *Weiberfasnacht,* or "Women's Carnival," begins at 11:11 a.m. on the Thursday before Shrove Tuesday. Many towns celebrate with costumes, parades, and floats. Those riding the floats toss handfuls of candy and flowers to the crowds that line the streets. Women often indulge themselves in behaviors that would be considered outrageous on other days. One traditional prank, now declining in popularity, involves snipping off a man's tie with a pair of scissors and then planting a kiss on his cheek. In Bonn women costumed as clowns, soldiers, devils, and witches storm city hall on the Thursday before Shrove Tuesday and run things for a day. In other places groups of women may take over pubs and streets, paying no attention to any command directed at them by a man. Later that evening many groups of female friends band together for a night on the town.

Carnival in Cologne

The citizens of Cologne boast that their Carnival celebrations are the most extravagant to be found in Germany. The earliest historical document to mention Cologne's Carnival celebrations dates back to 1340. The city's medieval Carnival celebrations featured masked processions organized by the guilds, associations of men following the same trade. Guild apprentices made up short humorous plays which they performed on city plazas and at the homes of local merchants. A folk figure known as *Bellen-Geck*, who personified Carnival, roamed city streets singing songs, delivering witty jabs at the failings of certain citizens, and posing riddles to bystanders.

Carnival in Cologne has survived centuries of attempts by politicians and priests to destroy it. In the sixteenth century a religious reform movement known as the Protestant Reformation influenced a number of its German adherents to campaign against Carnival. Indeed, in those regions of Germany that became predominantly Protestant, located primarily in the north and east, Carnival celebrations shriveled or disappeared. Cologne's celebrations survived and flourished, due at least in part to its location along the Rhine river in west central Germany. After the Thirty Years War (1618-48) politicians tried to outlaw Carnival fearing that the disorderly celebrations might inspire people to revolt against the government. The French emperor Napoleon I (1769-1821), whose troops conquered much of Germany in the late eighteenth and early nineteenth centuries, also tried to stop Carnival in Cologne, but soon found his soldiers would rather join the party than fight it. In the first half of the nineteenth century, during a period of political repression, Cologne's Carnival turned increasingly towards humorous social commentary, providing citizens a veiled yet significant means of expressing their political views.

Cologne's many Carnival societies organize its yearly celebrations. Throughout most of the year these groups function as social clubs. As the Carnival season nears, however, they begin planning the various entertainments that bring Cologne's Carnival to life. For example, each year the Carnival Societies of Cologne host approximately 800 Carnival "sessions," large parties with live entertainment that one may attend for the price of a ticket. The evening's entertainment includes humorous speeches by society members making fun of current events, well-known personalities, and politicians. Delivered from atop an upturned half of a barrel, these addresses are known as *büttenreden*, or "barrel speeches." As the evening progresses singers, dancers, comedians, clowns, and female impersonators furnish additional entertainment. Partygoers also look forward to the visit of Prince Carnival, accompanied by the Maiden and the Peasant. The citizens of Cologne vie with one another to be given the role of impersonating these folk figures during Carnival. The prince represents the spirit of Carnival, the Maiden signifies beauty, and the Peasant symbolizes the courage and strength of the people of Cologne. A successful party ends with audience members joining arms and belting out songs.

The sessions end by Women's Carnival Day. The "three crazy days" follow Women's Carnival Day. At this time Cologners take to the streets to celebrate Carnival with parades, drinking, dancing, and costumed hijinks of all kinds. On the Sunday before Shrove Tuesday the children of Cologne, dressed in costumes, march in special children's parades.

In Cologne people call the Monday before Shrove Tuesday *Rosenmontag*, or "Rose Monday." The celebration has nothing to do with roses, however. The name evolved from an older phrase describing the day as *Rasender Montag*, or "Raving Monday." On Rose Monday more than seven thousand people and three hundred horses participate in a giant parade that snakes its way through the city. It begins at 11:11 am and includes floats, bands, and people costumed as fools. Members of the Carnival societies ride atop these floats, pitching handfuls of candy, flowers, or small toys to the crowds lining the streets. About one million spectators enjoy the show. Similar Rose Monday parades also take place in Düsseldorf and Mainz.

Prince Carnival reigns over the celebrations in Cologne. Referred to as "His Crazy Highness," he and his companions take over city government on Shrove Tuesday. The prince's royal bodyguards, referred to as "the sparks," wear old-fashioned guard uniforms and carry wooden muskets, while the royal councilors don peaked hats and badges identifying themselves as members of the "Order of Fools."

Carnival in Munich

The city of Munich serves as the capital of Bavaria in southwest Germany. Munich's Carnival celebrations lack the sessions and barrel speeches popular in the Rhineland. Instead they reflect Venetian influence, especially in their elegant masked balls and parties *(for more on Carnival in Venice, see* **Italy, Carnival in**). In Munich the Carnival season begins on January 7, the day after Epiphany, but the festivities intensify as Ash Wednesday draws nearer. The last week of Carnival brings many town inhabitants out of their homes and into the city's nightclubs, where they drink beer and enjoy lively company until well after midnight. Others attend the many parties and masked balls that take place in Munich at this time of year. On the Sunday before Shrove Tuesday the people of Munich host a large parade known as *München Harisch,* or "Mad Munich." Many attend this event to see the gorgeous sixteenth- and seventeenth-century Venetian costumes worn by people in the parade. On Shrove Tuesday the *Marktfrauen,* or "market women," dress in humorous, clown-like costumes and perform a special dance in the market place.

Every seven years the citizens of Munich present the *Schäfflertanz,* or dance of the barrel-makers guild. This custom originated in 1463 when a deadly disease known as the plague ravaged Munich and the surrounding areas. After the outbreak had run its course the coopers, makers of wooden barrels and casks, were the first citizens to venture out of their homes. They danced and frolicked in the streets in order assure everyone that the city's thoroughfares were now free of disease. Every seven years the dance is performed at Carnival time in commemoration of those brave coopers. The most recent performance took place in 1998.

In Munich Carnival comes to a close with one last costume party on the evening of Shrove Tuesday. A person dressed as a fool represents Carnival itself and plays a starring role at this party. He permits himself to be placed in a mock coffin at the stroke of midnight. His followers carry the coffin out into the streets where those who mourn the end of Carnival throw their last sip of beer in its direction. A mock streetsweeper follows this procession, his presence signifying the removal of the last remnants of Carnival.

Further Reading

Brophy, James M. "Mirth and Subversion: Carnival in Cologne." *History Today* 47, 7 (1997): 42-48.

Griffin, Robert H., and Ann H. Shurgin, eds. *The Folklore of World Holidays.* Second edition. Detroit, MI: Gale Research, 1999.

Griffin, Robert H., and Ann H. Shurgin, eds. *Junior Worldmark Encyclopedia of World Holidays.* Volume 1. Detroit, MI: UXL, 2000.

Lord, Priscilla Sawyer, and Daniel J. Foley. *Easter the World Over.* Philadelphia, PA: Chilton Book Company, 1971.

Russ, Jennifer M. *German Festivals and Customs.* London, England: Oswald Wolff, 1982.

Schulte-Peevers, Andrea. "Cologne Carnival: A Trip to the Land of Fools, Floats, and Revelry." *German Life* (March 31, 1995).

Spicer, Dorothy Gladys. *Festivals of Western Europe.* 1958. Reprint. Detroit, MI: Omnigraphics, 1994.

Thonger, Richard. *A Calendar of German Customs.* London, England: Oswald Wolff, 1966.

Web Sites

"Karneval-Fastnacht-Fasching," an article on the various German Carnival celebrations that includes the sub-articles "Kölner Karneval," "The Swabian-Alemannic Fasnet," and "Fasching." Available through the "German Customs, Holidays and Traditions" web site, sponsored by German instructor Robert J. Shea: http://www.serve.com/shea/germusa/karneval.htm

The web site of the Tourist Office of the city of Cologne offers information about Carnival in Cologne at: http://www.koeln.de/portrait/e/events.html

Germany, Easter and Holy Week in

Over the centuries the German folk imagination has produced much Easter lore and numerous related customs. Many writers believe that the American **Easter Bunny** got its start in old German folklore concerning an Easter **hare**.

Palm Sunday

Holy Week begins with **Palm Sunday**, which Germans call *Palmsonntag*. Palm Sunday processions once marked the opening of Holy Week in Germany. At the rear of these processions came the *palmesel*, or "palm donkey," a wooden donkey on wheels with a carved figure of **Jesus** sitting on its back. Sometimes, in lieu of a palm donkey, the local priest might sometimes ride a real donkey at the tail end of the procession. The parade of churchgoers crossed through the village and circled the church before entering for **Sunday** morning services. This custom inspired Germans to describe those who are late to church or late in getting up on Palm Sunday as "palm donkeys."

Palm branches are an important Palm Sunday symbol, carried in religious processions in many different countries. Since few palm trees grow in Germany willow, birch, box, yew, hazel, and holly branches are used instead. In some places people decorate these branches. For example, in the Black Forest region people stripped branches and then festooned them with pussy willows, hearts, **crosses**, greenery, and ribbons. In Bavaria a traditional Palm Sunday decoration required twelve different kinds of branches to be joined together to make a "tree." Decorated with glass beads, the trees were brought to church to be blessed and later set up in fields where folklore insisted that they increased the chance of a good harvest. A decoration made

227

of tree branches and often shaped like a cross, called a *gemeindepalm* or "parish palm," stands in many German churches on Palm Sunday.

According to German folk tradition, "palm" branches that have been blessed in church have special powers. In some places people brought them home to keep ill fortune away from the household. In other locales tradition required more of a person. There people had to eat pussy willow buds to acquire their blessing. Another old tradition recommended scattering twigs from these Palm Sunday branches across one's fields as a means of turning away lightning strikes.

Crooked Wednesday

Germans sometimes refer to Wednesday of Holy Week as "Crooked Wednesday" (*see also* **Spy Wednesday**). The name recalls the Christian folk tradition identifying Wednesday as the day on which **Judas** turned Jesus over to the authorities.

Green Thursday

Germans call the Thursday of Holy Week, *Gründonnerstag*, or "Green Thursday" (*see also* **Maundy Thursday**). Some commentators believe, however, that Germans originally named the day "Crying Thursday" or "Mourning Thursday." They argue that the original name was based on an old medieval word, *greinen*, meaning "to cry." Eventually it slurred into *grün*, meaning "green." Another set of commentators believe that the name Green Thursday refers to the old custom of admitting penitents, who bore green branches as a sign of their joy, back into church on this day (*for more on penitence, see* **Repentance**). Some researchers believe that this custom gave rise to an old Latin name for the day, *Dies viridium* or "Day of the Green Ones."

German tradition calls for eating green foods, such as kale, spinach, cress, leeks, chives, and herbs, on Maundy Thursday. Folklore suggested that following this tradition brought good luck for the coming year. America's Pennsylvania Dutch, descendents of German immigrants, also followed the tradition of eating green foods on Maundy Thursday. In some parts of Germany people also eat "Judas ears," honey-filled rolls, on this day. Another old Green Thursday folk tradition declared it the proper day to bathe, do laundry, and clean the house in preparation for Easter. Indeed in some parts of Europe, the day was known as "Clean Thursday."

Good Friday

Germans have two names for **Good Friday**. The Old High German word *kara*, meaning "care," forms the basis of the name *Karfreitag*, Care Friday or Friday of Mourning. *Stiller Freitag*, another name for the day, means Quiet Friday. Many Germans observe this solemn holiday as a day of **fasting**. Good Friday has also long been associated with the performance of German **Passion plays**, folk plays dramatizing the events leading up to Jesus' crucifixion. Though few survived into the late twentieth century, the famous Passion play at Oberammergau in Bavaria still takes place every ten years.

Roman Catholic churches do not ring their **bells** on Good Friday. An old German custom invited lay people to replace the sound of church bells with wooden rattles, an invitation that many took up with gusto. In past times the noisy clatter of these rattles, instead of the chiming of church bells, called people to church services on this day. This custom inspired the people of Swabia to describe local loudmouths as having "a mouth like a Good Friday rattle."

German superstitions associated with Good Friday include the belief that it is a particularly good day to sow flowers. Another superstition affirms that hair cut on Good Friday will grow back luxuriously. One more bit of folklore associated with Good Friday teaches that if one cools hot iron in **water** on this day, the water will have the power to cure warts. Yet another old Good Friday folk tradition frowned on the drinking of alcohol, an abstinence which served to remind those who observed it that Jesus thirsted as he hung on the cross. In a similar vein folk custom forbade the slaughtering of animals on Good Friday. What's more, blacksmiths refused to touch hammer and nails on this day, remembering the awful purpose to which these had been put on the first Good Friday.

Holy Saturday

In some parts of Germany children once gathered to "hunt Judas" on **Holy Saturday** (*see also* **Judas, Burning of**). In Westphalia boys armed with wooden rattles performed this task rather noisily near midnight on Holy Saturday, whereas in Silesia children drove the local bell ringer, who played the role of Judas, out of town on Easter Sunday morning. Children also busied themselves in gathering wood for the Easter bonfire, a task which many began earlier in the week (*see also* **Easter Fires**). German folklore advised that the smoke from these bonfires improved the eyes of the elderly, who were therefore encouraged to attend these smoky events. Afterwards people brought the cinders and ashes home in the belief that they could ward misfortune away from the homestead, keep mice out of the fields, and protect cattle from disease.

Easter Sunday

Many egg-related games and customs are associated with **Easter Sunday** in Germany. In past centuries, courting couples used to exchange fancy **Easter eggs** as a token of their love. Another old custom encouraged children to go from house to house on Easter morning, singing for dyed eggs and fancy beads (*gebildbrote*). Today some German children prepare for the day by building a nest for the Easter Bunny to lay his eggs in. In some parts of Germany, however, a different kind of animal brings candies and dyed eggs to children. In Upper Bavaria the cockerel makes these deliveries, in Franconia and Thuringia it is the fox, in Bad Salzungen in the state of Hesse it's the crane, and in Hanover the cuckoo. Sometimes children make a gift of a special egg to their parents, writing on it a promise to do some household task that would please their mother and father. Easter egg hunts also take place on this day, as well as **egg-rolling** and **egg-tapping** games.

Many Germans go to church on Easter Sunday morning, although fewer attend Easter services than Christmas services. In past centuries pastors entertained the Easter morning congregation with funny sermons in order to elicit **laughter**, thereby sustaining the good humor viewed as appropriate to this celebration. This custom later came to be seen as irreverent and so disappeared.

German Easter decorations feature fresh spring flowers, especially the daffodil, and willow branches. **Egg trees**, branches or actual trees decorated with Easter eggs, also appear around Easter time. German immigrants brought this custom with them to the United States, where many Americans not of German descent adopted it as well. Special cakes and **breads** baked in the shape of a **lamb** often appear on German Easter tables. As Easter approaches, bakeries and confectioner's shops proudly display these symbols of the season. The lamb usually carries a religious banner bearing the image of a cross or lamb, while a ribbon and bell circles the lamb's neck.

An old piece of German folklore, also found in other European countries, teaches that Easter water confers health and beauty, as well as a certain magic. One old folk charm for beauty required a girl to rise early on Easter, fetch a bucket of fresh water, and bathe in it — all without saying a word. A similarly constructed Easter Sunday love charm promised girls that if on this day they brought a bucket of spring water home without looking back, talking, or being seen, they could see the face of their future love reflected in the water's surface. Another old wives' tale told that for a single instant between Holy Saturday and sunrise on Easter morning, rivers ran with **wine** in honor of the **Resurrection**. Farmers wishing to confer an Easter **baptism**, or *Ostertaufe*, on their crops collected fresh running water on Easter Sunday morning and sprinkled it over their fields, a practice which folklore suggested could enhance the harvest.

Another collection of German Easter lore concerns the power of the sun on Easter morning. An old luck charm advises that if one stands by an east-facing window at sunrise with an elder branch in hand, the first rays of the **Easter sun** will bring one luck. Another folk belief, common throughout Europe, suggests that the sun dances for joy on Easter morning. In past times people would rise early on Easter Sunday to greet the joyous holiday at sunrise and to perhaps catch a glimpse of this marvel (*see also* **Sunrise Service**).

Further Reading

Hudgins, Sharon. "A Special Flock." *The World and I* 16, 4 (April 2000): 134.

Lord, Priscilla Sawyer, and Daniel J. Foley. *Easter the World Over*. Philadelphia, PA: Chilton Book Company, 1971.

Russ, Jennifer M. *German Festivals and Customs*. London, England: Oswald Wolff, 1982.

Spicer, Dorothy Gladys. *Festivals of Western Europe*. 1958. Reprint. Detroit, MI: Omnigraphics, 1994.

Thonger, Richard. *A Calendar of German Customs*. London, England: Oswald Wolff, 1966.

Web Sites

"Easter," a brief article on German Easter customs posted by the Germany embassy in Ottawa, Canada: http://www.germanembassyottawa.org/easter/

The following searchable site offers a range of information on German culture: http://www.germany-info.org

Golden Rose

For 1,000 years the Roman Catholic popes have carried or blessed a golden rose on the fourth **Sunday** in **Lent**, known as **Laetare Sunday**. The rose symbolizes Christ, whom Christians believe to be, in fulfillment of biblical prophecy, the flower that sprang from the root of Jesse (Isaiah 11:1). After its use on Laetare Sunday the pope may then bestow the bejeweled, golden ornament on an individual, church, shrine, or city as a token of esteem and affection. The golden rose, and other customs associated with Laetare Sunday, introduce a note of gladness into an otherwise somber Lenten season and hint at Easter joy to come.

No one knows exactly when the customs surrounding the golden rose began. In the mid-eleventh century Pope Leo IX referred to the carrying of the golden rose on Laetare Sunday as an "ancient custom." In that era the Pope presided over Sunday morning mass at Santa Croce in Gerusalemme, or the Church of the Holy Cross in Jerusalem, on Laetare Sunday (*for more on the Roman Catholic religious service called the mass, see also* **Eucharist**). On his journey home to the Lateran Palace he held the golden rose in his right hand, while he blessed the crowd with his left. The fact that the first golden roses were not too heavy, being only a bit over six inches in length, made this custom possible. Over time the golden rose grew in size and became more elaborate in design. Instead of a single rose, the ornament grew to represent a bouquet of roses, along with a vase and a pedestal on which to place it. Craftsmen further embellished the golden rose by studding it with precious gems. Of course, after these developments occurred, the pope no longer carried it by himself in his left hand.

It is uncertain exactly when the popes began to lay a special blessing on the rose. At these ceremonies the pope offered prayers, sprinkled holy **water**, and burnt incense as means of conferring a holy blessing on the rose. In addition, some of these golden ornaments were made with tiny, hidden containers into which the pope poured musk and balsam. Scholars believe that the custom of bestowing the golden rose on churches, cities, shrines, or individuals as a token of the pope's esteem probably arose sometime after the establishment of the blessing ceremony. Records dating back to the twelfth century show that the most common recipients of the rose were kings and queens. In recent decades this precious token has often been awarded to Catholic queens.

The golden rose is blessed every year, whether it is given away or not. The pope exercises his own judgment in bestowing the golden rose. If he finds no one worthy of this special honor in any given year, then the golden rose is carefully stored for the pope's use the following year. If the pope gives the golden rose away, goldsmiths craft a new one for the following year.

Further Reading

"Golden Rose." In E. A. Livingstone, ed. *The Oxford Dictionary of the Christian Church*. Third edition. Oxford, England: Oxford University Press, 1997.

Rock, P. M. J. "Golden Rose." In Charles G. Herbermann et al., eds. *The Catholic Encyclopedia*. New York: Appleton, 1913. Available online at: http://www.newadvent.org/cathen/06629a.htm

Weiser, Francis X. *Handbook of Christian Feasts and Customs*. New York: Harcourt, Brace and World, 1952.

Good Friday

Black Friday, Great Friday, Holy Friday, Karfreitag, Langfredag, Long Friday, Pitkäperjanti, Sorrowful Friday, Viernes Santo

Christians commemorate the crucifixion of **Jesus** Christ on the Friday before Easter (*for more on crucifixion, see also* **Cross**). Known as "Good Friday," this day of observance came into being during the early Christian era. Solemn religious ceremonies and folk customs characterize the day in many parts of the world. Church services recall the account of Jesus' death given in Christian scripture in which soldiers loyal to the Jewish religious authorities capture Jesus on the evening of the **Passover** supper (*see also* **Maundy Thursday**). The next morning Jesus is questioned, beaten, and sentenced to death by the Roman governor Pontius **Pilate**. Roman soldiers place a crown of thorns upon his head and strip him of his clothing. Broken and bleeding, Jesus is led to a place called Golgotha, where they nail him to a cross. He dies on the cross that afternoon.

Symbols

The symbol most closely associated with the holiday is the cross or crucifix. A crown of thorns, recalling the crown of thorns placed on

Jesus' head by Roman soldiers in an attempt to torment and mock him, serves as another symbol of the holiday. A rooster, or cock, may also represent Good Friday. On the night of his arrest, Jesus predicted that his disciple **Peter** would deny him three times before the rooster crowed the following morning. When Jesus was arrested, his followers deserted him. Peter followed along behind the crowd that took Jesus away, however. Three bystanders recognized Peter as one of Jesus' disciples, but Peter argued with them, telling each of them that they were mistaken. At that point a rooster crowed, reminding Peter of Jesus' prediction. Thus the rooster not only recalls Peter's denial but also Jesus' foreknowledge of it. Other religious symbols of the holiday include representations of the **holy sepulchre** — that is, Jesus' tomb — and the *epitaphios*, a cloth embroidered with the image of Jesus reposing in death (*see also* **Shroud of Turin**). The **pelican** and the **passionflower** also remind Christians of Jesus' sacrifice of himself on Good Friday.

The liturgical color for Good Friday is black, symbolizing grief and death. Liturgical color schemes dictate the color of clerical robes and other church decorations in those churches that observe them.

In England **hot cross buns** were once closely associated with the holiday. Now they are available throughout **Lent**. Hot cross buns are also eaten in countries where the British have settled.

History

Early Christian communities celebrated Easter in different ways and on different dates. Moreover, they memorialized the story of Jesus' Passion — that is, the events leading up to and including his death — during the same festival that celebrated his **resurrection**. As a result, little can be said for certain about the exact origins of Good Friday.

Some scholars believe that the earliest Easter celebrations occurred in the second century in important ancient cities like Rome, Jerusalem, and Alexandria. These celebrations fell on the **Sunday** following Passover (*see also* **Easter Sunday**). In some communities that adopted this observance, a two-day **fast** preceded the Easter festival. If this is true, then fasting may be said to be the first religious custom associated with the Friday before Easter.

Other scholars, however, believe that the first Easter celebrations took place instead in second-century Asia Minor, a region now known as the modern nation of Turkey. Christians in this area placed special emphasis on the sacrificial death of Jesus Christ, a theme later assigned to Good Friday. They, like their counterparts in Rome, called the holiday *"Pascha,"* a Greek word inspired by the Aramaic pronunciation of the Hebrew word *Pesach*, which means Passover. Indeed, the Asia Minor Christians held Pascha on the same date that their Jewish neighbors celebrated Passover, on the fourteenth and fifteenth days of the Jewish month of Nisan. The observances included fasting, prayer, and readings from scripture, including the writings of the Jewish prophets and the Passover story as recounted in the Bible's Book of Exodus.

In the year 325 the Council of Nicaea, an important meeting of early Church leaders, attempted to unify these celebrations by setting a single date for the Easter festival (*see also* **Easter, Date of**). This decision not only helped to create the Easter festival we know today but also fostered the emergence of Good Friday as a separate and distinct observance. The best description of early Good Friday celebrations comes from Jerusalem, relayed to us in the diary of Egeria, a Spanish nun who made a pilgrimage to the Holy Land around the year 380.

According to Egeria, Christians in Jerusalem spent Good Friday at the Church of the Holy Sepulchre, a large compound of courtyards and chapels built over the site of Jesus' crucifixion, burial, and resurrection. They spent the morning engaged in a devotion we now call the **Veneration of the Cross**. From noon to three in the afternoon the faithful attended a series of Bible readings that included the writings of the Hebrew prophets, Christian texts affirming Jesus' fulfillment of these Old Testament prophecies, and the Passion story. Some researchers claim that special emphasis was placed on the Passion as told in the Gospel according to John. Another scripture service followed, which ended at about seven o'clock in the evening. Then the clergy began yet another ceremony memorializing Jesus' burial. Upon the conclusion of this event the clergy and those worshipers who were not already exhausted began a long vigil around the site of Jesus' tomb (*see also* Holy Sepulchre).

Good Friday celebrations continued to develop throughout the Middle Ages. Medieval Good Friday ceremonies emphasized human **sin**, the need for **redemption**, and Christ's suffering and sacrificial death. Therefore they took on a mournful tone. In western Europe Good Friday services centered around three ceremonies: the Veneration of the Cross, the vigil beside the holy sepulchre, and the **Eucharist**, performed with **bread** and **wine** consecrated on the previous day, **Maundy Thursday**. Medieval Christians also dramatized the sorrowful events of Good Friday with **Passion plays**, folk dramas retelling the events of the last days of Jesus' life. Unfortunately, both church and folk retellings of the Passion story often cast the blame for Jesus' death on the Jewish people. This interpretation of the events surrounding Jesus' death fueled anti-Jewish attitudes and actions, making **Holy Week** an especially dangerous time for this already persecuted minority.

Contemporary Religious Ceremonies

Roman Catholic Good Friday services frequently center around the Veneration of the Cross. During this ceremony worshipers approach a cross or crucifix, bow before it and kiss it. These gestures demonstrate their reverence for all that the cross represents. Although some Roman Catholic churches practice **veiling** during the last days of Lent, veils covering crosses or crucifixes are removed on Good Friday.

Another ceremony of Roman Catholic origin, the **Three Hours** service, is now observed in churches of many different denominations. This service considers the seven last utterances of Jesus as he hung on the cross.

In Hispanic countries Roman Catholics may also participate in a nighttime devotion called the *Pésame*, which focuses on the grief experienced by Jesus' mother (*for more on Pésame, see also* **Mary, Blessed Virgin**).

237

In parts of central, southern, and eastern Europe Roman Catholic churches offer an extra-liturgical devotion known as the vigil of the holy sepulchre. This devotional exercise begins at the end of Good Friday religious services. The presiding priest carries a figure representing the crucified Christ to a side altar, designated as the holy sepulchre. He places it there, just as Jesus' followers took his body down from the cross and placed it in the tomb. Parishioners visit the holy sepulchre and offer prayers throughout the rest of the day and on **Holy Saturday** as well.

Many Roman Catholics also participate in the **Stations of the Cross** on Good Friday. This devotional exercise, in which worshipers pray and meditate on fourteen scenes from the Passion story, dates back to the Middle Ages. Nevertheless, it achieved widespread popularity hundreds of years later in the sixteenth, seventeenth, and eighteenth centuries.

Orthodox churches often offer a service called the **Royal Hours** on the morning of Good Friday. During the afternoon the devout return for another service in which worshipers come forward to bow before and kiss the epitaphios, a cloth embroidered with the image of Jesus in death. Then the epitaphios is placed in a bier which parishioners have covered with flowers earlier in the day. On the evening of Good Friday, Orthodox worshipers attend another service in which the epitaphios, in its bier, is carried around the church in a candlelit procession. Because Orthodox Christians reckon each new day as beginning at sunset, this observance technically belongs to Holy Saturday. The afternoon service belongs to Holy Saturday, too, due to a longstanding tendency to celebrate the services of Holy Week in advance. The afternoon service commemorates the burial of Christ; the evening procession symbolizes Jesus' triumph over the power of death and darkness.

Fasting

The practice of fasting, a religious custom strongly associated with Good Friday, cuts across denominational boundaries. Although Roman Catholics eliminated many of their Lenten fasting customs in the last hundred years or so, Church authorities still require the faithful to fast on Good Friday. Observant Orthodox Christians fast throughout Lent. Those who do not observe a complete Lenten fast will often fast during Holy Week, especially on Good Friday. In Ethiopia some devout Orthodox Christians intensify their fast on Good Friday, going without food from Good Friday to Easter Sunday. Many other Christians, though not required to do so by their denominations, observe some kind of fast on Good Friday. In past times many Irish Christians practiced a "black fast" on this day, a regimen consisting of nothing more than tea and **water**.

Good Friday Customs

In Spain schools close during Holy Week and some shops observe shorter hours. Many businesses are closed on Good Friday. Spanish cities and towns frequently host processions on this day. Members of lay religious associations, called brotherhoods, carry floats depicting scenes from the Passion story on their shoulders. Hushed crowds of people line the streets in anticipation of the sober spectacle. Solemn religious processions also take place in Italy, Malta, and other southern European countries.

The city of Seville boasts the most famous Good Friday processions in Spain. Robed and hooded members of religious brotherhoods shoulder floats weighing thousands of pounds, carrying them in measured, swaying steps through the city streets. These floats feature life-sized wooden statues of figures from the Good Friday story. Real costumes made of silk, velvet, gold, and jewels adorn many of the figures, especially the revered images of the Virgin Mary. More robed and hooded marchers precede and follow behind the floats, those following often carrying large wooden crosses. Priests and elegantly attired civic leaders may also participate in these processions. Sometimes the spectacle moves onlookers so much that they offer a wailing kind of song, called a *saeta*, as the floats pass by (*see also* **Spain, Easter and Holy Week in**).

Mexican villagers observe Good Friday as a day of quiet. They view loud noises, **laughter**, running, swearing, and excitement as out of keeping with the spirit of the day. Churches remain darkened through-out the day, their interiors draped with black cloth. Many towns host somber parades representing Jesus' funeral procession. A figure of the crucified Christ is placed in a glass-faced coffin and carried through the streets. At some point along the route a statue of the Virgin Mary grieving for the death of her son is brought forward to meet the cas-ket. This meeting between the Virgin Mary and her crucified son con-stitutes the climax of the event (*see also* **Mexico, Easter and Holy Week in**).

In some European and Latin American countries people burn **Judas** in effigy on Good Friday (*see* **Judas, Burning of**). Judas was the disci-ple who turned Jesus over to the Jewish religious authorities, thereby starting the chain of events that led to Jesus' crucifixion.

In Europe Roman Catholic churches do not ring their **bells** on Good Friday. In some predominately Catholic countries church bells ring so frequently that children notice this sudden silence. Adults inform the curious among them that the bells have flown away to Rome to visit the pope.

In several Scandinavian countries, old folk beliefs encouraged the switching of children on Good Friday. Years ago in Sweden everyone, men and women, boys and girls, slapped each other with birch switches on Good Friday. This was done in remembrance that Christ was flogged on this day. Today vases filled with budding birch twigs sit in Swedish parlors at this time of year, a faint reminder of this old custom (*see also* **Sweden, Easter and Holy Week in**).

In past times English boys played **marbles** on Good Friday. Indeed, the six weeks of Lent became known as the marbles season in Eng-land. Some researchers believe that this folk custom, which may have come from Holland or Belgium, was inspired by the game of dice that the Roman soldiers played at the foot of the cross (Mark 15:24, Luke 23:35, John 19:24). Lent also once served as the tops season in England. Playing with tops was particularly popular on Good Friday, the end of the season. Skipping rope was an English Good Friday pastime especially associated with women and girls. This practice led

241

some to nickname the day "Long Rope Day." Some folklorists speculate that the custom may have become associated with Good Friday as a reminder of the fate that befell Judas, the disciple who betrayed Jesus. According to the Bible, he hung himself (Matthew 27:3-5). The citizens of Brighton were especially fond of skipping rope on Good Friday. The custom died out in the mid-twentieth century, however (*see also* **England, Easter and Holy Week in**).

In Bermuda children fly kites on Good Friday. Watching their kite ascending on the wind was supposed to provide children with a visual image of Jesus ascending to heaven (*see also* **Ascension Day**). In Poland and the former Yugoslavia children sit down with their grandparents to dye **Easter eggs** on Good Friday.

Good Friday Superstitions

Many superstitions have attached themselves to Good Friday. In past times blacksmiths hesitated to work on this day, out of respect for the terrible purpose that iron nails were put to on the first Good Friday. In medieval England monarchs blessed gold and silver "cramp rings" on Good Friday. These blessed rings were believed to protect the wearer against epilepsy and palsy. The custom dates back to the late Middle Ages but was discontinued by Elizabeth I (1533-1603).

In England people still eat hot cross buns on Good Friday. Studded with dried fruit and decorated with a cross made of icing, these buns were once the subject of much superstition. Some said these buns, and other bread baked on Good Friday, would never grow stale. Others thought the bread had the power to ward off ill luck. Still others mixed bun crumbs with water, creating a tonic said to cure intestinal illnesses.

French and English superstitions warned against washing clothes on Good Friday. Those who ignored this warning might find mysterious blood spots staining their newly laundered garments.

In some countries people believed that seeds sown on Good Friday would be certain to bloom. The English thought it a particularly good day to sow parsley, a plant associated with the devil. The holiness of the day could break the devil's hold upon the herb. In the western part of the United States potatoes were sown on Good Friday. The Pennsylvania Dutch, whose ancestors immigrated to the United States from Germany and Switzerland, claimed that Good Friday was an excellent day on which to plant seeds. One should not do any other garden work between Good Friday and Easter, however, out of respect for the belief that Jesus had been buried in the earth on those days.

The Pennsylvania Dutch also believed it bad luck to work on Good Friday. Folk superstition specifically warned women against baking on this day, though Friday normally served as baking day for Pennsylvania Dutch housewives. Eggs laid on Good Friday brought health and good luck to those who ate them. Sometimes people saved these eggs to eat for breakfast on Easter morning. Another superstition declared that rain always falls on Good Friday. On clear days the rain might only amount to a few drops that sprinkle the countryside unobserved.

German folk beliefs taught that Good Friday brought good luck in a number of endeavors. For example, hair cut on Good Friday would grow back in abundance and seeds planted would always sprout. Water used to cool hot iron on this day gained the power to cure warts. Finally, any rain that fell on Good Friday was thought to confer a blessing on the rest of the year.

In addition to the many superstitions associated with Good Friday, many legends have grown up around the events commemorated on this day. For example, several tales spin imaginative accounts of the **tree of the cross**. Various plant and animal legends tell of shrubs, flowers, and beasts whose encounter with Christ on Good Friday forever changed their appearance.

Names for Good Friday

Good Friday has been known by many names. The English phrase "Good Friday" came from the old German name for the observance, *Gottes Freytag,* or God's Friday. Today the Germans know the day as *Karfreitag,* which means Care Friday or Friday of Mourning. Nicknames for the day include Black Friday and Sorrowful Friday. In Norway it is called *Langfredag* and in Finland *Pitkäperjanti*, both of which mean Long Friday. The Swedes also know the day as Long Friday. Some suppose that this name came about in reference to the day's numerous and lengthy religious services; others speculate that it might refer to the suffering that Jesus endured on this day. Spanish speakers know the day as *Viernes Santo*, or Holy Friday. Orthodox Christians refer to the day as Holy Friday, Great Friday, or Holy and Great Friday.

Further Reading

Bradshaw, Paul F. "The Origins of Easter." In Paul F. Bradshaw and Lawrence A. Hoffman, eds. *Passover and Easter: Origin and History to Modern Times.* Two Liturgical Traditions series, volume 5. Notre Dame, IN: University of Notre Dame Press, 1999.

Downman, Lorna, Paul Britten Austin, and Anthony Baird. *Round the Swedish Year*. Stockholm, Sweden: Bokförlaget Fabel, 1961.

Harrowven, Jean. *Origins of Festivals and Feasts*. London, England: Kaye and Ward, 1980.

Henderson, Helene, and Sue Ellen Thompson, eds. *Holidays, Festivals, and Celebrations of the World Dictionary*. Second edition. Detroit, MI: Omnigraphics, 1997.

Hutton, Ronald. *Stations of the Sun*. Oxford, England: Oxford University Press, 1996.

Lord, Priscilla Sawyer, and Daniel J. Foley. *Easter Garland*. 1963. Reprint. Detroit, MI: Omnigraphics, 1999.

Lord, Priscilla Sawyer, and Daniel J. Foley. *Easter the World Over*. Philadelphia, PA: Chilton Book Company, 1971.

Monti, James. *The Week of Salvation*. Huntington, IN: Our Sunday Visitor Publications, 1993.

Myers, Robert J. *Celebrations: The Complete Book of American Holidays*. Garden City, NY: Doubleday and Company, 1972.

Pierce, Joanne M. "Holy Week and Easter in the Middle Ages." In Paul F. Bradshaw and Lawrence A. Hoffman, eds. *Passover and Easter: Origin and History to Modern Times.* Two Liturgical Traditions series, volume 5. Notre Dame, IN: University of Notre Dame Press, 1999.

Shoemaker, Alfred L. *Eastertide in Pennsylvania*. Kutztown, PA: Pennsylvania Folklife Society, 1960.

Thompson, Sue Ellen. *Holiday Symbols*. Second edition. Detroit, MI: Omnigraphics, 2000.

Weiser, Francis X. *The Easter Book.* New York: Harcourt, Brace and Company, 1954.

Wybrew, Hugh. *Orthodox Lent, Holy Week and Easter*. Crestwood, NY: St. Vladimir's Seminary Press, 1997.

Good Thief

St. Dismas

In the Gospel according to Luke, one of the accounts of **Jesus'** life recorded in the Christian Bible, Jesus speaks to two thieves who are being crucified alongside him (Luke 23:39-43). One of the thieves mocks Jesus' apparent helplessness, saying, "Are you not the Christ? Save yourself, and us" (*for more on the word Christ, see* Jesus). The second thief reacts differently. He reproaches his companion for these harsh words towards Jesus, saying, "Do you not fear God since you are under the same sentence of condemnation? And we indeed justly; for we are receiving the due reward of our deeds; but this man has done nothing wrong." Then he turns to Jesus and says, "Jesus, remember me when you come into your kingdom."

This humble speech has inspired generations of Christians to refer to this unnamed man as "the Good Thief." Jesus responds to the Good Thief's faith in him by saying: "Truly I say to you, today you will be with me in Paradise." The Good Thief's words and Jesus' response have inspired many Christians to view this story as an emblem of the relationship between **repentance** and **salvation**.

Legends

For centuries Christians have wondered about the identity of the two thieves crucified alongside Jesus. Since the Bible does not give their names or histories, storytellers have invented them. An ancient document known as The Acts of Pilate names the Good Thief Dysmas and his companion Gestas. These names changed slightly as they were passed down over the years, until they became Dismas and Gesmas. Although Dismas and Gesmas are the most common names assigned to the pair, others have been used. In the Arabic Infancy Gospel, an ancient document concerning Jesus' early years, the pair appear as Titus and Dumachus. Centuries later, in his 1851 poem "The Golden Legend," American poet Henry Wadsworth Longfellow (1807-1882) reused these names. The pair have also been called Zoatham and Camma, and Joathas and Maggatras.

The Arabic Infancy Gospel records a legend concerning the two thieves that links them with Jesus' infancy. According to this legend, when Jesus' mother and father fled into Egypt shortly after Jesus' birth, they were held up by bandits (*for more on Jesus' mother, see* **Mary, Blessed Virgin**). One of these highwaymen, however, recognized something special about the family and ordered the others to let them go. This man was the Good Thief, who would later die from crucifixion on the same day and in the same place as Jesus. In the Arabic Infancy Gospel the infant Jesus predicts as much, so confirming that he was no ordinary toddler. In one version of this document, the Good Thief's evil companion refuses to let the Holy Family go. He relents after the Good Thief bribes him with forty coins and grudgingly allows the Holy Family to escape unharmed.

Patronages and Relics

In time St. Dismas became the special patron of prisoners, those sentenced to execution, reformed thieves, undertakers, and funeral directors. Some theologians found the idea of elevating Dismas into sainthood a bit unsettling, since there was no proof that he had ever been **baptized**. They resolved this issue by concluding that the **water** that poured from Jesus' side when the Roman soldier pierced him with a spear (John 19:34) splashed onto the Good Thief and, in effect, baptized him. His feast day was assigned to March 25, which in early Christian times was believed by many to have been the actual date of the Crucifixion (*see also* **Annunciation; Easter, Date of**). Some

246

sources, however, record his feast date as March 26. The Church of Santa Croce in Gerusalemme, located in Rome, Italy, keeps a fragment of wood which, according to legend, came from the **cross** of the Good Thief.

Further Reading

Blackburn, Bonnie, and Leofranc Holford-Strevens. *The Oxford Companion to the Year*. Oxford, England: Oxford University Press, 1999.

Hackwood, Frederick William. *Christ Lore*. 1902. Reprint. Detroit, MI: Gale Research, 1969.

Web Sites

Page on St. Dismas, sponsored by the Catholic Forum at: http://www.cath olic-forum.com/saints/saintd11.htm

Page on St. Dismas, sponsored by Catholics Online at: http://saints.cath olic.org/saints/dismas.html

Gospel Accounts of Easter

Holy Week and **Easter Sunday** observances commemorate the events of the last days of **Jesus'** life, his death by crucifixion, and his **resurrection** (*for more on crucifixion, see* **Cross**). Each of the four Gospels—books in the Christian Bible that tell the story of Jesus' life—offers an account of these events. Although the gist of the story remains the same throughout the four Gospels, the details vary. These accounts may be found in the Gospel according to Matthew, Chapters 21-28, the Gospel according to Mark, Chapters 11-16, the Gospel according to Luke, Chapters 19-24, and the Gospel according to John, Chapters 12-21.

Greece, Easter and Holy Week in

The Greek word for Easter is *Pascha*, a Greek pronunciation of the Hebrew word for **Passover**, *Pesah* (*see also* **Easter, Origin of the Word**). Greeks also call the festival *Lambri*, meaning "the radiance" or "brightness." This name recalls the fires and lights used in the **Resurrection** service that commemorates **Jesus'** rising from the dead (*see also* **Easter Vigil**; **Easter Fires**). In Greece Easter is the most important holiday of the year. Greeks sometimes call it *Eorti Eorton*, "the festival of festivals."

Most Greeks are members of the Greek Orthodox Church. Orthodoxy is one of the three main branches of the Christian faith. Orthodox Christianity developed in eastern Europe, the Middle East, and north Africa. It split away from Western Christianity, which later divided into Roman Catholicism and Protestantism, about 1,000 years ago. Orthodox and other Eastern Christians follow a slightly different schedule of religious observances than do Western Christians. In addition, they maintain their own distinctive calendar system which causes their **Lent** and **Easter season** observances to fall on different dates than those celebrated by Western Christians (*see also* **Easter, Date of**).

Holy Week

Christians call the last week of Lent, that is, the seven days that precede Easter, **Holy Week**. Strictly observant Orthodox Christians **fast** throughout Lent, refraining from eating meat, fish, eggs, dairy products, olive oil, and alcoholic beverages. Many less observant Orthodox Christians, who do not fast throughout Lent, will observe the fast during Holy Week. Distinctive religious observances take place throughout Holy Week. In addition, Greek families put their homes through a special **spring cleaning** in preparation for Easter. This cleaning includes giving their homes a fresh coat of whitewash. Other Easter preparations include the purchase of decorated candles, wrapped with ribbons or molded into playful shapes, to carry during the Resurrection service. Godparents buy these candles for their godchildren. For those who would like a more permanent memento of the holiday, jewelry shops sell egg-shaped pendants, made of gold or enamel and marked with the current year.

Lazarus Saturday

Greeks and other Orthodox Christians observe the day before Holy Week begins as a religious holiday. Known as **Lazarus Saturday**, the day commemorates the raising of Lazarus from the dead (John 11:1-44). Orthodox church services held on that day retell the story of his coming back to life at Jesus' command. Some people refer to this miracle as the "first Easter." Indeed, Lazarus' raising provides Jesus' followers with a preview of the kind of miracle that will occur the following week on **Easter Sunday**.

Children celebrate Lazarus Saturday by singing folk songs about Lazarus from door to door. Called *lazarakia*, these songs describe the miracle of his return from the dead. Sometimes the children carry props said to represent Lazarus, such as a picture, doll, or even a staff or rod covered with flowers, ribbons, and cloth. On the island of Crete children display a more abstract emblem representing Lazarus, a **cross** made of reeds and decorated with lemon blossoms and pretty red flowers. In central Greece girls usually take responsibility for banding together to sing lazarakia. On the island of Cyprus boys do, often acting out the story told in the song. One child, draped with garlands of yellow flowers, lies down and pretends to be Lazarus. When the others call, "Lazarus, come out!" he jumps up from the ground. Songsters refresh themselves with special buns known as *lazari*. Some bakers form the buns by twisting lumps of dough, as if to represent a man twisted up in a sheet. Others form it into long thin strips, cross the ends, and decorate the resulting loop with a cross made out of currants, a raisin-like dried fruit. According to Greek folklore, a child who rolls one of these buns down a hill stands a good chance of finding a bird's nest where it comes to rest.

Palm Sunday

Fasting is relaxed on **Palm Sunday**, the first day of Holy Week, because it commemorates the joyful welcome that Jesus and his followers received as they entered the city of Jerusalem. Church services feature processions recalling that of Jesus and his followers, and worshipers are given small crosses twisted out of **palm** leaves attached to a sprig of bay or myrtle. Parishioners bring these ornaments, called *vayas*, home with them and tuck them inside the frame of an icon, a religious image used to focus prayer or worship. Old folk beliefs taught that the vayas protected against disease and other misfortunes. A pregnant woman, touched by a vaya, could expect an easier delivery, and in some places even farm animals were thought to benefit from the protection they bestowed.

Holy Tuesday

Church services on this day recall the woman who anointed Jesus' feet, sometimes identified as **Mary Magdalene** and sometimes as Mary of Bethany, another of Jesus' friends (John 12:3). Many women who don't normally attend church make an effort to attend this ceremony.

Holy Wednesday

On this day church services include special healing ceremonies in which worshipers are anointed with holy oil, a specially blessed, fragrant oil. As parishioners file out of the church the priest paints a cross on their foreheads, cheeks, chins, palms, and the backs of their hands with a swab dipped in holy oil.

Red Eggs

In Greece people dye their **Easter eggs** red. Several legends illustrate the significance of red Easter eggs to the Greek people. According to one of these tales, as Jesus hung on the cross a woman walked by carrying a basket of eggs. A drop of Jesus' **blood** fell onto the eggs, staining them all red. This miracle inspired the Greek people to dye all their Easter eggs red, in memory of the Crucifixion (*for more on* *crucifixion, see* Cross). Some people add that the red color of the egg represents the blood of the Crucifixion, the egg itself Jesus inside the tomb, and the cracking of the egg Jesus' resurrection and emergence from the tomb. Another old legend popular among the Orthodox credits Mary Magdalene with the invention of red Easter eggs, when an egg she was using to demonstrate the Resurrection to the emperor Tiberius miraculously turned red in her hand. In Greece the red egg has become an extremely popular Easter symbol. Red Easter egg toys for children also appear in shops at Easter time.

Some families take their red eggs to church to be blessed on **Maundy Thursday**, after which they are known as "evangelized eggs." In some areas old folk traditions called for housewives to dye one egg per family member and one for the Blessed Virgin Mary (*see* **Mary, Blessed Virgin**). After the eggs were eaten the shells were collected and buried at the foot of fruit trees in the belief that this would help them to bear more fruit.

Maundy Thursday

Greek tradition recommends that families bake Easter **breads** and dye their Easter eggs on Maundy Thursday. Because of its strong association with the dyed red eggs, Greeks sometimes call Holy Thursday "Red Thursday." According to one custom, the first egg to emerge from the dye is dedicated to the Blessed Virgin Mary. Folk tradition suggests that this egg might have the power to work miracles. Often families keep this egg or an Easter egg blessed at the Resurrection service in the *ikonostasi*, a shelf or niche where the family keeps devotional materials such as icons, incense, blessed palms from Palm Sunday, a Bible, and a cross. The Easter egg and other seasonal items, such as palm crosses, remain throughout the year, until they are disposed of on the following Maundy Thursday.

The morning church service on Maundy Thursday commemorates the Last Supper (*for more on the Last Supper, see* Maundy Thursday). The Bible tells that Jesus washed the feet of his disciples at the Last Supper, providing them with an example of how to treat others. Some Greek churches offer **footwashing** ceremonies on Holy Thursday in which the priest washes the feet of twelve men and boys. The people of Patmos stage a play called *Niptir*, or "Washing," in the town square which reenacts the famous footwashing scene. Some people wash the feet of their elders or other family members on Maundy Thursday, anointing them with scented oils.

The Last Supper is also famous for Jesus' sharing of bread and **wine** with his disciples, a gesture which the early Christians turned into a ceremony called the **Eucharist**. Since Maundy Thursday may be seen as the "birthday of the Eucharist," many people honor the day by participating in this ceremony.

Evening church services commemorate the Crucifixion (*see also* **Royal Hours**). Twelve Gospel passages, selections from the Bible that tell the story of Jesus' life, are read aloud and hymns are sung, including a long religious song called "The Virgin's Lament." Women and girls may stay up throughout the night, mourning the torture and death of Jesus.

Good Friday

Good Friday is a national holiday in Greece. The day's religious services commemorate the death of Jesus Christ and many of the day's folk customs echo the theme of death. Flags are flown at half-mast, people visit cemeteries, and church **bells** play funeral knells. In some towns people practice a folk custom called the **burning of Judas**, in which Jesus' disciple **Judas** is symbolically punished for having turned Jesus in to the religious authorities. Many devout people drink vinegar or eat foods prepared with vinegar on Good Friday, recalling that when Jesus thirsted on the cross, the guards offered him vinegar to drink (Matthew 27:48, Mark 15:36, Luke 23:36, John 19:29). Others observe a total fast.

On the morning of Good Friday the children and women of Greek parishes gather together to decorate the *kouvouklion*, a symbolic representation of Jesus' funeral bier. They cover it with flowers or flower petals donated by the people of the parish. In some places young girls sprinkle lemon leaves and rose petals over the bier. Later in the afternoon it will hold the *epitaphios*, a cloth embroidered with the image of Jesus reposing in death.

Afternoon services commemorate the removal of Jesus from the cross. During this service people come forward to kiss and bow before the epitaphios, using it as a devotional tool that allows them to express their feelings about Jesus' death. Sometimes children pass under the epitaphios in the form of a cross in order to receive a blessing from the cloth icon. As people leave the church clergy members offer them a flower from the kouvouklion. People part from each other with the pre-Easter greeting, *"Kali anastasi"* (good resurrection). The epitaphios remains in front of the church until the evening service. People come in throughout the afternoon to pay respects to the epitaphios in much the same way they would pay respects to the deceased at a funeral.

Evening services, which technically belong to **Holy Saturday**, commemorate Christ's burial and honor his dominion over death and darkness. This somber service features a candlelight procession, said to represent Jesus' funeral procession. Led by the priest and those who carry the kouvouklion containing the epitaphios, the congregation files out of the church and forms a procession that winds through the city streets, in some towns taking a tour through the cemetery, where the bier is carried over graves. Some families burn incense outside their homes to honor the passing of this procession. In many Greek cities, bands playing funeral marches accompany these sorrowful parades. In the Greek capital, Athens, the head of state and other important politicians participate in these processions. As the congregation returns to the church the bearers station themselves outside the front doors, raising the bier so that people must pass under it to reenter the church. Doing so is thought to confer a blessing. Before passing under the epitaphios worshipers blow out their candles, a gesture that signifies the death of Christ, and clergy members sprinkle rosewater, representing tears, on the congregation.

Holy Saturday

In Corfu people break crockery on Holy Saturday. The cracking and breaking apart of the pottery represents the opening of the tomb and Jesus' emerging from death to life. People also say that this custom punishes Judas for his betrayal of Christ, since every sharp edge of the broken crockery is thought to cut into him (*see also* Judas, Burning of). An old folk belief holds that the dead are released from the underworld on this day and permitted to return to earth. For the fifty days between Easter and **Pentecost** they live within spring flowers and communicate in secret ways with the living.

Many people spend part of the day preparing for the coming Easter feast. They bake breads and cakes, and buy or slaughter a **lamb** to be eaten at the festive meal on Easter Sunday. Greek custom also calls for visiting cemeteries on this day and for taking gifts of food to the recently bereaved and to the poor.

Morning church services on Holy Saturday commemorate Jesus' **Descent into Hell**, where he liberated the dead from captivity in the underworld. The mood of this service lightens considerably as it turns to consider the Resurrection. The clergy change their robes from dark to bright colors in the middle of the service, after which the priest scatters flower petals or bay leaves around the church while chanting, "Arise, O God, to the world." The leaves and petals represent Christ's triumph over death. One old Greek custom called for placing wagtails, a bird similar to a warbler, under a pile of bay leaves. When the priest called out, "Arise, O God, to the world," parishioners kicked away the covering of leaves and the birds flew away. The resulting commotion led Greeks to apply the phrase, "Arise, O God," to everyday speech, where it denotes a sudden noise or uproar of some kind.

Resurrection Service

Easter celebrations begin late at night on Holy Saturday with the Resurrection service, the most well attended church service of the entire year. Everyone who attends the Resurrection service brings a candle or buys one at the church. Some congregations decorate the church for this occasion with twigs of rosemary, signifying remembrance, strings of lights, and Greek flags. One popular tradition encourages people to wear **new clothes** to this service. Often people wear a single item of new clothing, such as a new pair of shoes. In response to this tradition an old Greek courting custom recommended that men send a new pair of shoes and a candle wrapped in white and pink ribbons to their betrothed at Easter time.

As the hour nears midnight the light inside the church dims until only an oil lamp near the altar continues to glow. At twelve the royal gates that close the altar off from the view of the congregation swing open and a priest emerges from behind the screen of icons holding a lighted candle and declaring, "Come receive the light from the unwaning light and glorify Christ who rose from the dead." He passes his light to a member of the congregation, who in turn passes it on until everyone's candle is lit. Next the priest leads the candle-bearing congregation in a procession around the church, which represents the arrival of the myrrh-bearing women at Jesus' tomb early on Sunday morning (*see also* Mary Magdalene). The priest proclaims the Resurrection outside the main doors of the church. Then the congregation reenters the building, now ablaze with lights, to conclude the service.

All Greece seems to erupt with noise in celebration of Jesus' midnight rising. Fireworks explode, car horns honk, church bells ring, and foghorns bellow. Amidst this joyful din the people exchange the customary Easter greeting, *"Christos Anesti"* (Christ is risen), and response, *"Alithos Anesti"* (Indeed he has risen). They may also kiss each other on the cheek.

Greek tradition also calls for families to bring a number of red eggs to the Resurrection service that they might be blessed. Afterwards the eggs are called "eggs of the Resurrection" or "eggs of the Good Word."

In Greek Orthodox churches the Resurrection service is punctuated with the singing of a joyful hymn strongly associated with Easter, "Christos Anesti" (Christ Is Risen). Red eggs may be distributed to the congregation as they leave the church. At the end of the service some people take their lighted candle home with them and use the flame to light the vigil lamp in front of their icons. Although the Saturday night service constitutes the main religious celebration of Easter, many Orthodox churches also offer an Easter Sunday service, known as the Great Vespers of Agape.

Easter Sunday

After returning home from the Resurrection service many families break their fast with a special Easter meal. Instead of offering a prayer before sitting down to eat, everyone sings "Christos Anesti" three times. This meal usually includes cheese, Easter eggs, *mayeritsa*, a lemony soup made from chopped lamb innards, and *tsoureki*, a sweet, braided Easter bread studded with red eggs. Many follow a tradition that states that the first food to cross one's lips after the long Lenten fast should be an Easter egg. According to this same tradition, the last food one eats before beginning the fast should be an Easter egg (*see also* **Cheese Week**).

The meal often begins with an **egg-tapping** game. In Greece egg tapping constitutes a popular **Easter Week** pastime. Greek families may place any egg that survives the egg-tapping contest intact in the home ikonostasi. In Greece egg tapping is such a common Easter game that the image of two red eggs knocking against one another appears on many Greek **Easter cards**. Winning the egg-tapping game is thought to bring good luck for the year. Some players make a wish before testing their egg against an opponent. Greek folklore teaches that the winner's wish will come true.

Activities on Easter Sunday afternoon revolve around the preparation and consumption of a huge Easter feast. A Greek Easter feast nearly always features roast lamb. Traditionalists prepare a whole lamb by roasting it on a spit. Other popular Easter foods include tsoureki, also called *lambropsoma*, roast chicken, *spanikopita*, or spinach pie, and *dolmades*, stuffed grape leaves. Some villages increase the festivity of the day by sponsoring community Easter barbecues. Many people continue Easter celebrations on **Easter Monday** and Tuesday.

Easter Week

Greeks call Easter Week, that is, the week following Easter, "Bright Week." Some people continue to offer the Easter greeting and response throughout this week. In Greek Orthodox churches the doors to the sanctuary remain open all week as a sign of Easter joy. The Sunday following Easter is known as *Antipascha*, a name signifying that the day closes the Pascha, or Easter, festival (*see also* **Low Sunday**).

Further Reading

Griffin, Robert H., and Ann H. Shurgin, eds. *Junior Worldmark Encyclopedia of World Holidays.* Volume 1. Detroit, MI: UXL, 2000.

Lord, Priscilla Sawyer, and Daniel J. Foley. *Easter the World Over*. Philadelphia, PA: Chilton Book Company, 1971.

Newall, Venetia. *An Egg at Easter*. Bloomington, IN: Indiana University Press, 1971.

Rouvelas, Marilyn. *A Guide to Greek Traditions and Customs in America*. Bethesda, MD: Nea Attiki Press, 1993.

Storace, Patricia. *Dinner with Persephone*. New York: Vintage Books, 1996.

Guatemala, Easter and Holy Week in

The city of Antigua hosts what some consider to be Guatemala's most impressive **Holy Week** observances. These observances revolve around a series of religious processions in which sacred statues are placed on platforms and carried through city streets on the shoulders of strong men. The processions begin during **Lent**, but intensify as Holy Week approaches.

The parades begin at eight in the morning and sometimes last all day. Bands of volunteers line the parade routes with *alfombras*, or "carpets," made from colored sawdust, sand, and flower petals. Some of these "carpets" are quite large, up to fifty feet in length. Whole families participate in their creation, the planning of which begins months in advance. Businesses and trade guilds may also create carpets. Once the design is selected, stencils are made and colors chosen. On the evening before the procession those responsible for the carpet may work through the night out on the street to complete their carpet. Many view their long hours of labor as an expression of their devotion to **Jesus**, or the saint whose image will pass over the carpet, or to God. Those who carry the heavy floats also consider their act an expression of religious devotion. Some are completing religious vows given in exchange for a favor or the forgiveness of **sins**. So many people want to help carry the floats that some processions stop every few blocks so new bearers can replace those who have already taken a turn.

Perhaps the most magnificent parade takes place on **Good Friday**. It features a life-sized statue of Jesus carrying his **cross**. The bearers begin the procession wearing purple robes. At three in the afternoon, the hour of Jesus' death, they change to black robes. Men dressed as Roman soldiers, some on foot, some on horseback, accompany the float. Those who accompany the procession are careful not to tread on the alfombras. Only those bearing the sacred images may step on them. Their passing destroys the fragile carpets, adding to the drama of the procession.

On the evening of Good Friday another religious procession centered on an image of Christ prepared for burial moves through the city streets. Incense-bearers and drummers accompany this solemn procession.

On **Holy Saturday** women with black lace draped over their heads serve as float bearers. Later that evening crowds of tourists and locals jam into the town's cathedral and the plaza in front of it for a candle-light service (*see also* **Easter Vigil**).

The final processions take place on **Easter Sunday**. The bearers wear white, symbolizing joy. Firecrackers explode as the celebrations draw to a close.

Further Reading

Evans, Larry L. "To Soften the Path: Sawdust Carpets in Guatemala's Easter Celebrations." *The World and I* 10, 4 (April 1995): 240.

Lord, Priscilla Sawyer, and Daniel J. Foley. *Easter the World Over*. Philadelphia, PA: Chilton Book Company, 1971.

Milne, Jean. *Fiesta Time in Latin America*. Los Angeles, CA: Ward Richie Press, 1965.

Web Sites

"La Semana Santa in Guatemala," an article about Holy Week observances in Guatemala by Tony Pasinski, posted by *Revue* magazine, a publication designed for Guatemala's resident English speakers at: http://www.revuemag.com/articles/1999/mar/semana.htm

"Easter in Antigua," a newspaper article by Claudia R. Capos, published by the *Buffalo News*, available online for a fee through Northern Light at: http://www.northernlight.com. Document ID: BM19980409010036523

Hare

The hare is a close relative to the **rabbit**. This shy, fleet-footed animal looms large in Middle Eastern, European, African, Asian, and American Indian folklore. Among these peoples the hare represents such diverse qualities as cleverness, quickness, femininity, fertility, sexuality, and self-sacrifice, and is often associated with the **moon** and eternal life. European folklore concerning the hare emphasizes its association with certain of these themes, namely fertility, sexuality, femininity, and the moon. Moreover, European folk beliefs attribute strange powers and a distinctive personality to this timid creature. The hare is closely associated with springtime, a season in which it is especially active. This association, as well as those mentioned above, probably explains how the hare, and later the rabbit, became a symbol of the Easter holiday.

The Moon, the Hare, and the Feminine

Many peoples throughout the world have linked the hare with the moon. While American children are told to look for the face of "the man in the moon," storytellers from many other cultures have for centuries told tales about the "hare in the moon." How did so many peoples come to associate the hare with the moon? Perhaps it came about because the hare, like the moon, hides during the day and is most often seen at twilight or during the night. Since many people believed that the hare never closed its eyes, not even to sleep, it may be that the hare's unblinking eye reminded them of the moon, the "eye in the sky" that watches while all else slumbers.

Mythologists suggest that the moon serves as a natural symbol of femininity since its monthly cycle mirrors that of the female reproductive system. Because the hare was thought to have an affinity with the moon, it often shared this association with the feminine. Another common association links the moon with birth, fertility, death, and rebirth. This connection, too, is suggested by the moon's monthly cycle of waxing, waning, disappearing, and reappearing. Stories of hares that willingly stayed in flaming fields or leapt into fires appear in a number of different cultures. Perhaps this association between the hare and death helped to link the animal symbolically with the moon in the folklore of many different lands.

Ancient Middle Eastern Folklore

As early as 2,000 years before Christ, the hare had become a symbol of death and rebirth in Mesopotamia and Syria. In ancient Egypt the hare was associated with the god Osiris who came to represent life, death, and immortality. Some evidence suggests that the moon became another minor emblem associated with Osiris.

Ancient Greek and Roman Folklore

The ancient Greeks associated the hare with Aphrodite, the goddess of love, and also with Eros, the god of sexual attraction. Indeed the ancient Greeks used hares as gifts signaling love and attraction. The hare's own reproductive practices probably suggested these associations, since the hare mates frequently throughout the spring and summer months. Indeed, the hare produces so many offspring that some ancient Greeks believed that the female hare could conceive while still pregnant. Dionysus, the Greek god best known as the patron of **wine**, might also be accompanied by a hare.

Scholars have discovered that the ancient Greeks and Romans often depicted the hare on gravestones and funeral art. According to one writer, this image represented the hope that love would conquer death. As belief in immortality became more widespread, the hare became an even more popular image in funeral art. The early Christians accepted this pre-existing symbolism and also used the image of the hare on their gravestones.

The Romans associated the hare with Diana, a goddess who presided over treaties, childbirth, and women in general, and one of whose symbols was the moon. The moon itself was seen as feminine by the Greeks and Romans. The hare shared this symbolic association with the feminine. In addition, the hare's great fertility made it a symbol of springtime in much of pre-Christian Europe.

The hare was also known for its fleetness of foot in the ancient world. This characteristic plays an important role in one of Aesop's Fables, a collection of moral tales attributed to an ancient Greek storyteller known as Aesop. In the famous tale known as "The Tortoise and the Hare," the quick-footed hare loses a race with the plodding tortoise due to over-confidence. The hare decides he can afford to take a nap before crossing the finish line, but he oversleeps, allowing the slow but diligent tortoise to win the race.

Ancient Northern European Folklore

Some folklorists have suggested that the ancient Norse goddess Freya was accompanied by magical hares. In Norse mythology Freya represented beauty, youth, and sexual attraction.

Medieval European Folklore

The hare continued to symbolize sexual desire throughout the Middle Ages. Though still widely known for its frequent matings and great fertility, medieval writers embellished the sexual reputation of the hare with many beliefs which we now know to be false. For example, some writings indicate that the hare was believed to change its sex at will. Other records reveal a belief in the ability of female hares to conceive without the aid of males, thus retaining their virginity even while bearing offspring.

Perhaps because of their earlier association with pagan goddesses, hares were also often thought to act as witches' familiars. Many people believed it possible for a witch to change her shape into that of a hare, in which capacity she often wreaked havoc on farmers' fields. In Germany, France, Holland and Ireland, the harvesting of the last stand of grain in the field was known as "cutting the hare."

The hare also acquired an association with ill luck, perhaps because of its connection to witchcraft, or perhaps because of the unusual sexual characteristics it was supposed to have. Many dreaded a chance meeting with one of these seemingly harmless animals. At some **May Day** celebrations hare-witches were ceremonially burned. In spite of these troubling associations, many medieval Europeans knew hares to be shy, fearful creatures. Thus writers and artists of the period often used the hare as a symbol of timidity.

Personality and Powers

In spite of its negative associations European folklore attributed powers to the hare that could be used for good. Amulets of hare's feet were at one time thought to confer potency or to have healing powers. The famous English diarist Samuel Pepys (1633-1703) once wrote that he recovered from a "colic" by means of a hare's foot. Later the hare's, or rabbit's, foot became a general good luck charm. Superstition dictated that the best time to cull a rabbit's foot was during a moonless night. Perhaps the old association between the hare and the moon lingered on, suggesting that the moon might look down with disfavor upon anyone whom she spotted harming a hare.

263

People also attributed distinct personality characteristics to the hare. Hares were believed to be sad and gloomy. Some avoided eating them for fear of picking up this tendency towards melancholy. Another folk belief attributed suicidal tendencies to the hare. Some farmers told of hares that stayed in burning fields until their skins were scorched.

Another set of European folk beliefs warned that in the springtime the hare turned from melancholy to madness. This belief may have been based on accurate observations of the hare's springtime mating habits. At this time of year hares suddenly leap straight up in the air, revealing their hiding places in the tall grass. Males competing for mates will often box with one another in this fashion. These habits gave rise to the expression "mad as a March hare." Perhaps they also inspired the word "harebrained."

Asian Folklore

The "hare in the moon" is a common theme in Asian folklore, as is the connection made between the hare, death, and immortality.

An ancient Chinese folktale explains how a hare came to reside on the surface of the moon. According to this legend the hare in the moon grinds the elixir of immortality while sitting at the foot of a cassia tree. One Chinese custom encourages children to celebrate the Mid-Autumn Festival by carrying hare-shaped lanterns to the tops of hills in the early evening, where they admire the moon's beauty and identify the immortal hare under the cassia tree in the light and dark shapes on the moon's surface. Indeed, in Chinese mythology hares symbolize longevity and are mystically linked to the moon. What's more, the hare is a symbol in the Chinese zodiac. Those born in the year of the hare are thought to share in its personality traits: kindness, diplomacy, good manners, a love of beauty, luck with money, and a boundless self-confidence which may turn into conceit.

Other peoples throughout Asia also see a hare rather than a man in the moon. The Japanese see a hare pounding rice cakes in the dark and light spots on the moon. A Buddhist folktale recounts that the Buddha, in an earlier incarnation as a hare, willingly gave his own

264

flesh to help feed a hungry soul. He gained immortality through this good deed, rising in the shape of a hare to the moon, where he is still visible to us today. A legend from India claims that a hare once performed a great act of compassion for the god Indra. The hare spied Indra, disguised as a famished pilgrim, praying for food. The hare had nothing but his body to give so he cast himself on the fire so that the pilgrim might eat. The god rewarded the hare by granting him immortal life on the moon.

African Folklore

In many cultures of the world the hare was celebrated for its cleverness. Nigerians, Dahomeans, and other Africans told many trickster tales featuring the hare, or rabbit. Trickster tales revolve around a mythic figure who achieves goals through trickery. These tricksters are usually strong-willed, adventurous, amoral, comical, irreverent, insatiable, and capable of both great cleverness and foolishness. Folklorists believe that African slaves brought folktales about clever hares to the United States, where they became part of African-American folklore. The Bre'r Rabbit tales, popularized by Joel Chandler Harris' retellings, are examples of this African-American rabbit lore. These tales tell how Bre'r rabbit gets the better of his neighbors and outwits all those who try to trap him.

American Indian Folklore

Many American Indians also told tales about the cleverness of the hare. Several Algonquin tribes of eastern North America told mythic tales about the Great Hare which portrayed him as a trickster god and culture hero who helped to shape and enlarge the earth. A tale known among one group of the Algonquins known as the Cree Indians told of how a resourceful hare gained immortality by traveling to the moon, where he still can be seen today. Other American Indian bands also see a hare in the moon. Many southeastern tribes portray the rabbit as a clever culture hero who brought the first fire to humankind. According to one tale Rabbit stole the first flames from across the ocean. He outran his pursuers and brought fire back across the sea to America, but ended up by setting the woods ablaze. Great Basin tribes tell similar stories about how Rabbit stole the sun.

Easter and the Hare

European folklore connected the hare to Easter by linking it to spring, fertility, and new life. The American **Easter Bunny** developed out of German folklore concerning the Easter Hare. The Easter bunny, and the Easter eggs it delivers, have become the predominant folk symbols of Easter in the United States.

Further Reading

Becker, Udo. "Hare." In his *The Continuum Encyclopedia of Symbols*. New York: Continuum, 1994.

Black, William George. "The Hare in Folk-Lore." *Folk-Lore Journal* 1, 1 (1883): 84-90.

Cavendish, Richard. "Hare." In his *Man, Myth and Magic*. Volume 8. New York: Marshall Cavendish, 1997.

Goodenough, Erwin R. *Jewish Symbols in the Greco-Roman Period*. Volume 8. New York: Pantheon Books, 1958.

Lau, Theodora. *The Handbook of Chinese Horoscopes*. Third edition. New York: HarperPerennial, 1995.

Layard, John. *The Lady of the Hare*. 1944. Reprint. New York: AMS Press, 1977.

Leach, Maria, ed. *Funk and Wagnalls Standard Dictionary of Folklore, Mythology, and Legend*. New York: Harper and Row, 1984.

Lord, Priscilla Sawyer, and Daniel J. Foley. *Easter the World Over*. Philadelphia, PA: Chilton Book Company, 1971.

Mercatante, Anthony. *The Facts on File Encyclopedia of World Mythology and Legend*. New York: Facts on File, 1988.

Pelton, Robert D. "Tricksters: African Tricksters." In Mircea Eliade, ed. *The Encyclopedia of Religion*. Volume 15. New York: Macmillan, 1987.

Ricketts, Mac Linscott. "Tricksters: North American Tricksters." In Mircea Eliade, ed. *The Encyclopedia of Religion*. Volume 15. New York: Macmillan, 1987.

Rowland, Beryl. *Animals with Human Faces*. Knoxville, TN: University of Tennessee Press, 1973.

Waida, Manabu. "Rabbits." In Mircea Eliade, ed. *The Encyclopedia of Religion*. Volume 12. New York: Macmillan, 1987.

Wood, Douglas. *Rabbit and the Moon*. New York: Simon & Schuster, 1998.

Hilaria

In the last several centuries before the fall of the Roman Empire (476 A.D.), Roman devotees of the goddess Cybele celebrated a festival of **laughter** and rejoicing on March 25. Known as Hilaria, the day commemorated the **salvation** of Attis, a young man devoted to the great goddess Cybele.

Cybele

Scholars believe that worship of Cybele began in an ancient kingdom known as Phrygia, located in what is now west-central Turkey. Phrygian civilization flourished between the twelfth and seventh centuries B.C. The great mother goddess Cybele dominated Phrygian religious life. The ancient Greeks borrowed the cult of Cybele from the Phrygians. They perceived a great similarity between Cybele and the Greek goddess Rhea, whom the Greeks called the mother of the gods, and eventually decided that the two were one. When the Romans began to worship Cybele, they also recognized her similarity to goddesses already known to them, but still tended to classify her as a foreign goddess. Wherever the cult of the Cybele spread, however, her role remained the same; she was recognized as the great mother goddess, the mother of gods, beasts, and human beings. Many also viewed her as the mother of the natural world. Some scholars interpret the wild, frenzied celebrations of followers as evidence of her close association with untamed nature.

Strategic concerns rather than purely devotional sentiments motivated the Romans to adopt the goddess Cybele. In 204 B.C. Carthaginian armies invaded what is now Italy. Although they had not yet reached Rome, inhabitants of that great city began to fear they soon would. Roman officials responded to the crisis in the following way. First they consulted certain religious texts known as the Sibylline books about how to stop the Carthaginians. The texts delivered the prophecy, "The mother is absent: seek the mother. When she comes she must be received with chaste hands." Seeking to clarify this cryptic message, Roman religious leaders sought further counsel with the Greek oracle at Delphi. It advised them to bring the Mother of the Gods, located on Mount Ida, home with them to Rome. Realizing that the oracle had referred them to the Phrygian goddess Cybele, Roman messengers traveled to Asia Minor and convinced Phrygian cult leaders on Mount Ida to let them bring a black rock sacred to Cybele home with them to Rome.

According to one ancient writer, when they arrived at Ostia, Rome's seaport city, the boat carrying the sacred rock ran aground. Try as they might, the men could not shift the boat out of the mud. The Romans began to despair when Claudia Quinta, a noblewoman accused of adultery, stepped forward. She declared, "If I am innocent of all charges, yield, goddess, to my chaste hands." The crowd watched in amazement as she drew the boat forward almost without effort. The Romans placed Cybele's sacred stone in the temple of Victory. Bumper crops and the retreat of the Carthaginians soon followed, and the Romans credited their new relationship with Cybele for these blessings. They called her *Mater Deum Magna Idaea*, Latin for "Great Idaean Mother of the Gods."

The Romans not only built a temple for Cybele but also established a festival for her. They held it on April 4, the day of her arrival in Rome. Called Megalesia, this festival grew to include a procession through the streets accompanied by wild strains of music and the frenzied dancing and startling cries of the goddess' eunuch priests, who beat themselves until they bled. Special sports matches, banquets, and plays also took place on that day.

Attis

One of the most important myths concerning Cybele told of her great fondness for a youth called Attis, who became her devotee. Numerous versions of the tale circulated throughout the ancient world. Many of them revolve around the revenge taken by the goddess when the young man's attention turns briefly to a human woman. In one telling of the tale, Attis' single-minded devotion to the goddess wavered long enough for him to become engaged to a princess. Enraged, Cybele caused him to go mad, and in his madness he castrated himself and died. Flowers sprang from his **blood** and his body turned into a pine tree. In other versions of the tale Attis is killed by a spear thrust, or by a wild boar. The story of Cybele and Attis changed as the centuries passed and as the myth migrated from one culture to another. In yet another version of the tale Cybele, remorseful over Attis' bloody death, succeeds in preserving him from decay by keeping him in a sort of semi-living state. In other tellings of the myth Attis is seen as a deity rather than a human being, and in still others Attis achieves immortality after his death.

269

March Celebrations in Honor of Attis and Cybele

In the first centuries of the current era Roman devotees of Cybele added another festival to their cult, this one honoring the life and death of Attis. This festival developed and expanded over time until it encompassed several distinct days of devotion and celebration. By the year 354 A.D., the festival had evolved into a two-week affair, which retold the story of Attis' life, death, and **resurrection**. It began on March 15, with a ceremony celebrating Attis' infancy. On March 22 festivities centered on the bearing of a freshly cut pine tree to the temple of Cybele. The pine tree figured in Attis' story in several ways. In some versions of his legend, he castrated himself and died under a pine tree. In others, he turned into a pine tree. Devotees began to mourn for the death of Attis on this day, and continued their mourning on March 23. On March 24, known as "the day of blood," temple priests whipped themselves until they bled and sprinkled the blood on Cybele's altar. The day's ceremonies also included the ritual burial of Attis. Devotees **fasted** on this day and continued to grieve for Attis.

On March 25 the whole tone of the festival suddenly switched from grief to gaiety, as followers of the god celebrated his revivification. They called this feast Hilaria, from the Latin word *hilaris,* meaning "cheerful." Feasts, masquerades, and all manner of merriment characterized the Hilaria festival.

On March 26 festival-goers enjoyed a quiet day of rest. Ceremonies resumed on March 27, when the black stone sacred to Cybele was taken from her temple and brought to the river to be cleansed. Dancing and singing crowds accompanied this joyous, flower-decked procession.

The Spring Equinox and Other Ancient Holidays

Roman astronomers recognized March 25 as the day of the **spring equinox**. This fact may have influenced followers of Cybele and Attis to schedule Hilaria on that day. Other ancient holidays celebrated on or around March 25 include **Passover, Pascha** or Easter, and the

Mesopotamian New Year festival (*see also* **Easter, Date of;** *for a contemporary festival related to the Mesopotamian New Year festival, see* **No Ruz**). These, too, may have influenced the celebration of Hilaria in some way.

Further Reading

Grimal, Pierre. *Dictionary of Classical Mythology*. A. R. Maxwell-Hyslop, translator. Oxford, England: Blackwell Reference, 1985.

James, E. O. *Seasonal Feasts and Festivals*. 1961. Reprint. Detroit, MI: Omnigraphics, 1993.

Lyttelton, Margaret, and Werner Forman. *The Romans, Their Gods and Their Beliefs*. London, England: Orbis, 1984.

Momigliano, Arnaldo. "Cybele." In Mircea Eliade, ed. *The Encyclopedia of Religion*. Volume 4. New York: Macmillan, 1987.

Perowne, Stewart. *Roman Mythology*. New York: Bedrick Books, 1969.

Vermaseren, Maarten J. *Cybele and Attis: The Myth and the Cult*. London, England: Thames and Hudson, 1977.

Willis, Roy, ed. "The Great Mother." In his *World Mythology*. New York: Henry Holt, 1993.

Hocktide

Binding Days, Hobtide,
Hock Days, Hoke Days

During the late Middle Ages English Easter celebrations continued long after **Easter Sunday** (*see also* **Easter Week**). They ended on the Monday and Tuesday following **Low Sunday**, or the second Monday and Tuesday after Easter. These two days were known as Hocktide, Hobtide, the Hoke Days, or the Hock Days, and served as an occasion for various financial and legal transactions as well as boisterous fun and games pitting one sex against the other.

History

The origin of the word "hocktide" continues to puzzle scholars, who have been unable to detect its meaning. The historical roots of these festive days have also eluded researchers. Some of the earliest writers to record the observance declared that it hailed from Anglo-Saxon times and commemorated a military victory against invading Danish soldiers during the reign of King Ethelred (d. 871). Other early commentators asserted that the festivities celebrated the death of Hardicanute (1019-1042), the last of the Danish kings to rule the English. Since the first recorded instance of Hocktide celebrations dates back only as far as 1406, these ancient origins seem doubtful. These explanations may have been inspired by a Hock Tuesday play presented at Coventry during the sixteenth century. The play tells the story of a band of wily Englishwomen who succeed in defeating and capturing Danish invaders where their menfolk had failed. In the sixteenth-century Protestant reformers sought to discontinue these yearly performances. Supporters countered their efforts by presenting the play to Queen Elizabeth I (1533-1603), who enjoyed and approved of it. Nevertheless, in the 1590s opponents eventually succeeded in permanently canceling the event.

Tuesday became the most important of the two days of Hocktide. Rent payments frequently came due on Hock Tuesday and on Michaelmas (September 29), a reminder of the ancient division of the year into two seasons, summer and winter. What's more, manorial courts often held session, many church officials collected money to pay parish expenses, and certain taxes came due on Hock Tuesday. But Hocktide was best known for a raucous folk custom, referred to as "hokking" in some old documents. This custom awarded men the right to waylay women on Hock Monday and hold them hostage until they paid a few coins for their ransom. Women received the same privilege on Hock Tuesday. Some people called Hocktide the "Binding Days" in reference to this custom. In certain places men detained women on Hock Tuesday and women detained men on Hock Monday. In a few locales only women enjoyed the customary right to collect Hocktide ransom.

Often both women and men contributed some part of their Hocktide ransom money to the local church. Parish records indicate that women often surpassed men in this unusual form of fund raising. Hocktide ransom money provided an important source of income in some parishes. Records from Lambeth reveal that at one point Hocktide money was the single largest source of parish income.

Quite a few of the historical records concerning Hocktide observances consist of complaints about disorderly behavior and excesses committed by enthusiastic Hocktide ransom collectors. By the seventeenth century many local authorities had succeeded in limiting or abolishing the right to make these collections. Religious authorities influenced by the ideas and attitudes fueling the Reformation, a sixteenth-century western European religious reform movement, eventually helped put a stop to Hocktide observances.

Nevertheless a trace of Hocktide jollity lingered on in a few locales. At the turn of the twentieth century lads in one Yorkshire village still extracted a form of Hocktide ransom by drawing a rope across a main street and permitting girls to pass only after they had yielded a kiss.

Current Customs

The citizens of the Berkshire town of Hungerford continue to observe Hock Tuesday. The town has preserved certain customs and civic activities long associated with the day, such as the meeting of the local Hocktide Court. This court elects minor local officials, including the "tithing" or "tutti" men, whose ancient duty was to protect local inhabitants and property during the coming year. Time-honored traditions permit the Tutti-men to collect a penny from each Hungerford commoner household as payment for their services. Women may give a kiss instead of a penny. Hungerford Hock Tuesday proceedings begin with the blowing of a replica of a horn given to the town by the English prince and duke of Lancaster, John of Gaunt (1340-1399), who granted the citizens of Hungerford a number of manorial privileges. While the court is in session the Tutti-men collect their staves, crowned with oranges and adorned with ribbons and flowers, and call on each commoner household in Hungerford to collect their traditional fee. The Orange Scrambler follows close behind, carrying a sack of oranges for distribution to the children of fee-paying families and to women who pay the fee with kisses instead of coins.

Afterwards the Tutti-men and the Orange Scrambler attend a civic luncheon. The luncheon includes a ritual known as "shoeing the wild mare." Two men wearing the traditional garb of a blacksmith seize all newcomers to the district and begin to drive nails into their shoes. They persist in these efforts until each newcomer cries "punch," signaling his readiness to buy a round of drinks for all present. The victim may elect instead to pay a fine of one pound. The crowd cheerfully welcomes into the community those who supply them with drinks. After lunch the Orange Scrambler and the Tutti-men toss the remaining oranges to a crowd of waiting children, who scramble to retrieve them.

Further Reading

Blackburn, Bonnie, and Leofranc Holford-Strevens. *The Oxford Companion to the Year*. Oxford, England: Oxford University Press, 1999.

Chambers, Robert. *The Book of Days*. Volume 1. 1862-64. Reprint. Detroit, MI: Omnigraphics, 1990.

Hole, Christina. *British Folk Customs*. London, England: Hutchinson and Company, 1976.

Howard, Alexander. *Endless Cavalcade*. London, England: Arthur Barker, 1964.

Hutton, Ronald. *Stations of the Sun*. Oxford, England: Oxford University Press, 1996.

Long, George. *The Folklore Calendar*. 1930. Reprint. Detroit, MI: Omnigraphics, 1990.

Web Site

Photos of Tutti Day in Hungerford on the Hungerford Chamber of Commerce web site: http://www.hungerford.co.uk/tutti_day.htm

Holy Grail

The legend of the Holy Grail flourished in late medieval Europe, becoming one of the most popular and enduring themes of medieval literature. Writers, traveling minstrels, poets, and storytellers spun many different versions of the tale, but most centered around the search for a mysterious vessel which could restore one's health or bring one closer to God. For medieval Christians such a receptacle immediately brought to mind the chalice of the **Eucharist**. Indeed later tales made this connection explicit. These tales identified the mysterious vessel as the chalice from which **Jesus** and his disciples drank at the Last Supper (*for more on the Last Supper, see* **Maundy Thursday**). According to legend Joseph of Arimathea used this same chalice to collect Christ's **blood** at the Crucifixion (*for more on crucifixion, see* **Cross**). Thus the Grail became not only the holiest of relics but also the supreme symbol of the Eucharist, the Christian ritual commemorating the events surrounding Jesus' death and **resurrection**. Because of its connection to the death and resurrection of Christ, the Holy Grail, like the Eucharist, may be thought of as an Easter symbol, one that centuries ago captured the imagination of a continent.

Chrétien de Troyes' Grail Legend

The earliest surviving legend concerning the Holy Grail was written by a French poet named Chrétien de Troyes around the year 1180. He called the tale *Perceval, ou Le Conte du Graal,* which means "Perceval, or the Story of the Grail." It recounts the story of a young knight named Perceval, who is innocent to the point of foolishness. In his aimless wanderings Perceval encounters a wise fisherman. This fisherman advises the youth to visit a mysterious castle surrounded by a wasteland. Perceval journeys to the castle and presents himself to its lord, who is called the "fisher king." An incurable wound confines the king to his couch.

While in the king's castle the young knight witnesses a strange procession, including a page with a white lance from which hangs a drop of blood, two pages carrying golden candelabras, a maiden carrying a glowing metal grail (a shallow bowl) set with gems, and another maiden carrying a platter of silver. Though he wonders at the meaning of this parade, Perceval says nothing. In failing to ask the question "Whom does the grail serve?" or "What ails thee, uncle?" the young knight has failed a magical test set for all who find the hidden castle of the fisher king. Those words, spoken by an innocent soul such as Perceval, could have broken the spell which kept the king's wound festering. The king cannot explain this to the young knight as he himself is struck speechless in the presence of the Grail as a penalty for his past **sins**. As a result of Perceval's failure the castle magically disappears and the young knight spends years looking for it.

Chrétien de Troyes died before he could finish the story. Nevertheless, his tale inspired a number of other writers, who retold it in their own ways. De Troyes used the word "grail," or *graal* in the Old French, to describe the mysterious shining vessel borne by the noble maiden. The word originally referred to a deep serving platter or shallow bowl. Later writers began calling this container the "Holy Grail" and identified it clearly as the chalice of the Last Supper. Other versions of the story defined the Grail as a precious stone, a cup, or a gem that fell from the crown of Lucifer, the devil, during his epic battle with God.

Wolfram von Eschenbach's Grail Legend

In 1207 a German poet and knight named Wolfram von Eschenbach (c. 1170–c. 1220) penned his version of the Grail story, called *Parzifal*, or Perceval. Von Eschenbach understood the Grail to be an emerald that fell from Lucifer's crown. In von Eschenbach's story this emerald bestows many miraculous blessings on those in its presence, including restoring youth, prolonging life, conferring spiritual perfection, and drawing one towards God. According to von Eschenbach a mysterious figure called the Grail King becomes the custodian of this holy object. Instead of dedicating himself to its protection, however, the Grail King gallops off in search of romance and adventure. Disregarding his sacred duty causes the king to be wounded in the course of his travels. The wounded Grail King returns to his castle to find that the territory that surrounds it has become a wasteland. Since the power of the Grail protects him, the wound cannot kill the Grail King but neither does it heal or grow less painful.

One day Perceval, an innocent and unsophisticated young knight from King Arthur's court, happens upon the realm of the Grail King. Perceval dines with the Grail King in the banquet hall, and notices the king's discomfort. Perceval almost asks, "What ails thee, uncle?" but restrains himself, having once been told by a mentor not to ask too many questions. Just as in de Troyes's story, Perceval fails a magical test when he censors his own spontaneous act of compassion. Perceval rides away from the castle the next day, and though he tries to return, he cannot find it.

Several years and many adventures later, Perceval encounters a dark-skinned Muslim youth named Feirefiz. Feirefiz spares Perceval's life in battle. Afterwards they discover that Feirefiz is Perceval's half-brother and the two become friends. These acts of compassion and reconciliation help Perceval in his quest to return to the Grail Castle. He does so, accompanied by Feirefiz. When Perceval sees the Grail being borne into the Great Hall by a beautiful maiden, he then turns and asks the king what ails him. This question heals the king's wound and restores life and vigor to his lands. When the king dies Perceval becomes the new Grail King, whereupon he is joined by his wife and sons.

Robert de Borron's Grail Legend

Early in the thirteenth century French poet Robert de Borron wrote a long poem entitled *Joseph d'Arimathie*, or "Joseph of Arimathea." This poem proclaims the Grail to be the chalice of the Last Supper and tells how Joseph of Arimathea became its keeper. Although the Bible informs us that Joseph of Arimathea was a follower of Jesus and that he buried Jesus' body in his own tomb (Matthew 27:57-59), it offers no further details on his life. De Borron supplied these details, explaining that after Jesus' death Joseph of Arimathea journeyed to England as a missionary, bringing the chalice of the Last Supper, or the Holy Grail, with him. He landed at Glastonbury, where he and his descendants established themselves as the mysterious keepers of the Grail.

The Quest for the Holy Grail

Around the year 1225 another Grail legend appeared on the scene. Scholars have not reached a consensus on who wrote this tale, titled *Queste de Saint Graal* (The Quest for the Holy Grail). The storyline strengthened the existing ties linking King Arthur and his knights to the story of the Holy Grail. In this Grail legend, the author introduces the pure knight Sir Galahad. All of King Arthur's knights venture forth in search of the Holy Grail, yet only Galahad is virtuous enough to come into its presence, and thus to receive its holy wisdom.

In this version of the story, the search for the Holy Grail becomes a quest for oneness with the Divine. The author implies that only those wholly motivated by virtue can hope to achieve this quest. Some scholars believe that the author of this tale was influenced by the teachings of St. Bernard of Clairvaux (1090-1153), who described the stages through which people move in seeking a mystical, or direct, relationship with God.

The hero, the sinless Sir Galahad, is the son of Sir Lancelot, who is inflamed by an illicit love for King Arthur's wife Guinevere. By making Galahad the hero of his story rather than Lancelot, the author of this tale contrasts the spiritual limitations of those enthralled by earthly loves with the spiritual achievements of those enthralled by the love of God.

Sir Thomas Malory's Legend of the Holy Grail

Around the year 1470 English writer Sir Thomas Malory presented his Grail legend along with other tales concerning King Arthur and his knights. Malory's work, called *Le Morte D'arthur*, or "The Death of Arthur," assigns a greater role to the foolish young knight Perceval than did the earlier story, *Queste de Saint Graal*. Both works, however, elevated him to a new status as one of King Arthur's knights. In Malory's tale Arthur's knights receive a vision of the Grail while assembled in the Great Hall at Camelot. All set out to find the holy vessel, but one by one, their character defects cause them to turn aside from the quest. Only the virtuous Sir Galahad, the ordinary Sir Bors, and the innocent Sir Perceval find the Holy Grail. Here Malory implies that the qualities that they represent — purity, humility, and openness — are the ones that allow us to draw close to God. Malory seems to rank purity the most important of these three virtues, since only Sir Galahad actually looked into the Grail and came to know all its secrets.

After finding the Grail the knights proceed to the mysterious city of Sarras, bringing the holy relic with them. There the three participate in a mystical celebration of the Eucharist, in which Christ himself appears as the celebrant. Galahad is crowned king of the Sarras, but dies a year later, at which time the Grail is taken up into heaven. Perceval then returns to Grail Castle. He finds the wasteland that had surrounded the castle restored to life and he becomes king of the renewed realm. Sir Bors makes his way back to Camelot to tell the tale of their adventures to the world.

Origins of the Grail Legends

Scholars have long pondered the meaning and the origins of the Grail legends and have come up with dozens of explanations for these tales. Many claim that their roots lie in Celtic mythology. These writers point to Celtic legends describing various magical cauldrons, platters that offer a never-ending supply of food, and a wounded king who lived in a wasteland. They argue that the Grail legends reworked these Celtic images, presenting them in a new, Christianized story. Other writers see elements of myths and rituals from the ancient Mediterranean and Middle Eastern world in the Grail legends.

Yet another group of researchers views the story as basically Christian. One of these scholars reminds us that during the era when legends concerning the Holy Grail spread throughout Europe church leaders were developing and proclaiming the concept of transubstantiation, a doctrine purporting to explain the mechanism by which the **wine** of the Eucharist became the blood of Christ (*see also* Eucharist). This line of thought suggests that a fascination with the mysteries of the Eucharist spread throughout European society at this time, inspiring the fanciful Grail tales and creating receptive audiences for these stories.

Search for the Holy Grail

Whatever their origins, these stirring legends convinced many that the Holy Grail actually existed and could be recovered. For centuries adventurers, military men, scholars, and politicians set out on their own quests to recover and possess this holiest of relics.

In 1099 a well-to-do Italian by the name of Guglielmo Embriaco journeyed to the Middle East to participate in the First Crusade, a series of battles in which European Christians attacked Muslim cities in the Middle East, hoping both to plunder them of their treasures and to place the territory under Christian rule. Embriaco and his followers helped to retake the city of Tyre. As a reward for his efforts, Embriaco appropriated for himself a green, hexagonally shaped bowl, said to have been carved from a single, large emerald. Many believed it to be the cup of the Last Supper, or the Holy Grail. Embriaco carted it back to his native city, Genoa, where it was dubbed the *Sacro Catino*, or "Holy Bowl," and held as a sacred relic in the cathedral of San Lorenzo.

In 1522 the Spanish attacked Genoa, supposedly with the intent of capturing the Sacro Catino. Spanish soldiers battered down the doors of the cathedral, but failed to discover the hiding place that the Italian clerics had devised for the holy relic. In 1806 another foreign invader succeeded where the Spanish had failed. The French military commander and emperor Napoleon Bonaparte (1769-1821) captured the city of Genoa, seized the Sacro Catino, and took it back to Paris with him. There scientists examined the bowl. They found it to be made of green glass rather than emerald, and dated it to about the first century. Not only did they destroy hopes that the Sacro Catino could be the Holy Grail, they also destroyed the Sacro Catino, breaking it into ten pieces while examining it. Nine of these pieces were eventually returned to Genoa.

Although many adventurers sought the Holy Grail in its native land, others suspected that the sacred cup left the Middle East soon after the death of Christ. Some believed the legend that Joseph of Arimathea brought it with him to Britain. At Glastonbury, the supposed site of his landing, local traditions suggested that the Holy Grail was buried somewhere on Glastonbury Tor, a rocky hill outside the town. Others whispered that it had been tossed into nearby "Chalice Well."

Another legend declared that the Holy Grail ended up in France, not Britain. It stated that after Jesus' death **Mary Magdalene** became the keeper of the Holy Grail, and that she brought it with her when she journeyed to France. Some speculated that by the Middle Ages the Grail had fallen into the hands of a religious sect known as the Cathars or Albigenses. In that era the Cathars established a fortress on the top of a mountain, known as Montségur, in the French region of Languedoc. When the armies of the Roman Catholic Church marched in to destroy the sect in the early thirteenth century, legend has it that several Cathar priests removed the sacred chalice from the fortress and hid it deep within one of the mountain's many caves.

The Nazis and the Holy Grail

Centuries later the notion that the cup of Christ lies hidden somewhere on Montségur launched what is perhaps the eeriest chapter in the long story of the hunt for the Holy Grail. During the 1930s, a top Nazi official named Heinrich Himmler (1900-1945) launched his own quest for the Holy Grail. Nazi leader Adolf Hitler (1889-1945) entrusted Himmler with the running of Germany's brutal Gestapo, or secret police force, as well as the S.S., an elite branch of the military. In his spare time Himmler enjoyed studying von Eschenbach's *Parzifal*, which states that the Grail Castle was built on top of *Munsalvaesche*, or "Mount Salvation." Himmler noted that the Cathars' medieval mountain stronghold, Montségur, bears a vaguely similar name. This piqued his interest in the Cathars and their teachings. The Cathars believed that life in this world was dominated by a struggle between the forces of good and evil, darkness and light. In this doctrine Himmler found support for the Nazi campaign to destroy the Jews, whom he identified with the forces of evil.

Himmler came to believe that possession of the Holy Grail would strengthen the Nazis' claim to rule Europe. Confident that the Nazis, as representatives of the forces of good and light, were the rightful heirs of the Holy Grail, Himmler joined forces with medieval historian Otto Rahn (1904-1939), also a member of the S.S. Rahn's studies had led him to conclude that the Grail was hidden somewhere on Montségur. In addition, Rahn proposed that the Holy Grail was not the chalice of the Last Supper, but rather a set of wood or stone tablets on which were written the mystical teachings of the pagan Aryan, or Germanic, peoples. This notion excited Himmler and others, who saw in it support for their belief in the superiority of the so-called Aryan race.

In 1931 Rahn traveled to France to seize the Grail and cart it away to Germany. Presenting himself to local people as a tourist, Rahn spent three months searching for the elusive prize but never found it. Nevertheless, in 1933 he published a book about the Cathars and the Holy Grail, entitled *Kreuzzug gegen den Gral* (Crusade against the Grail). The S.S. sent Rahn back to France in 1937. No one knows what he discovered on this trip, since he died shortly after returning from Montségur. The ornate sanctuary that Himmler had already begun to prepare for the Holy Grail remained empty.

Artistic Legacy of the Holy Grail

The legend of the Holy Grail has continued to inspire tale-tellers and artists down through the centuries. In *Idylls of the King* (1859-85) English poet Alfred, Lord Tennyson (1809-1892) presents readers with a new telling of the Grail story. Moreover, a number of important members of the Pre-Raphaelite Brotherhood, a group of nineteenth-century English artists, represented scenes from the Grail story in their work. For example, poet and painter Dante Gabriel Rossetti (1828-1882) depicted "How Sir Galahad, Sir Bors, and Sir Percival were fed by the Sanc Grael but Sir Percival's sister died by the way" (1864), and Edward Burne-Jones (1833-1898) designed a tapestry portraying "The Attainment of the Grail" (1898). Famous German composer Richard Wagner (1813-1883) based his opera *Parsifal* (1882) on Wolfram von Eschenbach's medieval Grail legend. American-born English poet T. S. Eliot (1888-1965) wove elements of the Grail story into his famous work *The Wasteland* (1922). Finally, the 1989 movie *Indiana Jones and the Last Crusade* tells the story of a twentieth-century Grail quest, in which an American archeology professor and his small band of companions prevent a battalion of Nazis from claiming the chalice of the Last Supper for the Third Reich. These and other artistic works, as well as the many historical and theoretical treatises concerning the chalice, continue to delight and intrigue the public. Through them the Holy Grail, that most precious icon of the mysteries surrounding Jesus' sacrificial death and resurrection, still beckons to the romantic and the pure in heart.

Further Reading

Angebert, Jean-Michel. *The Occult and the Third Reich.* Translated by Lewis A. M. Sumberg. New York: Macmillan, 1974.

Hutton, Ronald. *The Pagan Religions of the Ancient British Isles.* Oxford, England: Blackwell, 1993.

Kahane, Henry, and Renée Kahane. "Grail, The." In Mircea Eliade, ed. *The Encyclopedia of Religion.* Volume 6. New York: Macmillan, 1987.

Matthews, John. *The Grail: Quest for the Eternal.* New York: Crossroad, 1981.

Mystic Quests. Alexandria, VA: Time-Life Books, 1991.

Remy, Arthur F. J. "The Holy Grail." In Charles G. Herbermann et al., eds. *The Catholic Encyclopedia.* New York: Appleton, 1913. Available online at: http://www.newadvent.org/cathen/06719a.htm

Holy Saturday

Blessed Sabbath, Easter Eve, Great Saturday,
Holy and Great Saturday, Saturday of Glory,
Saturday of Light, Saturday of Mourning

Holy Saturday falls the day before Easter. It constitutes the last day of **Holy Week**. Although most western Europeans know the day as Holy Saturday, many eastern Europeans call it Great Saturday. German speakers refer to it as *Karsamstag*, "Saturday of Mourning." On the island of Malta it is known as *Sibt il Glorja*, "Saturday of Glory." Christians from Iran and Iraq speak of *Sabt al Noor*, or the "Saturday of Light." This last name refers to the ancient custom of celebrating the **Easter Vigil**, held late at night on Holy Saturday, with the lighting of countless lamps and candles.

Roman Catholic and Protestant churches usually do not offer religious services on this day. This silence reflects the belief that between his crucifixion on **Good Friday** and his **resurrection** on **Easter Sunday**, **Jesus** lay dead in the tomb (*for more on crucifixion, see* **Cross**). Easter Vigil services, held at night on Holy Saturday, are technically considered the start of Easter Sunday celebrations. Devout Christians have traditionally spent Holy Saturday in quiet meditation on the meaning of Jesus' death (*see also* **Holy Sepulchre**).

History

In early Christian times the faithful **fasted** and prayed on Holy Saturday in preparation for the evening's Vigil service. This service featured the **baptism** of newcomers to the Christian faith. In Rome candidates for baptism visited the bishop on Holy Saturday. They recited the Creed, a short summary of the Christian faith, in his presence as proof of their knowledge and understanding of Christian doctrine. Then the bishop exorcised the baptismal candidates of evil spirits and led a ceremony in which they formally rejected Satan and dedicated themselves to Jesus Christ. Afterwards the candidates returned home to pray and prepare themselves for their baptisms later that evening. In other places this recitation of the Creed took place on **Maundy Thursday**. This custom eventually died out as Christianity spread and adult baptisms decreased in number.

From early Christian times onward, Holy Saturday services have involved the lighting of numerous lamps, candles, or torches (*see also* **Easter Fires; Paschal Candle**). An early Christian writer recorded the fact that Emperor Constantine (d. 337) "transformed the night of the sacred vigil into the brilliance of day, by lighting throughout the whole city . . . pillars of wax, while burning lamps illuminated every house, so that this nocturnal celebration was rendered brighter than the brightest day" (Weiser, 134). St. Gregory of Nyssa (335-394) described Holy Saturday evening as the "glowing night which links the splendor of burning lamps to the morning rays of the sun, thus producing continuous daylight without any darkness" (Weiser, 134). This seeming contradiction, a night as bright as day, echoed the seeming contradiction at the heart of the Easter festival, that is, life emerging from death.

This light symbolism lost its impact in western Europe as religious officials began to offer the Easter Vigil service earlier in the day. Throughout the Middle Ages the vigil service slid slowly back into the daylight hours, moving from afternoon to midday, and, by the late sixteenth century, to morning. In the 1950s Roman Catholic authorities restored the Easter Vigil service to the evening of Holy Saturday.

Orthodoxy

Orthodoxy is one of the three main branches of the Christian faith. Orthodox Christianity split from Western Christianity — that is, Roman Catholicism, and later, Protestantism — about 1,000 years ago. Thus Orthodox traditions differ in some ways from those of Western Christians (*see also* **Easter, Date of**). For example, Orthodox Christians maintain the ancient Jewish custom of beginning each day at sundown. Therefore services held at Orthodox churches on the evening of Good Friday, in fact, mark the beginning of Holy Saturday in that faith tradition. Contemporary Orthodox Christians may attend several church services on Holy Saturday. Orthodox tradition holds that Jesus' **Descent into Hell**, that is, his journey to the netherworld to release the souls imprisoned by death, took place on Holy Saturday.

The service scheduled on the afternoon of Good Friday also belongs to Holy Saturday. It commemorates Jesus' burial and features a ceremonial cloth called the *epitaphios* embroidered with the image of Jesus reposing in death. At the end of the service the celebrant leads a short procession around the church carrying the Gospel book while others hold the epitaphios over it like a canopy. The procession ends at the *kouvouklion*, a ceremonial funeral bier that has been decorated with flowers. The priest lays the epitaphios down on the kouvouklion and then places the book on top of it. Clergy members and lay people approach the epitaphios one by one, bowing deeply before it and kissing both the cloth and the book. Clergy members offer each worshiper a flower from the kouvouklion. The bowing and kissing may be repeated up to three times. Parishioners take these flowers home with them and place them in the home *ikonostasi*, a special shelf or niche used to hold icons and other religious paraphernalia. The epitaphios remains on display in the church, inspiring worshipers to pray and to meditate on the death of Christ (*see also* **Sin; Repentance; Redemption; Salvation**).

The epitaphios and funeral bier will also play an important role in the solemn evening services that follow several hours later. The high point of this service comes when clergy members pick up the funeral bier and lead the worshipers, each one carrying a lit candle, in a procession around the interior of the church. The procession serves as an emblem of Jesus' victory over death and darkness (*see also* Descent into Hell). Many processions actually exit the building and circle the church grounds or go around an entire city block before returning to the church. In Greece and other predominately Orthodox countries these processions make even longer trips through village and city streets. In some towns the procession includes a tour through the local cemetery where the bearers guide the bier over gravestones. In Athens, the Greek capital, the head of state and other political leaders play important roles in this procession.

Upon returning to the church, those carrying the bier halt just outside the church doors, so that to gain re-admittance everyone must duck under the epitaphios. This mode of reentering the church is thought to confer a blessing. Before passing under the epitaphios worshipers blow out their candles, a gesture that signifies the death of Christ, and clergy members sprinkle rosewater, representing tears, on the congregation.

Orthodox services continue on the morning of Holy Saturday. These morning services begin by addressing Jesus' Descent into Hell to liberate the dead and his observance of the Jewish Sabbath by resting in the grave (*for more on Sabbath, see* **Sunday**). Unlike the somber ceremony of the previous evening, the mood of this morning service lightens as it turns to consider the Resurrection. The clergy change their robes from dark to bright colors in the middle of the service, after which the priest scatters flower petals or bay leaves around the church while chanting, "Arise, O God, to the world." The leaves and petals represent Christ's triumph over death. Although celebrated on the morning of Holy Saturday, this observance technically serves as the vespers, or evening, service for Easter Sunday and thus as the Easter Vigil. Indeed, it resembles the Easter Vigil service observed by many Western Christians. A second Easter service, often referred to as the Resurrection service, is offered late at night on Holy Saturday.

The Orthodox honor Holy Saturday with a variety of respectful names. They include Holy Saturday, Great Saturday, Holy and Great Saturday, and the Blessed Sabbath.

Folk Customs

Many people spend some part of Holy Saturday preparing for the Easter feast on the following day. In central Europe families prepare Easter **breads**, pastries, and meats on Holy Saturday. They boil and decorate **Easter eggs** on this day as well. In southern Germany old traditions encouraged housewives to bring baskets of Easter foods to church on Holy Saturday so that the priest might bless them (*see also* **Germany, Easter and Holy Week in**). In Poland schoolboys once engaged in an old Holy Saturday folk ritual known as "burying" the **Lenten** fare. After making off with a herring and a pot of rye gruel, typical Polish Lenten dishes, they "executed" the herring by means of a mock hanging and dashed the pot of gruel against a tree or rock. This informal rite expressed their delight about the end of the long Lenten fast (*see also* **Poland, Easter and Holy Week in**). In the mountains of Austria people light bonfires on the evening of Holy Saturday (*see also* Easter Fires). **Easter season** fires are also known in Germany, Sweden and the Netherlands, although there they may be lit on **Walpurgis Night** rather than on Easter eve.

In eastern Europe people prepare Easter baskets full of special Easter foods and decorated eggs on Holy Saturday. They bring the baskets to church where the priest blesses them. These baskets provide the family with breakfast on Easter Sunday morning. In Russia old traditions encouraged people to bring *paskha*, a special Russian Easter bread, to church on Holy Saturday for the priest's blessing (*see also* **Russia, Easter and Holy Week in**). In some regions priests visited homes on Holy Saturday, blessing the Easter feast that was already being set on the tables in preparation for the end of the Lenten fast. Families adorned these banquet tables with fresh spring flowers and dyed Easter eggs. According to old standards of Easter hospitality, each person who visited the home on that day was offered one of the family's painted Easter eggs.

Further Reading

Griffin, Robert H., and Ann H. Shurgin, eds. *The Folklore of World Holidays*. Second edition. Detroit, MI: Gale Research, 1999.

Hopko, Thomas. *The Orthodox Faith. Volume Two, Worship*. Syosset, NY: The Orthodox Church in America, 1972.

Monti, James. *The Week of Salvation*. Huntington, IN: Our Sunday Visitor Publications, 1993.

Rouvelas, Marilyn. *A Guide to Greek Traditions and Customs in America*. Bethesda, MD: Nea Attiki Press, 1993.

Spicer, Dorothy Gladys. *Festivals of Western Europe*. 1958. Reprint. Detroit, MI: Omnigraphics, 1994.

Tyrer, John Walton. *Historical Survey of Holy Week*. London, England: Oxford University Press, 1932.

Weiser, Francis X. *The Easter Book*. New York: Harcourt, Brace and Company, 1954.

Wybrew, Hugh. *Orthodox Lent, Holy Week and Easter*. Crestwood, NY: St. Vladimir's Seminary Press, 1997.

Web Site

"Holy Saturday," a document describing the beliefs and practices of Orthodox Christians concerning Holy Saturday, posted on the Orthodox Church in America web site: http://www.oca.org/pages/orth_chri/orthodox-faith/worship/holy-saturday.html

Holy Sepulchre

The phrase "holy sepulchre" refers to the tomb in which **Jesus'** body was laid after it was taken down from the **cross**. This journey, from the cross to the tomb, represents the last scene in the Passion story, that is, the story of the last days of Jesus' life (Matthew 27:59-61, Mark 15:46-47, Luke 23:53-56, John 19:38-42). During the Middle Ages Christians across western Europe began to incorporate commemorations of this event into their **Holy Week** devotions. These obser-

vances revolved around special tombs or altars constructed inside churches. Called "holy sepulchres" or "Easter sepulchres," these monuments still appear in Roman Catholic churches on **Good Friday**. Their presence inspires parishioners to pray and meditate on the death of Christ (*see also* **Sin**; **Redemption**; **Salvation**). Individual members of the congregation may spend time sitting quietly before these tombs, participating in a vigil that lasts from Good Friday through **Holy Saturday** (*for a similar Good Friday custom practiced by Orthodox Christians, see* **Epitaphios**).

History

Holy sepulchres and the ceremonies associated with them can be traced back to the tenth century, when they appeared in Germany and England. By the close of the Middle Ages they had spread throughout northern and central Europe. The ceremony whereby Jesus' body was laid in the sepulchre was usually called the *depositio*, a Latin word meaning "deposition" or "laying down." In this case the word refers to the removal of Jesus' body from the cross and to his subsequent burial. In most medieval rituals a cross or crucifix served to represent Jesus' body. Priests often sealed the remainder of the consecrated **Eucharist** in the tomb along with the crucifix. On **Easter Sunday** a clergy member removed the Eucharist and held it aloft before the congregation in a gesture representing the **Resurrection**. The holy sepulchres themselves were garnished with gold, purple or crimson cloth, and surrounded by a multitude of lit candles. Some churches placed statues of angels or soldiers around the Easter sepulchre. During the Middle Ages parishioners and clergy kept constant vigil at these tombs. This practice may have been fueled by the belief that the Second Coming of Jesus, an event which Christian scripture links with the end of the world, would occur on the night before Easter Sunday.

In the fifteenth century a new kind of deposition ceremony developed in Italy. Italian clerics replaced the cross or crucifix with a life-sized figurine of Jesus' body. Moreover, the procession from the cross to the tomb expanded, leaving the church and wending its way through town and village streets as would a real funeral procession.

These innovations soon spread to France and Spain, and from there to Spanish colonies in the Americas.

In the sixteenth century a religious reform movement called the Reformation rolled across Europe. The controversies stirred by this movement, which gave birth to Protestant Christianity, touched on many aspects of Christian worship, including established Roman Catholic beliefs concerning the Eucharist. As a result of these debates Roman Catholic churches began to emphasize the role of the Eucharist in the Good Friday deposition and vigil. For example, instead of placing the Eucharist inside the tomb, they began to set it on top of the tomb so it could be seen and venerated by worshipers. Resting inside a veiled monstrance—a glass-faced display case set atop a metal stand—and carried to the Easter sepulchre in a formal funeral procession, the Eucharist became a focal point of the deposition and vigil (*see also* **Veiling**).

Contemporary Customs

Today Good Friday observances at Roman Catholic churches still feature deposition ceremonies and vigils similar to those held hundreds of years ago. Some refer to the vigil as "the vigil of the holy sepulchre." Others know it as the "forty-hour vigil," since just about forty hours elapse from the moment of Jesus' death on Good Friday to his resurrection early on Easter Sunday morning. Extremely devout people will sometimes **fast** from all food for these forty hours.

In Latin America many Roman Catholic congregations disassemble their *monumentos*—shrines in which the Eucharist is placed on **Maundy Thursday**—on the morning of Good Friday. Parishioners then construct a life-sized reproduction of Jesus' crucifixion in the same spot. The people represented in this scene include Jesus, Jesus' mother the Virgin Mary, **Mary Magdalene**, and John, one of Jesus' disciples (*see also* **Mary, Blessed Virgin**). At three in the afternoon, at the close of the day's religious services, altar boys armed with flashing powder and noisemaking devices create a disturbance meant to suggest the mysterious upheavals that occurred at the moment of Jesus' death (Matthew 27:50-53, Luke 23:44-45). (*See also* **Three Hours**.) Then the priest ascends a ladder and reverently removes the figurine of Jesus' body from the cross. With great ceremony the corpse is carried to the shrine of the holy sepulchre. Devout parishioners visit and pray before the shrine throughout the afternoon, evening, and following day.

Similar ceremonies are observed in Europe. In many instances, however, the priest carries a crucifix or the Eucharist to the Easter sepulchre rather than a figurine representing Jesus' body. In Austria tradition dictates that soldiers in parade uniform maintain an honor guard around the holy sepulchre. Austrians interpret this gesture as an act of atonement for the disrespectful behavior of the Roman guards who waited at the foot of Jesus' cross.

Further Reading

Brewster, H. Pomeroy. *Saints and Festivals of the Christian Church*. 1904. Reprint. Detroit, MI: Omnigraphics, 1990.

Monti, James. *The Week of Salvation*. Huntington, IN: Our Sunday Visitor Publications, 1993.

Slim, Hugo. *A Feast of Festivals*. London, England: Marshall Pickering, 1996.

Urlin, Ethel L. *Festivals, Holy Days, and Saints' Days*. 1915. Reprint. Detroit, MI: Omnigraphics, 1992.

Weiser, Francis X. *The Easter Book*. New York: Harcourt, Brace and Company, 1954.

Holy Thursday

For the Thursday of Holy Week, *see* **Maundy Thursday**; for Ascension Thursday, *see* **Ascension Day**

Holy Week

Great Week, Holy and Great Week, Laborious Week, Palm Week, Paschal Week, Passion Week, Six Days of Pascha, Week of Lamentation, Week of Passion, Week of Remission, Week of Salvation

Holy Week falls the week before Easter. It lasts from **Palm Sunday**, the **Sunday** preceding Easter, to the following Saturday, known as **Holy Saturday**. During these seven days Christians commemorate the Passion, that is, the events that took place during the last days of **Jesus'** life. In those Christian denominations with strong liturgical traditions this week brings together some of the most thematically important services of the year. These services prepare worshipers to celebrate the most important festival of the year, Easter. In Roman Catholic churches, as well as in those Protestant churches that observe liturgical colors, priests wear red robes during Holy Week services. The color red symbolizes love and suffering, such as that displayed by Jesus in the Passion story.

History

The first historical reference to any kind of observance of Holy Week dates back to the third century. An old document from this era records the fact that certain Christian communities prepared for Easter by **fasting** during the week that preceded it. From the Monday after Palm Sunday through **Maundy Thursday** they ate only **bread**, salt, and **water**. On **Good Friday** and Holy Saturday, they abstained entirely from food, spending most of the day praying and reading the Bible.

By the fourth century historical evidence points to a more widespread observance of Holy Week. Around the year 380 a Spanish nun named Egeria made a pilgrimage to Jerusalem and recorded her experiences in her diary. Her writings tells us that by the late fourth century Jerusalem Christians had begun to observe Holy Week by commemorating the events that transpired during the last week of Jesus' life. In this way they attempted to relive the events leading up to Jesus' death as a preparation for celebrating his **resurrection**.

On Palm Sunday they recalled Jesus' triumphal entry into Jerusalem. On the following Wednesday church services reminded the faithful of **Judas'** arrangement with the religious authorities to betray Jesus (*see also* **Spy Wednesday**). On the next day, Maundy Thursday, various religious observances commemorated the Last Supper and Jesus' arrest in the Garden of Gethsemane. Good Friday was devoted to the remembrance of the Crucifixion (*for more on crucifixion, see* **Cross**). A late-night **Easter Vigil** service commemorating the Resurrection took place on Holy Saturday. Although Egeria tells us little about the Jerusalem vigil service, other sources confirm that by the late fourth century the **baptism** of new Christians had already become an important element of this service. Today's Holy Week observances commemorate the same events on the same days. Thus, by the end of the fourth century the outlines of Holy Week as we know it today were already in place.

Although for many years most scholars assumed that Holy Week celebrations evolved in Jerusalem, some now think that certain observances were imported from elsewhere. These scholars suspect that Christian communities in Constantinople (modern-day Istanbul, the capital of Turkey), and Alexandria, Egypt, were the first to celebrate **Lazarus Saturday** and Palm Sunday. They argue that pilgrims from these communities imported these festivals to Jerusalem. The Jerusalem community eventually adopted and combined them with services occurring during the latter part of Holy Week, giving rise to the sequence of rites that are familiar to us today.

In ancient times Holy Week observances varied from place to place. This variation continued into the Middle Ages, although the passing of time gradually brought with it increasing uniformity. It also inspired the invention of new devotional practices, such as **footwashing** on Maundy Thursday, and new folk customs, such as the baking and eating of **hot cross buns** on Good Friday. Over time certain ancient traditions disappeared in many places as well, including the **pardoning** of prisoners, a custom once practiced by some medieval monarchs. In spite of these additions and occasional subtractions, the religious themes associated with the days of Holy Week have remained fairly stable since early Christian times.

Orthodox Services

Orthodox Holy Week services differ slightly from those of Western Christians, that is, Roman Catholics and Protestants. Orthodoxy is one of the three main branches of the Christian faith. Orthodox Christianity developed in eastern Europe and the countries surrounding the eastern half of the Mediterranean Sea. Most members of this ancient faith tradition still hail from these eastern countries, although nowadays Orthodox Christian communities can also be found in the

West and include members from a wide variety of ethnic backgrounds. Orthodox Christians follow a different church calendar than that commonly adhered to by Western Christians (*see also* **Easter, Date of**). Therefore Orthodox and Western Christians often celebrate Holy Week at different times.

During the first half of Holy Week Orthodox church services emphasize the theme of judgment and the Second Coming of Christ. Western Christians meditate on these concepts during Advent, the four-week season of the church year that precedes Christmas. In Orthodox churches, vespers (evening) services during the first three days of Holy Week advise worshipers to live each day according to God's teachings since no one knows when judgment, or Christ, will come. These ceremonies are known as the "bridegroom services" in reference to the parable of the Wise and Foolish Bridesmaids (Matthew 25:1-13), a Bible passage featured in these services. Scholars of Orthodoxy trace this thematic development back to the ancient Christian belief that the Second Coming of Christ would occur at Easter time, most probably during the vigil service.

Names

Over the centuries Holy Week acquired a variety of names. In early Christian times some called it the "six days of **Pascha**," others called it the "Paschal Week," and still others "Great Week" or the "Week of Passion." Another old name for the observance, the "Week of Remission," referred to the ancient Maundy Thursday rite of conferring forgiveness on those undergoing public penance for their **sins** (*for more on penance, see* **Repentance**). Laborious Week, a reference to the fasting and other religious disciplines practiced during this period, constituted yet another old name for the festival. In medieval England it was known as "Palm Week" and, later, "Passion Week." The Germans dubbed this period of time *Karwoche*, or "Week of Lamentation." Spanish, French, and Italian speakers know this seven-day period as "Holy Week," a name also popular in the United States. Orthodox Christians favor "Great Week," "Holy and Great Week," or the "Week of Salvation."

For more on Holy Week customs and observances, *see also* **Alleluia**; Baptism; **Bells**; Cross; **Epitaphios**; **Easter Fires**; Easter Vigil; Fasting; Footwashing; **Descent into Hell**; **Holy Sepulchre**; Hot Cross Buns; **Judas, Burning of**; Mary, Blessed Virgin; Mary Magdalene; **Palm**; **Passion Play**; **Penitentes**; **Peter**; **Pilate, Pontius**; **Royal Hours**; **Stations of the Cross**; **Tenebrae**; **Three Hours**; **Triduum**; Veiling; **Veneration of the Cross**; Veronica

Further Reading

Bradshaw, Paul F. *The Search for the Origins of Christian Worship*. New York: Oxford University Press, 1992.

Davies, J. G. "The Origins of Holy Week and Its Development in the Middle Ages." In C. P. M. Jones, ed. *A Manual for Holy Week*. London, England: Society for Promoting Christian Knowledge, 1967.

"Holy Week." In E. A. Livingstone, ed. *The Oxford Dictionary of the Christian Church*. Third edition. Oxford, England: Oxford University Press, 1997.

Monti, James. *The Week of Salvation*. Huntington, IN: Our Sunday Visitor Publications, 1993.

O'Shea, W. J. "Holy Week." In *New Catholic Encyclopedia*. Volume 7. New York: McGraw-Hill, 1967.

Pierce, Joanne M. "Holy Week and Easter in the Middle Ages." In Paul F. Bradshaw and Lawrence A. Hoffman, eds. *Passover and Easter: Origin and History to Modern Times*. Two Liturgical Traditions series, volume 5. Notre Dame, IN: University of Notre Dame Press, 1999.

Talley, Thomas J. *The Origins of the Liturgical Year*. Collegeville, MN: Liturgical Press, 1986.

Wybrew, Hugh. *Orthodox Lent, Holy Week and Easter*. Crestwood, NY: St. Vladimir's Seminary Press, 1997.

Hot Cross Buns

Hot cross buns are a traditional **Good Friday** treat in England. These buns consist of sweetened **bread** dough enhanced with spices, citrus peel, and currants or raisins. After baking, the cooled buns are decorated with a **cross** made from sugar icing.

Among the English a preference for eating hot cross buns on Good Friday can be traced back at least as far as the eighteenth century. In 1733 *Poor Robin's Almanack* printed the following verse:

> Good Friday comes this month, the old woman runs
> With one or two a penny hot cross-buns
> Whose virtue is, if you believe what's said,
> They'll not grow mouldy like the common bread.
>
> (Weiser, 129)

In the nineteenth century researchers recorded many English folk beliefs concerning hot cross buns. According to these beliefs, these small loaves of bread would neither mold nor decay. Moreover they had the power to cure disease, especially intestinal disease. Some people hung hot cross buns in their homes all year long as a means of protecting the household against illness, lightning, fire, and other misfortunes. Street vendors sold dozens of these popular delicacies on Good Friday, attracting customers with ditties like the following:

> Hot cross buns, hot cross buns,
> One a penny, two a penny,
> Hot cross buns.
> If your daughters won't eat them,
> Give them to your sons;
> But if you have none of those little elves
> Then you must eat them all yourselves. (Weiser, 129)

Some researchers suspect that convictions concerning the power of bread stamped with a cross and baked on Good Friday can be traced back to the Middle Ages. During this era, bread baked for distribution during the **Eucharist** was imprinted with a cross. Some writers assert that in the late fourteenth century the monks of St. Alban's Abbey began promoting the consumption of hot cross buns on Good Friday by distributing buns stamped with a cross to the poor on that day. Moreover, throughout the latter half of the Middle Ages the Eucharist was placed in a special shrine called the **holy sepulchre** on Good Friday so that worshipers could pray and meditate on Christ's sacrificial death. After the Reformation, a sixteenth-century religious reform movement, this devotional practice declined in popularity. Some researchers suggest that nineteenth-century folk beliefs concerning the virtues of hot cross buns represent a remnant of earlier religious customs such as these.

By the twentieth century English bakeries began to produce hot cross buns throughout **Lent**. Today the buns can also be found in the United States and other countries to which the English have immigrated.

Further Reading

Hutton, Ronald. *Stations of the Sun*. Oxford, England: Oxford University Press, 1996.

Lord, Priscilla Sawyer, and Daniel J. Foley. *Easter the World Over*. Philadelphia, PA: Chilton Book Company, 1971.

Weiser, Francis X. *The Easter Book.* New York: Harcourt, Brace and Company, 1954.

Web Site

"One a Penny Poker," an article on hot cross buns posted in *Devon Life Online*, an electronic magazine about life in the English county of Devon: http://www.devonlife.co.uk/magazine/magarticles_folder/devon_customs/onepenny/oneapenny.html

Hungary, Easter and Holy Week in

Hungarian Easter celebrations blend many charming folk and religious traditions. The exchange of **Easter eggs** is such an important part of the festivities that Hungarians wish each other "Happy Easter and many red eggs!"

Palm Sunday

Hungarians substitute pussy willow branches for **palms** at their **Palm Sunday** services. Priests bless the branches which are then distributed to parishioners to take home with them. In past times Hungarian priests not only blessed branches on Palm Sunday, but also flowers. Thus arose the Hungarian folk name for the day *Virágvasarnap*, or "Flower Sunday." Another old custom called for a ritual battle between two folk figures, Prince Cibere and King Marrow Bone. King Bone represents indulgence while Cibere is the name of a sour bran soup eaten during the Lenten **fast**. On Shrove Tuesday Prince Cibere conquers King Bone, ushering in **Lent** and its accompanying fast. On Palm Sunday, King Bone reestablishes supremacy, signaling the coming end of the lean season of Lent.

Maundy Thursday

Hungarians call **Maundy Thursday** Green Thursday. Folk custom calls for eating green foods on this day. Church services include **footwashing** ceremonies that recall Christ's teachings at the Last Supper (*for more on the Last Supper, see* Maundy Thursday).

Good Friday

In some parts of Hungary people decorate their Easter eggs on **Good Friday**. In other regions, however, the eggs are usually finished by that day, along with other Easter preparations, including baking and

spring cleaning. An old folk tradition required that no fires be lit on this day and the next. The prohibition on lighting fires ended with the ringing of the **bells** for church services on **Holy Saturday**.

Holy Saturday

Many people still bring baskets of Easter food to church on Holy Saturday to receive the priest's blessing. The baskets often contain smoked ham, red Easter eggs, salt, and sometimes **wine**. This food is placed on the table at the feast that follows church services (*see also* **Easter Vigil**).

Easter Sunday

Hungarians call **Easter Sunday** *Húsvét*, meaning "Feast of Meat." Many homes serve a special meat loaf on this day, made of minced pork, ham, bread, eggs, and spices. Hungarians give one another Easter eggs as tokens of their affection on this day. Godparents often give decorated eggs to their godchildren. Little girls also exchange Easter eggs with friends on this day. One traditional method of doing so requires a girl to send a "bride's plate" to her friend, accompanied by eight or so other girls. The plate contains a bottle of wine, a large **pretzel**, and decorated Easter eggs. The recipient takes some of the eggs from the plate, replacing them with some of her own making, and sends the plate back to her girlfriend. Past customs also encourage Hungarian youths to decorate eggs to give to their sweethearts on this day. Girls often treasured these tokens of affection for many years. The girls in turn often gave twenty to thirty eggs to the men who courted them. In past times no one despaired if their egg-decorating skills were not up to snuff. Every village had at least one woman who specialized in the craft and would make Easter eggs for others.

Easter Eggs

Hungarians favor red Easter eggs. Indeed in Hungary people wish each other *"Boldog Húsvéti ünnepeket és sok piros tojást,"* meaning "Happy Easter and many red eggs!" According to Hungarian folklore, red, the color of blood, represents the essence of life itself. Red eggs are thus said to stand for eternal life, renewal, joy, freedom, love, spring, and **resurrection**. Old Hungarian folk beliefs assert that these red eggs attract good luck and protect recipients from harm, illness, and fire. The red egg is so prominent in Hungarian Easter celebrations that *piros tojás*, or "red egg," is a common way of referring to any Easter egg.

Hungarians also inscribe Easter eggs with elaborate traditional designs thought to be centuries old. These designs feature **crosses**, swastika crosses, and circles as well as stylized symbols representing the sun, wheels, rakes, hands, oak leaves, rams, and frogs. The circle signifies the Creator, the cross the union of heaven and earth, and the swastika the wheel of the sun, with its spokes representing the essential elements of creation: air, earth, water, and fire. It is also said to represent the protective arms of God stretched out over the world. Oak leaves stand for family unity. The rake, frog, cock's comb, seeds and dots suggest fertility, while the ram symbolizes renewal. Some folklorists suspect that these symbols, and indeed the custom of decorating eggs, may predate the arrival of Christianity in Hungary around the tenth century. One Hungarian researcher discovered a scratch-carved Easter egg in a grave dating back to ca. 400-700 A.D. Some scholars identify the custom of pressing a red egg into the hand of the deceased before burial as belonging to the ancient horsemen of central Asia, the ancestors of the Hungarian people.

Hungarian egg crafters use a variety of techniques to create fancy designs for their eggs (*for more on these techniques, see* Easter Eggs). Women tend to favor the wax resist or batik method. Men often prefer scratch-carving. Certain skilled blacksmiths and machinists have perfected the art of metal appliqué egg decorating, in which small metal ornaments, such as miniature horseshoes, tools, and spurs made of iron or lead are attached to the empty eggshell with tiny pins or nails.

Many of these elaborately decorated eggs became treasured possessions. The beauty and fragility of these works of folk art may have

303

inspired a well-known Hungarian expression. When someone takes great pains to care for something or someone, Hungarians say that they "take care of him/her/it as if he/she/it were an Easter egg."

Easter Monday

Hungarians call **Easter Monday** "Dousing Day" or "Water Plunge Monday." Folk tradition permits men and boys to douse women and girls with **water** on this day. In past times men interpreted this right rather roughly, sometimes dragging unwilling females into streams and ponds, or drenching them with well water. Folklore held that this treatment conferred good health, fertility, and the probability of being a good wife, which perhaps explains why women and girls responded to this soaking with hospitality, offering the men eggs, **bread**, or wine, and sometimes all three. Nowadays many men carry out the old custom in a more gentlemanly fashion, sprinkling women with water or even with cologne.

Further Reading

Lord, Priscilla Sawyer, and Daniel J. Foley. *Easter Garland*. 1963. Reprint. Detroit, MI: Omnigraphics, 1999.
Spicer, Dorothy Gladys. *Book of Festivals*. 1937. Reprint. Detroit, MI: Omnigraphics, 1990.

Web Site

"Hungarian Decorated Easter Eggs," "Easter in Hungary," and "Handled Like a Hímestojás," three articles by Emese Kerkay, posted by the American Hungarian Educators' Association at: http://www.magyar.org/ahfc/museum/husvet/

Italy, Carnival in

Many colorful and diverse **Carnival** celebrations take place throughout Italy. In spite of their diversity they all revolve around public events, such as parades, mock battles, open-air banquets, bonfires, and masquerades. The Italians call this holiday *Carnavale* or sometimes *la settimana grassa*, the "Week of Fat" or "Fat Week." It reaches its climax on **Shrove Tuesday**, or as the Italians say, *Martedì Grasso*, which means "Fat Tuesday." The Italian saying, *A Carnevale ogni scherzo vale*, "during Carnival every prank is fair," reflects the mischievous spirit of Carnival in Italy.

History

The people of Italy have been celebrating Carnival since the Middle Ages. These medieval celebrations gave participants an opportunity to feast, especially on food soon to be forbidden for **Lent**, and cavort through city streets, drinking, singing, dancing, flirting, and wearing masks. The anonymity afforded by the mask gave people the opportunity to dabble in sexual, and other, behavior they wouldn't normally engage in. People also enjoyed staging mock battles in which they threw oranges, eggs, or flour at one another. Around the seventeenth century festival-goers also began to throw candy-coated almonds or even beads made of plaster. Later, people tossed confetti and flowers at one another. By the eighteenth and nineteenth centuries some Italians wore wire face masks to protect themselves against all these flying objects.

Foods

In the past Carnival offered the people of Italy one last opportunity to use up forbidden foods, such as butter, eggs, and animal fat, before the beginning of the Lenten **fast**. These restrictions influenced the foods that became traditional Carnival dishes in Italy. In many regions of Italy people fry up sweetened strips of pastry for the festival. These traditional Carnival sweets acquired a variety of colorful names throughout the country, including "little lies" in the Piedmont region, "gossips" in Milan, and "nun's ribbons" in a number of different places. *Frittelle*, or "fritters," are another favorite Carnival sweet in Italy. In fact, the phrase *fare le fritelle*, or "to make fritters," means to enjoy Carnival. In many places favorite Carnival meals feature pork or sausage.

Carnival in Venice

Historical documents trace Carnival in Venice back to the Middle Ages. These early records reveal that medieval Venetians enjoyed masquerading during Carnival, but that some people took advantage of their disguises in order to break rules and commit crimes. Over the centuries many laws were passed to limit the times when and places at which one could wear masks. For example, a law passed in 1339 forbade people from roaming the city in disguise at night. In 1458 another edict restricted men from dressing as women in order to gain entry into convents for dishonest purposes. For many hundreds of years the love of the Venetian people for their masks and costumes proved stronger than these laws. In fact, masks were so popular among the Venetians that they were worn outside of the Carnival season at banquets. Carnival masking itself began as early as St. Stephen's Day, which falls on December 26. Masking was also associated with other festivals, such as **Ascension Day**. In the eighteenth century women wore masks while attending the theater. Masquerading died out in the nineteenth and twentieth centuries. Indeed Carnival in Venice itself came to an end under the rule of the Italian dictator Benito Mussolini (1883-1945), who outlawed the festival. When the people of Venice revived Carnival in 1979, the mask once again became an important element of the holiday and the primary symbol of Carnival in Venice.

In the year 1687 over 30,000 people visited Venice during Carnival. The well-to-do attended lavish costume parties and everyone, rich and poor, paraded down the main streets in costumes. People feasted in the main square until late into the night. In those days, people amused themselves by letting bulls loose in the city and chasing them through the streets. For those who found themselves trapped in the path of an angry bull, Venice's many canals offered a handy means of escape. In the nineteenth century Venetians abandoned the sport of bull-chasing. Other old Venetian Carnival customs include various acrobatic stunts, such as the building of large human pyramids outside the homes of top city officials and a trick called the "flight of the angel," whereby an acrobat descended from a tall bell tower by means of a rope, tossing confetti to the crowds below as he came down.

Nowadays thousands of people flock once again to Venice for Carnival. Sauntering through the city streets in costume and watching the fabulous masks and costumes of others still constitutes the primary pastime associated with this holiday. Festival-goers can see a wide range of contemporary and traditional costumes. In Venice traditional costumes include that of *La Bautta*, "the Domino," who wears a black hood, white mask, black three-cornered hat and black cape. *Il Dottore*, a pompous professor, is another popular character. Other traditional

307

costumes, popular throughout Italy, evolved from the stock characters of commedia dell'arte, a humorous kind of improvisational theater that began in the sixteenth century. These include Pierrot, a gloomy clown who wears a baggy white coat with big buttons, Harlequin, a rascally clown who wears clothes made of patches or diamond-shaped lozenges, and Punchinello, a hunchback.

The city also hosts many masked balls, some geared towards the famous and the wealthy, others more democratic in their guest list. On the last day of Carnival a public masquerade party is held on San Marcos square. Fireworks, music, dancing, and, of course, costume-watching entertain those who attend.

Ivrea

The town of Ivrea, located in the Piedmont region of Italy, celebrates the **Sunday**, Monday and Tuesday of Carnival with a giant food fight. The weapons are blood oranges, over sixty tons of them, shipped to the town from Sicily. Over the years the food fight has become an expression of neighborhood rivalry. Squads of invaders riding horse-drawn carts pelt buildings and people that they pass on their way through a given neighborhood. Defenders, stationed on the streets, protect their territory by hurling oranges at the carts and the people who ride them. Thrown with force, these juicy but substantial missiles cause bruises. Many people therefore opt out of this sport, wearing red knit caps to identify themselves as non-combatants.

In Ivrea a woman from the pages of local legend leads the celebrations. Named Violetta, but referred to most often as *La Mugnaia*, a nickname that identifies her as the daughter of the local miller, she lived during the twelfth century. In those days the local nobleman claimed the right to sleep with each new bride who lived in his territory on her wedding night. On her wedding day Violetta trudged up to the castle to comply with the nobleman's demands. She hid a knife in the folds of her clothing, however. As soon as she was alone with the tyrant, Violetta drew out the knife and killed him. Then she cut off his head and dangled it from the castle window to show the townspeople that their hated overlord was dead. After throwing the severed head into the river Violetta set fire to the castle and fled into the night. A three-day battle between the townspeople and the soldiers loyal to the old nobleman ensued. The people of Ivrea won their freedom. For this reason Ivreans still revere La Mugnaia as a heroine.

On the Saturday evening before **Ash Wednesday** a woman chosen to play the role of La Mugnaia leads a parade which kicks off Carnival in Ivrea. Other colorful characters from local and Italian history ride with her in the parade, including a man dressed as an early nineteenth-century French general, representing the period in history when Napoleon conquered this region of Italy. After the parade people disperse to attend the many Carnival parties held all over town. That same evening volunteers begin to prepare a huge meal for tomorrow's festival-goers. It consists mainly of *tofeja,* a bean dish seasoned with pork. In the town's main square 35 large cauldrons full of beans simmer slowly over fires all night long. People returning home from late-night parties often stop by to sample the dish.

The following day the people of Ivrea gather for a communal feast. La Mugnaia and the French General ladle the tofeja into bowls and act as host and hostess. Red **wine**, cheese, and chocolates accompany the meal. After the banquet another procession with La Mugnaia takes place. When the parade reaches the river the mayor tosses a brick from the decaying castle of the old nobleman into the water. This act recalls the image of La Mugnaia cutting off the nobleman's head and throwing it in the river.

A local legend also tells why beans became such a popular Carnival dish in Ivrea. It asserts that long ago the rich nobles who owned the land used to give away free beans once a year to the poor people who tilled their fields. Hunger pinched the farmers year round, however, making the yearly sack of beans seem a meager gift. One day some poor farmers threw the beans back at the landowners in disgust. Local lore identifies this incident as the first Carnival food fight in Ivrea. As late as 1872 well-to-do families tossed oranges, beans, and candy into the crowd during Ivrea's Carnival celebrations. One record indicates that these foodstuffs contributed substantially to the diet of the poor.

La Mugnaia appears again on **Shrove Tuesday**. She and the French General lead the ceremonies that bring Carnival to an end. On the previous day, the most recently married couples from each of the town's five neighborhoods shoveled the first earth from the spot on which the neighborhood's *scarli* would be planted. Scarli are tall wooden poles wrapped with heather and juniper greens and topped with a flag. On the evening of Shrove Tuesday, the scarli planted in the town's central plaza is the first to burn. La Mugnaia raises her sword in the air as a signal to the torchbearers to set the scarli on fire. If the flames reach as high as the flag atop the pole, then the neighborhood may expect good luck as well as many new marriages in the coming year. With a flute player piping out a mournful tune, the crowd walks to the next neighborhood to burn its scarli. After all the poles have burned the parade continues in silence, the only sound that of the General's sword as he drags it over the pavement. This funeral march memorializes the death of Carnival and the arrival of Lent.

On Ash Wednesday the citizens of Ivrea enjoy one last communal feast. This one features salt cod, a traditional Lenten food in southern Europe. Preparations begin four days before, when the dried, salted fish is put into water to soak. Soaking reconstitutes the fish and removes most of the salt. Volunteers fry the fish during the night on Shrove Tuesday. The following morning it is cooked with onions and a red or white sauce along with polenta. Many townspeople not only enjoy this feast on Ash Wednesday but also take some fish home and freeze it for use in the days or weeks to come.

Viareggio

Viareggio, located in the region of Italy known as Tuscany, hosts one of the most well-known Carnivals in Italy. The celebration as it is known today took shape in the late nineteenth century. In 1873 several local men staged the town's first Carnival parade. Riding atop a couple of ox-drawn carts strewn with garlands and **wine** bottles, some disguised themselves as Bacchus, the ancient Roman god of wine, while others, serving as coachmen, dressed as bears. Their modest effort proved so popular that the very next year a committee formed to produce a new parade. They added a fireworks display and a ceremony honoring the end of Carnival in which a dummy representing the festival is set on fire. Over the years the size of the floats and puppets have grown. Nowadays it's not uncommon to see floats carrying paper mâché figures several stories high. The artisans of Viareggio, who are called *maghi* or "magicians" for their amazing paper mâché sculptures, produce figures whose arms, legs, and eyes move, making them appear to be animated. They specialize in humorous representations of politicians, actors, intellectuals, and other famous people.

Viareggio's Carnival celebrations also feature many smaller parades that run through local neighborhoods. These neighborhood celebrations offer a wide variety of musical entertainments. As they say in Viareggio, *Carnevale é il vecchio, che la vita ci Ridá*, meaning "Carnival is the old fool who gives us life."

311

Verona

Verona's Carnival features a day devoted to the celebration of food. The parade that day is led by *Il Papa del Gnocco*, the Pope of Gnocci. Gnocci are a kind of potato and flour dumpling. Il Papa del Gnocco wields a scepter made to look like a giant fork spearing a giant gnocci. Parade floats celebrate local foodstuffs. After the parade the people who live in the neighborhood of San Zeno gather in the main plaza for a meal of gnocci, sausage, herring, and polenta.

Further Reading

Field, Carol. *Celebrating Italy*. New York: William Morrow and Company, 1990.

Griffin, Robert H., and Ann H. Shurgin, eds. *Junior Worldmark Encyclopedia of World Holidays*. Volume 1. Detroit, MI: UXL, 2000.

Lau, Alfred. *Carneval International*. Bielefeld, Germany: Univers-Verlag, n.d.

Lyden, Jacki. "Analysis: Battle of the Oranges in Carnival Celebration in Italy." Weekend Edition, National Public Radio (March 12, 2000). Transcript available for a fee online at http://www.elibrary.com; audiotape of segment available at http://www.npr.org (search on "Battle of Oranges").

Orloff, Alexander. *Carnival: Myth and Cult*. Wörgl, Austria: Perlinger, 1981.

Web Site

A history of Carnival in Venice available through the "Guest in Venice" web site, sponsored by Omnia Office at: http://www.guestinvenice.com/events/carnivalofvenice/uk/antico/storia/default.asp

Italy, Easter and Holy Week in

Italian tradition calls for giving one's home a thorough **spring clean-ing** during **Holy Week** in preparation for the priest's visit and Easter blessing. Easter baking and other Easter food preparation as well as religious devotions occupy many Italians during this week.

Palm Sunday

Italy's Roman Catholic churches hold **palm** processions on **Palm Sunday**. At Saint Peter's Basilica in Rome, the pope is carried aloft in a ceremony during which he blesses palm branches.

Maundy Thursday

Roman Catholic church services on **Maundy Thursday** feature **foot-washing** ceremonies. In Rome the pope washes the feet of thirteen men. Twelve of the men represent Jesus' twelve apostles, the thir-teenth represents an angel that, according to church tradition, ap-peared at the altar when Pope Gregory the Great officiated at the Last Supper service in the sixth century (*for more on the Last Supper, see* Maundy Thursday). In addition, churches prepare a special side altar, sometimes called a sepulchre, to house the remains of Thursday's **Eucharist**. At the end of the service the remains of the consecrated **bread** and **wine** are ceremoniously placed on this specially decorat-ed altar. Devout Italians may visit seven of these decorated altars on the evening of Holy Thursday (*see also* **Holy Sepulchre**).

Good Friday

Religious processions wind their way through the streets of many towns and villages on **Good Friday**. Some of these solemn parades focus on **Jesus'** death and feature representations of Jesus' funeral bier.

313

Many men are required to carry this often life-sized scene, mounted on top of a heavy platform. In addition to those who bear the platforms, others participate in the parade by carrying symbols of the Crucifixion, such as **crosses**, nails, crowns of thorns, and spears (*for more on crucifixion, see* Cross). Other Good Friday processions feature various scenes from the Passion story, that is, the story of Jesus' betrayal, judgment and execution (*see also* **Judas; Pilate, Pontius**). Still other parades focus on the Blessed Virgin Mary's grief and may feature life-sized statues of a tear-stained, black-robed Madonna accompanied by dozens or hundreds of black-garbed followers (*see* **Mary, Blessed Virgin**). In Sicily Good Friday processions depict the Virgin Mary's distressed search for her son, a legendary incident associated with the evening of Good Friday. These sorrowful parades may last all night and leave participants emotionally and physically drained.

Holy Saturday

Church services on **Holy Saturday** feature the blessing of **water**, the new fire ceremony, and the lighting of the **paschal candle** (*see also* **Baptism; Easter Fires**).

Easter Sunday

Many Italians associate Easter with spring vacations. The inclination to entertain oneself at Easter time is revealed in a common Italian saying, *Natale con i suoi, Pasqua con chi vuoi* (Christmas with your family, Easter with your own choice of friends).

Italians enjoy wearing **new clothes** on **Easter Sunday**. If one can't afford a new outfit, then a new pair of shoelaces or a new hair ribbon will do.

The Italian tradition of crafting elaborate and delicious chocolate **Easter eggs** stretches back several centuries. Italian parents, however, do not perpetuate the myth that these eggs are delivered by the **Easter Bunny**. Instead Italians openly frequent confectioners' shops to select from a wide variety of chocolate eggs, many with toys and trinkets inside. In addition to crafting eggs for children, confectioners also prepare chocolate Easter eggs for grownups. These eggs contain gifts suitable for adults, ranging from costume jewelry to plane tickets and even keys to a new car. Some exclusive shops will permit customers to submit their own gifts which the chocolate maker will then hide inside a custom-made Easter egg. The city of Turin has a reputation for producing some of Italy's finest and most exclusive chocolate Easter eggs.

The **lamb** continues to serve as an important Easter symbol in Italy. Not only do many Italians prefer roast lamb as the main course of their Easter feast, but many Italian Easter tables also feature lambs molded out of butter or marzipan.

Italy also boasts many regional Easter specialties. Sicilians enjoy *cassata*, an elaborate cake featuring sweetened ricotta cheese, candied pumpkin, sponge cake, and almond paste. The people of Piedmont favor a kind of pie combining rice and fresh, spring greens. In Liguria many families look forward to *torta pasqualina*, a tart combining vegetables and cheese in a crust of phyllo pastry. Italians also dye Easter eggs, sometimes nesting them in special Easter loaves. Italy's regional cuisines have produced a variety of Easter breads. In Genoa bakers prepare *pan dolce*, a sweet bread made with raisins, pine nuts, and candied fruit peel. Chefs from Lombardy invented *columba pasquale*, a sweet bread filled with candied orange peels, raisins, and almonds which is baked in special dove-shaped molds. This bread has become a popular Easter treat throughout Italy.

In the city of Florence many Italians gather on Easter Sunday morning to watch a six-hundred-year-old ritual known as the "burning of the cart." At around ten o'clock in the morning an ox-drawn cart lurches into the plaza in front of the city's cathedral. The oxen are then detached from the cart, which carries a beautifully decorated, multi-storied pyramid that is covered with fireworks. Assistants visit a nearby church where flints, which local legend identifies as coming from the tomb of Christ itself, are used to strike a flame. Then they ceremoniously carry the sacred flame back to the cathedral. Inside the cathedral a rocket made in the shape of a dove has been attached to a wire which runs from the cart through the cathedral doors and along the nave of the church. When the sacred flame lights its fuse, the dove rocket shoots along the wire out the church doors into the plaza and, hopefully, ignites the fireworks that festoon the cart. As the fireworks explode church **bells**, altar bells, and even cowbells begin to ring. The joyous din celebrates the **resurrection** of Jesus Christ.

Easter Monday

Italians call Easter Monday *Pasquetta*, or "Little Easter." Many Italians celebrate it with family walks and barbecues or picnics in the country-side (*see also* **Emmaus Walks**). A traditional appetizer associated with Easter Monday combines a hard-boiled egg, salt, and bitter greens. These foods, also consumed during the Jewish holiday of **Passover**, remind diners of the bitterness of the Jewish exile in Egypt, recounted in the Bible's Book of Exodus.

Further Reading

Field, Carol. *Celebrating Italy*. New York: William Morrow and Company, 1990.

Hudgins, Sharon. "Breads for Christ." *The World and I* 15, 4 (April 1999): 162.

Lord, Priscilla Sawyer, and Daniel J. Foley. *Easter the World Over*. Philadelphia, PA: Chilton Book Company, 1971.

Toor, Frances. *Festivals and Folkways of Italy*. New York: Crown, 1953.

Wolf, Burt. *Gatherings and Celebrations*. New York: Doubleday, 1996.

Web Site

"Easter without a Peep," a brief article on Italian Easter foods by Faith Heller Willinger, posted at: http://www.epicurious.com/g_gourmet/g04_italy/italy/easter.html

Jesus

The Christian religion takes as its focal point the life and teachings of Jesus of Nazareth. The Easter holiday, considered by many Christians to be the most important festival of the Christian year, celebrates Jesus' **resurrection**, that is, his rising to new life after having been executed by means of crucifixion (*for more on crucifixion, see* **Cross**). Who was Jesus and why is the commemoration of his death and resurrection the occasion of so much solemn ritual and festivity? Contemporary Christianity is a diverse religion which offers a number of different answers to these questions. Each sheds its own light on the meaning of the Easter festival.

Jesus of Nazareth lived in the first century in a land known today as Israel. He was born into a humble, Jewish family and apparently had a number of brothers, and perhaps sisters as well. At the time of Jesus' birth the Jewish people were subjects of the Roman Empire.

Little is known of Jesus' upbringing except that it took place in a town called Nazareth, a town located in Galilee, a poor region populated by peasant farmers, craftsmen, and fishermen struggling under heavy Roman taxes. Jesus grew up to become a spiritual teacher. Scholars deduce from his teachings that Jesus was well versed in the Hebrew scriptures. According to the Bible Jesus began his teaching career in the fifteenth year of the reign of Tiberius Caesar, which historians assume to have fallen somewhere between the years 27-29 A.D. His career ended when he was arrested and crucified by the Roman governor, Pontius **Pilate**.

The Resurrection

Beyond these simple facts, which most Christians and historians accept, lie other debated notions concerning Jesus' life and identity. For example, Christian scripture proclaims that Jesus rose from the dead on the third day after his death in an event known as the Resurrection. The disciples came to believe in Jesus' resurrection after they found his tomb empty and later encountered a living being, on several different occasions, whom they recognized as Jesus. Many Christians accept the biblical accounts of Jesus' resurrection as literally true. Others believe that the disciples did indeed experience Jesus' presence among them after his death, but think these encounters may not necessarily have involved the materialization of Jesus in the flesh. Still others interpret the biblical account of Jesus' resurrection as a kind of parable, meant to be understood metaphorically rather than literally. According to this line of thought, the biblical stories of Jesus' resurrection symbolize a state of mind found among his followers.

These differences in interpretation notwithstanding, the resurrection of Jesus Christ stands at the center of Christian theology. Many Christians view the Resurrection as an affirmation that through Jesus of Nazareth God is making a radical new offer of **salvation** to all of humanity. Moreover, the Resurrection helps to make sense of what Christians experience as Jesus' continuing presence among them. Finally, many Christians believe that the Resurrection not only provides evidence of the afterlife promised to all believers, but also confirms Jesus' identity as the Messiah or Christ.

The Messiah, The Christ

The word messiah comes from the Hebrew term *mashiah*, which means "anointed one." It refers to the ancient Jewish practice of anointing those who served as high priests and kings of Israel. The anointings took the form of special ceremonies in which the individual was rubbed with oil. This ritual represented the recognition that these individuals had been appointed by God to help his chosen people. The Hebrew scriptures, which Christians call the Old Testament, refer to kings such as Saul, David, and Solomon as messiahs. Even the Persian king Cyrus was called a messiah because he freed the Jewish people from slavery in Babylon. By the second century B.C. some Jews had blended the messiah concept with Old Testament prophecies concerning the rise of a descendent of King David who would restore Jerusalem and whose reign would be just and glorious. Thus for some Jews the meaning of the word "messiah" began to change from any high political or spiritual leader to a single future leader sent by God to rescue his people from political oppression. They referred to this just, merciful, wise, and glorious king as the Messiah.

Traditional Christian doctrine claims that Jesus of Nazareth was the Messiah. In the New Testament this word is usually translated as "Christ." The word Christ comes from the ancient Greek word *Christos*, which means "anointed one," reflecting the fact that some of the Christian scriptures were written in Greek. According to Christian scripture **Peter**, one of Jesus' disciples, recognized Jesus as the Messiah (Matthew 16:15-16, Mark 8:29, Luke 9:20, John 6:69). The first Christians also acknowledged Jesus as the Messiah or Christ. For example, the writings of the apostle Paul contain many references to Jesus as the Christ. This belief became central to the emerging Christian faith.

Some contemporary scholars, however, doubt that Jesus meant to claim the title of Messiah for himself. They note that in the Gospels (the books of the Christian Bible that recount the life and teachings of Christ) the title he most often claims is the "Son of Man." Moreover, on other occasions Jesus hesitates to accept the title of Messiah even when others identify him as such (Mark 8:30-31). The Bible does record one instance in which Jesus openly claims to be the Messiah (Mark 14:62), but some researchers suspect that this passage may have been embellished by the writer of this story, who, like other early Christians, already firmly believed that Jesus was the Messiah.

Another group of scholars believe that Christian scripture shows that Jesus definitely did identify himself as the Messiah. Some of them argue that his own actions demonstrate that he viewed himself in this way, especially his forgiving of sins and his blessing and inclusion of those considered socially and religiously unacceptable. Others interpret Jesus' apparent evasiveness in claiming the title of Messiah for himself as a device Jesus used to broaden people's understanding of his role, since many Jews at that time assumed the Messiah would serve his people as a kind of triumphant political leader. Other images Jesus employs to explain his role include prophet, shepherd, healer, and suffering servant. These scholars also find support for their viewpoint in Bible passages that identify Jesus as the Son of God.

The Son of God

Traditional Christian doctrine asserts that Jesus was the Son of God. In Hebrew scripture, a "son of God" is a person who plays a special role in bringing God's offer of salvation to humanity. Though these individuals enjoy a close relationship with God, they are not necessarily thought of as divine. The Old Testament identifies the people of Israel as sons of God (Exodus 4:22), implies that the king of the Israelites was customarily viewed as a son of God (Psalm 2:7), describes the angels as sons of God (Job 1:6), and proclaims that King David's son would be a son of God (2 Samuel 7:14). Many Christians interpret this line concerning King David's son as a reference to Jesus, who, though not David's son, was said to be a descendant of the great king. In a number of Bible passages Jesus implies that he is God's son, addressing God familiarly, as Father (Matthew 11:25-26, Mark 14:36), and claiming unique knowledge of God (Matthew 11:27).

After Jesus' death the idea that he was God's son became an important element of Christian belief. The meaning of the concept had changed, however, perhaps in light of the Resurrection and the early Christians's experience of Jesus' continuing presence among them. The statement that Jesus was the Son of God became an assertion that Jesus was divine. The Gospel according to John affirms Jesus' union with God throughout. It includes Jesus' affirmation that "the Father and I are one" (John 10:30). Christian doctrine eventually consolidated around the belief that Jesus was both fully human and fully divine, the only begotten Son of God. Some Christians do not interpret this doctrine as a proclamation of Jesus' divinity, however, but rather as an affirmation that Jesus was completely at one with God and that God chose Jesus to carry out his plan for humanity's **redemption** and salvation.

The Sacrifice, The Savior

An important and related element of Christian doctrine asserts that Jesus' death on the **cross** on **Good Friday** was a sacrifice made on behalf of all. This sacrifice not only atoned for the **sins** of the world, but also made any future **blood** sacrifices unnecessary (*for more on the concept of atonement, see* Redemption). At the Last Supper Jesus himself offered this interpretation of his death (*see* **Maundy Thursday**). This interpretation also fits with the timing of Jesus' death, which according to the Bible fell either on the first day of, or the day before, **Passover**. Passover celebrates the Israelites' escape from slavery in Egypt, an escape sanctioned by God and sealed with a sacrifice. Among the ancient Hebrews sacrificial animals had to be perfect, in good health, and unblemished. Jesus' spiritual perfection, as the Son of God, also supported the idea that his death was the supreme sacrificial offering, powerful enough to bring the era of sacrificial religion to a close and powerful enough to redeem the sins of his followers. Jesus' resurrection on the third day after his death affirmed his identity as the Christ and betokened the salvation that God would make possible through him. Indeed, the name Jesus, a Greek translation of the Hebrew name "Joshua," means "God saves."

Further Reading

Borg, Marcus J. *Meeting Jesus Again for the First Time*. New York: HarperSan-Francisco, 1994.

Borg, Marcus J., and N. T. Wright. *The Meaning of Jesus: Two Visions*. New York: HarperSanFrancisco, 1998.

Brown, Raymond. *The Death of the Messiah*. New York and London: Double-day and Geoffrey Chapman, 1994.

Carlston, Charles E. "Jesus Christ." In Paul J. Achtemeier, ed. *The Harper-Collins Bible Dictionary*. New York: HarperCollins, 1996.

Copan, Paul, ed. *Will the Real Jesus Please Stand Up? A Debate Between William Lane Craig and John Dominic Crossan*. Grand Rapids, MI: Baker, 1998.

Crossan, John Dominic. *Jesus: A Revolutionary Biography*. San Francisco, CA: HarperSanFrancisco, 1994.

Fitzmyer, Joseph A. "Messiah." In Paul J. Achtemeier, ed. *The HarperCollins Bible Dictionary*. New York: HarperCollins, 1996.

Fuller, Reginald H. "Son of God." In Paul J. Achtemeier, ed. *The HarperCollins Bible Dictionary*. New York: HarperCollins, 1996.

Gallaher Branch, Robin, and Lee E. Klosinsky. "Son." In David Noel Freed-man, ed. *Eerdmans Dictionary of the Bible*. Grand Rapids, MI: William B. Eerdmans Publishing, 2000.

"Jesus, Images of." In Leland Ryken, James C. Wilhoit, and Tremper Long-man III, eds. *Dictionary of Biblical Imagery*. Downers Grove, IL: InterVarsity Press, 1998.

"Jesus Christ." In E. A. Livingstone, ed. *The Oxford Dictionary of the Christian Church*. Third edition. Oxford, England: Oxford University Press, 1997.

Johnson, Luke Timothy. *The Real Jesus: The Misguided Quest for the Historical Jesus and the Truth of the Traditional Gospels*. New York: HarperSanFran-cisco, 1996.

Juel, Donald. "Christ." In David Noel Freedman, ed. *Eerdmans Dictionary of the Bible*. Grand Rapids, MI: William B. Eerdmans Publishing, 2000.

———. "Messiah." In David Noel Freedman, ed. *Eerdmans Dictionary of the Bible*. Grand Rapids, MI: William B. Eerdmans Publishing, 2000.

Maier, Paul J. *In the Fullness of Time: A Historian Looks at Christmas, Easter, and the Early Church*. Grand Rapids, MI: Kregel, 1991.

"Messiah." In E. A. Livingstone, ed. *The Oxford Dictionary of the Christian Church*. Third edition. Oxford, England: Oxford University Press, 1997.

Mowery, Robert L. "Son of God." In David Noel Freedman, ed. *Eerdmans Dictionary of the Bible*. Grand Rapids, MI: William B. Eerdmans Publishing, 2000.

Porter, J. R. *Jesus Christ: The Jesus of History, the Christ of Faith*. New York: Oxford University Press, 1999.

Powell, Mark Allan. *Jesus as a Figure in History*. Louisville, KY: Westminster John Knox Press, 1998.

Sanders, E. P. "Jesus Christ." In David Noel Freedman, ed. *Eerdmans Dictionary of the Bible*. Grand Rapids, MI: William B. Eerdmans Publishing, 2000.

Spong, John Shelby. *Resurrection: Myth or Reality?* New York: HarperSanFrancisco, 1994.

Witherington, Ben. *Jesus the Sage: The Pilgrimage of Wisdom*. Minneapolis, MN: Fortress Press, 1994.

Wright, N. T. *The Challenge of Jesus*. Downers Grove, IL: InterVarsity Press, 1999.

Wright, Thomas. *The Original Jesus*. Grand Rapids, MI: William B. Eerdmans, 1996.

Judas

Judas Iscariot was one of **Jesus'** twelve disciples. The four accounts of Jesus' arrest given in the Gospels (the books of the Christian Bible that recount the life and teachings of Christ) state that it was Judas who handed Jesus over to the Jewish religious authorities, thus beginning the chain of events that led to Jesus' crucifixion (*for more on crucifixion, see* **Cross**). After sharing the Last Supper with Jesus and the other disciples, Judas slipped away from them and sought out the chief priests (*for more on the Last Supper, see* **Maundy Thursday**). He led their soldiers and servants to the place where Jesus and the other disciples had assembled after dinner. In three of the four stories of Jesus' arrest, Judas greeted Jesus with a kiss, a gesture which identified Jesus to the mob that had come to arrest him. In the Gospel according to John, Jesus boldly confronts the crowd and makes himself known to them.

Why did Judas betray Jesus? Three of the four Gospel accounts of this event note that Judas arranged the betrayal beforehand, and state that the religious authorities paid him for disclosing information that would lead to Jesus' arrest (*see also* **Spy Wednesday**). Although the Gospel according to John does not include this information, it does claim that Judas kept track of all the disciples' funds, and that he made a habit of stealing small sums from this group account (John 12:6). John's Gospel concludes that the devil inspired Judas to desert Jesus (John 13:2), a perspective echoed in the Gospel according to Luke (Luke 22:3). Some researchers interpret these remarks as indications that the real conflict lay between Jesus and the devil, rather than Jesus and Judas.

The preceding interpretations of Judas' actions paint him as greedy and treacherous. By contrast, a few Bible commentators have offered explanations for Judas' actions that imply that Judas remained loyal to Jesus. For example, some writers have suggested that Judas decided

to notify the priests of Jesus' whereabouts after having been convinced that Jesus intended to die (Mark 14:4-11). Viewed in this light, Judas' act actually helps Jesus accomplish his own plan. Another viewpoint holds that Judas helped the chief priests because he believed that the encounter between Jesus and the religious authorities would inspire the common people to rise up in support of Jesus. This show of popular support would then force the priests to acknowledge Jesus' authority. Instead, however, the priests turn Jesus over to **Pilate**, the Roman governor, who decides to execute him. According to proponents of this viewpoint, shock and horror engulf Judas when he realizes that the events he set into motion were going to result instead in Jesus' torture and execution.

What became of Judas after Jesus had been taken away? The Gospel according to Matthew states that after Jesus had been arrested, Judas regretted his actions. He returned the thirty pieces of silver given to him by the chief priests. Then, in despair over Jesus' death sentence, he hung himself (Matthew 27:3-5). The Book of Acts describes Judas' fate in a different way. According to this text Judas used the money he got from the chief priests to buy some land. He didn't live to enjoy it, however. He fell down and burst open, spilling his entrails on the ground (Acts 1:18).

The Bible provides little other information on Judas' identity or his life before becoming one of Jesus' disciples. It gives his last name as Iscariot, a name whose meaning scholars debate. Many say that it comes from the Hebrew phrase, "man of Kerioth." If this is true, it signifies that Judas was the only one of Jesus' disciples from the land of Judea, the province in which the Jewish capital of Jerusalem was located. According to the Bible the other disciples came from a more remote region called Galilee. Other researchers claim that the name Iscariot bears a resemblance to the Greek word *sikarios*, which means assassin. Still others suggest that it means "man of Issachar." Yet another group contends that it comes from an Aramaic phrase meaning "man of the lie."

The story of Judas and Jesus has fascinated Christians for 2,000 years. Many have blamed Judas for Jesus' death, assuming that the faithless

Judas failed to recognize Jesus as the true Messiah and turned him in to the religious authorities in exchange for a cash reward (*for more on Messiah, see* Jesus). Tragically, many folk traditions and religious leaders over the centuries have identified Judas as a symbol of the Jewish people. Interpreted in this way, the story of Judas' betrayal served as a powerful means of whipping up anti-Jewish sentiment and excusing the deeds of those who acted out this hatred. Today many responsible Christian leaders are proposing different interpretations of Judas' actions. Some, as mentioned above, have suggested that Judas acted in good faith, believing that an encounter with the high priest would further Jesus' cause. Others have suggested that Jesus himself asked Judas to arrange this encounter. Still others, while retaining the notion that Judas betrayed Jesus, interpret Judas' act as symbolic of the human potential for **sin**, that is, unloving and unethical behavior, a potential found in people of all ethnic and religious backgrounds.

Further Reading

Brownrigg, Ronald. *The Twelve Apostles.* New York: Macmillan, 1974.

Flanagan, N. M. "Judas Iscariot." In *New Catholic Encyclopedia.* Volume 8. New York: McGraw-Hill, 1967.

"Judas Iscariot." In E. A. Livingstone, ed. *The Oxford Dictionary of the Christian Church.* Third edition. Oxford, England: Oxford University Press, 1997.

Keck, Leander, ed. *New Interpreter's Bible.* Volume 9. Nashville, TN: Abingdon Press, 1995.

Klassen, William. *Judas, Betrayer or Friend of Jesus?* Minneapolis, MN: Fortress Press, 1996.

Sheeley, Steven M. "Judas." In David Noel Freedman, ed. *Eerdmans Dictionary of the Bible.* Grand Rapids, MI: William B. Eerdmans Publishing, 2000.

Stein, Robert H. "Judas." In Paul J. Achtemeier, ed. *HarperCollins Bible Dictionary.* New York: HarperCollins, 1996.

Judas, Burning of

Judas was one of **Jesus'** twelve disciples. According to the Bible, when Jesus and the disciples traveled to Jerusalem to celebrate **Passover** Judas betrayed Jesus' whereabouts to the city's religious authorities. This act unleashed the chain of events ending in Jesus' crucifixion and death (*for more on crucifixion, see* **Cross**). As a means of symbolically punishing Judas for his misdeed, people in many parts of the world practice a folk custom known as the "burning of Judas" during **Holy Week**. In the days leading up to the ceremony participants prepare an effigy, or life-sized doll, of Judas. When this effigy is set ablaze, onlookers cheer. In some places the Judas doll is hanged or beaten rather than burned.

This vicious custom, once practiced in many corners of Europe, inflamed lingering prejudices against Jewish people, who, in Christian legends, were often represented by the figure of Judas. In Latin America, the practice took on a slightly different twist. In addition to venting their anger at Judas, many Latin Americans express their anger at unpopular or corrupt leaders by burning their effigies alongside that of Judas, or by making their Judas doll resemble one of these contemporary figures.

Latin America

In Mexico the burning of Judas takes place on **Holy Saturday**. Effigies of Judas and other unpopular public figures hang in plazas and on street corners. Mexican folk tradition calls for stuffing the heads of these dummies, made of straw, paper, and rags, with firecrackers. When the dummies are set ablaze, they burn furiously and their heads burst open, torn apart by exploding firecrackers. Children delight in the noisy, chaotic scene.

In past times Mexican folk artists often attached bags of candy, **bread**, clothes, umbrellas, and even bottles of alcohol to the Judas, so that these would be thrown into the crowd when the dummy exploded. They also crafted Judas dolls to look like unpopular political or religious figures. During times of political unrest this bit of folk protest prompted the government to outlaw the burning of Judas dolls that resembled a particular person or personified a certain social class. Nowadays Mexico City politicians appear to be more concerned about public safety than ridicule. Current citywide regulations prohibit exploding the Judases by means of fireworks.

The Peruvians burn Judas in effigy on **Good Friday**. The doll representing the despised disciple is tossed into the flames along with the effigies of unpopular politicians.

In Venezuela people burn Judas in effigy on the evening of **Easter Sunday**. Townspeople craft their Judas dolls to closely resemble a local or national leader, or any public figure whom they dislike. By doing so they provide themselves an opportunity to criticize this figure publicly, since, whatever its appearance, the effigy will be identified as "Judas." Just as in Mexico, these dolls are stuffed with fireworks. Before burning the effigies the townsfolk parade them through the streets and then display them in the town's plaza, where people may punch, slap, or insult the doll. The gathering crowd enhances their enjoyment of this parade and display by setting off fireworks and opening bottles of liquor saved for the occasion. Then a local person steps forward to read a list of accusations made against Judas and, by extension, against the local figure whom he represents. The citizens who write this list compose it in verse and weave much humor into their complaints. After this recitation someone sets flame to the doll. As the effigy burns, its firecracker-laced limbs explode. Onlookers laugh, cheer, and shout, heaping more abuse on Judas. More drinking and dancing round out the evening's entertainments.

Europe

Researchers believe that the Latin American customs described above have their roots in old Spanish traditions that were imported to the Americas during the colonial era. Judas burning was also practiced in Portugal.

Judas burning occurred in other European countries besides Spain. An old Czech folk tradition called for chasing Judas on Good Friday and burning Judas on Holy Saturday. Those who attended mass on Good Friday ran through the aisles after the service was over, sounding wooden noisemakers to chase away Judas. What's more, groups of boys rambled down streets and byways raising a racket, which in this case served to frighten away evil. On Holy Saturday Czech villagers made a straw-covered wooden cross and set it inside a stack of logs. This straw-and-wood construction represented Judas. After attending the **Easter Vigil**, boys lit lanterns from the **paschal candle** and then ran to set flame to the Judas bonfires. Judas burning and its related noisemaking customs died out among the Czechs in the early twentieth century.

Polish tradition taught that an effigy of Judas should be thrown from a high church steeple on **Spy Wednesday**. Youngsters then dragged the dummy through the streets, beat it with stones, and threw the remains of the doll in a river or pond.

Judas burning also occurred in a few places in England. In Liverpool's South End bands of children still practiced this custom in the late twentieth century. After procuring an old suit of men's clothes they fashioned a Judas dummy and stuck a pole up its back. Then they paraded it about the neighborhood, begging for pennies. After building up their tiny treasury they burned the Judas effigy in the middle of the street. Local policemen often broke up these proceedings as fire hazards.

In some parts of Greece villagers still burn or hang Judas in effigy on Easter Sunday or on Good Friday. A related Greek superstition teaches that when a piece of crockery breaks on Good Friday, every sharp edge cuts Judas. In some villages people purposefully broke pottery on this day in order to punish the treacherous disciple.

Africa

A variation of Judas burning also takes place among certain African Christians. In Nigeria people carry life-sized effigies of Judas through the streets on Good Friday, giving the community an opportunity to jeer at him. After these parades reach their destination someone steps forward to formally denounce Judas' treachery and to flog the effigy for Judas' crime.

See also **Czech Republic, Easter and Holy Week in; England, Easter and Holy Week in; Greece, Easter and Holy Week in; Mexico, Easter and Holy Week in; Poland, Easter and Holy Week in;** and **Spain, Easter and Holy Week in**

Further Reading

Clynes, Tom. *Wild Planet!* Detroit, MI: Gale Research, 1995.

Griffin, Robert H., and Ann H. Shurgin, eds. *The Folklore of World Holidays*. Second edition. Detroit, MI: Gale Research, 1999.

Hole, Christina. *British Folk Customs*. London, England: Hutchinson and Company, 1976.

Web Site

"The Chasing and Burning of Judas," an article about Judas burning in the Czech Republic, written by Petr Chudoba and posted under the "Holidays and Traditions" section on Local Lingo's Czech Republic site: http://www.localingo.com/countries/czech_republic/culture/judas.html

Laetare Sunday

Mid-Lent Sunday, Mothering Sunday, Refreshment Sunday, Rose Sunday, Sunday of the Rose

Roman Catholics and other Christians who follow the church calendar developed in western Europe celebrate the fourth Sunday in **Lent** as Laetare Sunday. In Latin, the official language of the Roman Catholic Church for most of its history, the word *laetare* means "rejoice!" The name Laetare Sunday comes from the words of the opening prayer for the **Sunday** mass (*for more on the Roman Catholic religious service known as the mass, see also* **Eucharist**), "Rejoice ye with Jerusalem."

History

Some writers believe that Laetare Sunday got its start from early Christian customs surrounding Easter **baptisms**. Candidates for baptism, or initiation into the Christian faith, prepared for the event throughout Lent. These preparations included **fasting** and penance, religious devotions designed to stimulate a change in heart and mind, as well as a study of Christian beliefs and practices (*for more on penance, see* **Repentance**). On the Wednesday after the fourth Sunday in Lent, the clergy entrusted the baptismal candidates for the first time with the Apostles' Creed, a summary of basic Christian beliefs. Thus the fourth Sunday in Lent took on a celebratory tone as the church rejoiced in anticipation of the addition of new members to the household of faith.

Even after early Christian baptismal customs were abandoned, the fourth Sunday in Lent continued to provide a small oasis of joy in the somber Lenten season. Priests wore rose-colored robes instead of the sober purple robes required throughout Lent. Organ music and flower decorations, forbidden during the rest of Lent, reappeared briefly on Laetare Sunday. In addition, in the Middle Ages a custom developed whereby the pope left morning mass on Laetare Sunday carrying a **golden rose** in his hand. The rose served as a symbol of joy, and later became a token of esteem that the pope bestowed upon cities, shrines, churches, and individuals. This led some Germans to call Laetare Sunday *Rosensonntag*, "Sunday of the Rose" or "Rose Sunday."

Roman Catholic officials reasoned that the customs associated with Laetare Sunday offered a brief respite from the solemn mood of the Lenten season. They hoped that this spot of refreshment would renew the weary and inspire them to persevere in their Lenten devotions. Orthodox, or Eastern, Christians also observe special mid-Lent customs that inspire the faithful to continue their Lenten disciplines (*see also* **Sunday of the Veneration of the Holy Cross**).

The Bible readings traditionally assigned to Laetare Sunday in the Roman Catholic Church frequently refer to Jerusalem. Researchers believe that early Catholic authorities assigned these readings for the day because the pope celebrated Laetare Sunday mass at a church in Rome known as the Church of the Holy Cross in Jerusalem (*see also* **Tree of the Cross**).

Mothering Sunday

By the seventeenth century people in some regions of England began to observe the fourth Sunday in Lent as "Mothering Sunday." Researchers have suggested several different origins for this holiday. One line of argument asserts that the observance began in the Middle Ages. On the fourth Sunday in Lent, or Mid-Lent Sunday, people customarily returned to the church in which they had been baptized and instructed as a child. These visits to one's "mother church" suggested the name "Mothering Sunday." According to custom, people brought gifts to put on the altar. They also visited their own mothers and brought them gifts as well. In time the church-related customs faded while the traditions linking the day with home and mother thrived.

Other scholars find scant historical evidence for the church visits and suggest instead that visits to one's home and mother characterized this observance from the start. In a poem entitled "Ceremony in Glocester" (1648), English poet-priest Robert Herrick (1591-1674) penned several lines of verse to describe the Mothering Sunday customs of his day:

> I'll to thee a simnell bring,
> 'Gainst thou go'st a-mothering,
> So that when she blesseth thee,
> Half that blessing thou'lt give to me. (Weiser, 1954: 73)

These folk customs may ultimately have been inspired by Laetare Sunday church services. At least one writer has suggested that one of the Bible readings previously assigned to the fourth Sunday in Lent in the Anglican Book of Common Prayer reminded the English to honor their mothers or their "mother church" on this day. This reading refers to Jerusalem as "the mother of us all" (Galatians 4:22-31).

Mothering Sunday declined in the early twentieth century. Live-in apprenticeships and domestic service jobs, both of which gave rise to situations in which large numbers of young people lived away from home, dwindled in this era, reducing the need for these home visits.

During World War II American soldiers stationed in England introduced their own Mother's Day customs. This cross-fertilization sparked a renewal of old, English Mothering Day practices.

Traditional Mothering Sunday gifts include flowers, a rich kind of plum cake known as simnel cake, and relieving one's mother of tiresome household chores for the day. The flower most closely associated with Mothering Sunday is the violet. In fact, an old English saying assures us that "he who goes a'mothering finds violets in the lane."

German Folk Customs

In Bavaria and other parts of Germany, mock battles between a youth representing winter and another representing summer take place on Laetare Sunday. In north Baden and south Hesse people celebrate the death of winter with children's parades. The children carry sticks decorated with violets, eggshells, and **pretzels**. Ceremonies symbolizing the "carrying away of death" are often part of these celebrations. This association between winter and death led people from these regions of Germany to call the day "Black Sunday" or "Death Sunday." Many considered it unlucky to have a child baptized on this day.

Old folk traditions such as these dramatize people's awareness of the shifting seasons. In fact, Laetare Sunday often falls around the date of the **spring equinox**, the twenty-four-hour period in which night and day are of equal length. Thus Laetare Sunday may be thought of as representing the time of year when summer, the season of light and warmth, defeats winter, the season of cold and dark.

Fountain Sunday

In Italy and France people called the fourth Sunday in Lent "Fountain Sunday." This name sprang from the folk custom of decorating wells and fountains with flowers and branches on this day, as a way of celebrating the defeat of winter and welcoming spring. Similar customs were practiced in many parts of central and southern Europe.

Refreshment Sunday

Laetare Sunday is also known as "Refreshment Sunday." Some hold that the name "Refreshment Sunday" came from the Gospel reading (a selection from the Christian Bible describing the life and teachings of Christ) traditionally assigned to that day in the Roman Catholic and Episcopal churches. It tells how Jesus worked a miracle to provide food for thousands of people who had followed him into the countryside to hear him teach (John 6:1-14). The Roman Catholic Church changed the readings assigned for this day in 1969.

Further Reading

Brewster, H. Pomeroy. *Saints and Festivals of the Christian Church*. 1904. Reprint. Detroit, MI: Omnigraphics, 1990.

Cowie, L. W., and John Selwyn Gummer. *The Christian Calendar*. Springfield, MA: G. and C. Merriam, 1974.

Hutton, Ronald. *Stations of the Sun*. Oxford, England: Oxford University Press, 1996.

"Laetare Sunday." In E. A. Livingstone, ed. *The Oxford Dictionary of the Christian Church*. Third edition. Oxford, England: Oxford University Press, 1997.

Urlin, Ethel. *Festivals, Holy Days, and Saints' Days*. 1915. Reprint. Detroit, MI: Omnigraphics, 1992.

Weiser, Francis X. *The Easter Book*. New York: Harcourt, Brace and Company, 1954.

———. *Handbook of Christian Feasts and Customs*. New York: Harcourt, Brace and World, 1952.

Web Site

"Frühling-Spring," an introduction to German folk customs associated with springtime. Posted by the German Embassy in Ottawa, Canada: http://www.germanembassyottawa.org/easter/index.html

Lamb

Contemporary American Easter decorations feature baby animals of all kinds, including lambs. These images remind us that Easter falls in the spring, a time when many animals give birth to their young. As an Easter symbol, however, the lamb signifies much more than springtime. Rather, it is an ancient symbol of **Jesus**, particularly his death and **resurrection**, whose roots date back hundreds of years before the start of the Christian religion.

Shepherds and Sheep in Jewish and Christian Religious Imagery

Early Christian artwork and texts depict Jesus both as a shepherd and as a lamb. Long before that time, though, the Jewish people spoke of God as a kind shepherd who protected and led his people. The famous opening lines of the twenty-third psalm make this connection clearly:

> The Lord is my shepherd, I shall not want;
> He makes me lie down in green pastures.
> He leads me beside still waters;
> He restores my soul.

In Christian scripture Jesus himself announces, "I am the good shepherd" (John 10:14). In these writings both faithful Jews and Christians are cast in the role of sheep. Today many people might find this imagery unflattering, since sheep seem to be stupid, passive creatures. In biblical times, however, people viewed sheep as highly valuable and beautiful. Various Bible stories associate lambs in particular with the qualities of gentleness, dependence, and innocence.

Jesus as the Sacrificial Lamb

Many phrases from Christian scripture describe Jesus as a lamb. The early Christians borrowed this image from the Jewish **Passover** festival. According to Christian scripture Jesus' death and resurrection took place during Passover, a holiday requiring faithful Jews to sacrifice a lamb to God and eat it during the Passover supper. The lamb recalled the original offering their ancestors made while slaves in Egypt, sacrificing a lamb to God and smearing its **blood** over their doorways as a sign of their faithfulness to the Lord. Afterwards they consumed the sanctified flesh of the lamb. The yearly Passover festival originated in biblical times as a means for Jews to express their gratitude to God for leading their ancestors out of slavery in Egypt over a thousand years before Christ was born. Through participation in the religious ceremonies associated with Passover Jews also reaffirmed their relationship with God. In Jesus' time religious custom required faithful Jews to bring a lamb to the Temple in Jerusalem where it was slain and the animals' blood sprinkled on the altar as an offering to God. Then worshipers took the sacrificial lamb home, where it was roasted and eaten by a gathering of family and friends.

Early Christians found the timing of Jesus' death and resurrection very significant. They began to think of Jesus as a kind of new sacrificial lamb, one whose voluntary suffering and death on the **cross** washed away their **sins** and led them from a kind of spiritual slavery towards a new relationship with God (*see also* **Redemption; Salvation**). Paul makes this comparison openly, declaring that "Christ our Passover lamb has been sacrificed" (1 Corinthians 5:7). The Gospel according to John also makes explicit references to Jesus as a Passover sacrifice. Early in this account of Jesus' life, John the Baptist recognizes Jesus as "the Lamb of God" (John 1:29). John's account of Jesus' death also makes it clear that the Roman soldiers presiding at the Crucifixion refrained from breaking Jesus' legs (John 19:32-33). This echoes the requirement found in Jewish scripture that the Passover lamb be roasted and eaten without breaking any of its bones.

Jesus' followers readily adopted this symbol, representing Jesus as a lamb in a variety of artwork. Many of these images refer explicitly to Jesus' death and resurrection. One standard image, known as the "Lamb of the Crucifixion" depicts a lamb carrying a cross on its back and bleeding from its chest into a chalice (*see also* **Eucharist; Holy Grail**). The "Lamb of the Resurrection" carries a triumphant banner with a large cross on it. In other images the lamb is used as a symbol of Jesus without any direct reference to the events commemorated at Easter. For example, the "Apocalyptic Lamb" shows a lamb carrying

the Book Sealed with Seven Seals and represents Christ as judge at the world's end. Another standard image depicts a lamb with a nimbus, or halo, behind its head standing on a hill from which flow four rivers. The lamb represents Christ, the hill the Church, and the four rivers the four Gospels or the four rivers of paradise. Artwork from the Roman catacombs, underground vaults where the early Christians buried their dead, offers other images of Jesus as a lamb. These images depict the lamb working the miracles performed by Jesus, according to Christian scripture, such as raising Lazarus from the dead (John 11:43-44) and feeding the five thousand (Matthew 14:21, Mark 6:44, Luke 9:14, John 6:10).

Lambs in European Folklore and Tradition

Traditional European folklore presented the lamb as a symbol of various human qualities and characteristics, especially purity and innocence. In the Middle Ages, paintings of St. Agnes (d. 304) often depicted her with a lamb. The lamb represented the saint's innocence, sweetness, patience, mercy, and humility.

Old folk beliefs and superstitions elaborated on the theme of the good lamb. According to some of these traditional beliefs, lambs and doves were the only two animals that the devil could not enter and use for his purposes. Some said that to see a lamb on Easter day brought good luck. Following this line of thought the Finns created small lamb-shaped ornaments to use as good luck charms. In England an old folk belief declared that the Lamb of the Resurrection appeared briefly in the center of the sun as it rose on Easter morning (*see also* **Easter Sun**). Some people therefore made it a practice to rise before dawn on Easter morning and to hike to the top of a hill in the hopes of glimpsing this miracle.

In many countries, such as those of eastern and southern Europe, lamb serves as the traditional main course of the Easter meal. Throughout Europe, candies and condiments, such as butter, may also be presented in the shape of a lamb at Easter. Central Europeans often serve a cake baked in the shape of a lamb at Easter time. The cooled cakes are frosted or dusted with confectioner's sugar and then often ornamented with a **bell** and ribbon round the lamb's neck as well as a religious banner. For the peoples of the Mediterranean, serving lamb at Easter time not only fulfills a symbolic role, but also a practical one. The often-rocky hills of the lands surrounding the Mediterranean Sea make perfect grazing grounds for sheep. The seasonal availability of lamb may also have supported its role as a traditional Easter food. Left to their own devices, sheep tend to be seasonal breeders. So in the days before modern animal husbandry techniques made lamb available year round, spring was the only time of the year during which people could enjoy fresh lamb.

Further Reading

Barth, Edna. *Lilies, Rabbits, and Painted Eggs*. New York: Houghton Mifflin/ Clarion Books, 1970.

Hudgins, Sharon. "A Special Flock." *The World and I* 16, 4 (April 2000): 134.

"Lamb." In Leland Ryken, James C. Wilhoit, and Tremper Longman III, eds. *Dictionary of Biblical Imagery*. Downers Grove, IL: InterVarsity Press, 1998.

Lord, Priscilla Sawyer, and Daniel J. Foley. *Easter Garland*. 1963. Reprint. Detroit, MI: Omnigraphics, 1999.

Møller-Christensen, V., and K. E. Jordt Jørgensen. *Encyclopedia of Bible Creatures*. Philadelphia, PA: Fortress Press, 1965.

Peifer, C. J. "Passover Lamb." In *New Catholic Encyclopedia*. Volume 10. New York: McGraw-Hill, 1967.

Rowland, Beryl. *Animals with Human Faces*. Knoxville, TN: University of Tennessee Press, 1973.

Weiser, Francis X. *The Easter Book*. New York: Harcourt, Brace and Company, 1954.

Last Supper

See **Maundy Thursday**

Laughter

Laughter may seem an inappropriate Easter symbol and custom to contemporary Christians. Yet up until the eighteenth century churches throughout central Europe rang with laughter on **Easter Sunday**. In order to evoke this mirth clergymen preached humorous sermons, told funny stories, or recited amusing poems. These jolly *Ostermärlein*, or Easter fables, contained moral teachings as well. The resulting laughter dispelled the somber mood which had prevailed throughout **Lent** and ushered in the joyful season of Easter. The hilarity also celebrated Christ's defeat of the devil and his victory over death.

The practice of eliciting Easter laughter began during the Middle Ages, reaching the height of its popularity between the fourteenth and the eighteenth centuries. The custom became so popular that printers issued several compilations of Easter fables during that era. In the seventeenth and eighteenth centuries, however, religious reformers began to criticize the practice. Eventually their viewpoint prevailed and people began to view Easter fables and Easter laughter as inappropriate and irreverent. The custom of celebrating Easter with laughter finally died out sometime between the late eighteenth and nineteenth centuries.

Further Reading

Russ, Jennifer M. *German Festivals and Customs*. London, England: Oswald Wolff, 1982.

Weiser, Francis X. *The Easter Book*. New York: Harcourt, Brace and Company, 1954.

Lazarus Saturday

Orthodox Christians celebrate Lazarus Saturday on the second Saturday before Easter. This observance commemorates Jesus' raising of Lazarus from the dead (John 11:1-44). According to the Bible this incident took place just before Jesus arrived in Jerusalem to celebrate **Passover**. Christians celebrate Jesus' entrance to Jerusalem on **Palm Sunday**, which falls on the **Sunday** before Easter. Orthodox Christians observe Lazarus Saturday on the day before Palm Sunday.

Orthodoxy is one of the three main branches of the Christian faith. Orthodox Christianity developed in eastern Europe, the Middle East, and north Africa. It split away from Western Christianity, which later divided into Roman Catholicism and Protestantism, about 1,000 years ago. Orthodox and other Eastern Christians follow a slightly different schedule of religious observances than do Western Christians. In addition, they maintain their own distinctive calendar system which causes their **Lent** and **Easter season** observances to fall on different dates than those celebrated by Western Christians.

History

Historical evidence suggests that devotion to Lazarus was common among the early Christians. Among Eastern Christians this devotion took the form of a festival celebrating his return from death. The observance of Lazarus Saturday can be traced back to ancient times. In the late fourth century a woman named Egeria journeyed to the Holy Land from western Europe. She kept a diary of her pilgrimage in which she recorded how Jerusalem Christians observed Lent and Holy Week. According to Egeria, Christians in Jerusalem celebrated the raising of Lazarus on the Saturday before Palm Sunday by walking in procession to the town of Bethany, where Lazarus had lived and died. There they visited the church that had been built over Lazarus' tomb.

343

Some scholars suspect that the earliest celebrations of Lazarus Saturday took place in the Christian communities of Constantinople, Turkey (modern-day Istanbul) and Alexandria, Egypt. They suggest that when Christians from these cities made pilgrimages to the Holy Land, they introduced these observances to the Jerusalem community, which later adopted them.

Religious Observance

Today Eastern Christians still observe Lazarus Saturday on the day before Palm Sunday. Orthodox church services held on that day retell the story of his coming back to life at Jesus' command. Some people refer to this miracle as the "first Easter." Indeed, Lazarus' raising provides Jesus' followers with a preview of the kind of miracle that will occur the following week on **Easter Sunday** (*see also* **Resurrection**).

Greek Folk Customs

In Greece, a country in which most people are Orthodox Christians, children celebrate Lazarus Saturday by singing folk songs about Lazarus from door to door. Called *lazarakia*, these songs describe the miracle of his rising from the dead. Sometimes the children carry props said to represent Lazarus, such as a picture, doll, or even a staff or rod covered with flowers, ribbons, and cloth. On the island of Crete children display a more abstract emblem representing Lazarus, a **cross** made of reeds and decorated with lemon blossoms and pretty red flowers. In central Greece girls usually take responsibility for banding together to sing lazarakia. On the island of Cyprus boys do, often acting out the story told in the song. One child, draped with garlands of yellow flowers, lies down and pretends to be Lazarus. When the others call, "Lazarus, come out!" he jumps up from the ground. Songsters refresh themselves with special buns known as *lazari*. Some bakers form the buns by twisting lumps of dough, as if to represent a man twisted up in a sheet. Others form it into a long thin roll, cross the ends, and decorate the resulting loop with a cross made out of currants, a raisin-like dried fruit. According to Greek folklore, a child who rolls one of these buns down a hill stands a good chance of finding a bird's nest where it comes to rest.

Eastern European and Middle Eastern Customs

Other eastern European nations share similar customs. In past times little Bulgarian girls decked themselves in bridal finery and went door to door singing songs about Lazarus. Householders gave them eggs or small coins in return. On the following day, Palm Sunday, slightly older girls continued the door-to-door serenades with songs that wished health, good fortune, romance, or happy marriages to the occupants. Another old Bulgarian custom taught boys and girls to reenact the Bible story concerning Lazarus' death. The boys, pretending to be Lazarus, feign death. The girls, acting as his sisters Mary and Martha, go from house to house asking, "When is the Lord coming to raise our brother from the dead?" Neighbors gave the children coins and cookies in exchange for this presentation.

In Romania folk tradition also encouraged little girls to dress in bridal clothes and go door to door singing songs about Lazarus and his sisters, Mary and Martha. Romanians call these girls *lazarines*. Similar customs prevailed in the former Yugoslavia, where small bands of children trouped from door to door singing songs about the miracle of Lazarus' rising from the dead. Adults rewarded them with fruit or candy. In Christian communities in the Middle Eastern nation of Syria, an old custom encouraged local school teachers to lead bands of students through the neighborhood chanting the story of Lazarus' rising from the dead. Householders presented the students with eggs or coins.

In some eastern European countries children gather pussy willow branches on Lazarus Saturday. The branches are blessed in church services that evening for use on the following day, Palm Sunday. In Russia parishioners took the blessed branches home with them and placed them next to their icons, religious images used in prayer and worship. Old Russian folklore recommended that parents switch their children with the willow wands, in order that they grow up "tall like the willow, healthy like water, and rich like the soil."

Further Reading

Bradshaw, Paul F. *The Search for the Origins of Christian Worship*. New York: Oxford University Press, 1992.

Griffin, Robert H., and Ann H. Shurgin, eds. *The Folklore of World Holidays.* Second edition. Detroit, MI: Gale Research, 1999.

Henderson, Helene, and Sue Ellen Thompson, eds. *Holidays, Festivals, and Celebrations of the World Dictionary.* Second edition. Detroit, MI: Omnigraphics, 1997.

Hopko, Thomas. *The Orthodox Faith. Volume Two, Worship.* Syosset, NY: The Orthodox Church in America, 1972.

"Lazarus." In E. A. Livingstone, ed. *The Oxford Dictionary of the Christian Church.* Third edition. Oxford, England: Oxford University Press, 1997.

Rouvelas, Marilyn. *A Guide to Greek Traditions and Customs in America.* Bethesda, MD: Nea Attiki Press, 1993.

Spicer, Dorothy Gladys. *Book of Festivals.* 1937. Reprint. Detroit, MI: Omnigraphics, 1990.

Lent

Great Lent

Many Christians observe an approximately forty-day period of preparation for Easter known as Lent. The call to **repentance**, that is, to a change of heart and mind that inspires one to live out God's teachings, echoes through this season of the church year. In response, Christians who observe Lent seek spiritual renewal through a variety of activities, including prayer and meditation, **fasting**, study, self-examination, and charitable works. The liturgical color for Lent is purple, which signifies humility and repentance.

For Western Christians, that is, Roman Catholics and Protestants, Lent begins on **Ash Wednesday**, forty-six days before Easter, and continues through **Holy Saturday**.

For Orthodox and other Eastern Christians, Lent begins on the evening of the seventh **Sunday** before Easter (*see also* **Forgiveness Sunday; Clean Monday**). Orthodoxy is one of the three main branches of the Christian faith. Orthodox Christianity developed in eastern Europe and the countries surrounding the eastern half of the Mediterranean Sea. Orthodox Christians follow a different church calendar than that commonly adhered to by Roman Catholics and Protestants (*see also* **Easter, Date of**).

Origins

Scholars agree that Lent came into being by the fourth century, but have yet to reach a consensus on its roots. Some of them argue that Lent grew out of what was originally a short fast in preparation for Easter. This fast may also have commemorated the sad events of **Good Friday**, the day on which **Jesus** was crucified, and Holy Saturday, the day on which he lay dead in the tomb. Fragments of the writings of early Christian leaders confirm the existence of these short fasts. Writing about Easter preparations in the year 190 A.D. a Christian leader named Irenaeus declared that "some think they ought to fast for one day, others for two days, and others even for several, while others reckon forty hours both of day and night to their fast." Not long afterward the Christian writer Tertullian compared the forty-hour fast taking place on Good Friday and Holy Saturday unfavorably with the longer fast observed by the Christian sect to which he belonged. Dionysius the Great, bishop of Alexandria (d. 264) recorded the fact that in his diocese some Christians did not observe a fast, and yet others fasted two, three, four, or six days in advance of Easter.

Many scholars interpret these early fasts as the beginnings of **Holy Week**, but do not believe that these pre-Easter observances expanded into the season we now call Lent. Instead they argue that early Christian customs surrounding **baptism** formed the backbone of the Lenten season.

The New Testament gives few clues as to the nature of the very first Christian baptisms, but seems to suggest that as soon as interested newcomers accepted the gospel of Christ they were baptized (Acts 8:35-39, 16:30-33). By the second century, however, documents produced by Christian writers tell of a period of preparation for baptism that included prayer, fasting, and religious instruction. Historical evidence shows that early Christian communities practiced baptism at different times of the year. By the third century, a decided preference to baptize at Easter emerged in a number of these scattered communities. By the fourth century, especially after the Council of Nicaea, an important meeting of early Christian leaders that took place in 325 A.D., Easter baptism became standard practice. This meant that the period of prayer, fasting, and religious instruction in preparation for baptism took place in the weeks preceding Easter.

Some scholars reason that as time went on people began to associate the devotions practiced by the baptismal candidates, or catechumens, with a preparation for Easter itself. This process may have been aided by the fact that baptizers and other community leaders were expected to set a good example by fasting along with the catechumens. In addition, beginning in the fourth century Christian leaders began to draw stronger parallels in their writings and teachings between baptism and the death and **resurrection** of Christ commemorated at Easter time. Drawing on images from Christian scripture they began to interpret baptism as a form of spiritual death and resurrection (Romans 6:1-11, Colossians 2:12). The closer the connection forged between baptism and Easter, the more logical it became for already-baptized Christians to prepare for Easter in much the same way that catechumens prepared for baptism.

Scholars still debate how Lent came to last forty days. One theory traces the origins of the forty-day fast to the early Christian community of Alexandria, Egypt. There, and possibly in other Christian communities, people practiced a forty-day fast following the feast of Epiphany, which falls on January 6. Among Eastern Christians, Epiphany commemorates Jesus' baptism in the river Jordan. According to the Bible, Jesus fasted for forty days in the desert following his baptism. After returning from the desert he launched his ministry (Matthew 4:1-11, Mark 1:12-13, Luke 4:1-13). The early Alexandrian Christians commemorated Jesus' ordeal with a forty-day fast beginning on the day after Epiphany. Catechumens were baptized at the end of this fast.

Some scholars believe that the forty-day fast practiced by the Alexandrian community may have inspired Christian leaders from other communities to adopt a forty-day fast as a preparation for baptism.

Nevertheless, Christian leaders outside the Alexandrian community shifted the fast to the forty days preceding Easter, thereby upholding an emerging preference for Easter baptism. In fact, the forty-day Lenten fast preceding Easter became commonplace by the fourth century. After that time Christian leaders drew more frequent parallels between the goals and meaning of the Lenten fast and Jesus' fast in the desert, as well as the forty-day trials endured by other important biblical figures, including Noah, Moses, and Elijah (Genesis 7:17, Exodus 34:28, 1 Kings 19:8).

Words for Lent

The first word used to describe this new season of the Christian year was the Greek word *tessarakoste*, meaning "fortieth." Christian leaders in western Europe adopted its Latin equivalent, *quadragesima*. In western Europe, the word quadragesima soon attached itself to the sixth Sunday before Easter, approximately the fortieth day before Easter, when western European Christians began the Lenten fast (*see also* **Pre-Lent**). This day became known as Quadragesima Sunday. The word for Lent in many European languages evolved from this old, Latin root word. For example, the Spanish word for Lent is *cuaresma*, the Italian *quaresima*, and the French *carême*. The English word "Lent" traces its roots back to another word altogether. It comes from the Anglo-Saxon term *lencten*, meaning "springtime." The word lencten itself may have come from an old Germanic root word meaning "long," a reference to the fact that the days lengthen in the spring.

Lent in the Early Middle Ages

Nearly as soon as the new Lenten season took shape, it began to change. By the fifth and sixth centuries, the rise in the number of infant baptisms diminished the importance of Lent as a season of study, prayer, and fasting in preparation for adult initiation into the Christian faith. In addition, the sheer number of new baptisms wore away at the custom of the Easter or **Pentecost** baptismal ceremony presided over by the bishop. In this way the strong links once forged between Easter and baptism slowly began to dissolve.

Instead, the devotions once practiced by aspiring Christians in preparation for baptism came to be seen as preparations that all Christians should make for Easter. One of the most important of these devotional practices was fasting. In the early days Christian communities showed little concern for the exact number of fast days contained in the six-week Lenten season. As fasting became a more important component of Lenten devotions, however, critics began to charge that beginning the fast on Quadragesima Sunday shortchanged the Lenten season. Even though Quadragesima Sunday falls forty-two days before Easter, Sundays did not count as true days of fast and penitence since they commemorate the resurrection of Christ. This left the season of Lent with only thirty-six days. Sometime during the seventh and eighth centuries Christian leaders across western Europe started to add four more days to the fast. This meant that Western Christians began Lent on the Wednesday following the seventh Sunday before Easter, a day which became known as Ash Wednesday.

In the early Middle Ages Lent increasingly came to be viewed as a season of repentance. The medieval view of repentance emphasized the admission of **sin**, the expression of sorrow, and the acceptance of punishment. Scholars speculate that during the early medieval era Lent served as a time during which those Christians who admitted to serious wrongdoing were publicly disciplined and reincorporated into the community. On the first day of Lent they confessed their sins before the entire congregation and expressed grief for their failings. Afterwards the priest sprinkled their heads with ashes and gave them a garment made of sackcloth, a rough kind of fabric, to wear. Thus attired they departed to complete the penance assigned to them. These penances might include prayer, charitable works, and manual labor. They might also include physical hardships, like sleeping on the ground and going barefoot throughout Lent. Penitents were also forbidden to cut their hair, bathe, and speak with others during Lent. For this reason they often served out this time in an isolated place, like a monastery. They returned to church again on **Maundy Thursday** to participate in a ceremony of reconciliation and to take the **Eucharist** again for the first time since the start of Lent. Because a person's spiritual errors were often thought to stain his or her relatives, entire families might undergo this process of atonement together (*see also* **Redemption**).

Some writers believe that the forty-day period of penance and isolation enforced on Lenten penitents may have indirectly inspired the medical practice called "quarantine," a period of mandatory isolation for the purposes of containing disease. Medical quarantines were invented in fourteenth-century Venice. Ships suspected of harboring disease were isolated for forty days before they were permitted to dock and unload. This practice was called *quarantina*, from the Italian word for forty, *quaranta*. The word "quarantine" has also been used by the Roman Catholic Church to refer to a forty-day period of penance.

Between the eighth and tenth centuries public confessions of the kind described above declined in popularity. Instead, people began to confess their sins privately to a priest. The several days preceding Lent became a popular time to complete this duty (*see also* **Shrovetide**). Lent itself provided a season in which to carry out the prescribed penance. In 1091 the Council of Benevento, a meeting of Church leaders, ordered that each and every Christian receive ashes at the start of Lent. This ritual, performed on Ash Wednesday, acknowledged that all human beings were sinners and ushered in Lent as a season of general repentance.

Fasting

Fasting, the oldest and most widespread Lenten custom, was practiced in an especially severe manner during the early Middle Ages, by both Western and Eastern Christians. Those following the fast ate only one meal a day sometime in the late afternoon. The meal contained no meat, fish, eggs, or dairy products. Even on Sundays meat was still forbidden. Beginning in the ninth century, however, Western Christians gradually began to loosen the strict requirements of the fast. The restriction against eating fish was lifted, and by the thirteenth century a light evening meal was permitted. By the fifteenth century even religious communities had moved the one daily meal closer to noon. Over time the prohibition against dairy products was abandoned. In the last several centuries the requirements of the Len-

351

ten fast have changed drastically for Roman Catholics. Meat became acceptable for the main Sunday meal, and then acceptable even for weekday meals, excluding Fridays. In 1966 Pope Paul VI almost completely eliminated fasting during Lent, retaining the custom only on Ash Wednesday and Good Friday, when meat is forbidden and only one full meal and two light meals should be taken. Observant Roman Catholics also abstain from eating meat on the Fridays of Lent.

The Orthodox Church, on the other hand, has maintained the rigorous fasting practices it inherited from medieval times. Strictly observant Orthodox Christians will abstain from eating meat, fish, dairy products, eggs, olive oil, **wine** and other alcoholic beverages for the duration of Lent. Other Orthodox Christians modify the official regime to suit their abilities and needs. Traditional Orthodox teachings, however, emphasize that Lent should be approached with joy rather than sorrow. Orthodoxy maintains that the repentance that God desires is not so much our grief over past sins, but rather our purification and renewed devotion, which fasting helps to bring about.

Orthodox Great Lent lasts slightly longer than Western Lent. It begins on the evening of the seventh Sunday preceding Easter, called Forgiveness Sunday. The first full day of Great Lent falls on the following day, Clean Monday. Many writers assert that in early medieval times, Eastern Christians fasted neither on Sundays nor on Saturdays, except on Holy Saturday. Thus Orthodox Christians began their Lent somewhat earlier than did Western Christians, in order to fill the tally of forty days. Contemporary Orthodox Christians maintain their fast throughout Lent, though fish may be eaten on the Feast of the **Annunciation** and, according to some, on **Palm Sunday**. Some Orthodox Christian authorities also permit a slight relaxation of the fast on Saturdays and Sundays, by permitting the consumption of wine and olive oil. In addition Orthodox Christians practice a kind of eucharistic fasting during the weekdays of Lent, celebrating the Divine Liturgy (*see also* Eucharist) only on Saturdays, Sundays, and the Feast of the Annunciation. Today the Orthodox fast begins a week before the official beginning of Orthodox Lent, with the removal of meat products from the diet (*see also* **Cheese Week**; Pre-Lent). Since the Orthodox

352

use a different set of rules to calculate the date of Easter, the Western and Eastern Lent periods usually fall during a different, but overlapping, series of weeks in the spring (*see also* **Easter, Date of**).

Orthodox Christians refer to the pre-Easter Lenten period as "Great Lent" in order to distinguish it from other lengthy fasts that occur during the church year. For example, very observant Orthodox Christians will also fast in the weeks preceding Christmas, an observance which is sometimes called "Little Lent" or "Christmas Lent."

Contemporary Observance

In recent decades Western Christians have placed less emphasis on fasting and traditional forms of penance, and more emphasis on study, prayer, worship, almsgiving, and other activities that foster spiritual renewal. Still, many Western Christians continue to view Lent as a time to practice self-discipline and austerity. The purpose of this austerity is to remove distractions that might prevent the faithful from focusing on the reality of their own shortcomings. Fasting and other kinds of self-discipline, themselves a form of austerity, are thought to strengthen the will and thereby increase one's ability to refrain from sin as well as one's inclination to devote oneself more fully to God. In many churches Lenten décor and music express the season's austerity. In some churches the organ is silent throughout Lent, no flowers are used in decorations, and the joyous exclamation **alleluia** is neither said nor sung. In some places the clergy **veils** religious images during the last days of Lent, thereby enforcing a kind of visual austerity. Although the Roman Catholic Church no longer requires Catholics to abstain from certain foods throughout the Lenten season, many still choose to give up a favorite food for Lent as a minor form of self-discipline. Some Anglicans and other Protestants also follow this custom.

In the Western Christian tradition the Lenten season is comprised of two distinct phases. The first five weeks call Christians to repentance. The last week, called Holy Week, focuses worshipers' attention on the events which took place in the last days of Jesus' life as a final preparation for Easter.

For more on Lenten practices, customs, and symbols, *see also* Ash Wednesday; **Descent into Hell**; **Fire Sunday**; **Golden Rose**; Good Friday; Holy Saturday; **Holy Sepulchre**; Holy Week; **Laetare Sunday**; **Lazarus Saturday**; Maundy Thursday; **Palm**; Palm Sunday; **Penitentes**; Pre-Lent; **Soul Saturdays**; **Spy Wednesday**; **Stations of the Cross**; **Sunday of the Veneration of the Holy Cross**; **Tenebrae**; and **Triduum**

Further Reading

Cowie, L. W., and John Selwyn Gummer. *The Christian Calendar*. Springfield, MA: G. and C. Merriam, 1974.

Garrett, Linda Oaks. "Repentance." In David Noel Freedman, ed. *Eerdmans Dictionary of the Bible*. Grand Rapids, MI: William B. Eerdmans Publishing, 2000.

Hopko, Thomas. *The Orthodox Faith. Volume Two, Worship*. Syosset, NY: The Orthodox Church in America, 1972.

Johnson, Maxwell E. "Preparation for Pascha? Lent in Christian Antiquity." In Paul F. Bradshaw and Lawrence A. Hoffman, eds. *Easter and Passover: The Symbolic Structuring of Sacred Seasons*. Two Liturgical Traditions series, volume 6. Notre Dame, IN: University of Notre Dame Press, 1999.

"Lent." In E. A. Livingstone, ed. *The Oxford Dictionary of the Christian Church*. Third edition. Oxford, England: Oxford University Press, 1997.

Matera, Frank J. "Repentance." In Paul J. Achtemeier, ed. *The HarperCollins Bible Dictionary*. New York: HarperCollins, 1996.

Metford, J. C. J. *The Christian Year*. London, England: Thames and Hudson, 1991.

Myers, Allen C., ed. "Redemption." In *The Eerdmans Bible Dictionary*. Grand Rapids, MI: William B. Eerdmans Publishing, 1987.

O'Shea, W. J. "Lent." In *New Catholic Encyclopedia*. Volume 8. New York: McGraw-Hill, 1967.

"Repentance." In E. A. Livingstone, ed. *The Oxford Dictionary of the Christian Church*. Third edition. Oxford, England: Oxford University Press, 1997.

Simpson, D. P. *Cassell's New Latin Dictionary*. New York: Funk and Wagnalls, 1959.

Skeat, W. W. *An Etymological Dictionary of the English Language*. Fourth edition, revised, enlarged, and reset. Oxford, England: Clarendon Press, 1958.

Slim, Hugo. *A Feast of Festivals*. London, England: Marshall Pickering, 1996.

Talley, Thomas J. *The Origins of the Liturgical Year*. Collegeville, MN: Liturgical Press, 1986.

Thurston, Herbert. "Lent." In Charles G. Herbermann et al., eds. *The Catholic Encyclopedia*. New York: Appleton, 1913. Available online at: http://www.newadvent.org/cathen/09152a.htm

Weiser, Francis X. *The Easter Book*. New York: Harcourt, Brace and Company, 1954.

———. *Handbook of Christian Feasts and Customs*. New York: Harcourt, Brace and World, 1952.

Wybrew, Hugh. *Orthodox Lent, Holy Week and Easter*. Crestwood, NY: St. Vladimir's Seminary Press, 1997.

Web Sites

"Great Lent," a page describing the beliefs and practices of Orthodox Christians concerning Lent, posted by the Orthodox Church in America: http://www.oca.org/pages/orth_chri/orthodox-faith/worship/great-lent.html

"Fasting," an essay by the Rev. George Mastrantonis describing Greek Orthodox fasting customs posted on the Greek Orthodox Archdiocese of America, New York, NY, web site at: http://www.goarch.org/access/orthodoxfaith/lent/fasting.html

"The Great Lent," an essay by the Rev. George Mastrantonis describing the history and customs of Lent in the Greek Orthodox Church, posted on the Greek Orthodox Archdiocese of America, New York, NY, web site at: http://www.goarch.org/access/orthodoxfaith/lent/great_lent.html

Lily

Although it has a long history as a Christian symbol, the lily became an Easter symbol relatively recently. As a Christian symbol the lily represents purity and virtue. Christian artists paired it perhaps most often with **Jesus'** mother, the Blessed Virgin Mary (*see* **Mary, Blessed Virgin**). Before the advent of Christianity the ancient Greeks and Romans associated the flower with the goddesses Hera and Juno.

More than one hundred years ago Americans began to use the lily as an Easter decoration and symbol.

Pagan Folklore

In ancient times the white lily was associated with several mother goddesses, including the Greek goddess, Hera, and her Roman counterpart, Juno. According to Greek mythology Hera, the queen of the gods, fell into many a jealous rage over the escapades of her flirtatious husband, Zeus. One day one of Zeus' human lovers bore him a son named Hercules. Zeus worried that his son's human ancestry might prevent him from inheriting the gift of immortality. He asked Hera to breastfeed the child in the hopes that drinking the milk of a goddess would confer eternal life upon him. The furious goddess refused to help her rival's son. So Zeus tricked Hera into breastfeeding the baby by giving her a powerful sleeping potion. When Hera fell into a deep slumber he brought the baby Hercules to her and let the infant suckle from the sleeping goddess' breast. The babe sucked so greedily that more milk than he could swallow gushed forth. The milk splashed across the heavens, forming a glowing white band stretched across the nighttime skies. The Romans called this celestial phenomenon the *Via Lactea*, which means the "Milky Road." We call it the "Milky Way." Some of the drops of milk fell all the way to earth. Upon hitting the ground they turned into beautiful white lily flowers.

Another version of the tale suggests that the red lily already flourished on the earth when Hercules was born. It claims that as Hera's milk rained down on the earth, each drop that hit a red lily turned it snow white. Yet another Greek legend suggests that jealousy over the beauty of the white lily brought the red lily and orange-colored tiger lily into existence. Hera claimed the white lily as her emblem while Aphrodite, the Greek goddess of love, whose Roman counterpart was called Venus, claimed the rose. The legend states that Aphrodite became jealous of Hera over the beauty and perfection of the lily. Hence she caused a large golden pistil to grow inside the flower to mar its perfect whiteness. The lily blushed with shame over its unseemly appearance, turning from white to orange and then red. This story hints at a certain sexual symbolism sometimes attributed to the lily due to the shape of its pistil. Indeed in Victorian times some people removed the pistils from lilies used in church decoration, for fear that the sight of them might unduly stimulate the congregation.

Christian Folklore

The lily has many meanings and associations in Christian tradition. Throughout the Bible lilies are praised for their beauty. Jesus called attention to the beauty of the lily in one of his parables, teaching his followers to trust that God will clothe them in greater splendor than he has the lilies of the field (Matthew 6:28-30, Luke 12:27-28). In Christian art the lily often stands for purity and virtue. Because she above all other women is thought to possess these qualities, the Virgin Mary is frequently shown with lilies. For example, in many European paintings of the **Annunciation** the angel Gabriel hands Mary a lily. In Semitic folklore the lily recalled Eve, whom the Bible identifies as the first woman God created. An old Semitic tale claimed each tear that Eve shed as she left the Garden of Eden turned into a lily when it hit the ground.

Other saints whose reputation for chastity and goodness earned them the honor of being depicted with the lily include St. Francis of Assisi, St. Anthony of Padua, St. Clare, and St. Dominic. The Virgin Mary's husband, St. Joseph, is often shown with the lily as well, which may represent the notion that he and Mary lived together without ever consummating their marriage. Another tale declares that the lily became associated with St. Joseph because of an incident that occurred at the time of his betrothal. The high priest entrusted with making a suitable match for the virtuous maiden Mary summoned all the men who sought her hand and had them leave their staves overnight in the temple sanctuary. When the high priest went to retrieve them the following morning he found that Joseph's staff had sprouted beautiful white lilies, signifying his worthiness to wed Mary.

Another Christian legend gives the lily a role in the events leading up to Jesus' crucifixion (*for more on crucifixion, see* **Cross**). The main purpose of the tale, however, seems to be explaining why lily flowers droop on the end of their stalks and why red lilies grow in Palestine. The legend claims that as Jesus walked in the Garden of Gethsemane on the night before his death the flowers bowed their heads as he passed by in recognition of his sorrow. The vain lily did not, thinking that the sight of its beauty would comfort him. Jesus paused for a moment to look upon the lovely white lily. When the lily saw the humility in his gaze it was overcome with shame for its own conceit. It blushed a deep shade of orange-red and drooped its head. It has remained that way ever since.

The Easter Lily

The lily family contains thousands of species divided up into about two hundred and fifty different genera. Daffodils, tulips, hyacinths, and amarylli are members of the lily family. In addition to flowers, many common foods belong to the lily family, including onions, garlic, and asparagus.

Images of the Madonna lily have graced hundreds of years of European religious artwork. This beautiful flower blooms in the summer and therefore never became an Easter symbol. The flower that Americans know as the Easter lily is, in fact, a native of Japan. Travelers brought this new species of lily back to England in 1819. In the 1850s commercial cultivation of the exotic new blooms began in the British colony of Bermuda. They soon acquired a variety of names, including trumpet lily, gun lily, blunderbuss lily, and Bermuda lily. Botanists dubbed the new species *Lilium longiflorum*.

In the 1880s an enthusiastic American gardener named Mrs. Thomas P. Sargent discovered these new lilies on a trip to Bermuda. Returning to Philadelphia with lily bulbs, she introduced the plant to American flower fanciers. Churchgoers looking for a fragrant, white flower that could be forced to blossom at Easter time quickly popularized the imported blooms as Easter decorations.

In the early part of the twentieth century America imported most of its lily bulbs from Japan. When World War II cut off this trade route, American flower growers began to cultivate the bulbs themselves. Today most Easter lilies sold in the United States come from bulbs grown on farms in northern California and in Oregon.

The lily's long history as a Christian symbol of purity and goodness and its white color probably figured into its appeal as an Easter symbol. White is the liturgical color of Easter, that is, the color of priests' robes and church decorations at Easter time in those churches that observe these seasonal color changes. In the language of church symbolism white represents joy, glory, light, and purity. Hence the Easter lily's large white flowers can serve as living emblems of these qualities. Flowers themselves function as age-old symbols of springtime, but also as symbols of new life, a principal theme of the Easter festival (*see also* **Resurrection**).

Further Reading

Beals, Katharine M. *Flower Lore and Legend*. 1917. Reprint. Detroit, MI: Gale Research, 1973.

Clement, Clara Erskine. *A Handbook of Christian Symbols*. 1886. Reprint. Detroit, MI: Gale Research, 1971.

Heath, Sidney. *The Romance of Symbolism*. 1909. Reprint. Detroit, MI: Gale Research, 1976.

Lehner, Ernst, and Johanna Lehner. *Folklore and Symbolism of Flowers, Plants and Trees*. 1960. Reprint. Detroit, MI: Omnigraphics, 1990.

Lord, Priscilla Sawyer, and Daniel J. Foley. *Easter Garland*. 1963. Reprint. Detroit, MI: Omnigraphics, 1999.

Metford, J. C. J. *Dictionary of Christian Lore and Legend*. London, England: Thames and Hudson, 1983.

Myers, Robert J. *Celebrations: The Complete Book of American Holidays*. Garden City, NY: Doubleday and Company, 1972.

Low Sunday

Alb Sunday, Antipascha, Dominica in albis, Laud Sunday, Octave of Easter, Quasimodo Sunday, White Sunday

Low Sunday is the **Sunday** after Easter. In early Christian times it marked the end of the ceremonies surrounding Easter **baptisms**. During that era many adult converts to the Christian religion were baptized at the **Easter Vigil** service. After their baptisms the priest or his assistants dressed them in white robes. These robes symbolized their joy and their new membership in the Christian church. In the week following **Easter Sunday** they returned to church daily for further instruction in Christian doctrine and ceremony. They wore their white robes during these church visits. On the Sunday after Easter they appeared in church dressed in their white robes for the last time. After the close of the service they returned the robes and began their roles as ordinary members of the congregation.

As time passed priests baptized more and more people on days other than Easter. Accordingly, the baptismal customs associated with **Easter Week** faded away. They did leave one mark on the holiday, however. In western Europe, the Sunday after Easter was long known as *Dominica in albis*, a Latin phrase meaning "Sunday in albs" or "Alb Sunday." The name calls attention to the albs, or white robes, worn by the newly baptized and is therefore sometimes translated as "White Sunday." This day has also been called "Quasimodo Sunday" after the Latin phrase from the introit, a short prayer assigned to the day's church services. The Latin version of this prayer begins, *Quasi modo geniti*, meaning "As newborn babes," a phrase taken from Christian scripture (1 Peter 2:2). Today most English speakers call the Sunday following Easter Low Sunday. Most scholars believe the name evolved from "Laud Sunday." In Latin *laud* means "praise." It is the first word of a hymn sung before the Gospel reading, a selection from Christian scripture describing the life and teachings of **Jesus**, set for this day. Others suspect that Low Sunday might have developed from "Close Sunday," a name which refers to the close of Easter Week festivities.

Low Sunday serves as the last day of the Easter octave. In the language of the church an octave is an **eight**-day period defined by a festival and the seven days that follow it. Around the year 389 the Roman emperor made it easier for the newly baptized to attend to their religious duties during this week by declaring it a holiday. Indeed, people celebrated Easter Week both as a holiday and a holy time. Many refrained from working and attended church daily during this week. The celebrations following Easter gradually diminished, however. By the late eleventh century Church authorities expected the faithful to attend church only three times during this week. By the turn of the twentieth century only **Easter Monday** remained as a day of obligatory church attendance for Roman Catholics. In 1911 Roman Catholic authorities released the faithful from this last Easter Week obligation.

Many call the week following Easter Sunday "Easter Week." The week has also been called "White Week" in reference to the white garments worn by the newly baptized, or the "Week of New Garments."

361

The Greeks call the week following Easter "Bright Week." They sometimes call the Easter festival itself *Lambri*, meaning "Bright," a name
that evokes the fires and lights associated with the Easter Vigil service (*see also* **Easter Fires**). In Greek Orthodox and other Orthodox
churches the doors to the sanctuary remain open during this week in
honor of the **Resurrection**. Among the Orthodox the Sunday after
Easter is sometimes referred to as *Antipascha*, a name signifying that
the day closes the *Pascha*, or Easter, festival. The Orthodox also call the
day "St. Thomas Sunday," since church services on this day retell the
story of St. Thomas the Apostle's encounter with the risen Christ.

Further Reading

Blackburn, Bonnie, and Leofranc Holford-Strevens. *The Oxford Companion to
the Year*. Oxford, England: Oxford University Press, 1999.

Cowie, L. W., and John Selwyn Gummer. *The Christian Calendar*. Springfield,
MA: G. and C. Merriam, 1974.

Johnson, E. "Easter and Its Cycle." In *New Catholic Encyclopedia*. Volume 5.
New York: McGraw-Hill, 1967.

Metford, J. C. J. *The Christian Year*. London, England: Thames and Hudson,
1991.

Rouvelas, Marilyn. *A Guide to Greek Traditions and Customs in America*. Bethesda, MD: Nea Attiki Press, 1993.

Weiser, Francis X. *The Easter Book*. New York: Harcourt, Brace and Company,
1954.

Web Site

"Post-Easter Sundays," a document describing the beliefs and practices of
Orthodox Christians concerning the Sundays between Easter and Pentecost.
Posted on the Orthodox Church in America web site: http://www.oca.org/
pages/orth_chri/orthodox-faith/worship/post-easter-sundays. html

Marbles

In past times **Ash Wednesday** kicked off the English marbles season. Throughout **Lent** men and boys played competitive marble games with one another. The marbles season ended on **Good Friday**, which was known as Marble Day in Surrey and Sussex, regions where the game was particularly popular. After that time anyone caught playing marbles might be forced to forfeit them. Some researchers believe that the practice of playing marbles on Good Friday may have come from Holland or Belgium. At least one writer suspects that the game of dice that the Roman soldiers played at the foot of the **cross** (Mark 15:24, Luke 23:35, John 19:24) inspired the association between marbles and Good Friday.

The village of Tinsley Green, near Crawley in Sussex, hosts a marbles championship every year on Good Friday. The competition dates back to the year 1600, when, according to legend, a local girl convinced her suitors to compete for her favor by playing a game of marbles. Today the tournament winner is declared the "Champion of Great Britain" and receives a silver cup.

Further Reading

Harrowven, Jean. *Origins of Festivals and Feasts*. London, England: Kaye and Ward, 1980.

Hole, Christina. *British Folk Customs*. London, England: Hutchinson and Company, 1976.

Howard, Alexander. *Endless Cavalcade*. London, England: Arthur Barker, 1964.

Mardi Gras
Carnival, Fat Tuesday

The French call the last day of **Carnival** *Mardi Gras*, which means "Fat Tuesday." This name traveled across the Atlantic Ocean with French settlers and planted itself in the Louisiana Territory, a part of the United States first colonized by the French. Two large coastal cities developed in this region, Mobile, in what was later to become the state of Alabama, and New Orleans, in the state of Louisiana. The United States government purchased the Louisiana Territory in 1803, after which Anglo-American settlers joined the Creoles, colonists of French and Spanish descent who had already made their home there. Large numbers of African-American slaves also lived in New Orleans. These three groups all contributed elements to New Orleans's Mardi Gras festival.

Contemporary Mardi Gras celebrations are characterized by a series of ornate parades, featuring elaborately decorated floats carrying costumed revelers who throw souvenirs to the crowd. In addition, many people wander the streets in costumes ranging from the extremely simple and skimpy to the extremely elaborate. Much of the fun derived by festival-goers consists in just watching the costumed spectators pass by. Finally, some New Orleanians round out their Mardi Gras experience by attending fancy masquerade balls and banquets.

Early Street Masquerades and Costume Balls

The earliest documents to mention Carnival in Louisiana date back to the late eighteenth century. Some commentators point out, however, that Carnival is not routinely mentioned in historical documents until the early nineteenth century. They therefore conclude that New Orleans's Mardi Gras established itself in that era.

Street masquerades and costume balls were the first customs associated with Mardi Gras in New Orleans. A startled visitor recorded his experience of New Orleans's street Carnival in the year 1835:

> Men and boys, women and girls, bond and free, white and black, yellow and brown, exert themselves to invent and appear in grotesque, quizzical, diabolical, horrible, humorous, strange masks and disguises. Human bodies are seen with heads of beasts and birds; snake's heads and bodies with arms of apes; man-bats from the moon; mermaids, satyrs, beggars, monks, and robbers, parade and march on foot, on horseback, in wagons, carts, coaches, cars &c, in rich confusion up and down the street, wildly shouting, singing, laughing, drumming, fiddling, fifing, and all throwing flour broadcast as they went their reckless way. (Gill, 36)

Not everyone came to Mardi Gras simply to put on a costume and have a good time parading through the streets. By the middle of the nineteenth century ruffians and prostitutes used the general mayhem of Mardi Gras to stage various illegal acts. Many law-abiding citizens stayed indoors during Carnival for fear of being assaulted and robbed.

In contrast to the rowdy Carnival of the streets, nineteenth-century New Orleans also hosted plenty of masked balls. These ranged, however, from exclusive high society affairs to dance hall parties that one could attend for the price of an entrance ticket. Historical evidence for the balls of Louisiana's Carnival season dates back to the time of the American Revolution. The season lasted from Epiphany, or Twelfth

Night, which falls about two weeks after Christmas, to Carnival Tuesday. The public balls were often the scenes of coarse behavior and sometimes even violence, and by the middle of the nineteenth century they were discontinued. Private balls remained, however, and were especially popular among the well-to-do. These private balls continue today. The most exclusive affairs are those thrown by the oldest of the Carnival krewes, the social clubs that sponsor the Mardi Gras parades.

Mobile's Carnival and Cowbellion Society

Many Mardi Gras scholars point out that the first Carnival parades in the region were held in Mobile, Alabama, rather than New Orleans, Louisiana. In 1831 a group of intoxicated young men broke into a Mobile hardware store on New Year's eve and, seizing a supply of rakes and cowbells, marched through the city streets raising a racket. When asked who they were and what they were doing, the leader of the group quipped, "We're the Cowbellion de Rakin Society." Oddly enough this custom, which soon became associated with Carnival, may have its roots in old European Christmas customs. The leader of the motley group of paraders on that New Year's eve was himself of German extraction and had been reared in Pennsylvania Dutch country, where noisemaking and masking were customs associated with Christmas and New Year's. In any case, the group repeated its performance the following year, and soon the torchlit spree became a tradition. By the 1840s it had become a parade complete with floats. The tradition gave rise to Mobile's yearly Mardi Gras parades, which, though older than New Orleans's, are not as well known.

The Founding of New Orleans's Carnival Krewes

Around the mid-nineteenth century a group of well-to-do businessmen introduced a new element to New Orleans's Mardi Gras celebrations. The core of this group hailed from Mobile and had been members of the Cowbellion de Rakin Society. In 1857 they formed a secret society called the Mystick Krewe of Comus whose main purpose was to design elaborate Mardi Gras floats and ride them in a parade throughout the city. In doing so they sought to draw attention away from the sleazy aspects of Mardi Gras and to instead add a note of refinement. The Krewe of Comus performed their parade at night-time, their donkey-drawn carts illuminated by dozens of torches carried by African-American men. Members of the Krewe rode atop the floats in costumes, poses, and settings that illustrated their chosen theme. They took their parade themes from classical mythology and literature, and thus tried to set a civilized tone that would distinguish them from the wild revels in the streets. Indeed, the name "Comus" comes from a masque written by the famous English poet John Milton (1608-1674), and the first parade floats created by the Krewe of Comus featured characters from Milton's poem *Paradise Lost* (1674).

In the year 1872 two more krewes appeared on the New Orleans Mardi Gras scene, the Krewe of Rex and the Krewe of Momus. The Krewe of Rex was formed to honor the visit of the Russian grand duke Alexander III (1845-1894), the younger son of Tsar Alexander II. While in New York the Grand Duke had met and fallen in love with actress Lydia Thompson, whose stage show included the song "If I Ever Cease to Love." As the Rex parade passed the viewing stand the bands marching in the parade played "If I Ever Cease to Love" in the Grand Duke's honor. This tune has since established itself as the theme song of New Orleans's Mardi Gras. The Krewe of Rex gave birth to another Mardi Gras tradition that year. The man playing Rex wore a costume made of purple, gold, and green cloth. These became the official colors of Mardi Gras. Purple symbolizes justice, gold power, and green faith.

Throughout most of the nineteenth century New Orleans's Creole citizens did not mingle very easily with the city's Anglo-American population. The Mystick Krewe of Comus was composed primarily of Anglo-Americans. Krewe members adopted the French custom of masking yet they performed it in an orderly and regimented fashion heretofore unknown in New Orleans. Moreover, although they introduced the first Carnival float to New Orleans's Mardi Gras celebrations, they borrowed an established Creole custom in celebrating the success of their parade with a masked ball and banquet. As the krewes began to multiply and grow in popularity Creoles joined them in larg-

367

er numbers, and the two elements of the city's elite began to socialize and do business together.

African-American Celebrations

Right from the start African Americans found themselves excluded from the Carnival krewes. Rather than accept this exclusion from official Carnival celebrations as defeat, they invented their own Mardi Gras traditions. In 1909 a group of black citizens got together and formed the Zulu Social Aid and Pleasure Club (named for a South African tribe), also known as the Krewe of Zulu. The Zulu parades mocked racial stereotypes and poked fun at Rex and the other pompous white krewes. Each year a king presided over Zulu's celebrations. In 1949 Louis Armstrong, the famous jazz trumpeter, himself a native of New Orleans, filled this role.

In addition, some African Americans formed their own loose-knit Carnival associations which bore invented Indian names. These black Indian krewes, or tribes, were unlike their white counterparts in that they were loosely organized under the direction of a big chief, paraded only in their own neighborhoods, and did not follow a set parade route and schedule. Krewe members sewed elaborate feathered and beaded costumes based loosely on the stylized Plains Indians costumes promoted by Buffalo Bill's wild west show. This tradition continues today, though few tourists venture away from the main parade routes to see the brilliant costumes displayed by the Mardi Gras Indians.

Finally, African-American-influenced music, such as jazz and blues, has gained widespread popularity and can be heard all over the city during Mardi Gras.

More New Krewes

Over the years more and more Carnival krewes formed, many also named after gods, goddesses, and other mythological figures. In 1941 the Krewe of Venus, the first all-female Krewe, appeared. In the 1960s and 1970s Mardi Gras began to expand from New Orleans proper into the suburbs. The addition of new krewes, whose membership was open to a wider range of people, helped to democratize the festival. These new krewes ignored some of the old Mardi Gras traditions and began to create their own. For example, the super krewes of Bacchus and Endymion started to hire celebrities to reign as their king or queen. The parades put on by these two extremely large krewes take place on the Saturday and **Sunday** before Mardi Gras. The two super krewes entertain festival-goers with about 75 floats and 60 marching bands.

Today New Orleans and its suburbs boast 57 registered Carnival krewes. Members pay large sums each year to fund their krewe's costumes, floats, throws, ball, and banquet. Indeed, because New Orleans's Mardi Gras is largely paid for by the krewes, it has been called the "greatest free show on earth." The krewes have ensured that the parades, with their elaborate floats and costumes, constitute the highlight of New Orleans's Mardi Gras. Although the Mardi Gras parade season lasts twelve days, the most impressive parades take place on the Saturday, Sunday, Monday, and Tuesday before **Ash Wednesday**.

Krewe Cuts

The old krewes founded in the nineteenth century established a tradition of social exclusivity, drawing their members by invitation only from among families known to them and from a narrow range of ethnic, economic, and religious groups. They excluded blacks and Jews entirely. In the early 1990s a campaign led by city councilwoman Dorothy Mae Taylor challenged this exclusivity. She argued that membership in these elite Carnival krewes opened doors to many business opportunities and so membership restrictions served as a form of racial discrimination. The city council eventually passed a law requiring Carnival krewes to open their doors to all who can afford the membership fees. The law still permits the krewes to limit membership to a single sex, however. Of the old-line krewes only Rex agreed to comply with the new regulations. Comus, Momus, and Proteus opted to withdraw from the parades rather than integrate at the city's command. In the year 2000, Proteus decided to comply with the regulations and returned to the festivities.

Kings and Queens

The krewes' introduction of glamorous and organized Mardi Gras parades and parties not only contrasted with the disorder of street Carnival celebrations but also with their egalitarian nature. The processions and balls sponsored by the krewes were both orderly and exclusive. Even those invited to attend these affairs found themselves slotted into various ranks and categories that reflected and reinforced New Orleans's social hierarchies. For example, each year the Krewe of Rex, whose name means "king" in Latin, selects one member to reign as king. Other important krewe members are given titles of lesser nobility. Not long after Rex began this custom, their king was acknowledged by all as the king of New Orleans's Mardi Gras celebrations. Other krewes also treat the man selected to impersonate their figurehead as their king. In the 1880s the Krewe of Comus began to select a high society woman to rule with Comus as his queen. She in turn could choose members of her royal court. Soon other krewes, such as Rex, Momus, and Proteus, added this feature to their processions and masked balls. Later the roles of queen and court lady were relegated to young debutantes, with the honor of being selected as Queen of Comus understood to be the jewel in the crown of the debutante season.

Carnival Throws

In the early nineteenth century people on the street followed the old European custom of throwing things at one another during Carnival. Many threw flour, but some tossed more obnoxious substances like dirt, bricks and lye, a chemical that burns the skin. This practice led to the passage of a local law prohibiting throwing things during Carnival. The custom proved stronger than the law, however, and by the middle of the century some Creoles were riding through the city streets in carriages during Mardi Gras throwing candy and flowers to ladies and children on balconies. During the 1870s some krewes began to scatter candies and peanuts to parade watchers. Others picked friends and relatives out of the crowds and tossed party favors in their direction. In the 1920s the Krewe of Rex stepped up the custom of throwing favors into the crowd. They began to shower parade-goers with necklaces made of glass beads. This custom soon caught on with the other krewes and still lives today, though now the beads are made of plastic.

During the 1960s the krewes began to toss fake plastic coins which they called "doubloons." Nowadays in addition to these items the krewes scatter many different favors over the crowd, including plastic whistles, tiny stuffed animals, plastic cups, and even computer disks. People who line the parade route compete with one another in grabbing and collecting the trinkets thrown from the floats. Crying "Throw me something, mister," they hope to encourage the costumed krewe members aboard the floats to launch a handful of favors in their direction.

The production of Mardi Gras favors has become a big business. In 1991 the largest Mardi Gras supply house sold 41 million strings of beads. It has been estimated recently that in a single parade season the 2,300 krewe members of Bacchus and Endymion alone gave away 1.5 million plastic cups, 2.5 million doubloons and over 28 million strings of beads.

Old and New Traditions

The people of New Orleans still observe Epiphany, on January 6, as the start of the Carnival season. Mardi Gras balls and parties begin on this day and continue until Fat Tuesday. King's cake, originally an Epiphany treat, has become a food closely associated with the Carnival season. When cooks prepare this rich cake they mix a tiny trinket, usually in the shape of a baby, into the batter. People serve the cake at Mardi Gras parties. According to tradition, the person who gets the baby in their slice of cake throws the next party. It has been estimated that half a million king cakes are sold in Louisiana each year, and fifty thousand more are shipped out of state.

Also on Epiphany, the Phunny Phorty Phellows temporarily take over the St. Charles Avenue streetcar. This group consists of about fifty men and women who ride the streetcar in costume while munching on king cake and listening to the dixieland band that accompanies them. They enhance this enjoyable experience by tossing a variety of Mardi Gras throws to passersby. Their annual outing is a relatively new Mardi Gras tradition.

Another new tradition bespeaks the growing fame and popularity of New Orleans's Mardi Gras outside of New Orleans. In 1998 the Krewe of the Americas sponsored its first Mardi Gras parade. This krewe caters to people who are not from New Orleans, but would still like to march in a parade.

Finally, many citizens gather at the Spanish plaza on Mardi Gras eve to hail the ceremonial arrival of Rex, the King of Carnival. According to a time-honored Mardi Gras tradition, Rex and his entourage roll into New Orleans by riverboat and disembark to the acclaim of the gathered crowd.

Tourists and Commercialism

In the year 2000 an estimated two million tourists came to New Orleans for Carnival. Their spending generated about one billion dollars of income for the city. New Orleans is a relatively poor city that increasingly depends on tourist income. Unfortunately, many tourists come to Mardi Gras seeking to participate in its more decadent customs, such as excessive drunkenness, illegal drug use, public nudity, and illicit sex. This frustrates many locals, who see a creeping increase in this kind of behavior during Mardi Gras, but feel unable to lobby against it for fear of hurting the city's festival revenue. They long for the Mardi Gras of their childhood, remembered as a time when most festival-goers were families with children, who brought lawn chairs and barbecue grills out to the sidewalk and spent the day picnicking and watching floats. Nowadays, some worry about exposing their children to the festival.

Some locals also fear increasing commercialism will change the nature of Mardi Gras. In recent years corporate sponsors have sought advertising space on the floats or along the parade routes. In New Orleans, city law prohibits the use of floats for political or business advertising, but in the suburbs these laws don't apply and certain suburban krewes have leased floats to various business interests. Still, some observers believe they have spotted the beginning of a trend back toward smaller krewes, which they hope will not only steer Carnival floats away from commercialism but also yield more family-oriented and more sophisticated floats.

Further Reading

Burdeau, Cain. "Mardi Gras' Excesses Rain on Locals' Parade." *Christian Science Monitor* (February 26, 2001): 3.

Christianson, Stephen G., ed. *The American Book of Days*. Fourth edition. New York: H. W. Wilson, 2000.

Flake, Carol. *New Orleans*. New York: Grove Press, 1994.

Gill, James. *The Lords of Misrule*. Jackson, MS: University of Mississippi Press, 1997.

Griffin, Robert H., and Ann H. Shurgin, eds. *Junior Worldmark Encyclopedia of World Holidays*. Volume 1. Detroit, MI: UXL, 2000.

Kinser, Samuel. *Carnival American Style*. Chicago: University of Chicago Press, 1990.

Lohman, Jon. "It Can't Rain Every Day: The Year-Round Experience of Carnival." *Western Folklore* 58, 3 (1999): 279-98.

Myers, Robert J. *Celebrations: The Complete Book of American Holidays*. Garden City, NY: Doubleday and Company, 1972.

Web Sites

For more information concerning Mardi Gras in New Orleans, see the following page, posted by the New Orleans's Metropolitan Convention and Visitors Bureau: http://www.nawlins.com/new_site/visitor/vismardi.cfm

The Louisiana State Museum's Mardi Gras exhibit offers a range of information on and images of Mardi Gras: http://lsm.crt.state.la.us/mgras/mardigras.htm

For more on the Mardi Gras Indians, see: http://mardigrasneworleans.com/mardigrasindians/

Arthur Frommer's Budget Travel Online offers a useful description of Mardi Gras in New Orleans: http://www.frommers.com/destinations/neworleans/0020010042.cfm

Mary, Blessed Virgin

Jesus' mother, the Blessed Virgin Mary, appears in only one of the four biblical accounts of Jesus' crucifixion and **resurrection** (*for more on crucifixion, see* **Cross**). The Gospel according to John claims that she was present during the agonizing hours that Jesus spent on the cross (John 19:25). In spite of the scant attention that the Bible gives to Mary's role in the Easter story, the image of Mary witnessing and grieving over her own son's execution has gripped the imagination of countless Christians over the centuries (*see also* **Seven Sorrows, Feast of the**). During the Middle Ages this scene from Mary's life fascinated western European Christians. Painters and sculptors produced numerous images depicting Mary in her grief. This image was often referred to by its Latin name, *Mater Dolorosa*, meaning Sorrowing Mother. Musicians and poets also elaborated on this image in verse and song. The "Stabat Mater," a famous Latin hymn that invites listeners to enter into Mary's grief as she stood at the foot of the cross, achieved widespread popularity during this era.

This avid interest in Mary's reaction to her son's suffering and death gave rise to a variety of tales that elaborated on the sparse biblical account of her deeds on Good Friday. For example, one medieval legend concerning the events of the first Good Friday pictured Mary, distressed and perhaps confused with grief, wandering through the night in search of her dead son. A legendary incident also established itself firmly in the devotional exercise known as the **Stations of the Cross**. This religious exercise took root in Europe during the Middle Ages but reached the height of its popularity centuries later. One of the stations depicts an encounter between Mary and Jesus in the streets of Jerusalem as Jesus, bent under the weight of his cross, staggers towards the site of his own crucifixion.

In another devotional exercise found among Roman Catholics of Hispanic or Italian descent, people gather together on the evening of Good Friday to meditate on the sorrows of the Virgin Mary as she grieves for her dead son. This observance, which Hispanics call the *Pésame* or the *Soledades*, may take a variety of forms. In some church ceremonies, a figure of the crucified Christ will be removed from the cross, anointed with oils, and placed inside the tomb. Ritualized expressions of sympathy and solidarity are then offered to the grieving mother. In other places the observance revolves around a silent nighttime procession in which participants, holding lit candles, imagine themselves accompanying Mary in her grief. Some contemporary Pésame ceremonies offer participants a chance to speak, linking the grief in their own lives with that of the Virgin Mary.

Further Reading

Cohen, Hennig, and Tristram Potter Coffin, eds. *The Folklore of American Holidays*. Third edition. Detroit, MI: Gale, 1999.

Monti, James. *The Week of Salvation*. Huntington, IN: Our Sunday Visitor Publications, 1993.

Pelikan, Jaroslav. *Mary Through the Centuries*. New Haven, CT: Yale University Press, 1996.

Reumann, John. "Mary." In Mircea Eliade, ed. *The Encyclopedia of Religion*. Volume 9. New York: Macmillan, 1987.

Mary Magdalene

Mary Magdalene was a follower of **Jesus** Christ. Various passages from Christian scripture demonstrate that she remained faithful to him even during his final hours. Not only did she wait at the foot of the **cross**, but she also attended his burial. Furthermore, each of the four biblical accounts of the first Easter records her presence at the discovery of Jesus' empty tomb. Thus her devotion earned her the extraordinary privilege of being one of the first to witness and proclaim the **Resurrection**.

Mary Magdalene in the Bible

Christian scripture contains twelve separate references to Mary Magdalene. The Gospel according to Luke identifies her as a woman from whom Jesus cast out seven demons. It continues by noting that Mary Magdalene, along with several other women whom Jesus had healed, traveled about with him and the disciples, supporting them from their own resources (Luke 8:2-3).

All the other Bible passages that refer to Mary Magdalene come from accounts of Jesus' crucifixion and resurrection recorded in the Gospels of Matthew, Mark, Luke and John, scriptural accounts of Jesus' life. Matthew, Mark, and John record her presence at the site of Jesus' crucifixion (Matthew 27:56, Mark 15:40, John 19:25). Matthew and Mark mention that she was present at Jesus' entombment as well (Matthew 27:61, Mark 15:47). Finally, all four Gospel writers agree that she rose early on the **Sunday** morning after the Crucifixion and went to Jesus' tomb, bringing with her the ointments required to give Jesus' body a proper burial. Thus Mary was among the first witnesses of the Resurrection. Mark says the risen Christ appeared first to Mary Magdalene (Mark 16:9-10). Matthew declares that he appeared first to Mary Magdalene and another, unspecified Mary (Matthew 28:1-10). Luke claims that Mary Magdalene, Joanna, and Mary the mother of James received the first news of the Resurrection from an angel at the site of Jesus' empty tomb. His account also specifies that after the women received this news the risen Christ himself appeared to **Peter** and another male disciple as they were walking to a village called Emmaus (*see also* **Emmaus Walk**). John asserts that the risen Christ first appeared to Mary Magdalene alone.

Thus the biblical portrait of Mary Magdalene depicts her as the foremost witness to the Resurrection. As the first to witness to the Resurrection Mary also became the first to proclaim the news of the risen Christ. In John and Matthew the risen Jesus himself commands her to spread word of his resurrection to the apostles.

The biblical portrait of Mary portrays her as someone whose faith in Jesus never wavered. This record of unwavering devotion may be compared to that of the disciples, most of whom appear to have deserted Jesus during his trial and execution. Peter denied his relationship with Jesus after Jesus had been seized by the religious authorities. Matthew records that only a handful of Jesus' female followers accompanied him to the cross and lists Mary Magdalene's name first among them (Matthew 27:55-56) (*see also* **Mary, Blessed Virgin**). Mark's account of the Crucifixion mentions three women by name and again Mary Magdalene's name heads the list. He also records the presence of unspecified others who had followed Jesus to Jerusalem (Mark 15:40). Luke states that Jesus' "acquaintances" as well as his female followers witnessed the Crucifixion, although he doesn't offer any names (Luke 23:49). John's account of those who followed Jesus to the cross names several women, including Mary Magdalene, and alludes to only one, unnamed male disciple (John 19:26-27).

The Bible reveals only one more detail about the life of Mary Magdalene. The name "Magdalene" identifies Mary as a resident of Magdala, a small town on the shores of Lake Galilee. Scholars believe that the word "Magdala" comes from *migdol* or *migdal*, the Hebrew word for "tower." Thus St. Jerome (c. 347-419 or 420) called her "Mary of the Tower," and argued that her name reflected her steadfast faith. Mary's surname set her apart from the other women who surrounded Jesus. The others are usually identified as the mother, sister, or wife of someone else. The fact that Mary Magdalene was identified by her place of origin suggests that she may have been an unusually independent woman, perhaps an unmarried woman of means who used her income to follow and support Jesus.

Mary Magdalene in the Christian East

The image of Mary Magdalene that developed among Orthodox Christians differed quite strongly from the one advanced by Western Christians, that is, Roman Catholics and Protestants. Orthodoxy is one of the three main branches of the Christian faith. Orthodox Christianity developed in eastern Europe and the countries surrounding the eastern half of the Mediterranean Sea. Orthodox Christians follow a different church calendar than that commonly adhered to by Roman Catholics and Protestants (*see also* **Easter, Date of**).

Orthodox Christians retained an image of Mary Magdalene similar to that portrayed in the Bible. She is honored as a witness to the Resurrection and accorded the titles of "Myrrhbearer" and "Equal to the Apostles." In the late fourth century Orthodox Christian leaders dedicated the second Sunday after Easter to Mary Magdalene and the other women who brought burial spices and ointments to Jesus' tomb. It is called the "Sunday of the Myrrophores," or Sunday of the Myrrh Bearers.

A well-known legend among Orthodox Christians tells that after Jesus' **ascension** Mary Magdalene traveled about spreading word of Jesus' resurrection. When she arrived in Rome she visited the emperor Tiberius in order to lodge a complaint against **Pilate** and to bear witness to the Resurrection. During her audience with the Emperor she picked up an egg from a nearby table in order to illustrate the concept of resurrection. Tiberius scoffed at her, however, declaring that a man once dead couldn't rise again to new life any more than the egg in her hand could turn red. At once the egg flushed a deep, **blood** red. In Orthodox religious art Mary Magdalene is often portrayed holding a red egg. Greeks and other Orthodox Christians still follow an old tradition of celebrating Easter, the Feast of the Resurrection, with eggs dyed a deep, blood red.

Mary Magdalene in Western Europe

During the first several centuries after Christ's death, western European Christians began to construct a very different view of Mary Magdalene. During this era speculations about her past started to overshadow the actual biblical record of Mary's character. As commentators searched the Bible for more evidence of her background, they began to merge Mary Magdalene with several other women who knew Jesus. For example, the unnamed woman who washes and anoints Jesus' feet in a story from the Gospel according to Luke was often thought to be Mary Magdalene (Luke 7:36-50). Luke describes this woman as "a woman of the city" and "a sinner." Christian authorities in western Europe quickly assumed that this meant that the woman was sexually involved with more than one man, or perhaps a prostitute. Several sentences later, Luke introduces Mary Magdalene, a sequence of events which led many to conclude that the immoral woman and Mary Magdalene were one and the same person. The fact that in biblical times the citizens of the town of Magdala had acquired a reputation for immoral and irreverent behavior may also have influenced Bible commentators to assume that Mary Magdalene and the sinful woman were the same person. In this way western European Christians came to view Mary Magdalene as a notorious prostitute who had been cured of her inclination to pursue this way of life by Jesus Christ.

Christian officials in western Europe also assumed that Mary Magdalene and a woman identified in the Bible as Mary of Bethany were the same person. Mary of Bethany is perhaps best known for her rapt attention to Jesus' teaching as demonstrated in a story told in the Gospel according to Luke (10:38-42). In another passage Mary of Bethany also anoints Jesus' feet (John 12:3).

By blending together aspects of three women who at one time or another anointed Jesus, western European Christians created an imaginary history for Mary Magdalene. According to this history she had been a prostitute who, after having admitted her sins to Jesus, had been cured and forgiven by him. Thereafter she dedicated herself to mourning her misguided past and leading a pious and retiring life of devotion to Christ. Thus western European Christians viewed her as the primary model of **repentance** presented in Christian scripture. In fact, the English word "maudlin," meaning foolishly sentimental and given to tears, evolved from the word "Magdalene" and reflects the predominant image of her in Western Christianity. For close to two thousand years this vision of Mary eclipsed the biblical record of her deeds and character.

In western Europe the cult of Mary Magdalene reached its zenith in the late Middle Ages. Its increasing appeal may have been enhanced by a renewed emphasis on the virtues of repentance among western European preachers during that era. Artists continued to provide memorable representations of Mary Magdalene long after her cult declined in popularity, however. In western European religious art Mary Magdalene usually appears with the jar of ointment that she used to anoint Jesus and long, flowing golden hair, a symbol of her sexuality.

In recent decades Western Christians have begun to reevaluate their image of Mary Magdalene. In 1969 Roman Catholic Church authorities officially declared that Luke's penitent sinner, Mary of Bethany, and Mary Magdalene were not the same person.

Further Reading

Brewster, H. Pomeroy. *Saints and Festivals of the Christian Church*. 1904. Reprint. Detroit, MI: Omnigraphics, 1990.

Gaventa, Beverly Roberts. "Mary." In David Noel Freedman, ed. *Eerdmans Dictionary of the Bible*. Grand Rapids, MI: William B. Eerdmans Publishing, 2000.

Haskins, Susan. *Mary Magdalene: Myth and Metaphor*. New York: Harcourt Brace and Company, 1993.

Jansen, Katherine Ludwig. *The Making of the Magdelen*. Princeton, NJ: Princeton University Press, 2000.

"Mary Magdalene, St." In E. A. Livingstone, ed. *The Oxford Dictionary of the Christian Church*. Third edition. Oxford, England: Oxford University Press, 1997.

Munro, Winsome. "Mary." In Paul J. Achtemeier, ed. *The HarperCollins Bible Dictionary*. New York: HarperCollins, 1996.

Portraro, Sam. *Brightest and Best: A Companion to the Lesser Feasts and Fasts.* Cambridge, MA: Cowley, 1998.

Schlumpf, Heidi. "Who Framed Mary Magdalene?" *U.S. Catholic* (April 2000). Available online at: http://www.uscatholic.org/2000/04/0004cov.htm

Web Sites

For an Orthodox perspective on Mary Magdalene, see the web site of *Orthodox America*, a magazine for American Orthodox Christians: http://www. roca. org/OA/9/9k.htm

For another Orthodox perspective on Mary Magdalene, see the page sponsored by the Greek Orthodox Archdiocese of Australia: http://cygnus.uwa. edu.au/~jgrapsas/pages/Magdalene.htm

Maslenitsa

Butter Week, Maslyanitsa

Russians celebrate the week before the beginning of **Lent** as *Maslenitsa* (or *Maslyanitsa*), which means "Butter Week" (*see also* **Cheese Week**). Russian Orthodox Christians ease into their Lenten **fast** during this week by removing meat from their diet. Butter, milk and cheese remain, however, and offer many rich menu possibilities which Russians take advantage of during Butter Week. At the end of the week, when Lent officially begins, observant Orthodox Christians complete their Lenten fasting regimen, removing both meat and dairy products from their diet for the duration of Lent.

Customs

In past times traditional Butter Week entertainments included strolling through public places in fine clothes or in masks and costumes, courting and flirting with the opposite sex, visiting friends and relatives, enjoying rich foods, and taking sleigh rides, sometimes accompanied by a basket of *blinis* to munch on. Other activities associated with Maslenitsa include attending plays put on by troupes of travel-ing actors, playing winter games, such as sliding down specially con-structed hills of ice, and participating in rituals marking the death of winter. During the Communist era (1917-91) many of these customs began to die out. Today enjoying winter games and amusements, vis-iting friends and family, and consuming stacks of blinis are the most characteristic activities of the holiday.

Certain holiday activities used to be associated with specific days of the week. For example, some people visited the gravesites of their relatives on the first **Sunday** of Maslenitsa, bringing with them bas-kets of blinis that had been blessed in church. Monday, Tuesday, and Wednesday of Butter Week were once viewed as the ideal time for newlyweds to visit their in-laws. Other people associate this custom with the following Thursday.

These days people indulge in sweet foods on Wednesday of Butter Week. Outdoor games and activities begin in earnest on Thursday and include sledding, snowball fights, singing, dancing, and sleigh rides. At the end of the week's festivities, many communities con-struct a straw figure dubbed "Prince Carnival." They pull him through the streets in a sleigh on the last day of Maslenitsa, begging him to stay and so to extend the festival. But Lent cannot be postponed, and so they sit Prince Carnival upon his throne, place his throne upon a woodpile, and set flame to it on the last evening of Butter Week.

The last day of Butter Week is known as **Forgiveness Sunday**. An old Russian folk tradition required people not only to ask forgiveness of family members, friends, and neighbors, but also to visit the ceme-tery in order to ask forgiveness from the dead. The living embraced one another as a sign of **pardon**. The dead were offered blini.

Blinis

Blinis have become a symbol of this Russian **Carnival** celebration, so important are they to its proper observance. Russian cooks make bli-nis by preparing a thin batter which they then pour into a hot frying pan. The resulting crepes, or pancakes, should be thin, golden brown, and about the size of a saucer. After removing them from the pan they roll the blini up around a variety of rich fillings. These fillings include sturgeon, caviar (fish eggs), pickled herring, sour cream and jam, butter, mushrooms and onions, and much more. Russians consume these small delicacies by the dozens during Maslenitsa.

Legend and Origin

A Russian legend offers a fanciful explanation for the origins of this holiday. Long ago a peasant man walking in the woods encountered a merry young girl named Maslenitsa. To his great surprise he discovered that the fresh, red-cheeked beauty was the daughter of Frost, a minor yet forbidding deity personifying winter. The man begged the girl to return home with him to his village. The villagers were enduring a bitterly cold winter that year, and he thought the magical young lady might brighten their spirits. Maslenitsa did indeed return to the village with the peasant man. The villagers found warmth, joy, and hope in her presence. So great was their relief that they danced and laughed to the point of exhaustion. As Maslenitsa's visit neared its end, however, their spirits sank with fear of the dreadful cold. Their desperation wrung Maslenitsa's heart, and so she gave them a charm against the cold. She suggested that they prepare batter, fry it in the shape of the sun and feast on the resulting pancakes. Upon seeing this tribute, she advised, the sun would not leave them but stay and grow stronger. The charm worked and ever after the Russian people have celebrated the end of winter and the first flush of spring with a festival named in Maslenitsa's honor.

Folklorists believe that Russian Butter Week customs and celebrations predate the arrival of Christianity in Russia at the end of the tenth century. They suspect that in pre-Christian times the festival celebrated the first signs of the arrival of spring. Some interpret the traditional festival foods, blini and sunny-side-up fried eggs, as symbols of the sun. Today Russians still welcome the arrival of spring during Maslenitsa. At the end of the festival some country people make large scarecrow-like dolls stuffed with straw to represent winter and toss them onto lit bonfires. This act symbolizes the death of winter and the birth of spring. Spreading the ashes of this blaze over one's fields is said to improve the harvest. Some people toss the remaining Maslenitsa food onto the bonfire as well as any wooden objects that have broken over the past year. In other areas people build a snow fortress, sometimes over a frozen river. On the last day of the festival people besiege and occupy the fortress. This act, too, signals the defeat of winter and the arrival of spring.

Further Reading

Griffin, Robert H., and Ann H. Shurgin, eds. *The Folklore of World Holidays*. Second edition. Detroit, MI: Gale Research, 1999.

Lord, Priscilla Sawyer, and Daniel J. Foley. *Easter the World Over*. Philadelphia, PA: Chilton Book Company, 1971.

Matloff, Judith. "Bingeing on Hot Buttered Blini in Frigid Moscow." *Christian Science Monitor* (February 3, 1999). Available online through Northern Light for a fee at: http://www.northernlight.com. Document ID: BM19990 203010020782

Papashvily, Helen, and George Papashvily. *Russian Cooking*. Revised edition. Alexandria, VA: Time-Life Books, 1977.

Solovyova, Julia. "Holiday Mixes Paganism, Christianity." *The Moscow Times* (February 16, 1999). Available online through Northern Light for a fee at: http://www.northernlight.com. Document ID: EB19990216710000175

Utenkova, Yelena. "Hold the Aunt Jemima: These are Blini." *Russian Life* (March 1, 1996).

Web Site

"Russian Folk Holidays and Traditions," a page sponsored by the city government of Moscow, Russia: http://www.moscow-guide.ru/Culture/Folk.htm

Mass

See **Eucharist**

Maundy Thursday

Clean Thursday, Great Thursday, Green Thursday,
Holy and Great Thursday, Holy Thursday, Red Thursday,
Sharp Thursday, Sheer Thursday, Shrift Thursday,
Thursday of the Mystical Supper

Maundy Thursday falls during **Holy Week**, on the Thursday before Easter. It commemorates the events that occurred at the Last Supper, the last meal that **Jesus** ate with his followers before his arrest, trial, and crucifixion. According to three of the four biblical accounts of this evening, the meal was a **Passover** supper. Many of the folk and religious customs associated with the day refer to the events that took place at this supper. Some scholars believe that the English word "maundy" comes from the Latin word *mandatum*, or commandment, which refers to the commandment Jesus gave to his followers during the Last Supper. Others believe that the word maundy came from the English custom whereby the king or queen distributed goods to poor people on this day in a basket known as a "maund."

The Last Supper

Jesus shared the Last Supper with twelve of his most devoted follow-ers (called the disciples or apostles): **Peter**, John, Matthew, James (son of Zebedee), Andrew, Philip, Bartholomew, Thomas, James (son of Alphaeus), Thaddaeus, Simon, and **Judas**. At the Last Supper Jesus did more than just share a meal with his followers, however. He left them with several last teachings. The first concerned the meaning of his upcoming death. Jesus gave them this teaching in a symbolic way. He took **bread**, asked for God's blessing, and broke it, distributing it among his disciples. He told him that the bread was his body. Then he passed them a cup of **wine**, identifying it as his **blood**, and asked them to drink it (Matthew 26:26-29, Mark 14:22-25, Luke 22:16-19). In keeping with the Gospels of Matthew, Mark, and Luke, the early Christians interpreted Jesus' words and deeds at the Last Supper in terms of the Passover themes of sacrifice, **redemption**, and **salvation**. What's more, they identified Jesus' death as a sacrifice made for their sakes in order to cleanse them of their **sins** and open the door to a new kind of relationship with God. They created a ceremony called the **Eucharist** as a way of commemorating Jesus' sacrifice and as a way of inviting others to participate in the bread and wine of the Last Supper. The Eucharist became the most important ritual in Christian communal worship.

Because it commemorates the Last Supper, Maundy Thursday is sometimes called the "birthday of the Eucharist." Orthodox Christi-ans sometimes refer to Maundy Thursday as "Holy and Great Thurs-day of the Mystical Supper." They also refer to it simply as "Holy and Great Thursday," "Holy Thursday," or "Great Thursday."

After breaking bread with his followers Jesus gave them a command-ment and set them a powerful example of how to behave towards one another. In the Gospel according to John, Jesus declares:

> A new commandment I give to you, that you love one anoth-er; even as I have loved you, that you also love one another. By this all men will know that you are my disciples, if you have love for one another (John 13:34-35).

387

Jesus demonstrated the kind of love and service he wanted his disciples to offer one another by washing their feet (*see also* **Footwashing**). Afterwards he explained:

> "Do you know what I have done to you? You call me Teacher and Lord; and you are right, for so I am. If I then, your Lord and Teacher, have washed your feet, you also ought to wash one another's feet. For I have given you an example, that you also should do as I have done to you. Truly, truly, I say to you, a servant is not greater than his master; nor is he who is sent greater than he who sent him. If you know these things, blessed are you if you do them." (John 13:12-17)

Jesus' Prayer in the Garden of Gethsemane

After supper Jesus and his disciples went to the Garden of Gethsemane, located across the Kidron Valley on the Mount of Olives. There, while his followers slept, Jesus prayed to God about the future that he foresaw. He asked God to take away the suffering that he was about to endure (*see* **Good Friday**). In spite of his own desire to escape harm, he ended his prayer by affirming his willingness to carry out God's will, whatever that might be. Shortly thereafter, Jesus was arrested by a band of armed men, led to the Garden of Gethsemane by Jesus' disciple Judas, who identified Jesus to the mob by kissing him on the cheek.

Early History

Historical records reveal that as far back as the fourth century Christians celebrated Maundy Thursday with elaborate ceremonies. According to Egeria, a fourth-century Spanish nun who kept a diary concerning her pilgrimage to the Holy Land, Jerusalem Christians honored the day with three distinct religious services. They celebrated the Eucharist twice during the afternoon. The first service officially closed the **Lenten fast** and the second commemorated the Last Supper. Later that evening the Christian community reassembled again outside Jerusalem on the Mount of Olives to begin a late-night service remembering again Christ's words at the Last Supper, his prayers in the Garden of Gethsemane and his arrest and trial before the Roman governor Pontius **Pilate**. This service took place in stages as the congregation made its way back to Jerusalem, stopping for Bible readings at sites along the way where key events in the story took place (*for more on this service, see* **Royal Hours**).

The Orthodox churches of the Christian East inherited the tradition of this late-night service and procession. Orthodox Christians living outside of Jerusalem, however, replaced the procession with a lengthy church service. Orthodoxy is one of the three main branches of the Christian faith. Orthodox Christians, found mainly in eastern Europe and the countries surrounding the eastern half of the Mediterranean Sea, maintain customs and rituals distinct from those of Western Christians, that is, Roman Catholics and Protestants. During the days of the predominantly Orthodox Byzantine Empire (330-1453), the emperor himself used to attend this late-night church service in the cathedral of Constantinople, a city now known as Istanbul, Turkey. For that reason the service became known as the Royal Hours. Today most Orthodox churches offer this service on the morning of Good Friday. The service consists of selections from the Bible describing Jesus' last days on earth, usually referred to as the Passion. These are divided up into twelve chapters and are either read or sung, accompanied by prayers, hymns, and other texts.

In western Europe the religious customs and traditions of Rome exercised far more influence than those of Jerusalem. By the fourth century, Roman Christians celebrated Maundy Thursday with a ceremony devoted to the reconciliation of penitents (*see also* **Repentance**). This process began about six weeks earlier. Those who had committed what were considered serious offences in the Christian community confessed these deeds publicly at church services that marked the beginning of Lent (*see also* **Ash Wednesday**). They spent the Lenten season completing the religious exercises and enduring the hardships assigned to them to cleanse them of their sins and renew their devotion to God. They were forbidden to attend church again until Maundy Thursday. They reappeared on that day to participate in the religious ceremony whereby penitents were reconciled with the church. After kneeling in the doorway of the church for the first part of the service, they were eventually permitted to approach the bishop or priest to receive forgiveness for their sins. After the service they retired to bathe and shave, since these activities had been forbidden them during Lent. The ceremony of reconciliation marked the end of the Lenten season. Indeed, Maundy Thursday was viewed as the last day of Lent rather than the first day of the **Triduum** throughout the Middle Ages.

In the days of the early church, when many adults were baptized at Easter time, candidates for **baptism** were expected to appear before the bishop or his representative on Maundy Thursday and recite the Creed, a summary of Christian doctrine. In Rome church officials transferred this custom to **Holy Saturday**. This recitation proved that they had been sufficiently instructed in the Christian faith and were ready for baptism. This custom disappeared as infant baptisms gradually replaced those of adult converts. Nevertheless, in Roman Catholic and Anglican cathedrals, special oils used in baptismal ceremonies are still consecrated on Maundy Thursday, an echo of the day's ancient ties to the preparation of baptismal candidates.

Medieval History

Long after public confessions and reconciliations of the kind described above had been abandoned, ordinary people carried on the tradition of bathing and cleaning their clothes on Maundy Thursday. People called the day "Clean Thursday" in reference to these customary Easter preparations. In times past bathing and cleaning one's clothes were more difficult, time-consuming tasks than they are today and therefore these tasks were undertaken less frequently. In recognition of the special exertions involved, the church granted some exemptions from the strict Lenten fasting rules on this day. In fourteenth-century England men also shaved and trimmed their beards on Maundy Thursday. Hence people dubbed it "Sheer," "Shrift," or "Sharp" Thursday. The custom of bathing, shaving, and washing on Maundy Thursday in preparation for Easter faded over time. Nevertheless, in some places Maundy Thursday still serves as a day on which to wash altar cloths and clean the church in preparation for Easter.

In German-speaking countries folk tradition renamed Maundy Thursday "Green Thursday." Researchers have come up with several explanations for this name. One theory traces it back to the reconciliation of penitents that used to take place on this day. The penitents carried green branches as a sign of their joy. Indeed, *Dies viridium,* an old Latin name for the day which means "Day of the Green Ones," came from this custom. In the symbolic code of the western European church, green represents hope and victory. The green twig in particular symbolizes a long struggle crowned by victory (*see also* **Palm Sunday**). Until the thirteenth century priests wore green vestments on Maundy Thursday. Today two liturgical colors are used in Maundy Thursday services. Before the Eucharist priests wear red vestments, symbolizing the suffering love that sustains martyrdom. For the Eucharist itself priests change to white robes, representing joy, in this case, the joy inspired by the gift of the Eucharist.

Another theory concerning the origins of the name "Green Thursday" suggests that it evolved from an older name, "Mourning Thursday." The two names are not as far apart in German as they are in English since the German word for mourning is *grunen* and the German word for green is *grün.*

Contemporary Church Customs

Although some old religious customs associated with the day have been abandoned, others remain. Still more have been added in recent times. For example, many Roman Catholic and Anglican churches and religious institutions offer footwashing ceremonies on Maundy Thursday. These ceremonies date back to the seventh century, but were inspired by the words and deeds of Jesus himself as recorded in the Bible. The ritual offers participants the opportunity to give and receive the kind of humble love and service that Jesus gave to his followers. In these ceremonies a member of the clergy washes the feet of people in the community or congregation. In some Christian denominations clergy members wash the feet of all who wish to participate in the ceremony. In another variation of this ceremony a priest bathes the feet of twelve boys or men. Seated in a half circle around the priest, the boys and men represent Jesus' twelve apostles. In some places folk dramas amplify the religious ritual. Each year the Greek town of Patmos stages a folk play dramatizing the washing of the disciples' feet. Participants stage the play, titled *Niptir*, or "Washing," in the town square.

Many Protestant churches celebrate the Lord's Supper on Maundy Thursday. Some hold special "Upper Room" services on this day. Parishioners eat a meal composed of many foods that Jesus and his disciples may have included in their Passover meal. They eat in silence, while listening to readings from the Bible. The name given to this service refers to the place where Jesus shared the Last Supper with his disciples, described in the Bible simply as an "upper room."

According to an old church custom dating back to the eighth century, **bells** ring for the last time before Easter on Maundy Thursday. In the absence of the bells the beginning and ending of religious services and devotions were announced by the sounding of a wooden clapper board, an ancient device used in churches before the introduction of bells in the fifth century. In the Catholic countries of Europe the sudden silence of the church bells puzzled children. Adults often told them that the bells had flown off to Rome to visit the pope and spend the night at St. Peter's before returning on Easter morning. French parents even hinted that it was the returning bells that brought children their **Easter eggs**.

In some churches the altar is ceremonially stripped of all its cloth coverings at the end of Maundy Thursday services. Other cloth hangings are also removed. This stripping leaves the church with a stark appearance, thus preparing it for the mournful services that take place the following day on Good Friday. It also gives those in charge of cleaning and decorating the church an opportunity to wash everything thoroughly in preparation for Easter. This custom fits well with the day's nickname, "Clean Thursday," although most writers believe that this name came about from an old tradition encouraging people to bathe and clean their clothes on Maundy Thursday in preparation for Easter. In the Middle Ages the floors and walls of the church were scrubbed on Maundy Thursday. Moreover, altar tables were ceremonially washed with **water** and wine, an act that symbolized Christ's blood washing the world clean from sin.

In Roman Catholic and Anglican cathedrals holy oil that will be used in the coming year is blessed at a special service on Maundy Thursday. Clergy members use this oil for special religious services, including baptisms, confirmations, ordinations, and for anointing the dying and those in ill health. The blessing of holy oil on Maundy Thursday can be traced back to the fifth century.

Orthodox Maundy Thursday services commemorate the Last Supper and Jesus' command to his disciples that they love one another. Since Orthodoxy follows the ancient Jewish custom of reckoning the start of each new day at sunset, their Maundy Thursday services begin on Wednesday evening. In some Orthodox churches Wednesday evening services are accompanied by the anointing of the sick, a ceremony in which priests pray over persons seeking physical and spiritual healing, and anoint them with holy oil.

Beginning of the Triduum

Maundy Thursday begins the Triduum, the last three days of Holy Week. Although many reckon the Triduum simply as the Thursday, Friday, and Saturday that precedes Easter, technically the Triduum begins on the evening of Maundy Thursday and continues through the daylight hours of **Easter Sunday**. **Tenebrae** services, an ancient monastic ceremony of psalms, chants, Bible readings, and hymns, may be offered during the Triduum in Roman Catholic and Episcopal churches.

Special Altars

Roman Catholics have long maintained a tradition whereby a portion of the Eucharist prepared on Maundy Thursday is venerated and preserved for use on the following day. In the past great ceremony and elaborate decorations attended this devotion. At the end of the mass the priest reverently placed the consecrated host in a special container (*for more on the Roman Catholic religious service known as the mass, see* Eucharist). Then followed a solemn procession to a specially decorated corner of the church, called a "repository" or the "altar of repose," where the container would be displayed.

In Latin American and southern European countries the container was placed at a great height, often with the use of a special scaffolding. Then the scaffolding was decorated with candles, **lilies**, orchids, **palms**, and other suitable materials. Latin Americans and southern Europeans call these displays *monumentos*, or "tombs," a reference to Jesus' upcoming death. In other European countries the repository was adorned with gold, silver, jewels, flowers, candles, and images of angels, and was called a "sepulchre," "throne," "paradise," or "garden." In the Middle Ages one devotional practice urged people to visit and offer prayers before seven *monumenti* on the evening of Maundy Thursday. Some contemporary Roman Catholics carry on the practice of visiting as many altars of repose as possible on Maundy Thursday. Today the displays surrounding the altar of repose are apt to be less elaborate than those of previous generations. Roman Catholic officials discourage worshipers from referring to these decorated repositories as "tombs," since the commemoration of Jesus' death and burial will not come until the following day, Good Friday (*see also* **Holy Sepulchre**).

Other Customs Associated with the Day

Many Greeks dye their Easter eggs on this day. Only bright red dye is used, representing the blood of Christ (*for more on egg symbolism in Orthodoxy, see* **Mary Magdalene**). In reference to these eggs Greeks have nicknamed the day "Red Thursday." Another Greek custom associated with the day is the cleaning of the home *ikonostasi*, a shelf or niche where the family keeps devotional materials such as icons, religious images used in prayer and worship, incense, blessed palms from Palm Sunday, a Bible, and a cross. Often families keep a red Easter egg in the ikonostasi throughout the year. The Easter eggs, palm crosses, and other seasonal material from the previous year are disposed of on Holy Thursday (*see also* **Greece, Easter and Holy Week in**).

In central Europe folk customs encouraged the eating of green foods on Green Thursday. Spinach, kale, leeks, green salads, and soups made with green vegetables or herbs are especially popular on this day. This custom is carried out in some Slavic countries as well. It can also be found among the Pennsylvania Dutch, whose ancestors immigrated to the United States from Germany and Switzerland.

Symbols

The Eucharist serves as an important religious symbol of Maundy Thursday. Blessed bread and wine, the gifts of the Eucharist, may also represent the holiday.

In Roman Catholic churches, as well as those Protestant churches that observe liturgical colors, priests wear red robes at the start of Maundy Thursday services. Liturgical colors govern the changing hues of clerical robes and other church decorations throughout the year. In the liturgical color scheme red represents love and suffering. At the celebration of the Eucharist the priest changes to white robes, symbolizing joy. This switch reflects the honor given to Maundy Thursday as the birthday of the Eucharist and the joy with which Christians receive this gift from Christ.

Further Reading

Blackburn, Bonnie, and Leofranc Holford-Strevens. *The Oxford Companion to the Year*. Oxford, England: Oxford University Press, 1999.

Cowie, L. W., and John Selwyn Gummer. *The Christian Calendar*. Springfield, MA: G. and C. Merriam, 1974.

Leclerq, H. "Maundy Thursday." In Charles G. Herbermann et al., eds. *The Catholic Encyclopedia*. New York: Appleton, 1913. Available online at: http://www.newadvent.org/cathen/10068a.htm

Lord, Priscilla Sawyer, and Daniel J. Foley. *Easter Garland*. 1963. Reprint. Detroit, MI: Omnigraphics, 1999.

Metford, J. C. J. *The Christian Year*. London, England: Thames and Hudson, 1991.

Monti, James. *The Week of Salvation*. Huntington, IN: Our Sunday Visitor Publications, 1993.

Myers, Robert J. *Celebrations: The Complete Book of American Holidays*. Garden City, NY: Doubleday and Company, 1972.

Niemann, Paul J. *The Lent, Triduum, and Easter Answer Book*. San Jose, CA: Resource Publications, 1998.

Pierce, Joanne M. "Holy Week and Easter in the Middle Ages." In Paul F. Bradshaw and Lawrence A. Hoffman, eds. *Passover and Easter: Origin and History to Modern Times*. Two Liturgical Traditions Series, volume 5. Notre Dame, IN: University of Notre Dame Press, 1999.

Rouvelas, Marilyn. *A Guide to Greek Traditions and Customs in America*. Bethesda, MD: Nea Attiki Press, 1993.

Slim, Hugo. *A Feast of Festivals*. London, England: Marshall Pickering, 1996.

Urlin, Ethel L. *Festivals, Holy Days, and Saints' Days*. 1915. Reprint. Detroit, MI: Omnigraphics, 1992.

Weiser, Francis X. *The Easter Book*. New York: Harcourt, Brace and Company, 1954.

Wybrew, Hugh. *Orthodox Lent, Holy Week and Easter*. Crestwood, NY: St. Vladimir's Seminary Press, 1997.

May Day

May Day, celebrated on May 1, is an ancient European folk holiday of uncertain origins. Some writers trace it back to ancient Roman festivals. Others believe that it evolved out of ancient Celtic or northern European observances (*see also* **Beltane**). The folklore of northern Europe reveals that ethnic groups from Russia to Ireland celebrated the arrival of May by gathering flowers and greenery from meadows and woodlands. They used this foliage to decorate their homes and yards. In some countries boys left branches, decorated trees, or poles outside the homes of girls they knew. Other May Day customs found in many European countries include erecting and decorating maypoles to serve as the center of May Day festivities, dancing, and the crowning of a May king or May queen.

Origins

Some writers believe that May Day celebrations started in ancient Rome. The Romans celebrated the festival of Floralia during the last days of April and the first days of May. This holiday celebrated the blossoming of flowers and welcomed the arrival of spring. Romans observed the occasion with bouts of drinking and rowdy, flirtatious games. Celebrations also included the release of **hares** and goats, both symbols of lust, as well as tossing flowers, beans, and greenery at other people. Prostitutes adopted Floralia as a festival with special significance for their trade. In addition, dramas and games were held at the temple of Flora in Rome. To honor the goddess people wrapped the columns of the temple in flower garlands while women and girls dressed in white sprinkled fresh flower petals all around. One holiday tradition held that the first person to place a wreath of flowers on the statue of Flora would have good luck in the months to come. Children followed a tradition of their own, fashioning little dolls that represented the goddess and decking them with flowers.

May first was sacred to the goddess Bona Dea. Little is known about her and her festival. Some say she was the mother or sister of Faunus (Pan), a demi-god associated with the flocks. It may be that she was a kind of mother goddess that presided over the fertility of the earth. Only women were permitted to attend her sacred rites.

Bringing in the May

In England one of the older customs connected with May Day was known as "going a-Maying" or "bringing in the May." Boys and girls of courtship and marriage age would rise early on May Day morning and go into the woods in search of flowers and greenery, often while it was still dark. They brought armloads of foliage and blossoms back into town, strewing them about as holiday decorations. The earliest document to refer to this custom dates back to 1240. About one hundred years later the famous English writer Geoffrey Chaucer (1342-1400) noted that on May Day "forth goeth all the court, both most and least, to fetch flowers fresh," documenting the fact that in his day the nobility as well as the commoners went a-Maying. The English poet Edmund Spenser offers a somewhat longer description of the custom in his 1579 work *The Shepherd's Calendar*:

> Siker this morrow, no longer ago,
> I saw a shole of shepherds outgo
> With a singing, and shouting, and jolly cheer;
> Before them yode a lusty Tabrere,
> That to the many a horn-pipe play'd
> Whereto they dancen each one with his maid.
> To see these folks make such jouissance,
> Made my heart after the pipe to dance.
> Then to the greenwood they speeden them all,
> To fetchen home May with their musical:
> And home they bring him in a royal throne
> Crowned as king; and his queen attone
> Was Lady Flora, on whom did attend
> A fair flock of fairies, and a fresh bend
> Of lovely nymphs — O that I were there

꿨ꑤꑤꑤꑤꑤꑤꑤꑤꑤꑤꑤꑤꑤꑤꑤꑤꑤꑤꑤꑤꑤꑤꑤꑤꑤꑤꑤꑤꑤꑤꑤꑤꑤꑤꑤꑤꑤ

To helpen the ladies their May-bush to bear!
(Chambers, 1: 571)

During the sixteenth century a religious reform movement known as the Protestant Reformation gave birth to a sect of conservative Protestants known as Puritans. English Puritans complained about these May Day customs, grumbling that many a sexual encounter took place during these May morning or May eve outings to the woods. Their campaign against the custom may have succeeded in discouraging some from participating in May Day activities in the mid-seventeenth century, years during which they achieved a good deal of political power. Nevertheless, the old enthusiasm for bringing in the May returned later in the century as their influence waned. The custom finally began to die out in the nineteenth century, probably as a result of the effects of urbanization and industrialization on the countryside and rural populations.

Offerings, Garlands, and Baskets

These trips to the woods furnished participants with the materials needed for another English May Day custom, the May offering. In some places, upon returning from the woods those who had gone a-Maying left greenery and branches outside the doors of village residents. These offerings had symbolic meanings known to local people. In the Cambridgeshire Fens boys left sloe branches at the doors of popular girls, blackthorn at the homes of flirtatious girls, elder for promiscuous girls, and nettles outside the homes of those considered scolds. In Northhamptonshire an offering of hawthorn branches signaled affection or approval, while sloe, crab-apple, nettles or thistles conveyed dislike or disapproval. In some areas May-ers brought offerings of flowers and greenery from door to door, singing traditional May carols and hoping in exchange for a tip of food, drink, or money. Young men might combine the delivery of May offerings with small destructive acts aimed at those people against whom they bore a grudge. These acts of revenge included trampling gardens, pulling up fence stakes, and overturning carts. This tradition of May Day mischief continues today in the Yorkshire region.

In past times many young women wove blossoms and leaves into May garlands which they sold from door to door. In England the weaving and distribution of garlands on May Day can be traced back to the fifteenth century. The custom died out in the 1950s, when widespread affluence eliminated the financial motivation for the practice.

Boys in many parts of Europe gathered greenery on May eve to leave at the homes of local girls. In Switzerland boys left small pine trees festooned with ribbons and flowers under their girlfriends' windows. They called this offering a *maitannli*, or May pine tree. German lads left similar trees, called *Maien*, outside the homes of girls they loved. In Switzerland unpopular or conceited girls might find an ugly straw dummy outside their windows instead of a pretty May tree. Czech boys practiced a similar custom with local girls, leaving their sweethearts either a decorated pole or a small pine tree adorned with colored eggshells and ribbons (*see also* **Egg Lore**). Macedonian lads wove wreaths of flowers and fragrant leaves and left them at the doors of their girlfriends' houses. Spanish boys brought tree branches adorned with flowers to their sweethearts' windows.

In Ireland people decorated bushes with ribbons, eggshells, and flowers in honor of May Day. In France small decorated trees or poles, called "Mays," appeared everywhere on May Day.

In the United States girls once gathered flowers and presented them to one another in May baskets. According to folk tradition these baskets, made from paper or cardboard, must be hung on the front door of the girl's home without the occupants seeing who delivered it. This custom, especially popular in the eastern United States, has now fallen out of fashion. Other largely defunct American May Day customs include dances held on school lawns and, in some colleges, the election of May queens.

In Hawaii May 1 is known as Lei Day. People observe it by wearing flower garlands called leis, a Hawaiian symbol of goodwill and friendship.

The Maypole

In past centuries the maypole, a tall pole set upright in the ground at some central location, staked out the ground where May Day dancing, games, and revelry would take place. These activities provided ample opportunity for young men and women to meet and flirt with one another.

Before these May Day frolics could take place, however, a tree had to be selected, cut down, stripped of its branches and leaves, dragged into town, and heaved upright. This required teamwork because people wanted tall maypoles, which naturally had to be made from tall, heavy trees. In England historical records dating back several centuries reveal that once the pole was brought into town people set about festooning it with flower garlands, greenery, flags, and streamers. Many German villagers preferred to make their maypoles out of spruce trees skinned of all but their topmost branches. They then decorated the poles with ribbons and a May wreath, frequently entwined with sausages, sweets, and gifts, thereby enticing adventurous youths into attempting to climb the pole. Each town or village took pride in its maypole. Sometimes local rivalries spurred young men from one locale to steal another town's maypole.

Although it is often assumed to be an ancient British custom, the earliest English documents referring to circular dances in which participants weave a garland of ribbons round a maypole date back only as far as the nineteenth century. Similar circular dances round a beribboned maypole can be found in Germany, Austria, the Czech Republic, and parts of Spain, as well as in Venezuela and Mexico's Yucatan Peninsula. These dances can also be found at May fairs in the United States.

In England historical documents referring to maypoles date back to the second half of the fourteenth century, though they may have been in use earlier than that time. The Puritans, who were suspicious of holiday merry-making generally, also disliked maypoles, viewing them as lures in the direction of idol worship. In 1644 Puritans in England outlawed maypoles in their country. The poles were reinstated, however, when the Puritans lost power later in the century. From then on, maypoles were a common sight across England until the late eighteenth century, when interest in them began to die out. When the wooden poles decayed and fell down they were not replaced.

The English Puritans who immigrated to America to found New England's Plymouth colony brought their disapproval of May Day with them. In the year 1627, an Anglican who dwelt among them, one Thomas Morton, raised an eighty-foot maypole at his plantation in honor of the holiday. Decorated with flowers, antlers, and ribbons, the maypole scandalized his Puritan neighbors. They whispered that Morton had even danced around the pole in the company of Indian women. Puritan leader John Endecott would have none of it. He publicly renamed Merry Mount, Morton's plantation, "Mount Dragon," in reference to a Philistine idol mentioned in the Bible. The too-merry Morton was then accused of trading arms with the natives and shipped back to England. In 1628 William Bradford, the Puritan governor of the recently founded English colony in Massachusetts Bay, complained about the jollity that took place round the maypole in his community. Puritan officials succeeded in having the pole torn down.

Many theories as to the significance of the maypole have been advanced by folklorists and other commentators. For example, some have argued that the maypole and the ceremonies surrounding it represent a vestige of ancient tree worship. Others contend that the pole symbolizes the male sexual organ and so pays tribute to sexuality and fertility. Little evidence exists to back up any of these claims. It seems safe to say, however, that the maypole, like many other May Day customs, helped people to express their happiness at seeing nature in full bloom.

May Kings and Queens

In England local people often chose a May king to preside over the games and revels taking place during this festive month. In other places a May queen presided over these activities, although this was rarer. Often chosen for her looks, the May queen might be asked to impersonate a May spirit or goddess in her manner and attire as she walked in a May Day procession. In the nineteenth century French girls sometimes selected one of their playmates to deck with flower garlands and present as a May queen. English girls of the same era might present a doll as the May queen. In some parts of England both a May king and May queen shared the duties associated with this role. May kings and queens were also known in other European countries.

Fairies, Witches, and Bonfires

Irish folklore whispered that fairies fought each other over the ripening crops on May eve. Spirits of the dead also wandered abroad on this night, according to Irish folklore. To ward off harm from these supernatural creatures Irish people sometimes left them offerings of food. In many other European countries witches were thought to walk about on this night. In countries where these notions were prevalent people often celebrated May eve with bonfires (*for more on these beliefs and practices, see* Beltane; **Walpurgis Night**).

May Dew and May Water

In past times one commonly held European and North American folk belief advised young women that washing their faces in May Day dew would preserve their complexion, impart beauty, and confer health and luck. In some places getting one's head wet with May eve dew was believed to prevent headaches during the year to come. In certain parts of Germany people suspected May **water** to possess special, magical properties. In Brittany and on the Somme (France) people once made pilgrimages to wells and fountains in the month of May. Old folk beliefs once popular in the region surrounding Paris, France, advised that May milk drunk at dawn surpassed all other kinds of milk.

Labor Day

Over 160 nations observe May Day as a holiday honoring workers. As such, it constitutes the second most celebrated holiday in the world.

Although the United States does not observe May 1 as Labor Day, historians trace the history of a holiday honoring workers back to late nineteenth-century America. During this era American labor organizers fought to replace the ten-hour or longer work day with a standard eight-hour day. An important organization representing workers, the National Federation of Organized Trades and Labor Assemblies, called for a general strike on May 1,1886, with the goal of persuading employers to adopt the eight-hour work day. On May 1 striking workers held peaceful protests. These demonstrations continued in Chicago, however, amidst growing tensions fueled by a split in the labor movement between trade unionists and socialists. On May 4 strikers gathered outside the McCormick reaper factory on Haymarket Square to protest the police violence which had caused the deaths of several workers on the previous day. When the police arrived someone threw a bomb. The explosion resulted in the deaths of seven officers and the injuries of many other policemen and civilians. Seven anarchists (radical leftists) from Chicago's labor movement were arrested and convicted of the crime, in spite of the fact that no evidence was produced to connect them with the bomb blast. This miscarriage of justice as well as the eventually successful campaign for the eight-hour day stamped May first with a permanent connection to workers' issues in the minds of many people.

At its 1889 convention in Paris, France, the International Socialist Congress declared May 1 to be International Labor Day. As the labor movement gained respect and strength throughout the world, labor advocates in many different countries instituted May Day as a legal holiday honoring workers. Many Communist countries celebrated May Day as a major patriotic holiday with military and other parades.

St. Tammany's Day

In Maryland May 1 was once known as St. Tammany's Day. Tammany, Taminend or Tamina was a Delaware Indian chief who lived during the colonial era. He befriended William Penn (1644-1718) and signed a treaty with him. In the years preceding the American Revolution certain colonists, disgusted with the British and their patriotic societies, formed their own political club. The British named their political societies after Christian saints, such as St. George and St. Andrew. To give their club a distinctly American flavor, the colonists decided to let Tammany serve as their patron saint. The Tammany Society went on to wield a good deal of power in American politics, especially in New York City.

Superstitions

A myriad of superstitions have attached themselves to this day. In the British Isles it was once thought unlucky to lend fire on this day. Those who came asking for it were thought to be witches (*for more on related fire practices, see* Beltane).

In some regions of the United States folklore taught that May Day dew could remove freckles. Southern folklore recommended curing a sore throat by opening one's mouth in the direction of the May Day sunrise and letting the first beam of light shine into one's throat. Southern lore also offered many May Day love charms for girls who were curious about the identity of their future mates. A young lady who wore white dogwood blossoms pinned to her blouse on May Day could be sure that the first man she met wearing a white hat would be her future husband. Another bit of lore advised inquisitive girls to leave their handkerchiefs out on the grass on May eve. The next morning they were sure to find that a snail had crawled across them, leaving behind a trail resembling the initials of their future husbands. Another snippet of southern lore recommended standing with one's back towards a spring on May Day morning and looking at it over one's shoulder with the aid of a mirror. These actions should cause the image of one's future husband to rise out of the water.

Further Reading

Blackburn, Bonnie, and Leofranc Holford-Strevens. *The Oxford Companion to the Year*. Oxford, England: Oxford University Press, 1999.

Chambers, Robert. *The Book of Days*. Volume 1. 1862-64. Reprint. Detroit, MI: Omnigraphics, 1990.

Christianson, Stephen G., ed. *The American Book of Days*. Fourth edition. New York: H. W. Wilson, 2000.

Cohen, Hennig, and Tristram Potter Coffin, eds. *The Folklore of American Holidays.* Third edition. Detroit, MI: Gale, 1999.

Cooper, J. C. *The Dictionary of Festivals.* London, England: Thorsons, 1990.

Griffin, Robert H., and Ann H. Shurgin, eds. *The Folklore of World Holidays.* Second edition. Detroit, MI: Gale Research, 1999.

Henderson, Helene, and Sue Ellen Thompson, eds. *Holidays, Festivals, and Celebrations of the World Dictionary.* Second edition. Detroit, MI: Omnigraphics, 1997.

Hutton, Ronald. *Stations of the Sun.* Oxford, England: Oxford University Press, 1996.

James, E. O. *Seasonal Feasts and Festivals.* 1961. Reprint. Detroit, MI: Omnigraphics, 1993.

Leach, Maria, ed. *Funk and Wagnalls Standard Dictionary of Folklore, Mythology and Legend.* New York: Harper and Row, 1984.

Russ, Jennifer M. *German Festivals and Customs.* London, England: Oswald Wolff, 1982.

Scullard, H. H. *Festivals and Ceremonies of the Roman Republic.* Ithaca, NY: Cornell University Press, 1981.

Mexico, Easter and Holy Week in

Villages and towns all across Mexico honor **Holy Week** and Easter by reenacting the Passion story, that is, the events that took place during the last few days of **Jesus'** life. These reenactments usually involve religious processions that take place on various days during Holy Week. In many places sacred statues are removed from churches and carried on floats throughout the town. Sometimes people dress as characters from the Bible and follow behind the floats. In other places people honor the final days of Holy Week with **Passion plays**, a form of street theater in which local people play out scenes from the story of Jesus' arrest, trial, and crucifixion (*for more on crucifixion, see* **Cross**). **Good Friday** events often include **penitentes**, people carrying out religious vows to undergo physical suffering as an expression of regret for some past misdeed. A folk custom known as the **burning of Judas** occurs in many places on **Holy Saturday**. **Easter Sunday** often passes quietly compared to what has gone before, with many people celebrating Jesus' **resurrection** by attending religious services and enjoying a large meal with their families. In villages people may gather for communal feasts, fireworks displays, singing, and dancing.

Holy Week in Taxco

The town of Taxco, in southern Mexico, is famed throughout the country for its Holy Week processions. They begin on **Palm Sunday**, when inhabitants of a nearby village walk in procession to Taxco, bearing a litter on which they have placed a statue of Jesus riding a donkey. As they enter Taxco twelve men dressed as Jesus' disciples join the procession, which continues to the Church of Santa Prisca for the Blessing of the **Palms**.

The following day, Monday of Holy Week, the people of Taxco parade the statues of San Miguel and the Nativity through the streets of town, accompanied by rows of men, women, and children carrying lit candles. Many who follow the procession bear staffs decorated with brightly colored tissue paper and gourds. People from nearby towns join in this procession, bearing their own holy images on litters. The citizens of Taxco mount another religious procession on the evening of Holy Tuesday, this one focused around three images of Jesus found in local churches. Drummers, musicians playing the *chirimía*, a local version of the flute, and church choirs singing sacred music precede the floats carrying the statues. The *almas encadenadas*, or "chained souls," follow this procession. Dressed in mourning and dragging ankle chains, they represent souls condemned to a period of suffering after death as payment for their misdeeds on earth.

A special church service called *Las Tinieblas*, the darkness, begins at 3:00 p.m. on the afternoon of Holy Wednesday (*see also* **Spy Wednesday**). This service commemorates the gloomy hours before Jesus' arrest, when he prayed in the Garden of Gethsemane while his companions slept. It also honors the trials that Jesus endured during his years of teaching. Later that evening another religious procession wends it way through the streets of Taxco, this one featuring images of the Virgin of Fatima (*see also* **Mary, Blessed Virgin**), the Blessed Trinity, Adam and Eve, Our Lord of Calvary, and Our Lord of the Portada.

On **Maundy Thursday** little girls dressed as angels keep vigil in the garden attached to the Church of Santa Prisca, which on this day represents the Garden of Gethsemane to the people of Taxco. They decorate the garden with fresh greenery and caged songbirds so that it resembles a small paradise. According to Roman Catholic custom, church **bells** stop ringing on Maundy Thursday. Instead, the harsh sound of *matracas*, wooden rattles, call worshipers to the late afternoon service, which commemorates the Last Supper (*see also* **Foot-washing**; *for more on the Last Supper, see* Maundy Thursday). After the service *sayones*, men dressed like Roman soldiers, begin to pour into the streets. Many of these men undertake this role every year in order to carry out a vow made to God. Around 7:00 p.m. the man who plays the role of Jesus Christ enters the Garden of Gethsemane. Another man playing the role of **Judas** enters, too, and kisses Jesus on one cheek. At this point the sayones enter and take Jesus away to jail, where he is kept in chains. At 11:00 that evening a man playing the role of Pontius **Pilate** sentences Jesus to crucifixion and washes his hands, a gesture which signifies his refusal to take responsibility for what has just happened.

While town inhabitants reenact the drama of Jesus' arrest and trial, people from nearby villages have been streaming into town carrying images of the Crucifixion. Flowers and lanterns festoon the litters that bear these sacred images. Devotees with lit candles walk behind each float. *Encruzados*, "crucified ones," known elsewhere as penitentes, also appear in these processions. They wear long black skirts and hoods which fall down to their shoulders and march with their arms stretched out so that their bodies form the shape of a cross. They carry bundles of thorns strapped across their shoulders and outstretched arms and sometimes also wear belts made of horsehair to increase their suffering.

On Good Friday townspeople reenact Jesus' journey to the site of his execution as well as his crucifixion. First, a band of children carries Jesus' cross through the streets. Then the man playing Jesus must hoist the cross across his own shoulders and carry it to the place where the mock crucifixion takes place. Jesus' body is removed from the cross at around four in the afternoon, after which follows an elaborate funeral procession. The encruzados, drained from the torments to which they have subjected themselves, trudge wearily behind the funeral procession.

Easter in Taxco

The people of Taxco begin to celebrate Jesus' resurrection on Saturday morning. Church bells swing back and forth, announcing the joyous news. The sayones, still in costume, register nervousness and fear upon hearing the news. The final religious procession takes place on Easter Sunday. This procession features the image of the resurrected Jesus.

Mexico City's Passion Play

Mexico City's Passion play lasts several days. It covers an area of four kilometers (about two and one-half miles), features several thousand participants, and draws crowds of three to four million people. The citizens of eight Mexico City neighborhoods spend months preparing the props, sets, wardrobe, makeup, and street decorations, as well as planning to manage the large numbers of people who attend the event. The Passion play takes place in a district of Mexico City known as Iztapalapa. Mexican officials boast that this event may be considered the largest pageant of popular culture in the world.

The Iztapalapa Passion play began in 1833, when residents of Iztapalapa decided to reenact the Passion in order to express their gratitude to Jesus for stopping a cholera epidemic. Although the event has grown over the years, a number of families have maintained the right to certain roles and functions in the event, and some of them even have old documents assigning their ancestors the same roles. An organizing committee, however, elects the individuals who fill the important roles of Jesus, the Blessed Virgin Mary, and the twelve disciples (*see also* Mary, Blessed Virgin; **Peter**). In order to qualify for the role of Jesus a man must be recognized as pure and devout, possess a good reputation, live locally, and have parents born in Iztapalapa. He must also be willing to acquire the strength and endurance necessary to carry a 100-kilogram (about 45 pounds) cross for four kilometers. Moreover, when approached by members of the crowd desiring healings or miracles, he must respond kindly. Physical and spiritual training for this formidable task begins months in advance. The young women of Iztapalapa vie for the role of Jesus' mother. To qualify for the role they must not only possess certain physical characteristics, but also possess a spotless reputation and be of high moral character.

Although based loosely on the story told in the Bible, the Iztapalapa Passion play also includes legendary events and characters. The players reenact the Last Supper and Jesus' betrayal on Maundy Thursday. On Good Friday, Christ carries his cross to the scene of the crucifixion. He is accompanied by thousands of people carrying out vows to complete an act of penance during this procession (*for more on penance, see* **Repentance**). These people, called Nazarenes, wear purple robes, carry their own crosses, wear crowns of thorns, and walk the procession in bare feet (*see also* Penitentes). A number of young women express their piety by walking the procession costumed as companions to Mary. The drama concludes with Jesus' crucifixion, while Judas hangs himself from a nearby tree. In 1999, officials estimate that about 4,600 people participated in the staging of the Passion play, more than 2,500 Nazarenes followed Christ to the site of the crucifixion, and three million people watched some or all of the spectacle.

Further Reading

Lord, Priscilla Sawyer, and Daniel J. Foley. *Easter the World Over*. Philadelphia, PA: Chilton Book Company, 1971.

Marcus, Rebecca B., and Judith Marcus. *Fiesta Time in Mexico*. Champaign, IL: Garrard, 1974.

Milne, Jean. *Fiesta Time in Latin America*. Los Angeles, CA: Ward Richie Press, 1965.

Web Site

See also "Semana Santa in Mexico," an article by May Herz, available from *Inside Mexico*, a company dedicated to producing quality educational materials on Mexican culture: http://www.inside-mexico.com/featuresemana.htm

Moon

The moon peeps in and out of the story of Easter. Not only was the moon a potent symbol of death and rebirth in the ancient world, but **Jesus'** death also took place at the time of the full moon. Today Christians still watch the moon to determine the date of Easter (*see also* **Easter, Date of**).

Moon Symbols and Celebrations in the Ancient World

In the ancient world many cultures viewed the moon as a symbol of fertility, death, and rebirth. These concepts are illustrated in the moon's changing phases. Each month the moon waxes, wanes, disappears, and returns to the sky. Indeed, in the ancient Mediterranean world a number of deities associated with fertility, death, and the afterlife claimed the moon as one of their symbols. These deities include the Egyptian god Osiris, the Greek god Dionysus, and the Babylonian goddess Ishtar (or Innana). The moon was also frequently associated with **water** and with women, feminine principles, or goddesses. Perhaps this association came about because the length of the moon's cycle, 29.5 days, mirrors that of the menstrual cycle (*for more on moon symbolism, see also* **Hare**).

The communal celebrations and sorrows of ancient peoples (and other groups who live in greater contact with the natural world than we do today) often waxed and waned in accordance with the moon's cycle. These peoples frequently greeted the return of the new, crescent moon with relief and the arrival of the full moon with celebration.

411

They often experienced the waning moon as a time of uneasiness and the dark of the moon as a fearful interlude.

The Jewish culture in which Jesus was raised fits this pattern of lunar celebration in part. The ancient Hebrews created a luni-solar calendar, which used both the lunar cycle of 29.5 days and the solar cycle of a year to measure time. Each month began on the day a new moon was sighted. This day was celebrated as a festival, Rosh Hodesh. This observance is mentioned in certain Bible texts (for example, Numbers 10:10, 28:14), which indicate that the ancient Hebrews commemorated each new moon with sacrifices and celebrations. Some Jews still observe Rosh Hodesh today. Several Jewish holidays, including **Passover**, were timed to occur at the full moon (the others are Sukkot and Tu Bishvat). According to the ancient Jewish tradition recorded in the Bible, the first day of Passover falls on the fourteenth day of the Jewish month now called Nisan (Exodus 12:6). This date places the festival close to the time of the **spring equinox**.

The Moon in the Easter Story

Christian scriptures indicate that Jesus was captured and killed at the time of Passover, therefore at the time of the full moon. Three of the four biblical accounts of Jesus' death, those recorded in the Gospels of Matthew, Mark, and Luke, agree that the Last Supper took place on the first day of Passover (*for more on the Last Supper, see* **Maundy Thursday**). That same night **Judas** Iscariot betrayed Jesus and handed him over to the servants and followers of Jerusalem's religious authorities. These texts imply that Jesus was tried and executed the following day. The Gospel according to John records slightly different dates, however. John declares that Jesus was captured on the night before Passover and that he was crucified on the following day, just as the Jews were making their preparations for the Passover meal that they would consume later that evening (*for more on crucifixion, see* **Cross**).

People listening to accounts of Jesus' death and **resurrection** in the ancient world, where the moon and its cycle were already well-known symbols of death and rebirth, might find it easy to apply further lunar symbolism to the Easter story. All Gospel accounts of Jesus' crucifixion declare that he was buried on the day of his death and remained in the tomb for the following day, which was the Sabbath (*for more on the Sabbath, see* **Sunday**). They also agree that he rose from the dead early in the morning on the day after the Sabbath. These two dark days in which Jesus was dead and sealed in the tomb find their parallel in the days of the month in which there is no moon. After this apparent "death," the moon comes back to life, reappearing to the naked eye as a slender crescent on the third day after it disappeared. Jesus also reappeared on the third day, emerging from the tomb fully alive on **Easter Sunday**. Centuries later an early Christian writer found the moon's monthly cycle to be an apt symbol of the Christian belief in resurrection. He noted:

> Luna per omnes menses nascitur, crescit, perficitur, minuitur, consumitur, Innovatur. . . . Quod in luna per menses, hoc in resurrectione semel in toto tempore. (Eliade, 175)

> [The moon during every month is born, grows, reaches its full size, diminishes, is consumed and is renewed. What happens to the moon throughout the months, happens in resurrection but once for all time. (Translated by Nancy Stork)]

The Timing of Easter

Christian authorities sometimes refer to feasts such as Easter, which do not always occur on the same date every year, as "movable feasts." Most of these movable feasts are related to Easter, and their timing is thus affected by the cycles of the moon. Indeed, Easter may be thought of as Christianity's great lunar festival.

The reason for the shifting date of Easter boils down to the fact that the solar cycle of one year is not divisible by an even number of lunar cycles. It takes the earth 365.2422 days to complete its revolution around the sun. We call this period of time a "year." It takes the moon 29.5 days to complete its cycle, going from dark to full to dark again. The Jews, and many other peoples, called this period of time a "month." Indeed, the word "month" comes from the ancient Indo-European root word meaning "moon." During the 365.2422 days that

413

it takes the earth to complete one solar cycle, the moon completes twelve cycles and is 11.25 days into a thirteenth cycle. Because we do not begin a new lunar cycle on the same day we begin a new solar cycle, the various phases of the moon fall on different dates from year to year. The holidays attached to specific dates of the solar year, such as Christmas, fall on the same date each year. The date of Easter, however, is set by both the moon and the sun, and so it shifts about on the calendar.

Christian scripture asserts that Jesus was crucified and resurrected at the time of the Jewish Passover. When early Church authorities met at the Council of Nicaea (325 A.D.) they worked out a system of determining the date of Easter that would place it at approximately this time of year. They decreed that Easter should always fall on a Sunday and that it should not coincide exactly with Passover. Eventually Christian religious authorities agreed that Easter would fall on the first Sunday following the first full moon which occurs on or after the spring equinox (*see also* Easter, Date of). The spring equinox, the twenty-four-hour period in which day and night are of equal lengths, marks the end of the first quarter of the solar year. This rule means that in countries following the Western Christian tradition Easter may occur on any Sunday between March 22 and April 25. Of course, the timing of Easter affects the timing of the whole cycle of related Christian holidays and observances, including **Ash Wednesday**, **Lent**, **Holy Week**, **Ascension Day**, and **Pentecost**.

Moon Lore and Moon Science

For centuries folk beliefs have asserted that the moon affects the behavior of humans, plants, and animals. Most of this lore, while fascinating in and of itself, does not pertain to the Easter story. One bit of moon lore can be tied to the holiday, however. For example, much folklore insists that the full moon inspires irrational behavior in human beings. In fact, the Latin word for moon, *luna*, can be found in our English word "lunatic." Although today we use the word lunatic to describe a person whose behavior is irrational at all times, the word was originally used to describe people who "went crazy" at the time of the full moon.

Several scientific studies support this supposed connection between the full moon and disorderly or erratic behavior. One of them found that murder rates in two major U.S. cities increased noticeably around the time of the full moon. Other studies have shown that hospital emergency rooms see more patients at the full moon than at any other time in the lunar cycle and that psychiatric units admit more patients at this time. The story of Jesus' betrayal, arrest, trial, punishment, and crucifixion, which took place at the time of the full moon, fits this pattern well. These violent events exploded out of an unstable mixture of human motivations and emotions, including fear, greed, anger, blame-shifting, and power-mongering. A believer in lunar folklore might not be surprised to find out that they took place at the time of the full moon.

Further Reading

Bellenir, Karen. *Religious Holidays and Calendars*. Second edition. Detroit, MI: Omnigraphics, 1998.

Bram, Jean Rhys. "Moon." In Mircea Eliade, ed. *The Encyclopedia of Religion*. Volume 10. New York: Macmillan, 1987.

Cain, Kathleen. *Luna: Myth and Mystery*. Boulder, CO: Johnson Books, 1991.

Eisenberg, Azriel. *The Story of the Jewish Calendar*. New York: Abelard-Schuman, 1958.

Eliade, Mircea. *Patterns in Comparative Religion*. Cleveland, OH: Meridian, 1963.

Katzeff, Paul. *Full Moons*. Secaucus, NJ: Citadel Press, 1981.

Niemann, Paul J. *The Lent, Triduum, and Easter Answer Book*. San Jose, CA: Resource Publications, 1998.

Rees, Elizabeth. *Christian Symbols, Ancient Roots*. London, England: Jessica Kingsley, 1992.

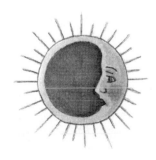

New Clothes

The custom of wearing new clothes on **Easter Sunday** dates back to ancient times. Most commentators trace it back at least as far as the fourth century, when Easter became the most popular time of year for **baptisms**. The ritual of baptism introduces new members to full participation in the Christian faith. In ancient times candidates for baptism were expected to disrobe before undergoing the required immersion in **water**. Afterwards they put on new, white robes as a sign of their change in status. They wore these robes in church during the following week.

By the start of the Middle Ages, the custom of the Easter baptism was already fading. Yet the association of Easter with newness, and renewal, remained. It may have been strengthened by the fact that Easter falls during the spring season, the time when both plants and animals bring forth new life. Moreover the Easter festival itself celebrates the renewal of life in the face of death (*see also* **Resurrection**).

Finally, in medieval times, some European countries observed New Year's Day on March 25 (*see also* **Annunciation; Spring Equinox**). Folklorists suspect that all these associations between Easter and newness encouraged the custom of wearing new clothes at Easter time.

Wearing new clothes at Easter eventually came to be seen not only as a religious custom and symbol, but also as a means of insuring good luck. An old Irish saying advises, "For Christmas, food and drink; for Easter, new clothes." *Poor Robin's Almanac* once warned, "At Easter let your clothes be new, or else be sure you will it rue." In Ireland some children wore **crosses** made of ribbons on their right arms, perhaps serving as a substitute for those who could not afford new garments. Italian folk custom dictated that if a man sent a woman a new pair of gloves for Easter it signified his desire to marry her. If the woman wore the gloves it signaled her intention to accept such an offer. An American superstition counseled that wearing three new items of clothing on Easter Sunday would attract good luck for the rest of the year.

In past times central Europeans not only showed off their finery in church, but also strolled about town and even into the countryside afterwards. Similar outings on **Easter Monday**, called **Emmaus walks**, may have inspired the American **Easter parade**.

Further Reading

Myers, Robert J. *Celebrations: The Complete Book of American Holidays*. Garden City, NY: Doubleday and Company, 1972.

Schmidt, Leigh Eric. *Consumer Rites*. Princeton, NJ: Princeton University Press, 1995.

Weiser, Francis X. *The Easter Book.* New York: Harcourt, Brace and Company, 1954.

No Ruz

Farmer's Day, Jamshed Navroz, Nauroz, Nav Roz, Nawruz, Nevrus, Novrus Bairam

The people of Iran, formerly Persia, celebrate New Year's Day in the spring. Their new year festival, called *No Ruz* or *Nawruz*, falls at the time of the **spring equinox** (around March 21 in the Northern Hemisphere). Some of the folk customs associated with No Ruz resemble folk practices associated with Christian Easter celebrations. The peoples of Iraq, Turkey, central Asia, Azerbaijan, Afghanistan, and Pakistan, as well as the Kurds and some Indians also celebrate No Ruz. The Parsis of India know the festival as *Jamshed Navroz*. The Turks dub it *Nevrus*, and the people of Afghanistan call it *Nauroz*. In Kashmir people have named the holiday *Nav Roz*, and in Turkmenistan it's *Novrus Bairam*.

History

Scholars believe that the people of ancient Mesopotamia (which lies mostly in modern-day Iraq) celebrated their new year festival at the time of the spring equinox. The festival also honored the yearly renewal of the world by the god Marduk, who kept the forces of chaos and destruction at bay. Although the ancient Mesopotamian civilization eventually declined, the holiday survived by transforming itself to fit the changing religious and cultural beliefs of the region. With the rise of the Zoroastrian religion the old festival acquired new significance. It not only celebrated the start of a new year, but also commemorated the creation of the world as we know it and venerated God, who in the Zoroastrian religion was known as Ahura Mazda, the Lord of Wisdom. Researchers have determined that the Achaemenid kings (c. 550–330 B.C.) celebrated this great festival. In the seventh century the rise of Islam eclipsed the Zoroastrian religion in the region. Persians, as well as other Middle Easterners and Asians, kept the holiday after converting to Islam in the seventh and eighth centuries. Nevertheless, No Ruz lost its previous religious associations and became simply a new year celebration.

Although Islam became the dominant faith in the Middle East, Zoroastrianism survived as a minority religion, especially in India, where its modern-day adherents are known as Parsis. The Parsis have maintained their own version of the No Ruz festival, which features religious rituals focused on the ceremonial reading of sacred texts. Parsis also extend good wishes to one another on No Ruz. In addition, they practice a special kind of handshake, called *hamazor*, in which the right hand of one person is clasped between the palms of another.

A Fresh Start

The customs and symbols of the No Ruz festival emphasize newness, freshness, growth, and renewal. In Iran homes are given a thorough cleaning in preparation for the holiday, and people put on **new clothes** (*see also* **Spring Cleaning**). Families decorate their homes with plates of sprouting wheat, dishes of colored eggs, and bowls of **water** in which they place a green leaf (*see also* **Easter Eggs; Egg Lore**). People light candles, often placing them in front of a mirror to magnify the light given off by the flame, and let them burn until completely melted down. In some families these candles are carried about the home accompanied by prayers for the blessing of the dwelling place and its occupants.

Charity

In Iran food, clothing, *halva* (a sweet made from sesame seeds), and money are distributed to the needy at local cemeteries on the Thursday before No Ruz. Families with a comfortable standard of living donate these items. According to old superstitions, bringing these gifts to the graveyard pays one's debts to the dead and, hopefully, curries their favor. This custom also insures that everyone, rich and poor, can celebrate the festival.

Fire

Fire plays another important role in the No Ruz festival. People light outdoor bonfires on the Wednesday before the holiday (*see also* **Easter Fires**). They give thanks for the previous year and perform an old folk charm thought to bring health and good luck for the coming year. While someone jumps over the blaze, their companions sing to the fire asking it to confer its redness (a sign of good health) and take away yellowness (a sign of illness or ill fortune). Some commentators see in this practice a link back to the Zoroastrian religion, in which sacred fires are kept constantly burning in fire temples. In Zoroastrianism fire represents the divine.

The Seven Symbols

Another popular Persian No Ruz custom consists of setting a table with the seven symbols of the holiday. Each of the objects begins with the Farsi letter *seen*, the equivalent of our "s." According to legend, Zoroaster, the founder of the Zoroastrian religion, offered these same substances to the deity Ahura Mazda. Oftentimes this table is set weeks before No Ruz so that it may serve as a festive reminder and symbol of the upcoming holiday. The seven symbols are *Samanu* (a Persian sweet), a coin (*sekeh*), green vegetables (*sabzee*), a hyacinth flower (*sonbol*), garlic (*seer*), dried fruit (*senjed*), and vinegar (*serekh*). These objects represent truth, justice, good thoughts and actions, abundance, virtue, immortality, and generosity.

New Year's Eve and Day

On New Year's eve Persian families set a special, ceremonial table. They lay the dish of sprouting grain and the seven symbols in front of a mirror, which is lit by a number of burning candles, one for each member of the household. A copy of the Qur'an (the holy book of Islam), a bowl of milk, a bowl of yogurt, and some coins also grace the ceremonial table. While waiting for the new year to begin, adults recite the Qur'an or say prayers, a custom which is believed to bless the home and attract good fortune. Many families also set off fireworks on New Year's eve. When the new year begins the families eat sweetmeats, which symbolize a happy new year.

On New Year's day Persian children receive gifts of coins, cake, and dyed and decorated hard-boiled eggs. The eggs represent fruitfulness and the renewal of the earth.

The Thirteen Days of No Ruz

In Iran the No Ruz season lasts for thirteen days. Some families make sure to usher in this festive season with a reading from the Qu'ran. During No Ruz people wear new clothes, give one another gifts, often sweets and coins, and visit family and friends. Another No Ruz custom takes place thirteen days after the holiday. On this day people try to spend as much time as possible picnicking and playing sports or games. The number thirteen brings bad luck in Persian culture. Folk tradition therefore teaches that keeping active outdoors on this day helps one avoid picking up bad luck for the coming year. Persians call the custom "Dodging the Unlucky Number."

Afghanistan

Afghanis celebrate No Ruz with their own distinctive customs. Women make a special dessert with dried fruit and nuts. They also bake cookies to share with friends and neighbors. Kite flying is a popular holiday pastime. In Afghanistan No Ruz may also be called "Farmer's Day." It marks the first day of spring and people celebrate by attending agricultural fairs and livestock competitions.

Special *buzkashi* matches take place in honor of the holiday. Afghanis play this violent sport on horseback with whips. Players lash their mounts and their opponents indiscriminately as each team battles to take control of the carcass of a goat (or calf) and drag it down the field, around a goal post, and back to a central area. Afghani celebrations also include a special ceremony at the tomb of Hazrat Ali in Mazar-i-Sharif. Thousands visit this shrine in the hope of gaining religious merit and healing illnesses.

The Karakalpaks

The Karakalpak people in the central Asian countries of Uzbekistan, Kazakhstan, Russia, and Turkmenistan also celebrate No Ruz. They honor the holiday by dressing in their finest clothes. Children perform skits in schools. Townspeople gather in the central square for games, contests, speeches, and food. At home people celebrate by making and eating *sumalak*, a sweet pudding made from young wheat plants. The tender stalks must be boiled for a day and a night to yield the pudding. Several families band together to prepare a large amount of this time-consuming dish. Everyone takes a turn feeding the fire and stirring the pot. Sumalak symbolizes the No Ruz holiday to the Kara-kalpak people. They not only consider it highly nutritious, but also savor it as the first taste of the new foods that the coming spring harvest will bring.

Further Reading

Cooper, J. C. *The Dictionary of Festivals*. London, England: Thorsons, 1990.

Eliade, Mircea. *Patterns in Comparative Religion*. Cleveland, OH: Meridian, 1963.

Griffin, Robert H., and Ann H. Shurgin, eds. *The Folklore of World Holidays*. Second edition. Detroit, MI: Gale Research, 1999.

Gulevich, Tanya. "Zagmuk." In her *Encyclopedia of Christmas*. Detroit, MI: Omnigraphics, 2000.

Henderson, Helene, and Sue Ellen Thompson, eds. *Holidays, Festivals, and Celebrations of the World Dictionary*. Second edition. Detroit, MI: Omnigraphics, 1997.

Web Sites

"Iranian New Year No Ruz," an article by Massoume Price concerning the history and customs of this festival, posted at: http://www.iranonline.com/festivals/Iranian-new-year/index.html

"Nowrooz Holiday Celebrates Life," a Radio-Free Europe article by Abbas Djavadi and Bruce Pannier, posted at: http://www.rferl.org/nca/features/1998/03/F.RU.980320132251.html

The Republic of Turkey's Ministry of Culture offers a web page describing No Ruz celebrations in Turkey and Central Asia at: http://www.kultur.gov.tr/english/main-e.html (click on "Art-Culture," then "Folk Cultures," then "Nevruz")

Pace Egging

In past centuries children or young men in northern England and Scotland went pace egging on **Easter Monday**. The word pace comes from *Pascha*, the ancient Greek word for Easter which also became the Latin term for the observance. The word Pascha in turn came from *Pesach*, the Aramaic pronunciation of the Hebrew word for **Passover**. Pace egging was also once practiced in Belgium, Denmark, and the Netherlands on various days during the **Easter season**.

Egg Payments and Egg Begging

In medieval and Renaissance times eggs were a valuable source of food and thus sometimes used in lieu of money to pay certain fees. In the thirteenth century English peasants brought eggs to the lord of the local manor at Easter. People also used eggs to make their Easter offering to the church. Country people continued to do so until the eighteenth century in some districts, while the well-to-do offered cash.

The English pace-egging customs familiar to folklorists grew out of older egg-begging customs. These egg-begging customs can be traced back to the sixteenth century. In those days humble people practiced various kinds of begging customs at Christmas time, the object of which was to secure enough food to enjoy a Christmas feast. In some parts of England similar customs spread to Easter and the several days preceding it, when youngsters would go door-to-door reciting folk rhymes encouraging householders to donate an egg, a bit of bacon, a wedge of cheese, or other savory item to their Easter feast. Contemporary American children practice a similar kind of door-to-door begging at Halloween.

Pace Egging

By the eighteenth century inhabitants of some regions of England called this custom "peace egging," a variant of "pace egging." In some places pace eggers sported homemade costumes. These costumes consisted of burned cork smeared across the face, paper streamers pinned to one's clothes, or a simple mask. In other regions youngsters improved the costumes somewhat and added a bit of a folk play revolving around such comic characters as Old Tosspot, Lord Nelson, and Betsy Brownbags. Thus pace egging came to resemble Christmas time mumming, another begging custom whose participants disguised their identities with masks and costumes.

Pace egging was particularly popular in northwestern England, where pace-egg plays quickly caught on. The lads who participated in this custom were known as "pace eggers" or "jolly boys." The following traditional pace-egging verses reflect the food-collecting concerns that inspired the invention of the custom:

> We are two-three jolly boys, all of one mind,
> We are come a-pace-egging, and we hope you'll prove kind.
> We hope you'll prove kind with your eggs and strong beer,
> And we'll come no more a-pace-egging until another year .
> (Hole, 150)

Please, good mistress, an Easter egg,
Or a flitch of bacon
Or a little trundle cheese
Of your own making. (Hole, 151)

Please, Mrs. Whiteleg,
Please to give us an Easter egg
If you won't give us an Easter egg
Your hens will all lay addled eggs,
And your cocks all lay stones. (Hole, 151)

Around the mid-nineteenth century many pace eggers switched their activities to Easter Monday. By this time the custom served less as a means of obtaining food for an Easter feast and more as a way of having fun and enjoying a few free drinks. During the early twentieth century the custom died out in most parts of Britain. In Yorkshire and Cheshire a few groups of children may still present pace-egg plays on Easter Monday, though some folklorists view this as a self-conscious attempt to revive an essentially extinct folk custom.

Further Reading

Hole, Christina. *British Folk Customs*. London, England: Hutchinson and Company, 1976.

Howard, Alexander. *Endless Cavalcade*. London, England: Arthur Barker, 1964.

Hutton, Ronald. *Stations of the Sun*. Oxford, England: Oxford University Press, 1996.

Paczki Day
Fat Thursday, Tlusty Czwartek

In past times Poles observed a **fast** which prohibited the consumption of butter and lard throughout the forty days of **Lent**. They celebrated *Zapusty*, or **Carnival**, in the last few days before Lent, indulging in rich, buttery foods that would soon be off limits and engaging in all sorts of amusements thought to be out of keeping with the solemn spirit of Lent. One type of pastry in particular, a large jelly-filled donut called *paczki*, became a holiday favorite. Making paczki served as a means of using up the last remnants of soon-to-be-forbidden foods. Eventually these sweet treats came to be seen as emblematic of the joyful excesses of the last days of Carnival.

In Poland people eat paczki on the Thursday before **Ash Wednesday**, the first day of Lent. They call this day *Tlusty Czwartek*, or Fat Thursday *(for more on Fat Thursday, see also* **Shrovetide***)*. In past times people also celebrated the day with parties and masked balls.

Polish Americans uphold the custom of eating paczki in preparation for Lent. They celebrate Paczki Day on the last day of Carnival, however. The pastries are widely available in Polish-American bakeries on that day, and may even be found in supermarkets in areas that boast large Polish-American populations. Polka dances may also be organized in celebration of Paczki Day.

In past times Polish Carnival celebrations included some very boisterous customs. On Shrove Tuesday, the last day of Carnival, some people waited by the church doors to catch those young adults of marriageable age who had not yet found a spouse. They tried to pin a smelly, unattractive bit of garbage, such as a chicken foot or a herring skeleton, to their backs without them knowing it. Sometimes they also pinned rude verses to their clothing making fun of their failure to find a mate. Another old Shrove Tuesday custom encouraged young men to round up a bunch of young women and hold a mock livestock auction. Before bidding on the women, the men examined their eyes and teeth, just as they would do before buying cattle. Lively and humorous banter accompanied this event. At Easter time the young women were expected to reward those who had bid for them with a gift of **Easter eggs**. If no one bid on her, a girl considered herself disgraced. In another old Shrove Tuesday custom husbands and wives gathered in local taverns to watch the women dance. The higher the women leaped, the higher the hemp crops would grow. If a man thought his wife could leap higher, he bought her another mug of beer and asked to her to dance some more. In some places Poles constructed a straw figure named Marzanna, who represented winter, and drowned her on Shrove Tuesday. In other places this event took place during the first half of Lent, often on **Laetare Sunday**.

For more on Easter in Poland, *see also* **Poland, Easter and Holy Week in**

Further Reading

Lord, Priscilla Sawyer, and Daniel J. Foley. *Easter the World Over*. Philadelphia, PA: Chilton Book Company, 1971.

Nowakowski, Jacek, and Marlene Perrin. *Polish Touches*. Iowa City, IA: Penfield Press, 1996.

Spicer, Dorothy Gladys. *Book of Festivals*. 1937. Reprint. Detroit, MI: Omnigraphics, 1990.

Web Sites

"Paczki Day," a page on the Polish Easter Traditions web site, posted by Dr. Ann Hetzel Gunkel, a professor of philosophy and cultural studies at Columbia College in Chicago: http://acweb.colum.edu/users/agunkel/homepage/easter/easter.html

"Paczki Day," a brief article on Paczki Day that includes recipes, posted at the *Polish-American Journal's* web site at: http://www.polamjournal.com/Library/Holidays/paczki/body_paczki.html

Palm

In **Jesus'** day many Mediterranean and Middle Eastern peoples used the palm branch or palm tree as a symbol. The early Christians adopted these symbols from the cultures that surrounded them and reinterpreted them. In early Christian art the palm branch often represents martyrdom. It may also stand for heaven, peace, and victory. During the **Lent** and **Easter seasons**, however, the palm branch calls to mind **Palm Sunday** and all the events that the day commemorates.

Palm Sunday

Palm Sunday falls on the **Sunday** before Easter, which is the sixth and last Sunday of Lent. It constitutes the first day of **Holy Week**, a week of observances commemorating the last events in Jesus' life. Palm Sunday celebrates Jesus' arrival in Jerusalem. According to the Bible crowds gathered to welcome him, hailing him as a prophet, that is, someone who understands and speaks for God. As he rode by, mounted on a donkey, they greeted him with cries of "Hosanna," an exclamation praising God, which means "Save, we pray." Many reverenced him by taking off their own cloaks and throwing them in his path or by cutting green branches for him to ride on (Matthew 21, Mark 11, Luke 19). In the account of this event given in the Gospel according to John, people waved palm branches as Jesus rode by (John 12:12-15).

The Ancient Hebrews

The ancient Hebrews considered the palm a beautiful and noble tree, and associated it with joy, fertility, and God's blessing. In ancient times the Jews adopted the custom of carrying palm fronds, woven together with other branches, during the Feast of the Tabernacles. They also built and lived in huts made of palm leaves for the duration of this week-long celebration. During this joyous festival, also called Sukkot, they gave thanks to God for the harvest and rejoiced in their deliverance from exile and slavery.

Peoples of the Ancient Mediterranean and Middle East

The peoples of the ancient Middle East, including the Babylonians, Egyptians, Jews, and Assyrians, found many uses for the palm tree. The palm tree not only provided cool shade in the hot Middle Eastern climate, but also furnished food in the form of dates. Over the centuries the peoples of the Middle East discovered how to construct walls and fences with palm branches, weave palm fronds into roof thatching, mats and baskets, and spin the stringy material that grows at the crown of the tree into rope. They fermented palm sap to create an alcoholic beverage and pressed date kernels to obtain oil.

In ancient times the palm was considered beautiful and stately. Egyptian buildings often featured stylized columns modeled on the palm tree. Moreover, the builders of Egyptian, Assyrian, and Phoenician temples embellished their work with the image of the palm tree. According to the Bible, Jewish craftsmen adorned the temple built by King Solomon with carvings of cherubim, flowers, and palm trees (1 Kings 6:29).

The palm served as a spiritual symbol for a number of ancient peoples. The ancient Greeks sometimes used the palm tree as an emblem of the sun god, Apollo. The Greek word for palm, *phoenix*, tied it closely to the mythological bird believed to have eternal life. Some writers assert that various Middle Eastern peoples, including the Egyptians, Babylonians, and Assyrians, considered the palm sacred in some way.

429

Because it was known for its beautiful palm trees, the Greeks and Romans named the land of Phoenicia (which lies mostly in modern Lebanon) after the Greek word for palm. Indeed the ancient Phoenician cities of Tyre and Sidon minted coins stamped with the image of the palm tree. Numerous ancient Jewish coins also feature palm trees.

The ancient Romans themselves used the palm branch as a symbol of victory. Roman soldiers paraded with palm branches as a way of announcing their military conquests. After the defeat of the Jewish uprising against Rome in 70 A.D., the Romans issued a coin picturing a weeping woman underneath a palm tree.

Christians

The early Christians also used the palm branch as a symbol. They borrowed the Roman interpretation of the palm branch as an emblem of victory but added their own twist to this interpretation. For the early Christians the palm branch represented a victory of the spirit rather than a military victory. As such the palm branch quickly became a symbol of martyrdom. It was also used to represent heaven, peace, and hope. In early Christian artwork the image of the palm tree sometimes stood for the Tree of Life and was used as an emblem of Christ (*see also* **Cross; Tree of the Cross**).

By the Middle Ages lengthy palm processions were an important feature of Palm Sunday celebrations. In western Europe medieval pilgrims often carried palm branches as symbols of their status as pilgrims, perhaps echoing this seasonal custom.

Further Reading

Becker, Udo. "Palm Tree." In his *The Continuum Encyclopedia of Symbols*. New York: Continuum, 1994.

Heath, Sidney. *The Romance of Symbolism*. 1909. Reprint. Detroit, MI: Gale Research, 1976.

Knapp, Justina. *Christian Symbols and How to Use Them*. 1935. Reprint. Detroit, MI: Gale Research, 1974.

Lehner, Ernst, and Johanna Lehner. *Folklore and Symbolism of Flowers, Plants and Trees*. 1960. Reprint. Detroit, MI: Omnigraphics, 1990.

Murphy, F. X. "Palm." In *New Catholic Encyclopedia*. Volume 10. New York: McGraw-Hill, 1967.

"Palm." In Richard Cavendish, ed. *Man, Myth and Magic*. Volume 14. New York: Marshall Cavendish, 1997.

"Palm." In Leland Ryken, James C. Wilhoit, and Tremper Longman III, eds. *Dictionary of Biblical Imagery*. Downers Grove, IL: InterVarsity Press, 1998.

Webber, F. R. *Church Symbolism*. 1938. Second edition, revised. Reprint. Detroit, MI: Omnigraphics, 1992.

Palm Sunday

Dimanche des Rameaux (Branch Sunday), Domingo de las Palmas (Sunday of the Palms), Domingo de Ramos (Branch Sunday), Fig Sunday, Flowering Sunday, Hosanna Sunday, Pascua Florida (Flowery Easter), Pasques Fleuris (Flowery Easter), Passion Sunday, Willow Sunday, Willowswitch Sunday

Palm Sunday falls on the **Sunday** before Easter, which is the sixth and last Sunday of **Lent**. It constitutes the first day of **Holy Week**, a week of observances commemorating the last events in **Jesus'** life. On Palm Sunday Christians remember Jesus' triumphal arrival in Jerusalem. According to the Bible crowds gathered to welcome him, hailing him as a prophet, that is, someone who understands and speaks for God. As he rode by, mounted on a donkey, they greeted him with cries of "Hosanna," a Hebrew phrase meaning "Save, we pray" or "Save now." Many reverenced him by taking off their own cloaks and throwing them in his path or by cutting green branches for him to ride on (Matthew 21, Mark 11, Luke 19). In the account of this event given in the Gospel according to John, people waved **palm** branches as Jesus rode by (John 12:12-15). The ancient Hebrews considered the palm a beautiful and noble tree, and associated it with joy, fertility, and God's blessing. The ancient Romans viewed the palm branch as a symbol of victory. The early Christians borrowed

431

this symbolism from the Romans. Nevertheless, they put their own stamp on it, using the palm branch not only as an emblem of victory but also of martyrdom.

Since ancient times Palm Sunday church services have included Bible readings recounting the Passion story. This story tells what happened to Jesus in Jerusalem. Less than one week after a crowd cheered his arrival, a disciple betrayed him, the Roman governor Pontius **Pilate** sentenced him to death, and a crowd witnessed his crucifixion (*see also* **Judas**; *for more on crucifixion, see* **Cross**).

The palm procession, a reenactment of the joyous welcome given to Jesus as he rode into Jerusalem, constitutes one of the day's oldest customs. It dates back to ancient times. The palm branch came to represent both the joy and triumph of this occasion and thus became a symbol of the holiday. In many churches palm branches or crosses woven from palm fronds are blessed and distributed to worshipers. Roman Catholic and Episcopal churches store the remainder of the blessed palms until **Ash Wednesday** of the following year, when they are burned to make the ashes that the clergy daub onto the foreheads of those who attend Ash Wednesday services. The liturgical color for Palm Sunday is red, signifying martyrdom, love, and suffering.

History

The oldest known account of a Palm Sunday service dates back to about 380 A.D. It reveals the palm procession to be the oldest custom associated with the day. According to Egeria, a late fourth-century pilgrim to the Holy Land, Jerusalem Christians celebrated Palm Sunday with a procession that led from the Mount of Olives into the city. They gathered on the Mount of Olives around five in the afternoon to listen to a reading from one of the Gospel accounts of Jesus' entry into Jerusalem. Then the bishop, representing Jesus, led them down the hill into the city. Egeria notes that many in the crowd carried palm or olive branches.

Though Egeria's account provides us with the earliest description of a Palm Sunday service, some scholars suspect that earlier celebrations took place in the Christian communities of Alexandria, Egypt, and Constantinople (modern-day Istanbul), Turkey. They suspect that when Christians from these cities made pilgrimages to the Holy Land, they introduced these observances to the Jerusalem community, which later adopted them.

The most striking element of these early observances was the palm procession. The Palm Sunday procession spread to western Europe in the early Middle Ages. The procession, as well as the ceremonial blessing of palm branches at the altar appeared in Spain some time between the fifth and seventh centuries. Similar rites were probably adopted in Rome sometime around the eighth century.

As the palm procession spread throughout Europe people altered it to suit the local landscape. The processions usually began from some holy place, such as a church or shrine just outside the town, and led to the city's cathedral or principal church. In some places, especially France and England, the clergy carried the Blessed Sacrament, or **Eucharist**, at the head of the procession. In other places people marched behind a cross, the Bible, or saints' relics. In still other areas a *Palmesel* or *Palmchristus* led the way. These wooden statues depicting Jesus mounted on a donkey can be traced back to the tenth century and were especially popular in Germany. Bystanders watching these processions often took active roles as well, strewing branches, clothes, carpets, or flowers in the path of the parade. In Biberbach, Germany, before the Protestant Reformation, choir members echoed the actions of Jesus' first followers, who threw their cloaks to the ground for him to walk on, by removing their surplices and tossing them in the path of the Palmesel.

Orthodox Christians also celebrate Palm Sunday with processions. Orthodoxy is one of the three main branches of the Christian faith. It developed in eastern Europe, the Middle East, and north Africa. Orthodoxy and Roman Catholicism split apart from each other about 1,000 years ago, thus the two groups developed different religious customs. In Constantinople, the capital of the Greek-speaking Byzantine Empire, palm processions can be traced back to the ninth or tenth centuries. A document from the fourteenth century reveals that the Byzantine emperor himself marched in this procession, accompanied by the Orthodox patriarch, or bishop, of Constantinople, and numerous other church and state officials. By the evening of the previous day, **Lazarus Saturday**, people had strewn the parade route with palm, myrtle, and laurel branches, as well as flowers. The columns that lined the route were similarly decorated.

In many western European countries these elaborate Palm Sunday processions shrank and declined after the Reformation, the sixteenth-century religious reform movement that gave birth to Protestant Christianity. In many regions they became short parades around the churchyard or even shorter processions within the church itself. As many cemeteries were housed in the churchyard in past eras, these processions gave the congregation a special opportunity to pray beside the graves of the departed. Today, even though cemeteries are often located far from home and church, the custom of visiting family graves on Palm Sunday persists in England, France, Belgium, and the United States.

In addition to the palm procession, the blessing of the palms constitutes another distinctive feature of Palm Sunday religious services. This ceremony can be traced back as far as the sixth century. By the late Middle Ages it had become a long and detailed ritual. In that era the blessed palms not only represented Jesus' triumphal entry into Jerusalem, but also came to be seen as objects that offered protection against the devil. In England palm crosses were once sold as cures for diseases.

Modern Revisions

In the 1950s Roman Catholic officials shortened and changed the palm blessing ceremony in order to refocus worshipers' attention on the event the holiday commemorates: Jesus' entry into Jerusalem and the beginning of Holy Week. In the 1960s the reforms brought about by Vatican II, a series of important meetings of Roman Catholic leaders, led Church authorities to officially change the name of the sixth

Sunday in Lent from Palm Sunday to **Passion Sunday**. This decision reflects the desire of Church officials to place greater emphasis on the story of the last days in Jesus' life than on the blessing of the palms. Indeed, this story, referred to as the Passion story, is read or sung at Palm Sunday services in Roman Catholic churches, as well as those Protestant churches that have retained elements of Roman Catholic tradition in their worship services. If the Passion story is to be sung, an old liturgical tradition recommends that the part of the narrator be assigned to someone with a tenor voice, the part of Jesus to a bass voice, and the other parts to alto voices.

Other Names for Palm Sunday

One old folk name for the day, Hosanna Sunday, comes from the cry of the people as they welcomed Jesus into Jerusalem. Most other folk names, however, refer to plants used to celebrate the festival. Since palm trees don't grow in cold, northern climates, many northern Europeans had to adapt their Palm Sunday customs to suit the climate and vegetation of their land. The Italians substituted olive branches for palm branches, and the Irish yews. In Russia, Germany, Poland, Lithuania, and England worshipers made do with willow branches. Indeed, in Russia the use of willow branches inspired people to call the festival "Willow Sunday." The Spanish refer to the day as *Domingo de Ramos*, or "Branch Sunday," in reference to the use of green branches as a religious symbol. The French also call the day Branch Sunday, or *Dimanche des Rameaux* in French. "Flowery Easter" serves as both an old Spanish and a French name for the holiday. This translates to *Pascua Florida* in Spanish and *Pasques Fleuris* in French. The name recalls the old custom of blessing flowers as well as palm branches, in addition to the custom of entwining flowers amid the fronds of the blessed palm branches.

Pascua Florida, the old Spanish name for the holiday, engraved itself onto the map of the United States when Spanish explorer Ponce de León caught sight of the North American continent on March 20, 1513. It was Palm Sunday, so he named the lush, green land "Florida" in honor of the day and in recognition of the land's fertility.

Palm Sunday in Jerusalem

Christians in Jerusalem still observe Palm Sunday with a procession from the Mount of Olives to Jerusalem, retracing the route by which Jesus was supposed to have entered the city. Researchers believe that Jesus entered the city by the old Zusan Gate, which the Romans demolished in 70 A.D. Another gate, called the Golden Gate, replaced it. In the ninth century, however, the Muslim rulers of Jerusalem walled up the Golden Gate in an effort to safeguard the city against invaders. In spite of the difficulties in retracing Jesus' original route, thousands of pilgrims from around the world come to Jerusalem each year to participate in this endeavor. In recent years Christian Palestinian children have had the honor of leading the worshipers towards Jerusalem. The procession descends from the Mount of Olives, passes the Garden of Gethsemane, and crosses the Kidron Valley before entering the walled Old City. Today's worshipers still carry palm branches in imitation of those Jerusalemites who originally welcomed Jesus into the city 2,000 years ago.

Palm Sunday in Spain

In many Spanish towns and villages, people observe the day with special religious processions. Frequently children carrying palm branches lead these parades. Some processions feature large floats called *pasos*, which display scenes from the last days of Jesus' life depicted with life-sized wooden statues. Teams of men, and occasionally women, carry these floats, which can weigh more than two tons (*see also* **Spain, Easter and Holy Week in**).

Palm Sunday in Austria, Germany, and the former Yugoslavia

In Austria palm branches are blessed at church services and distributed to parishioners. One old custom encouraged Austrian farmers to transfer this blessing to their homesteads by singing and praying as they walked through their buildings and fields, leaving a sprig of blessed palm in each place. According to Austrian folklore the sprigs

437

afford protection against disease and ill weather. Another old custom taught children to festoon palm branches with **pretzels** and to carry them through the streets in honor of the day.

In Germany's Black Forest region people decorated poles with pussy willows, leaves, streamers, hearts, and crosses, and carried them into church to be blessed. Poles studded with glittering glass beads were also brought in for a blessing. Later, farmers installed these poles in their fields as a means of protecting and blessing their crops. In some areas of Germany the Palmesel can still be found leading Palm Sunday processions to church. Blessed willow wands or palm branches are brought home and used for decorations. German folklore teaches that the branches may transfer the blessing to the home. In some areas twigs from these branches were at one time planted in gardens in the hopes of protecting them from lightning (*see also* **Germany, Easter and Holy Week in**).

In the former Yugoslavia willow branches are blessed in church services. Old folk customs encouraged parishioners to bring the blessed willows home with them and parade them through their fields as a means of imparting a blessing on them. Afterwards the branches might be displayed above doors and on barns. Another set of old folk traditions advised young women to toss freshly gathered blossoms into their bath **water**. This Palm Sunday flower bath was supposed to help them maintain their beauty throughout the year. In addition, girls were taught to sow flax and flower seeds on this day, while boys cut green branches to make garlands and crowned their girlfriends with willow wreaths.

Palm Sunday in Mexico

Mexicans call Palm Sunday *Domingo de las Palmas*, or "Sunday of the Palms." Many gather together large bunches of palms, flowers, and bay branches to bring with them to church. Afterwards they bring these bouquets home with them. Mexican folklore teaches that blessed Palm Sunday flowers can ward off diseases (*see also* **Mexico, Easter and Holy Week in**).

Palm Sunday in Greece

In northern Greece Orthodox priests bless laurel and myrtle branches during the Palm Sunday religious services. Laurel, or bay, branches are an old Greek emblem of triumph. In addition, parishioners fashion palm fronds into baskets, crosses, stars, and half-**moon** shapes. The priest also blesses these and gives one to everyone attending the service. People take them home and place them next to their icons, religious images used in prayer and worship. Religious processions may also take place inside churches, reminding worshipers of the triumphal welcome given to Jesus as he rode into Jerusalem on the first Palm Sunday. The strict Lenten **fast** practiced by Orthodox Christians may be slightly relaxed in honor of the day to include fish (*see also* **Greece, Easter and Holy Week in**).

Palm Sunday in the Netherlands

In the Netherlands children celebrate by making a Palm Sunday ornament called a *Palmpaas*, or "Easter Palm." The palmpaas usually consists of a rod or staff attached to a hoop from which dangle all sorts of Easter emblems and good things to eat, including eggshells, paper flags, chocolate eggs, raisins, figs, oranges, and cakes (*see also* **Easter Eggs**). Children go door to door displaying their homemade palmpaas and begging for eggs.

Palm Sunday in England and Wales

In England, as in many other northern European countries, palm processions declined in popularity after the Reformation. Nevertheless, the old association between Palm Sunday and greenery remained, giving rise to a new tradition whereby boys and men collected willow, box, or hazel branches in the days preceding Palm Sunday. These branches were thought to bring good luck and were used as home decorations. In past times some people called Palm Sunday "Fig Sunday" in reference to the custom of eating figs or fig pudding on that day. In some areas special fig fairs were held as a means of supplying consumers with the fruit. Some writers assert that the day acquired that name from an association with a story told by Jesus in the Bible known as the Parable of the Barren Fig (Matthew 21:18-22, Mark 11:12-14). The Welsh call Palm Sunday "Flowering Sunday," perhaps because of the custom of strewing family gravesites with flowers and greenery on that day (*see also* **England, Easter and Holy Week in**).

Palm Sunday in Poland, Russia, the Ukraine, and Finland

An informal Polish name for Palm Sunday is "Flower Sunday." Poles bring home pussy willow wands that have been blessed by the priest. They are put in vases of water to encourage Easter blooms. Old folk customs instructed the man and woman of the house to switch one another with these wands. The beating of a man was said to help his crops to grow, the beating of a woman was said to make her fertile. Russians and Ukrainians held similar beliefs about Palm Sunday willow wands (*see also* **Poland, Easter and Holy Week in; Russia, Easter and Holy Week in; Ukraine, Easter and Holy Week in**).

The Finns sometimes call the day "Willowswitch Sunday" in reference to an old custom whereby children go door to door with willow switches with which they swat the woman of the house. Farm women in turn hit their sheep and cows with a willow switch. According to Finnish folk beliefs, this switching was supposed to impart health. Farm families saved the switches to use again when it was time to take the animals into open pasture (*see also* **Finland, Easter and Holy Week in**).

Further Reading

Bradshaw, Paul F. *The Search for the Origins of Christian Worship*. New York: Oxford University Press, 1992.

Hogan, Julie. *A Treasury of Easter Celebrations*. Nashville, TN: Ideals Publications, 1999.

Hole, Christina. *British Folk Customs*. London, England: Hutchinson and Company, 1976.

Lord, Priscilla Sawyer, and Daniel J. Foley. *Easter Garland*. 1963. Reprint. Detroit, MI: Omnigraphics, 1999.

———. *Easter the World Over*. Philadelphia, PA: Chilton Book Company, 1971.

Mershman, Francis. "Palm Sunday." In Charles G. Herbermann et al., eds. *The Catholic Encyclopedia*. New York: Appleton, 1913. Available online at: http://www.newadvent.org/cathen/11432b.htm

Metford, J. C. J. *Dictionary of Christian Lore and Legend*. London, England: Thames and Hudson, 1983.

Monti, James. *The Week of Salvation*. Huntington, IN: Our Sunday Visitor Publications, 1993.

O'Shea, W. J. "Palm Sunday." In *New Catholic Encyclopedia*. Volume 10. New York: McGraw-Hill, 1967.

"Palm." In Leland Ryken, James C. Wilhoit, and Tremper Longman III, eds. *Dictionary of Biblical Imagery*. Downers Grove, IL: InterVarsity Press, 1998.

"Palm Sunday." In E. A. Livingstone, ed. *The Oxford Dictionary of the Christian Church*. Third edition. Oxford, England: Oxford University Press, 1997.

Pierce, Joanne M. "Holy Week and Easter in the Middle Ages." In Paul F. Bradshaw and Lawrence A. Hoffman, eds. *Passover and Easter: Origin and History to Modern Times.* Two Liturgical Traditions series, volume 5. Notre Dame, IN: University of Notre Dame Press, 1999.

Rouvelas, Marilyn. *A Guide to Greek Traditions and Customs in America*. Bethesda, MD: Nea Attiki Press, 1993.

Spicer, Dorothy. *Book of Festivals*. 1937. Reprint. Detroit, MI: Omnigraphics, 1990.

Urlin, Ethel. *Festivals, Holy Days, and Saints' Days*. 1915. Reprint. Detroit, MI: Omnigraphics, 1992.

Weiser, Francis X. *The Easter Book*. Harcourt, Brace and Company, 1954.

Pancake Day

In England Shrove Tuesday, the last day before **Lent**, is also known as "Pancake Day" (*for more on Shrove Tuesday, see* **Shrovetide**). Hundreds of years ago the English observed a strict **fast** throughout Lent, during which they ate neither meat nor dairy products. They hurried to consume all these foods in the last several days before Lent, lest they go to waste during the fast. One of the quickest ways to use up butter, milk, and eggs was to make and eat pancakes. Hence Shrove Tuesday became "Pancake Day."

In medieval times church **bells** tolled on Shrove Tuesday reminding people to confess their **sins** to a priest before the start of Lent. In England, the Reformation, a sixteenth-century religious reform movement, reduced the importance of the **pre-Lenten** confession. The bell-ringing custom remained, however, although people reinterpreted its meaning. They began to hear the clanging bells as a reminder to use up all their butter, milk, and eggs before the start of Lent. Thus the Shrove Tuesday bell became known as the "pancake bell."

In the year 1621, English writer John Taylor penned a humorous description of these proceedings:

> . . . by that time that the clock strikes eleven, which (by the help of a knavish sexton) is commonly before nine, then there is a bell rung, called the Pancake-bell, the sound whereof makes thousands of people distracted, and forgetful of manners or of humanity; then there is a thing called wheaten flour, which the sulphury, Necromantic cooks do mingle with water, eggs, spice and other tragical, magical enchantments, then they put it by little and little into a frying-pan of boiling suet, where it makes a confused, dismal hissing (like the Lemean snakes in the reeds of Acheron, Styx or Phlegeton) until at last, by the skill of the cooks it is transformed into the form

of a Flap-Jack, which in our translation is called a Pancake, which ominous incantation the ignorant people do devour very greedily. (Hutton, 152)

In past times English lads went door to door on Shrove Tuesday, begging for pancakes and other soon-to-be-forbidden treats. Folklorists have preserved one of the rhymes that accompanied this annual outing:

Dibbity, dibbity, dibbity, doe,
Give me a pancake and I'll go;
Dibbity, dibbity, dibbity, ditter,
Please to give me a bit of a fritter. (Lord and Foley, 63)

Perhaps this old begging custom inspired Westminster School's "Pancake Greeze," an event which continues to this day. At 11 a.m. on Shrove Tuesday the school cook tosses a large pancake up over a crowd of students chosen to represent their grades. The boys scramble for possession of the flapjack and the one emerging with the cake —or the largest piece of it—receives a monetary reward from the school dean. The cook also receives a reward for his participation in this annual event.

Pancake Race

The annual pancake race that takes place in the town of Olney, England, is perhaps the most famous pancake-related event that occurs on Shrove Tuesday. According to local legend, this race began in the year 1445 when a housewife engaged in making pancakes heard the church bells summoning worshipers to confession. Not wanting to be late for church, but at the same time not wanting to leave her pancake uncooked, she wrapped a scarf around her head and dashed off to church, still wearing her apron and still flipping her pancake in the skillet. This unusual feat attracted the attention of the neighbors. In succeeding years they followed her example, and a local tradition was born. Each year the housewives of Olney race each other to the village church, wearing housedresses, aprons, and headscarves, and carrying a skillet containing a flapjack, which they are required to flip

443

three times during the race. The prize for winning is a kiss from the verger, or church caretaker.

In 1950 the housewives of Liberal, Kansas, decided to take up Shrove Tuesday pancake racing. They challenged the women of Olney to a competition to see whose winner turned in the best time. Liberal's pancake race has thrived since that day, and a friendly rivalry has grown up between the two pancake-loving towns. Liberal racers follow the same rules and receive the same prize as do their colleagues in England. These two well-known events have inspired other communities and church congregations to sponsor pancake races on Shrove Tuesday.

Although few English people maintain the strict Lenten fasting that gave rise to these events, many still crave pancakes on Shrove Tuesday. This customary dish is also consumed in the United States, where some churches hold "pancake suppers" on this day.

Further Reading

Hole, Christina. *Easter and Its Customs*. New York: M. Barrows and Company, 1961.
Hutton, Ronald. *Stations of the Sun*. Oxford, England: Oxford University Press, 1996.
Lord, Priscilla Sawyer, and Daniel J. Foley. *Easter the World Over*. Philadelphia, PA: Chilton Book Company, 1971.

Web Sites

For the history of the pancake race in Liberal, Kansas, see the following page, written by local resident Virginia Leete: http://www.pancakeday.com/History.html

The following site, posted by the town of Olney, England, furnishes a description and photos of the pancake race at: http://www.olney.co.uk/pancake99/gallery/pancake99.htm

Pardon

The golden threads of forgiveness, pardon, and release weave in and out of the events commemorated during **Holy Week**. Pontius **Pilate** pardons **Barabbas**. **Jesus** forgives his tormentors and pardons the **Good Thief** (Luke 23:32-43). After his death Jesus releases the souls of the departed from captivity in the underworld (*see also* **Descent into Hell**). In addition, the early Christians quickly came to see Jesus' death itself as a sacrifice that offered both forgiveness and **redemption** to the whole human race.

In recognition of the importance of these themes to the spiritual message of the Easter festival, the early Christians pardoned and released criminals during Holy Week. St. John Chrysostom (c. 347-407) mentioned this practice in his writings, drawing a parallel between these earthly pardons and Jesus' Descent into Hell, an event commemorated on **Holy Saturday**. St. Gregory of Nyssa (c. 335-c. 394) recorded the fact that some Christians expanded the concept of the Easter pardon by freeing slaves at this time of year.

Centuries later French monarchs still granted an Easter pardon on **Good Friday**, releasing one prisoner whose crime was otherwise unpardonable. Some called this period of the year the "reign of Christ" in reference to the spirit of forgiveness evidenced in these kinds of actions. In the eleventh century the citizens of Aquitaine, a region of southwestern France, were expected to uphold the "truce of God" from the evening prayer service on **Spy Wednesday** until the morning of **Easter Monday**. The local laws imposed strict punishment on any who dared commit an act of violence or revenge during these holy days.

In a few countries Christians still observe the old tradition of granting Easter pardons (*see also* **Forgiveness Sunday**). In Colombia this custom is called the "Feast of the Prisoners" and is practiced on **Maundy**

Thursday in the town of Popayán. On this day a small band of politicians, priests, and children, accompanied by the army band, march out to the local jail. There they prepare a banquet for the prisoners from the cartloads of food that they brought with them in the procession. After the feast, officials select one prisoner from among those who have served most of their sentence. For the rest of the day he sits on a street corner, under guard, while passersby offer him gifts of food and money. At evening time the guards set him free (*see also* **Colombia, Easter and Holy Week in**).

Further Reading

Griffin, Robert H., and Ann H. Shurgin, eds. *Junior Worldmark Encyclopedia of World Holidays*. Volume 1. Detroit, MI: UXL, 2000.

Monti, James. *The Week of Salvation*. Huntington, IN: Our Sunday Visitor Publications, 1993.

Slim, Hugo. *A Feast of Festivals*. London, England: Marshall Pickering, 1996.

Weiser, Francis X. *The Easter Book*. New York: Harcourt, Brace and Company, 1954.

Pascha

Christian scripture asserts that **Jesus'** death and **resurrection** took place during the Jewish **Passover** festival. Indeed, early Christians interpreted the end of Jesus' life in light of the biblical story of Exodus, which explains the events behind the celebration of Passover. In this way they came to understand Jesus as a new kind of sacrificial **lamb**, one whose willingness to die for their sakes washed away their **sins**, thereby delivering them from a form of spiritual bondage and leading them towards a new relationship with God (*see also* **Redemption**). They began to celebrate this understanding in a new ceremony called the **Eucharist**, and in a new festival called *Pascha*.

Easter in the Context of Passover

Christian scripture — in particular, passages from the Gospels of Mark, Matthew, and Luke — describes Jesus' last meal with his friends as a Passover supper. At this meal Jesus asked his followers to remember him by breaking **bread** and drinking **wine** together in his name. In response to this request, Christians later created a special religious ritual called the Eucharist. This ceremony is celebrated weekly in many churches around the world, recalling the words and deeds of Jesus at that Passover supper (*see also* **Maundy Thursday**).

According to the Gospels of Mark, Matthew, and Luke, Jesus' arrest took place later that night. His trial and crucifixion occurred the following day, still the first day of Passover according to the Jewish calendar (*for more on crucifixion, see* **Cross**). The Gospel of John records slightly different dates. According to John, the Last Supper took place the day before Passover, as did Jesus' trial and crucifixion (*for more on the Last Supper, see* Maundy Thursday). Some scholars have pointed out that in John's account, Jesus is dying on the cross at the same time that the Passover lambs are being killed in the Temple. Thus in John's account Jesus is cast as the new sacrificial lamb in a very direct way. The Gospel of John introduces this theme much earlier, when John the Baptist recognizes Jesus as "the Lamb of God" (John 1:29). John also recounts that the Roman soldiers presiding at the Crucifixion refrained from breaking Jesus' legs (John 19:32-33). This echoes the requirement found in Jewish scripture that the Passover lamb be roasted and eaten without breaking a bone.

Scholars believe that John's Gospel was written sometime between 75 and 100 A.D. Nevertheless, the earliest Christian scripture to refer to Jesus as the Passover lamb was written by Paul decades earlier. Writing around the middle of the first century Paul draws the connection directly, declaring that "Christ, our Paschal lamb, has been sacrificed" (1 Corinthians 5:7).

The Christian Pascha

In Christian scripture and the writings of early Christians, the Jewish Passover is referred to as Pascha, a Greek pronunciation of the He-

447

brew word *Pesah*. In these early Christian texts the term Pascha refers not only to the Jewish Passover festival, the sacrificial lamb, and the Passover meal, but also to the emerging Christian festival later called Easter. This usage reflects the view that Jesus' death on the cross represented a new Passover sacrifice and Exodus experience for all who would later follow him. By the mid-second century this interpretation had become widespread in Christian circles.

In English the word "Easter" eventually replaced the Greek term Pascha as the name of the festival (*see also* **Easter, Origin of the Word**). Other European languages still retain traces of the original Greek term in their word for Easter, however. The Spanish refer to the festival as *Pascua*, the Italians call it *Pasqua*, the French *Pâques*, the Portuguese *Páscoa*, the Romanians *Paste*, and the Greeks and Russians *Pascha*.

By the second half of the second century, Christians were regularly observing a yearly Passover festival in commemoration of Christ's death and resurrection. They celebrated from sunset to midnight on the fifteenth of the month of Nisan (according to the Jewish calendar). Documents from that era suggest that the observance consisted of **fasting**, chanting, scripture reading (especially the twelfth chapter of Exodus), the Eucharist, and a homily. By the end of the second century Christian communities adopted the practice of baptizing new members during this yearly ceremony (*see also* **Baptism**).

The Timing of Passover and Easter

By the start of the third century, the framework of what was later to become **Holy Week**, Easter, and **Easter Week** (the week following Easter) had been established. Yet controversy simmered about the date on which to celebrate the Christian Pascha. Some communities, especially those in Asia Minor and Syria, wanted to continue celebrating it on the same evening that the Jews celebrated their Passover meal. Others lobbied for celebrating the festival on the **Sunday** following the fourteenth of Nisan. This sentiment may have been fueled by the fact that many of the new converts were from Greek and Roman backgrounds and so were accustomed to a fixed solar rather than a shifting lunar calendar. In addition, Christian scripture records the Resurrection as having occurred on the day after the Jewish Sabbath, that is, on a Sunday. All four Gospel accounts agree on this matter (*see also* **Eight**).

The debate concerning the date of the Christian Pascha was eventually resolved at the Council of Nicaea (325 A.D.). This important meeting of the leaders of the early Christian Church produced the Nicene Creed, a fundamental statement of the Christian faith, and other important decisions regarding Christian faith and practice. The Council decreed that Pascha would fall on the Sunday following the full **moon** that occurred on or after the **spring equinox**. In those days, however, significant differences existed in the calendrical calculations and astronomical observations of timekeepers from different parts of the ancient Mediterranean and Middle Eastern world. As a result the bishops also had to contend with the fact that Roman astronomers claimed that the spring equinox fell on March 25, while Alexandrian (Egyptian) astronomers argued that it fell on March 21. The Council members sided with the Alexandrians in this matter, proclaiming that for the purposes of calculating the date of Easter, the spring equinox would be reckoned as falling on March 21 (*see also* **Easter, Date of**).

The Nicene Council's decision concerning the timing of Easter disconnected the scheduling of the Christian Pascha from the Jewish festival calendar and launched it as an independent holiday. This decision helped to establish the Christian calendar. After Council members anchored Easter to a certain time of year the holiday began to provide a stable hub around which a new cycle of Easter-related festivals were developed (*see also* **Ascension Day**; **Ash Wednesday**; Lent; Holy Week; **Pentecost**).

Further Reading

Baldovin, John F. "Easter." In Mircea Eliade, ed. *The Encyclopedia of Religion*. Volume 4. New York: Macmillan, 1987.

Bradshaw, Paul F., and Lawrence A. Hoffman, eds. *Passover and Easter: Origin and History to Modern Times*. Two Liturgical Traditions series, volumes 5 and 6. Notre Dame, IN: University of Notre Dame Press, 1999.

Finn, Thomas M. "Pasch, Paschal Controversy." In Everett Ferguson, ed. *The Encyclopedia of Early Christianity*. Volume 2. New York: Garland, 1997.

Jacobs, Louis. "Passover." In Mircea Eliade, ed. *The Encyclopedia of Religion*. Volume 11. New York: Macmillan, 1987.

James, E. O. *Seasonal Feasts and Festivals*. 1961. Reprint. Detroit, MI: Omnigraphics, 1993.

Mac Rae, G. W. "Passover, Feast of." In *New Catholic Encyclopedia*. Volume 10. New York: McGraw-Hill, 1967.

"Passover." In E. A. Livingstone, ed. *The Oxford Dictionary of the Christian Church*. Third edition. Oxford, England: Oxford University Press, 1997.

Peifer, C. J. "Passover Lamb" and "Passover Meal." In *New Catholic Encyclopedia*. Volume 10. New York: McGraw-Hill, 1967.

Senn, Frank C. "Should Christians Celebrate the Passover?" In Paul F. Bradshaw and Lawrence A. Hoffman, eds. *Passover and Easter: The Symbolic Structuring of Sacred Seasons*. Two Liturgical Traditions series, volume 6. Notre Dame, IN: University of Notre Dame Press, 1999.

Paschal Candle

Easter Candle

Fire, light, and brightness have served as Easter symbols since early Christian times (*see also* **Easter Fires**). Biblical accounts of the **Resurrection** encourage this association, since they all agree that **Jesus'** followers discovered his empty tomb, and in some instances witnessed the risen Christ, on **Easter Sunday** morning at sunrise. The early Christians celebrated Easter with a late-night vigil service. It began near midnight on **Holy Saturday** and continued into the early hours of **Sunday**. Given the darkness of the hour the provision of light for this service was a simple necessity. Nevertheless the light itself became a symbol of the risen Lord. By the sixth century, many western European Christians began to interpret the one large candle used to illuminate the texts being read aloud during the **Easter Vigil** as a special symbol of Christ. Thus this candle became known as the paschal candle. The word "paschal" evolved from the Greek word *Pascha*, which means Easter. Pascha in turn came from *Pesah*, the Hebrew word for **Passover**.

In Roman Catholic, Anglican and Lutheran churches, the Easter Vigil service begins with the lighting of the paschal candle. Paschal candles may be found in other Protestant churches as well. According to tradition the candle must be lit with newly kindled fire, rather than from an already-established flame. The kindling of the new fire generally takes place out of doors. The congregation, carrying unlit candles of their own, gathers round the flames. The priest begins the Easter Vigil service by inviting the congregation to worship and laying a blessing on the new fire. Then the priest inscribes a cross and the Greek letters alpha and omega into the wax of the candle. Alpha and omega, the first and last letters of the Greek alphabet, refer to lines from the Bible's Book of Revelation that use these letters to describe God as both the source and destination of all things (Revelation 1:8, 21:6,

22:13). The priest also carves the number representing the current year into the wax. Afterwards he or she pushes five grains of incense, representing the five wounds of Christ, into the wax. Then the priest lights the wick with the newly kindled fire. Acolytes, young people who assist the priest during religious services, light their candles from the paschal candle and begin to pass the flame along to others. After everyone's candle is lit the congregation and clergy form a procession into the church, led by the deacon carrying the glowing paschal candle. The deacon then places the paschal candle in a stand near the lectern, where its light will illuminate the Bible passages that will be read out loud during the service.

The illuminated paschal candle greets worshipers at all Sunday services between the Easter Vigil and **Pentecost**. Its light represents the presence of the risen Christ. Before 1970 Roman Catholic clergy removed the paschal candle on **Ascension Day**. The extinguishing of the paschal candle on this day symbolized the fact that after the Ascension the resurrected Jesus would no longer appear to his disciples on earth clothed in human flesh. The Roman Catholic Church currently specifies that the paschal candle should remain in use through the feast of Pentecost. This change represents the recognition that the candle stands for the Risen Christ, whose presence is celebrated throughout the **Easter season**, rather than the historical Jesus, who departed on Ascension Day.

In addition to its special markings, the paschal candle can be identified by its size. It may measure several feet in height, and is usually placed in a special, tall candlestick standing on the floor, which gives it the appearance of being even bigger. In past times some churches and cathedrals produced enormous paschal candles. Church documents from the eighth to twelfth centuries record candles that range from just under two feet to five feet tall. By the eighteenth century several French churches and cathedrals prided themselves on paschal candles that stood about twenty-five feet high. England's Salisbury cathedral once boasted of paschal candles that soared up thirty-six feet in height.

History

In explaining the origins of the paschal candle some researchers point to an ancient Christian service called the *Lucernarium,* a ceremonial lighting of the lamps in preparation for the evening prayer service. As time passed the Lucernarium became a service in its own right which included chanting, prayer, and psalms. Scholars believe that the early Christians based the Lucernarium on Jewish lamp-lighting rituals. In time, however, the Christian observance disappeared. Some commentators think that the ceremony that surrounds the lighting of the paschal candle on Easter eve is all that remains of this ancient observance.

The first historical document referring to a special paschal candle dates back to the year 378 A.D. By the fifth century many references to the paschal candle can be found in Church documents from Spain and Italy. Christians quickly interpreted the candle as a symbol of Christ. To many the enormous candle also recalled the pillar of fire that led the Israelites out of slavery in Egypt (Exodus 13:21). In the eighth century a scholarly English monk named St. Bede (672 or 673–735) recorded the fact that in Rome priests carved the number representing the current year onto the paschal candle. By the tenth century historical documents refer to the insertion of five grains of incense into the candle. Several interpretations of this practice have been offered over the centuries, but most commentators now agree that the grains serve to represent the five wounds of Christ. The inscription of the alpha and omega on the candle can be traced back to the twelfth century. In the twelfth century Roman Catholic authorities officially incorporated the paschal candle into the Roman liturgy.

The method of kindling the new fire used to light the candle has varied through the ages. In some parts of Europe the clergy once used powerful lenses to intensify the rays of the sun to such a degree that they could kindle flame. This method depended on the fact that during the Middle Ages people began to celebrate the Easter Vigil on Saturday afternoon or morning rather than Saturday night. In other zones they hid a candle in a special location in the church on **Maundy Thursday** and used that flame to light the paschal candle. In still other areas they used flint, which when struck with force often gives off a spark. Some deemed this method especially appropriate in light of Bible passages in which Jesus describes himself as a "cornerstone" (Matthew 21:42, Mark 12:10, Luke 20:17). With this passage in mind the stony flint could serve as a symbol of the Christ, whose words and deeds spark the process of spiritual illumination among his followers.

Further Reading

MacGregor, A. J. *Fire and Light in the Western Triduum*. Collegeville, MN: Liturgical Press, 1992.

Metford, J. C. J. *The Christian Year*. London, England: Thames and Hudson, 1991.

Monti, James. *The Week of Salvation*. Huntington, IN: Our Sunday Visitor Publications, 1993.

O'Shea, W. J. "Easter Vigil." In *New Catholic Encyclopedia*. Volume 5. New York: McGraw-Hill, 1967.

Web Site

"How Do We Use a Paschal Candle?" by Scott C. Weidler, posted on the Evangelical Lutheran Church of America's web site at: http://www.elca.org/dcm/worship/qa/paschalcandle.html

Passionflower

Christ's Bouquet, Christ's Crown, Crown of Thorns, Jesus' Passion, Maypop, Mother-of-God's Star, Our Lord's Flower

The passionflower hails from the tropical zones of South and North America. Known to botanists by the scientific name *Passiflora*, the passionflower has acquired many other folk names, many of which refer in some way to the Easter story. These names include passionflower, **Jesus'** passion, Christ's bouquet, Our Lord's flower, crown of thorns, Christ's crown, maypop, and Mother-of-God's star.

In the sixteenth century Spanish missionaries who had journeyed to the New World (the Americas) along with the conquistadors saw this plant for the first time and marveled at its beauty. These religious men named the new specimen "passionflower" because they perceived many symbols of Jesus' passion, that is, the story of the last days of his life, in its large, colorful blossoms. For example, they interpreted the flower's ten petals as symbols of the ten loyal apostles. This reckoning excluded the apostle **Judas** who betrayed Jesus, and the apostle **Peter**, who denied him.

The passionflower raises a striking corona, often red in color, above the center corolla. This reminded the missionaries of the crown of thorns placed on Jesus' head by the Roman guards. Some said that the numerous long, thread-like divisions of the corona represented the 72 thorns of the crown. Others felt that they represented the countless followers of Jesus. The flower's five stamens suggested the five wounds that Jesus received on the cross. The three styles at the center of the flower symbolized the three nails used to crucify him. The blossom's single ovary was said to represent either the vinegar-soaked sponge that Jesus was offered on the **cross**, or the single hammer used to drive in the nails.

Further Reading

Ewert, Neil. *The Lore of Flowers*. Poole, Dorset, England: Blandford Press, 1982.

Lehner, Ernst, and Johanna Lehner. *Folkore and Symbolism of Flowers, Plants and Trees*. 1960. Reprint. Detroit, MI: Omnigraphics, 1990.

Lord, Priscilla Sawyer, and Daniel J. Foley. *Easter Garland*. 1963. Reprint. Detroit, MI: Omnigraphics, 1999.

Web Site

A commercial site offering botanical information and results of scientific research concerning the passionflower, print references, and further web links: http://rain-tree.com/maracuja.htm

Passion Play

In the late Middle Ages many western European towns and cities hosted Passion plays on **Good Friday**. These plays told the story of **Jesus'** Passion, that is, the events that took place during the last days of Jesus' life. Passion plays began to die out in the sixteenth century. The custom survives, however, in Latin America, where it was introduced by the Spanish. It has also endured in certain regions of Germany. The inhabitants of the Bavarian town of Oberammergau produce a famous, old Passion play every ten years. Folk dramas of this kind can be found in a few other German towns as well as in a handful of Austrian and Swiss villages. Several dozen American towns have also adopted this old European custom. Furthermore, many American churches sponsor Easter pageants in which children act out the story of Jesus' death, **resurrection**, and **ascension**. These pageants may be thought of as modern American versions of the medieval European Passion play.

Mystery Plays

Passion plays belong to a category of folk drama known as mystery plays. Mystery plays evolved out of certain dramatic elements of medieval church services. In the Middle Ages western European clergy began to teach the Christian religion by dramatizing scenes from Bible stories during religious services. They offered these dramatizations on feast days, acting out certain aspects of the story behind the holiday. Eventually these biblical skits became known as "mystery plays," since they concerned the mysterious working of God on earth. These dramatizations began in churches with clergy members acting out all the roles. The playlets proved popular and soon townspeople and wandering actors started to produce the dramas themselves. They began to stage the new plays in the town square and thus attracted larger and more boisterous crowds. Moreover they translated the stories from Latin, the language of the Church, to local languages, and lengthened the dramas by adding new roles and dialogue. Much of this added material was coarse and humorous. Church officials found the new dramas irreverent and eventually condemned them. Nevertheless, the plays flourished until about the sixteenth century.

Passion Plays

The earliest known Passion play, written in Latin by the Benedictine monks of Monte Cassino, Italy, dates back to the twelfth century. The first Passion plays written in vernacular languages appear about two hundred years later in Germany and France. These fourteenth-century plays may have been inspired by the establishment of the feast of Corpus Christi, officially embraced by the Roman Catholic Church in the thirteenth century but not widely celebrated until the fourteenth century. This holiday, which falls on the Thursday after Trinity Sunday, or the second Thursday after **Pentecost**, honors the Last Supper and the gift of the **Eucharist** (*for more on the Last Supper, see* **Maundy Thursday**). The Last Supper plays a crucial role in the Passion, so people began to celebrate the festival by dramatizing elements of the Passion story. These Passion plays soon migrated to Good Friday, the day on which Christian churches commemorate Jesus' crucifixion (*for more on crucifixion, see* **Cross**).

Even before this development, however, western European Christians had incorporated dramatic elements into their Good Friday celebrations. These included a long, melodious lament, called the *planctus*, describing the sorrow of the Virgin Mary as she stood at the foot of her son's cross (*see also* **Mary, Blessed Virgin**). By the twelfth century priests chanted the planctus before the cross at Good Friday religious services. Moreover, Christ's reproaches to his persecutors as he hung on the cross, called the *improperia*, was set to music and sung by choirs. In the thirteenth century other incidents from the Passion story, including Jesus' trial, his journey to the site of the Crucifixion, and his slow death on the cross were added to these sung and chanted dramas. The addition of these dramatic elements to Good Friday church services also contributed to the birth of the Good Friday Passion play.

Good Friday Passion plays reached the height of their popularity during the fifteenth and sixteenth centuries. They began to die out in the sixteenth century, along with other kinds of mystery plays. Researchers often attribute this decline to the effect of the Reformation, a sixteenth-century religious reform movement which eventually wielded great influence over the religious beliefs and behaviors of western Europeans.

Oberammergau's Passion Play

Remarkably, in Oberammergau, Germany, the custom of staging a Passion play on Good Friday has survived until present times. The Oberammergau tradition dates back to the time of the Thirty Years' War in the early seventeenth century. In the year 1632 Swedish troops destroyed much of the Bavarian countryside. An even more frightening devastation followed in their wake: an outbreak of an incurable and often-fatal disease known as the plague. As this menace reached nearer and nearer the mountain village of Oberammergau, the town council swore a solemn oath to God. They pledged that the town's citizens and their descendents would stage an elaborate Passion play once every ten years if the town were spared from the plague. Tradition has it that not one soul was lost to the deadly disease in Oberammergau after the pledge was made.

The town's citizens have lived up to the vow made by their ancestors. The first play was staged in 1634. In 1680 the town's citizens began to present the plays in years divisible by ten. In the past 375 years they have only failed to present two of the scheduled plays. In 1870 the Franco-Prussian War interrupted their plans to stage the drama and in 1940 another war, World War II, again prevented them from carrying out this ancestral duty. They postponed the 1920 play until 1922 due to severe economic conditions in Germany. In 1934 they produced a special play to commemorate the three-hundredth anniversary of their forebears' deliverance from the plague. Germany's recently appointed chancellor, Adolf Hitler, attended this performance of the play. Publicity posters for that year downplayed the drama's religious message and instead pitched it as a folk play about the Fatherland, or the "blessed powers of the earth," an interpretation more in keeping with the ideology of Hitler's Nazi political party.

In recent years the Oberammergau play has undergone several rewrites aimed at paring away various anti-Jewish elements contained in the traditional texts. The old script blamed the Jewish people for Jesus' death (*see also* **Judas**). The new script encourages the audience to examine their own shortcomings instead of placing blame on others (*see also* **Sin**). For example, the opening lines of the play include the following statement by the narrator: "Let no one try to find blame in others; let each of us recognize his own guilt in these events." Moreover, nowadays Jesus' disciples are shown dressed in Jewish clothing, instead of classical Roman garb, and the crowd that condemns Jesus before Pontius **Pilate** is shown to be religiously and ethnically mixed rather than composed completely of Jews.

Today's Passion play requires the participation of about half the town's 4,000 inhabitants. In the year 2000 about half a million visitors from around the world attended the town's Passion play, which ran from May till October. Each performance begins at 9:30 in the morning and ends after 6:00 p.m. Mercifully, the producers schedule a three-hour lunch break about halfway through the performance.

Mexico City's Passion Play

Mexico City's Passion play lasts several days. It covers an area of four kilometers (about two and one-half miles), features several thousand participants, and draws crowds of three to four million people. The citizens of eight Mexico City neighborhoods spend months preparing the props, sets, wardrobe, makeup, and street decorations, as well as preparing to manage the large numbers of people who attend the event. The Passion play takes place in a district of Mexico City known as Iztapalapa. Mexican officials boast that this event may be considered the largest pageant of popular culture in the world.

The Iztapalapa Passion play began in 1833, when residents of Iztapalapa decided to reenact the Passion in order to express their gratitude to Jesus for stopping a cholera epidemic. Although the event has grown over the years, a number of families have maintained the right to certain roles and functions in the event, and some of them even have old documents assigning their ancestors to the same roles. An organizing committee, however, elects the individuals who fill the important roles of Jesus, the Blessed Virgin Mary, and the twelve disciples. In order to qualify for the role of Jesus a man must be widely recognized as pure and devout, possess a good reputation, live locally, and have parents born in Iztapalapa. He must also be willing to acquire the strength and endurance necessary to carry a 100-kilogram (about 45 pounds) cross for four kilometers. Moreover, when approached by members of the crowd desiring healings or miracles, he must respond kindly. Training for this formidable task begins months in advance.

Although based loosely on the story told in the Bible, the Iztapalapa Passion play also includes legendary events and characters. The players reenact the Last Supper and Jesus' betrayal on Maundy Thursday. On Good Friday, Christ carries his cross to the scene of the crucifixion. He is followed by thousands of young men carrying out vows to complete an act of penance during this procession (*for more on penance, see* **Repentance**). These men, called Nazarenes, follow behind Christ in bare feet, carrying their own crosses and wearing crowns of thorns (*see also* **Penitentes**). Young women may walk in the procession, too, as a means of expressing their piety. The drama concludes with Jesus' crucifixion, while Judas hangs himself from a nearby tree. In 1999, officials estimate that about 4,600 people participated in the staging of the Passion play, more than 2,500 Nazarenes followed Christ to the site of the crucifixion, and three million people watched some or all of the spectacle.

Further Reading

Byrne, Lavinia. "Confronting the Truth Over Coffee with Christ." *Financial Times* (June 17-18, 2000): 9.

Conte, Jeanne. "Passion 2000: Oberammergau's Easter Play." *The World and I* 15, 4 (April 2000): 175.

"Drama, Christian." In E. A. Livingstone, ed. *The Oxford Dictionary of the Christian Church.* Third edition. Oxford, England: Oxford University Press, 1997.

Dunn, E. C. "Passion Play." In *New Catholic Encyclopedia*. Volume 10. New York: McGraw-Hill, 1967.

Hogan, Julie. *Treasury of Easter Celebrations*. Nashville, TN: Ideals Publications, 1999.

Monti, James. *The Week of Salvation*. Huntington, IN: Our Sunday Visitor Publications, 1993.

"Mystery Play." In Phyllis Hartnoll, ed. *The Oxford Companion to the Theatre*. Fourth edition. Oxford, England: Oxford University Press, 1983.

"Oberammergau." In E. A. Livingstone, ed. *The Oxford Dictionary of the Christian Church*. Third edition. Oxford, England: Oxford University Press, 1997.

"Passion Play." In Phyllis Hartnoll, ed. *The Oxford Companion to the Theatre*. Fourth edition. Oxford, England: Oxford University Press, 1983.

Russ, Jennifer M. *German Festivals and Customs*. London, England: Oswald Wolff, 1982.

Salzer, Anselm. "Passion Plays." In Charles G. Herbermann et al., eds. *The Catholic Encyclopedia*. New York: Appleton, 1913. Available online at: http://www.newadvent.org/cathen/11531a.htm

Web Sites

See also "Semana Santa in Mexico," an article by May Herz, available from *Inside Mexico*, a company dedicated to producing quality educational materials on Mexican culture: http://www.inside-mexico.com/featuresemana.htm

See also the Oberammergau Passion play's web site at: http://www.passions spiele2000.de/passnet/english/index_e.html

Passion Sunday
Black Sunday, Care Sunday, Carling Sunday, Judica Sunday, Quiet Sunday, Silent Sunday

Christians use the word "passion" to describe the suffering endured by **Jesus** during the last few days of his life, especially the Crucifixion (*see also* **Cross**). This usage harks back to the origins of the word. Although we associate the English word passion with strong emotion, it in fact comes from the Latin *passio*, which means "suffering." In past times the fifth **Sunday** in **Lent** was known as Passion Sunday. This name came from one of the Bible readings assigned to that day in Roman Catholic churches, which compared the animal sacrifices made by ancient Jewish priests with Jesus' sacrifice of his own life (Hebrews 9:12-15). This reading reminded the congregation of Jesus' sacrificial death, to be commemorated the following week on **Good Friday**. Indeed, Passion Sunday inaugurated a special season within Lent known as Passiontide. During Passiontide, the last two weeks of Lent, church services turned towards the consideration of Jesus' last days on earth.

Throughout the first four weeks of Lent clergy members exhorted worshipers to reflect on their own relationship with God. By contrast, during Passiontide church services encouraged the faithful to meditate on the Passion story. Several Passiontide customs marked this change of direction. The Gloria, a hymn proclaiming God's glory, was omitted from worship services during Passiontide. This omission symbolized the fact that during his last days on earth Jesus was not glorified by those he sought to teach, but rather tormented and abandoned.

A custom known as **veiling** also helped to set the mood of Passiontide. Veils, or lengths of cloth, were cast over crucifixes, sculptures, and religious images in churches. These veils were purple, in keeping with the system of liturgical colors that governs the hue of priests' robes and church decorations throughout the year in Roman Catholic churches. Purple represents **repentance** in this system of church color symbolism. Some evidence suggests, however, that before the sixteenth century red, a color associated with martyrdom, may have served as the liturgical color of Passiontide. Some writers believe that the practice of veiling evolved from the last line of the Gospel reading assigned to the fifth Sunday in Lent. Gospel readings come from the section of the Christian Bible that tells the story of Jesus' life. The Gospel reading assigned to this Sunday declares that after a dispute with religious authorities Jesus left the temple and hid himself (John 8:59). Some writers suggest that the custom of veiling provided a visual representation of Jesus' disappearance. Crucifixes were unveiled on Good Friday, sculptures and other religious images during the late-night **Easter Vigil** on **Holy Saturday**.

The customs associated with Passion Sunday inspired a number of folk names for the observance. In northern England Passion Sunday was called "Carling Sunday" from the custom of consuming carlings, or parched peas, on that day. In past times innkeepers often provided free carlings to their customers on Passion Sunday and housewives fried carlings in butter at home. The name "Care Sunday" may also have evolved from this practice, which died out in the twentieth century. Others suspect the name Care Sunday refers to cares, or sorrows, of Jesus, which are commemorated during Passiontide. The Germans called the day "Black Sunday " in reference to the custom of veiling religious images. In Slavic countries the fifth Sunday in Lent was known as "Silent Sunday" or "Quiet Sunday." Others called the day "Judica Sunday" in reference to the first line of the opening prayer, or introit, assigned to that Sunday's mass (*for more on the Roman Catholic religious service known as the mass, see also* **Eucharist**). In Latin it read *Judica me, Deus,* which means, "Judge me, God."

Passion Sunday and Passiontide were observed by Roman Catholics, Anglicans, and others who followed the church calendar rooted in Roman Catholic tradition. Orthodox and other Eastern Christians did not share this observance. In 1969 the Roman Catholic Church discontinued the celebration of Passion Sunday and Passiontide. Church officials changed the Bible readings assigned to the fifth Sunday in Lent and shifted the consideration of Christ's passion to Holy Week. Holy Week begins on the sixth Sunday in Lent, known to many as **Palm Sunday**. Although the name Palm Sunday is still widely used, Roman Catholic officials now prefer to call the sixth Sunday in Lent "Passion Sunday."

Further Reading

Alston, G. Cyprian. "Judica Sunday." In Charles G. Herbermann et al., eds. *The Catholic Encyclopedia.* New York: Appleton, 1913. Available online at: http://www.newadvent.org/cathen/08553a.htm

Cowie, L. W., and John Selwyn Gummer. *The Christian Calendar*. Springfield, MA: G. and C. Merriam, 1974.

Hole, Christina. *British Folk Customs*. London, England: Hutchinson and Company, 1976.

Monti, James. *The Week of Salvation*. Huntington, IN: Our Sunday Visitor Publications, 1993.

Niemann, Paul J. *The Lent, Triduum, and Easter Answer Book*. San Jose, CA: Resource Publications, 1998.

"Passion, The." In E. A. Livingstone, ed. *The Oxford Dictionary of the Christian Church*. Third edition. Oxford, England: Oxford University Press, 1997.

"Passion Sunday." In E. A. Livingstone, ed. *The Oxford Dictionary of the Christian Church*. Third edition. Oxford, England: Oxford University Press, 1997.

"Passiontide." In E. A. Livingstone, ed. *The Oxford Dictionary of the Christian Church*. Third edition. Oxford, England: Oxford University Press, 1997.

Slim, Hugo. *A Feast of Festivals*. London, England: Marshall Pickering, 1996.

Urlin, Ethel. *Festivals, Holy Days, and Saints' Days*. 1915. Reprint. Detroit, MI: Omnigraphics, 1992.

Weiser, Francis X. *The Easter Book*. New York: Harcourt, Brace and Company, 1954.

Passover

Pesah, Feast of Unleavened Bread, the Season of Our Freedom

Passover is a Jewish holiday that falls in the spring. It commemorates the liberation of the ancient Hebrews from slavery in Egypt some 3,300 years ago. Throughout the centuries Jews have honored Passover as one of their most important holidays. In addition, Passover also shaped the Christian holiday of Easter (*see also* **Pascha**). Scholars remind us that **Jesus** was in Jerusalem at the time of his arrest, trial, and crucifixion because he had come there to celebrate Passover (*for more on crucifixion, see* **Cross**). When the early Christians began to commemorate the events surrounding Jesus' death as yearly holidays they scheduled these observances around the time of Passover.

Timing of Passover

According to the Jewish calendar Passover begins on the fifteenth day of the month of Nisan. The Jewish calendar begins each new month on the night of the new **moon**. Since the moon takes 29.5 days to complete its cycle from new to full and back to new again, the fifteenth of Nisan always falls on the night of a full moon. Passover is also timed to occur after the **spring equinox**. In Israel and for Reform Jews, the holiday lasts seven days, ending on the twenty-first of Nisan. Other Jews living outside of Israel celebrate for eight days.

The Jewish calendar also takes into account the solar cycle of 365.2422 days, the number of days it takes the earth to revolve around the sun. This cycle creates the seasons of the year. During the 365.2422 days it takes the earth to revolve once around the sun, the moon completes twelve cycles and is 11.25 days into a thirteenth cycle. In order to keep the lunar months from falling behind the solar seasons of the year, the Jewish calendar adds an extra month every third year. In this way the holidays occur in the same season each year, although they are not always celebrated on the same dates. Thus the first day of Passover may fall anywhere between March 27 and April 24.

Passover as Recounted in the Book of Exodus

The story of the Jews' escape from slavery in Egypt is recorded in the second book of the Bible which is called Exodus. In chapter twelve God commands the Jews to celebrate a ceremonial meal each year on the night of the fifteenth of Nisan, in commemoration of their liberation from Egyptian slavery (Exodus 12:6). This meal marks the beginning of Passover. According to the Jewish calendar, days begin and end at sunset. Therefore, the afternoon preceding this feast falls on the fourteenth of Nisan, but the evening celebration itself falls during the first hours of the fifteenth of Nisan.

The first chapters of Exodus tell of the many plagues that God set upon the people of Egypt in order to convince the Egyptian pharaoh, or king, to let the Hebrews go. In the tenth and last of these torments God instructed the angel of death to kill the eldest child of every

465

Egyptian family, as well as all the firstborn animals, in a single night. Earlier God had told Moses how to protect Jewish families from this terrible persecution. Moses commanded each Jewish family to sacrifice a **lamb** on the afternoon preceding the massacre and to smear some of the lamb's **blood** above the door of their home. In this way the angel knew which homes were Jewish and therefore which houses to pass over. This act of divine vengeance finally convinced the Egyptian pharaoh to free the Jewish slaves.

As soon as they received word of the pharaoh's decision to let them go, the Jews began their journey out of Egypt. They left in a hurry, without waiting for their **bread** dough to rise. Afterwards, the pharaoh changed his mind about freeing the Jewish slaves and led the Egyptian army in pursuit of them. The fleeing slaves couldn't pause their journey long enough to make proper bread, so they instead survived by baking flat, unrisen bread. The teachings Moses relayed to the Jews in the book of Exodus instruct those celebrating Passover to refrain from eating leavened bread for the entire seven days of the festival (Exodus 12:18). This statute recalls the conditions of the Jews' escape from Egypt.

The Celebration of Passover in Biblical Times

Some scholars suspect that the festival we now call Passover was created by combining two pre-existing festivals. The first was a spring festival involving the sacrifice and consumption of a young animal as a means of asking God to bless and increase their herds. The second festival, called the Feast of Unleavened Bread, was a week-long observance in which people refrained from eating leavened bread. It may have originally begun as a spring harvest festival. According to these scholars, the Jewish people merged these two festivals sometime after their escape from Egypt. What's more, they assigned the new festival a radically different significance. The new holiday was still referred to as the Feast of Unleavened Bread (Exodus 12:17, 23:15), but also acquired a new name *Pesah*, from an old Hebrew word meaning to limp or to jump. Some writers suggest that this name referred to the angel of death "passing over" the homes of the Hebrew slaves in Egypt. Hence, Pesah has been translated into English as "Passover."

The yearly Passover festival became a means for Jews to express their gratitude to God for leading their ancestors out of slavery in Egypt. Through participation in the religious ceremonies associated with Passover Jews also reaffirmed their relationship with God. These ceremonies changed over time. In the sixteenth chapter of the biblical book of Deuteronomy the Jewish people are commanded to offer their Passover sacrifices at a site which God has made a "dwelling for his name," that is, the Temple in Jerusalem (Exodus 16:2). By the time that Jesus was born Passover had already become a well-established pilgrim festival. Every year thousands of Jews made their way to Jerusalem to offer their sacrificial lamb at the Temple. Religious custom required faithful Jews to bring a lamb to the Temple, where it was slain. The priests sprinkled the animals' blood on the altar as an offering to God. Then worshipers took the sanctified lamb home, where it was roasted and eaten by a gathering of family and friends.

After the destruction of the Temple and the fall of Jerusalem in 70 A.D., this sacrificial rite vanished as did the pilgrimage to Jerusalem. Instead Passover became a festival focused around home observance.

The Contemporary Celebration of Passover

Passover begins with a ritual meal, called a "Seder," a word meaning "order" or "arrangement" in Hebrew. Some Jews living outside of Israel celebrate the Seder on both the fifteenth and the sixteenth of Nisan, following old calendar traditions. The meal is composed of certain symbolic foods and eaten with certain gestures and phrases. Readings from the Haggadah, an anthology of texts concerning the Seder that dates back to the Middle Ages, accompany the meal. The readings include hymns and poems, stories about the Jews' escape from Israel, and explanations of the rituals being observed. The central theme of the Haggadah is that God alone delivered the Jewish people from slavery (*see also* **Salvation**).

The foods composing a Seder meal include a green vegetable, a symbol of spring and of rebirth, which is dipped in salt **water** before consumption. The salt water itself represents the sweat and tears of the Jewish slaves in Egypt. The meal also contains *haroset*, a dish of chopped apples and nuts, representing the mortar that the Hebrew slaves made for the Egyptians, and bitter herbs, signifying the bitterness of slavery. Other traditional Seder foods include a roasted lamb shank bone, representing the original Passover sacrifice, and a roasted egg, representing the sacrifices Jews later made at the Temple in Jerusalem. Participants also drink from four cups of **wine** throughout the ceremony. A fifth cup of wine is placed on the table for the prophet Elijah, who is said to attend every Seder ceremony in spirit.

The meal is accompanied by matzoh, a kind of unleavened bread or cracker, which serves as a symbol of freedom. Today observant Jews follow an elaborate procedure to insure that their homes contain not one speck of leavened food for the duration of the Passover festival. Each room of the house is searched for crumbs and thoroughly scoured. Many families maintain a special set of dishes and utensils for use at Passover. Others put their everyday kitchenware through a special ritual cleaning designed to eliminate every particle of leavened food which may be clinging to them. Leavened breads and other foods forbidden during the holiday are sealed away or removed from the household. Although the first and last days of Passover are observed with rest, festivity and religious rites, the remaining days of the festival are observed primarily by refraining from eating leavened foods.

The Passover festival is sometimes referred to as "the Season of Our Freedom." This name reflects the main themes of the festival — the liberation of ancient Hebrews from their bondage in Egypt, and their rise as a free and independent people (*see also* **Redemption**).

Further Reading

Bloch, Abraham P. *The Biblical and Archeological Background of the Jewish Holy Days*. New York: Ktav, 1978.

Eisenberg, Azriel. *The Story of the Jewish Calendar*. New York: Abelard-Schuman, 1958.

Jacobs, Louis. "Passover." In Mircea Eliade, ed. *The Encyclopedia of Religion*. Volume 11. New York: Macmillan, 1987.

James, E. O. *Seasonal Feasts and Festivals*. 1961. Reprint. Detroit, MI: Omnigraphics, 1993.

Mac Rae, G. W. "Passover, Feast of." In *New Catholic Encyclopedia*. Volume 10. New York: McGraw-Hill, 1967.

"Passover." In E. A. Livingstone, ed. *The Oxford Dictionary of the Christian Church*. Third edition. Oxford, England: Oxford University Press, 1997.

Peifer, C. J. "Passover Lamb" and "Passover Meal." In *New Catholic Encyclopedia*. Volume 10. New York: McGraw-Hill, 1967.

Raphael, Chaim. *A Feast of History: The Drama of Passover Through the Ages*. London, England: Weidenfeld and Nicolson, 1972.

Steingroot, Ira. *Keeping Passover*. New York: HarperSanFrancisco, 1995.

Strassfeld, Michael. *The Jewish Holidays*. New York: Harper and Row, 1985.

Werblowsky, R. J. Zwi, and Geoffrey Wigoder. "Pesah." In their *The Oxford Dictionary of the Jewish Religion*. Oxford, England: Oxford University Press, 1997.

Wigoder, Geoffrey. "Passover." In his *Encyclopedia of Judaism*. New York: Macmillan, 1989.

Web Site

For more on the rites and customs of Passover, see the following web site sponsored by the Union of Orthodox Jewish Congregations in America: http://www.ou.org/chagim/pesach/default.htm

Peacock

The peacock, or male peafowl, is known in many lands as one of the most beautiful and exotic of all birds. Its train of long, shiny blue, green, and brown tail feathers can reach lengths of up to six feet. Its chest feathers startle the eye with their unusual, metallic shade of blue. Originally native to India, Sri Lanka, and Java, the bird is now found in zoos and gardens throughout the world. Traders brought this magnificent bird to the lands surrounding the Mediterranean Sea during ancient times. The ancient Romans adopted the bird as a symbol of the immortality bestowed upon the empress after her death. The early Christians in their turn viewed the peacock as a symbol of the **resurrection** of Christ as well as the immortality of his followers.

The Peacock in Ancient Greece and Rome

The ancient Greeks declared the peacock sacred to the goddess Hera, the queen of all the gods. The Romans later claimed the bird as an emblem of the goddess Juno, Hera's Roman counterpart. The bird also came to stand for the apotheosis of the Roman empress after her death, that is, her transformation into an immortal goddess. (The emperor's apotheosis was symbolized by an eagle). When an empress died a peacock was released from the bonfire in which her body was to be burnt, symbolizing her transformation into a goddess. Peacocks can be found on Roman funeral art, an assertion that the dead rose again to eternal life.

The Peacock as a Jewish and Christian Symbol

The ancient Hebrews also used the peacock in their religious art. Although its exact meaning remains uncertain, experts suspect that the ancient Jews saw the peacock as a symbol of the afterlife.

Folklore dating back to ancient times asserted that the flesh of the peacock was not susceptible to decay, like that of all other animals. It was also widely believed that the bird yearly shed its gorgeous tail feathers, only to gain an even more brilliant train of feathers for the coming year. This folklore led the early Christians to adopt the peacock for their religious art. The yearly renewal of its feathers and the supposed preservation of its flesh made it a natural symbol of the Christian doctrine of the resurrection of the dead. The early Christians depicted the peacock in the Roman catacombs, the underground vaults where they buried their dead. The bird is also frequently represented in Byzantine church art.

This aura of sacredness clung to the peacock until the Middle Ages. In that era knights and squires took their oaths on the king's peacock. Indeed, "By the peacock" was a common exclamation in those days. Still today, when the pope rides in his processional chair, as he does on **Easter Sunday**, he is flanked by two chamberlains, carrying great fans of ostrich feathers onto which have been added the tips of peacock feathers.

Christian artists have also used the peacock and its feathers as an emblem of the glories of heaven. Sometime artists depicted angels with peacock feathers in their wings. The round "eye spots" in the bird's tail feathers have also been interpreted as the all-seeing eyes of the church.

Further Reading

Evans, E. P. *Animal Symbolism in Ecclesiastical Architecture*. 1896. Reprint. Detroit, MI: Gale Research, 1969.

Hulme, F. Edward. *The History, Principles and Practice of Symbolism in Christian Art*. 1891. Reprint. Detroit, MI: Gale Research, 1969.

Ingersoll, Ernest. *Birds in Legend, Fable and Folklore*. 1923. Reprint. Detroit, MI: Singing Tree Press, 1968.

Knapp, Justina. *Christian Symbols and How to Use Them*. 1935. Reprint. Detroit, MI: Gale Research, 1974.

Lord, Priscilla Sawyer, and Daniel J. Foley. *Easter Garland*. 1963. Reprint. Detroit, MI: Omnigraphics, 1999.

Møller-Christensen, V., and K. E. Jordt Jørgensen. *Encyclopedia of Bible Creatures*. Philadelphia, PA: Fortress Press, 1965.

Webber, F. R. *Church Symbolism*. 1938. Second edition, revised. Reprint. Detroit, MI: Omnigraphics, 1992.

Pelican

The Pelican in Her Piety

In the days before biology was well understood people often spun imaginative tales to explain the behavior or appearance of various animals. These folktales often interpreted what was unknown in terms of familiar cultural and religious beliefs. In this way the natural world became an extension of the human world, full of symbols that reminded people of their own way of life and the things they held sacred.

The pelican became a symbol of Christ because the way in which it feeds its young reminded people of **Jesus'** sacrificial death on the **cross**. The pelican scoops fish out of the sea and holds them in a pouch of skin hanging beneath its lower beak. It feeds its young by opening its beak and permitting them to grab bits of the bloody mass of fish collected there. This method contrasts with the way in which most adult birds feed their young, which is by placing bits of food in the youngsters' open beaks. Tellers of traditional tales connected the image of the baby birds feeding on what appeared to be their mother's flesh and **blood** to the story of Christ's death.

A Folktale and a Christian Symbol

An old, well-known European folktale explained that while pruning their own feathers pelicans purposely draw blood into their beaks in order to feed their offspring with this life-giving fluid. The legend concluded by noting that this self-sacrificing behavior leaves behind a permanent red mark on the bird's beak. Indeed, one species of pelican has a reddish beak tip, a fact which may have inspired the folktale.

This story portrays the pelican as a symbol of Jesus Christ in his role as redeemer (*see also* **Redemption**). Just as the pelican nourishes its children with its own blood, so, too, did Jesus sacrifice his own life for the benefit of his followers. Christians commemorate this event, the death of Jesus by crucifixion, on **Good Friday** (*for more on crucifixion, see also* **Cross**). Just as Christ was crucified by the people whom he hoped to serve, baby pelicans appear to rip at the flesh of their own mother. At the Last Supper, which took place on the night before his execution, Jesus spoke in veiled terms of his approaching death. He asked his followers to eat **bread** and drink **wine** in remembrance of his body and blood which he would soon offer for their sakes (*see also* **Eucharist; Maundy Thursday**). Thus blood became an important symbol of Jesus' sacrifice. By pondering the mystery of the pelican's apparently bloody beak in light of Christian blood symbolism, storytellers turned the humble sea bird into a symbol of Christ.

The Pelican in Art and Literature

Christians have seen the pelican as a symbol of Christ the redeemer ever since the time of St. Augustine (354-430). By the late Middle Ages the bird had also come to represent the Eucharist. This symbolism was so widely acknowledged in past eras that artists and writers made frequent reference to it. The Italian writer, Dante (1265-1321), referred to Jesus as "our pelican." Thomas Aquinas (1225-1274), a medieval saint and philosopher, called Jesus "our pelican of piety" in

one of his poems. In his famous play *Hamlet*, English writer William Shakespeare (1564-1616) penned these lines for the moody prince:

> To his good friends thus wide I'll ope my arms,
> And, like the kind, life-rend'ring pelican,
> Refresh them with my blood. (Hulme, 188)

Pelicans can also be found in many church decorations and other works of religious art. In Christian art the image of the pelican feeding its brood on its own blood is often referred to as "the pelican in her piety."

Other Versions of the Folktale

According to Christian belief, Jesus' death and **resurrection** have not only offered humanity a new, more spiritual way of life, but have also opened the door to a blissful afterlife (*see also* Resurrection; **Salva-**

tion). Several alternate versions of the pelican tale reflect this doctrine. One proclaimed that the bird could revive its dead offspring by feeding them with its own blood. Yet another version of the pelican legend asserted that the mother pelican fed her offspring on her own blood in times of famine, dying so that they could live (*see also* Redemption). Both of these tales again recall the sacrifice of Jesus and its life-bestowing consequences.

Further Reading

Heath, Sidney. *The Romance of Symbolism.* 1909. Reprint. Detroit, MI: Gale Research, 1976.

Hulme, F. Edward. *The History, Principles and Practice of Symbolism in Christian Art.* 1891. Reprint. Detroit, MI: Gale Research, 1969.

Ingersoll, Ernest. *Birds in Legend, Fable and Folklore.* 1923. Reprint. Detroit, MI: Singing Tree Press, 1968.

Møller-Christensen, V., and K. E. Jordt Jørgensen. *Encyclopedia of Bible Creatures.* Philadelphia, PA: Fortress Press, 1965.

Webber, F. R. *Church Symbolism.* 1938. Second edition, revised. Reprint. Detroit, MI: Omnigraphics, 1992.

Penitentes

The Spanish word *penitentes* means "penitents" or "those who repent." In Spain and in some areas of the world colonized by the Spanish, a few people, often referred to as penitentes, observe old **Good Friday** traditions by inflicting physical suffering on themselves. They voluntarily undergo this suffering, or penance, for a variety of reasons (*for more on penance, see* **Repentance**). Some seek to express repentance for their own misdeeds, others to fulfill a promise made to God, **Jesus**, or the Virgin Mary in exchange for granting a particular favor, and still others to imitate the suffering of Jesus and thereby deepen their relationship with him (*see also* **Mary, Blessed Virgin**).

History

During the late Middle Ages, lay religious associations advocating penitential exercises involving physical suffering gained favor with many western Europeans. During the late fifteenth century, religious brotherhoods dedicated to the Passion of Christ, that is, the story of his suffering during the last days of his life, emerged in Spain. During **Holy Week** members of these associations walked in procession through the streets whipping themselves as an expression of repentance and piety. Other religious associations also established themselves around this time and adopted similar penitential practices. Some historians credit Franciscan and Dominican monks for fostering a religious mentality which encouraged lay Spaniards to undertake these kinds of physically painful penances.

Spain

In southern Spain religious brotherhoods, called *cofradías*, still play a large role in Holy Week observances. They sponsor religious processions in which they carry floats depicting scenes from the last days of Jesus' life through the streets. Other members of the cofradía, dressed in long robes and pointed hoods, walk in front of or behind the floats. Those who precede the float are called *nazarenos*, or "Nazarenes." While most of the nazarenos do not perform acts of physical penance, some do opt to walk barefoot through the city streets in these processions, during which the participants may be on their feet for up to twelve hours. Those who follow the floats, called *penitentes*, undertake various pain-inducing disciplines as a means of expressing repentance for their **sins**. Self-flagellation is a thing of the past in Spain, however. Instead contemporary penitentes may walk barefoot or in chains, and many carry heavy wooden **crosses** for the duration of the procession. Carrying the floats also constitutes a physical hardship since those who do so spend hours crowded into the small space beneath it, made relatively airless by heavy cloth draperies. Moreover, the floats weigh hundreds if not thousands of pounds and therefore each man shoulders a heavy burden (*see also* **Spain, Easter and Holy Week in**).

Southwest United States

During the sixteenth and seventeenth centuries the Spanish founded many colonies in different parts of the world. In some of these places Spanish missionaries and colonists planted the seed of similar religious practices. For example, in southern Colorado and New Mexico, areas once ruled by the Spanish, a secretive religious brotherhood called the *Hermanos Penitentes*, or "Penitent Brothers," emerged. The early history of the brotherhood remains unclear but some writers suspect a connection with the Third Order of St. Francis, an assembly of lay people associated with the Franciscan religious orders. Prior to the nineteenth century Roman Catholic authorities assigned very few priests to this area. During the nineteenth century, however, priests and other Church authorities arrived in greater numbers, determined to exert control over the population. They found the Brotherhood an entrenched element of local religious life. In addition to performing many acts of charity, the brotherhoods carried out Holy Week observances in which their members inflicted suffering upon themselves and each other as a means of penance and as an imitation of the sufferings of Christ. For example, they whipped themselves or, according to some reports, even volunteered to undergo crucifixion on Good Friday *(for more on crucifixion, see* Cross). Church authorities condemned the various chapters of the Brotherhood but were unable to eliminate them.

Today these associations, whose membership and traditions remain to some extent secret, still exist in New Mexico and Colorado. Their Holy Week observances are said to include several painful penitential exercises, including the carrying of heavy wooden crosses in lengthy processions, the infliction of small flesh wounds, and whippings. In addition, some participants crawl on their knees throughout the procession or wear a crown of thorns. Crucifixions, in which a man is tied rather than nailed to a cross, are said to take place on Good Friday. All this suffering has a spiritual aim. Members of the penitential brotherhoods believe that penance in the form of physical suffering brings them closer to **salvation**.

477

Latin America

Mexico City's **Passion play** provides young men with an opportunity to act as "Nazarenes" on Good Friday. The Nazarenes have vowed to follow Christ in a reenactment of the Passion story, trudging the four-kilometer (about two and one-half miles) route towards the site of the crucifixion barefoot, carrying heavy crosses and wearing crowns of thorns. Doing so for three consecutive years completes their penance. In 1999 more than 2,500 Nazarenes participated in the Good Friday procession (*see also* **Mexico, Easter and Holy Week in**).

In Colombia many penitentes march in Good Friday religious processions commemorating the Crucifixion. They express repentance for their sins or compassion for the pain inflicted on Jesus by bringing suffering on themselves. They may walk barefoot or in chains, whip themselves, or carry heavy crosses made of wood (*see also* **Colombia, Easter and Holy Week in**).

Philippines

The Philippines, the only predominantly Christian country in Asia, was also colonized by the Spanish. Today *flagellantes*, people who whip themselves, still take to the streets on Good Friday. Moreover, a handful of people go even further and have themselves crucified on Good Friday as a means of atoning for their sins. Roman Catholic Church authorities disapprove of these bloody displays of folk piety but have been unable to stop them. Unlike the secretive New Mexico rites, however, the Filipino rituals occur in public places. Hundreds of tourists come to gawk at these displays of intense physical suffering.

In some parts of the Philippines, however, old penitential practices have been modified to suit current values. In the town of Palo, for example, a modern version of the penitentes, called *tais-dupol*, replaced the flagellantes in the late nineteenth century. The tais-dupol participate in a city-wide enactment of the Passion. This event takes place on Good Friday. Garbed in blue and white robes and hoods, they precede the religious processions, clearing the streets and holding back the crowds. Although they perform these duties barefoot, there is little else about the experience that might cause unusual physical suffering. This role is usually sought by young, single men who see it as an act of devotion that expresses their repentance for various misdeeds (*see also* **Philippines, Easter and Holy Week in**).

Further Reading

Arpon, Alvin Gz. "Pamalandong: Good Friday in Palo." *Philippines Today* 3 (June 2000). Available online at: http://www.pia.ops.gov.ph/philtoday/pt03/pt0316.htm

Clynes, Tom. *Wild Planet!* Detroit, MI: Gale Research, 1995.

Cohen, Hennig, and Tristram Potter Coffin, eds. *The Folklore of American Holidays*. Third edition. Detroit, MI: Gale, 1999.

Espinosa, Aurelio. "Hermanos Penitentes, Los." In Charles G. Herbermann et al., eds. *The Catholic Encyclopedia.* New York: Appleton, 1913. Available online at: http://www.newadvent.org/cathen/11635c.htm

Mitchell, Timothy. *Passional Culture: Emotion, Religion and Society in Southern Spain*. Philadelphia, PA: University of Pennsylvania Press, 1990.

Weigle, Marta. *The Penitentes of the Southwest*. Santa Fe, NM: Ancient City Press, 1970.

Pentecost

Binkosti, Blumenfest (Flower Feast), Domineca Spiritului Santu (Sunday of the Holy Spirit), Feast of the Holy Ghost, Id El-'Uncure (Feast of the Solemn Assembly), Pentecosté, Pentecôte, Pentekoste, Pentiqosti, Pfingsten, Pintse, Pünkösd, Red Feast, Slavnost Letnice (Summer Feast), Whitsunday, Zielone Swieta (Green Holyday)

The resurrected **Jesus** appeared to his disciples several times before ascending into heaven (*see also* **Ascension Day; Resurrection**). Before doing so he promised that the Holy Spirit—sometimes called the Holy Ghost—would soon appear to inspire and uphold them (Acts 1:8). The Christian feast of Pentecost commemorates the coming of the Holy Spirit. According to the Bible, this occurred fifty days after **Passover**, on the Jewish feast of **Shavuot** (Acts 2). A loud noise like the sound of a strong wind accompanied the coming of the Spirit, as did tongues of flame, which rested on the disciples. The Holy Spirit filled Jesus' followers with such wisdom and power that they spontaneously began to preach in foreign languages that they had never studied and did not know. Then **Peter** stood up and addressed the crowd that had gathered to watch this miracle. According to Christian scripture, his appeal to them to repent and be **baptized** was so powerful that three thousand people became Christians on that day (*see also* **Repentance**). For this reason Pentecost is sometimes called "the birthday of the church." In the Western Church calendar, observed by Roman Catholics and Protestants, it can fall anywhere between May 10 and June 13. Eastern Christians, who use a different calendar system, celebrate it between May 24 and June 27 (*see also* **Easter, Date of**).

On Pentecost the **paschal candle** is lit for the last time. This emblem of the risen Christ stands beside the altar from Easter to Pentecost. Its disappearance signals the end of the period of the Christian year specifically dedicated to celebrating the presence of the risen Lord among his disciples (*see also* **Easter Season**). Customs often practiced in religious services as a means of evoking the atmosphere of the first Pentecost include the use of various foreign languages and the making of hissing, wind-like sounds.

History

The word Pentecost comes from *Pentekoste*, the Greek word for fiftieth. The early Christians rejoiced for fifty days following **Easter Sunday**, commemorating Jesus' resurrection and ascension, as well as the outpouring of the Holy Spirit on his disciples. They celebrated each of these days as if it were a **Sunday**. Thus they neither fasted nor knelt to pray throughout the entire fifty days. They called this period of time Pentecost. Some scholars believe that this festive season may have been inspired by a Jewish observance known as *Sefirat Haomer*, or "Counting the Omer" (*for more on this observance, see* Shavuot).

The first references to the celebration of Pentecost in the writings of the early Christians date back to the second century. Because some writers fail to mention it at all, however, certain scholars conclude that it was not observed throughout the whole of the Christian church. During the fourth century Christians began to emphasize the fiftieth day of Pentecost. By the last two decades of the fourth century the fiftieth day had become a festival in its own right. Nevertheless, its significance varied from region to region. In Rome, Constantinople (now Istanbul, Turkey), Milan (Italy), and Spain, Christians commemorated the gift of the Holy Spirit on the fiftieth day of Pentecost. In other places, notably Jerusalem, Christians celebrated both the Ascension and the outpouring of the Holy Spirit on this day. Eventually, the word Pentecost came to refer only to the fiftieth day after Easter, which became a special feast day celebrating the coming of the Holy Spirit. For many centuries Christian clergy preferred to baptize newcomers to the Christian religion on the feast of Pentecost and on Easter Sunday.

Although the word Pentecost eventually came to refer primarily to the fiftieth day after Easter, Christians still recognize the days between Easter Sunday and Pentecost as a special, holy time of year. The English dubbed this period of time Eastertide, a season of the church year dedicated to the celebration of the Resurrection and the presence of the resurrected Christ among his followers (*see also* Easter Season).

Christians also use the word Pentecost to refer to a season of the church year. The season stretches from the feast of Pentecost to the beginning of Advent. The church year ends at the close of the Pentecost season and starts again with Advent. Advent begins on the Sunday closest to November 30. It constitutes a four-week period of preparation for the celebration of the birth of Jesus at Christmas time.

Symbols

The story of the first Pentecost inspired the symbols and many of the customs of this holiday. In Christian art fire, or tongues of flame, often stand for Pentecost and the coming of the Holy Spirit. This symbolic use of flames fits well with the fire symbolism running throughout the Bible. In the Bible fire often signals God's presence and represents his power to purify. The liturgical color for Pentecost is red, symbolizing fire. Liturgical colors, hues that have been assigned certain symbolic meanings in Christian worship, are attached to the festivals and seasons of the church year. Church decorations and priests' robes will feature these colors throughout the year. In church symbolism the color red usually symbolizes love and sacrifice, a combination often associated with martyrdom. At Pentecost, however, red signifies the tongues of flame said to have appeared over Jesus' disciples as they received the inspiration of the Holy Spirit.

Folklore from a number of European countries presents flowers and greenery as Pentecost symbols. Red flowers, such as roses and peonies, have especially strong associations with the holiday.

Wind constitutes another Pentecost symbol. It, too, stands for the Holy Spirit, especially for its power and universal presence. Biblical writers saw wind as a symbol of God's great might. Wind also called to mind the essence of life itself, which God "breathed" into Adam after creating him out of clay (Genesis 2:7). In Christian scripture, or the New Testament, wind sometimes stands for God's Holy Spirit, which breathes spiritual vitality into human beings.

The dove serves as yet another emblem of Pentecost. This symbol for the Holy Spirit does not appear in scriptural accounts of the first Pentecost, but rather in other passages concerning Jesus' baptism (Matthew 3:16, Mark 1:10, Luke 3:22, John 1:32). At that moment the Holy Spirit, in the shape of a dove, descended from heaven and alighted on him. Filled with the Holy Spirit, Jesus began his teaching and healing career. The vivid imagery of the descending dove has impressed itself on the imaginations of countless Christians over the centuries. It became one of the most popular Christian symbols for the Holy Spirit. In central and eastern Europe families often hang a carved wooden dove, sometimes encased in a glass ball, over their dining tables on Pentecost. In Germany church services may include the lowering of a carved dove from the ceiling. These ornaments call to mind the presence of the Holy Spirit. In church services the presence of the Holy Spirit may also be represented by the use of several different languages.

Medieval Customs

In medieval times religious services employed these Pentecost symbols in a striking way. At the point in the service when the priest intoned, *"Veni Sancte Spiritus"* (Come, Holy Spirit), the choir made hissing or rattling noises in imitation of a great wind. In some countries, like France, this effect was achieved by sounding trumpets rather than by hissing. In those days many churches had holes in their roofs, known as "Holy Ghost holes." As the hissing noise continued a great disk, suspended on a rope, descended from the Holy Ghost hole. This disk bore the emblem of a white dove surrounded by golden rays on a blue background. As the disk neared the congregation red flowers and petals rained down from the Holy Ghost hole, representing the tongues of flame that rested over Jesus' disciples. In some places lighted wicks and straws were tossed down the Holy Ghost hole instead of flowers. Although people may have enjoyed this touch of realism, the danger of setting the congregation on fire led to the eventual cancellation of this custom. In the thirteenth century roses fell from the Holy Ghost hole in many French churches. In certain places Church officials enhanced Pentecost services by releasing white doves, which were permitted to fly freely about the church.

In medieval England Pentecost served as the occasion for cathedrals to collect small fees toward the upkeep of their buildings. People who were fortunate enough to live in a house with at least one chimney were expected to make these yearly donations to the cathedral in their diocese. On Pentecost they walked in procession behind their local priest to present these offerings at the cathedral. People dubbed these small donations "Pentecostals," "Whitsun-farthings" or "smoke farthings." Parish churches raised money by selling specially brewed beer at events known as **Whitsun ales**. In England the Monday and Tuesday following Pentecost Sunday were also holidays. People celebrated the Whitsun holidays, as they were called, with feasts, dances, and outdoor games.

483

Flowers and Greenery

In some European countries people decked churches and homes with greenery and flowers in celebration of Pentecost. Some commentators believe that this custom may have been transferred to Pentecost from **May Day**, a folk holiday celebrating the arrival of spring. Indeed May Day, celebrated on May first, often falls in close proximity to Pentecost. Some folk names for Pentecost reflect the importance of flowers and greenery in setting the tone of the holiday. For example, Poles and Ukrainians sometimes refer to the holiday as *Zielone Swieta*, or "Green Holyday." Germans dubbed the festival *Blumenfest*, or "Flower Feast." Czechs coined yet another folk name for the holiday, *Slavnost Letnice*, or "Summer Feast."

Rural German customs also bespeak a strong connection between Pentecost and the celebration of spring. Pentecost falls during the time of the year when cattle are driven to their summer grazing grounds. In many areas these animals were festooned with ribbons, leaves, and cowbells. The German phrase "dressed like a Whitsun ox"—applied to someone who was overdressed—recalls this old custom. Expeditions into the woods to gather greenery for Pentecost decorations might also include dressing someone as "the wild man" or "the green man" by covering him or her in a costume of moss and leaves. In Silesia, a region of Germany, people waited until Pentecost to erect their maypoles.

Whitsun Brides and Grooms

The folk traditions of rural Sweden furnish another example of a May Day custom that seems to have migrated to Pentecost in some places. In past times village Swedes celebrated Pentecost by choosing a local young woman to be the "Whitsun bride." In many other European countries a similar figure, called the May queen, was associated with May Day celebrations. Sometimes a Whitsun bridegroom reigned alongside the bride. The Whitsun bride visited neighborhood homes, along with her ladies-in-waiting. The Whitsun bride and her entourage entertained each household with a song, dance, or clever speech. Householders in return might be expected to offer the girl a gift of eggs (*see also* **Egg Lore**). In spite of the privileges associated with the position, many young women and men resisted acting the role of the Whitsun bride or groom. Their resistance may have reflected their awareness of the superstition that the Whitsun bride and groom would never marry, having already been pledged to the season of spring itself.

Noise

In past times people in some parts of Europe ushered in Pentecost with loud noises. In German-speaking countries people shot off guns or cracked whips in honor of the holiday. Pentecost shooting was known as *Pfingstschiessen* and whip-cracking as *Pfingstschnalzen*. Some folklorists think this custom may have originated in the belief that loud noises drive away evil spirits. In later times, however, Germans viewed the din as a boisterous salute to the holiday.

Dawn, Dew, and Wind

Another old Pentecost folk tradition requires the truly devout to rise early on Pentecost morning and climb to the tops of mountains and hills in order to pray. This custom was called "catching the Holy Ghost." Prayers uttered at sunrise on Pentecost were thought by some to be particularly powerful. The dew that falls at dawn on Pentecost was also thought to have special curative properties. In some parts of northern Europe people once walked barefoot on the grass to receive the blessing afforded by Pentecost dew. Or they wiped pieces of **bread** in the dew and later fed them to their animals as a means of protecting them against accidents and illnesses. Kite flying is another custom connected with Pentecost, most likely resulting from the strong association between kites and the wind.

White Sunday

The English invented another name for Pentecost, that is, Whitsunday. Whitsunday comes from the phrase "White Sunday," or *Hwita Sunnandaeg* in Old English. Most folklorists believe that this name was inspired by the fact that in early times Pentecost was an important occasion for baptisms. Candidates for baptism dressed in special, white robes, thus suggesting the folk name "White Sunday." Another, fanciful explanation of the word "Whitsunday" suggests that "Whit" signifies "wit," and refers to the knowledge and speaking abilities conferred upon Jesus' disciples by the Holy Spirit.

Red Sunday

Red, the liturgical color for Pentecost, has also impressed itself on the folk imagination. In some parts of Europe the "Red Feast" became a folk name for the holiday. In German-speaking regions people called the red peony, which blossoms about the time of festival, the *Pfingstrose*, or "Rose of Pentecost," and the oriole, a bright, red bird, the *Pfingstvogel*, or "Pentecost bird."

More Names for the Holiday

In many European languages the official name for the feast evolved from its oldest title, *Pentekoste*, the Greek word for "fiftieth." For example, in French it's *Pentecôte*, in Spanish *Pentecostés*, in German *Pfingsten*, and in Syrian *Pentiqosti*. The Slovenians call the holiday *Binkosti*, the Hungarians *Pünkösd*, the Danish *Pintse*. Many eastern Europeans call it the "Feast of the Holy Ghost" and the Romanians know it as *Domineca Spiritului Santu*, or "Sunday of the Holy Spirit." Among certain Middle Eastern Christians the festival is referred to as *Id El-'Uncure*, or "Feast of the Solemn Assembly."

Further Reading

Bradshaw, Paul F. *The Search for the Origins of Christian Worship*. New York: Oxford University Press, 1992.

Cowie, L. W., and John Selwyn Gummer. *The Christian Calendar*. Springfield, MA: G. and C. Merriam, 1974.

Downman, Lorna, Paul Britten Austin, and Anthony Baird. *Round the Swedish Year*. Stockholm, Sweden: Bokförlaget Fabel, 1961.

Griffin, Robert H., and Ann H. Shurgin, eds. *The Folklore of World Holidays*. Second edition. Detroit, MI: Gale Research, 1999.

Harper, Howard. *Days and Customs of All Faiths*. 1957. Reprint. Detroit, MI: Omnigraphics, 1990.

Hutton, Ronald. *Stations of the Sun*. Oxford, England: Oxford University Press, 1996.

Ingersoll, Ernest. *Birds in Legend, Fable and Folklore*. 1923. Reprint. Detroit, MI: Singing Tree Press, 1968.

Metford, J. C. J. *The Christian Year*. London, England: Thames and Hudson, 1991.

"Pentecost." In Leland Ryken, James C. Wilhoit, and Tremper Longman III, eds. *Dictionary of Biblical Imagery*. Downers Grove, IL: InterVarsity Press, 1998.

Slim, Hugo. *A Feast of Festivals*. London, England: Marshall Pickering, 1996.

Talley, Thomas J. *The Origins of the Liturgical Year*. Collegeville, MN: Liturgical Press, 1986.

———. "Christian Worship." In Mircea Eliade, ed. *The Encyclopedia of Religion*. Volume 15. New York: Macmillan, 1987.

Tyson, Joseph B. "Pentecost." In Paul J. Achtemeier, ed. *The HarperCollins Bible Dictionary*. New York: HarperCollins, 1996.

Urlin, Ethel L. *Festivals, Holy Days, and Saints' Days*. 1915. Reprint. Detroit, MI: Omnigraphics, 1992.

Weiser, Francis X. *The Holyday Book*. New York: Harcourt, Brace and Company, 1956.

Peter

Jesus' disciple Peter plays a small but important role in the Easter story. After the Last Supper, as Jesus and his disciples make their way to the Mount of Olives, Peter boasts that he will never forsake Jesus (*for more on the Last Supper, see* **Maundy Thursday**). Jesus sadly predicts that before the night is over Peter will deny him three times (Matthew 26:33-35). When the supporters of the Jewish high priest come to arrest Jesus, Peter cuts off the ear of one of the high priest's servants in an attempt to defend his master. Jesus rebukes him, telling him to put away his sword. In one biblical account of Jesus' arrest, that found in the Gospel according to Matthew, Peter follows the mob that takes Jesus to the high priest's house. While the high priest questions Jesus, Peter lurks in the shadows of the courtyard, waiting to see how things turn out (Matthew 26:69-75). Three different people see him there and accuse him of being one of Jesus' companions. Peter denies each accusation. Then he hears a cock crow, signaling the beginning of the new day, and he remembers Jesus' prediction. Filled with remorse, he weeps.

Although Peter's faith fails him during the darkest hour, Christian scripture tends to portray him as an eager and earnest follower of Jesus. In fact his loyalty sometimes leads him into statements or actions that Jesus condemns (Mark 8:29-33, John 13:8-9, Matthew 26:51-52, John 18:10). Nevertheless many scholars think that Peter was one of Jesus' closest companions. Originally a fisherman from Galilee, Peter along with his brother Andrew left their former lives to become Jesus' disciples. Some sources indicate that Peter may have been the first disciple that Jesus called. Jesus not only gave him a new occupation, but also a new name. Peter's given name was Simon, but according to Christian scripture Jesus renamed him *Kepha* or *Kephas*, which is Aramaic for "rock" (Matthew 16:18, Mark 3:16, John 4:42). Since the Christian scriptures were written in Greek, they record the Greek version of this name, *Petros*, or in English, Peter. Jesus gave him that name for a purpose. He proclaimed that Peter was to be the rock on which he would build his church. The stories concerning Peter in the Book of Acts reveal the insight and inspiration with which Peter preached, healed, and led the Christian community after Jesus' death.

Christian scripture gives evidence both of Peter's virtues and his faults. Many Christians find that this combination of devotion and weakness, insight and error, makes Peter an approachable and yet inspiring model of Christian spiritual growth.

Peter's role in the Easter story didn't end at the time of Jesus' arrest. According to certain Bible passages, Peter was the first person to see the resurrected Jesus (1 Corinthians 15:5, Luke 24:1-34). Other passages, however, claim that the risen Jesus first appeared to **Mary Magdalene**. In one of the biblical accounts of Jesus' **resurrection**, that found in the Gospel according to Luke, the risen Jesus reveals himself first to Peter and another, unnamed disciple on the **Sunday** of the Resurrection. As the men walk from Jerusalem to a village called Emmaus they meet a man along the road who becomes their companion (*see also* **Emmaus Walk**). He is the resurrected Jesus, although the disciples don't recognize him as such. As they journey towards Emmaus Jesus explains the meaning of the Hebrew prophecies concerning the Messiah. Once they arrive in the village the men sit down to break **bread** together, and the risen Jesus offers a blessing. Only then do the disciples recognize him. In that instant, Jesus disappears.

After Jesus' death Peter served as a leader and a missionary in the new, Christian church. Christian scripture and tradition provides some evidence that he played an important role in the founding of the church in Rome and that he may have ended his days there. According to Christian tradition he was condemned to die because of his religious beliefs. Legend has it that Peter was crucified head downwards at his own request. He chose this position because he thought himself unworthy to die in the same manner as had Jesus Christ. As early as the second century Roman Christians revered a specific site as the location of Peter's burial. Many believe that this same site now lies under St. Peter's Basilica in Rome, Italy. Today Christian pilgrims still journey to the famous Basilica to pay tribute to St. Peter.

Christians have viewed Peter in many ways over the years. Many Christians understand him to have been given special authority in the church as a leader among the apostles. This view is based on one of Jesus' speeches, recorded in the Gospel according to Matthew (Matthew 16:18). Roman Catholic doctrine holds him to have been the first bishop of Rome, or pope. It further proclaims that because Peter enjoyed a special kind of authority, all who serve as pope also have special authority over the entire church. Protestants and Eastern Christians disagree.

In Christian art Peter is often portrayed as the keeper of the keys of heaven. He also appears next to churches, holding a book, or seated as a bishop, settings that symbolize the work he undertook after Christ's death. Occasionally artists depict him weeping alongside a rooster in reference to his role in the Easter story.

Further Reading

Davids, Peter H. "Peter." In David Noel Freedman, ed. *Eerdmans Dictionary of the Bible*. Grand Rapids, MI: William B. Eerdmans Publishing, 2000.

Grant, Michael. *Saint Peter*. New York: Scribner, 1995.

McDue, James F. "Peter the Apostle." In Mircea Eliade, ed. *The Encyclopedia of Religion.* Volume 11. New York: Macmillan, 1987.

Neyrey, Jerome H. "Peter." In Paul J. Achtemeier, ed. *The HarperCollins Bible Dictionary*. New York: HarperCollins, 1996.

"Peter, St." In E. A. Livingstone, ed. *The Oxford Dictionary of the Christian Church*. Third edition. Oxford, England: Oxford University Press, 1997.

Walsh, John Evangelist. *The Bones of St. Peter*. Garden City, NY: Doubleday, 1982.

Philippines, Easter and Holy Week in the

When the Spanish came to the Philippines in the sixteenth century, they brought the Roman Catholic religion with them. Although Spanish rule crumbled in 1898, the religion remained. Today eighty percent of Filipinos are Roman Catholic. Indeed the Philippines is the only predominantly Christian country in Asia. Visitors often remark on the intensity of Filipino Easter and **Holy Week** observances. These observances engulf participants in both the grief and the rapture of the Easter story.

Lent

During **Lent** Filipinos stage **Passion plays**. In Marinduque the play reenacts the legend of the unnamed Roman soldier who thrust his spear into **Jesus'** side as he hung on the **cross** (John 19:34). The legend elaborates on the incident mentioned in the Bible by naming the soldier Longinus. It further asserts that Longinus, blind in one eye, experienced a miraculous healing when **blood** dripping from Christ's wounds splashed onto his blind eye and restored his vision. Longinus then became a devoted Christian who was eventually put to death by his fellow soldiers for his faith in Christ.

In Marinduque, those citizens who play the part of the Roman soldiers, called *moriones*, wear enormous wooden masks with long black beards, open mouths, big black eyes, and pink or red flesh. The moriones also wear colorful helmets called *turbantes*. This costume helps to disguise the identity of the participants, who take part in the play as a means of expressing religious devotion rather than having fun or showing off. In the Marinduque Passion play, the soldiers capture Longinus three times and each time he manages to escape. The fourth time they seize him Longinus does not escape. The moriones escort him to a scaffold, but Longinus continues to declare his faith in Christ.

491

The moriones behead Longinus, place him on a stretcher, and carry him through the town.

Palm Sunday

Palms are blessed in Filipino churches on **Palm Sunday**. The joy of Jesus' triumphal entry into Jerusalem quickly fades, however, as the observances of Holy Week turn to consider the events associated with Jesus' imprisonment and execution.

Maundy Thursday

On **Maundy Thursday** some people practice a custom called *visita iglesia*, which entails visiting as many churches as they can. Others sing the Passion story, that is, the story of Jesus' arrest, trial and execution.

Good Friday

Holy Week observances climax on **Good Friday**, with the commemoration of Jesus' crucifixion (*for more on crucifixion, see* Cross). In some places processions of **penitentes** trudge through the streets beating themselves with whips until they draw blood. They do this in completion of a promise made to God in exchange for some favor or the forgiveness of **sins**. Each year a few people undertake even greater suffering by having themselves crucified. They remain on the cross only a few minutes before being taken down. Nevertheless this spectacle of suffering attracts crowds of locals and tourists. While some denounce these bloody customs as barbaric, others point to their cultural significance for poor Filipinos. They say that during the centuries of foreign rule Filipino peasants embraced the story of Jesus' anguish as emblematic of their own sufferings at the hands of Spanish landlords and religious authorities. In recent years the urban poor have used these customs to draw attention to their plight. Roman Catholic religious officials have spoken out against the crucifixions but have been unable to put an end to this folk custom.

Other less dramatic Good Friday customs include participating in the **Stations of the Cross**, meditating on the seven last utterances of

Christ, watching Passion plays, and singing or reciting the Passion story (*for more on the seven last utterances of Christ, see* **Three Hours**).

Easter Sunday

Many Filipinos celebrate **Easter Sunday** by attending the *salubong* (meeting) of the risen Jesus and his mother, Mary (*see also* **Mary, Blessed Virgin**). At dawn a figure representing Jesus is placed on top of a carriage and taken to one end of town, while a statue of the Blessed Virgin Mary is taken to the other end of town. As the two statues move back into town people line up behind them forming a procession. In some places women and girls follow the Blessed Virgin while men and boys follow Jesus. The two statues meet at a place designated as "Galilea." The meeting of these two figures unleashes the joy of Easter. Children dressed as angels burst into song, the veil covering Mary's face falls away, and a flock of doves takes flight. After the two images meet the procession turns toward the church and people enter to attend Easter morning mass.

Further Reading

Henderson, Helene, and Sue Ellen Thompson, eds. *Holidays, Festivals, and Celebrations of the World Dictionary*. Second edition. Detroit, MI: Omnigraphics, 1997.

Mendoze, Lunita. *Festivals of the World: Philippines*. Milwaukee, WI: Gareth Stevens Publishing, 1999.

Tope, Lily Rose R. *Philippines*. New York: Marshall Cavendish, 1991.

Web Site

"Religion-Philippines: Holy Week of Folk Rituals, Gory Spectacle," an article by Johanna Sun, and available through the Inter Press Service at: http://www.oneworld.org/ips2/apr98/04_45_007.html

Phoenix

Ancient legends preserve the tale of the immortal phoenix, a marvelous bird that rises from the ashes of its own funeral pyre. According to these legends, when the bird senses that it is close to death it builds a bonfire from scented woods and myrrh and takes its place amidst the flames. After its body is consumed, a new phoenix emerges from the ashes of the old one. Early Christian thinkers quickly adopted this pre-existing symbol of rebirth and immortality as a symbol of the **resurrection** of Christ and his followers.

Variations of the Tale

The legend of the phoenix developed in ancient Egypt and was adopted by the ancient Greeks. To the Egyptians the bird stood for the sun, which rises anew each day. Some also associated the bird with Osiris, the Egyptian god who died and was resurrected. The Egyptians believed this red-gold bird dwelt somewhere in Arabia, or perhaps India, and that it had a lifespan of about five hundred years.

Several different versions of the phoenix legend circulated through-out the ancient Mediterranean world. According to one, when the bird knew itself to be dying it journeyed to Heliopolis, an important Egyptian city. There it built a nest of fragrant woods and spices on the altar of the Temple of the Sun. Fire consumed both the nest and the phoenix, but a baby bird miraculously emerged from the smoking remains. In several days the young phoenix grew strong enough to fly away from the temple. Some versions of the tale specify that the young bird grew from a worm which crawled out of the body of the dead bird. Other versions of the legend omit all mention of Helio-polis, suggesting instead that the bird constructed its funeral pyre at some unspecified place in the desert, using the heat of the sun and the fanning of its own wings to set the wood ablaze. Some tale tellers added that the young bird that rose from the ashes of these lonely funeral bonfires then journeyed to Heliopolis clutching a ball of myrrh in which it had entombed the body of its dead parent.

The tale of the phoenix was well known in the ancient Mediter-ranean world. The Jews told a folktale about this bird, too. They said it was the only bird in the Garden of Eden that did not eat the forbid-den fruit. Thus the phoenix alone retained the gift of eternal life.

The Egyptians called this legendary bird a *bennu*, while the Greeks referred to it as a "phoenix." The ancient Greeks used a nearly identi-cal word for "**palm** tree." Some writers have noted that the ashes of the date palm tree make good fertilizer for palm seedlings. They spec-ulate that this agricultural fact might have given rise to the myth of the baby bird which emerges from the ashes of its parent. In any case, date palm trees also served as symbols of eternal life among the early Christians. They often appeared together with phoenixes in early Christian artwork.

An Early Christian Symbol

The pagan Romans used the phoenix as a symbol of immortality on funeral urns. The early Christians adopted the phoenix as a symbol of their own belief in the resurrection of the dead. Phoenixes are de-picted on the walls of some of Rome's earliest catacombs, underground vaults in which the early Christians buried their dead. They also appear on the walls of early Christian churches, often with star-shaped disks of light behind their heads. The popularity of this symbol declined during Renaissance times, although it is still occasionally seen on robes worn by the clergy during religious services.

Further Reading

Evans, E. P. *Animal Symbolism in Ecclesiastical Architecture*. 1896. Reprint. Detroit, MI: Gale Research, 1969.

Heath, Sidney. *The Romance of Symbolism*. 1909. Reprint. Detroit, MI: Gale Research, 1976.

Hulme, F. Edward. *The History, Principles and Practice of Symbolism in Christian Art*. 1891. Detroit, MI: Gale Research, 1969.

Knapp, Justina. *Christian Symbols and How to Use Them*. 1935. Reprint. Detroit, MI: Gale Research, 1974.

Leach, Maria, ed. *Funk and Wagnalls Standard Dictionary of Folklore, Mythology and Legend*. New York: Harper and Row, 1984.

Lord, Priscilla Sawyer, and Daniel J. Foley. *Easter Garland*. 1963. Reprint. Detroit, MI: Omnigraphics, 1999.

Webber, F. R. *Church Symbolism*. 1938. Second edition, revised. Reprint. Detroit, MI: Omnigraphics, 1992.

Pig

The pig is a traditional European symbol of good luck and abundance. The invention of ceramic coin jars for children, traditionally made in the shape of a pig and therefore known as "piggy banks," was inspired by this symbolism. In past times this symbolism also inspired girls to wear pig-shaped charms on charm bracelets. Men once wore similar charms on their watch chains.

In many European countries a traditional Easter feast features pork (*see also* **Lamb**). Some explain this preference for pork at Easter time with reference to the pig's role as a symbol of abundance. Others, however, believe that this custom began in medieval times as a jab at the Jews for their refusal to accept **Jesus** as the Messiah (*for more on Messiah, see* Jesus). Traditional Jewish dietary laws prohibit Jews from eating pork. Christians, however, understood themselves to have been released from the obligation to follow these laws through the sacrificial death and **resurrection** of Jesus Christ. So they celebrated Easter by eating pork. Many Europeans still enjoy feasting on pork at Easter time. In the United States ham serves as a traditional Easter dish.

Further Reading

Myers, Robert J. *Celebrations: The Complete Book of American Holidays.* Garden City, NY: Doubleday and Company, 1972.

Weiser, Francis X. *The Easter Book.* New York: Harcourt, Brace and Company, 1954.

Pilate, Pontius

The mighty Roman Empire ruled **Jesus'** homeland during his lifetime. Politicians sent from Rome served as provincial governors backed up by battalions of Roman soldiers. The fifth Roman governor of the province of Judea held that post between 26 and 36 A.D. His name was Pontius Pilate and he lived in the Judean capital of Jerusalem. History remembers him for one act alone. According to the Bible he sentenced Jesus to death by crucifixion on a spring day about two thousand years ago (*for more on crucifixion, see* **Cross**; *see also* **Good Friday**).

Pilate's Role in the Easter Story

All four biblical accounts of Jesus' trial—found in the Gospels according to Matthew, Mark, Luke, and John—tell of Pilate's encounter with Jesus (Mark 15:1-15, Matthew 27:1-2, 11-26, Luke 23:1-25, John

18:28-19:16). In general they paint a picture of a man who registers astonishment at Jesus' failure to defend himself, who believes Jesus to be innocent of any wrongdoing, but who nevertheless caves in to public pressure to execute him. Interesting differences between the accounts emerge when they are examined more closely.

Pilate's wife enters the story in only one of the four accounts. In the Gospel according to Matthew she dreams about Jesus on the night before his death and warns her husband to have "nothing to do with that righteous man" (Matthew 27:19). Pilate tries to avoid convicting Jesus, arguing with the crowd that is calling for Jesus' crucifixion and asking them to explain what harm Jesus has done. He eventually hands Jesus over to be flogged and crucified. Before he does so, he proclaims himself clean, or innocent, of Jesus' **blood**, and demonstrates this to the crowd by washing his hands. The crowd roars back, "His blood be on us and on our children" (Matthew 27:25). In Christian art, Pilate is often depicted washing his hands. Moreover, the expression "to wash one's hands" of something, meaning to deny one's responsibility about something, is still in common usage.

King Herod, governor of Galilee, appears only in Luke's account of the meeting between Christ and Pilate. In an attempt to avoid condemning Jesus himself, Pilate sends him to see Herod, who happens to be in Jerusalem at the time. Herod returns Jesus to Pilate, who eventually gives in to the demands of those who want him crucified.

John's Gospel gives a longer version of Pilate's encounter with Jesus. In this account Pilate appears especially intrigued by Jesus' answers to his questions concerning Jesus' identity and mission. Pilate orders Jesus flogged in an attempt to appease the mob with something short of Jesus' death. He tries to reason with the horde clamoring for Jesus' crucifixion but they in return question his loyalty to the Roman emperor. Finally Pilate bows to the will of the crowd and orders Jesus' execution.

Another View of Pilate

Pilate appears in only a few ancient texts besides the Bible. Ancient Jewish documents paint a different picture of Pilate than that shown in Christian scripture. They complain about his crass violations of Jewish religious customs and portray him as prone to violence as a means of rule. According to one of these texts Pilate was recalled to Rome in 36 A.D. for excessive use of force against his subjects.

Pilate in Christian Legend

Nothing is known about the later part of Pilate's life. One early Christian text suggested that he eventually committed suicide. Another speculated that the emperor Nero (37-68 A.D.) had him beheaded. This lack of knowledge created a void into which rushed Christian storytellers, eager to supply the missing details. Instead of portraying the man responsible for signing Jesus' death warrant as evil, however, some early Christian legends showed Pilate in an even more favorable light than does the Bible. Scholars explain this trend as an outgrowth of the increasing friction between the Jewish community and those Jews and Gentiles who wished to follow Jesus. Thus the campaign to purify Pilate's image was in large part motivated by the desire of certain Christians to portray Jews in a bad light.

In some legends Pilate converts to Christianity after Jesus' crucifixion. In one tale Pilate ends his life as a martyr for the Christian cause. A legend attributed to the Coptic Christians of north Africa claims that after Jesus' death Pilate and his wife became Christians. This so annoyed his former Jewish and Roman supporters that they crucified him. But one crucifixion was not enough. They cut him down from the first cross and then attached him to the same cross on which Jesus had been crucified (*see also* **Tree of the Cross**). Even then he was not allowed to die, but taken down once more and sent to Rome, where he was beheaded. The Coptic Christians of north Africa eventually proclaimed Pilate both a Christian martyr and a saint, along with his wife, whom Christian tradition assigned the name Procula. Procula also became a saint in the Greek Orthodox Church.

Early Christian legends may have minimized the role of Pontius Pilate in Jesus' death for fear that portraying him as guilty of Christ's death would encourage Roman officials to view the new, Christian religion as a threat to their authority. In the early fourth century, after

Roman authorities adopted an official policy of toleration towards the Christian religion, Christian storytellers no longer found it necessary to shift the blame for Jesus' death away from the Romans and onto the Jews. After this time, western European legends concerning Pontius Pilate began to portray him in a more negative light.

Further Reading

Cheney, Emily. "Pilate, Pontius." In David Noel Freedman, ed. *Eerdmans Dictionary of the Bible*. Grand Rapids, MI: William B. Eerdmans Publishing, 2000.

García-Treto, Francisco O. "Pilate Pontius." In Paul J. Achtemeier, ed. *The HarperCollins Bible Dictionary*. New York: HarperCollins, 1996.

"Pilate, Pontius." In E. A. Livingstone, ed. *The Oxford Dictionary of the Christian Church*. Third edition. Oxford, England: Oxford University Press, 1997.

Wroe, Ann. *Pontius Pilate*. New York: Random House, 1999.

Poland, Easter and Holy Week in

In past times Poles **fasted** diligently throughout **Lent** and celebrated Easter with joy and feasting. Although the Roman Catholic Church eliminated much of the Lenten fast in the twentieth century, Poles still celebrate Easter with food and festivity.

Holy Week

In Poland the last week of Lent, **Holy Week**, is known as *Wielki Post* or "Great Week." During this week Polish families prepared their homes for Easter. Traditionally women gave their homes a thorough **spring cleaning**, shopped, baked, and cooked for the Easter feast. They also prepared *pisanki*, elaborately decorated **Easter eggs** (*for more on pisanki, see* Easter Eggs). Men cleaned the yard, farm buildings, and livestock in preparation for *Wielkanoc*, the great Easter festival (*for Polish carnival celebrations, see* **Paczki Day**).

Palm Sunday

Niedziela Kwietna, or Flower Sunday, is an old Polish name for **Palm Sunday**. This name sprang from the custom of bringing bouquets of flowers, pussy willows, and evergreens to church to be blessed. The flowers and greenery served as a substitute for **palm** branches, the traditional symbol of the holiday, which do not grow well in Poland and other northern European countries.

Palm Sunday services in Poland's Roman Catholic churches feature processions in which worshipers carry willow branches or sticks decorated with flowers. Weeks before Palm Sunday people cut willow branches, take them home, and place them in pots of **water**. This causes the branches to bud in time for Palm Sunday. In the past parents encouraged their children to swallow one of the fuzzy little buds which, according to folklore, would prevent sore throats and perhaps even keep the youngsters in good health throughout the year. Another old folk custom advised parents to strike their children on the legs with the pussy willow branches in order to make them good and pure. A related bit of folklore proposed that tapping men on the legs with pussy willows would encourage their crops to grow, while tapping women on the legs could make them fertile.

Inhabitants of the town of Kalwaria Zebrzydowska stage the nation's best-known **Passion plays** on Palm Sunday. Both local residents and religious pilgrims take part, dressed as Romans, disciples of **Jesus**, and as Pharisees (Jewish religious officials in biblical times). Thousands of people attend the performance, which is held at a monastery on the side of a hill. The small town also boasts impressive palm processions, featuring artificially constructed palm branches reaching up to thirty feet in length.

Holy Wednesday

Old folk traditions associated with the Wednesday of Holy Week taught Polish youngsters to build straw dummies representing **Judas**, the disciple who handed Jesus over to the religious authorities (*see also* **Spy Wednesday**). They hurled these effigies from church steeples, dragged them through the streets, beat them with stones, and tossed their remains into a pond or lake to "drown" (*see also* **Judas, Burning of**). In some places this custom takes place on **Maundy Thursday**.

Maundy Thursday

Many Poles attend church services on this day. In Roman Catholic churches these services feature **footwashing** ceremonies. At the close of the service the remains of the consecrated **Eucharist** are put in a special container which is placed on a beautifully decorated altar, sometimes referred to as a sepulchre. Many parishes vie with each other to see who can create the most memorable display. Devout Poles may uphold the old custom of visiting seven different churches in order to view seven of these altars on the evening of Maundy Thursday (*see also* **Holy Sepulchre**).

In past times many Polish families did their Easter baking on Maundy Thursday. According to another old custom people lit fires for the poor to warm themselves by and provided them with food on Maundy Thursday. When church **bells** stop ringing on the Thursday of Holy Week, Polish parents traditionally told their youngsters that the bells had flown away to Rome.

Good Friday

Solemn church services mourning the death of Jesus take place on **Good Friday**. These services feature a devotional activity known as the **Veneration of the Cross**.

On Good Friday many churches display life-sized images of Jesus lying in the tomb. These tableaux often include figures of angels, lit candles, flowers, and the three crosses of Mount Calvary, where Jesus was crucified alongside two thieves (*see also* **Good Thief**; *for more on crucifixion, see* **Cross**). Devout Poles often consider a visit to these displays an important devotional exercise, especially on **Holy Saturday**.

Devout Poles may observe a strict fast on Good Friday, consuming neither food nor beverages. Some will eat only simple, cold foods like **bread** and cold baked potatoes. Some cover the mirrors in their homes with a black veil to remind them that they are in mourning for the death of Jesus Christ (*see also* **Veiling**). Good Friday was the day traditionally reserved for the decoration of pisanki, or Easter eggs.

Holy Saturday

On this day Poles prepare baskets of Easter foods which are taken to church later that evening to be blessed (*see also* **Easter Vigil**). Each of these foods symbolizes an aspect of the Easter festival. The Easter eggs represent life and rebirth. The Polish sausage (*kielbasa*) or ham stands for the lifting of the old dietary laws that restricted Jews from eating pork. Horseradish or pepper symbolizes the bitter herbs eaten by Jews during **Passover**. A **lamb**, made from cake, butter or plaster, represents Jesus as the sacrificial "lamb of God." Bread reminds Poles of the biblical teaching that Jesus is the "bread of life." **Wine** signifies the **blood** of Christ, shed during the Crucifixion. Vinegar recalls the vinegar offered to Jesus as he hung on the cross. Salt, together with bread, denotes hospitality. Before placing these foods in the basket Poles line the basket with a white napkin. They cover the foods with another linen or lace napkin and decorate it with sprigs of boxwood.

In past times Poles extinguished all their home fires on Holy Saturday. They relit them with the candle brought back from the Easter Vigil service (*see also* **Easter Fires**). Many Poles still bring back holy water, specially blessed water, from this service. They traditionally used this water to confer blessings on family members, crops, and livestock.

Easter Sunday

On Easter Sunday Poles offer one another the traditional Polish Easter greeting, "A joyful **alleluia** to you." On **Easter Sunday** morning Poles celebrate by ringing church bells, silenced since Maundy Thursday. This celebration may also include various kinds of bangs and explosions, understood as symbolic of Jesus' rising from the dead.

Easter Sunday religious services usually feature a procession around the church with the Blessed Sacrament (or Eucharist) carried underneath a canopy. Poles hurry home after Easter morning church services to start their Easter feast. They often begin the banquet by sharing wedges of blessed Easter eggs and exchanging Easter blessings with one another. Many Polish Easter tables feature a centerpiece in the shape of a lamb, made from sugar, cake, or plaster. Indeed, the image of a lamb carrying a banner stamped with a cross is an important Easter symbol in Poland.

Easter Monday

Poles celebrate **Easter Monday**, or Dyngus Day, with a folk custom that encourages men to drench women with water. Some researchers believe that this custom dates back to pre-Christian times when it was viewed as a means of ensuring purity, fertility, and cleanliness. The word *dyngus* is of uncertain origin, but one writer believes it may come from a root word meaning "worthy" or "bicker." In the old days young men accomplished their Easter Monday task with pails, or by dragging young women to nearby ponds, streams, or horse troughs and throwing them in. Nowadays some youth merely sprinkle girls with water, but other more boisterous lads have taken to drenching anyone they meet, using watering cans, squirt guns, and any other method they find handy. Easter Monday is so closely associated with these customs that Poles often call the holiday *Lany Poniedzialek* (Wet Monday) or *Swietego Lejka* (St. Drencher's Day). The very next day tradition permitted girls free reign to drench the boys with water (*for more on this custom, see* Easter Monday).

In Poland people once practiced *chodzenie* on Easter Monday. Young people gathered together in groups and went door to door singing songs and reciting bits of folk poetry. Some attempted to combine this custom with water throwing, threatening to drench householders who did not offer them anything in return for their efforts. Good-humored families usually presented the Easter carolers with a few treats, including Easter eggs, a taste of homemade liquor, small change, a piece of cake, or a bite of sausage. Polish folk tradition permitted chodzenie throughout the **Easter season**, a fifty-day period beginning on Easter Sunday and ending on **Pentecost**.

Further Reading

Griffin, Robert H., and Ann H. Shurgin, eds. *Junior Worldmark Encyclopedia of World Holidays.* Volume 1. Detroit, MI: UXL, 2000.

Lord, Priscilla Sawyer, and Daniel J. Foley. *Easter the World Over*. Philadelphia, PA: Chilton Book Company, 1971.

Nowakowski, Jacek, and Marlene Perrin. *Polish Touches*. Iowa City, IA: Penfield Press, 1996.

Web Sites

For more on Lent, Carnival and Easter in Poland, see "Polish Easter Traditions," a web site designed by Dr. Ann Hetzel Gunkel, a professor of philosophy and cultural studies at Columbia College in Chicago: http://acweb. colum.edu/users/agunkel/homepage/easter/easter.html

"A Guide to Polish Easter Traditions" by Robert Strybel, posted at the *Polish-American Journal* web site at: http://www.polamjournal.com/Library/Holidays/ Easter/easter.html

The Polish Genealogical Society's customs and traditions page at: http:// www.pgsa.org/traditions.htm

"The Origins of Dyngus," an article by Czeslaw M. Krysa, posted at the *Polish-American Journal* web site at: http://www.polamjournal.com/Library/ Holidays/Easter/easter.html

The *Polish News'* "Did You Know That . . .; Everything You Ever Wanted to Know about Poland: Special Easter Edition" by Robert Strybel at: http:// www.polishnews.com/polonica/diduknow15.shtml

Pomegranate

In Christian art the pomegranate is often used as a symbol of **Jesus'**
resurrection as well as the promised resurrection of his followers. It
is frequently shown as a gift from the child Jesus to his mother Mary
(*see also* **Mary, Blessed Virgin**). Artists using the pomegranate as a
symbol of the Resurrection have depicted it with seeds bursting forth
from a split rind. This image recalls the way in which a living Jesus
burst out of the tomb on Easter morning.

Other Meanings in Christian Art

Artists have also used the pomegranate to represent other aspects of
the Christian religion. Sometimes pomegranates stand for the church
and its congregations. A single pomegranate husk encloses many
seeds, just as a unified church is composed of many different individuals and congregations. The pomegranate has also been used by Christian artists as a symbol of fertility and of hope.

An Ancient Symbol

Long before it was adopted as a Christian symbol, the peoples of the
ancient Mediterranean world had turned the pomegranate into a
symbol of fertility, death, and rebirth. The ancient Semites viewed the
pomegranate as a symbol of life and fruitfulness. One legend suggested that the pomegranate was the forbidden fruit eaten by Adam
and Eve in the Garden of Eden.

The ancient Greeks declared pomegranates sacred to Aphrodite, the
goddess of love and sexuality. Pomegranates were said to spring up
from the blood of Dionysus, the god of **wine**. The ancient Greeks also associated pomegranates with the story of Persephone, the goddess of spring. Captured by Hades, the god of the underworld, Persephone was about to be rescued from the realm of the dead when she

ate several pomegranate seeds. Consuming these seeds tied her permanently to the underworld. Although Hades permitted the young goddess to leave, each year Persephone had to return to the underworld for several months, at which time winter fell upon the land.

A Modern Greek Symbol

This association with life, death, and fertility continues in contemporary Greek tradition. Greek Orthodox mourners often sprinkle pomegranate seeds on the special dishes of *kollyva*, sweetened, boiled wheat, prepared to commemorate the resurrection of the dead at Greek funerals and later memorial services (*see also* **Soul Saturday**). According to contemporary Greek folklore, the boiled wheat berries stand for eternal life and the pomegranate seeds represent abundance.

Further Reading

Bailey, Henry Turner. *Symbolism for Artists*. 1925. Reprint. Detroit, MI: Gale Research, 1972.

Clement, Clara Erskine. *A Handbook of Christian Symbols*. 1886. Reprint. Detroit, MI: Gale Research, 1971.

Goldsmith, Elisabeth. *Ancient Pagan Symbols*. 1929. Reprint. Detroit, MI: Gale Research, 1976.

Leach, Maria, ed. *Funk and Wagnalls Standard Dictionary of Folklore, Mythology and Legend*. New York: Harper and Row, 1984.

Lehner, Ernst, and Johanna Lehner. *Folklore and Symbolism of Flowers, Plants and Trees*. 1960. Reprint. Detroit, MI: Omnigraphics, 1990.

Rouvelas, Marilyn. *A Guide to Greek Traditions and Customs in America*. Bethesda, MD: Nea Attiki Press, 1993.

Webber, F. R. *Church Symbolism*. 1938. Second edition, revised. Reprint. Detroit, MI: Omnigraphics, 1992.

Pre-Lent

A generation or two ago many American Christians, notably Roman Catholics and Episcopalians, observed a period of spiritual preparation for **Lent** known as pre-Lent. According to the Western Christian tradition, pre-Lent begins on the ninth **Sunday** before Easter and ends two and one-half weeks later on **Ash Wednesday**. Although this observance was recently struck off the Roman Catholic liturgical calendar, Orthodox and other Eastern Christians still celebrate pre-Lent. In the Eastern Christian tradition pre-Lent begins on the tenth Sunday before Easter and lasts a full three weeks.

History

Some writers believe that pre-Lent dates back to early Christian times. One of the earliest mentions of the observance in any historical document comes from the writings of St. Maximus of Turin (d. 408-423 A.D.). He suggested that the especially religious could demonstrate their devotion by beginning their Lenten **fast** during pre-Lent. In 541 the fourth Council of Orleans discussed the religious observance of pre-Lent. Some writers argue that one of the sixth-century popes, perhaps Pope Pelagius I (d. 561) or Pope John III (d. 574), ordered special penitential observances during pre-Lent in an effort to invoke God's protection during an era when rampaging armies devastated Italy and threatened Rome. Others believe that Pope Gregory I, also known as St. Gregory the Great (540-604), helped to formalize the observance of pre-Lent by writing special intercessions, or prayers, to be said during this period.

The Three Sundays of Western Pre-Lent

In the West the three Sundays of pre-Lent acquired a series of tongue-twisting Latin names. The first of these, known as Septuagesima Sunday, fell nine Sundays before Easter. The word Septuagesima means "seventieth." The second was called Sexagesima Sunday and the third was known as Quinquagesima Sunday. Sexagesima means "sixtieth" and quinquagesima means "fiftieth."

For Western Christians pre-Lent lasted about two and one-half weeks. It ended on the Wednesday following Quinquagesima Sunday, which is called Ash Wednesday. The following Sunday, the first Sunday in Lent, was once called Quadragesima, or "fortieth," Sunday. Quadragesima Sunday occurs approximately forty days before Easter. Once established, the name Quadragesima Sunday suggested that the preceding Sundays be given a series of numerical names, even though Sexagesima Sunday and Septuagesima Sunday do not fall exactly sixty and seventy days before Easter. The desire to sketch out a roughly seventy-day period of preparation for Easter may also have figured into the adoption of these names. According to the Bible the ancient Israelites spent seventy years as captives in Babylon. To those familiar with this story an approximately seventy-day period of preparation for Easter might suggest a similar sequence of exile and hardship followed by divine deliverance (*see also* **Redemption**). Other writers have speculated that ancient Christian fasting customs helped to establish the period of pre-Lent. In some quarters of the church, Thursdays, Saturdays, and Sundays were never observed as fast days. Therefore, in order to end up with an approximately forty-day fast in anticipation of Easter, the fast would have to begin on the Monday following Septuagesima Sunday.

Traditional Observance

To lay people and monastics alike the religious services that occurred during the three Sundays of pre-Lent took on a special character, one that emphasized devotion, penance, and atonement (*for more on penance and atonement, see* **Repentance**). Special religious customs helped to set the tone of these masses (*for more on the Roman Catholic religious service known as the mass, see* **Eucharist**). For example, clergy and worshipers abstained from speaking the word **alleluia**, a joyous exclamation meaning "praise the Lord," during pre-Lent. This abstinence continued on into Lent. Moreover, no flowers adorned the altar during pre-Lent, a formal prayer known as the Gloria was omitted, and priests

509

wore somber, purple robes. The color purple represents repentance in the color symbolism of the Western Church. In addition, the clergy and some of the laity began to wean themselves from foods forbidden during the Lenten fast in this preparatory period.

People also sought out priests during the last several days of pre-Lent in order to make formal confessions of their **sins** and to receive absolution, or forgiveness. In England this custom gave rise to the name **"Shrovetide"** for the last several days of pre-Lent as well as the name "Shrove Tuesday" for the very last day of this preparatory season. The word "shrove" is an archaic English word meaning "wrote." In medieval times after a priest heard a confession he frequently wrote out a prescription for an appropriate penance, a series of religious rituals that expresses a person's remorse for his or her errors and hopefully inspires renewed devotion. After going through this process of making confession, receiving penance, and accepting absolution a person was said to be "shriven" of their sins.

The religious customs of pre-Lent conflicted with folk customs popular at that time of year. The especially pious may have begun their Lenten fast in pre-Lent, but many others feasted on rich foods, such as meat, butter, oil, eggs, and cheese. For example, the English dubbed Shrove Tuesday **Pancake Day**, and in northern England people referred to the last Monday of pre-Lent as "Collop Monday." On that day tradition dictated that one dine on collops, or pieces of meat, which were often fried with eggs and butter. Similar customs existed throughout Europe and gave rise to other charming folk names for the last days of this season. The Russians called the last week of pre-Lent "Butter Week," as they sated themselves on butter-rich dishes during these days (*see also* **Maslenitsa**). The French and Germans also gorged themselves with rich foods on the last day of pre-Lent. Hence, they called the day "Fat Tuesday," which translates to *Mardi Gras* in French and *Fetter Dienstag* in German. This impulse to indulge in rich foods may have been spurred by anticipation of the upcoming fast. Or people may have been motivated by the desire to use up foods that could not be eaten during Lent. *Poor Robin's Almanack* for the year 1684 offered this description of the frantic kitchen activity that characterized the day:

But hark, I hear the pancake bell,
And fritters make a gallant smell;
The cooks are baking, frying, boyling,
Stewing, mincing, cutting, broyling,
Carving, gormandising, roasting,
Carbonading, cracking, slashing, toasting.
                    (Lord and Foley, 63)

In Ireland Quinquagesima Sunday was known as "Whispering Sunday." This name grew out of folk traditions that encouraged matchmaking during pre-Lent. Since this activity was frowned on and marriage forbidden during Lent, Quinquagesima Sunday marked one of the last days that "whispering" of this sort could take place before Easter. In a similar vein, the Tuesday before Ash Wednesday was known as "Sulky Tuesday," named after the sulky looks of girls who had failed to find a husband. Matchmaking was not the only pleasurable activity the Irish indulged in during pre-Lent. Some people called Quinquagesima Sunday "Tippling Sunday" in reference to the custom of celebrating the last Sunday before Lent with hearty drinking.

In addition to these folk customs a wild celebration known as **Carnival** dominated the streets of many European countries during the last days of pre-Lent. These street celebrations offered a startling contrast to the somber mood prevailing in the churches. Carnival celebrations later spread to Latin America, the Caribbean, and the southern United States (*see also* **Mardi Gras**).

Cancellation and Continued Observance

The Roman Catholic Church discontinued the observance of pre-Lent in 1969. Nevertheless the three Sundays of pre-Lent still appear in the Book of Common Prayer used by the Church of England. The Book of Common Prayer currently used by the American Episcopal Church, however, makes no reference to the three Sundays of pre-Lent. Those Western Christians who still observe the season use the time to plan appropriate Lenten disciplines, including fasting regimens, study or meditation projects, and charitable works.

Orthodox Pre-Lent

Orthodox Christians still maintain a pre-Lent season. Orthodoxy is one of the three main branches of the Christian faith. Orthodox Christianity developed in eastern Europe and the countries surrounding the eastern half of the Mediterranean Sea. Most members of this ancient faith tradition still hail from these eastern countries although Orthodox Christian churches can also be found in the West. Orthodox Christians follow a different church calendar than that commonly adhered to by Western Christians, that is, Roman Catholics and Protestants (*see also* **Easter, Date of**). Orthodox pre-Lent lasts for a full three weeks. The purpose of this observance is to help the faithful begin Lent with the proper attitude. The Gospel readings assigned to each of the four Sundays that bracket this three-week period exemplify elements of this attitude. The Gospels — the first four books of the New Testament, or Christian Bible — offer four accounts of the life and death of Christ, as told by Matthew, Mark, Luke, and John.

The first Sunday of pre-Lent occurs ten weeks before Orthodox Easter and is known as the Sunday of the Publican and Pharisee. The name comes from the Gospel reading assigned for this Sunday (Luke 18:10-14). The story of the Publican and the Pharisee celebrates the virtue of humility before God.

The story of the Prodigal Son is told on the second Sunday of pre-Lent, commonly known as the Sunday of the Prodigal Son (Luke 15:11-32). This story emphasizes the need to return to God as well as God's eagerness to accept all those who approach Him. "Meat Week" begins on the evening of the Sunday of the Prodigal Son. During this week observant Orthodox Christians feast on meat, since the rules of the Lenten fast decree that meat be eliminated from their diet the following week.

The third Sunday of pre-Lent is called Last Judgment Sunday. The Gospel reading assigned for this day proclaims that the righteous will reap heavenly rewards while the selfish and indifferent will face punishment for their lack of compassion (Matthew 25:31-46). This reading reminds Orthodox Christians to commit themselves anew to good deeds, especially deeds of mercy. This Sunday is also known as "Meatfare Sunday," since it is the last day of Meat Week, and the last day on which Orthodox Christians may eat meat before **Easter Sunday**. The week following Meatfare Sunday is known as **Cheese Week** or Butter Week since it is the last week during which observant Orthodox Christians may eat cheese and dairy products before the beginning of the Lenten fast. During Cheese Week a festive mood similar to that of western European Carnival prevails in lands populated by Orthodox Christians.

The Saturday that precedes Last Judgment Sunday constitutes the first of the four yearly **Soul Saturdays**. These Saturdays occur during the pre-Lent, Lent, and Easter seasons and are marked by special religious observances dedicated to the memory of the departed. The second Soul Saturday falls the following week, the last Saturday of pre-Lent.

The fourth and last Sunday of pre-lent is known as **Forgiveness Sunday**. Forgiveness Sunday falls on the seventh Sunday before Orthodox Easter. Worship services recall the story of Adam and Eve's expulsion from Paradise as well as Jesus' teaching on forgiveness and fasting (Matthew 6:14-18). The Gospel reading assigned for this Sunday reminds Orthodox Christians of the necessity of giving and receiving forgiveness. Forgiveness Sunday is also known as "Cheesefare Sunday," since it is the last day on which observant Orthodox Christians eat cheese and other dairy products before the beginning of the Lenten fast.

Orthodox Christians have maintained the Jewish custom of beginning each day on the evening that precedes it. Therefore Lent begins on the evening of Forgiveness Sunday, after vespers, the evening prayer service. For the next seven weeks strictly observant Orthodox Christians will consume no meat, eggs, dairy products, olive oil, fish, **wine**, or alcohol. The following day, known as **Clean Monday**, constitutes the first full day of Lent.

Further Reading

Blackburn, Bonnie, and Leofranc Holford-Strevens. *The Oxford Companion to the Year*. Oxford, England: Oxford University Press, 1999.

Brewster, H. Pomeroy. *Saints and Festivals of the Christian Church.* 1904. Reprint. Detroit, MI: Omnigraphics, 1990.

Cowie, L. W., and John Selwyn Gummer. *The Christian Calendar.* Springfield, MA: G. and C. Merriam, 1974.

Harper, Howard. *Days and Customs of All Faiths.* 1957. Reprint. Detroit, MI: Omnigraphics, 1990.

Lord, Priscilla Sawyer, and Daniel J. Foley. *Easter the World Over.* Philadelphia, PA: Chilton Book Company, 1971.

Mathewes-Green, Frederica. *Facing East.* New York: HarperSanFrancisco, 1997.

Metford, J. C. J. *The Christian Year.* London, England: Thames and Hudson, 1991.

Rouvelas, Marilyn. *A Guide to Greek Traditions and Customs in America.* Bethesda, MD: Nea Attiki Press, 1993.

"Septuagesima." In E. A. Livingstone, ed. *The Oxford Dictionary of the Christian Church.* Third edition. Oxford, England: Oxford University Press, 1997.

Slim, Hugo. *A Feast of Festivals.* London, England: Marshall Pickering, 1996.

Weiser, Francis X. *The Easter Book.* New York: Harcourt, Brace and Company, 1954.

———. *Handbook of Christian Feasts and Customs.* New York: Harcourt, Brace and World, 1952.

Wybrew, Hugh. *Orthodox Lent, Holy Week and Easter.* Crestwood, NY: St. Vladimir's Seminary Press, 1997.

Web Site

"Pre-Lent," a document describing the beliefs and practices of Orthodox Christians concerning pre-Lent, posted on the Orthodox Church in America web site: http://www.oca.org/pages/orth_chri/orthodox-faith/worship/pre-lent.html

Pretzel

Nowadays people don't think of the common, everyday pretzel as an **Easter season** food. Nevertheless, for centuries the pretzel qualified as an acceptable food during the forty-day **fast** that precedes Easter (*see also* **Lent**). The pretzel dates back to ancient times. The earliest known image of a pretzel comes from a fifth-century manuscript housed in the Vatican.

Observant Christians in the Roman Empire considered pretzels a suitable Lenten food for two reasons. First, because pretzel dough contains only flour, salt, and **water**, these **bread** snacks fulfilled the strict requirements of the Lenten fast. Second, by virtue of their shape, they symbolized the proper activity of an observant Christian during Lent: prayer. In those days many Christians prayed by crossing their arms in front of them and placing the fingertips of each hand on the shoulders of the opposing arms. The bow-shaped pretzel, still common today, represents the crossed arms of a person in prayer. The Romans called these treats *bracellae*, meaning "little arms" in Latin. Later, the Germans transformed this word into *brezel* or *prezel*. English speakers in turn translated the German word as "pretzel." By the Middle Ages pretzels had become a popular Lenten food in many parts of Europe.

In past times **Ash Wednesday** witnessed the arrival of the pretzel vendor on the streets of Germany, Austria, and Poland. As an act of Lenten charity pretzels were sometimes distributed free to poorer folk. Central Europeans often washed down their pretzels with beer. The Poles enjoyed these crunchy snacks with a dish of beer soup. In Austria children sometimes dangled them from the ends of **palm** branches on **Palm Sunday**. Pretzels continued to be widely identified with Lent until the nineteenth century. As western Europeans began to discard the food restrictions once associated with Lent, pretzels lost their association with the season and gradually became a year-round snack food.

Further Reading

Hogan, Julie. *Treasury of Easter Celebrations*. Nashville, TN: Ideals Publications, 1999.

Weiser, Francis X. *The Easter Book*. New York: Harcourt, Brace and Company, 1954.

Rabbit

As Easter approaches images of rabbits pop up everywhere, in advertising displays, on greeting cards, and in candy shops. The rabbit indeed has become a symbol of the holiday. America inherited this symbol from its European immigrants. A slight change accompanied this transfer of folklore, however. In Europe's German-speaking lands, the **hare**, not the rabbit, delivers colored eggs and sweets to children at Easter time. In the United States people have tended to lump hares and rabbits together. In fact they are separate species. This confusion over names has resulted in much of the imported European folklore concerning the hare transferring itself to the American rabbit (*see also* **Easter Bunny**).

Hares and Rabbits

Although hares and rabbits are similar in appearance and are closely related, important differences separate the two species. Hares belong to the genus *Lepus*. They have large ears, short tails, and long, strong hind legs and feet. Due to the fact that their eyes are placed so far back on their head, they can see in front, behind, and overhead all at the same time. Hares move about by hopping. They can cover 12 feet in a single, long jump, but when escaping predators they have been known to propel themselves as far as 20 feet in a single leap. Hares can run faster than almost any other animal, and have been clocked at speeds of up to 45 miles per hour. Even when running at top speed, hares can turn sharp corners without slowing down or come to a sudden, complete stop.

Hares have one unusual habit. They sometimes leap several feet straight up in the air in order to survey their surroundings. This leaping behavior is exaggerated in the month of March, when the mating season begins. The males often leap high into the air, as they fight one another for the right to mate with the females. Sometimes males and females court by leaping at and boxing with one another. These behaviors gave rise to the saying "mad as a March hare." Perhaps they also inspired the expression "harebrained," meaning rash or giddy.

Unlike hares, true rabbits are native only to Europe and Africa, although human beings have spread them around the world. Biologists classify these mammals as belonging to the genus *Orycytologus* and the species *cuniculus*. They differ from hares in a number of ways. Rabbits are sociable animals that live in crowded underground burrows called "warrens." Hares live on their own in "forms," or nests, hidden in tall grass. Rabbits scurry into their underground dens to escape predators while hares outrun them. Moreover, rabbits are runners whereas hares are leapers. Hares are wild animals, while rabbits have been successfully domesticated. Unlike hares, rabbits are born without fur and with closed eyes. Rabbits dislike getting their fur wet, but hares don't seem to mind water and are excellent swimmers.

Americans tend to confuse hares, rabbits, and related species, calling all of them "rabbits." For example, the Jackrabbit and the Snowshoe Rabbit, found in the north and west of the United States, are, in fact, hares. Many call the eastern cottontail a rabbit, although it actually belongs to a different genus and species than does the European rabbit. Biologists know it as *Sylvilagus floridanus*.

Contemporary American Folklore

This confusion of names may help to explain why the old, European folklore concerning hares attached itself to the animal known generically to Americans as the rabbit. For example, Americans view the hare, or rabbit, as a symbol of sexuality. Indeed, *Playboy* magazine calls its models "bunnies" and uses the figure of a rabbit's ears as a symbol on its merchandise. Rabbits continue to enjoy a well-deserved reputation for fertility. This reputation links the rabbit symbolically to springtime, the season of new life and new growth. Many Americans see the Easter Bunny primarily as a symbol of springtime.

Although European folklore has pictured the hare as both lucky and unlucky, Americans tend to view rabbits as lucky animals. A rabbit's foot is a well-known good luck charm, and untold numbers of these severed appendages dangle from key chains and car rearview mirrors. Rabbits may also be invoked for good luck at the beginning of a new month, or new **moon**. The word "rabbits" or "white rabbits" must be the very first words spoken during this period in order to acquire the luck. For example, upon waking up on the first day of a new moon, one should exclaim, "White rabbits!" Some people add that in order to ensure the turn of luck the last words one speaks before going to sleep on the previous night should be "Black rabbits!"

In recent times the rabbit has taken on a relatively new identity as a suitable childhood companion and child-friendly animal. Nineteenth- and twentieth-century writers and tellers of folktales helped to shape this image of the rabbit in the United States and Europe. A number of classic children's stories and folktales from this era introduce rabbits as main characters. Examples include Lewis Carroll's *Alice's Adventures in Wonderland* (1865), featuring the White Rabbit and the March Hare, Beatrix Potter's *Tale of Peter Rabbit* (1901), Margery Williams's *The Velveteen Rabbit* (c. 1922), Thornton W. Burgess's *Adventures of Peter Cottontail* (1941), Robert Lawson's *Rabbit Hill* (1944), Richard Adams's *Watership Down* (1972), and Joel Chandler Harris's Bre'r

Rabbit tales (retellings of African-American folktales published around the turn of the twentieth century). These stories portray rabbits as cozy, clever, or magical animals. The Easter Bunny shares in these qualities. To some extent so, too, does the animated cartoon character Bugs Bunny, another favorite with children. Perhaps these imagined character traits inspire children's continuing affection for these fictional rabbits and their mythological companion, the Easter Bunny.

Further Reading

Bare, Colleen Stanley. *Rabbits and Hares*. New York: Dodd, Mead and Company, 1983.

Cavendish, Richard, ed. "Rabbit." In his *Man, Myth, and Magic*. Volume 9. New York: Marshall Cavendish, 1970.

Lord, Priscilla Sawyer, and Daniel J. Foley. *Easter the World Over*. Philadelphia, PA: Chilton Book Company, 1971.

Porter, Keith. *Discovering Rabbits and Hares*. New York: Bookwright Press, 1986.

Rowland, Beryl. *Animals with Human Faces*. Knoxville, TN: University of Tennessee Press, 1973.

Redemption
Atonement

It has been said that the Bible tells the story of God's efforts to save humanity with the human tendency towards **sin** as the central problem to be overcome (*see also* **Salvation**). According to biblical ways of thinking, sin ruptures one's relationship with God. Therefore human beings stand in need of a means by which they can heal, or reconcile, this relationship. Christians believe that **Jesus'** death by crucifixion on **Good Friday** reconciled humanity with God (*for more on crucifixion, see also* **Cross**). This process of reconciliation is often referred to as redemption.

The word redemption comes from the verb "to redeem," which means to recover, to buy back, to liberate from bondage, to pay a ransom for something or someone, or to rescue. As used in the Bible, the word redemption generally refers to a liberation or a recovery of something of value, usually with the implication that a price must be paid for such deliverance. The word redemption occurs far more often in the Old Testament, or Hebrew scriptures, than it does in the New Testament, or Christian scriptures. Nevertheless, Christianity grew out of ancient Judaism and it inherited a good portion of Jewish religious thought, including some of its teachings concerning redemption. In the New Testament the concept of redemption is closely linked with that of salvation.

Redemption and Sacrifice among the Ancient Hebrews

The ancient Jews believed that they had a covenant, or agreement, with God that spelled out how they had to live in order to please God and to continue to receive his help. The Hebrew scriptures, which Christians call the Old Testament, recall many instances when the entire nation or a particular individual broke this agreement by committing deeds not in accordance with Jewish religious teaching. These deviations, or sins, disturbed Israel's or the individual's harmonious relationship with God. Jewish religious authorities taught that one's standing with God could be restored through a combination of **repentance** and sacrifice.

Like most other peoples of the ancient world, the Jews practiced sacrifice as a means of worshiping God. The ancient Jews sacrificed a variety of animals, all of which had to be in perfect health and without scar or blemish. After the priests killed the sacrificial animals they sprinkled their **blood** on the altar as an offering to God. Sometimes priests or worshipers ate all or part of the sacrificial animal (*see also* **Passover**). Usually the animal's carcass was burned to complete the sacrifice. The ancient Hebrews also sacrificed grains, oil, **wine**, and incense.

In general, these sacrifices were understood as gifts given to God and were thought to honor God. Sacrifices were also made for specific purposes. Sometimes people offered sacrifices to God as a means of expressing their gratitude or their devotion. In addition, sacrifices were used to seal religious covenants, such as when the Israelites accepted the obligation to live according to the Ten Commandments revealed to their leader, Moses, by God (Exodus 24:3-8). The ancient Hebrews also presented God with sacrifices when the nation had failed to live according to God's teachings. Individuals might make sacrifices when they had broken religious rules concerning purity, honest testimony, and respect for holy things. Some scholars suggest that the ancient Hebrews believed that God accepted the sacrifice as a substitute for punishing the offender. Others are less sure of the exact reasoning behind these offerings. Whatever the logic behind these acts, the ancient Hebrews viewed sacrifice as a means of atoning for their misdeeds. Here the word "atone" means to return to a state of being at one with God. This process of atonement was also called redemption.

Christian Views of Redemption

Christian scripture reveals that Jesus accepted Jewish sacrificial practices, but criticized those people who used them as a substitute for repentance (Matthew 5:23-25, 23:23-24). Nevertheless, Christians did not reproduce Jewish sacrificial customs. They believed that Jesus' death on Good Friday was itself a sacrifice, an astounding event which brought the era of sacrificial religion to a close.

Christians trace this belief back to biblical accounts of the Last Supper, the last meal that Jesus ate with his followers before his arrest, trial, and execution (*for more on the Last Supper, see* **Maundy Thursday**). These accounts are found in the Gospels of Matthew, Mark, Luke, and John, which offer descriptions of Jesus' life and death. At the Last Supper Jesus took **bread**, asked for God's blessing, and broke it, distributing it among his disciples. He told them that the bread was his body. Then he passed them a cup of wine, identifying it as his blood and asked them to drink it (Matthew 26:26-29, Mark 14:22-25, Luke 22:16-19). In Matthew's account Jesus calls his blood "my blood of the covenant, which is poured out for many for the forgiveness of sins" (Matthew 26:28, *see also* Mark 14:24). Here Jesus identifies his upcoming death as a sacrificial offering, made to seal a new covenant between Jesus' followers and God. He also states that this offering will have the power to confer the forgiveness of sins, or, in other words, to redeem his followers from the consequences of their sins.

According to three of the four Gospel accounts of this event, the Last Supper was a Passover meal. The fourth account, given in the Gospel according to John, suggests that Jesus died on the cross at the same time that the **lambs** were being slaughtered in the Temple in preparation for the Passover meal. The early Christians found the timing of Jesus' death very significant. It further convinced them to view his death as a sacrificial offering made to rescue them from slavery to sin, just as God had rescued the Hebrews from slavery to the Egyptians during the first Passover.

The early Christians created a ceremony called the **Eucharist** as a way of commemorating Jesus' sacrifice and as a way of inviting all to participate in the bread and wine of the Last Supper. The Eucharist is the central and most important ritual in Christian communal worship.

Christian scripture tends to place greater emphasis on the price paid for redemption than does Jewish scripture. The early Christians quickly came to the conclusion that Jesus paid this price once for all in undergoing death by crucifixion on Good Friday (1 Corinthians 15:3; 2 Corinthians 5:14,15,19). Although Christians believe that Jesus was a human being, Christian scripture also calls him the Son of God (John 3:16) and asserts that he lived without sin (Hebrews 4:15). According to Christian theology Jesus' spiritual perfection made him the one and only person whose sacrificial death could have redeemed humanity and brought an end to the practice of sacrifice itself.

In the Gospel according to Mark, Jesus begins his ministry by urging people to repent, that is, to return to God's teachings (Mark 1:15). Jesus' emphasis on personal repentance finds echo in Christian teachings that insist that repentance stands alongside Christ's sacrificial death as a requirement for redemption.

Further Reading

Alsup, John E. "Redemption." In Paul J. Achtemeier, ed. *The HarperCollins Bible Dictionary*. New York: HarperCollins, 1996.

Anderson, Gary A. "Sacrifices and Offerings." In David Noel Freedman, ed. *Eerdmans Dictionary of the Bible*. Grand Rapids, MI: William B. Eerdmans Publishing, 2000.

"Atonement." In E. A. Livingstone, ed. *The Oxford Dictionary of the Christian Church*. Third edition. Oxford, England: Oxford University Press, 1997.

"Blood." In Leland Ryken, James C. Wilhoit, and Tremper Longman III, eds. *Dictionary of Biblical Imagery*. Downers Grove, IL: InterVarsity Press, 1998.

Harvey, John D. "Redemption." In David Noel Freedman, ed. *Eerdmans Dictionary of the Bible*. Grand Rapids, MI: William B. Eerdmans Publishing, 2000.

Matera, Frank J. "Reconciliation." In Paul J. Achtemeier, ed. *The HarperCollins Bible Dictionary*. New York: HarperCollins, 1996.

Mulzac, Kenneth D. "Atonement." In David Noel Freedman, ed. *Eerdmans Dictionary of the Bible*. Grand Rapids, MI: William B. Eerdmans Publishing, 2000.

Myers, Allen C., ed. "Atonement," "Redemption," and "Sacrifices and Offerings." *The Eerdmans Bible Dictionary*. Grand Rapids, MI: William B. Eerdmans Publishing, 1987.

Rattray, Susan. "Worship." In Paul J. Achtemeier, ed. *The HarperCollins Bible Dictionary*. New York: HarperCollins, 1996.

"Redemption." In E. A. Livingstone, ed. *The Oxford Dictionary of the Christian Church*. Third edition. Oxford, England: Oxford University Press, 1997.

"Redemption." In Leland Ryken, James C. Wilhoit, and Tremper Longman III, eds. *Dictionary of Biblical Imagery*. Downers Grove, IL: InterVarsity Press, 1998.

"Sacrifice." In E. A. Livingstone, ed. *The Oxford Dictionary of the Christian Church*. Third edition. Oxford, England: Oxford University Press, 1997.

"Sacrifice." In Leland Ryken, James C. Wilhoit, and Tremper Longman III, eds. *Dictionary of Biblical Imagery*. Downers Grove, IL: InterVarsity Press, 1998.

Repentance

Since the early Middle Ages **Lent**, the approximately six-week period that precedes Easter, has been observed as a season of repentance. For centuries the faithful have carried out acts of penance, that is, exercises designed to express or cultivate repentance, during this season of the church year. An examination of the origin and development of this biblical concept sheds much light on the historical development of the Lenten season and its customs.

Repentance in the Hebrew Scriptures

In the Hebrew scriptures, which Christians call the Old Testament, the word used for repentance was *shub*, a term which expresses the idea of turning around or turning back. For the writers of these texts the concept of repentance meant forsaking wrongdoing in order to return to the upright way of life that is pleasing to God. The ancient Jews cultivated repentance through a variety of religious practices, including wearing clothes made out of sackcloth (a coarse fabric), smearing ashes on their heads and faces, **fasting**, confessing their errors, and wailing with remorse. These customs served as public admissions of wrongdoing as well as expressions of grief and regret. Some of the Hebrew prophets, such as Amos, Hosea, and Isaiah, warned that these practices must not be used as a substitute for the kind of spiritual transformation that results from heart-felt repentance. These prophets called on the nation of Israel to return to the virtues beloved by God. Other prophets, especially Jeremiah and Ezekiel, directed the same message at individuals who had fallen into **sin**, urging them to return to God's teachings.

Repentance in the Christian Scriptures

Writing in ancient Greek the authors of the Christian New Testament translated this concept of spiritual transformation and return to God's ways as *metanoia*, a word which literally means "change of mind." These writers meant something more profound than what we would call a change of mind, however. Instead they were referring to a total transformation in outlook, affecting the heart, mind, and spirit. Thus in the New Testament the concept of repentance takes on a slightly different shape, one that places less emphasis on guilt and regret and more emphasis on breaking through to a new way of understanding God, oneself, and the world. In other words, the New Testament view of repentance equates it with conversion.

Several passages from Christian scripture link repentance with **baptism**, the ritual whereby the early Christians confirmed the conversion of newcomers and welcomed them into the faith tradition. Before the advent of Christianity, the ancient Jews used baptism as a cleansing ritual and later employed it as a means of initiating new members into the Jewish faith. In the opening scenes of the New Testament John the Baptist urges the Hebrew people to undergo the ritual of baptism as a means of expressing their repentance and accepting God's forgiveness for their sins. Contemporary Christian theologians still equate baptism with the forgiveness of sin. After being baptized by John, **Jesus** began his own ministry, repeating John's call to repentance and reform (Mark 1:14-15). Later New Testament passages clearly link baptism into the Christian faith with repentance (Acts 2:38).

Repentance and Lent

By the fourth century many Christian communities had developed a preference for baptizing new members at Easter. In the weeks preceding Easter candidates for baptism prepared for this spiritual rebirth by fasting, praying, and receiving religious instruction. Devout members of the Christian community fasted and prayed alongside these newcomers to set them a good example and to inspire them. As Christianity became the religion of the majority, however, more and more people were baptized as infants and children and so did not undergo these preparations. Nevertheless, the Lenten season continued to be viewed as a time of fasting and prayer in preparation for the greatest feast of the Christian year, Easter.

Although Easter baptisms became less common as the number of Christians grew, Easter preparations continued to develop along much the same lines as before. These Lenten devotional practices, however, once associated with conversion and baptism, became ever more closely associated with repentance and the confession of sin. This change in the Church's observance of the Lenten season coincided with the appearance and spread of a new, Latin translation of the Bible. In the late fourth century Christian authorities in western Europe ordered that the Bible be translated from Greek into Latin, Latin being a more familiar language to the people of western Europe.

The Latin Bible replaced the Greek word *metanoia* with the Latin word *paenitentia*. The word *paenitentia* originally meant "regret." It is related to the Latin word *poena*, meaning punishment or penalty. Adopted for usage by the Church, the word paenitentia meant "repentance" and came to imply both sorrow for wrongs committed as well as punishment or penalty paid for them. Presumably both the grief and the punishment would steer the penitent towards spiritual transformation. We get our English words "penance" and "repentance" from the Latin word paenitentia. The English word "penitentiary," meaning "prison," also comes from this Latin root.

In western Europe, where Latin was the official language of a united Church for more than 1,000 years, the Latin word paenitentia, with its emphasis on sorrow and punishment, established itself as the theme of the Lenten season by the early Middle Ages. This view of repentance found clear expression in early medieval customs concerning the reconciliation of wrongdoers with the Christian community. This process began at the start of Lent when erring community members publicly confessed their sins (*see also* **Ash Wednesday**). Priests assigned penance to those whose sins were deemed severe. These penances often included dressing in sackcloth and ashes, sleeping on the ground, going barefoot, secluding oneself in a remote place such as a monastery, keeping long periods of silence, refraining from bathing and shaving, and engaging in prayer, charitable works, and manual labor. Wrongdoers were expected to persist in these devotional acts throughout Lent before finally gaining re-admittance to church and re-acceptance in the community.

Although western European Christians abandoned most of these Lenten customs long ago, Roman Catholics and some Protestants retained the Lenten fast until recent times. Today Roman Catholics still fast on Ash Wednesday and **Good Friday**. In addition, they are expected to make a formal confession, a process now referred to as the rite or sacrament of reconciliation, sometime during Lent.

By contrast, Orthodox and other Eastern Christians have preserved their ancient Lenten fasting customs. Nevertheless, the Orthodox understand Lent to be a joyful rather than a sorrowful season. This attitude stems from their understanding of repentance, which is closer to the Greek metanoia than the Latin paenitentia. For Orthodox Christians repentance means turning to God in a process that entails a rigorous search for self-knowledge, the recognition and confession of sin, and a deep desire to change. Orthodox Christians view fasting and other spiritual disciplines observed during Lent as ways of seeking self-correction, purification, and enlightenment during this holy season.

Further Reading

Garrett, Linda Oaks. "Repentance." In David Noel Freedman, ed. *Eerdmans Dictionary of the Bible*. Grand Rapids, MI: William B. Eerdmans Publishing, 2000.

Hopko, Thomas. *The Lenten Spring*. Crestwood, NY: St. Vladimir's Seminary Press, 1998.

Matera, Frank J., ed. "Repentance." In Paul J. Achtemeier, ed. *The Harper-Collins Bible Dictionary*. New York: HarperCollins, 1996.

Myers, Allen C., ed. "Repentance." In *The Eerdmans Bible Dictionary*. Grand Rapids, MI: William B. Eerdmans Publishing, 1987.

Porter, T. A. "Repentance." In *New Catholic Encyclopedia*. Volume 12. New York: McGraw-Hill, 1967.

Rahner, Karl, and Herbert Vargrimler, eds. "Metanoia." In their *Dictionary of Theology*. Second edition. New York: Crossroads, 1981.

"Repentance." In E. A. Livingstone, ed. *The Oxford Dictionary of the Christian Church*. Third edition. Oxford, England: Oxford University Press, 1997.

"Repentance." In Leland Ryken, James C. Wilhoit, and Tremper Longman III, eds. *Dictionary of Biblical Imagery*. Downers Grove, IL: InterVarsity Press, 1998.

Resurrection

Easter celebrates the resurrection of **Jesus** Christ. Indeed the "Feast of the Resurrection" is another name for the festival. The verb "to resurrect" means to raise from the dead. According to Christian scripture God raised Jesus from the dead on the third day after his crucifixion (*for more on crucifixion, see* **Cross**). This event, referred to simply as the Resurrection, astonished Jesus' followers (*see also* **Mary Magdalene; Peter**). More importantly, it convinced them that through the life, death, and resurrection of Jesus Christ, God was offering humanity a new means of **salvation**.

During Jesus' lifetime some Jews believed that the dead would be resurrected to face judgment for their deeds on earth. The Jewish doctrine of resurrection differed from other contemporary doctrines concerning the afterlife, such as the Greek belief in the immortality of the soul. The notion of resurrection insists that the body rises along with the soul or spirit, in other words, that the total person enters the afterlife. Furthermore, it implies that life after death is a gift from God, since it is God that raises the dead to new life. By contrast, belief in an eternal soul suggests instead that the soul is by nature immortal. According to this belief system the soul lives on after the body's

death as a matter of course. Behind the doctrine of resurrection lies a positive evaluation of life in the physical body, since God sustains both the body and the spirit after death.

Over the centuries Christian theologians have disputed the exact manner in which the body joins the soul in the afterlife. Many Christian thinkers follow the lead of St. Paul, who asserted that the physical body becomes a spiritual body, which God will raise up to eternal life:

> . . . flesh and blood cannot inherit the kingdom of God, nor does the perishable inherit the imperishable. Lo! I tell you a mystery. We shall not all sleep, but we shall all be changed, in a moment, in the twinkling of an eye, at the last trumpet. For the trumpet will sound, and the dead will be raised imperishable, and we shall be changed. For this perishable nature must put on the imperishable, and the mortal nature must put on immortality. (1 Corinthians 15:50-53)

Christian scripture asserts that God resurrected Jesus from the dead on the **Sunday** after his crucifixion and that he appeared to his followers on a number of occasions before finally ascending into heaven (*see also* **Ascension Day**). In one passage Jesus invites his disciple Thomas to touch the wounds inflicted during the Crucifixion in order to verify Jesus' identity (John 20:27). In another story Jesus eats a meal with his disciples, proving that he is not a disembodied ghost but rather a resurrected man (John 21:12-13). Nevertheless these passages also imply that some change had indeed taken place in Jesus' physical nature. For example, his followers sometimes failed to recognize the risen Jesus at first. Moreover, the risen Jesus did things that ordinary human beings could not do, such as suddenly appearing in a locked room (John 20:19) and disappearing into thin air (Luke 24:31). Thus Christian scripture teaches that resurrection is not merely the same thing as resuscitation or reanimation of the physical body but rather involves a transformation of that body.

These encounters with the risen Jesus transformed the previously dispirited disciples into energetic and effective leaders and teachers of the new, Christian religion. They also shaped some of the fundamental doctrines of that religion. Jesus' resurrection not only convinced his followers that the resurrection of the dead would actually happen, but also led them to believe a new era had begun in God's efforts to save humanity (Acts 17:31). Jesus' resurrection was seen as a token of what was to come for all of humankind (1 Corinthians 15:22). It was also interpreted as an affirmation of Jesus' role as savior (*see also* Salvation). Animated by these encounters and these beliefs, the disciples founded the Christian religion. New believers joined themselves to Christ in **baptism**, which was viewed as a death of the old self, in order to share in his resurrection (Romans 6:4-11, 1 Peter 3:21). Resurrection was understood both literally and metaphorically to include spiritual transformation while on earth as well as life after death.

Over the centuries Christian artists have conveyed the concept of resurrection in visual images. Standard symbols have emerged, including the **butterfly**, the **peacock**, the **phoenix**, and the number **eight**, which also stands for eternal life.

Further Reading

"Easter." In E. A. Livingstone, ed. *The Oxford Dictionary of the Christian Church*. Third edition. Oxford, England: Oxford University Press, 1997.

Fuller, Reginald H. "Resurrection." In Paul J. Achtemeier, ed. *The Harper-Collins Bible Dictionary*. New York: HarperCollins, 1996.

Myers, Allen C., ed. "Resurrection." In *The Eerdmans Bible Dictionary*. Grand Rapids, MI: William B. Eerdmans Publishing, 1987.

"Resurrection." In Leland Ryken, James C. Wilhoit, and Tremper Longman III, eds. *Dictionary of Biblical Imagery*. Downers Grove, IL: InterVarsity Press, 1998.

"Resurrection of Christ, The." In E. A. Livingstone, ed. *The Oxford Dictionary of the Christian Church*. Third edition. Oxford, England: Oxford University Press, 1997.

"Resurrection of the Dead." In E. A. Livingstone, ed. *The Oxford Dictionary of the Christian Church*. Third edition. Oxford, England: Oxford University Press, 1997.

Seely, David Rolph. "Resurrection." In David Noel Freedman, ed. *Eerdmans Dictionary of the Bible*. Grand Rapids, MI: William B. Eerdmans Publishing, 2000.

Rogation Days

The Rogation Days fall on April 25 and on the Monday, Tuesday, and Wednesday that precede **Ascension Day**. The Church established these days of prayer, **fasting**, and processions as a formal means of asking God for a good harvest, protection against natural disasters, and forgiveness of **sins**.

Origins

Most scholars agree that the early Christians based the Rogation Days on an ancient Roman spring festival called Robigalia. The name Robigalia comes from *robigo*, the Latin word for rust, a crop disease. The Romans dedicated Robigalia to various ceremonies aimed at protecting the ripening spring crops from this disease. They celebrated it on April 25 by marching in procession down the via Flaminia to the Milvian bridge. There they offered the entrails of a dog and a sheep to the god Robigus in the hope that he would then spare their crops.

Roman Christians imitated many of these practices. On April 25 they held similar processions but concluded by praying to their own God to preserve the crops. In the sixth century Pope Gregory the Great (c. 540-604) standardized this observance.

In the year 470 a French bishop called for three days of prayer, fasting, and processions in order to protect his earthquake-ravaged diocese from further tremors. He scheduled these days of prayer and penance for the Monday, Tuesday, and Wednesday preceding Ascension Day (*for more on penance, see* **Repentance**). This observance spread throughout France and reached Rome around the ninth century. In Rome the pope combined these ceremonies with those already occurring on April 25. He mandated that the most important religious services take place on April 25 and the other, lesser services on the three days preceding the Ascension.

English speakers call these four days of prayer and processions the Rogation Days. The word rogation comes from the Latin word *rogare*, meaning "ask" or "plead." April 25 is known as the Major Rogation, and the other days as the Minor Rogations. St. Mark's Day is also observed on April 25, although this observance is not related to the Rogation Days. In addition, although the **Sunday** before Ascension Day was not one of the original Rogation Days, the spirit of the Rogation Days influenced the way in which it was observed and inspired people to call it Rogation Sunday.

Beating the Bounds

In medieval England the Rogation Days were observed with processions that began in the local church and proceeded to outline the boundaries of the parish, pausing occasionally for the recitation of prayers. Priests and cross-bearers led these long walks in the countryside. Accordingly, the English sometimes called the Rogation Days the "Walking Days" from the Old Anglo-Saxon name for the observance, *Gang Daegas*, meaning approximately "Day of Going About." They also called them the "Cross Days," a reference to the **cross** carried at the head of the processions. Scholars trace the custom of prayerful perimeter-walking back to the Roman festival of Ambargalia, in which the Romans paced the perimeter of their fields asking the gods to bless them with fertility. In any case, those who participated in the Rogation Day walks were expected to fast before the procession, and to treat the event as a sober religious exercise rather than a holiday in the countryside. Nevertheless, people tended to turn the event into an expression of pride in their parish. On occasion, an excess of "team spirit" led some parish groups to attack others that they encountered.

After the Reformation — a western European religious reform movement that began in the sixteenth century — some of the newly formed Protestant denominations attempted to eliminate folk customs associated with the Rogation Days. In England Rogation processions were curtailed, though not completely eliminated. At a later date, however, people revived them. Some writers believe that the processions served an important social as well as religious function by teaching youth the parish boundary lines in an era when maps were not in common circulation. Youngsters accompanying the procession were often bumped against stone boundary markers, tossed into streams that divided one parish from another, or forced to climb hedges, walls, or even houses built over the boundary lines. Some writers speculate that this painful process gave rise to the folk name for the custom, "beating the bounds." Presumably this ordeal left the boys with a permanent if somewhat unpleasant memory of the exact location of the parish boundaries. On the other hand, the name may come from the common custom of beating the boundary markers with wooden wands so as to impress their location upon the memory. Indeed some parish processions did not subject participants to painful ordeals other than the walk itself, which could be quite taxing. In many locations adults and children who took part in these excursions were rewarded with coins, sweets, fruit, nuts, **bread**, cheese, or ale along the way.

The beating of the bounds during the Rogation Days reached the height of its popularity around 1700 and then entered a long, slow decline. Folklorists attribute this decline to the enclosure of what had once been open fields, as well as waning belief in the effectiveness of the processions as a means of finding favor with God. In recent years these old Rogationtide processions have experienced a modest revival. Priests lead parish children in yearly Ascension Day processions in the university town of Oxford. In Chudleigh, near Exeter, ambitious parishioners beat the bounds of their parish every seven years. The expedition takes the party over a twenty-one-mile route, requiring at least one volunteer to swim the river Teign and the entire party to board a bus in order to cross a busy highway. The arduous nature of the task seems to have inspired the seven-year delay between processions.

Rural Life Sunday and the Cancelling of the Rogation Days

Since 1929 many churches in the United States have observed Rogation Sunday as Rural Life Sunday, or Soil Stewardship Sunday. Services on this day examine the religious aspects of rural life. In 1969 the Roman Catholic Church cancelled the Rogation Days. In their place Church authorities instituted days of prayer for human needs, human works, and the fruits of the earth. Local bishops may now set appropriate dates for these observances in their dioceses.

Further Reading

Blackburn, Bonnie, and Leofranc Holford-Strevens. *The Oxford Companion to the Year*. Oxford, England: Oxford University Press, 1999.

Harper, Howard. *Days and Customs of All Faiths*. 1957. Reprint. Detroit, MI: Omnigraphics, 1990.

Henderson, Helene, and Sue Ellen Thompson, eds. *Holidays, Festivals, and Celebrations of the World Dictionary*. Second edition. Detroit, MI: Omnigraphics, 1997.

Hole, Christina. *British Folk Customs*. London, England: Hutchinson and Company, 1976.

Hutton, Ronald. *Stations of the Sun*. Oxford, England: Oxford University Press, 1996.

James, E. O. *Seasonal Feasts and Festivals*. 1961. Reprint. Detroit, MI: Omnigraphics, 1993.

Metford, J. C. J. *The Christian Year*. London, England: Thames and Hudson, 1991.

Miller, J. H. "Rogation Days." In *New Catholic Encyclopedia*. Volume 12. New York: McGraw-Hill, 1967.

Niemann, Paul J. *The Lent, Triduum, and Easter Answer Book*. San Jose, CA: Resource Publications, 1998.

O'Connor, Joseph E. "Rogation Days." In Charles G. Herbermann et al., eds. *The Catholic Encyclopedia*. New York: Appleton, 1913. Available online at: http://www.newadvent.org/cathen/13110b.htm

"Rogation Days." In E. A. Livingstone, ed. *The Oxford Dictionary of the Christian Church*. Third edition. Oxford, England: Oxford University Press, 1997.

Scullard, H. H. *Festivals and Ceremonies of the Roman Republic*. Ithaca, New York: Cornell University Press, 1981.

Royal Hours

The Royal Hours is an Orthodox service traditionally held late at night on **Maundy Thursday**. The service retells the Passion story, that is, the story of the last days of **Jesus'** life, in which he was betrayed, arrested, beaten, and crucified (*for more on crucifixion, see also* **Cross**). Orthodox Church authorities follow the ancient Jewish tradition of beginning each new day at sundown. Therefore, a church service held on the evening of Maundy Thursday would actually be associated with the following day, **Good Friday**. Today many Orthodox churches offer the Royal Hours service on the morning of Good Friday.

Orthodoxy is one of the three main branches of the Christian faith. Orthodox Christianity developed in eastern Europe, the Middle East, and north Africa. It split away from Western Christianity, which later divided into Roman Catholicism and Protestantism, about 1,000 years ago. Orthodox and other Eastern Christians follow a slightly different schedule of religious observances than do Western Christians. In addition, they maintain their own distinctive calendar system which causes their **Lent** and **Easter season** observances to fall on different dates than those celebrated by Western Christians (*see also* **Easter, Date of**).

History

The Royal Hours service can be traced back to the small Christian community of fourth-century Jerusalem. Around the year 380 A.D. Egeria, a western European pilgrim to the Holy Land, wrote a description of **Holy Week** services in Jerusalem. According to Egeria, members of the Christian community gathered together late at night on Thursday of Holy Week. They met at the Church of Eleona, built over the site where Jesus was said to have given his last teachings, located on the Mount of Olives, a hill outside Jerusalem. They listened to Bible readings telling the first part of the Passion story. The congregation then made its way to Jerusalem in stages, stopping for Bible readings at sites en route where key events in the story took place. Next they visited the Ibomon church, also on the Mount of Olives, built over the site where the **Ascension** was supposed to have taken place. Then they proceeded to the Garden of Gethsemane, the site where, according to the Bible, Jesus was arrested. They arrived there around three in the morning. After offering prayers and listening to selections from the scriptures, they set off for their homes in the city of Jerusalem, singing hymns as they marched through the pre-dawn darkness. Scholars believe that the readings used in this service included fifteen psalms and seven passages from the Gospels, the books in the Christian Bible describing the life and teachings of Jesus. These readings began with the story of the Last Supper and ended with Jesus' trial before **Pilate** (*for more on Last Supper, see* Maundy Thursday). The worshipers continued their devotions on Friday with religious services held at the site of Jesus' crucifixion (*see also* **Stations of the Cross**).

By the tenth century the Jerusalem service had developed into a more complete representation of the Passion story. The procession began on Mount Sion, where the Last Supper was believed to have taken place, and then crossed the Kidron Valley and the Mount of Olives before entering the Garden of Gethsemane. Then the group came to the city of Jerusalem, stopping at a site near the house of Caiphas, the Jewish high priest, that was associated with **Peter's** repentance (Matthew 26:75, Mark 14:72, Luke 22:61-62, John 18:27). They proceeded to Pilate's residence and from there walked to the site of the Crucifixion, over which the Church of the Holy Sepulchre had been built. Twelve readings — eleven from the Gospels and one from the Hebrew scriptures, or Old Testament — accompanied this procession.

This late-night Holy Thursday service was also well known among Orthodox Christians outside Jerusalem by the tenth century. Worshipers listened to the same Bible readings, but enhanced the experience by offering prayers and singing hymns instead of processing to the holy sites connected with the Passion story. The Byzantine emperor himself used to attend this service in his capital city of Constantinople, now called Istanbul (Turkey). The emperor's attendance inspired what is now a common name for the service, the "Royal Hours." The word "hours" in this context refers to the canonical hours, prayer services held at specific times of the day or night. The Royal Hours began with matins, a service held either at midnight or at daybreak.

Russian Orthodox Christians also adopted the Royal Hours service. In the days when Russia was ruled by tsars, folk customs encouraged those who had attended the service to try to carry home a lighted candle with which to kindle the taper or lamp that stood beside their icons, religious images used in prayer and worship (*see also* **Russia, Easter and Holy Week in; Ukraine, Easter and Holy Week in**).

Contemporary Services

Today many Orthodox churches offer Royal Hours services on the morning of Good Friday. The service features the twelve Gospel readings that retell the Passion story as well as passages from the Old Testament, Psalms, and Christian Epistles. It combines the first, third, sixth, and ninth canonical hours, services usually offered at six a.m., nine a.m., noon, and three p.m. and often called by their Latin names *prime, terce, sext,* and *none.* The congregation holds candles in their hands which they light during each of the twelve Gospel readings and then extinguish. After the service the *kouvouklion*, a representation of Jesus' burial bier, is brought before the worshipers. Orthodox churches also hold religious services on the afternoon of Good Friday, in which the *epitaphios*, or winding sheet—a cloth onto which has been embroidered an image of Christ's burial—is symbolically removed from the cross and placed in the funeral bier. The ceremony surrounding the epitaphios may be thought of as the Orthodox parallel to the Roman Catholic ceremony around the **holy sepulchre**, or the Roman Catholic devotion known as the **Veneration of the Cross**.

Further Reading

Monti, James. *The Week of Salvation.* Huntington, IN: Our Sunday Visitor Publications, 1993.

Rouvelas, Marilyn. *A Guide to Greek Traditions and Customs in America*. Bethesda, MD: Nea Attiki Press, 1993.

Weiser, Francis X. *The Easter Book*. New York: Harcourt, Brace and Company, 1954.

Wybrew, Hugh. *Orthodox Lent, Holy Week and Easter*. Crestwood, NY: St. Vladimir's Seminary Press, 1997.

Web Site

"Holy Friday," a document describing the beliefs and practices of Orthodox Christians concerning Good Friday, posted on the Orthodox Church in America web site: http://www.oca.org/pages/orth_chri/orthodox-faith/worship/holy-friday.html

Russia, Easter and Holy Week in

Before enduring the rigors of **Lent**, Russians enjoy a week-long **Carnival** celebration known as **Maslenitsa**, or "Butter Week." At the close of the festival observant Orthodox Christians will begin a strict Lenten **fast**, in which both meat and dairy products are removed from the diet.

Most Russian Christians belong to the Russian Orthodox Church. Orthodoxy is one of the three main branches of the Christian faith. Orthodox Christianity developed in eastern Europe, the Middle East, and north Africa. It split away from Western Christianity, which later divided into Roman Catholicism and Protestantism, about 1,000 years ago. Orthodox and other Eastern Christians follow a slightly different schedule of religious observances than do Western Christians and preserve many distinct customs. In addition, they maintain a separate calendar system which usually causes their Lent and **Easter season** observances to fall on different dates than those celebrated by Western Christians.

539

Holy Week

Russian families begin a major housecleaning campaign during **Holy Week** so that the house will sparkle when the Easter feast arrives (*see also* **Spring Cleaning**). Women and girls beat rugs, polish brass, sweep, mop, launder, paint, and prepare **new clothes** for Easter. Baking and other culinary preparations for the Easter feast also take place during Holy Week. Devout Orthodox Christians will continue to fast during Holy Week, and many others who have not observed the rigorous dietary regimen during the rest of Lent will fast during this week.

Palm Sunday

Youngsters gather willow branches in preparation for **Palm Sunday**, when they are used in church services (*see also* **Palm**). Those who attend services often bring blessed willow branches home from church and place them beside their icons, religious images used in prayer and worship.

Maundy Thursday

People who attend church services on **Maundy Thursday** may attempt to carry a lit candle home from church. Those who manage to keep the flame alive make the sign of the **cross** with the candle above their front door. Upon entering the house they use the flame to light the candles standing before their icons.

Holy Saturday

Preparations for the Easter feast are finalized on this day. Many people bring baskets of special Easter foods to church to receive the priest's blessing. In the old days priests visited the homes of their more influential parishioners on **Holy Saturday** in order to bless their Easter table. Those who plan to attend the late-night **Resurrection** service set their tables before leaving for church (*for more on this service, see* **Easter Sunday**).

540

Easter Sunday

In the Russian Orthodox Church the Resurrection service, which begins late at night on Holy Saturday and continues on into the early morning hours of Easter Sunday, celebrates the Easter miracle. It resembles in some ways the **Easter Vigil** service observed by Roman Catholics and certain Protestants. More people attend the Divine Liturgy on this evening than on any other day of the year.

This dramatic service features a candle-lighting ceremony which begins around midnight. At this hour the priest emerges from behind the screens that enclose the altar holding a single lit candle. The flame represents the risen Christ. As he holds the candle before the congregation the priest declares, "Come ye and receive light from the unwavering Light; and glorify Christ, who has risen from the dead." Then he passes the flame to several worshipers, who in turn light their neighbors' candles until everyone in the church is carrying a glowing candle. Next the priest leads the candle-bearing congregation in a procession around the church, which represents the arrival of the myrrh-bearing women at **Jesus'** tomb early on **Sunday** morning (*see also* **Mary Magdalene**). The priest announces what the women discovered: the tomb is empty and Jesus has been raised from the dead! Upon hearing this joyous proclamation members of the congregation turn to one another and give the Easter greeting, *"Khristos voskres"* (Christ is risen!) to which the proper response is *"Voistinu voskres"* (Indeed, he is risen!). They complete this greeting by kissing each other three times on the cheek, alternating from right to left to right. Especially observant Russian Orthodox will greet friends and family members in the same way throughout the fifty-day Easter season, though others may continue this practice for only a few days after Easter.

In past times many country people visited the local graveyard after the Resurrection service, still carrying their lighted candles from church. Thus they brought the good news of the Resurrection to their departed relatives. Sometimes they hung little porcelain **Easter eggs** from the arms of the cemetery crosses, thereby including the dead in the joyous celebration of Easter.

541

Russian tradition calls for the Easter feast to begin directly after the Resurrection service. This means that the meal begins well past midnight and ends in the early hours of the morning. Traditional Russian Easter fare includes roasted meat, for example, roast suckling **pig**. The meal will also include many toasts, usually with a powerful Russian liquor called *vodka*, although other alcoholic beverages may be drunk as well. **Egg-tapping** games also accompany the Easter feast. Russians top off the Easter banquet with *paskha*, a sweet, creamy dairy dish made from pot cheese, butter, sugar, eggs, vanilla, and dried fruit and nuts, as well as *kulich*, a tall, sweet **bread**, studded with dried fruit. This cake-like bread is baked in coffee cans in order to ensure that it reaches a dramatic height, which creates a visual symbol of Jesus' rising from death. After letting the cake cool bakers cover it with white icing. An Easter bread called paskha may also be served. Many cooks put the finishing touch on Easter foods like paskha and kulich by decorating them with the initials "X B," which stand for *Khristos voskres*.

During the Soviet era (1917-91), Communist political authorities disapproved of Easter celebrations. Though they did not succeed in preventing people from baking at Easter time, they did encourage people to call their holiday bread "spring cake" instead of kulich, since the latter name was associated with the ancient Easter holiday. After the fall of communism Russians stopped using the term "spring cake" and went back to using the word kulich to describe their special Easter bread.

Russian folk tradition proclaims Easter a time to free birds from cages and to make charitable donations to prisoners. Russians also visit friends and family on Easter Sunday, dressing in their finest clothes and partaking of one another's Easter fare. Russian etiquette requires that each person present offer every other person the Easter greeting. Many Russians also exchange Easter eggs with one another on this holiday. The most popular color for Russian Easter eggs is red. The red color is said to represent the **blood** of Christ. Many Russians also enjoy painting elaborate designs on their eggs, especially images of Jesus Christ. Girls may be presented with small porcelain charms made in the shape of an Easter egg. These are collected and worn on necklaces. In past times the Russian nobility exchanged bejeweled eggs made out of precious metals. The most famous of these, made by goldsmith Karl Fabergé, are still prized by today's jewelry collectors (*for more on these eggs, see* Easter Eggs).

Another old Russian tradition casts open church belfries to all who want to ring the **bells** on Easter Sunday. This privilege extends throughout **Easter Week**. In past times the constant ringing of church bells during this week inspired people to call it the "Week of Chimes." The Soviet government outlawed this festive custom in 1929. In addition, government officials destroyed almost all of Russia's church bells. According to one writer, before the Russian revolution in 1917 the nation boasted eighty thousand bell towers, each housing between five and one hundred bells. Only two bell towers, one in the town of Vologda and the other in Rostov, survived the Soviet period with all their bells intact. Since the fall of communism in 1991, however, Russian foundries have been casting new bells to replace those previously destroyed. What's more, the school for bell ringers in Arkhangel'sk is now training a whole new generation of bell ringers to carry on Russia's bell traditions.

Further Reading

Lord, Priscilla Sawyer, and Daniel J. Foley. *Easter the World Over*. Philadelphia, PA: Chilton Book Company, 1971.

Papashvily, Helen, and George Papashvily. *Russian Cooking*. Revised edition. Alexandria, VA: Time-Life Books, 1977.

Pavlova, Elena. "The Week of Chimes: Reviving an Easter Tradition in Russia." *The World and I* 11, 5 (May 1996): 202.

Utenkova, Yelena. "Kulich: The King of Easter Cuisine." *Russian Life* (April 1, 1996).

Web Site

"Christ Is Risen! A Russian Easter Celebration," posted by Clever Hedgehog Translation Services at: http://www.cleverhedgehog.com/paskha.htm

Salvation

The discovery of **Jesus' resurrection** on Easter morning had a profound impact on the small circle of his followers and on the first Christians. It convinced them that a new era had dawned, an era in which God was making salvation possible through Jesus and his teachings.

Salvation in the Hebrew Scriptures

The meaning of the words "salvation" and "save" evolve as one reads through the Bible. In the earliest Hebrew scriptures, which Christians call the Old Testament, "to save" means to rescue or to deliver. God, kings, and judges are called "savior" for leading the Hebrews out of dangerous, oppressive, or distressing situations. In these texts not only does salvation refer to escape from danger, but also to movement towards a state of well-being, prosperity, and expanded possibilities. Various kinds of reconciliations between God and humanity are also referred to as salvation. In these early writings salvation is something that happens over and over again to the Jewish people. These texts give little evidence of belief in a long-lasting or eternal state of salvation or an afterlife.

Later Old Testament writers begin to imagine a final deliverance for the Jewish people. This deliverance would end the period of history in which the Jews found themselves, a period characterized by the threat of one after another disaster, conquest, or conflict. Furthermore, it would usher in the glorification of Israel. In this future era of salvation the scattered Jewish people would be gathered together to enjoy peace, justice, and abundance. Some texts link the coming of this era with the conversion and subjugation of the Gentiles, that is, the non-Jewish peoples. These later Old Testament writings also begin to suggest a belief in an afterlife characterized by the resurrection of the body and spirit. During Jesus' lifetime many Jews believed in the resurrection of the dead.

Salvation in the Christian Scriptures

Written in Greek, the Christian scriptures, or New Testament, also use a word whose root meaning is "rescue" to convey the concept of salvation. In some instances the word "save" is used as a straightforward synonym for rescue or deliver (Matthew 27:40, 49). Most New Testament references to salvation, however, imply it to be a state of liberation, peace, wholeness, and closeness to God. This definition of salvation implies that the saved live untroubled by **sin** and its consequences, a state which the New Testament also refers to as **redemption**. Nevertheless, salvation is not to be taken for granted. New Testament writers warn that every individual must take responsibility for monitoring their relationship with God, keeping watch over their own salvation (Philippians 2:12). (*See also* **Repentance**.)

In the New Testament salvation is a gift from God, therefore only God and Jesus Christ are referred to as "savior." Jesus functions alongside God as savior because, according to Christian doctrine, he is the Son of God, a human man through whom God acted and spoke in such a clear way that his followers concluded that Jesus shared in God's divine essence in a way that other human beings do not. Thus Jesus served as God's chosen messenger, appointed to teach the world through word and example how to attain salvation. This idea finds expression in the very meaning of Jesus' name, which means "God saves" or "God is salvation" in Hebrew.

The New Testament view of salvation expands and combines pre-existing Jewish beliefs concerning salvation, life after death, and the destiny of the Jewish people. In several accounts of his healing miracles, Jesus speaks of healing as salvation (Matthew 9:21-22, Mark 5:23). Some passages in the New Testament equate salvation with eternal life (Romans 5:9-10, 21). The word salvation may also refer to a future point in history when God fulfills his final plans for humanity (Matthew 19:23-29). This image of salvation harks back to earlier Jewish beliefs concerning the final deliverance and triumph of the Jewish people. The writers of the New Testament understood God's future plans for humanity's salvation to include the resurrection of Jesus' faithful followers (Philippians 3:20). Yet salvation is not limited to the future. The New Testament presents salvation as a process that extends from the past through the present and into the future.

The New Testament writings of the first Christian leaders reveal that the resurrection of Jesus Christ became the focal point for early Christian beliefs concerning salvation. Jesus' resurrection was seen as a token of the future resurrection of all the faithful (1 Corinthians 15). The fact that Jesus' resurrection had already happened meant that humanity's final salvation had been transformed from a promise into a reality. It could no longer be spoken of as taking place in a future era, but rather had already begun to happen. For Jesus' followers, his resurrection initiated a new era in God's efforts to save humanity. Previously the Jews had understood God's offer of salvation to be limited to the nation of Israel. The writers of the New Testament explain that through the life, death, resurrection and teachings of Jesus Christ, God extended his offer of salvation to the whole world (John 3:16-17).

Further Reading

Alsup, John E. "Salvation." In Paul J. Achtemeier, ed. *The HarperCollins Bible Dictionary*. New York: HarperCollins, 1996.

Fuller, Reginald H. "Savior." In Paul J. Achtemeier, ed. *The HarperCollins Bible Dictionary*. New York: HarperCollins, 1996.

Light, Gary W. "Salvation." In David Noel Freedman, ed. *Eerdmans Dictionary of the Bible*. Grand Rapids, MI: William B. Eerdmans Publishing, 2000.

Myers, Allen C., ed. "Salvation." In *The Eerdmans Bible Dictionary*. Grand Rapids, MI: William B. Eerdmans Publishing, 1987.

Neyrey, Jerome H. "Eternal Life." In Paul J. Achtemeier, ed. *The HarperCollins Bible Dictionary*. New York: HarperCollins, 1996.

"Salvation." In Leland Ryken, James C. Wilhoit, and Tremper Longman III, eds. *Dictionary of Biblical Imagery*. Downers Grove, IL: InterVarsity Press, 1998.

Sand Dollar

Holy Ghost Shell

Some people consider the sand dollar a natural symbol of the birth and death of **Jesus** Christ. For this reason it acquired the folk name Holy Ghost Shell. A little poem by an anonymous author, entitled "Legend of the Sand Dollar," explains this symbolism:

> There's a pretty little legend
> That I would like to tell
> Of the birth and death of Jesus
> Found in this lowly shell.

> If you examine closely
> You'll see that you find here
> Four nail holes and a fifth one
> Made by a Roman spear.

On one side the Easter **lily**
Its center is the star
That appeared unto the shepherds
And led them from afar.

The Christmas poinsettia
Etched on the other side
Reminds us of his birthday
Our happy Christmastide.

Now break the center open
And here you will release
The five white doves awaiting
To spread good will and peace.

This simple little symbol
Christ left for you and me
To help us spread his gospel
Through all eternity.

Further Reading

Lord, Priscilla Sawyer, and Daniel J. Foley. *Easter Garland*. 1963. Reprint. Detroit, MI: Omnigraphics, 1999.

Web Site

Many versions of this poem can be found online. The one reprinted above comes from: http://www.seashells.org/legendsanddollar.htm

Seven Sorrows, Feast of the
Friday of Sorrows

In the Middle Ages many Western Christians felt a great devotion to the Blessed Virgin Mary and a great sympathy for her suffering at the time of **Jesus'** crucifixion and death (*see* **Mary, Blessed Virgin**; *for more on crucifixion, see* **Cross**). In the fifteenth century the people of Germany began to honor the Virgin Mary's sorrow with a special day of religious devotion. This feast day fell during the **Easter season**. Other communities also celebrated the feast, assigning a date during the Easter season or sometime after the feast of **Pentecost**. Towards the end of that century some communities had widened the scope of this feast to include the seven great sorrows that marked Mary's life. This commemoration of the seven sorrows caught on as the feast began to spread across Catholic Europe. During the seventeenth century some of the groups that adopted the festival began to celebrate it during **Lent**, usually during the week before **Holy Week**. In 1729 Pope Benedict XIII made the observance—called the Feast of the Seven Sorrows of the Blessed Virgin Mary—universal throughout the Roman Catholic Church, fixing its celebration on the Friday before **Palm Sunday**.

The following incidents, recorded in scripture and legend, constitute the seven great sorrows of Mary's life: the prophecy she received from Simeon (Luke 2:3-35), the flight into Egypt (Matthew 2:14), the loss of the child Jesus in Jerusalem (Luke 2:43-49), the sight of her son on his way to be crucified, her vigil at the foot of the cross while Jesus was dying (John 19:25), the removal of Jesus' body from the cross, and Jesus' burial. Sometimes Christian artists represent the seven sorrows by portraying Mary with seven swords or daggers piercing her heart.

In the year 1668 a religious order known as the Servites gained the privilege of celebrating the Seven Sorrows of Mary on the third **Sunday** in September. In the early nineteenth century Pope Pius VII declared this September celebration valid for the entire Roman Catholic Church.

The Feast of the Seven Sorrows became an important day in the Lenten calendar of many Latin American countries. People observed it by decorating and visiting shrines devoted to Mary as the Sorrowful Mother. The festival also retained a good deal of popularity in central Europe, where it was known as the Friday of Sorrows. Many popular devotions took place on this day, and in some places it was customary to eat soup made from seven bitter herbs, including watercress, parsley, leeks or chives, spinach, nettle, sour clover, and primrose or yellow cowslip.

The two festivals dedicated to the Seven Sorrows of the Blessed Virgin Mary continued to be celebrated until the 1960s, when the reforms instituted by Vatican II, a series of important meetings of Roman Catholic leaders, eliminated the Lenten festival. The September holiday remains although the date has shifted. The 1969 calendar of the Roman Catholic Church named the holiday the Feast of Our Lady of Sorrows and recorded the date of its celebration as September 15.

Further Reading

Holweck, F. G. "Feasts of the Seven Sorrows of the Blessed Virgin Mary." In Charles G. Herbermann et al., eds. *The Catholic Encyclopedia*. New York: Appleton, 1913. Available online at: http://www.newadvent.org/cathen/1415b.htm

Rouillard, P. "Marian Feasts." In *New Catholic Encyclopedia*. Volume 9. New York: McGraw-Hill, 1967.

"Seven Sorrows of the Blessed Virgin Mary." In E. A. Livingstone, ed. *The Oxford Dictionary of the Christian Church*. Third edition. Oxford, England: Oxford University Press, 1997.

Weiser, Francis X. *The Easter Book*. New York: Harcourt, Brace and Company, 1954.

Shavuot

Atzeret, Day of First Fruits, Feast of Weeks, Hag Hakatzir, Harvest Feast, Pentecost, Yom Habikkurim

Shavout is a Jewish holiday that takes place seven weeks after **Passover**. According to the Jewish calendar the festival falls on the sixth day of the month of Sivan. Its date in the civil, or Gregorian, calendar moves around from year to year due to differences in the two time-reckoning systems (*for more on the Gregorian and Jewish calendar systems, see* **Easter, Date of**). The word Shavuot means "weeks." This name comes from the Hebrew Bible, which refers to the observance as the "Feast of Weeks." In biblical times the holiday celebrated the spring harvest. Hebrew scripture also calls the festival *Hag Hakatzir*, or "Harvest Feast" (Exodus 23:16). In later times the holiday also came to commemorate God's giving of the Torah, the first five books of the Bible, to the Jewish people. Jews who live in Israel and Reform Jews outside Israel celebrate the festival for one day only. Orthodox and Conservative Jews celebrate Shavuot for two whole days.

Shavuot in Ancient Times

In biblical times Shavuot served as an occasion to thank God for the spring crops. In fact, it coincided with the end of the barley harvest and the beginning of the wheat harvest. On Shavuot worshipers gave the priests at the Temple in Jerusalem two loaves of **bread**, made from their finest spring wheat, to offer to God in a ritual of thanksgiving. People also expressed gratitude for the bounty of the earth by offering God the first fruits of the harvest. Animal sacrifices were also required. Thus the festival acquired another name, *Yom Habikkurim* or "Day of First Fruits."

Shavuot was one of three Jewish agricultural festivals that required the faithful to make a pilgrimage to Jerusalem. After the destruction of the Temple in 70 A.D. and the dispersion of the Jewish people, the holiday could no longer be honored in the same way. So the rabbis, Jewish clergymen, turned to Jewish scripture and, after years of study, gleaned from it another interpretation of the festival. They realized that the ancient Israelites arrived at Sinai seven weeks after escaping from Egypt. Once there Moses, the Jewish leader, climbed Mount Sinai and received the Ten Commandments from God. He brought these down from the mountain and the Jewish people accepted them wholeheartedly in return for God's special care and protection. Afterwards God gave Moses other teachings contained in the Torah. Since the ancient Jewish people had already established the Passover festival in commemoration of their ancestors' escape from Egypt, it made sense that any festival occurring seven weeks later must commemorate the giving of the Torah. This interpretation of the holiday prevailed by the third century. It gave rise to yet another name for the festival. In the diverse body of Jewish writings known as the Talmud, Shavuot is sometimes called *Atzeret*, or "conclusion," since it completes the story commemorated in the Passover festival.

Counting the Omer

Shavuot falls seven weeks, or fifty days, after Passover. Thus some people referred to the festival as **Pentecost**, a name which comes from the Greek word meaning "fiftieth." On the sixteenth day of the

Jewish month of Nisan—the second day of Passover—Jewish priests ceremonially offered sheaves of barley, called *omer*, to God by waving them around in the Temple. Some understood this ritual to be a prayer for the protection of the barley harvest. Since biblical times Jews have observed the forty-nine days between Passover and Shavuot by formally counting them off. These forty-nine days of counting acquired their own name, *Sefirat Haomer* or "Counting the Omer." Observant Jews still carry out this practice in the form of a blessing recited every evening. In ancient times the forty-nine days between the first day of Passover and Shavuot coincided with the spring harvest. In searching for the deeper meaning of the forty-nine-day observance, some commentators also point out that the period comprised seven weeks of seven days. The number seven has special significance in Jewish spirituality since Hebrew scripture states that God created the world in seven days and instituted the Sabbath on the seventh day, commanding the Jewish people to observe it as a holy day of rest (*for more on the Christian significance of the Sabbath, see* **Sunday**). In biblical writings the number seven often symbolizes completeness.

Many contemporary celebrations place more emphasis on Shavuot than on Counting the Omer. Nevertheless, some scholars believe that in ancient times the entire fifty days of Sefirat Haomer and Shavuot were thought to be holy.

Contemporary Religious Observance

Contemporary religious services feature a reading of that portion of the Torah that describes the encounter between God, Moses, and the Israelites gathered at Mount Sinai. Many congregations stand when the Ten Commandments are read aloud, in a gesture that reenacts the scene at Mount Sinai and signifies their own acceptance of God's commands. In Israel religious services also include a reading of the Book of Ruth. This story tells how Ruth, a young Moabite woman, left her family and her native country after her husband's death. Ruth casts her lot with that of her Jewish mother-in-law, returning with the older woman to the Jewish homeland. Once there Ruth embraces the Jewish religion and way of life, marries a well-to-do Jewish man, and has children. This story highlights the Shavuot theme of commitment to God's teachings. Much of the story's action takes place during the spring harvest season, which may provide another reason for its association with Shavuot. Finally, Ruth was the grandmother of the Jewish hero King David, who, according to tradition, was born and died on Shavuot. Jewish communities outside of Israel also associate the Book of Ruth with Shavuot, but their synagogues generally reserve this reading for the second day of the festival.

Folk Customs

Some of the folk customs associated with Shavuot recognize its ancient role as a harvest festival. For example, homes and synagogues may be decorated with flowers and greenery, evoking spring's bounty. Other customs pay tribute to the holiday's religious significance. One such custom calls for the eating of dairy foods on Shavuot. Over the years Jewish commentators have proposed many explanations for this custom. Some say that dairy foods contain a natural sweetness which calls to mind the sweetness of the Torah. It has also been said that the custom derives from a line in the Song of Songs, which says, "honey and milk are on your tongue." Some Jewish thinkers interpret this line as a reference to the Torah. Others say that when the Israelites received the Torah, they were like newborn babes in their relationship with God. Therefore Jews eat dairy products on Shavuot in remembrance of this period of spiritual infancy. Still another explanation for the custom suggests that when the Israelites returned from Mount Sinai, they were too tired to cook a meat meal, so they ate cold dairy foods instead. Another twist on this tale argues that the Israelites had just received the kosher dietary laws, but hadn't time to prepare the kosher cooking utensils required by these laws, and so had to make a meal of cold dairy products.

Shavuot has become a holiday that symbolizes the importance of Torah study and Jewish education. Some holiday customs reflect this theme. In France, Germany, and parts of eastern Europe parents brought young children to Hebrew school for the first time on Shavuot. The teachers gave the youngsters slates marked with the Hebrew alphabet and covered with honey and sweets. Thus the children came to know the sweetness of Torah study. In past times certain pious Jews used to spend the entire night in Torah study. Today some synagogues offer a modified version of this custom by organizing Torah and Talmud study sessions on the evening of Shavuot. Shavuot has also become a recognized occasion for ceremonies surrounding Jewish education. Hebrew school graduation exercises and confirmation ceremonies, whereby Jewish teens affirm their willingness to become adult members of the Jewish community, often take place on Shavuot.

Further Reading

Fellner, Judith B. *In the Jewish Tradition*. New York: Smithmark, 1995.

Goodman, Philip. *The Shavuot Anthology*. Philadelphia, PA: Jewish Publication Society of America, 1974.

Henderson, Helene, and Sue Ellen Thompson, eds. *Holidays, Festivals, and Celebrations of the World Dictionary*. Second edition. Detroit, MI: Omnigraphics, 1997.

Klagsbrun, Francine. *Jewish Days*. New York: Farrar, Straus, Giroux, 1996.

Seidman, Hillel. *The Glory of the Jewish Holidays*. New York: Shengold, 1968.

"Seven." In Leland Ryken, James C. Wilhoit, and Tremper Longman III, eds. *Dictionary of Biblical Imagery*. Downers Grove, IL: InterVarsity Press, 1998.

Strassfeld, Michael. *The Jewish Holidays*. New York: Harper and Row, 1985.

Talley, Thomas J. *The Origins of the Liturgical Year*. Collegeville, MN: Liturgical Press, 1986.

Tyson, Joseph B. "Pentecost." In Paul J. Achtemeier, ed. *The HarperCollins Bible Dictionary*. New York: HarperCollins, 1996.

Weber, Vicki L., ed. *The Rhythm of Jewish Time*. West Orange, NJ: Behrman, 1999.

Web Site

For more on the customs and significance of Shavuot, see the following website, sponsored by the Union of Orthodox Jewish Congregations of America: http://www.ou.org/chagim/shavuot/

555

Shroud of Turin
Holy Shroud

The Shroud of Turin is an aging strip of linen cloth that bears the imprinted image of a man who appears to have been beaten and crucified (*for more on crucifixion, see* **Cross**). This image resembles a photographic negative in that the areas one might expect to be dark are light and the areas that one might expect to be light are dark. For centuries the Shroud of Turin has been venerated as the burial shroud of **Jesus** Christ. How did the image get on the cloth? Many devout Christians believe that the cloth captured the radiance of Jesus' **resurrection**. Skeptics suggest that a clever medieval artist transferred the image onto the cloth and then sold it as a religious relic. Scientists have discovered many interesting things about the shroud but still do not agree about its origins.

Description

The Roman Catholic cathedral in Turin, Italy, currently houses the shroud. This strip of linen measures 14 feet 3 inches (464 centimeters) long and 3 feet 7 inches (138 centimeters) wide. It bears two brownish images of a naked man, both his front and back sides. These two figures lie head to head, as if a dead man were placed lengthwise on one end of the cloth and the other end pulled over his head and body. These likenesses do not appear to have been painted on the cloth, and researchers cannot yet tell what they are made of. They have, however, determined that authentic **blood** stains mark the image in certain places. Trickles of blood run down the forehead. Small rivulets of blood also run down the arms, coming from apparent wounds in the wrists. Larger blood stains saturate an area on the right side of the chest and an area corresponding to where the victim's feet would have been. Moreover, the victim's back in particular shows marks that correspond well with those that would have been inflicted by a beating from a Roman *flagrum*, a whip of leather thongs tipped with balls of lead. The cloth also bears scorch and **water** marks from a fire that it survived in the year 1532. All these wounds correspond with the story of Jesus' death as told in the Bible.

Jesus' Shroud in the Bible

Biblical accounts of Jesus' death confirm that he was wrapped in a linen burial cloth. All four Gospels — books in the Christian Bible that summarize Jesus' life and teachings — agree that he was crucified on a Friday by soldiers carrying out an order given by the Roman governor Pontius **Pilate**. He died that afternoon and was removed from the cross shortly thereafter. Because the Jewish Sabbath started at sundown, and it was against Jewish custom to bury the dead on the Sabbath, Jesus' corpse was disposed of quickly (*for more on Sabbath, see* **Sunday**). Joseph of Arimathea, a secret follower of Jesus, wrapped him in a linen shroud and sealed him in a stone tomb (Matthew 27:59, Mark 15:46, Luke 23:53, John 19:40). Christians commemorate these sad events on **Good Friday**.

The Gospel according to John offers one further mention of Jesus' shroud (John 20:1-18). On the **Sunday** following Jesus' burial, **Mary Magdalene** went to Jesus' tomb and found that the stone that sealed the entrance had been rolled away. She ran to fetch **Peter** and another disciple, and the three of them returned to the tomb. Peter and the other disciple entered the tomb and found the linen burial cloths as well as a napkin that had been on Jesus' head, but no body. After the men departed, the resurrected Jesus appeared to Mary Magdalene. These events are commemorated on **Easter Sunday**.

The History of the Shroud of Turin

The first documented appearance of the shroud now housed in Turin's cathedral dates back to the 1350s. In the early years of that decade a French knight, Geoffrey de Charny, the squire of the French village of Lirey, built a church in which to house what he claimed to be the burial shroud of Christ. The bishop of Troyes, Pierre D'Arcis, pronounced the cloth a fake and claimed that the artist who did it had confessed to the deed. Clement VII (reigned 1378-94), the Avignon antipope, declared that the image could be used as an object of devotion, so long as it was not presented as the true shroud of Christ. Later popes, however, presumed the relic to be authentic. In 1452 Marguerite de Charny, who did not have an heir, turned the shroud over to the duke of Savoy. In 1478 the Savoys moved the relic from Chambéry (France) to the family's new stronghold in Turin. The last of the dukes of Savoy, Umberto II, willed it to the Vatican upon his death in 1983.

The Mandylion and the Shroud

If the cloth housed in Turin's cathedral is the burial shroud of Jesus Christ, where was it before 1350? Some shroud researchers believe they may have found the answer to that question. They suggest that the Turin shroud is, in fact, the Mandylion, an exact image of Jesus Christ miraculously imprinted upon a piece of cloth (*see also* **Veronica**). Legends about the Mandylion were popular in eastern Christian lands and date back at least as far as the fourth century. This cloth was originally believed to belong to King Abgar V of Edessa (4 B.C.–50 A.D.), who was healed by viewing it and so converted to Christianity. In 942 a cloth said to be the Mandylion was brought from Edessa to Constantinople (now Istanbul, Turkey), the capital of the Christian east. Scattered historical references from the next four centuries make mention of Constantinople's miraculous cloth, bearing an image of Jesus "not made by human hands." Some researchers suggest that the old Orthodox Good Friday custom of displaying a cloth icon of Jesus reposing in death can be traced back to the veneration accorded the Mandylion in this era (*see also* **Epitaphios**).

In 1204 soldiers from western Europe, taking part in a war of conquest known as the Crusades, sacked the city of Constantinople. The Mandylion disappeared without a trace. Certain writers suggest that the Knights Templar stole the Mandylion and brought it back to western Europe with them.

Science and the Shroud

Skeptics dismiss the idea that the Turin shroud dates back to ancient times, let alone that it once served as Jesus' burial cloth. The best piece of evidence in their arsenal is the carbon 14 testing done on the shroud in 1988. Three separate laboratories analyzed a small sample of the cloth and concluded that the linen was made between 1260 and 1390. Many scientists decided that these results confirmed the shroud to be a medieval forgery. Yet others were not convinced. They reminded the public that carbon 14 dating often comes with a wide margin of error. In 1993 Dr. Leoncio Garza-Valdes proposed that tiny micro-organisms build up on the surfaces of old artifacts such as the shroud. He showed how these micro-organisms can leave behind a biofilm which affects the accuracy of carbon 14 dating, making objects test newer than they actually are.

In the meantime, other shroud researchers were making interesting discoveries about the image itself. For example, the image on the shroud has certain three-dimensional properties which become visible when viewed through a relatively new piece of scientific equipment called a VP-8 image analyzer. Shroud supporters ask how a medieval artist could possibly have created an image akin to a photographic negative more than five hundred years before the invention of photography and then encoded it with 3-D information.

Artists, too, have commented on the uniqueness of the shroud. They point out that the shroud man appears to have been crucified with nails through his wrists. Standard medieval images of the crucified Jesus showed the nails piercing his hands. Indeed, not until the 1960s did historians realize that Roman soldiers nailed their crucifixion victims to the cross through their wrists, not their hands. How could a medieval artist have anticipated this knowledge? What's more, artists can find no sign of brushstrokes on the shroud, and no evidence that the image was painted or dyed onto the linen. Then there's the light. It doesn't appear to be coming from any particular direction. Photographs — whether illuminated by the sun or some man-made light source — appear brighter in some areas and darker, or shadowed, in others. In order to achieve their three-dimensional effect, realistic paintings imitate this fact of life. The shroud image resembles a modern x-ray more than a painting or photo in this regard, in that it seems to have been created by an unknown light source that radiated from the body to the cloth. Some researchers have concluded that the pattern of light and dark areas on the image correspond to the distance of the supposed body from the shroud; the closer the contact between the body and the cloth, the darker the imprint on the cloth.

Other scientific experiments have proven that the shroud contains microscopic grains of pollen from plants that grow in Israel and Turkey. Shroud supporters believe this proves that the shroud passed through those two countries at some point in its history.

Shroud skeptics return again and again to the evidence provided by the carbon 14 testing to settle the issue of the shroud's authenticity. Yet if the shroud is a medieval forgery, by what means did the clever artist create such an image? No one has yet been able to answer that question in a completely satisfactory manner. Some writers propose that a secretive medieval artist actually invented a primitive form of photography and developed the image of a corpse onto a piece of linen. Experiments along these lines have not yet furnished results that reproduce all the qualities of the shroud image. With the experts in disagreement, the public can only wait and see if the science of the twenty-first century unravels the mystery of the Shroud of Turin.

Further Reading

Drews, Robert. *In Search of the Shroud of Turin*. Totowa, NJ: Rowman and Allanheld, 1984.

Gove, Harry E. *From Hiroshima to the Iceman: The Development and Applications of Accelerator Mass Spectrometry*. Philadelphia, PA: Institute of Physics Publishing, 1999.

Guiley, Rosemary Ellen, ed. "Shroud of Turin." In her *Harper's Encyclopedia of Mystical and Paranormal Experiences*. New York: HarperSanFrancisco, 1991.

Wilson, Ian, and Barrie Schwortz. *The Turin Shroud: The Illustrated Evidence*. London, England: Michael O'Mara, 2000.

Web Sites

The following web site on current shroud research was put together by Barry Schwortz, a photographer who was invited to photograph the shroud as part of the official 1978 research team: http://www.shroud.com

The Archdiocese of Turin maintains its own web site on the shroud: http://sindone.torino.chiesacattolica.it/en/welcome.htm

The Skeptical Shroud of Turin web site is sponsored by the Committee for the Scientific Investigation of Claims of the Paranormal: http://humanist.net/shroud/

Shrovetide

Shrovetide is another name for **Carnival**. While Carnival offers people an opportunity to eat rich foods and celebrate with abandon before beginning the solemn season of **Lent**, the old-fashioned English word "Shrovetide" calls to mind the religious duties once associated with this time of year. In past times people sought out priests during the last several days of Carnival in order to make formal confessions of their **sins** and to receive absolution, or forgiveness. The word "shrove" is an archaic English word meaning "wrote." In medieval times after a priest heard a confession he frequently wrote out a prescription for an appropriate penance, that is, a series of religious rituals that expressed a person's remorse for his or her errors and inspired renewed devotion (*for more on penance, see* **Repentance**). After going through this process of making confession, receiving penance, and accepting absolution, a person was said to be "shriven" of their sins. Hence the last several days of Carnival, when priests shrove their parishioners of their sins, were dubbed Shrovetide.

In some places Shrovetide began on the **Sunday** before **Ash Wednesday**, the first day of Lent. It ended on the Tuesday before Ash Wednesday. People called this day Shrove Tuesday because it was the last day to confess one's sins before the start of Lent. In other places Shrovetide lasted longer, beginning on the Thursday before Ash

Wednesday, sometimes called "Fat Thursday." Shrovetide coincides with the last few days of **pre-Lent**. This three-week period of preparation for Lent is no longer observed by most Western Christians, that is, Roman Catholics and Protestants, but is still acknowledged by Eastern Christians, that is, those Christians whose traditions of worship originated in eastern Europe, the Middle East, and north Africa.

Further Reading

Blackburn, Bonnie, and Leofranc Holford-Strevens. *The Oxford Companion to the Year*. Oxford, England: Oxford University Press, 1999.
Metford, J. C. J. *The Christian Year*. London, England: Thames and Hudson, 1991.

Sin

The concept of sin plays a large role in a number of Easter-related observances. According to Christian doctrine **Jesus'** sacrificial death on the **cross** on **Good Friday** rescued his followers from the consequences of their sins. In the **Eucharist**, a ceremony that takes place every **Sunday** in some churches, Christians remember the events surrounding Jesus' crucifixion and recommit themselves to the new covenant, or relationship, with God brought about through these events. Finally, the concepts of sin and **repentance** have shaped the way in which many Christians observe **Lent**, the approximately six-week season that precedes **Holy Week** and Easter.

Today the word "sin" is commonly understood to refer to an immoral or unethical act. Frequently sin is seen as shameful. Biblical concepts of sin appear to have been broader and somewhat more subtle than this everyday understanding. The Hebrew scriptures, which Christians call the Old Testament, rely on several different words to describe human failings, all of which have been translated into modern English as "sin." For example, these texts often lament humanity's tendency towards *'awon*, which means "wickedness" but which evokes the concept of bending or twisting. They also denounce what they see as *paša*, meaning rebellion or breaking of the law. A third common term for these kinds of errors, *hata*, signifies missing the mark or straying from the path. They also apply the words *šagag*, to err or to go astray, and *ta'â*, to err or to wander. Writing in ancient Greek, the authors of the New Testament, or Christian scriptures, usually describe these same human failings by invoking the concept of *hamartía*, a term used to describe an arrow that misses its target. They also speak of *ponerós*, evil, *adikía*, injustice or unrighteousness, *parábasis*, transgression, and *anomía*, lawlessness. These words, too, have been translated into English as "sin."

Some contemporary Christian theologians describe sins as those human actions not in accordance with God's loving purposes for Creation. Others understand sin as human failure or refusal to live the life intended for them by God. At the heart of these and other theological definitions of sin lies the notion of human withdrawal from God. Since sin separates people from God, it also distances them from the possibility of **salvation**. Biblical writers often describe sin in terms of slavery, debt, or death. The Bible repeatedly observes that in spite of its unpleasantness human beings tend to lapse into sin. Selfishness or lack of trust in God usually motivates these lapses. Because sin results in estrangement, or distance from God, the healing of sin requires a process of reconciliation, or restoration of one's relationship with God. Christians call this process **redemption**. They believe that this process, begun by God, centers around the life, teachings, and sacrificial death of Jesus Christ. During his life Jesus taught his followers how to have a closer relationship with God (*see also* Repentance). Moreover, Jesus offered his own suffering and death by crucifixion as a sacrifice for the sins of his followers (*for more on the concept of sacrifice, see* Redemption). According to Christian theology, this sacrificial act reconciled humanity and the whole of Creation with God.

Further Reading

Efird, James M. "Sin." In Paul J. Achtemeier, ed. *The HarperCollins Bible Dictionary*. New York: HarperCollins, 1996.

Jefford, Clayton N. "Sin." In David Noel Freedman, ed. *Eerdmans Dictionary of the Bible*. Grand Rapids, MI: William B. Eerdmans Publishing, 2000.

Myers, Allen C., ed. "Sin." In *The Eerdmans Bible Dictionary*. Grand Rapids, MI: William B. Eerdmans Publishing, 1987.

"Sin." In E. A. Livingstone, ed. *The Oxford Dictionary of the Christian Church*. Third edition. Oxford, England: Oxford University Press, 1997.

"Sin." In Leland Ryken, James C. Wilhoit, and Tremper Longman III, eds. *Dictionary of Biblical Imagery*. Downers Grove, IL: InterVarsity Press, 1998.

Soul Saturday
Memorial Saturday, Psychosavato, Saturday of Souls

On four Saturdays of each year Greek Orthodox churches hold special church services dedicated to the memory of departed loved ones. The Orthodox call each of these days "Soul Saturday," "Saturday of Souls," or "Memorial Saturday." The Greek name for these observances is *Psychosavato*. The four Soul Saturdays fall during the **pre-Lent**, **Lent**, and Easter seasons. Orthodox and other Eastern Christians follow a different church calendar than that commonly adhered to by Western Christians, that is, Roman Catholics and Protestants (*see also* **Easter, Date of**). For the Orthodox Lent begins on the evening of **Forgiveness Sunday**, seven Sundays before Easter. In Greek Orthodox churches the first Soul Saturday occurs two Saturdays before the beginning of Lent, the second on the Saturday before Forgiveness Sunday, the third on the first Saturday in Lent, and the fourth on the Saturday before **Pentecost**. Other Orthodox churches may schedule these observances on different Lenten Saturdays.

Orthodox Christians hold Soul Saturday services on Saturdays in remembrance that Jesus lay dead in his tomb on the Saturday before the Resurrection (*see also* **Holy Saturday**). During the service the names of deceased parishioners are read out loud and prayers are offered for them. After church worshipers eat *kollyva*, a special dish that Greeks and other Orthodox Christians make for funerals and other memorial services. Kollyva is made from boiled wheat, raisins, nuts, sugar, spices, and other ingredients. According to Greek folklore, each ingredient in this dish represents an aspect of the afterlife. The wheat stands for eternal life, the raisins for sweetness, the sugar for heaven, the **pomegranate** seeds for abundance, and the parsley for the fertile earth. Each family who attends the service may bring a platter of kollyva with them to church. The families decorate their offerings of kollyva with a **cross** and the initials of the deceased, although it is customary to mix all the kollyva together after the service. This gesture represents the mingling of souls that takes place in heaven. As people partake of the mixed kollyva they greet one another with the phrase, "May God forgive the souls of the dead."

Orthodox Christians may also observe Soul Saturday by visiting the graves of the departed. This manner of observance provides family members with a good opportunity to clean and decorate grave sites. In Greece women usually perform this chore. Family members may also bring candles and kollyva to the grave site.

Further Reading

Rouvelas, Marilyn. *A Guide to Greek Traditions and Customs in America*. Bethesda, MD: Nea Attiki Press, 1993.

Storace, Patricia. *Dinner with Persephone*. New York: Vintage Books, 1996.

Spain, Easter and Holy Week in

Easter is the most important holiday of the year in Spain. Many shops and offices shorten their business hours during **Holy Week** and don't open at all on **Good Friday**. In many towns and cities religious processions, not cars, jam the streets on the Friday of Holy Week. While some Spaniards consider Easter an important time of the year to attend to one's religious devotions, others take advantage of the time off from work and school to enjoy a spring vacation.

Spanish Holy Week observances generally revolve around a series of religious processions featuring floats depicting scenes from the Passion story, that is, the story of **Jesus'** arrest, trial, and execution. Religious statues, removed from their shrines in local churches and placed on top of platforms, form the basis of these scenes. Groups of men, and occasionally women, carry the resulting floats on their shoulders. Special religious services often accompany these processions, which take place throughout Holy Week.

Holy Week activities begin on **Palm Sunday**, which Spaniards call *Pascua Florida*, or "Flowery Easter." This name may have developed from the custom of blessing green branches and flowers at church services on this day. In time it came to refer to all of Holy Week. This is a popular day for Spanish children to undergo the ritual of confirmation, thus becoming full members of the Roman Catholic Church. Holy Week observances reach their climax on Good Friday, with the commemoration of Jesus' death by crucifixion (*for more on crucifixion, see* **Cross**). In recent years clergy members and others have attempted to increase the attention paid to Jesus' **resurrection**, celebrated on **Easter Sunday**. In some towns new Easter Sunday processions, with floats depicting the risen Christ, have been added to the traditional Holy Week parades. Apart from events such as these, Easter Sunday often passes quietly as a day spent at home with friends and family.

Holy Week in Seville

The people of Seville, a city in southern Spain, are famous throughout the country for the zeal with which they celebrate Holy Week. The town hosts between fifty and sixty religious brotherhoods whose members decorate and carry the floats that make up the somber religious processions. These organizations date back to the Middle Ages, when they were associated with the guilds, groups of men who pursued the same trade. Each brotherhood is named for a particular aspect of the Passion or for some biblical character associated with the Passion. Some say the Brotherhood of the Holy Cross of Jerusalem, Jesus the Nazarene and Holy Mary of the Conception, founded in 1340, is the oldest brotherhood in Seville. Each brotherhood possesses an image of the scene or biblical character it is named after, and these life-sized statues form the basis of the brotherhood's Holy Week floats. Some brotherhoods possess more than one image.

Spanish artisans have taken great care in the creation of these images so that they appear life-like, thereby moving the people to greater devotion. Tears made of glass slip down the cheeks of statues depicting the Virgin Mary, whose eyebrows and tresses may be made from real human hair (*see also* **Mary, Blessed Virgin**). Some brotherhoods possess images that are hundreds of years old and have attracted a following beyond the membership of the brotherhood. One such image is the Virgin of Good Hope, whom Sevillians call, affectionately, *La Macarena*. Real jewels and precious metals adorn her robes. La Macarena takes to the streets on the evening of Good Friday, mourning for her dead son. The platform she rides upon measures nine feet wide, twenty feet long, and fifteen feet high. It weighs about half a ton.

Members of the religious brotherhoods carry the floats. These men, called *costaleros*, place bags of sawdust on their shoulders to cushion them against the float's enormous weight. The costaleros cannot be seen by the crowd as the folds of rich material draped along the edges of the float hang to the ground. The size and weight of the float determines the number of bearers necessary to carry the load. Large floats may require thirty to forty people to lift them up, and the largest may require up to fifty costaleros to bear the load. Since the bearers cannot see where they are going, one man, called the *capataz*, directs them along the route. From time to time, an extra will replace one of the men underneath the float, who may be temporarily overcome by heat and exhaustion in the crowded, dark, and relatively airless space underneath the platform. The costaleros must walk in step with one another so that the float progresses with a smooth motion that Sevillians find pleasing. At key points in the procession the bearers rock the float so that it sways from side to side, giving the appearance that the image is dancing.

Those members of the brotherhoods who are not carrying the floats still have a role to play during the processions. They may join the processions as *nazarenos*, "nazarenes," or **penitentes**. Nazarenos and penitentes wear long-sleeved, full-length robes and pointed hoods over their heads. These hoods completely cover their faces and shoulders, hiding their identity from onlookers. The resulting anonymity insures that the humble desire to do penance or express religious devotion inspires people to take on these roles, rather than the prideful desire to be recognized as taking part in an important religious spectacle. An internal support inside the nazarenos' hoods makes them stand up straight, something like a traditional "dunces' cap." The penitentes' hoods lack this internal support, and so flop down across the backs of their heads and shoulders. The penitentes and nazarenos also differ in the manner in which they participate in the procession. The penitentes take part as a means of doing penance (*for more on penance, see* **Repentance**). They carry heavy wooden crosses on their shoulders and sometimes walk barefoot or with their ankles chained together. Although the nazarenos don't take on these torments, their participation is also grueling, since processions usually last eight to twelve hours.

The first element in each procession is a large cross, called the "guide cross." Rows of nazarenos come next, followed by the float depicting Christ. The penitentes march behind the float of Christ. If a float bearing the image of the Blessed Virgin Mary also appears, it will follow behind the float depicting Jesus. Hundreds, and in some cases thousands, of people participate in each procession. Crowds line each side of the street during these solemn parades. The beauty and drama of the event so moves some of them that they shout out their compliments to the floats. Some even sing a short, wailing kind of song called a *saeta*, which summarizes the depth of their feelings about the event.

Easter Season in Seville

The joy repressed during Holy Week celebrations bursts forth a week or two after Easter, in *La Feria de Sevilla*, Seville's annual fair, also called *La Feria del abril*, or April Fair. This week-long event began in the nineteenth century as a horse and cattle fair. Buyers and sellers celebrated deals with little drinks purchased from wooden fairground booths. In time the importance of the livestock deals faded while the fairground celebrations grew. Finally the festivities took on a life of their own, completely divorced from the buying and selling of animals. Today Sevillians celebrate the April Fair by dressing in old-fashioned flamenco costumes, which means long, tight-fitting ruffled dresses for the women and close-fitting black trousers, short jackets, and hats for the men. The sons and daughters of well-to-do families, gorgeously costumed, ride horses through the streets. Large fairground tents known as *casetas* spring up in a section of town called *Los Remedios*. Sponsored by associations, clubs, and individuals, the casetas contain tables, chairs, bars, and even small stages so that guests may enjoy food, drink, and the Flamenco music and dance strongly associated with this region of Spain.

Further Reading

Epton, Nina. *Spanish Fiestas*. New York: A. S. Barnes and Company, 1968.

Lord, Priscilla Sawyer, and Daniel J. Foley. *Easter the World Over*. Philadelphia, PA: Chilton Book Company, 1971.

Mitchell, Timothy. *Passional Culture: Emotion, Religion and Society in Southern Spain*. Philadelphia, PA: University of Pennsylvania Press, 1990.

———. *Violence and Piety in Spanish Folklore*. Philadelphia, PA: University of Pennsylvania Press, 1988.

Web Sites

"Semana Santa — Holy Week — Easter," posted through Andalucia.com, the web site for *Andalucia Magazine*: http://www.andalucia.com/magazine/english/ed2/semana-santa.htm

Holy Week in Seville, several pages sponsored by ALTUR, an organization promoting tourism in the region of Andalucia, Spain: http://www.altur.com/eng/pseville/seville/holidays.shtml

Spring Cleaning

Old European folk traditions taught people to prepare for Easter by giving their homes a thorough cleaning. They rolled up rugs, carried them outside and beat them to remove dirt and dust. Sofas, upholstered chairs, and mattresses were also aired out and beaten. Families washed windows, laundered curtains, and waxed floors. In some places people scheduled this cleaning for the Monday, Tuesday, and Wednesday of **Holy Week**. In medieval times the Thursday of Holy Week, called "Clean Thursday" in some places, served as the day on which to bathe, wash clothes, and perform other personal grooming chores in preparation for Easter (*see also* **Maundy Thursday**).

Several other religious and folk traditions recommend house cleaning as a means of preparing for a major spring holiday. Jewish religious teachings insist that the faithful clean their homes thoroughly in preparation for **Passover**. Tradition requires them to pay particular attention to removing all traces of leavened foods, down to the smallest crumb. Persians and other Middle Easterners who celebrate the new year festival called **No Ruz** also prepare by cleaning their homes. Rooted in the ancient Zoroastrian religion, the No Ruz festival, celebrated around the time of the **spring equinox**, originally commemorated the creation of the world as we know it and honored the god Ahura Mazda.

These spring house cleanings may be viewed as part of a purification process that prepares people to invite the sacred into their lives during these holy festivals. In contemporary American culture the idea of spring cleaning, severed from its religious roots, has passed into the realm of folk tradition. Especially in cold northern climates, the lengthening days and warmer weather make spring an especially good time for any cleaning process that involves going outdoors. If cold weather has kept the family cooped up inside all winter long, then the interior of the home may need a good cleaning as well.

Further Reading

Griffin, Robert H., and Ann H. Shurgin, eds. *The Folklore of World Holidays*. Second edition. Detroit, MI: Gale Research, 1999.

Weiser, Francis X. *The Easter Book.* New York: Harcourt, Brace and Company, 1954.

Web Site

"Iranian New Year No Ruz," an article by Massoume Price, posted at: http://www. iranonline.com/festivals/Iranian-new-year/index.html

Spring Equinox
Vernal Equinox

As winter melts into spring the days begin to lengthen and the nights get shorter. This process continues until, during one twenty-four-hour period, night and day are the same length. This event is known as the vernal, or spring, equinox. The word equinox comes from astronomy. It refers to those two twenty-four-hour periods in each year in which the day lasts as long as the night. Indeed, the word equinox is composed of two Latin root words meaning "equal night." In the Northern Hemisphere the equinox that occurs around March 21 heralds the arrival of spring. In the Southern Hemisphere this same day is known as the fall, or autumn, equinox and announces the beginning of autumn. In September the situation reverses itself. In the Northern Hemisphere the fall equinox arrives around September 23. This same date brings the spring equinox to the Southern Hemisphere.

Axis, Orbit, and Equinox

Scientists have determined that this slow shift in the length of earth's days and nights is caused by the tilt of the planet's axis. Each day the earth completes one full rotation on its axis, the imaginary line connecting the North and South Poles. As each continent turns to face the sun its inhabitants experience daylight, and as it turns away from the sun they experience night. All the while the earth rotates on its axis it is also moving in a long, slow, circular orbit around the sun. The earth's axis does not cross the plane of the earth's orbit around the sun at a perpendicular angle, however. Instead the earth tilts 23.5 degrees to one side. The degree and direction of this tilt remains constant as the earth orbits the sun. It takes the earth an entire year to complete its orbit around the sun.

Although the tilt of the earth remains the same, the position of the earth relative to the sun changes. In the Northern Hemisphere the winter solstice, the shortest day and longest night of the year, occurs when the earth reaches that point in its orbit in which the imaginary line connecting the earth and the sun is directly in line with the earth's axis. This gives the tilt of the earth its maximum effect on the length of the planet's days and nights because it angles the North Pole directly away from the sun and the South Pole towards it. Thus on this day people in the Northern Hemisphere experience the longest night and shortest day of the year.

As the earth continues its orbit around the sun, the days begin to lengthen. The tilt of the earth remains the same, but the path of the earth's orbit around the sun slowly moves it towards a position in which the Poles point neither towards nor away from the sun. Instead the earth's axis runs exactly parallel to the sun. When the planet reaches this position the tilt of the earth's axis has no effect on how much sunlight each region of the globe receives. During this twenty-four-hour period day and night are of equal length every place on the earth. In the equatorial zones the sun treads a path across the sky that takes it directly overhead, eliminating all shadows. In the Northern Hemisphere this day is called the spring equinox.

As the earth continues its orbit it arrives, three months later, at another location at which the earth's axis points towards the sun. This time, however, the tilt of the earth angles the North Pole towards the sun and the South Pole away from it. People in the Northern Hemisphere experience the summer solstice, the longest day and shortest night of the year, while people in the Southern Hemisphere welcome the winter solstice. Three months later the earth finds itself at the other position in its yearly orbit in which the earth's axis runs parallel to the sun. In the Northern Hemisphere the days have been getting shorter since the summer solstice. Therefore northerners experience this twenty-four-hour period of equal daylight and darkness as the autumn equinox, while southerners enjoy the arrival of the spring equinox.

Holidays

Throughout history and in many different cultures people have rejoiced at the arrival of the spring equinox with its promise of light, warmth, and the renewal of nature's bounty. Holidays cluster around the date, many of which emphasize the theme of renewal. The ancient Mesopotamians established their new year festival at this time of year, which later civilizations transformed into **No Ruz**. The ancient Jews celebrated their release from slavery in Egypt with the **Passover** festival, also scheduled close to the spring equinox. The Romans observed **Hilaria** at this time of year, a festival commemorating the **salvation** of Attis, a youth devoted to the goddess Cybele. Christians observe two holy days near the spring equinox—Easter, honoring the **resurrection** of **Jesus** Christ, and the **Annunciation**, commemorating the Blessed Virgin **Mary**'s conception of the Christ child.

Further Reading

Krupp, E. C. *Beyond the Blue Horizon*. New York: HarperCollins, 1991.

Upgren, Arthur. *The Night Has a Thousand Eyes: A Naked-Eye Guide to the Sky, Its Science, and Lore*. New York: Plenum Press, 1998.

Web Site

"From Stargazers to Starships," a web site authored by NASA employee David P. Stern that teaches basic astronomy, physics, and the history and applications of space flight: http://www-spof.gsfc.nasa.gov/stargaze/Sintro.htm

Spy Wednesday
Black Wednesday, Crooked Wednesday

In Ireland the Wednesday before Easter is known as Spy Wednesday. The name comes from the Bible passage read in church on that day, which explains the role that **Judas** Iscariot played in bringing about **Jesus'** death. According to the calendar of the Roman Catholic Church, Spy Wednesday marks the last full day of **Lent** and **Holy Week**. The **Triduum** begins on the evening of the following day, **Maundy Thursday**, and continues through **Easter Sunday**.

Judas Iscariot was one of Jesus' twelve disciples. Although Judas was not a spy in the sense in which we use the word today, spies do perform the same kinds of treacherous acts that Judas did. In exchange for a sum of money Judas betrayed Jesus' whereabouts to the religious authorities who sought his death. Then Judas returned to Jesus' side, pretending continued admiration and faithfulness. In Germany people once called the day Crooked Wednesday, while Czech folk tradition dubbed the day Black Wednesday. These names, too, convey a sense of something having gone wrong. In past times Polish schoolboys dragged effigies of Judas through the street on this day (*see* **Judas, Burning of**).

The idea that Judas betrayed Jesus on a Wednesday gave this day a special place in the Christian calendar. Indeed, the early Christians fasted on Wednesdays throughout the year in remembrance of this sad event. Around the year 400 Western Christians, that is, Roman Catholics, abandoned the Wednesday **fast** in exchange for a Saturday fast, which is also no longer practiced. Orthodox and other Eastern Christians maintained the ancient tradition of the Wednesday fast, however. Even today, strictly observant Orthodox Christians continue to fast on Wednesdays in remembrance of Judas' act of treachery.

Further Reading

Blackburn, Bonnie, and Leofranc Holford-Strevens. *The Oxford Companion to the Year*. Oxford, England: Oxford University Press, 1999.

Metford, J. C. J. *The Christian Year*. London, England: Thames and Hudson, 1991.

Monti, James. *The Week of Salvation*. Huntington, IN: Our Sunday Visitor Publications, 1992.

Niemann, Paul J. *The Lent, Triduum, and Easter Answer Book*. San Jose, CA: Resource Publications, 1998.

Slim, Hugo. *A Feast of Festivals*. London, England: Marshall Pickering, 1996.

Stations of the Cross
Way of the Cross

The Stations of the Cross, or Way of the Cross, is a prayer and meditation practice particularly popular among Roman Catholics. The stations consist of fourteen scenes from **Jesus'** trial and crucifixion (*for more on crucifixion, see* **Cross**). These are generally represented in artwork or visual symbols of some kind. As worshipers pass by each station they meditate on Jesus' suffering and sacrificial death. They also reflect on the example each incident sets for Christians living today and offer prayers. In Jerusalem Christians observe the Stations of the Cross by walking through the city itself, stopping to pray and meditate at sites where the fourteen incidents may have taken place. Many consider walking the Stations of the Cross to be an especially appropriate way to observe **Good Friday**.

History

Devotion to the Stations of the Cross began in Jerusalem. An old Christian legend traces this observance back to Jesus' mother, the Virgin Mary, who was said to revisit the scenes of her son's suffering daily after his death (*see* **Mary, Blessed Virgin**). In the late fourth

575

century Egeria, a western European pilgrim to the Holy Land, recorded the fact that Jerusalem Christians honored Good Friday with a procession from the Mount of Olives, just outside Jerusalem, to Jerusalem's Church of the Holy Sepulchre, built over the supposed site of Jesus' crucifixion and burial (*see also* **Royal Hours**). From that period until the arrival of the European Crusaders around the turn of the twelfth century, historical records are spotty. Nevertheless, a tenth-century document recorded a Good Friday procession that stopped at six sites between the Mount of Olives and the Church of the Holy Sepulchre.

In the very last years of the eleventh century men from all over Europe, responding to a call from Pope Urban II, formed military battalions and converged on the Holy Land. Their stated mission was to wrest military and political control of Palestine away from its Muslim inhabitants and to install Christian rulers dedicated to safeguarding Christian holy sites and guaranteeing Europeans access to them. Called the Crusades, this series of military campaigns lasted till the thirteenth century. When the Crusaders arrived in Jerusalem, they found no public processions on Good Friday. Instead Jerusalem Christians prayed in the chapels of the Church of the Holy Sepulchre on that day. The church, a site of intense Christian devotion since early times, was itself a ruin. Destroyed in 1009, it had been only partially reconstructed. The energetic Crusaders rebuilt the Church of the Holy Sepulchre and erected many new churches over sites associated with the events in Christian scripture before leaving Palestine at the end of the thirteenth century.

In that same century Franciscan monks arrived in the Holy Land. By the fourteenth century they had been entrusted by the pope to care for sites of Christian devotion in Palestine. The Franciscan monks also dedicated themselves to aiding Christian pilgrims in the Holy Land. They served as guides to many generations of European Christians who continued to make pilgrimages to Jerusalem long after the Crusaders had departed. Visitors in the twelfth, thirteenth, and fourteenth centuries reported walking a route called the *Via Sacra*, a Latin phrase meaning "Sacred Road," which took them past many Christian shrines.

Meanwhile, both the Crusaders and the Christian pilgrims brought their devotion to Jerusalem's holy sites back to Europe. They developed the idea of reproducing these sites in their home towns for devotional purposes. Though the Stations of the Cross were known in Europe during the late Middle Ages, the exercise did not achieve widespread popularity until the sixteenth, seventeenth, and eighteenth centuries. During the sixteenth century Franciscan monks all across Europe began to promote prayerful meditation on the Way of the Cross as a means of deepening one's relationship with Christ. As a result of their efforts many towns and cities set about reproducing Jesus' route from trial to crucifixion. Artists created scenes illustrating the events associated with Jesus' sufferings. In some towns the stations took the form of a series of stage settings constructed along a little path. In other places a number of chapels attached to a large church would be dedicated to the stations. These series of tableaux went by a variety of names, including the Way of the Cross, the Way of Affliction, the Mournful Way, the Very Painful Way, the Seven Falls, the Seven Pillars, and the Sorrowful Journey. In each city, however, one might find different scenes from Jesus' last days represented among the Stations of the Cross. What's more, one might find a different number of scenes represented, ranging anywhere from five to twelve (*for a related custom, see also* **Passion Play**).

From about the seventeenth century onward Franciscan monks in Jerusalem, custodians of many of the holy sites associated with Jesus' life, actively promoted the Stations of the Cross in that holy city. They led pilgrims along what they supposed to be the actual route of Jesus' journey from the site of his trial to the site of his crucifixion. This route became known as the *Via Dolorosa*, a Latin phrase meaning the Sorrowful Road, a name by which it is still known today. In 1725 a Franciscan named Eleazar Horn sketched a map of Jerusalem identifying the location of fourteen Stations of the Cross. This map had the effect of stabilizing both the number of stations included in the devotion and the incidents represented. Nowadays pilgrims to Jerusalem observe some of the stations in different locations, but meditate on the same fourteen incidents. Every Friday afternoon Franciscan monks can still be found leading pilgrims along the Way of the Cross through Jerusalem's crowded streets.

Contemporary Customs

Of the fourteen scenes which compose the Stations of the Cross, nine come from the Bible and five from medieval folklore. The scenes are as follows:

1. **Pilate** sentences Jesus to death
2. Jesus is given his cross
3. Jesus falls for the first time
4. Jesus meets his mother
5. Simon of Cyrene carries the cross for Jesus
6. **Veronica** wipes Jesus' face
7. Jesus falls for the second time
8. Jesus meets the women of Jerusalem
9. Jesus falls for the third time
10. Roman soldiers strip Jesus of his clothes
11. Roman soldiers nail Jesus to the cross
12. Jesus dies on the cross
13. Jesus is taken down from the cross
14. Jesus is sealed in the tomb

The five folkloric incidents are Jesus' three falls, his meeting with Veronica, and his meeting with his mother. Together the stations portray a painful journey towards an agonizing death borne with humility and patience on behalf of others. As worshipers stop at each station they consider the spiritual lesson contained in each vignette and the example set by Christ. They offer prayers concerning the application of the lesson in their own lives and in the world. Some churches that reproduce the Stations of the Cross for their own congregations today add a fifteenth station representing Jesus' **resurrection**. Many devout Christians have written prayers and meditations to accompany the stations. Often a guide leads a group of worshipers in these set prayers and meditations as they move from station to station.

Today the Stations of the Cross may be found in many different places and formats. In addition to those that are available year-round,

churches may set up the stations for **Lent** or **Holy Week**. One can even experience online versions of the stations on the World Wide Web. Throughout the year pilgrims to Jerusalem still walk the Way of the Cross in the same streets that Jesus may well have trod in his last few hours, some carrying a large wooden cross as a means of entering into the experience more fully. In Rome Pope John Paul II arrives at the Coliseum each year on Good Friday, shoulders a large wooden cross, and leads thousands of worshipers in the Stations of the Cross. By so doing he upholds a papal tradition dating back to the mid-eighteenth century.

Further Reading

Ball, Ann. *A Handbook of Catholic Sacramentals*. Huntington, IN: Our Sunday Visitor, 1991.

Monti, James. *The Week of Salvation*. Huntington, IN: Our Sunday Visitor Publications, 1993.

Peterson, John. *A Walk in Jerusalem*. Harrisburg, PA: Morehouse Publishing, 1998.

Weiser, Francis X. *The Easter Book*. New York: Harcourt, Brace and Company, 1954.

Web Sites

Catholic Online offers a simple electronic version of the Stations of the Cross at the following address: http://www.catholic.org/prayer/station.html

Creighton University's Online Ministries presents the Stations of the Cross as a personal meditation. Includes images, prayers, history, and an explanation of how and why to do the stations: http://www.creighton.edu/Collaborative Ministry/stations.html

The following site, sponsored by Christus Rex and the Franciscan Friars of the Custody of the Holy Land, takes the viewer through the Stations of the Cross with photos of the sites in Jerusalem where, according to Christian tradition, the events took place: http://www.christusrex.org/www1/jvc/TVC main.html

A searching, contemporary version of the stations, in which each station is identified as a site in an ordinary California town (San Mateo). Designed by United Church of Christ minister Jim Burklo: http://www.stanford.edu/~burklo2/stations.html

Sunday

The Lord's Day

Christians gather for communal worship on Sunday. The first Christians adopted this practice as a means of commemorating the **Resurrection**, which took place on a Sunday. Early Christian worship services centered around a communal meal. This communal meal eventually evolved into a ritual known as the **Eucharist**, a ritual still at the heart of the Sunday worship service in a number of Christian denominations. The Eucharist reminds Christians both of **Jesus'** sacrificial death on **Good Friday** and of his resurrection on **Easter Sunday**. Thus, for many Christians, Sunday services throughout the year echo the themes celebrated during the yearly Easter festival.

History

The first Christians, most of whom were Jewish by birth, observed the Jewish Sabbath on Saturdays and met for communal Christian worship on Sunday. The Sabbath is an ancient institution dating back to the foundations of Judaism. The word Sabbath means "to stop" or "that which stops." Genesis, the first book of the Bible, tells how God created the world in six days and rested on the seventh. The Jews patterned their calendar around this story, inventing the seven-day week, which eventually became an important unit of time throughout the Western world. Just as God rested on the seventh day, so did the ancient Jews. This day of rest also reminded the Hebrews that God rescued them from a life of hard labor as slaves in Egypt (*see also* **Passover**). Jewish laws forbade all kinds of work and travel on Saturday, the Sabbath day. Breaking these laws was a serious offense against God. The earliest known Sabbath observances consisted mainly of refraining from anything that might be considered work. This break in normal work routines created a good opportunity for prayer and worship, obligations that were later added to the Sabbath.

All four biblical accounts of Jesus' resurrection agree that it occurred on the day after the Jewish Sabbath, that is, on the first day of the Jewish week. This remarkable event so astounded the first Christians, however, that it shattered their view of the endlessly repeating cycle of the seven-day week. They began to view the day of the Resurrection as the **eighth** day of the week, because on that day God had added something utterly new to his Creation by raising Jesus from the dead. This symbolic eighth day of the week, in fact, coincided with the first day of the Jewish week. The early Christians found this overlap between the Jewish first day and the Christian eighth day extremely meaningful. In their eyes the first day of the Jewish week represented the beginning of the world and the creation of light, as told in the first chapter of the book of Genesis. The eighth day of the Christian week represented the beginning of a new kind of light and a new kind of creation, namely, the new relationship between God and humanity made possible through the death and resurrection of Jesus Christ. The association between the Resurrection and the eighth day convinced the early Christians to schedule their weekly worship services on Sunday rather than Saturday. They referred to their day of worship as the Lord's Day.

Scholars of Christianity trace the custom of Sunday worship back to the first century. They find hints of the practice in Christian scripture dating to that era (John 20:19, Acts 20:7, 1 Corinthians 16:2). At that time Christians from Jewish backgrounds continued to observe the Sabbath every Saturday. They also met for communal worship on Sundays. Justin Martyr penned the following description of these early Sunday worship services around the year 150:

> And on the day called Sunday there is an assembly in one place of all who live in cities or in the country, and the memoirs of the apostles or the writings of the prophets are read as long as time permits: then, when the reader has ceased, the president gives his exhortation to the imitation of these good things. Then we all stand up together and offer prayers and, as we before said, when our prayer is ended, bread is brought and wine and water, and the president in like manner sends

up prayers, and thanksgivings according to his ability and the congregation assents saying the Amen. And the participation of the things over which thanks have been given is to each one, and to those who are absent a portion is sent by the hands of the deacons. And they who are well-to-do, and willing, give each one as he wills, according to his discretion, and what is collected is deposited with the president, and he himself succours the orphans and widows and those who are in want through sickness or other cause, and those who are in bonds, and the strangers who are sojourning: and in a word he takes care of all who are in need. And we all have our common meeting on Sunday because it is the First Day, on which God, having changed darkness and matter made the world, and Jesus Christ our Saviour on the same day rose from the dead. (Hodgkins, 18-19)

As more non-Jews joined the Christian movement debate arose over whether or not they should practice Jewish religious customs, like observing the Sabbath. Most Christian authorities believed that they were not required to do so. These authorities reasoned that Jesus' life, sacrificial death, and resurrection had given Christians a new way of relating to God, one that dissolved many of the old obligations of the Jewish religion. Eventually, non-Jewish Christians outnumbered Jewish Christians and the Christian observance of the Saturday Sabbath faded, replaced by Sunday worship services.

During the fourth and fifth centuries Christianity became the dominant religion of the Roman Empire. This newfound political power inspired new legislation. From the fourth century onwards, both religious and political authorities began to restrict people from working on Sunday. Yet apart from this restriction, the old, Jewish Sabbath customs were not revived, nor did Christians come to view Sunday as the Sabbath.

During the sixteenth century a western European religious reform movement called the Reformation gave birth to Protestant Christianity. In England and Scotland Protestants veered away from the Christian consensus concerning the old Sabbath customs. They began to insist that Christians not only refrain from all ordinary chores and activities, but also behave piously on Sunday, which they began to call the Sabbath. The Puritans brought these beliefs to colonial America, where they gave rise to the so-called "blue laws." The blue laws forbade people to work on Sundays, as well as restricting a host of activities deemed unsuitable for the Sabbath by these conservative Protestant Christians. In mid-nineteenth century America another Protestant group, the recently formed Seventh-day Adventists, began to observe the Saturday Sabbath, a practice which they believe to be more in keeping with biblical teachings.

Further Reading

Blackburn, Bonnie, and Leofranc Holford-Strevens. *The Oxford Companion to the Year*. Oxford, England: Oxford University Press, 1999.

Bradshaw, Paul F. *The Search for the Origins of Christian Worship*. New York: Oxford University Press, 1992.

Coble, Ann. "Lord's Day" and "Sabbath." In David Noel Freedman, ed. *Eerdmans Dictionary of the Bible*. Grand Rapids, MI: William B. Eerdmans Publishing, 2000.

Collins, Adela Yabro. "Lord's Day." In Paul J. Achtemeier, ed. *The Harper-Collins Bible Dictionary*. New York: HarperCollins, 1996.

Hodgkins, William. *Sunday — Christian and Social Significance*. London, England: Independent Press, 1960.

North, R. "Sabbath." In *New Catholic Encyclopedia*. Volume 12. New York: McGraw-Hill, 1967.

"Sabbatarianism." In E. A. Livingstone, ed. *The Oxford Dictionary of the Christian Church*. Third edition. Oxford, England: Oxford University Press, 1997.

"Sabbath." In E. A. Livingstone, ed. *The Oxford Dictionary of the Christian Church*. Third edition. Oxford, England: Oxford University Press, 1997.

Swartly, Willard M. "Sabbath." In Everett Ferguson, ed. *Encyclopedia of Early Christianity*. Volume 2. New York: Garland, 1997.

Talley, Thomas J. "Christian Worship." In Mircea Eliade, ed. *The Encyclopedia of Religion*. Volume 15. New York: Macmillan, 1987.

Sunday of the Veneration of the Holy Cross

Sunday of the Adoration of the Holy Cross, Sunday of the Cross

Both Western and Eastern Christians mark the middle of **Lent** with special services. Roman Catholics and others who follow the Western liturgical calendar celebrate the third **Sunday** in Lent as **Laetare Sunday**. Orthodox and other Eastern Christians observe the Veneration of the Holy Cross on the third full Sunday in their Lenten season (*see also* **Easter, Date of**).

Orthodoxy is one of the three main branches of the Christian faith. Orthodox Christianity developed in eastern Europe and the countries surrounding the eastern half of the Mediterranean Sea. Orthodox Christians follow a different church calendar than that commonly adhered to by Western Christians, that is, by Roman Catholics and Protestants.

The Sunday of the Veneration of the Holy Cross kicks off the fourth week of Orthodox Lent and marks the halfway point in this season of **fasting**, prayer, and charity. Sunday morning religious services focus on the meaning of the **cross**. During church services a cross is carried to the center of the church and surrounded by the smoke of burning incense. Worshipers come forward to bow before the cross and kiss it. Parishioners are reminded of **Jesus'** single-minded determination to carry out his mission on earth, ending with his death on the cross. The cross therefore serves worshipers as a symbol of Christ's steadfastness. In addition, it represents Christ's offer of **salvation**, made through his sacrificial death and **resurrection** (*see also* **Redemption; Sin**). Thus the cross stands not only for death but also for new life. It thereby recalls both the Easter message and the promise of the Easter feast that crowns the strenuous Lenten season.

The cross remains in the middle of the church throughout the following week. Parishioners may continue to focus their devotions on it, thereby finding the strength to continue their Lenten disciplines (*for a similar custom practiced by Western Christians, see* **Veneration of the Cross**).

Further Reading

Rouvelas, Marilyn. *A Guide to Greek Traditions and Customs in America*. Bethesda, MD: Nea Attiki Press, 1993.

Wybrew, Hugh. *Orthodox Lent, Holy Week and Easter*. Crestwood, NY: St. Vladimir's Seminary Press, 1997.

Web Site

"Sundays of Lent," a document describing Orthodox Lenten services, posted on the Orthodox Church in America web site: http://www.oca.org/pages/orth_chri/orthodox-faith/worship/sundays-of-lent.html

Sunrise Service

According to Christian scripture, **Jesus'** followers discovered his empty tomb at dawn on **Easter Sunday** morning. Thus Christians have long associated the dawn hour with the **Resurrection**. In past centuries European folklore claimed that the sun danced for joy as it rose on Easter Sunday morning (*see also* **Easter Sun**). In many European towns and villages people rose early on Easter morning in order to see this marvelous sight. They gathered together on hilltops or wide, flat plains to begin the long-awaited Easter celebrations at the first glimpse of the sun. In the United States today many Protestant churches hold special sunrise services at dawn on Easter morning.

The history of the American Easter sunrise service stretches back before the founding of the United States of America. Moravian communities were the first to hold regularly scheduled sunrise services on American soil. The Moravians, also known as the American Branch of the Renewed Church of the Unity of the Brethren, or Unitas Fratrum, are members of an evangelical Protestant denomination that originated in Germany in the fifteenth century. The first Moravians immigrated to the American colonies in the eighteenth century. In 1752 a group of young men, residents of the Moravian community of Salem, North Carolina, gathered together to pray on the evening of **Holy Saturday**. As the dawn hour approached they recalled that Jesus' female followers rose early on Easter Sunday morning to visit Jesus' tomb and thus received the first news of the Resurrection (*see also* **Mary Magdalene**). This example inspired them to end their observances at the local graveyard. There, as the first rays of the Easter sun glimmered on the eastern horizon, they sang hymns of praise to God in celebration of the Resurrection. This event quickly evolved into a tradition that the community still upholds.

Today preparations for the Easter sunrise services in Winston-Salem begin around two a.m. on Easter Sunday morning. Members of brass bands assemble outside at this early hour and prepare to play Easter music in the last few hours before dawn. This joyful noise wakens worshipers, who assemble outside the Moravian church before daybreak. The minister announces, "The Lord is risen!" to which the multitude replies, "He is risen indeed!" After singing a few Easter hymns the congregation forms a long procession to the Moravian cemetery, accompanied by the brass bands. The morning's service concludes in the graveyard as the sun gradually illuminates the tombs of the departed. Other towns settled by Moravians, such as Bethlehem, Pennsylvania, host similar sunrise services on Easter morning.

The Easter sunrise service has become a common feature in many American Protestant churches. Unlike the Moravian observances, however, these services generally do not take place in cemeteries. In those regions that can expect mild weather at Easter time, sunrise services are often held out of doors so that worshipers may experience the moment of sunrise as a living symbol of the Resurrection (*for more on dawn and the east as Christian symbols, see* **Easter, Origin of the Word**). Local congregations often retire to nearby beauty spots, neighborhood parks, city plazas, hilltops, meadows, and mountaintops to convene their Easter sunrise service. Well-known Easter sunrise services can be found in some of America's most beautiful parks, such as Grand Canyon National Park, Yosemite National Park, and Mount Rushmore National Memorial. Services are also held at such nationally recognized locations as New York's Central Park and the Tomb of the Unknown Soldier in Arlington National Cemetery. In Hollywood, California, tens of thousands of people attend a sunrise service in the Hollywood Bowl, a huge outdoor amphitheater. A full symphony orchestra accompanies the massive choir that sings during this event.

The citizens of the easternmost state of Maine claim the honor of being the first Americans to witness the Easter dawn. Special Easter services are held atop Cadillac Mountain in Maine's Acadia National Park, a location said to receive the first rays of the sunrise as it sweeps across the American continent. America's Easter sunrise celebrations may well conclude with those held in Hawaii, the westernmost state, especially with the ceremony held at Punchbowl National Memorial

Cemetery, just outside Honolulu. The sun must rise high in the sky before these worshipers catch a glimpse of it, since this service is held inside the crater of an inactive volcano.

Further Reading

Hark, Max J. "Moravian Sunrise Service." In Alfred Shoemaker's *Easter in Pennsylvania*. Kutztown, PA: Pennsylvania Folklife Society, 1961.

Henderson, Helene, and Sue Ellen Thompson, eds. *Holidays, Festivals, and Celebrations of the World Dictionary*. Second edition. Detroit, MI: Omnigraphics, 1997.

Hogan, Julie. *Treasury of Easter Celebrations*. Nashville, TN: Ideals Publications, 1999.

Lord, Priscilla Sawyer, and Daniel J. Foley. *Easter Garland*. 1963. Reprint. Detroit, MI: Omnigraphics, 1999.

Web Site

"Moravian History, Terms, and Facts," a page posted by the Moravian Gift and Book Shop of Winston-Salem, North Carolina, an arm of the Board of Education of the Moravian Church: http://www.newsalem.com/mbg/facts. htm

Sweden, Easter and Holy Week in

Swedes associate Easter time with the return of the sun and the coming of spring. They celebrate Easter by filling vases with budding birch twigs, sometimes decorated with colored feathers. In the past people whisked each other with these birch twigs on **Good Friday**, some say in remembrance of the whipping endured by **Jesus** before his crucifixion (*for more on crucifixion, see also* **Cross**). Nowadays people simply hope that the birch buds blossom in time to make a pretty display for Easter. The Swedish phrase for "Happy Easter" is *glad Påsk*.

Holy Week

In the past Swedes treated **Holy Week** as a sad, solemn time. No weddings or christenings took place during this week and many businesses and places of entertainment closed on **Good Friday**. These customs have begun to break down in recent years.

Palm Sunday

Although the **palm** branch is the traditional symbol for **Palm Sunday**, Swedes make do with willow branches, since few palms grow as far north as Sweden. Many Swedes display these willow branches in their homes and offices.

Holy Wednesday

An old custom associated with Holy Wednesday encouraged people to play a certain kind of practical joke on one another. They attempted to attach a silly or unpleasant object to a person's clothing without the person noticing. If the person walked around with the object all day before becoming aware of it, then the joke was a success (*for more on Holy Wednesday, see* **Spy Wednesday**).

Maundy Thursday

Swedish folklore taught that witches were especially active during Holy Week, and above all on **Maundy Thursday**. On this day they journeyed to a place called *Blåkulla* for a private celebration of their own (*see also* **Walpurgis Night**). People hid their broomsticks and billygoats on this day, fearing that a witch in sudden need for transportation might steal them and, by means of a spell, fly away on them to Blåkulla. Witches transformed ordinary brooms into flying brooms by wiping them with a magical ointment. One recipe for flying ointment called for metal shavings taken from church **bells**. Frightening folktales whispered that gangs of witches gathered in bell towers during Holy Week to harvest this magic ingredient.

These now-extinct folk beliefs left behind an unusual children's custom. In Sweden girls go door-to-door on Maundy Thursday dressed as witches. These charming **Easter witches** bestow Easter greetings and hope in exchange to receive a sweet of some kind. In some places this custom takes place on **Holy Saturday**.

Other folk beliefs associated with Maundy Thursday include the notion that a woman who spun thread on this day would be sure to endure a painful childbirth and the belief that drawing **water** from a well about an hour before dawn could protect one from sunburn during the coming year. Later in the day many Swedes ate green soup, made from soup stock and green vegetables (*for more on this custom, see* Maundy Thursday).

Good Friday

Another old folk teaching, also found in Finland, warned that witches were especially active on Good Friday and Holy Saturday, the two days that Jesus Christ spent in the grave (*see also* **Finland, Easter and Holy Week in**). People protected themselves from evil enchantments on these dangerous days by burning bonfires, painting crosses on their doors, hanging crossed pairs of scythes in their barns, shooting off firearms, and other activities thought to frighten away witches. Nowadays neighborhood children dressed up as Easter witches are all that remains of these folk beliefs.

591

In northern Sweden boys once tormented girls on Good Friday by chasing them and whipping them with birch twigs. They stopped when the girls offered them a drink. On **Easter Sunday** and Monday the tables turned and girls pursued and slapped boys with birch twigs.

Swedes still enjoy traditional Good Friday foods. These include beer soup, green peas, and fried salt herring.

Holy Saturday

Swedes begin to eat their **Easter eggs** on the evening of Holy Saturday. Although the eggs may be decorated, the designs usually aren't as elaborate as those found in other European countries (*for more on these elaborate designs, see* Easter Eggs).

Easter Sunday

In past times some Swedes hesitated before lighting a fire in their fireplaces on Easter Sunday. Folklore taught that witches often got caught in chimneys on their way home from Blåkulla, and few people wanted to face a singed and angry witch on Easter morning. The only way to make absolutely certain that your chimney did not have some kind of supernatural creature lurking within it on Easter morning was to burn wood from nine different kinds of trees. According to some writers, the Easter bonfires held in western Sweden on this day are another remnant of these old, Swedish beliefs about witches (*see also* **Easter Fires**).

Further Reading

Downman, Lorna, Paul Britten Austin, and Anthony Baird. *Round the Swedish Year*. Stockholm, Sweden: Bokförlaget Fabel, 1961.

Lord, Priscilla Sawyer, and Daniel J. Foley. *Easter the World Over*. Philadelphia, PA: Chilton Book Company, 1971.

Web Site

An article entitled "Påsk — Easter," posted by Sweden's Lulea University at: http://www.luth.se/luth/present/sweden/history/folklore/easter.html

Switzerland, Carnival in

The city of Basel hosts the most famous **Carnival** celebrations in Switzerland. The citizens of Basel celebrate their Carnival during **Lent**. It begins on the Monday after **Ash Wednesday**. Some writers explain this unusual starting date by suggesting that when Basel became mostly Protestant its people decided to assert their independence from the rules and regulations of the Roman Catholic Church. These rules dictated that Carnival come before Lent and that Lent begin on Ash Wednesday. In other Swiss cities populated primarily by Roman Catholics, Carnival does indeed take place the week before Ash Wednesday, making it possible for tourists to travel from Carnival to Carnival during in the weeks that precede and follow the start of Lent.

Throughout the rest of the German-speaking world, Carnival is *Fastnacht*, or "Fast's Eve." In 1925 Basel's Carnival committee decided that they would spell the word *"Fasnacht,"* that is, without the "t." Basel's Carnival celebrations are also distinguished by an orderliness and seriousness that some say typifies the spirit of the city.

History

Historical records concerning Carnival in Basel date back to 1376, making it one of the oldest documented Carnivals in Europe. In the sixteenth century, alarmed by the violence and disorder of Carnival celebrations, Church authorities attempted to outlaw masks during the festival. By and large the town's inhabitants ignored this rule. Young people, costumed as skeletons, ghosts, and witches, wandered the city streets looking for people to play practical jokes on. One favorite prank involved beckoning an unsuspecting person out of his or her home, after which the Carnival pranksters would wipe them with tar, sprinkle them with ashes, and toss them into a fountain. Under the cover of costume and mask, some Carnival-goers looted stores that weren't tightly locked up, especially sausage shops, as sausages were considered a traditional Carnival food. Hoop and saber dances were held in public places, provoking over-enthusiastic participants to start fights which sometimes ended in death. Guilds, associations of men following the same trade, paraded through the streets during Carnival, while outside of town people lit great bonfires and engaged in mock battles with sticks. Town authorities eventually created separate days of celebration for women and children, in order to protect them from rude and violent elements of Basel's Carnival celebrations.

Many of the traditions that typify Basel's contemporary Carnival evolved during the eighteenth and nineteenth centuries. These include lantern parades and fife and drum bands, both innovations borrowed from the French. The introduction of the *vogel gryff* or "griffin" also dates back to this era. The vogel gryff ceremony takes place about a month before Carnival. It begins with the arrival by river raft of a man representing a forest spirit or wild man. Dressed in a leafy green costume with a frightening brass mask, he carries a small pine tree that has been torn up by the roots. Four fools, as well as drummers and flag bearers, accompany him. When he lands in Basel he is greeted by two other folk figures, a griffin and a lion. These costumed citizens perform special dances before the homes of notable townspeople. Children attempt to snatch the apples dangling from the wild man's costume, risking a swat from his pine tree if he catches them. In past times apple-snatching was a rougher sport, as the lion would defend the wild man's apples by tossing any child he caught into a nearby fountain. The vogel gryff ceremony is not accepted by many Baslers as part of their authentic Carnival tradition, however, due to its relatively recent introduction.

Morgestraich

Not only does Basel's Carnival begin on an unusual date, it begins at an unusual time. The opening ceremony, called the *Morgestraich* or "morning call," starts at four a.m. In spite of the early hour, the town's inhabitants line the streets waiting for the sound of the church **bells** that kick off the parade. At four a.m. the lights go off all over the city, fife and drum bands begin to march, and the parade starts, illuminated by large lanterns made from cloth stretched tight over wooden frames. The cloth is then painted with the theme of each Carnival society's presentation. Society members wear costumes and masks topped with their own individual lanterns.

One writer explains the Morgestraich as a result of a humorous meeting between a band of early morning Carnival masqueraders accompanied by a fife and drum ensemble and a troop of soldiers called out for an early morning drill. According to this theory, the citizens of Basel then decided to memorialize this humorous encounter the following year, thus giving birth to a tradition. Another writer argues that both the Morgestraich and the late starting date of Carnival can be explained by the fact that in the early sixteenth century the city's Protestant rulers wanted to get rid of all customs associated with Roman Catholicism. Carnival, however, was too popular to destroy, so they simply shifted the date to coincide with the local ceremony honoring the induction of the city's young men into the military. The date of this ceremony fell during Lent, thereby tweaking Roman Catholic religious sensibilities and disassociating Basel's Carnival from its Roman Catholic roots. A trace of the military heritage of Basel's Carnival remains in the Morgestraich and its dawn march to the sound of fife and drum bands.

Traditional Costumes

Certain costumes have become traditional favorites for Basel Carnival-goers. These include *Alte Tante*, an interfering aunt, *Fasnachtsfrau*, an old, gossipy woman, and *Waggis*, a foolish fellow from the countryside.

Parades and Pies

Basel's parades continue for the next three days. One hundred and fifty "cliques," or Carnival societies, take part in these parades. They represent 10,000 to 20,000 people, about ten percent of the town's population. After, and sometimes during the parades, marchers and musicians duck into local eating establishments to refresh themselves. There they order *mehlsuppe*, a roasted flour soup, and *swiebelewähe*, onion pie, both of which are traditional Carnival dishes. Hot spiced **wine**, called *glühwein*, is another Carnival favorite. The largest parades take place on Monday afternoon. These parades include floats from which Carnival society members throw confetti, mimosas, and oranges.

Humor

Rhymes satirizing local events and personalities, known as *zeedel*, are handed out to spectators along Monday's parade route. Written in the local dialect of German, they may be unintelligible to German speakers from other countries. Later that evening local actors go from tavern to tavern performing *Schnitzelbängg*, funny, rhyming recitations concerning local events. The Basel Fasnacht committee awards prizes to the Schnitzelbängg that best captures the wit and irony that characterizes Basel Carnival humor.

"Intriguing," or *intrigieren*, offers Baslers a less-structured and more personal form of Carnival humor. This custom gives Carnival-goers a chance to draw attention to and embarrass a friend or acquaintance by approaching them under the cover of a mask and whispering suggestive gossip about them. In Basel good manners dictate that intriguers avoid vulgar or truly cruel statements. Sometimes the intriguer brings accomplices who grab the victim and stuff confetti inside his or her clothing.

Guggenmusik

On Tuesday *guggenmusik* bands wander through the streets, temporarily replacing the fife and drum corps. These humorous brass bands, composed of accomplished as well as very amateur musicians, appeared in the nineteenth century. Some of the less accomplished musicians play old, damaged instruments, repaired and ornamented with lengths of hose and extra horns. These bands begin tunes together but quickly slide into discord and disarray. Somehow, the better musicians of the bunch manage to guide the piece to a successful close.

Children's Carnival

A special children's carnival, or *Kinderfasnacht*, also takes place on Tuesday. Costumed children parade through the streets as their proud parents look on from the sidelines.

Last Day

On Wednesday, the last day of Carnival, everyone takes to the streets, including the guggenmusik bands, the fife and drum corps, the intriguers, the Snitzelbängg troupes, and the masqueraders. Wagons roll through the streets, from which oranges and blossoms are thrown to the crowds. Carnival enthusiasts keep the party going through the night. It ends with a dawn soccer match and **egg-tapping** contest on the Andreas Platz. Some Baslers argue that Carnival really ends with the event that follows, the *Kehruus*, or "sweeping out." This city-wide cleanup involves sweeping up the tons of Carnival confetti that now litter the streets.

Order and Tradition

The people of Basel value orderliness as well as neatness. In fact, members of the Carnival committee draw up guidelines for crowd behavior and appropriate costumes which are distributed to festival-goers on the first day of Carnival. Custom dictates that all masking cease at dawn on Thursday morning. Those violating this tradition, or appearing in costumes not in keeping with the guidelines established by the Carnival committee, may face boos and protests from other Carnival-goers.

Further Reading

Lau, Alfred. *Carneval International*. Bielefeld, Germany: Univers-Verlag, n.d.
Orloff, Alexander. *Carnival: Myth and Cult*. Wörgl, Austria: Perlinger, 1981.
Rubin, Rich. "A Joyful Madness: Carnival in Basel." *German Life* (February-March 1999). Available online at: http://www.germanlife.com/

Web Site

The Basel Fasnacht Committee has a web site that provides a guide to the Carnival at: http://www.fasnacht.ch

Tenebrae

Some Roman Catholic and Anglican churches offer Tenebrae services during the **Triduum**, that is, the last three days before Easter. This solemn evening service commemorates **Jesus'** crucifixion, death, and entombment (*for more on crucifixion, see* **Cross**). Tenebrae services are generally divided up into three distinct sections called "nocturnes." Each nocturne is composed of psalms, chanted verses, and Bible readings. The name Tenebrae, which means "darkness" in Latin, refers to several aspects of this observance. For example, as the service proceeds, the light in the church grows dimmer, until the congregation is left in complete darkness. This dimming of the lights symbolizes Jesus' suffering, abandonment, death, and burial. It may also allude to the biblical assertion that darkness fell over the land during the last **three hours** of Jesus' suffering on the cross (Matthew 27:45, Mark 15:33, Luke 23:44).

Both the themes addressed during the service and the symbolic use of candles make this observance a literal and symbolic descent into darkness. The service begins with candles glowing on the altar, which are sometimes placed in a kind of elaborate candelabra known as a "Tenebrae hearse." The clergy extinguish one candle after another as the service progresses. Most commentators suggest that this process represents the way in which Jesus' followers deserted him one, by one during his trial, execution, and burial. Finally one candle remains, representing Christ. Near the end of the service this candle is hidden, symbolizing Jesus' death and burial. After the final prayers are said, the candle reappears briefly, its faint glow permitting worshipers to make their way out of the church.

The Tenebrae hearse has an interesting history. The English word "hearse" evolved from *hirpex*, a Latin word meaning "harrow," an agricultural tool used to break up the soil. English speakers borrowed the word from the French, who transformed it into *herse*. To people who spent their days working the land, the triangular candelabra, with its two ascending rows of candles, resembled a harrow and so acquired the same name. They used the same word to describe a wooden framework used to hold the burial cloths over caskets. Like the candelabra this framework was fitted with candles that resembled the spikes of a harrow. Eventually the word hearse came to be used in the sense we use it today, as a vehicle that carries coffins to funerals and burial grounds.

Another Tenebrae tradition calls for the making of a loud noise at the end of the service. This sound represents the earthquake that took place when Jesus died (Matthew 27:54). Some writers believe that this interpretation came about after the fact, as people sought to attribute meaning to the sound of prayer books snapping shut, a sound which the darkness seemed to amplify. Other researchers suggest that the loud noise originally came from the crack of a wooden clapper signaling the end of the service. These clappers were pressed into service from **Maundy Thursday** to Easter, since church tradition forbade the joyous sound of **bells** during this sad time.

Tenebrae services can be traced back to the eighth century, and may have been in existence as early as the sixth century. Originally the service was performed in the middle of the night, since it combines matins and lauds, monastic prayer services traditionally offered at midnight and right before daybreak, respectively. Later, however, the service was pushed back to the previous evening in order that lay people might attend. The gradual extinguishing of candles originally took place only on **Good Friday**. By the twelfth century this practice had been adopted for all Tenebrae services during the Triduum. The number of candles used at these services varied until the late Middle Ages, when fifteen was determined to be the appropriate number. The readings traditionally used for the service date back to the eighth century and consist of selections from the Bible's Book of Lamentations, the writings of St. Augustine, and the letters of St. Paul. After Vatican II, a series of important meetings of Roman Catholic Church leaders that took place between 1962 and 1965, the service was rewritten to include other materials.

Further Reading

Monti, James. *The Week of Salvation*. Huntington, IN: Our Sunday Visitor Publications, 1993.

Stevens, D. "Tenebrae." In *New Catholic Encyclopedia*. Volume 13. New York: McGraw-Hill, 1967.

"Tenebrae." In E. A. Livingstone, ed. *The Oxford Dictionary of the Christian Church*. Third edition. Oxford, England: Oxford University Press, 1997.

Thurston, Herbert. "Tenebrae." In Charles G. Herbermann et al., eds. *The Catholic Encyclopedia*. New York: Appleton, 1913. Available online at: http://www.newadvent.org/cathen/14506a.htm

Weiser, Francis X. *The Easter Book*. New York: Harcourt, Brace and Company, 1954.

Three Hours

According to the Bible **Jesus** was crucified sometime on the morning of **Good Friday** (*for more on crucifixion, see* **Cross**). At noon the skies darkened and at three in the afternoon Jesus died (Matthew 27:45-50, Mark 15:33-37, Luke 23:44-45). Three Hours services commemorate the agony that Jesus endured during the last three hours of his life. They also provide an opportunity for worshipers to meditate on the seven statements that Jesus made from the cross. These statements are found in the four Gospels — books in the Christian Bible describing the life and teachings of Christ. They are:

1. "Father, forgive them; for they know not what they do." (Luke 23:34)
2. To the **Good Thief** crucified at Jesus' side: "Truly, I say to you, today you will be with me in paradise." (Luke 23:43)
3. To **Mary, Blessed Virgin**: "Woman, behold, your son." To his disciple John: "Behold your mother." (John 19:26-27)
4, *"Eloï, eloï, lama sabachthani?"* (My God, my God, why hast thou forsaken me?) (Mark 15:34, Matthew 27:46)
5. "I thirst." (John 19:28)
6. "It is finished." (John 19:30)
7. "Father, into thy hands I commit my spirit!" (Luke 23:46)

Most Three Hours services take place on Good Friday between noon and three o'clock.

History

Father Alonso Messia, a Roman Catholic priest from Peru, invented the Three Hours devotion in the seventeenth century. This devotion began at noon, when a large crucifix and a number of lighted candles were placed on the altar. The first of Jesus' seven statements was read aloud, after which a priest delivered a sermon on the subject. After listening to this address the worshipers sang hymns, prayed together, and observed a period of silence. This cycle was repeated for each of the seven statements. At three p.m. the priest announced Jesus' death. Worshipers concluded the observance by reciting the Creed, a summary of fundamental Christian beliefs, and asking forgiveness for their **sins**.

Although Messia receives the credit for having invented this ceremony, it resembles one of the Good Friday services observed by Jerusalem Christians in the late fourth century. Egeria, a western European pilgrim to the Holy Land during that era recorded the outlines of this observance in her diary. According to Egeria the Christian community in Jerusalem gathered together at Golgotha, the site of Jesus' crucifixion, at noon on Good Friday. There they participated in a three-hour service that included readings from Hebrew and Christian scripture, prayers, and hymns. The passages from Hebrew scripture, which Christians call the Old Testament, were paired with readings from Christian scripture, or the New Testament. These pairings were designed to demonstrate the fulfillment of biblical prophecies in the life and death of Jesus. The service ended with a reading of the Passion according to St. John. Tears slid down the faces of many worshipers as they listened to this account of Jesus' last days. Afterwards the congregation prayed together and then dispersed.

After its introduction in Peru, the Three Hours devotion spread to other Latin American countries, including Ecuador, Chile, Colombia, and Mexico. It also migrated across the Atlantic Ocean to Italy and Spain. Eventually it made its way to the United States and England. In Europe famous composer Franz Joseph Haydn (1732-1809) wrote a piece of music called "Seven Last Words" (1809) especially for the service. Charles Gounod (1818-1893) also wrote music to accompany the service.

Although it achieved its initial popularity among Roman Catholic congregations, Protestants, too, eventually adopted the Three Hours service. In many Protestant churches it has become the main Good Friday observance.

Contemporary Services

Today's Three Hours services vary somewhat in their format. They may include musical offerings performed by trained musicians, special meditations, and other devotional acts not included in older variations of the observance. Nevertheless, the outlines of the service remain the same. Three Hours services generally take place between noon and three p.m. on Good Friday, and provide an opportunity for worshipers to consider Jesus' words and deeds during his last hours on earth.

Further Reading

Harper, Howard. *Days and Customs of All Faiths*. 1957. Reprint. Detroit, MI: Omnigraphics, 1990.

Metford, J. C. J. *The Christian Year*. London, England: Thames and Hudson, 1991.

Monti, James. *The Week of Salvation*. Huntington, IN: Our Sunday Visitor Publications, 1993.

Seidenspinner, Clarence. *Great Protestant Festivals*. New York: Henry Schuman, 1952.

Weiser, Francis X. *The Easter Book.* New York: Harcourt, Brace and Company, 1954.

Tree of the Cross

What kind of tree was used to make the **cross** on which **Jesus** was crucified? What happened to the cross after Jesus died? These questions inspired centuries of storytellers to spin tales that filled the gaps in our knowledge with fanciful images and fables. Some tell which species of tree was used to fashion Jesus' cross. Others claim that the cross was made of one of the sacred trees described in the Bible as the Tree of the Knowledge of Good and Evil and the Tree of Life. Still others glorify the miraculous powers of the true cross, the actual wooden cross on which Jesus died. Over the centuries the tree has served as a sacred symbol in many different cultures. Some mystical interpretations of the cross echo the meaning folklorists have assigned to these other sacred trees.

The Tree of the Cross

A number of old Christian legends identify the kind of wood used to make Jesus' cross. For example, one legend states that the Romans made the cross out of a dogwood tree. As the soldiers approached, the dogwood quivered with reluctance to serve so terrible a purpose. God rewarded the dogwood for its tenderness by turning it into a small, crooked, and delicate tree whose limbs could never again be used to make a cross. Another legend suggests that the only tree willing to serve as the wood for Jesus' cross was the mistletoe. As punishment for its participation in the Crucifixion the mistletoe became a shriveled and scraggly bush, unable to live on its own and instead reduced to life as a parasite on other trees.

The True Cross

According to legend, St. Helena, mother of the Roman emperor Constantine, journeyed to the Holy Land in the year 326. There she sought and found the true cross. The story claims that St. Helena found several crosses buried underneath the Temple of Venus, a pagan monument constructed over the site of Jesus' crucifixion. The bishop of Jerusalem suggested that the body of a dead man be laid against each of the crosses in order to discern which was the true cross. Nothing happened when the corpse was laid on the first two, but when the body touched the third cross, the dead man sprang to life. Other variations of the tale state that a sick woman was healed the instant she touched the true cross.

The legend continues by declaring that St. Helena left part of the true cross in Jerusalem, took a piece of it back to Constantinople with her, and sent a piece on to Rome. There the Romans built the Church of Santa Croce in Gerusalemme, or the Church of the Holy Cross in

Jerusalem, expressly for the purpose of housing this holy artifact (*see also* **Golden Rose**). This artifact, which many believed to be the true cross, quickly became the holiest and most sought after of Christian relics. Fragments of wood said to have come from the true cross were soon distributed throughout Europe. Many tales sprang up concerning the miraculous powers of these fragments. Scholars believe that the **Good Friday** devotion known as the **Veneration of the Cross** may have been inspired by St. Helena's apparent discovery of the true cross and the spread of its relics throughout Europe.

Biblical Trees and the Cross

Another genre of legend attempts to give the tree used to make Jesus' cross a spiritual pedigree. These legends suggest that the tree was a descendant of the Tree of the Knowledge of Good and Evil whose fruit Adam and Eve ate in the Garden of Eden. God had forbidden them to eat this fruit, so as a punishment for their disobedience he expelled them from the Garden.

According to one version of the legend, years later, when Adam was sick and dying, he sent his son Seth back to the Garden to obtain a healing balm. Upon arriving at the gates of the Garden of Eden Seth relayed his father's request to the angel guarding the door. Although the angel refused to give Seth the balm, he did give him three seeds from the Tree of Knowledge. (In some versions of the tale the seeds come from the Tree of Life.) Along with these seeds the angel relayed the promise of humanity's future **salvation**. Seth returned to Adam with the seeds and the promise. Upon hearing the angel's message Adam laughed for this first time since his expulsion from the garden. Shortly thereafter Adam died, and Seth buried him with the three seeds under his tongue, according to the angel's instructions. So it was that a great tree grew out of Adam's grave.

As the years rolled by the tree figured in the lives of many important biblical figures. Moses' staff came from a sapling cut from the root of this tree. King David replanted it in his garden where it grew into a mighty tree. Solomon ordered the tree cut down, hoping to use it as a beam in his magnificent palace, but the workmen found the log either too long or too short for every purpose and so threw it into a ditch where it became a natural log bridge for those who wished to cross. The Queen of Sheba almost set foot on this bridge when she recognized it and understood its destiny. She waded across the stream rather than set foot on it. At her urging King Solomon adorned the log with gold and silver and installed it as a lintel in his palace. His wicked grandson later stripped the log of its valuables and tossed into a pool where it sank. It resurfaced in the last year of Jesus' life. One Friday morning Roman soldiers hauled it out of the water and used it to fashion a cross with which to crucify Jesus of Nazareth.

This legend heightens the connection between Adam's **sin** and Jesus' sacrificial death. The same tree that tempted Adam into sin became an instrument of salvation by providing the wood for the cross. Further, the image of Jesus hanging on a cross made from the wood of the Tree of the Knowledge of Good and Evil suggests that Jesus himself is the fruit of that tree. This image in turn opens up a new way of understanding the **Eucharist**. If Jesus is the fruit of the Tree of Knowledge then partaking of the **bread** and **wine** of the Eucharist, presented as Jesus' body and **blood**, offers Christians a taste of the once-forbidden fruit of that tree.

Christian artists in the Middle Ages frequently pictured the cross as a kind of tree. These images draw a connection between the fruitfulness associated with trees and the Crucifixion, presenting viewers with a visual image of the new life arising out of Jesus' sacrificial death. In some instances, the cross was depicted as the Tree of Life. According to the Bible, the Tree of Life also stood in the Garden of Eden. Its fruit granted immortality to those who consumed it. In portraying the cross as the Tree of Life artists again echoed the idea that Jesus' death granted humanity access to eternal life.

Other Sacred Trees

In biblical times other Middle Eastern peoples besides the Hebrews told stories about the Tree of Life. This tree, signifying the source of life itself, can be found in the religious art and stories of the ancient

Egyptians, Assyrians, and Mesopotamians. Furthermore, examples of sacred trees can be found in the mythology of peoples from around the globe. Frequently the tree stands for the cosmos, that is, for all of creation. Or it may stand for the central axis of the world. Just as the central axis of a tree runs from underneath the ground to the skies, so the central axis of the world tree is said to unite heaven and earth.

Some mystical interpretations of the Christian cross echo the ideas discussed above. Because the cross extends in all four directions some Christians have understood it to represent the totality of existence. Others have interpreted the vertical bar as a symbol of eternity while the cross bar represents time. Still others have viewed the vertical beam as representing heaven and the horizontal beam earth. Interpreted in this light the cross represents the intersection of time with eternity and the meeting of heaven and earth.

Further Reading

Baring-Gould, Sabine. *Curious Myths of the Middle Ages*. 1866-68. Reprint. New York: University Books, 1957.

Becker, Udo. "Tree, Tree Cross." In his *The Continuum Encyclopedia of Symbols*. New York: Continuum, 1994.

Cirlot, J. E. *A Dictionary of Symbols*. New York: Barnes and Noble Books, 1993.

Eliade, Mircea. *Patterns in Comparative Religion*. Cleveland, OH: Meridian, 1963.

Every, George. *Christian Legends*. New York: Peter Bedrick Books, 1987.

Goldsmith, Elisabeth. *Ancient Pagan Symbols*. 1929. Reprint. Detroit, MI: Gale Research, 1976.

Hackwood, Frederick William. *Christ Lore*. 1902. Reprint. Detroit, MI: Gale Research, 1969.

Hogan, Julie. *Treasury of Easter Celebrations*. Nashville, TN: Ideals Publications, 1999.

"Tree, Trees." In Leland Ryken, James C. Wilhoit, and Tremper Longman III, eds. *Dictionary of Biblical Imagery*. Downers Grove, IL: InterVarsity Press, 1998.

Triduum

The word triduum means "three days" in Latin. In the language of the Roman Catholic Church a triduum is a three-day period of prayer and worship during which worshipers give thanks to God for help received, ask for God's favor and assistance, honor religious festivals, or commemorate important events. The most important regularly occurring triduum of the year precedes and includes **Easter Sunday** and is known as the Easter, or Holy, Triduum. During these three days, which begin on the evening of **Maundy Thursday** and last through evening on Easter Sunday, numerous church services and devotional exercises focus worshipers' attention on **Jesus'** death and **resurrection** (*see also* **Easter Vigil**; **Epitaphios**; **Good Friday**; **Holy Saturday**; **Holy Sepulchre**; Maundy Thursday; **Passion Play**; **Royal Hours**; **Stations of the Cross**; **Sunrise Service**; **Tenebrae**; **Three Hours**; **Veneration of the Cross**).

The Easter Triduum was once known as "the still days." This nickname can be traced back to eighth-century England. One religious writer of the time attributes the name to the notion that Jesus lay "still" in the grave between his death and resurrection. In medieval times this name might also call to mind the fact that all commerce came to a halt during the Triduum, as people devoted these three days to worship, prayer, and celebration. As far back as the eighth century Roman Catholic custom called for the silencing or "stilling" of **bells** at the start of the Easter Triduum. The harsh cracks of wooden clappers replaced the ringing church bells that usually announced the beginning and end of religious services. Inquisitive children who wondered what had happened to the church bells were sometimes told that they had flown away to Rome to visit the pope. Church bells boomed out again during the late-night Easter Vigil service on Holy Saturday, when the prohibition on bell ringing was lifted.

Further Reading

Monti, James. *The Week of Salvation*. Huntington, IN: Our Sunday Visitor Publications, 1993.

Mulhern, P. "Triduum." In *New Catholic Encyclopedia*. Volume 14. New York: McGraw-Hill, 1967.

Niemann, Paul J. *The Lent, Triduum, and Easter Answer Book*. San Jose, CA: Resource Publications, 1998.

Trinidad, Carnival in

Carnival in Trinidad has been called the biggest party on earth. Indeed, approximately one-tenth of the island's population participates in the costume parades that take place on Carnival Monday and Tuesday. Thousands of others play in calypso or steel drum bands that accompany the parades, dance in the streets, or participate in Carnival in other informal ways. The Carnival season begins after Christmas and lasts until **Ash Wednesday**, with the most intense celebrations taking place on the last two days of this period. Calypso bands, steel drum music, elaborate and imaginative processions of masqueraders, and various competitions for the best singers, songs, costumes, and bands are the most characteristic elements of the Trinidad Carnival.

History

In 1498 Christopher Columbus became the first European to visit the island of Trinidad. Spanish settlers began to arrive shortly thereafter. Trinidad's native population soon died out from overwork and ill treatment received at the hands of the European colonists. When native workers became scarce the Europeans brought slaves from Africa to work on their plantations. Spanish, French, and English colonists arrived in turn, determined to make their fortune in the New World. After slavery was abolished the British brought East Indians to Trinidad to serve as manual laborers. This mix of African, Asian, and European cultures gave birth to Trinidad's distinctive Carnival celebrations.

French settlers, who began to arrive in 1783, introduced Carnival to Trinidad. The celebrations of these well-to-do planters emphasized elegant costume parties and dances. Free blacks took part in these revels, but the influence of African culture was minimal. This state of affairs began to change after the abolition of slavery in 1833. From the 1840s onward elements of African culture began to play an increasingly important role in the festival. Eventually the formal Carnival parties favored by the European settlers became a thing of the past.

The Africans and their descendants instead introduced the element of street theater to the celebrations by wearing their costumes in public and engaging in spontaneous horseplay with bystanders. Some of the costumes they favored mocked the ways of both wealthy and working-class Europeans, while others recalled bits of African and European folklore. One such character, called "Dame Lorraine," required the masquerader to don wide flowing skirts, carry a fan, and flirt with people in the streets. Another character, a richly costumed swaggering fellow named Pierrot Grenade was based on a European clown. Other characters, such as the "moko jumbie," a man walking on stilts, evolved from west African folklore. This costume offered a special advantage, as moko jumbies customarily used their newfound height to solicit tips from those watching Carnival celebrations from their balconies. Drunken sailors, Indians, minstrels, devils, the burrokeet (a donkey and rider), Jammet (a figure who is both male and female), bats, and midnight robbers rounded out the cast of traditional Carnival characters. Today these traditional costumes have fallen out of favor with most masqueraders, but can still be seen here and there at Carnival time.

Carnival Music

Calypso music, inseparably associated with Carnival in Trinidad, also evolved from a combination of African and European influences. Its roots lie in the songs of praise and criticism sung by musically talented slaves to amuse their patrons. The slaves hid direct criticism in jaunty tunes and witty words so as to avoid punishment. Today's calypso singers often improvise their lyrics and many songs address contemporary social concerns and issues in a pointed and yet light-hearted way. Guitars and maracas accompany a vocalist, tapping out a rhythm that often runs counter to that established by the singer. In the mid-twentieth century another important kind of Carnival music emerged from the folk culture of Trinidad. In experimenting with the bottoms of old, discarded oil drums, a by-product of the nation's emerging oil industry, street musicians discovered that they made a pleasing sound when struck like a drum. What's more, they found that when hit in different places the steel drums produced different tones, permitting the drummer to tap out a tune. At Carnival time dozens of drummers gather together to form large steel drum bands that accompany Trinidad's costume parades.

Fetes

As Carnival Monday and Tuesday approach promoters begin to schedule fetes (from the French word for party, *fête*) with increasing frequency. These leisurely musical events feature a long lineup of calypso bands and singers. In between acts people munch on food that they brought from home, sip drinks, and assess the strengths and weaknesses of the performers. Fetes usually last many hours.

Mas Bands

Trinidadians refer to the practice of masquerade as "mas." Participating in the parades of costumed dancers and musicians that take over the streets during Carnival is known as "playing mas." The groups themselves are called "mas bands." The months of preparation required to organize these parades takes place at a temporary headquarters known as a "mas camp." Those who run the mas camp may have been working out the theme and costumes for this year's mas band since the close of the previous Carnival season. In the past groups of family members, friends, and neighbors organized themselves into mas bands and spent months working on their elaborate costumes. Today many prefer to pay money to march in a professionally organized mas band that has already designed a set of costumes around a specific theme. These fabulous costumes dazzle the eye and make Trinidad's Carnival among the most glamorous in the world. Some costumes require hundreds and perhaps even thousands of hours to complete. Insects, animals, figures from folklore and history, ancient cultures, outer space, and other fantasy themes provide the inspiration for many of today's costume designers.

In the past mas bands numbered forty, fifty, or sixty people. Nowadays a band of that size would be considered quite small. Bands ranging from several hundred to over a thousand people are considered medium sized. The largest bands are composed of seven to eight thousand people. These large-scale bands reflect the increasing importance of professional designers in Trinidad's Carnival celebrations.

On the Monday and Tuesday before Ash Wednesday, each band's king or queen will lead them along the parade route. A truck equipped with loudspeakers precedes each band, blaring out the year's favorite Carnival tunes. Really large mas bands may have several trucks stationed at intervals along the long procession of masked dancers, so that every segment of the mas band can hear the music. Other mas bands dance to the sounds of marching steel drum bands.

Carnival Kings and Queens

The prettiest and most elaborate costumes in each mas band are those worn by the band's king and queen. These costumes may extend far beyond the body of the person playing the king and queen, sometimes measuring thirty feet in height or width. Various wires and supports hold the costume together and some of it may rest on wheels in order to lessen the amount of dead weight carried by the person wearing the costume. In the past king costumes may have weighed close to two hundred pounds while queen costumes have been known to exceed fifty pounds. New, lightweight materials are helping costume designers take the burden off these Carnival kings and queens.

In spite of the difficulties involved in playing the role of king and queen, many Trinidadians view it as the opportunity of a lifetime to play a starring role in a festival that has come to define the culture of the island.

Carnival Saturday

On Saturday evening a steel drum band competition takes place in Port of Spain's Queen's Park Savannah, a park with a large grassy expanse that will become the staging ground for many Carnival events. The winning group will be declared the band of the year. More than one hundred bands take part in this competition. For months beforehand, pan yards — empty lots converted into outdoor rehearsal halls for the local steel drum band — reverberate with the sounds of their nightly practice sessions.

In recent years promoters in Port of Spain have scheduled a special kiddies' Carnival event on Saturday morning. About seventy or eighty mas bands take part in this event. The tots parade through the city's streets in matching costumes in much the same way that the adults will do several days later. The children's bands are smaller, however, numbering less than one hundred participants each.

Dimanche Gras

On Dimanche Gras, or "Fat Sunday," two more competitions take place in Queen's Park Savannah. Calypso singers perform before a panel of judges to see whose tune will be selected as the top song of the competition and thus come to define the year's Carnival celebrations. In addition, the kings and queens of each mas band parade before the judges to see whose costume and interpretive dancing will win them the title of best Carnival king and queen.

J'ouvert

J'ouvert is a contraction of a French phrase meaning "day opens." This prelude to the costumed processions that take place during the daylight hours on Carnival Monday and Tuesday begins in the wee hours of Monday morning. J'ouvert, sometimes referred to as "dirty mas," contrasts with the "pretty mas" parades that follow it. People roam the dark streets in sketchy suggestions of costumes, chase each other and throw dirt and other messy substances at one another. Men dress in such a way as to exaggerate their sexuality or dress as women. Other popular J'ouvert costumes include devils and demons. Many drink to excess and chase the opposite sex. People band together in informal parades, accompanying their charge through the streets by drumming on metal tins, car hubs, or steel drums. Trucks equipped with loudspeakers roll down the avenues blaring out calypso, or soca, music and gathering a string of wild revelers in their wake.

Carnival Monday

Many people who participate in J'ouvert will be back later on Monday morning to march in the first parades. These sally forth around midday. Not every member of a mas band will participate in the Monday march. Some save their strength for Tuesday. In addition many will not wear their full costume. Especially fragile pieces will be saved for Carnival Tuesday, when the parades will pass by the judges' stand. The masqueraders stay on their feet for hours dancing to the calypso or soca music that precedes them, shuffling, or "chipping," when they get too tired to dance. Most bands break up at eight or nine p.m.

Carnival Tuesday

The processions begin somewhat earlier in the morning on Shrove Tuesday, or Carnival Tuesday (*for more on Shrove Tuesday, see* **Shrovetide**). Many hit the streets by eight a.m. in order to get a good position in the lineup of bands that will pass by the judges' stand. Band members will spend all day dancing and chipping behind their king and queen. Forward movement sometimes slows to a standstill because once mas bands arrive at the judges' stand, they stop to put on performances. These stoppages back up the parade route for the remaining bands. Thousands dressed in street clothes cavort behind the masquerade bands. By evening time even people who spent the afternoon watching the spectacle from the sidelines have joined the dancing in the streets. By dark the masqueraders are entering the "last lap" of Carnival, when the mas bands march back to mas camp for one last party. Many participants never make it that far, however, having dropped out from exhaustion somewhere along the route. Carnival celebrations end abruptly at midnight. Many feel that it is inappropriate to be seen in a costume after that hour.

Ash Wednesday

In past times many Trinidadians observed Ash Wednesday as the first, solemn day of the **Lenten fast**. Nowadays, however, many head for the beach to relax after the excitement of Carnival. The bouncy calypso music heard everywhere and the crowds of exhausted partygoers give these beach scenes the feel of an extended but much more low-key Carnival celebration.

Further Reading

Ellis, Royston. *Festivals of the World: Trinidad*. Milwaukee, WI: Gareth Stevens, 1999.

Griffin, Robert H., and Ann H. Shurgin, eds. *Junior Worldmark Encyclopedia of World Holidays*. Volume 1. Detroit, MI: UXL, 2000.

Hill, Errol. *The Trinidad Carnival*. Austin, TX: University of Texas Press, 1972.

Mason, Peter. *Bacchanal! The Carnival Culture of Trinidad*. Philadelphia, PA: Temple University Press, 1999.

Web Site

The "Visit Trinidad and Tobago" web site, sponsored by the Tourism and Industrial Development Company of Trinidad and Tobago, Ltd., offers a number of pages on Carnival customs and history: http://www.visittnt.com/ToDo/Events/Carnival

Ukraine, Easter and Holy Week in the

Ukrainians celebrate **Holy Week** and Easter with stories, customs, foods, prayers, and dances. Ukrainian **Easter eggs**, called *pysanky*, are famous throughout the world for the beauty of their intricate designs.

Palm Sunday

The willow branch symbolizes **Palm Sunday** for the people of the Ukraine. Since few **palm** trees grow in their country Ukrainians long ago substituted willows for the more traditional palm branch as a symbol of the holiday. Old religious traditions call for the blessing of willow branches on Palm Sunday. Another old custom required children to swallow one bud from the branch of a blessed pussy willow as a means of preventing sore throats. This custom has fallen out of favor, but many Ukrainians still preserve the old tradition of striking each other with willow branches on this day. They accompany this gentle whisking, called "God's wounds," with folk blessings, such as "Be as tall as the willow, as healthy as the water and as rich as the earth," and folk verses like "It is not I that strikes, it is the palm. Six nights hence—the great night! A week hence—the great day!" Ukrainians call Palm Sunday *Kvitna*, "Flower," or *Verbna*, "Willow" Sunday.

Maundy Thursday

Ukrainians have many folk names for **Maundy Thursday**, the Thursday of Holy Week. It is known as *Chystyi*, "clean" or "pure," *Bilyi*, "white," *Strasnyi*, "passion," *Velykyi*, "great," and *Zhyvnyi*, "nourishing," Thursday. Several old folk customs connected with this day feature sacred flames. In past times many young men lit bonfires on this evening to light the way for ghosts returning to their family and as a means of cleansing the neighborhood from evil influences. At church services people held burning "passion candles" during twelve Gospel readings, selections from the Christian Bible describing the life and teachings of Christ. They carried these burning candles home with them and used the flame to burn a **cross** into a beam of the house. People kept these candles throughout the year, lighting them during thunderstorms to ward away lightning bolts and during times of danger to keep the family safe. According to folk belief, these candles also had the power to heal illnesses, hasten difficult deliveries, and soothe the dying. Some housewives dedicated part of the day to the creation of pysanky—elaborately decorated, multi-colored eggs (*for more on pysanky, see* Easter Eggs).

Good Friday

Many Ukrainians **fast** on **Good Friday**, avoiding both meat and dairy products. Some will eat only after they make their visit to the *plaschanytsia*, or Holy Shroud, displayed in Ukrainian churches on this day (*for more on this custom, see* **Epitaphios**). In past times many Ukrainians prepared their Easter **breads** on this day. Ukrainian Easter breads include two traditional favorites, *paskha*, a sweet, dairy-rich holiday bread, and *babka*, a kind of coffee cake.

Holy Saturday

Ukrainian folk tradition calls for final Easter preparations to be made on **Holy Saturday**. Family members dye plain, single-colored Easter eggs, called *krashanky*, and some design pysanky as well. Ukrainians play egg games with krashanky and eat them on **Easter Sunday**. In past times people threw the empty shells into streams and ponds as a means of honoring the departed. Youngsters were told to rub red krashanky against their cheeks to make them rosy. Ukrainians treasure pysanky, and those received as gifts may be preserved for many years. Bonfires may be lit on the evening of Holy Saturday, usually on the church grounds or on top of a nearby hill (*see also* **Easter Fires**).

Easter Eggs

Ukrainian folklore offers many stories concerning the origins of pysanky. One tale says that Simon of Cyrene, the man who carried **Jesus'** cross for a while (Luke 23:26), spread the custom of coloring eggs for Easter. According to the folktale Simon was an egg peddler. After his encounter with Jesus, Simon found that his eggs always took on bright, cheerful hues. Another Ukrainian tale states that when Jesus hung on the cross, each drop of his **blood** that hit the ground became a red egg. As Jesus' mother Mary wept at the foot of the cross, her tears splashed onto some of the eggs, leaving behind intricate designs (*see* **Mary, Blessed Virgin**). Yet another Ukrainian story suggests that one winter the weather was so harsh that birds plummeted from the sky, overcome by the cold. Some peasants felt pity for the birds and took them into their homes until spring came. Several days after their release the birds returned to their foster homes, each one bearing a beautifully decorated egg as a token of their gratitude.

According to one old Ukrainian tradition a young woman who wanted to get married should drop a pysanky inscribed with her name into a nearby stream. The man who found it would almost certainly return it to her and perhaps even decide to wed her. Another tradition encouraged children to build nests for the **Easter Bunny** to lay his eggs in. Thoughtful youngsters lined the nests with grass or moss and also provided tender young shoots for the **rabbit** to eat.

Easter Baskets

It may take several days for a Ukrainian housewife to prepare the basket of traditional Easter foods brought to church on Holy Saturday or early on Easter Sunday to receive the priest's blessing. These foods include ham, sausages, cheese, plain and decorated eggs, butter, horseradish, and paskha. Ukrainian folk tradition accords each food a symbolic meaning. The meats recall the animals used for sacrificial purposes in the Hebrew scriptures, or Old Testament, as well as Jesus' sacrifice of his own life on the cross. Butter and cheese represent abundance and peace. The eggs stand for the tomb out of which Jesus emerged as well as for new life. The candle embedded in the paskha symbolizes the light of the resurrected Christ. After placing these foods in their baskets Ukrainian women cover them with beautifully embroidered cloths. Many of these cloths are family heirlooms. These foods will form part of the feast that takes place on Easter Sunday.

Easter Sunday

Ukrainians call Easter Sunday *Velykden*, or "Great Day." Easter church services often take place late at night on Holy Saturday or early on Easter morning (*see also* **Easter Vigil**; **Sunrise Service**). People bring baskets of Easter foods to church with them, which the priests bless after the service. After the blessing people turn to one another and offer the Easter greeting, *"Khrystos Voskres"* (Christ is risen) and the response, *"Voistyno Voskres"* (He is risen indeed!). Many accompany this greeting with the traditional three kisses on the cheek. Often friends and family exchange pysanky at this time. In past times people frequently went to the graveyard directly after the service, bringing the glad news of the **Resurrection** to their departed loved ones.

In the old days, the head of the household often visited the barn and beehives with a basket of food before sitting down with his family to breakfast on Easter morning. Thus he included the family's domesticated animals in the Easter feast and celebration. Many Ukrainians retain the old tradition of sharing an Easter egg as the first course of the Easter feast and as a means of marking the end of the Lenten fast. Other foods likely to be included in the Easter feast are *kovbasa*, a kind of sausage, *borsch*, a soup made from beets and beef, pork or ham, *pirozhki*, pastries stuffed with cheese or meat, babka, and paskha.

In past times people would gather in the churchyard on Easter Sunday. They performed *hahilky*, ritual round dances, with each other and took part in games and other festivities. Old Ukrainian folk tradition encourages the continuous ringing of church **bells** on Easter Sunday. Boys and men took turns with this prestigious task. Nowadays many Ukrainian churches still feature folk dancing on Easter Sunday, usually special performances by the parish's youth group.

Easter Monday

Ukrainians call **Easter Monday** "Wet Monday." The name refers to the custom of dousing girls and women with **water** on this day. This custom is especially popular with young men, who often wait to catch their sweethearts by surprise with a bucket full of water. Ukrainians also refer to Easter Monday as "Wandering Monday" because folk tradition encourages families to pay visits to relatives and godparents on this day.

Further Reading

Griffin, Robert H., and Ann H. Shurgin, eds. *Junior Worldmark Encyclopedia of World Holidays.* Volume 1. Detroit, MI: UXL, 2000.

Lord, Priscilla Sawyer, and Daniel J. Foley. *Easter the World Over.* Philadelphia, PA: Chilton Book Company, 1971.

Tracz, Orysia Paszczak. "Ukrainian Easter Tradition: Velykden — Great Day." *Ukrainian Weekly* 63, 17 (April 23, 1995): 11.

Wax, Emily. "A Ukrainian Easter, the Holiday Helps Immigrants Hold on to Their Heritage." *Newsday* (April 11, 1999): G14.

Web Site

"Ukrainian Easter Customs and Traditions," an article by Lubow Wolynetz, curator of the Folk Art Collection for the Ukrainian Museum, New York City, at: http://www.brama.com/art/easter.html

Veiling

In some Roman Catholic and Episcopal churches, **crosses**, statues, and religious images are covered with a piece of cloth known as a veil during the last days of **Lent**. These Lenten veils are usually purple, the liturgical color of Lent, which signifies **repentance** (*for more on the concept of repentance, see* Lent). In some places white veils may be used instead.

Veiling the Altar

The meaning and practice of Lenten veiling has changed substantially since it was first begun in the tenth or eleventh century. In those days the Lenten veil consisted of a large piece of white or purple cloth hung like a drapery to hide the sanctuary, or altar, from the sight of the assembled congregation. The veil typically bore symbols and images representing the suffering that **Jesus** endured during his last days on earth. In medieval times the veils remained in place throughout Lent. They were usually constructed so that they parted in the middle. During important parts of the service, such as the Gospel reading (a selection from the Christian Bible describing the life and teachings of Christ), the veil was partially opened and afterwards shut again. Lenten veiling was practiced in western Europe and was especially popular in Germany, France, and England. In some places people called the veils "hunger cloths." Since medieval Christians observed Lent by **fasting**, the name "hunger cloth" may reflect their interpretation of the Lenten veil as a means of enforcing a kind of visual fast that went hand in hand with their reduced intake of food.

During the Middle Ages the Lenten veil remained in place from the beginning of Lent until Wednesday of **Holy Week** (*see also* **Spy Wednesday**). Until recent times the Bible reading scheduled for that day was the story of the last days of **Jesus'** life as told in the book of the Christian Bible known as the Gospel according to Luke. In Luke's account, at the moment of Jesus' death the veil hiding the innermost sanctuary of the great Jewish Temple in Jerusalem was torn in two (Luke 23:44-46; *see also* Matthew 27:51, Mark 15:38). In the medieval church the Lenten veil parted dramatically at this point in the service, revealing a full view of the sanctuary for the first time since the start of Lent.

In the Jewish religion as practiced in Jesus' day, the veil hanging in the Temple at Jerusalem prevented people from casting their eyes directly on the holiest of objects kept in the sanctuary. Only the high priest could pass beyond the veil, and he did so only once a year, on the festival called the "Day of Atonement," or Yom Kippur. Christian commentators assert that the rending of the Temple veil at the moment of Jesus' death represents the new relationship with God made possible through Christ. Whereas the rituals of the ancient Jews concerning the Temple veil might be interpreted to mean that God was too holy to be approached by ordinary people and therefore inaccessible, Christianity would teach that every believer has direct access to God and that God wants everyone to approach him. The tearing of the Temple veil in the Gospel accounts of Jesus' death symbolizes this teaching. Medieval Christians saw this teaching enacted in symbolic form with the parting of the Lenten veil on Wednesday of Holy Week.

In most places the custom of veiling the sanctuary during Lent disappeared around the end of the Middle Ages. As late as 1894, however, this kind of Lenten veiling was still practiced at the cathedral in the Spanish city of Seville. The Spanish added an extra flourish to this old custom. One visitor to Seville in the 1890s reported that at the moment during the service that the Lenten veil parted, a small canon mounted near the altar fired, shattering the silence and illuminating the gloom of the vast cathedral with a series of sudden, explosive flares.

Veiling Statues, Crucifixes, and Other Religious Images

The custom of placing individual veils over statues, crucifixes, and religious imagery also dates back to the tenth century. A thirteenth-century Church document specified that these veils should remain in place from the first Monday in Lent until **Easter Monday**, that is, the day after Easter. As time went on, however, the custom of veiling religious statues, imagery, and crucifixes shifted to the last two weeks of Lent, a period known as Passiontide. The Gospel reading previously assigned to **Passion Sunday**, the first day of Passiontide, tells that after a dispute with religious authorities Jesus left the Temple and hid himself (John 8:59). Passiontide veiling came to be seen as an emblem of this story. Many interpret the veiling of images as a symbol of Jesus' disappearance and the veiling of his glory during his last days on earth. According to custom the veils covering crucifixes are removed on **Good Friday**, and the veils covering other religious imagery are removed during the late-night **Easter Vigil** service on **Holy Saturday**.

In the early 1960s, as a result of a series of important meetings of Roman Catholic leaders known as Vatican II, Pope John XXIII officially changed many aspects of Roman Catholic religious services. The bishops of each nation were given the power to continue or discontinue the practice of veiling religious images, statues, and crucifixes during Lent. In those parishes that do maintain this old custom, it is now begun during the vespers, or evening, service preceding **Palm Sunday** and continued until the late-night Easter Vigil service on Holy Saturday.

Further Reading

Metford, J. C. J. *The Christian Year*. London, England: Thames and Hudson, 1991.

Monti, James. *The Week of Salvation*. Huntington, IN: Our Sunday Visitor Publications, 1993.

Niemann, Paul J. *The Lent, Triduum, and Easter Answer Book*. San Jose, CA: Resource Publications, 1998.

"Veil." In Leland Ryken, James C. Wilhoit, and Tremper Longman III, eds. *Dictionary of Biblical Imagery*. Downers Grove, IL: InterVarsity Press, 1998.

Weiser, Francis X. *The Easter Book*. New York: Harcourt, Brace and Company, 1954.

Veneration of the Cross

Creeping to the Cross

Many Roman Catholic churches practice a devotion known as the Veneration of the Cross on **Good Friday**. The clergy and congregation approach a **cross** or crucifix one by one, and offer a gesture of respect to all that it represents. This gesture usually includes kneeling or bowing before the cross and then kissing it. In medieval England and Germany people expressed their humility before **Jesus'** suffering and sacrificial death by approaching the cross on their hands and knees. This practice may have inspired an old folk name for the ceremony: "Creeping to the Cross" *(for a similar custom practiced by Eastern Christians, see* **Sunday of the Veneration of the Holy Cross** *and* **Epitaphios***)*.

The Veneration of the Cross on Good Friday can be traced back to fourth-century Jerusalem. The diary of Egeria, a Spanish nun who made a pilgrimage to Jerusalem in the late fourth century, records that Jerusalem Christians attended this ceremony on Good Friday. During church services the local bishop presented worshipers with what was believed to be the true cross, that is, the actual wooden cross upon which Jesus was crucified (*see also* **Tree of the Cross**; *for more on crucifixion, see* Cross). The congregation then came forward one by one to bow before this sacred relic, touch it to their eyes and forehead, and to kiss it. Religious officials supervised the ceremony closely, for fear that under the cover of kissing the cross pilgrims would take a bite out of it, thereby securing a valuable souvenir of their trip to the Holy Land.

According to legend, St. Helena (c. 248–c. 328) discovered the true cross in 326. Soon afterwards Christian leaders in Rome sought and obtained a fragment of this holy relic, which they housed in the Church of Santa Croce in Gerusalemme. Along with the relic came the Jerusalem community's ceremony of the Veneration of the Cross. From Rome the ceremony spread throughout Europe. It was known in England in the late tenth century, when Aelfric, archbishop of Canterbury, urged Christians to "greet God's cross with a kiss" in observance of Good Friday.

The Veneration of the Cross flourished throughout medieval Europe. During the sixteenth and seventeenth centuries, however, various Christian leaders began to criticize the practice. These leaders spearheaded the Reformation, a religious reform movement which swept across western Europe giving birth to Protestant Christianity. In general, Protestants abandoned the Veneration of the Cross. Roman Catholics, however, maintained the practice.

In today's Roman Catholic rite the priest solemnly unveils a crucifix in three stages, or carries it to the altar in a procession divided up into three stages (*see also* **Veiling**). There he holds it up before the congregation declaring, "This is the wood of the cross, on which hung the savior of the world." The assembled parishioners reply, "Come, let us worship." The priest then genuflects — bends one knee down or touches the knee to the floor — before the crucifix, and kisses Jesus' feet. The congregation follows behind the priest, one by one approaching the crucifix and reverencing it in the same fashion.

Further Reading

Chirat, H. "Cross, Finding of the Holy." In *New Catholic Encyclopedia*. Volume 4. New York: McGraw-Hill, 1967.

Hutton, Ronald. *Stations of the Sun*. Oxford, England: Oxford University Press, 1996.

Monti, James. *The Week of Salvation*. Huntington, IN: Our Sunday Visitor Publications, 1993.

"Veneration of the Cross." In E. A. Livingstone, ed. *The Oxford Dictionary of the Christian Church*. Third edition. Oxford, England: Oxford University Press, 1997.

Weiser, Francis X. *The Easter Book*. New York: Harcourt, Brace and Company, 1954.

Veronica

The pious legend of St. Veronica tells of an act of compassion that this woman performed for **Jesus** on **Good Friday**. According to the legend Veronica watched Jesus laboring to carry his cross to the site of the Crucifixion. Moved by his suffering and helpless to do more to aid him, she offered him her handkerchief to wipe the **blood** and sweat from his face. When he returned it, she found impressed upon the cloth an exact image of his face. This legend became extremely popular in the Middle Ages. It is represented in the sixth of the **Stations of the Cross**, a popular devotional exercise often performed during **Lent**.

True Images

The story of Veronica and her handkerchief does not appear in the Bible. Scholars believe that it got its start several centuries after Christ's death, when various stories concerning actual images of Jesus' face, supposedly made during his lifetime, circulated among Christian communities. Naturally such an image would be eagerly sought after by Jesus' followers. As the centuries rolled by many Christians raised their hopes even higher. They dreamt of finding what they called a "true image" of the Savior, not simply a likeness of Jesus created by an artist, but rather an exact replication of his features miraculously impressed upon a material object by the power of God (*see also* **Shroud of Turin**). By the Middle Ages a legend arose about just such an image which came into the hands of the woman we call Veronica.

History and Relics

The legend of Veronica developed during the Middle Ages. Several variations of the tale circulated throughout Europe. The version of the story told above can be traced back to fourteenth-century France. This version eventually became the most popular telling of the tale. In another variation of the story Veronica was said to have convinced St. Luke to paint her a portrait of Jesus. The likeness was good, but not exact, and Veronica was not satisfied. Later she acquired a true image when Jesus came to her house for a meal. Before eating he washed his face and dried it upon a towel. The towel retained a perfect impression of his features. Jesus told her to keep the miraculous portrait which could work miracles. Several years after Jesus' death Veronica traveled to Rome at the request of the emperor Tiberius (42 B.C.-37 A.D.). The Emperor touched the image imprinted on Veronica's towel and was instantly cured of a disease.

A cloth said to bear a "true image" of Jesus' face was known in Rome as early as the eighth century. Veneration of this relic of the life of Christ reached its height in the fourteenth and fifteenth centuries. Several other cities and cathedrals also claimed to possess pieces of cloth bearing true images of Christ's face. These cloths were referred to as "veronicas," from the Latin phrase *vera icon* meaning "true image."

From Berenice to Veronica

How did the woman with the cloth image of Jesus come to be called Veronica? Many writers have supposed that legend dubbed this woman "Veronica" because the name means true image. The actual origins of Veronica and her cloth are somewhat more complicated, however. The legend of Veronica identifies her as a woman who appears in a biblical story concerning Jesus' career as a healer. It claims that she is the hemorrhaging, or bleeding, woman who was cured by touching Jesus' robe (Matthew 9:20-22, Mark 5:25-34, Luke 8:43-48). As early as the fourth century, Christian literature identified this woman as Berenice, a version of the Greek name Pherenice, meaning "bearer of victory." Eventually western Europeans began to refer to her by the Latinized form of this name, Veronica. In the Middle Ages Christian lore began to assert that this same woman also possessed a cloth that bore a true image of Jesus.

Interpreting the Legend

How is it that the bleeding woman became the subject of the Veronica legend? No certain proofs exist, but scholars speculate that the meaning of the name "Veronica" in Latin suggested to many people that she possessed the much-sought-after true image of Christ's face. Also, the selection of the hemorrhaging woman as the one who later comforts Christ with her handkerchief gives the story of this woman's encounters with Jesus a certain symmetry. The Bible tells that the woman we call "Veronica" once reached out to touch Jesus' clothing in the hope of stopping her bleeding. The legend reverses this image. It suggests that on the day of the crucifixion Jesus' reached out to accept the cloth offered to him by Veronica so that he might staunch the sweat and blood of his own injuries.

The legend focuses our attention on the miraculous appearance of a true image of Jesus' face on Veronica's handkerchief. Indeed this legendary handkerchief was considered a priceless relic of the life of Christ during the Middle Ages. This miracle almost overshadows the appearance of another likeness of Christ also depicted in the story. Veronica's act of compassion itself might also be said to be a "true image" of Christ, wrought in the living flesh of one of his followers. Viewed in this way the legend depicts several "true images" of Christ, the first image presented in the person of Jesus himself, the second appearing in Veronica's heart when she was moved by Jesus' suffering, the third in her act of mercy, and the fourth upon the cloth.

Artistic Legacy

For hundreds of years Christians found the legend of Veronica a meaningful and moving tale. Many old churches throughout Europe display paintings or carvings from the legend of Veronica on their walls. Moreover, many famous European artists painted Veronica and her miraculous cloth, including El Greco (1541-1615), Hieronymous Bosch (1450-1516), Rogier Van der Weyden (1399?-1464), and Francisco de Zurbarán (1598-1664).

Further Reading

Degert, Antoine. "Veronica, St." In Charles G. Herbermann et al., eds. *The Catholic Encyclopedia*. New York: Appleton, 1913. Available online at: http://www.newadvent.org/cathen/15362a.htm

Hackwood, Frederick W. *Christ Lore*. 1902. Reprint. Detroit, MI: Gale Research, 1969.

Kuryluk, Ewa. *Veronica and Her Cloth: History, Symbolism and Structure of a "True" Image*. Cambridge, MA: Basil Blackwell, 1991.

Meagher, P. K. "Veronica." In *New Catholic Encyclopedia*. Volume 14. New York: McGraw-Hill, 1967.

"Veronica, St." In E. A. Livingstone, ed. *The Oxford Dictionary of the Christian Church*. Third edition. Oxford, England: Oxford University Press, 1997.

Walpurgis Night

Walpurgis Night falls on the evening of April 30. In past times many people feared that witches were especially active on this day and evening (*see also* **Easter Witches**). Northern and central European folklore warned that these menacing figures prowled in the twilight dusk, waiting until the dark hours of the night to gather together for a wild feast and frolic. Rumors circulated as to the exact location of this fearsome gathering. Many believed that it might lie on Mount Brocken (Brockenberg), in Germany's Harz Mountains. On Walpurgis Night people took extra precautions to prevent passing witches from harming their families, homes, and fields. Folk tradition taught that loud noises frightened away witches. Therefore, people rang church **bells**, slammed doors, hit pots and pans, and cracked whips. They also lit bonfires and torches, raised **crosses**, and decorated their homes with rosemary and birch boughs, all of which were thought to repel witches.

Little remains of these Walpurgis Night beliefs today. In past times, however, they were so common that they inspired the great German writer Johann Wolfgang von Goethe (1749-1832) to depict a Walpurgis Night witches' sabbath in his famous play, *Faust* (1808-32). In the play the devil, who goes by the name of Mephistopheles, takes Faust to this sinister event. In addition, vivid images of a midsummer's night witches' festival on Mount Brocken spurred Russian composer Modest Mussorgsky (1839-1881) to write his well-known piece, *Night on Bald Mountain* (1867), also known as *Saint John's Night on Bare Mountain*.

The Scandinavian and German-speaking countries produced most of Europe's Walpurgis Night witch lore. Nevertheless, in some other European countries the evening was also thought to have an eerie quality about it. In England and Ireland, old folk traditions taught special methods for protecting oneself from witchcraft on this night. Irish lore hinted that the fairies fought one another over the ripening crops on this evening.

Why April 30?

Some folklorists point out that Walpurgis Night falls on the evening before **May Day**, a day long associated in folklore with the death of winter, the birth of spring, and the celebration of nature. Walpurgis Night itself falls exactly six months from Halloween, another evening associated with uncanny forces and supernatural encounters in European folklore. Some folklorists speculate that in past times people viewed these two dates as turning points in the cycle of the year, and thus as times when the walls dividing the natural and the supernatural worlds waned thin.

Contemporary Customs

In the Czech Republic people still light large bonfires on the evening of April 30. In the old days, people believed that the bonfires protected them from witches. Not only could witches harm people and livestock, but they also caused winter and cold weather to linger on.

Czech folklore advised that burning an effigy of a witch — that is, a life-sized dummy made to resemble a witch — hastened the coming of warm weather. Today people no longer fear witches. Nevertheless, the old custom of lighting a May eve bonfire remains. People kindle the flames close to nightfall and sit close beside them, singing songs and roasting sausages in the flames. When it's dark they toss an ugly effigy of a witch into the flames. In the Czech Republic this once-fearful evening has become an occasion for some outdoor fun.

Swedes still celebrate Walpurgis Night, although contemporary Swedish festivities have little to do with witches. Instead they commemorate the death of winter and the birth of spring. University students, in particular, participate in Walpurgis Night observances, sometimes by gathering for rallies at which a speaker solemnly and formally announces the arrival of spring. In Sweden the lengthening days serve as a better guide to the changing seasons than does the weather. In this far northern land snow may still blanket the ground on April 30. In keeping with ancient traditions, the Swedes continue to light bonfires on this evening, often on hilltops or on mounds. These days, however, the fires aren't stoked by anxious farmers seeking protection from malicious witchcraft, but rather by young lovers hoping the flames will enhance the spell that attracts them to one another.

Finns celebrate May eve, which they call Vappu, with singing, dancing, and revelry in the streets. In Helsinki students, and former students, wear their traditional white caps for this night of lively street activity and parties. Some may even swim across the moat that surrounds the statue of Havis Amanda in order to adorn her with a cap. On May Day students and workers stage parades.

Finally, Walpurgis Night celebrations have become an important tourist attraction in Germany's Harz Mountains. In a bid to attract travelers to the region, promoters have stamped the image of the witch on everything from hotel brochures to beer steins. The village of Schierke, located at the foot of Mount Brocken, hosts about six thousand people each year for their Walpurgis Night celebrations. The day begins with a children's costume parade, in which kindergartners dress as

witches and devils. Later that evening people assemble in a local park which takes on the appearance of a fairground, complete with booths selling local crafts, drinks, and foods. Fair-goers enter into the spirit of the event, dressing as witches, goblins, vampires, and valkyries, the magical maiden-warriors from Scandinavian mythology. The evening's festivities take place around a huge bonfire and include a pantomime play as well as a fireworks display. Rival celebrations take place in other villages of the region.

Walpurga

Most writers state that Walpurgis Night takes its name from the saint whose feast is celebrated on the following day. St. Walburg or Walpurga (c. 710-779) grew up to become a nun and, upon the invitation of her brother, Willibald, bishop of Eichstätt (700-787), took up the post of abbess of Heidenhem, near Nuremberg, Germany. She died on February 25, 779, but on May 1, 870, religious authorities transferred her remains to Eichstätt, where a church had been built in her name. Her feast day is celebrated on May 1 in honor of this event. Walpurga is the patroness of the diocese of Eichstätt and also the city of Antwerp, Belgium. Folk belief has credited her with the power to ward off magical harms as well as the ability to protect the harvest.

A few writers suggest instead that a little-known minor deity, also known as Walpurga, gave her name to the mythical festival of witches on Mount Brocken. According to local folklore Walpurga, who was associated with the woods and springtime, could tell the future with her three-cornered mirror and carried a magical spindle and thread. These attributes may signify her to be a variant of Holde, or Frau Holle, another, more popular German goddess. According to one tale the Wild Hunt, a troop of ghostly figures that rides the night skies during winter, chased Walpurga during the last nine nights before May Day. Walpurga sought protection from mortals during these nights, often entering the homes of kindly villagers through a window thoughtfully left open. Like Holda, Walpurga was believed to reward those who helped her.

Further Reading

Blackburn, Bonnie, and Leofranc Holford-Strevens. *The Oxford Companion to the Year*. Oxford, England: Oxford University Press, 1999.

Casanova, Gertrude. "Walburga, St." In Charles G. Herbermann et al., eds. *The Catholic Encyclopedia*. New York: Appleton, 1913. Available online at: http://www.newadvent.org/cathen/15526b.htm

Frazer, James George. *The New Golden Bough*. Theodor H. Gaster, ed. New York: S. G. Phillips, 1959.

Griffin, Robert H., and Ann H. Shurgin, eds. *The Folklore of World Holidays*. Second edition. Detroit, MI: Gale Research, 1999.

Harvey, Steenie. "Season of the Witch." *The World and I* 16, 4 (April 2001): 260.

Henderson, Helene, and Sue Ellen Thompson, eds. *Holidays, Festivals, and Celebrations of the World Dictionary.* Second edition. Detroit, MI: Omnigraphics, 1997.

Ince, Sarah. *The Magical Year.* Richmond, VA: Time-Life Books, 1992.

Nollen, Tim. *Festivals of the World: Czech Republic.* Milwaukee, WI: Gareth Stevens, 1999.

Web Sites

This web page, part of German instructor Robert J. Shea's site on German folk customs, offers additional Walpurgis Night folklore: http://www.serve.com/shea/germusa/walpurgi.htm

Another informative page on St. Walpurga, sponsored by Catholic Community Forum: http://www.catholic-forum.com/saints/saintw02.htm

Water

Scholars of world mythology point out that water serves as one of humankind's most familiar and yet most powerful symbols. Moreover, many religious and folk beliefs, tales, and practices imply that water carries within it the mysterious spirit of the Divine. Water purifies, blesses, heals, and makes fruitful in many folk and religious customs. World folklore contains numerous tales concerning the "fountain of youth," a mythical spring that restores youth and vigor. Various folk traditions have identified the locations of healing wells whose waters cure disease, confer fertility, or provide an especially powerful channel through which to contact the Divine. People toss coins into "wishing wells" in many lands, observing old superstitions that credit these wells with the power to bestow luck or grant wishes. Folk stories whisper of magical liquids that restore health or even impart immortality (*see also* **Holy Grail**). Throughout the world people bathe, dip, and sprinkle themselves and others with water in religious rituals designed to bring about beneficial changes to body, mind, or spirit. Religious and folk customs connected to Easter reflect some of these ancient and widespread symbols and beliefs.

Water Symbolism in the Bible

In the Bible God or the Holy Spirit often works through or with water. The first book of the Bible, Genesis, tells how God created the earth out of water and unformed matter and later destroyed it in a mighty flood. Thus water serves not only as the creative source from which new forms rise but also an end which engulfs them and dissolves them once again into formless matter. According to Mircea Eliade, a noted scholar of comparative religion, this theme appears in many of the world's religious traditions.

The Bible also relies on water imagery to describe the workings of God or the Holy Spirit. For example, one Hebrew prophet spoke of God "pouring out" his Spirit and his blessing upon Israel (Isaiah 44:3). Moreover, biblical descriptions of the presence of God's Spirit within the individual often compare it to a well, spring, or fountain. In Christian scripture we find that like God himself, **Jesus** can command the waters (Luke 8:22-25, Matthew 14:22-33). In addition, Jesus describes himself to his followers as a source of water from which they may drink and slake their thirsts (John 7:37-39, 4:13-14). Here Jesus is offering himself as a wellspring of the Holy Spirit, or a source of spiritual refreshment.

In Jewish and Christian religious traditions water rituals may be used to cleanse the spirit. The Hebrew Bible prescribes a variety of ritual washings designed to return both body and spirit to a state of cleanliness. In the Christian New Testament, John the Baptist, a Jewish prophet whose ministry preceded that of Jesus, immersed his followers in flowing water to cultivate a change in their spirits. These **baptisms** in the river Jordan signified **repentance** and conferred the forgiveness of **sins**.

Easter Baptisms

Because of the close connections drawn between God and water in Hebrew scripture and religious culture, John's river baptisms may indeed have proved powerful spiritual experiences for his followers. The Christian baptisms later instituted by the Church also drew on biblical water symbolism. Christian baptism not only offered its participants the forgiveness of sins, but also signified their acceptance of a new relationship with God through Christ and bestowed upon them the presence of the Holy Spirit. Among the early Christians this ritual required three full immersions in water. Early Christian leaders were quick to interpret these immersions as a form of spiritual death and rebirth. This interpretation drew on the water symbolism established in the Bible in which God both destroys and creates with water. In biblical spirituality God not only acts through water, but also God acts like water. This symbolic equation may well have given early Christian baptismal candidates a heightened sense of the baptismal drenchings as an act of giving oneself over to God.

The early Christian interpretation of baptism as a kind of spiritual death and rebirth also relied heavily on the parallels drawn between it and the death and **resurrection** of Christ (Romans 6:3-4). Thus baptism signified the end of the convert's old life and the beginning of a new one as a follower of Jesus Christ. Early Christians emphasized this comparison by baptizing new members into the faith during the **Easter Vigil**, the late-night service on **Holy Saturday** which commemorated Jesus' death and resurrection. Today Easter still serves as a traditional time for baptisms in a number of Christian denominations.

Easter Water Customs

In addition to baptism, a number of other water-related rites and customs take place at Easter time. These practices also draw on established Christian and folk symbolism concerning water. On **Maundy Thursday** many Roman Catholic and Episcopalian churches observe an ancient **footwashing** rite called the *mandatum*, from the Latin word for "command." This custom echoes Jesus' profound act of humility in washing the feet of his followers at the Last Supper as well as his commandment that his followers wash one another's feet (*for more on Last Supper, see* Maundy Thursday). On Holy Saturday many Roman Catholic churches distribute holy water (specially blessed water) to their parishioners. The parishioners take this Easter water with them and use it to impart blessings on themselves, their families, and their homes. Finally, every **Sunday** in churches throughout the world water is used to prepare the **Eucharist**. In this ceremony, which commemorates Christ's words and deeds at the Last Supper, members of the congregation come forward for a sip of **wine** mixed with water.

Old European folk beliefs suggest that all running water receives God's blessing on **Easter Sunday** in commemoration of the Resurrection. In the Middle Ages women of central and eastern Europe washed their faces in streams and rivers on Easter Sunday to receive this blessing (*see also* **Czech Republic, Easter and Holy Week in**). This custom was also known in France and was eventually transported to French Canada. In Germany old folk traditions recommended that horses be led into flowing waters on Easter Sunday as a means of insuring their good health (*see also* **Germany, Easter and Holy Week in**). Folk traditions popular throughout Europe advised people to visit a body of flowing water on Easter in order to collect and save a bottle of nature's own Easter water. Many people believed this Easter water had healing powers. Throughout Europe people blessed their farm animals with this water. In Austria and Germany couples on their way to be wed sprinkled one another with drops of Easter water. Irish folklore suggested that Easter water could protect against witches and other evil creatures (*for more Easter water customs, see* **Easter Monday**; *for more on witches, see* **Easter Witch**).

Further Reading

Ball, Ann. *A Handbook of Catholic Sacramentals*. Huntington, IN: Our Sunday Visitor, 1991.

Bird, Phyllis A. "Water." In Paul J. Achtemeier, ed. *The HarperCollins Bible Dictionary*. New York: HarperCollins, 1996.

Cavendish, Richard. "Water." In his *Man, Myth and Magic*. Volume 20. New York: Marshall Cavendish, 1997.

Eliade, Mircea. *Patterns in Comparative Religion*. Cleveland, OH: Meridian, 1963.

Gratsch, E. J. "Water." In *New Catholic Encyclopedia*. Volume 14. New York: McGraw-Hill, 1967.

Jenney, Timothy P. "Water." In David Noel Freedman, ed. *Eerdmans Dictionary of the Bible*. Grand Rapids, MI: William B. Eerdmans Publishing, 2000.

Niemann, Paul J. *The Lent, Triduum, and Easter Answer Book*. San Jose, CA: Resource Publications, 1998.

Rattue, James. *The Living Stream: Holy Wells in Historical Context*. Rochester, NY: Boydell Press, 1995.

Rees, Elizabeth. *Christian Symbols, Ancient Roots*. London, England: Jessica Kingsley, 1992.

"Water." In Leland Ryken, James C. Wilhoit, and Tremper Longman III, eds. *Dictionary of Biblical Imagery*. Downers Grove, IL: InterVarsity Press, 1998.

Weiser, Francis X. *The Easter Book*. New York: Harcourt, Brace and Company, 1954.

Whitsun Ale

In late medieval and Renaissance England some parish churches financed themselves by holding church ales. These community parties, held at the local church, featured the sale of beer brewed specially for the occasion. Sometimes the parties included food as well. Most church ales were held on holidays and so provided people a way to celebrate as well as furnishing the local church with needed income. These events took place most frequently at Whitsuntide (**Pentecost** and the week that followed), but might also occur around Easter, **May Day**, Christmas, and on patron saint days. The English often referred to Pentecost as Whitsunday, so these Pentecost parties became known as Whitsun ales.

One writer of the time described a Whitsun ale in Cornwall (southwestern England) as follows:

> For the church-ale, two young men of the parish are yerely chosen by their last foregoers to be wardens, who, dividing the task make collection among the parishioners, of whatso-

ever provision it pleaseth them voluntarily to bestow. This they employ in brewing, baking, and other acates [purchased provisions], against Whitsuntide, upon which holidays the neighbours met at the church house, and there merily feed on their owne victuals, each contributing some petty portion to the stock, which, by many smalls, groweth to a meetly greatness; for there is entertayned a kind of emulation between these wardens, who, by his graciousness in gathering, and good husbandry in expending, can best advance the churche's profit. Besides, the neighbour parishes at those times lovingly visit one another, and frankly spend their money together. The afternoons are consumed in such exercises as olde and yonge folk (having leysure) doe accustomably weare out the time withall. When the feast is ended, the wardens yeeld in their accounts to the parishioners; and such money as exceedeth the disbursement is layd up in store, to defray any extraordinary charges arising in the parish, or imposed on them for the good of the countrey or the prince's service; neither of which commonly gripe so much, but that somewhat stil remayneth to cover the purse's bottom.

(Hackwood, 51-52)

In the sixteenth century a religious reform movement known as the Protestant Reformation gave birth to Protestant Christianity. In England one of the new sects, a group of conservative Protestants called Puritans, objected to many folk customs connected with holiday celebrations, among them church ales. They denounced the events as irreverent intrusions onto holy ground that encouraged drunkenness, disorder, and sexual misconduct. Their campaign against Whitsun ales may have dampened England's enthusiasm for the events. The decline of the Whitsun ale was secured, however, by the fact that by the late seventeenth century church ales had ceased to be an important source of parish funding. Although churches stopped sponsoring these events, people in many parishes continued to gather together for a Whitsun feast, which they organized and paid for themselves.

641

Further Reading

Hackwood, Frederick W. *Inns, Ales, and Drinking Customs of Old England.* London, England: T. Fisher Unwin, 1909.

Hutton, Ronald. *Stations of the Sun.* Oxford, England: Oxford University Press, 1996.

Wine

The Christian ceremony known as the **Eucharist** commemorates the events that took place at the Last Supper (*for more on the Last Supper, see* **Maundy Thursday**). Christian scripture offers several accounts of this supper, **Jesus'** last meal before his death (Matthew 26:26-30, Mark 14:22-26, Luke 22:14-20). At this meal, which many believe to have been a **Passover** Seder, Jesus took **bread**, identified it as his body and passed it to his disciples to eat. Then he gave them wine, which he told them was his **blood**. Today Christians reenact this meal in a church ceremony known as the Eucharist or the Lord's Supper. In this ceremony worshipers take a sip of wine and a bite of bread identified as Jesus' body and blood (*see also* **Good Friday**). Before serving the wine to the congregation, clergy members mix it with **water**. This mixture of water and wine represents Jesus' blood to contemporary worshipers, just as it did to Jesus' disciples at the Last Supper. Today some Protestant churches substitute grape juice for wine.

Wine as an Ancient and Modern Jewish Symbol

The Bible presents wine in a positive light. The Psalmist praises God for the gift of wine, which can "gladden the heart" (Psalm 104:15). Indeed wine is often served at celebrations. In general the Bible associates wine with well-being, joy, and blessings. These associations still permeate the celebration of the Jewish Sabbath (*for more on Sabbath, see* **Sunday**). This home religious observance focuses around the evening meal, turning it into a special occasion for expressing one's gratitude to God and for rejoicing with one's family. At the start of the meal the oldest male present recites a prayer of blessing over a full cup of wine. The cup is then passed around the table so that everyone may take a sip of the blessed wine.

Various passages in the Hebrew scriptures, or Old Testament, compare wine with blood. One such passage describes wine as the "blood of grapes" (Genesis 49:11). Blood was an important element in ancient Jewish religious sacrifices. It was offered in acceptance of covenants, or agreements, between God and humanity, as well as in seeking atonement, or reconciliation, with God (*see also* **Sin**; **Redemption**). The ancient Jews also offered wine in certain religious sacrifices. Therefore, when Jesus used wine to represent his blood at the Last Supper, he was drawing on religious imagery that would have been familiar to his followers. Wine is still an important element in the Jewish Passover Seder, where it accompanies blessings and hymns.

Wine and Water

Throughout the ancient Mediterranean world people drank wine on a daily basis, often mixed with water. Among the Romans as well as the Jews an everyday mealtime beverage consisted of two or three parts water to one part of wine. Some scholars believe that this everyday mixture was used at religious rituals as well. Thus the wine served at Passover celebrations was mixed with water as was the wine served at early Christian celebrations of the Eucharist.

This mixture of wine and water also recalls passages from Christian scripture. The Gospel according to John declares that after Jesus died a Roman soldier pierced his side with a spear, bringing forth a flow of "blood and water" (John 19:34). The appearance of water as well as blood may have symbolic significance, since throughout the New Testament, and especially in the writings of John, water imagery is used to describe the workings or the presence of God's Holy Spirit. In the third century St. Cyprian came up with a theological interpretation of the eucharistic formula of wine and water. He declared that the wine represented Christ, the water his followers, and the mixture of the two their union. Other commentators drew links between the miracle at the wedding in Cana, where Jesus turned water into wine (John 2:1-11), and the eucharistic practice of mixing wine and water.

Wine Controversies

In nineteenth-century America members of a number of evangelical Protestant denominations, such as the Methodists, Baptists, and Disciples of Christ, began to criticize what they saw as the widespread abuse of wine and other alcoholic beverages in American society. In sermons, speeches, and written documents they denounced wine and spirits as evil influences which led those who consumed them towards violence, poverty, familial discord, and other forms of social and moral decay. Many of these people also believed that drinking wine and other alcoholic beverages undermined one's physical health. Religious figures from these denominations beseeched their followers to abstain from all alcoholic beverages. Eventually these negative attitudes towards wine led clergy in many evangelical Protestant denominations to substitute grape juice for wine in the celebration of the Eucharist. This change reflects the depth of their alarm since it directly contradicts Christian scripture. In the Bible passages concerning the Last Supper Jesus clearly identifies his blood as "wine."

Their fervent dislike and distrust of alcohol led many evangelical Protestants to campaign for laws making it difficult or impossible for anyone to obtain alcoholic beverages. By the 1920s social reformers who supported this agenda had succeeded in bringing about a national Prohibition law. During the Prohibition era (1920-33) the eighteenth amendment to the Constitution of the United States made the production and sale of alcoholic beverages illegal throughout the land. An exception was made for wine used for religious rituals, such as the Eucharist, however. So throughout the Prohibition era Roman Catholics, Episcopalians, Lutherans, and other Christians who wished to maintain the use of wine in the celebration of the Eucharist continued to do so.

Although the eighteenth amendment to the Constitution was repealed in 1933, some evangelical Protestants continued to speak out against the evils of alcohol. As a result many evangelical Protestant and other churches still serve grape juice instead of wine in their celebrations of the Eucharist.

Further Reading

"Blood." In Leland Ryken, James C. Wilhoit, and Tremper Longman III, eds. *Dictionary of Biblical Imagery*. Downers Grove, IL: InterVarsity Press, 1998.

Cole, R. Dennis. "Wine." In David Noel Freedman, ed. *Eerdmans Dictionary of the Bible*. Grand Rapids, MI: William B. Eerdmans Publishing, 2000.

Ferguson, Everett. "Wine." In his *Encyclopedia of Early Christianity*. Volume 2. New York: Garland, 1997.

Fuller, Robert C. *Religion and Wine: A Cultural History of Wine Drinking in the United States*. Knoxville, TN: University of Tennessee Press, 1996.

Jenney, Timothy P. "Water." In David Noel Freedman, ed. *Eerdmans Dictionary of the Bible*. Grand Rapids, MI: William B. Eerdmans Publishing, 2000.

Myers, Allen C., ed. "Wine." In *The Eerdmans Bible Dictionary*. Grand Rapids, MI: William B. Eerdmans Publishing, 1987.

"Wine." In Leland Ryken, James C. Wilhoit, and Tremper Longman III, eds. *Dictionary of Biblical Imagery*. Downers Grove, IL: InterVarsity Press, 1998.

Bibliography

This biliography lists all books and articles consulted for this volume.

Abbas, Jailan. *Festivals of Egypt*. Cairo, Egypt: Hoopoe Books, 1995.

Achelis, Elisabeth. *The Calendar for Everybody*. 1943. Reprint. Detroit, MI: Omnigraphics, 1990.

Achtemeier, Paul J., ed. *The HarperCollins Bible Dictionary*. New York: HarperCollins, 1996.

Aivazian, Sirarpi Feredjian. "Pilgrimage: Eastern Christian Pilgrimage." In Mircea Eliade, ed. *Encyclopedia of Religion*. Volume 11. New York: Macmillan, 1987.

"Alleluia." In E. A. Livingstone, ed. *The Oxford Dictionary of the Christian Church*. Third edition. Oxford, England: Oxford University Press, 1997.

Alston, G. Cyprian. "Judica Sunday." In Charles G. Herbermann et al., eds. *The Catholic Encyclopedia*. New York: Appleton, 1913. Available online at: http://www.newadvent.org/cathen/08553a.htm

Alsup, John E. "Redemption." In Paul J. Achtemeier, ed. *The HarperCollins Bible Dictionary*. New York: HarperCollins, 1996.

————. "Salvation." In Paul J. Achtemeier, ed. *The HarperCollins Bible Dictionary*. New York: HarperCollins, 1996.

Angebert, Jean-Michel. *The Occult and the Third Reich*. Trans. by Lewis A. M. Sumberg. New York: Macmillan, 1974.

Arpon, Alvin Gz. "Pamalandong: Good Friday in Palo." *Philippines Today* 3 (June 2000). Available online at: http://www.pia.ops.gov.ph/philtoday/pt03/pt0316/htm

"Ascension of Christ." In E. A. Livingstone, ed. *The Oxford Dictionary of the Christian Church*. Third edition. Oxford, England: Oxford University Press, 1997.

"Ash Wednesday." In E. A. Livingstone, ed. *The Oxford Dictionary of the Christian Church*. Third edition. Oxford, England: Oxford University Press, 1997.

"Ashes." In Leland Ryken, James C. Wilhoit, and Tremper Longman III, eds. *Dictionary of Biblical Imagery*. Downers Grove, IL: InterVarsity Press, 1998.

"Atonement." In E. A. Livingstone, ed. *The Oxford Dictionary of the Christian Church*. Third edition. Oxford, England: Oxford University Press, 1997.

Aveni, Anthony. *Empires of Time*. New York: Kodansha Books, 1995.

Bailey, Henry Turner. *Symbolism for Artists*. 1925. Reprint. Detroit, MI: Gale Research, 1972.

Baldovin, John F. "Easter." In Mircea Eliade, ed. *The Encyclopedia of Religion*. Volume 4. New York: Macmillan, 1987.

Ball, Ann. *A Handbook of Catholic Sacramentals*. Huntington, IN: Our Sunday Visitor, 1991.

Bare, Colleen Stanley. *Rabbits and Hares*. New York: Dodd, Mead and Company, 1983.

Baring-Gould, Sabine. *Curious Myths of the Middle Ages*. 1866-68. Reprint. New York: University Books, 1957.

Barth, Edna. *Lilies, Rabbits, and Painted Eggs*. New York: Houghton Mifflin/Clarion Books, 1970.

Beals, Katharine M. *Flower Lore and Legend*. 1917. Reprint. Detroit, MI: Gale Research, 1973.

Becker, Udo. "Butterfly." In his *The Continuum Encyclopedia of Symbols*. New York: Continuum, 1994.

———. "Hare." In his *The Continuum Encyclopedia of Symbols*. New York: Continuum, 1994.

———. "Palm Tree." In his *The Continuum Encyclopedia of Symbols*. New York: Continuum, 1994.

———. "Tree, Tree Cross." In his *The Continuum Encyclopedia of Symbols*. New York: Continuum, 1994.

Bellenir, Karen. *Religious Holidays and Calendars*. Second edition. Detroit, MI: Omnigraphics, 1998.

Bigelow, A. L. "Bells." In *New Catholic Encyclopedia*. Volume 2. New York: McGraw-Hill, 1967.

Billson, Chas. J. "The Easter Hare." *Folk-Lore* 3, 4 (1892): 441-66.

Bird, Phyllis A. "Water." In Paul J. Achtemeier, ed. *The HarperCollins Bible Dictionary*. New York: HarperCollins, 1996.

Black, William George. "The Hare in Folk-Lore." *Folk-Lore Journal* 1, 1 (1883): 84-90.

Blackburn, Bonnie, and Leofranc Holford-Strevens. *The Oxford Companion to the Year*. Oxford, England: Oxford University Press, 1999.

Bloch, Abraham P. *The Biblical and Archeological Background of the Jewish Holy Days*. New York: Ktav, 1978.

"Blood." In Leland Ryken, James C. Wilhoit, and Tremper Longman III, eds. *Dictionary of Biblical Imagery*. Downers Grove, IL: InterVarsity Press, 1998.

Borg, Marcus J. *Meeting Jesus Again for the First Time*. New York: HarperSanFrancisco, 1994.

Borg, Marcus J., and N. T. Wright. *The Meaning of Jesus: Two Visions*. New York: HarperSanFrancisco, 1998.

Bradshaw, Paul F. *The Search for the Origins of Christian Worship*. New York: Oxford University Press, 1992.

―――. "Easter in Christian Tradition." In Paul F. Bradshaw and Lawrence A. Hoffman, eds. *Easter and Passover: Origin and History to Modern Times*. Two Liturgical Traditions series, volume 5. Notre Dame, IN: University of Notre Dame Press, 1999.

―――. "The Origins of Easter." In Paul F. Bradshaw and Lawrence A. Hoffman, eds. *Passover and Easter: Origin and History to Modern Times*. Two Liturgical Traditions series, volume 5. Notre Dame, IN: University of Notre Dame Press, 1999.

Bradshaw, Paul F., and Lawrence A. Hoffman, eds. *Passover and Easter: Origin and History to Modern Times*. Two Liturgical Traditions series, volume 5. Notre Dame, IN: University of Notre Dame Press, 1999.

―――. *Passover and Easter: The Symbolic Structuring of Sacred Seasons*. Two Liturgical Traditions series, volume 6. Notre Dame, IN: University of Notre Dame Press, 1999.

Bram, Jean Rhys. "Moon." In Mircea Eliade, ed. *The Encyclopedia of Religion*. Volume 10. New York: Macmillan, 1987.

Brewster, H. Pomeroy. *Saints and Festivals of the Christian Church*. 1904. Reprint. Detroit, MI: Omnigraphics, 1990.

Brophy, James M. "Mirth and Subversion: Carnival in Cologne." *History Today* 47, 7 (1997): 42-48.

Brown, Raymond. *The Death of the Messiah*. New York and London: Doubleday and Geoffrey Chapman, 1994.

Brownrigg, Ronald. *The Twelve Apostles*. New York: Macmillan, 1974.

Burdeau, Cain. "Mardi Gras' Excesses Rain on Locals' Parade." *Christian Science Monitor* (February 26, 2001): 3.

Byrne, Lavinia. "Confronting the Truth Over Coffee with Christ." *Financial Times* (June 17-18, 2000): 9.

Cabrol, Fernand. "Octave." In Charles G. Herbermann et al., eds. *The Catholic Encyclopedia*. New York: Appleton, 1913. Available online at: http://www.newadvent.org/cathen/11204a.htm

Cain, Kathleen. *Luna: Myth and Mystery*. Boulder, CO: Johnson Books, 1991.

Carey, Greg. "Emmaus." In David Noel Freedman, ed. *Eerdmans Dictionary of the Bible*. Grand Rapids, MI: William B. Eerdmans Publishing, 2000.

Carlston, Charles E. "Jesus Christ." In Paul J. Achtemeier, ed. *The Harper-Collins Bible Dictionary*. New York: HarperCollins, 1996.

Casanova, Gertrude. "Walburga, St." In Charles G. Herbermann et al., eds. *The Catholic Encyclopedia*. New York: Appleton, 1913. Available online at: http://www.newadvent.org/cathen/15526b.htm

Cavendish, Richard. "Hare." In his *Man, Myth and Magic*. Volume 8, New York: Marshall Cavendish, 1997.

———. "Water." In his *Man, Myth and Magic*. Volume 20. New York: Marshall Cavendish, 1997.

Chambers, Robert. *The Book of Days*. 2 volumes. 1862-64. Reprint. Detroit, MI: Omnigraphics, 1990.

Cheney, Emily. "Pilate, Pontius." In David Noel Freedman, ed. *Eerdmans Dictionary of the Bible*. Grand Rapids, MI: William B. Eerdmans Publishing, 2000.

Child, Heather, and Dorothy Colles. *Christian Symbols, Ancient and Modern*. New York: Charles Scribner's Sons, 1972.

Chirat, H. "Cross, Finding of the Holy." In *New Catholic Encyclopedia*. Volume 4. New York: McGraw-Hill, 1967.

Christianson, Stephen G., ed. *The American Book of Days*. Fourth edition. New York: H. W. Wilson, 2000.

Cirlot, J. E. *A Dictionary of Symbols*. New York: Barnes and Noble Books, 1993.

Clancy, P. M. J. "Fast and Abstinence." In *New Catholic Encyclopedia*. Volume 5. New York: McGraw-Hill, 1967.

Clark, Cindy Dell. *Flights of Fancy, Leaps of Faith*. Chicago: University of Chicago Press, 1995.

Clement, Clara Erskine. *A Handbook of Christian Symbols*. 1886. Reprint. Detroit, MI: Gale Research, 1971.

Clynes, Tom. *Wild Planet!* Detroit, MI: Gale Research, 1995.

Coble, Ann. "Lord's Day" and "Sabbath." In David Noel Freedman, ed. *Eerdmans Dictionary of the Bible*. Grand Rapids, MI: William B. Eerdmans Publishing, 2000.

Cohen, Hennig, and Tristram Potter Coffin, eds. *The Folklore of American Holidays*. Third edition. Detroit, MI: Gale, 1999.

Cole, R. Dennis. "Wine." In David Noel Freedman, ed. *Eerdmans Dictionary of the Bible*. Grand Rapids, MI: William B. Eerdmans Publishing, 2000.

Coleman, Satis N. *Bells, Their History, Legends, Making, and Uses*. 1928. Reprint. Detroit, MI: Tower Books/Gale, 1971.

Collins, Adela Yabro. "Lord's Day." In Paul J. Achtemeier, ed. *The Harper-Collins Bible Dictionary*. New York: HarperCollins, 1996.

Conte, Jeanne. "Passion 2000: Oberammergau's Easter Play." *The World and I* 15, 4 (April 2000): 175.

Cooper, J. C. *The Dictionary of Festivals*. London, England: Thorsons, 1990.

———. *An Illustrated Encyclopedia of Traditional Symbols*. London, England: Thames and Hudson, 1978.

Copan, Paul, ed. *Will the Real Jesus Please Stand Up? A Debate Between William Lane Craig and John Dominic Crossan*. Grand Rapids, MI: Baker, 1998.

Cowie, L. W., and John Selwyn Gummer. *The Christian Calendar*. Springfield, MA: G. and C. Merriam, 1974.

"Cross." In Richard Cavendish, ed. *Man, Myth and Magic*. Volume 4. New York: Marshall Cavendish, 1997.

Crossan, John Dominic. *Jesus: A Revolutionary Biography*. San Francisco, CA: HarperSanFrancisco, 1994.

Crossan, John Dominic [Dominic M.]. "Barabbas." In *New Catholic Encyclopedia*. Volume 2. New York: McGraw-Hill, 1967.

Davids, Peter H. "Peter." In David Noel Freedman, ed. *Eerdmans Dictionary of the Bible*. Grand Rapids, MI: William B. Eerdmans Publishing, 2000.

Davies, J. G. "The Origins of Holy Week and Its Development in the Middle Ages." In C. P. M. Jones, ed. *A Manual for Holy Week*. London, England: Society for Promoting Christian Knowledge, 1967.

Degert, Antoine. "St. Veronica." In Charles G. Herbermann et al., eds. *The Catholic Encyclopedia*. New York: Appleton, 1913. Available online at: http://www.newadvent.org/cathen/15362a.htm

Downman, Lorna, Paul Britten Austin, and Anthony Baird. *Round the Swedish Year*. Stockholm, Sweden: Bokförlaget Fabel, 1961.

"Drama, Christian." In E. A. Livingstone, ed. *The Oxford Dictionary of the Christian Church*. Third edition. Oxford, England: Oxford University Press, 1997.

Duncan, David Ewing. *Calendar*. New York: Avon, 1998.

Dunn, E. C. "Passion Play." In *New Catholic Encyclopedia*. Volume 10. New York: McGraw-Hill, 1967.

"East." In Leland Ryken, James C. Wilhoit, and Tremper Longman III, eds. *Dictionary of Biblical Imagery*. Downers Grove, IL: InterVarsity Press, 1998.

"Easter." In E. A. Livingstone, ed. *The Oxford Dictionary of the Christian Church*. Third edition. Oxford, England: Oxford University Press, 1997.

Edsman, Carl-Martin. "Fire." In Mircea Eliade, ed. *The Encyclopedia of Religion*. Volume 5. New York: Macmillan, 1987.

Efird, James M. "Sin." In Paul J. Achtemeier, ed. *The HarperCollins Bible Dictionary*. New York: HarperCollins, 1996.

Eisenberg, Azriel. *The Story of the Jewish Calendar*. New York: Abelard-Schuman, 1958.

Eliade, Mircea. *Patterns in Comparative Religion*. Cleveland, OH: Meridian, 1963.

Eliade, Mircea, ed. *The Encyclopedia of Religion*. 16 volumes. New York: Macmillan, 1987.

Ellis, Royston. *Festivals of the World: Trinidad*. Milwaukee, WI: Gareth Stevens, 1999.

Epton, Nina. *Spanish Fiestas*. New York: A. S. Barnes and Company, 1968.

Espinosa, Aurelio. "Hermanos Penitentes, Los." In Charles G. Herbermann et al., eds. *The Catholic Encyclopedia*. New York: Appleton, 1913. Available online at: http://www.newadvent.org/cathen/11635c.htm

Evans, E. P. *Animal Symbolism in Ecclesiastical Architecture*. 1896. Reprint. Detroit, MI: Gale Research, 1969.

Evans, Larry L. "To Soften the Path: Sawdust Carpets in Guatemala's Easter Celebrations." *The World and I* 10, 4 (1995): 240.

Every, George. *Christian Legends*. New York: Peter Bedrick Books, 1987.

Ewert, Neil. *The Lore of Flowers*. Poole, Dorset, England: Blandford Press, 1982.

"Fasting." In Leland Ryken, James C. Wilhoit, and Tremper Longman III, eds. *Dictionary of Biblical Imagery*. Downers Grove, IL: InterVarsity Press, 1998.

"Fasts and Fasting." In E. A. Livingstone, ed. *The Oxford Dictionary of the Christian Church*. Third edition. Oxford, England: Oxford University Press, 1997.

"Feet." In Leland Ryken, James C. Wilhoit, and Tremper Longman III, eds. *Dictionary of Biblical Imagery*. Downers Grove, IL: InterVarsity Press, 1998.

Fellner, Judith B. *In the Jewish Tradition*. New York: Smithmark, 1995.

Ferguson, Everett. "Baptism" and "Baptistery." In his *Encyclopedia of Early Christianity*. Volume 1. New York: Garland, 1997.

———. "Bread." In his *Encyclopedia of Early Christianity*. Volume 1. New York: Garland, 1997.

———. "Eucharist." In his *Encyclopedia of Early Christianity*. Volume 1. New York: Garland, 1997.

———. "Footwashing." In his *Encyclopedia of Early Christianity*. Volume 1. New York: Garland, 1997.

———. "Wine." In his *Encyclopedia of Early Christianity*. Volume 2. New York: Garland, 1997.

Festivals and Holidays. New York: Macmillan, 1999.

Field, Carol. *Celebrating Italy*. New York: William Morrow and Company, 1990.

Finn, Thomas. "Pasch, Paschal Controversy." In Everett Ferguson, ed. *Encyclopedia of Early Christianity*. Volume 2. New York: Garland, 1997.

"Fire." In Leland Ryken, James C. Wilhoit, and Tremper Longman III, eds. *Dictionary of Biblical Imagery*. Downers Grove, IL: InterVarsity Press, 1998.

Fitzmyer, Joseph A. "Messiah." In Paul J. Achtemeier, ed. *The HarperCollins Bible Dictionary*. New York: HarperCollins, 1996.

Flake, Carol. *New Orleans*. New York: Grove Press, 1994.

Flanagan, N. M. "Judas Iscariot." In *New Catholic Encyclopedia*. Volume 8. New York: McGraw-Hill, 1967.

Frazer, James George. *The New Golden Bough*. Theodor H. Gaster, ed. New York: S. G. Phillips, 1959.

Fuller, Reginald H. "Resurrection." In Paul J. Achtemeier, ed. *The HarperCollins Bible Dictionary*. New York: HarperCollins, 1996.

———. "Savior." In Paul J. Achtemeier, ed. *The HarperCollins Bible Dictionary*. New York: HarperCollins, 1996.

———. "Son of God." In Paul J. Achtemeier, ed. *The HarperCollins Bible Dictionary*. New York: HarperCollins, 1996.

Fuller, Robert C. *Religion and Wine: A Cultural History of Wine Drinking in the United States*. Knoxville, TN: University of Tennessee Press, 1996.

Gallaher Branch, Robin, and Lee E. Klosinsky. "Son." In David Noel Freedman, ed. *Eerdmans Dictionary of the Bible*. Grand Rapids, MI: William B. Eerdmans Publishing, 2000.

Gammie, John G. "Fasting." In Paul J. Achtemeier, ed. *The HarperCollins Bible Dictionary*. New York: HarperCollins, 1996.

García-Treto, Francisco O. "Pilate Pontius." In Paul J. Achtemeier, ed. *The HarperCollins Bible Dictionary*. New York: HarperCollins, 1996.

Garrett, Linda Oaks. "Repentance." In David Noel Freedman, ed. *Eerdmans Dictionary of the Bible*. Grand Rapids, MI: William B. Eerdmans Publishing, 2000.

Gaventa, Beverly Roberts. "Mary." In David Noel Freedman, ed. *Eerdmans Dictionary of the Bible*. Grand Rapids, MI: William B. Eerdmans Publishing, 2000.

Gelling, Peter, and Hilda Ellis Davidson. *The Chariot of the Sun*. New York: Frederick A. Praeger, 1969.

Gill, James. *The Lords of Misrule*. Jackson, MS: University of Mississippi Press, 1997.

"Golden Rose." In E. A. Livingstone, ed. *The Oxford Dictionary of the Christian Church*. Third edition. Oxford, England: Oxford University Press, 1997.

Goldsmith, Elisabeth. *Ancient Pagan Symbols*. 1929. Reprint. Detroit, MI: Gale Research, 1976.

Goldwasser, Maria Julia. "Carnival." In Mircea Eliade, ed. *The Encyclopedia of Religion*. Volume 3. New York: Macmillan, 1987.

Goodenough, Erwin R. *Jewish Symbols in the Greco-Roman Period*. Volume 8. New York: Pantheon Books, 1958.

Goodman, Philip. *The Shavuot Anthology*. Philadelphia, PA: Jewish Publication Society of America, 1974.

Grant, Michael. *Saint Peter*. New York: Scribner, 1995.

Gratsch, E. J. "Water." In *New Catholic Encyclopedia*. Volume 14. New York: McGraw-Hill, 1967.

Greene, Debra Illingworth. "Easter: Promise of New Life." *The Lutheran* (April 1999). Available online at: http://www.thelutheran.org/9904/page35.html

Griffin, Robert H., and Ann H. Shurgin, eds. *The Folklore of World Holidays*. Second edition. Detroit, MI: Gale Research, 1999.

———. *Junior Worldmark Encyclopedia of World Holidays*. Volumes 1 and 2. Detroit, MI: UXL, 2000.

Grimal, Pierre. *Dictionary of Classical Mythology*. A. R. Maxwell-Hyslop, translator. Oxford, England: Blackwell Reference, 1985.

Gulevich, Tanya. *Encyclopedia of Christmas*. Detroit, MI: Omnigraphics, 2000.

Hackwood, Frederick W. *Christ Lore*. 1902. Reprint. Detroit, MI: Gale Research, 1969.

———. *Inns, Ales, and Drinking Customs of Old England*. London, England: T. Fisher Unwin, 1909.

Hark, Max J. "Moravian Sunrise Service." In Alfred Shoemaker's *Easter in Pennsylvania*. Kutztown, PA: Pennsylvania Folklife Society, 1961.

Bibliography

Harper, Howard. *Days and Customs of All Faiths.* 1957. Reprint. Detroit, MI: Omnigraphics, 1990.

Harrowven, Jean. *Origins of Festivals and Feasts.* London, England: Kaye and Ward, 1980.

Hartnoll, Phyllis, ed. *The Oxford Companion to the Theatre.* Fourth edition. Oxford, England: Oxford University Press, 1983.

Harvey, John D. "Redemption." In David Noel Freedman, ed. *Eerdmans Dictionary of the Bible.* Grand Rapids, MI: William B. Eerdmans Publishing, 2000.

Harvey, Steenie. "Season of the Witch." *The World and I* 16, 4 (April 2001): 260.

Haskins, Susan. *Mary Magdalene: Myth and Metaphor.* New York: Harcourt Brace and Company, 1993.

Hatchett, Marion J. *Commentary on the American Prayer Book.* New York: HarperSanFrancisco, 1995.

Heath, Sidney. *The Romance of Symbolism.* 1909. Reprint. Detroit, MI: Gale Research, 1976.

Hellwig, Monica K. "Eucharist." In Mircea Eliade, ed. *The Encyclopedia of Religion.* Volume 5. New York: Macmillan, 1987.

Henderson, Helene, and Sue Ellen Thompson, eds. *Holidays, Festivals, and Celebrations of the World Dictionary.* Second edition. Detroit, MI: Omnigraphics, 1997.

Hill, Errol. *The Trinidad Carnival.* Austin, TX: University of Texas Press, 1972.

Hinson, E. Glenn. "Fasting." In Everett Ferguson, ed. *Encyclopedia of Early Christianity.* Volume 1. New York: Garland, 1997.

Hodgkins, William. *Sunday — Christian and Social Significance.* London, England: Independent Press, 1960.

Hogan, Julie. *Treasury of Easter Celebrations.* Nashville, TN: Ideals Publications, 1999.

Hole, Christina. *British Folk Customs.* London, England: Hutchinson and Company, 1976.

———. *Easter and Its Customs.* New York: M. Barrows and Company, 1961.

———. *English Custom and Usage.* 1941-2. Reprint. Detroit, MI: Omnigraphics, 1990.

Holweck, F. G. "Feasts of the Seven Sorrows of the Blessed Virgin Mary." In Charles G. Herbermann et al., eds. *The Catholic Encyclopedia.* New York: Appleton, 1913. Available online at: http://www.newadvent.org/cathen/1415b.htm

Bibliography

"Holy Week." In E. A. Livingstone, ed. *The Oxford Dictionary of the Christian Church*. Third edition. Oxford, England: Oxford University Press, 1997.

Hopko, Thomas. *The Lenten Spring*. Crestwood, NY: St. Vladimir's Seminary Press, 1998.

———. *The Orthodox Faith. Volume Two, Worship*. Syosset, NY: The Orthodox Church in America, 1972.

Hopley, Claire. "Lenten Delights." *The World and I* 16, 3 (March 2001): 112.

Horsley, Richard A., and Neil Asher Silberman. *The Message and the Kingdom*. New York: Grosset/Putnam, 1997.

"Hospitality." In Leland Ryken, James C. Wilhoit, and Tremper Longman III, eds. *Dictionary of Biblical Imagery*. Downers Grove, IL: InterVarsity Press, 1998.

Howard, Alexander. *Endless Cavalcade*. London, England: Arthur Barker, 1964.

Hudgins, Sharon. "Breads for Christ." *The World and I* 14, 4 (1999): 162.

———. "A Special Flock." *The World and I* 15, 4 (2000): 134.

Hulme, F. Edward. *The History, Principles and Practice of Symbolism in Christian Art*. 1891. Reprint. Detroit, MI: Gale Research, 1969.

Hutton, Ronald. *The Pagan Religions of the Ancient British Isles*. Oxford, England: Blackwell, 1993.

———. *Stations of the Sun*. Oxford, England: Oxford University Press, 1996.

Ince, Sarah. *The Magical Year*. Richmond, VA: Time-Life Books, 1992.

Ingersoll, Ernest. *Birds in Legend, Fable and Folklore*. 1923. Reprint. Detroit, MI: Singing Tree Press, 1968.

Jacobs, Louis. "Passover." In Mircea Eliade, ed. *The Encyclopedia of Religion*. Volume 11. New York: Macmillan, 1987.

James, E. O. *Seasonal Feasts and Festivals*. 1961. Reprint. Detroit, MI: Omnigraphics, 1993.

Jansen, Katherine Ludwig. *The Making of the Magdalene*. Princeton, NJ: Princeton University Press, 2000.

Jefford, Clayton N. "Sin." In David Noel Freedman, ed. *Eerdmans Dictionary of the Bible*. Grand Rapids, MI: William B. Eerdmans Publishing, 2000.

Jenney, Timothy P. "Water." In David Noel Freedman, ed. *Eerdmans Dictionary of the Bible*. Grand Rapids, MI: William B. Eerdmans Publishing, 2000.

"Jesus, Images of." In Leland Ryken, James C. Wilhoit, and Tremper Longman III, eds. *Dictionary of Biblical Imagery*. Downers Grove, IL: InterVarsity Press, 1998.

"Jesus Christ." In E. A. Livingstone, ed. *The Oxford Dictionary of the Christian Church*. Third edition. Oxford, England: Oxford University Press, 1997.

Johnson, E. "Easter and Its Cycle." In *New Catholic Encyclopedia*. Volume 5. New York: McGraw-Hill, 1967.

Johnson, Luke Timothy. *The Real Jesus: The Misguided Quest for the Historical Jesus and the Truth of the Traditional Gospels*. New York: HarperSanFrancisco, 1996.

Johnson, Maxwell E. "Preparation for Pascha? Lent in Christian Antiquity." In Paul F. Bradshaw and Lawrence A. Hoffman, eds. *Passover and Easter: The Symbolic Structuring of Sacred Seasons*. Two Liturgical Traditions series, volume 6. Notre Dame, IN: University of Notre Dame Press, 1999.

"Judas Iscariot." In E. A. Livingstone, ed. *The Oxford Dictionary of the Christian Church*. Third edition. Oxford, England: Oxford University Press, 1997.

Juel, Donald. "Christ." In David Noel Freedman, ed. *Eerdmans Dictionary of the Bible*. Grand Rapids, MI: William B. Eerdmans Publishing, 2000.

———. "Messiah." In David Noel Freedman, ed. *Eerdmans Dictionary of the Bible*. Grand Rapids, MI: William B. Eerdmans Publishing, 2000.

Kahane, Henry, and Renée Kahane. "Grail, The" In Mircea Eliade, ed. *The Encyclopedia of Religion*. Volume 6. New York: Macmillan, 1987.

Katzeff, Paul. *Full Moons*. Secaucus, NJ: Citadel Press, 1981.

Keck, Leander, ed. *New Interpreter's Bible*. Volume 9. Nashville, TN: Abingdon Press, 1995.

Kinser, Samuel. *Carnival American Style*. Chicago: University of Chicago Press, 1990.

Klagsbrun, Francine. *Jewish Days*. New York: Farrar, Straus, Giroux, 1996.

Klassen, William. *Judas, Betrayer or Friend of Jesus?* Minneapolis, MN: Fortress Press, 1996.

Knapp, Justina. *Christian Symbols and How to Use Them*. 1935. Reprint. Detroit, MI: Gale Research, 1974.

Krupp, E. C. *Beyond the Blue Horizon*. New York: HarperCollins, 1991.

Krysa, Czeslaw M. "How to 'Write' and [sic] Easter Egg. Pisanki Comes from the Polish Word 'Pisac,' Meaning 'to Write'." *Polish-American Journal* 86, 3 (March 1, 1997): 9. Available online at: http://www.polamjournal.com/ Library/Holidays/Easter/easter.html

Kselman, John S. "Easter." In Paul J. Achtemeier, ed. *The HarperCollins Bible Dictionary*. New York: HarperCollins, 1996.

Kuryluk, Ewa. *Veronica and Her Cloth: History, Symbolism and Structure of a "True" Image*. Cambridge, MA: Basil Blackwell, 1991.

"Laetare Sunday." In E. A. Livingstone, ed. *The Oxford Dictionary of the Christian Church*. Third edition. Oxford, England: Oxford University Press, 1997.

Lagerkvist, Pär. *Barabbas*. New York: Vintage Books, 1951.

"Lamb." In Leland Ryken, James C. Wilhoit, and Tremper Longman III, eds. *Dictionary of Biblical Imagery*. Downers Grove, IL: InterVarsity Press, 1998.

Latham, James E. "Bread." In Mircea Eliade, ed. *The Encyclopedia of Religion*. Volume 2. New York: Macmillan, 1987.

Lau, Alfred. *Carneval International*. Bielefeld, Germany: Univers-Verlag, n.d.

Lau, Theodora. *The Handbook of Chinese Horoscopes*. Third edition. New York: HarperPerennial, 1995.

Layard, John. *The Lady of the Hare*. 1944. Reprint. New York: AMS Press, 1977.

"Lazarus." In E. A. Livingstone, ed. *The Oxford Dictionary of the Christian Church*. Third edition. Oxford, England: Oxford University Press, 1997.

Leach, Maria, ed. *Funk and Wagnalls Standard Dictionary of Folklore, Mythology and Legend*. New York: Harper and Row, 1984.

Leclerq, H. "Maundy Thursday." In Charles G. Herbermann et al., eds. *The Catholic Encyclopedia*. New York: Appleton, 1913. Available online at: http://www.newadvent.org/cathen/10068a.htm

Lee, Tan Chung. *Festivals of the World: Finland*. Milwaukee, WI: Gareth Stevens Publishing, 1998.

Lehner, Ernst, and Johanna Lehner. *Folklore and Symbolism of Flowers, Plants and Trees*. 1960. Reprint. Detroit, MI: Omnigraphics, 1990.

"Lent." In E. A. Livingstone, ed. *The Oxford Dictionary of the Christian Church*. Third edition. Oxford, England: Oxford University Press, 1997.

Light, Gary W. "Salvation." In David Noel Freedman, ed. *Eerdmans Dictionary of the Bible*. Grand Rapids, MI: William B. Eerdmans Publishing, 2000.

"Light." In Leland Ryken, James C. Wilhoit, and Tremper Longman III, eds. *Dictionary of Biblical Imagery*. Downers Grove, IL: InterVarsity Press, 1998.

Livingstone, E. A., ed. *The Oxford Dictionary of the Christian Church*. Third edition. Oxford, England: Oxford University Press, 1997.

Lohman, Jon. "It Can't Rain Every Day: The Year-Round Experience of Carnival." *Western Folklore* 58, 3 (1999): 279-98.

Long, George. *The Folklore Calendar*. 1930. Reprint. Detroit, MI: Omnigraphics, 1990.

Lord, Priscilla Sawyer, and Daniel J. Foley. *Easter Garland*. 1963. Reprint. Detroit, MI: Omnigraphics, 1999.

———. *Easter the World Over*. Philadelphia, PA: Chilton Book Company, 1971.

Luciow, Johanna, Ann Kmit, and Loretta Luciow. *Eggs Beautiful: How to Make Ukrainian Easter Eggs*. Minneapolis, MN: Ukrainian Gift Shop, n.d.

Lyden, Jacki. "Analysis: Battle of the Oranges in Carnival Celebration in Italy." Weekend Edition, National Public Radio (March 12, 2000). Transcript available for a fee online at http://www.elibrary.com; audiotape of segment available at http://www.npr.org (search on "Battle of Oranges").

Lynch, J. E. "Fast and Abstinence." In *New Catholic Encyclopedia*. Volume 16. New York: McGraw-Hill, 1967.

Lyttelton, Margaret, and Werner Forman. *The Romans, Their Gods and Their Beliefs*. London, England: Orbis, 1984.

MacCulloch, J. A. *The Harrowing of Hell*. Edinburgh, Scotland: T. and T. Clark, 1930.

MacGregor, A. J. *Fire and Light in the Western Triduum*. Collegeville, MN: Liturgical Press, 1992.

Mac Rae, G. W. "Passover, Feast of." In *New Catholic Encyclopedia*. Volume 10. New York: McGraw-Hill, 1967.

Maier, Paul J. *In the Fullness of Time: A Historian Looks at Christmas, Easter, and the Early Church*. Grand Rapids, MI: Kregel, 1991.

Marcus, Rebecca B., and Judith Marcus. *Fiesta Time in Mexico*. Champaign, IL: Garrard, 1974.

"Mary Magdalene, St." In E. A. Livingstone, ed. *The Oxford Dictionary of the Christian Church*. Third edition. Oxford, England: Oxford University Press, 1997.

Mason, Peter. *Bacchanal! The Carnival Culture of Trinidad*. Philadelphia, PA: Temple University Press, 1999.

Mason, Steve A. "Sacrifices and Offerings." In David Noel Freedman, ed. *Eerdmans Dictionary of the Bible*. Grand Rapids, MI: William B. Eerdmans Publishing, 2000.

Matera, Frank J. "Reconciliation." In Paul J. Achtemeier, ed. *The HarperCollins Bible Dictionary*. New York: HarperCollins, 1996.

———. "Repentance." In Paul J. Achtemeier, ed. *The HarperCollins Bible Dictionary*. New York: HarperCollins, 1996.

Mathewes-Green, Frederica. *Facing East*. New York: HarperSanFrancisco, 1997.

Matloff, Judith. "Bingeing on Hot Buttered Blini in Frigid Moscow." *Christian Science Monitor* (February 3, 1999). Available online for a fee through Northern Light at http://www.northernlight.com. Document ID: BM1999020301 0020782

Matthews, John. *The Grail: Quest for the Eternal*. New York: Crossroad, 1981.

McBrien, Richard P. "Alleluia." In his *The HarperCollins Encyclopedia of Catholicism*. New York: HarperSanFrancisco, 1995.

———. "Ascension, Feast of." In his *The HarperCollins Encyclopedia of Catholicism*. New York: HarperSanFrancisco, 1995.

McDue, James F. "Peter the Apostle." In Mircea Eliade, ed. *The Encyclopedia of Religion*. Volume 11. New York: Macmillan, 1987.

McNicol, Allan J. "Lord's Supper." In David Noel Freedman, ed. *Eerdmans Dictionary of the Bible*. Grand Rapids, MI: William B. Eerdmans Publishing, 2000.

Meagher, P. K. "Veronica." In *New Catholic Encyclopedia*. Volume 14. New York: McGraw-Hill, 1967.

Mercatante, Anthony. *The Facts on File Encyclopedia of World Mythology and Legend*. New York: Facts on File, 1988.

Mershman, Francis. "Palm Sunday." In Charles G. Herbermann et al., eds. *The Catholic Encyclopedia*. New York: Appleton, 1913. Available online at: http://www.newadvent.org/cathen/11432b.htm

Meslin, Michael. "Baptism." In Mircea Eliade, ed. *The Encyclopedia of Religion*. Volume 2. New York: Macmillan, 1987.

"Messiah." In E. A. Livingstone, ed. *The Oxford Dictionary of the Christian Church*. Third edition. Oxford, England: Oxford University Press, 1997.

Metford, J. C. J. *The Christian Year*. London, England: Thames and Hudson, 1991.

———. *Dictionary of Christian Lore and Legend*. London, England: Thames and Hudson, 1983.

———. "Descent of Christ into Hell." In his *Dictionary of Christian Lore and Legend*. London, England: Thames and Hudson, 1983.

Millen, Nina. *Children's Festivals from Many Lands*. New York: Friendship Press, 1964.

Miller, Charles H. "Emmaus." In Paul J. Achtemeier, ed. *The HarperCollins Bible Dictionary*. New York: HarperCollins, 1996.

Miller, J. H. "Cross." In *New Catholic Encyclopedia*. Volume 4. New York: McGraw-Hill, 1967.

———. "Rogation Days." In *New Catholic Encyclopedia*. Volume 12. New York: McGraw-Hill, 1967.

Milne, Jean. *Fiesta Time in Latin America*. Los Angeles, CA: Ward Richie Press, 1965.

Mitchell, Timothy. *Passional Culture: Emotion, Religion and Society in Southern Spain*. Philadelphia, PA: University of Pennsylvania Press, 1990.

————. *Violence and Piety in Spanish Folklore*. Philadelphia, PA: University of Pennsylvania Press, 1988.

Møller-Christensen, V., and K. E. Jordt Jørgensen. *Encyclopedia of Bible Creatures*. Philadelphia, PA: Fortress Press, 1965.

Momigliano, Arnaldo. "Cybele." In Mircea Eliade, ed. *The Encyclopedia of Religion*. Volume 4. New York: Macmillan, 1987.

Monti, James. *The Week of Salvation*. Huntington, IN: Our Sunday Visitor Publications, 1993.

Mowery, Robert L. "Son of God." In David Noel Freedman, ed. *Eerdmans Dictionary of the Bible*. Grand Rapids, MI: William B. Eerdmans Publishing, 2000.

Mulhern, P. "Triduum." In *New Catholic Encyclopedia*. Volume 14. New York: McGraw-Hill, 1967.

Mulzac, Kenneth D. "Atonement." In David Noel Freedman, ed. *Eerdmans Dictionary of the Bible*. Grand Rapids, MI: William B. Eerdmans Publishing, 2000.

Munoa, Phillip. "Ascension." In David Noel Freedman, ed. *Eerdmans Dictionary of the Bible*. Grand Rapids, MI: William B. Eerdmans Publishing, 2000.

Munro, Winsome. "Mary." In Paul J. Achtemeier, ed. *The HarperCollins Bible Dictionary*. New York: HarperCollins, 1996.

Murphy, F. X. "Palm." In *New Catholic Encyclopedia*. Volume 10. New York: McGraw-Hill, 1967.

Myers, Allen C. "Atonement," "Redemption," and "Sacrifices and Offerings." *The Eerdmans Bible Dictionary*. Grand Rapids, MI: William B. Eerdmans Publishing, 1987.

————. "Repentance." In *The Eerdmans Bible Dictionary*. Grand Rapids, MI: William B. Eerdmans Publishing, 1987.

————. "Resurrection." In *The Eerdmans Bible Dictionary*. Grand Rapids, MI: William B. Eerdmans Publishing, 1987.

————. "Salvation." In *The Eerdmans Bible Dictionary*. Grand Rapids, MI: William B. Eerdmans Publishing, 1987.

————. "Sin." In *The Eerdmans Bible Dictionary*. Grand Rapids, MI: William B. Eerdmans Publishing, 1987.

————. "Wine." In *The Eerdmans Bible Dictionary*. Grand Rapids, MI: William B. Eerdmans Publishing, 1987.

Myers, Allen C., ed. *The Eerdmans Bible Dictionary*. Grand Rapids, MI: William B. Eerdmans Publishing, 1987.

Myers, Robert J. *Celebrations: The Complete Book of American Holidays*. Garden City, NY: Doubleday and Company, 1972.

"Mystery Play." In Phyllis Hartnoll, ed. *The Oxford Companion to the Theatre*. Fourth edition. Oxford, England: Oxford University Press, 1983.

Mystic Quests. Alexandria, VA: Time-Life Books, 1991.

National Conference of Catholic Bishops. *Holy Days in the United States*. Washington, D.C.: United States Catholic Conference, 1984.

Newall, Venetia. *An Egg at Easter*. Bloomington, IN: Indiana University Press, 1971.

Neyrey, Jerome H. "Ascension." In Richard P. McBrien, ed. *The HarperCollins Encyclopedia of Catholicism*. New York: HarperSanFrancisco, 1995.

———. "Eternal Life." In Paul J. Achtemeier, ed. *The HarperCollins Bible Dictionary*. New York: HarperCollins, 1996.

———. "Peter." In Paul J. Achtemeier, ed. *The HarperCollins Bible Dictionary*. New York: HarperCollins, 1996.

Niemann, Paul J. *The Lent, Triduum, and Easter Answer Book*. San Jose, CA: Resource Publications, 1998.

Noggin, J. F. "Bread, the Liturgical Use of." In Charles G. Herbermann et al., eds. *The Catholic Encyclopedia*. New York: Appleton, 1913. Available online at: http://www.newadvent.org/cathen/02749a.htm

Nollen, Tim. *Festivals of the World: Czech Republic*. Milwaukee, WI: Gareth Stevens, 1999.

North, R. "Sabbath." In *New Catholic Encyclopedia*. Volume 12. New York: McGraw-Hill, 1967.

Nowakowski, Jacek, and Marlene Perrin. *Polish Touches*. Iowa City, IA: Penfield Press, 1996.

"Oberammergau." In E. A. Livingstone, ed. *The Oxford Dictionary of the Christian Church*. Third edition. Oxford, England: Oxford University Press, 1997.

O'Connor, Joseph E. "Rogation Days." In Charles G. Herbermann et al., eds. *The Catholic Encyclopedia*. New York: Appleton, 1913. Available online at: http://www.newadvent.org/cathen/13110b.htm

Orloff, Alexander. *Carnival: Myth and Cult*. Wörgl, Austria: Perlinger, 1981.

O'Shea, W. J. "Easter Vigil." In *New Catholic Encyclopedia*. Volume 5. New York: McGraw-Hill, 1967.

———. "Holy Week." In *New Catholic Encyclopedia*. Volume 7. New York: McGraw-Hill, 1967.

———. "Lent." In *New Catholic Encyclopedia*. Volume 8. New York: McGraw-Hill, 1967.

————. "Palm Sunday." In *New Catholic Encyclopedia*. Volume 10. New York: McGraw-Hill, 1967.

"Palm." In Richard Cavendish, ed. *Man, Myth and Magic*. Volume 14. New York: Marshall Cavendish, 1997.

"Palm." In Leland Ryken, James C. Wilhoit, and Tremper Longman III, eds. *Dictionary of Biblical Imagery*. Downers Grove, IL: InterVarsity Press, 1998.

"Palm Sunday." In E. A. Livingstone, ed. *The Oxford Dictionary of the Christian Church*. Third edition. Oxford, England: Oxford University Press, 1997.

Papashvily, Helen, and George Papashvily. *Russian Cooking*. Revised edition. Alexandria, VA: Time-Life Books, 1977.

"Passion, The." In E. A. Livingstone, ed. *The Oxford Dictionary of the Christian Church*. Third edition. Oxford, England: Oxford University Press, 1997.

"Passion Play." In Phyllis Hartnoll, ed. *The Oxford Companion to the Theatre*. Fourth edition. Oxford, England: Oxford University Press, 1983.

"Passion Sunday." In E. A. Livingstone, ed. *The Oxford Dictionary of the Christian Church*. Third edition. Oxford, England: Oxford University Press, 1997.

"Passiontide." In E. A. Livingstone, ed. *The Oxford Dictionary of the Christian Church*. Third edition. Oxford, England: Oxford University Press, 1997.

"Passover." In E. A. Livingstone, ed. *The Oxford Dictionary of the Christian Church*. Third edition. Oxford, England: Oxford University Press, 1997.

Pavlova, Elena. "The Week of Chimes: Reviving an Easter Tradition in Russia." *The World and I* 11, 5 (May 1996): 202.

Peifer, C. J. "Passover Lamb" and "Passover Meal." In *New Catholic Encyclopedia*. Volume 10. New York: McGraw-Hill, 1967.

Pelikan, Jaroslav. *Mary Through the Centuries*. New Haven, CT: Yale University Press, 1996.

Pelton, Robert D. "Tricksters: African Tricksters." In Mircea Eliade, ed. *The Encyclopedia of Religion*. Volume 15. New York: Macmillan, 1987.

"Pentecost." In Leland Ryken, James C. Wilhoit, and Tremper Longman III, eds. *Dictionary of Biblical Imagery*. Downers Grove, IL: InterVarsity Press, 1998.

Perkins, Pheme. "Barabbas." In Paul J. Achtemeier, ed. *The HarperCollins Bible Dictionary*. New York: HarperCollins, 1996.

Perowne, Stewart. *Roman Mythology*. New York: Bedrick Books, 1969.

"Peter, St." In E. A. Livingstone, ed. *The Oxford Dictionary of the Christian Church*. Third edition. Oxford, England: Oxford University Press, 1997.

Peterson, John. *A Walk in Jerusalem*. Harrisburg, PA: Morehouse Publishing, 1998.

Bibliography

Pierce, Joanne M. "Holy Week and Easter in the Middle Ages." In Paul F. Bradshaw and Lawrence A. Hoffman, eds. *Passover and Easter: Origin and History to Modern Times.* Two Liturgical Traditions series, volume 5. Notre Dame, IN: University of Notre Dame Press, 1999.

"Pilate, Pontius." In E. A. Livingstone, ed. *The Oxford Dictionary of the Christian Church.* Third edition. Oxford, England: Oxford University Press, 1997.

Porter, J. R. *Jesus Christ: The Jesus of History, the Christ of Faith.* New York: Oxford University Press, 1999.

Porter, Keith. *Discovering Rabbits and Hares.* New York: Bookwright Press, 1986.

Porter, T. A. "Repentance." In *New Catholic Encyclopedia.* Volume 12. New York: McGraw- Hill, 1967.

Portraro, Sam. *Brightest and Best: A Companion to the Lesser Feasts and Fasts.* Cambridge, MA: Crowley, 1998.

Potts, Donald R. "Blood." In David Noel Freedman, ed. *Eerdmans Dictionary of the Bible.* Grand Rapids, MI: William B. Eerdmans Publishing, 2000.

Powell, Mark Allan. *Jesus as a Figure in History.* Louisville, KY: Westminster John Knox Press, 1998.

Primiano, Leonard Norman. "All Fools' Day." In Mircea Eliade, ed. *The Encyclopedia of Religion.* Volume 1. New York: Macmillan, 1987.

Quinn, J. D. "Ascension of Jesus Christ." In *New Catholic Encyclopedia.* Volume 1. New York: McGraw-Hill, 1967.

Quinn, J. D., J. H. Rohling, and P. Verdier. "Descent of Christ into Hell." In *New Catholic Encyclopedia.* Volume 4. New York: McGraw-Hill, 1967.

"Rabbit." In Richard Cavendish, ed. *Man, Myth and Magic.* Volume 9. New York: Marshall Cavendish, 1970.

Rader, Rosemary. "Fasting." In Mircea Eliade, ed. *The Encyclopedia of Religion.* Volume 5. New York: Macmillan, 1987.

Rahner, Karl, and Herbert Vargrimler, eds. "Metanoia." In their *Dictionary of Theology.* Second edition. New York: Crossroads, 1981.

Raphael, Chaim. *A Feast of History: The Drama of Passover Through the Ages.* London, England: Weidenfeld and Nicolson, 1972.

Rattray, Susan. "Worship." In Paul J. Achtemeier, ed. *The HarperCollins Bible Dictionary.* New York: HarperCollins, 1996.

Rattue, James. *The Living Stream: Holy Wells in Historical Context.* Rochester, NY: Boydell Press, 1995.

"Redemption." In E. A. Livingstone, ed. *The Oxford Dictionary of the Christian Church.* Third edition. Oxford, England: Oxford University Press, 1997.

"Redemption." In Leland Ryken, James C. Wilhoit, and Tremper Longman III, eds. *Dictionary of Biblical Imagery*. Downers Grove, IL: InterVarsity Press, 1998.

Rees, Elizabeth. *Christian Symbols, Ancient Roots*. London, England: Jessica Kingsley, 1992.

Remy, Arthur F. J. "The Holy Grail." In Charles G. Herbermann et al., eds. *The Catholic Encyclopedia*. New York: Appleton, 1913. Available online at: http://www.newadvent.org/cathen/06719a.htm

"Repentance." In E. A. Livingstone, ed. *The Oxford Dictionary of the Christian Church*. Third edition. Oxford, England: Oxford University Press, 1997.

"Repentance." In Leland Ryken, James C. Wilhoit, and Tremper Longman III, eds. *Dictionary of Biblical Imagery*. Downers Grove, IL: InterVarsity Press, 1998.

"Resurrection." In Leland Ryken, James C. Wilhoit, and Tremper Longman III, eds. *Dictionary of Biblical Imagery*. Downers Grove, IL: InterVarsity Press, 1998.

"Resurrection of Christ, The." In E. A. Livingstone, ed. *The Oxford Dictionary of the Christian Church*. Third edition. Oxford, England: Oxford University Press, 1997.

"Resurrection of the Dead." In E. A. Livingstone, ed. *The Oxford Dictionary of the Christian Church*. Third edition. Oxford, England: Oxford University Press, 1997.

Reumann, John. *The Supper of the Lord*. Philadelphia, PA: Fortress Press, 1985.

———. "Mary." In Mircea Eliade, ed. *The Encyclopedia of Religion*. Volume 9. New York: Macmillan, 1987.

Ricketts, Mac Linscott. "Tricksters: North American Tricksters." In Mircea Eliade, ed. *The Encyclopedia of Religion*. Volume 15. New York: Macmillan, 1987.

Ries, Julien. "Cross." In Mircea Eliade, ed. *The Encyclopedia of Religion*. Volume 4. New York: Macmillan, 1987.

Rock, P. M. J. "Golden Rose." In Charles G. Herbermann et al., eds. *The Catholic Encyclopedia*. New York: Appleton, 1913. Available online at: http://www.newadvent.org/cathen/06629a.htm

"Rogation Days." In E. A. Livingstone, ed. *The Oxford Dictionary of the Christian Church*. Third edition. Oxford, England: Oxford University Press, 1997.

Rogers, Eric N. *Fasting: The Phenomenon of Self-Denial*. New York: Thomas Nelson, 1976.

Bibliography

Roth, Cecil, ed. *The Standard Jewish Encyclopedia*. Garden City, NY: Doubleday and Company, 1959.

Rouillard, P. "Marian Feasts." In *New Catholic Encyclopedia*. Volume 9. New York: McGraw-Hill, 1967.

Rouvelas, Marilyn. *A Guide to Greek Traditions and Customs in America*. Bethesda, MD: Nea Attiki Press, 1993.

Roux, Jean-Paul. "Blood." In Mircea Elide, ed. *The Encyclopedia of Religion*. Volume 12. New York: Macmillan, 1987.

Rowland, Beryl. *Animals with Human Faces*. Knoxville, TN: University of Tennessee Press, 1973.

Rubin, Rich. "A Joyful Madness: Carnival in Basel." *German Life* (February-March 1999). Available online at: http://www.germanlife.com/

Russ, Jennifer M. *German Festivals and Customs*. London, England: Oswald Wolff, 1982.

Ryken, Leland, James C. Wilhoit, and Tremper Longman III, eds. *Dictionary of Biblical Imagery*. Downers Grove, IL: InterVarsity Press, 1998.

"Sabbatarianism." In E. A. Livingstone, ed. *The Oxford Dictionary of the Christian Church*. Third edition. Oxford, England: Oxford University Press, 1997.

"Sabbath." In E. A. Livingstone, ed. *The Oxford Dictionary of the Christian Church*. Third edition. Oxford, England: Oxford University Press, 1997.

"Sacrifice." In E. A. Livingstone, ed. *The Oxford Dictionary of the Christian Church*. Third edition. Oxford, England: Oxford University Press, 1997.

"Sacrifice." In Leland Ryken, James C. Wilhoit, and Tremper Longman III, eds. *Dictionary of Biblical Imagery*. Downers Grove, IL: InterVarsity Press, 1998.

"Salvation." In Leland Ryken, James C. Wilhoit, and Tremper Longman III, eds. *Dictionary of Biblical Imagery*. Downers Grove, IL: InterVarsity Press, 1998.

Salzer, Anselm. "Passion Plays." In Charles G. Herbermann et al., eds. *The Catholic Encyclopedia*. New York: Appleton, 1913. Available online at: http://www.newadvent.org/cathen/11531a.htm

Sanders, E. P. "Jesus Christ." In David Noel Freedman, ed. *Eerdmans Dictionary of the Bible*. Grand Rapids, MI: William B. Eerdmans Publishing, 2000.

Schlumpf, Heidi. "Who Framed Mary Magdalene?" *U.S. Catholic* (April, 2000). Available online at: http://www.uscatholic.org/2000/04/0004cov.htm

Schmidt, Leigh Eric. *Consumer Rites*. Princeton, NJ: Princeton University Press, 1995.

Schoenberg, M. W. "Crucifixion." In *New Catholic Encylopedia*. Volume 4. New York: McGraw-Hill, 1967.

Schulte-Peevers, Andrea. "Cologne Carnival: A Trip to the Land of Fools, Floats, and Revelry." *German Life* (March 31, 1995).

Scott, Miriam Van. *Encyclopedia of Hell*. New York: St. Martin's Press, 1998.

Scullard, H. H. *Festivals and Ceremonies of the Roman Republic*. Ithaca, NY: Cornell University Press, 1981.

Seely, David Rolph. "Resurrection." In David Noel Freedman, ed. *Eerdmans Dictionary of the Bible*. Grand Rapids, MI: William B. Eerdmans Publishing, 2000.

Seidenspinner, Clarence. *Great Protestant Festivals*. New York: Henry Schuman, 1952.

Seidman, Hillel. *The Glory of the Jewish Holidays*. New York: Shengold, 1968.

Senn, Frank C. "Should Christians Celebrate the Passover?" In Paul F. Bradshaw and Lawrence A. Hoffman, eds. *Passover and Easter: The Symbolic Structuring of Sacred Seasons*. Two Liturgical Traditions series, volume 6. Notre Dame, IN: University of Notre Dame Press, 1999.

"Septuagesima." In E. A. Livingstone, ed. *The Oxford Dictionary of the Christian Church*. Third edition. Oxford, England: Oxford University Press, 1997.

"Seven." In Leland Ryken, James C. Wilhoit, and Tremper Longman III, eds. *Dictionary of Biblical Imagery*. Downers Grove, IL: InterVarsity Press, 1998.

"Seven Sorrows of the Blessed Virgin Mary." In E. A. Livingstone, ed. *The Oxford Dictionary of the Christian Church*. Third edition. Oxford, England: Oxford University Press, 1997.

Sheeley, Steven M. "Judas." In David Noel Freedman, ed. *Eerdmans Dictionary of the Bible*. Grand Rapids, MI: William B. Eerdmans Publishing, 2000.

Shoemaker, Alfred L. *Eastertide in Pennsylvania*. Kutztown, PA: Pennsylvania Folklife Society, 1960.

Simpson, D. P. *Cassell's New Latin Dictionary*. New York: Funk and Wagnalls, 1959.

"Sin." In E. A. Livingstone, ed. *The Oxford Dictionary of the Christian Church*. Third edition. Oxford, England: Oxford University Press, 1997.

"Sin." In Leland Ryken, James C. Wilhoit, and Tremper Longman III, eds. *Dictionary of Biblical Imagery*. Downers Grove, IL: InterVarsity Press, 1998.

Skeat, W. W. *An Etymological Dictionary of the English Language*. Fourth edition, revised, enlarged, and reset. Oxford, England: Clarendon Press, 1958.

Slim, Hugo. *A Feast of Festivals*. London, England: Marshall Pickering, 1996.

Smith-Christopher, Daniel J. "Fasting." In David Noel Freedman, ed. *Eerdmans Dictionary of the Bible*. Grand Rapids, MI: William B. Eerdmans, 2000.

Solovyova, Julia. "Holiday Mixes Paganism, Christianity." *The Moscow Times* (February 16, 1999). Available online through Northern Light for a fee at http://www.northernlight.com. Document ID: EB19990216710000175

Spicer, Dorothy Gladys. *Book of Festivals*. 1937. Reprint. Detroit, MI: Omnigraphics, 1990.

———. *Festivals of Western Europe*. 1958. Reprint. Detroit, MI: Omnigraphics, 1994.

Spong, John Shelby. *Resurrection: Myth or Reality?* New York: HarperSanFrancisco, 1994.

Stein, Robert H. "Bread." In Paul J. Achtemeier, ed. *The HarperCollins Bible Dictionary*. New York: HarperCollins, 1996.

———. "Judas." In Paul J. Achtemeier, ed. *The HarperCollins Bible Dictionary*. New York: HarperCollins, 1996.

Steingroot, Ira. *Keeping Passover*. New York: HarperSanFrancisco, 1995.

Stevens, D. "Tenebrae." In *New Catholic Encyclopedia*. Volume 13. New York: McGraw-Hill, 1967.

Storace, Patricia. *Dinner with Persephone*. New York: Vintage Books, 1996.

Strassfeld, Michael. *The Jewish Holidays*. New York: Harper and Row, 1985.

"Supper." In Leland Ryken, James C. Wilhoit, and Tremper Longman III, eds. *Dictionary of Biblical Imagery*. Downers Grove, IL: InterVarsity Press, 1998.

Swartly, Willard M. "Sabbath." In Everett Ferguson, ed. *Encyclopedia of Early Christianity*. Volume 2. New York: Garland, 1997.

Talley, Thomas J. *The Origins of the Liturgical Year*. Collegeville, MN: Liturgical Press, 1986.

———. "Christian Worship." In Mircea Eliade, ed. *The Encyclopedia of Religion*. Volume 15. New York: Macmillan, 1987.

"Tenebrae." In E. A. Livingstone, ed. *The Oxford Dictionary of the Christian Church*. Third edition. Oxford, England: Oxford University Press, 1997.

Thompson, Sue Ellen. *Holiday Symbols*. Second edition. Detroit, MI: Omnigraphics, 2000.

Thonger, Richard. *A Calendar of German Customs*. London, England: Oswald Wolff, 1966.

Thurston, Herbert. "Ash Wednesday." In Charles G. Herbermann et al., eds. *The Catholic Encyclopedia*. New York: Appleton, 1913. Available online at: http://www.newadvent.org/cathen/01775b.htm

————. "Lent." In Charles G. Herbermann et al., eds. *The Catholic Encyclopedia*. New York: Appleton, 1913. Available online at: http://www.new advent.org/cathen/09152a.htm

————. "Symbolism." In Charles G. Herbermann et al., eds. *The Catholic Encyclopedia*. New York: Appleton, 1913. Available online at: http://www.new advent.org/cathen/14373b.htm

————. "Tenebrae." In Charles G. Herbermann et al., eds. *The Catholic Encyclopedia*. New York: Appleton, 1913. Available online at: http://www.new advent.org/cathen/14506a.htm

Toor, Frances. *Festivals and Folkways of Italy*. New York: Crown, 1953.

Tope, Lily Rose R. *Philippines*. New York: Marshall Cavendish, 1991.

Tracz, Orysia Paszczak. "Ukrainian Easter Tradition: Velykden — Great Day." *Ukrainian Weekly* 63, 17 (April 23, 1995): 11.

"Tree, Trees." In Leland Ryken, James C. Wilhoit, and Tremper Longman III, eds. *Dictionary of Biblical Imagery*. Downers Grove, IL: InterVarsity Press, 1998.

Trenchard, Warren C. "Barabbas." In David Noel Freedman, ed. *Eerdmans Dictionary of the Bible*. Grand Rapids, MI: William B. Eerdmans Publishing, 2000.

Turner, Alice K. *The History of Hell*. New York: Harcourt Brace and Company, 1993.

Tyack, George S. *A Book about Bells*. 1898. Reprint. Detroit, MI: Omnigraphics, 1991.

Tyrer, John Walton. *Historical Survey of Holy Week*. London, England: Oxford University Press, 1932.

Tyson, Joseph B. "Pentecost." In Paul J. Achtemeier, ed. *The HarperCollins Bible Dictionary*. New York: HarperCollins, 1996.

Upgren, Arthur. *The Night Has a Thousand Eyes: A Naked-Eye Guide to the Sky, Its Science, and Lore*. New York: Plenum Press, 1998.

Urlin, Ethel L. *Festivals, Holy Days, and Saints' Days*. 1915. Reprint. Detroit, MI: Omnigraphics, 1992.

Utenkova, Yelena. "Hold the Aunt Jemima: These are Blini." *Russian Life* (March 1, 1996).

————. "Kulich: The King of Easter Cuisine." *Russian Life* (April 1, 1996).

"Veil." In Leland Ryken, James C. Wilhoit, and Tremper Longman III, eds. *Dictionary of Biblical Imagery*. Downers Grove, IL: InterVarsity Press, 1998.

"Veneration of the Cross." In E. A. Livingstone, ed. *The Oxford Dictionary of the Christian Church*. Third edition. Oxford, England: Oxford University Press, 1997.

Bibliography

Vermaseren, Maarten J. *Cybele and Attis: The Myth and the Cult.* London, England: Thames and Hudson, 1977.

"Veronica, St." In E. A. Livingstone, ed. *The Oxford Dictionary of the Christian Church.* Third edition. Oxford, England: Oxford University Press, 1997.

"Vigil." In E. A. Livingstone, ed. *The Oxford Dictionary of the Christian Church.* Third edition. Oxford, England: Oxford University Press, 1997.

Waida, Manabu. "Rabbits." In Mircea Eliade, ed. *The Encyclopedia of Religion.* Volume 12. New York: Macmillan, 1987.

Walsh, John Evangelist. *The Bones of St. Peter.* Garden City, NY: Doubleday, 1982.

"Water." In Leland Ryken, James C. Wilhoit, and Tremper Longman III, eds. *Dictionary of Biblical Imagery.* Downers Grove, IL: InterVarsity Press, 1998.

Watts, Alan W. *Easter.* New York: Henry Schuman, 1950.

Wax, Emily. "A Ukrainian Easter, the Holiday Helps Immigrants Hold on to Their Heritage." *Newsday* (April 11, 1999): G14.

Weakland, R. M. "Alleluia." In *New Catholic Encyclopedia.* Volume 1. New York: McGraw-Hill, 1967.

Weaver, Robert S. *International Holidays.* Jefferson, NC: McFarland, 1995.

Webber, F. R. *Church Symbolism.* 1938. Second edition, revised. Reprint. Detroit, MI: Omnigraphics, 1992.

Weber, Vicki L., ed. *The Rhythm of Jewish Time.* West Orange, NJ: Behrman, 1999.

"Wednesday." In E. A. Livingstone, ed. *The Oxford Dictionary of the Christian Church.* Third edition. Oxford, England: Oxford University Press, 1997.

Weigle, Marta. *The Penitentes of the Southwest.* Santa Fe, NM: Ancient City Press, 1970.

Weiser, Francis X. *The Easter Book.* New York: Harcourt, Brace and Company, 1954.

———. *Handbook of Christian Feasts and Customs.* New York: Harcourt, Brace and World, 1952.

———. *The Holyday Book.* New York: Harcourt, Brace and Company, 1956.

Werblowsky, R. J. Zwi, and Geoffrey Wigoder. "Pesah." In their *The Oxford Dictionary of the Jewish Religion.* Oxford, England: Oxford University Press, 1997.

Wigoder, Geoffrey. "Fasting and Fast Days." In his *Encyclopedia of Judaism.* New York: Macmillan, 1989.

———. "Passover." In his *Encyclopedia of Judaism.* New York: Macmillan, 1989.

Bibliography

Williams, Sam K. "The Lord's Supper." In Paul J. Achtemeier, ed. *The Harper-Collins Bible Dictionary*. New York: HarperCollins, 1996.

Willis, Roy. "The Great Mother." In his *World Mythology*. New York: Henry Holt, 1993.

"Wine." In Leland Ryken, James C. Wilhoit, and Tremper Longman III, eds. *Dictionary of Biblical Imagery*. Downers Grove, IL: InterVarsity Press, 1998.

Witherington, Ben. *Jesus the Sage: The Pilgrimage of Wisdom*. Minneapolis, MN: Fortress Press, 1994.

Wolf, Burt. *Gatherings and Celebrations*. New York: Doubleday, 1996.

Wood, Douglas. *Rabbit and the Moon*. New York: Simon & Schuster, 1998.

Wright, N. T. *The Challenge of Jesus*. Downers Grove, IL: InterVarsity Press, 1999.

Wright, Thomas. *The Original Jesus*. Grand Rapids, MI: William B. Eerdmans, 1996.

Wroe, Ann. *Pontius Pilate*. New York: Random House, 1999.

Wybrew, Hugh. *Orthodox Lent, Holy Week and Easter*. Crestwood, NY: St. Vladimir's Seminary Press, 1997.

Zenon, Elyjiw. "Ukrainian Pysanky: Easter Eggs as Talismans." *Ukrainian Weekly* 13, 16 (April 16, 1995): 11.

Bibliography

Web Sites

Listed below are more than eighty web sites related to Easter and Carnival, organized according to the following categories: Easter, Holy Week, and Lent Around the World; Easter History; Easter and the Calendar; Carnival; Folk Holidays; Folk Customs, Observances, and Symbols; and Religious Customs, Observances, and Related Bible Figures. These web addresses were checked just prior to press time and found valid.

Easter, Holy Week, and Lent Around the World

Bulgaria

The following page gives excerpts from the writings of Kuzman Shapkareff (published in 1885) concerning Holy Week and Easter traditions in Bulgaria:

http://www.b-info.com/places/Bulgaria/Easter/

Czech Republic

"Easter in the Czech Republic," a series of articles posted by Radio Prague, the international service of Czech Radio:

http://voskovec.radio.cz/easter/

A series of articles on various aspects of Lent, Holy Week, and Easter by Petr Chudoba, posted under the "holidays and traditions" section of Local Lingo's Czech Republic site:

http://www.locallingo.com/countries/czech_republic/culture

England

"One a Penny Poker," an article on hot cross buns posted in *Devon Life Online*, an electronic magazine about life in the English county of Devon:
   http://www.devonlife.co.uk/magazine/magarticles_folder/devon_customs/onepenny/oneapenny.html

This web site, maintained by Tissington Hall, in Tissington, England, describes various aspects of the local well-dressing ceremony:
   http://www.tissington-hall.com/well_dressing.htm

The Ecclesiological Society, an organization whose members share a common passion for the history of church services, church architecture, and church furnishings, has posted the following web site, describing the appearance of England's surviving Easter sepulchres, as well as the Holy Week customs associated with them:
   http://www.ecclsoc.org/eastersepul.html

Finland

"Finnish Easter Traditions," an article by Sirpa Karjalainen, Assistant of Ethnology at the University of Helsinki, posted on the Virtual Finland web site:
   http://www.finland.fi/finfo/english/paaseng.html

Germany

"Frühling-Spring," an article on German Lent, Easter, Easter season, and Pentecost customs posted by the German Embassy in Ottawa, Canada:
   http://www.germanembassyottawa.org/easter/

The following, searchable site offers a range of information on German culture, including Easter celebrations:
   http://www.germany-info.org

Guatemala

"La Semana Santa in Guatemala," an article about Holy Week observances in Guatemala by Tony Pasinski, posted by *Revue* magazine, a publication designed for Guatemala's resident English-speakers:
   http://www.revuemag.com/articles/1999/mar/semana.htm

Web Sites

Hungary

"Hungarian Decorated Easter Eggs," "Easter in Hungary," and "Handled Like a Hímestojás," three articles by Emese Kerkay, posted by the American Hungarian Educators' Association at:
http://www.magyar.org/ahfc/museum/husvet/

Italy

"Easter Without a Peep," a brief article on Italian Easter foods by Faith Heller Willinger, posted at:
http://www.epicurious.com/g_gourmet/g04_italy/italy/easter.html

Lithuania

The Lituanian Folk Culture Centre, located in Vilnius, Lithuania, has reprinted a number of excerpts from Juozas Kudrika's book, *The Lithuanians* (1991), on its web site. The following page concerns Easter celebrations in Lithuania:
http://www.lfcc.lt/publ/thelt/node19.html#SECTION0019

The Lithuanian-American Community, Inc., a non-profit organization dedicated to serving the educational, social and cultural needs of Lithuanian Americans, has reprinted various excerpts from the book *Lithuanian Customs and Traditions* (third edition, c. 2001) by Danute Brazyte Bindokiene, on its web site. The Easter page links to separate pages on Easter eggs and Holy Week:
http://www.lithuanian-american.org/educat/tradicijos/velykos.html

Mexico

"Semana Santa in Mexico," an article by May Herz, available from *Inside Mexico*, a company dedicated to producing quality educational materials on Mexican culture:
http://www.inside-mexico.com/featuresemana.htm

The following site, sponsored by Mexico Connect, an e-zine dedicated to promoting Mexico as a country of business opportunity, offers photos and brief descriptions of Holy Week and Easter customs in Mexico. Gives links to additional articles on Easter celebrations in Mexico:
http://www.mexconnect.com/mex_/feature/easterindex.html

Philippines

"Pamalandong: Good Friday in Palo," by Alvin Gz. Arpon, published in *Philippines Today* 3 (June 2000). Available on the web at:
   http://www.pia.ops.gov.ph/philtoday/pt03/pt0316.htm

"Religion-Philippines: Holy Week of Folk Rituals, Gory Spectacle," an article by Johanna Sun, available through the Inter Press Service at:
   http://www.oneworld.org/ips2/apr98/04_45_007.html

Poland

This site, compiled by Dr. Ann Hetzel Gunkel, a professor of philosophy and cultural studies at Columbia College in Chicago, offers information on Polish Carnival, Lent, and Easter celebrations:
   http://acweb.colum.edu/users/agunkel/homepage/easter/easter.html

The *Polish American Journal*'s web site offers a collection of articles concerning Polish holidays, including Easter and Carnival:
   http://www.polamjournal.com/Library/Holidays/

"Dyngus and Lany Poneidzialek," an article by Robert Strybel published in the *Am-Pol Eagle*, a newspaper serving western New York's Polish-American population, posted at:
   http://www.dyngusday.com/

The Polish Genealogical Society's customs and traditions page at:
   http://www.pgsa.org/traditions.htm

The *Polish News'* special Easter edition, "Did You Know That," by Robert Strybel, at:
   http://www.polishnews.com/polonica/diduknow15.shtml

Russia

"Russian Folk Holidays and Traditions," a page sponsored by the city government of Moscow, Russia:
   http://www.moscow-guide.ru/Culture/Folk.htm

"Christ Is Risen! A Russian Easter Celebration," posted by Clever Hedgehog Translation Services at:
   http://www.cleverhedgehog.com/paskha.htm

Spain

"Semana Santa — Holy Week — Easter," posted on Andalucia.com, the web site for *Andalucia Magazine*:

http://www.andalucia.com/magazine/english/ed2/semana-santa.htm

"Holy Week in Seville," sponsored by ALTUR, an organization promoting tourism in the region of Andalucia, Spain:

http://www.altur.com/eng/pseville/seville/holidays.shtml

Ukraine

"Ukrainian Easter Customs and Traditions," an article by Lubow Wolynetz, curator of the Folk Art Collection for the Ukrainian Museum, New York, NY:

http://www.brama.com/art/easter.html

"Pysanky — Easter Eggs," a page sponsored by the Ukrainian Museum, New York, NY:

http://www.ukrainianmuseum.org/pysanky.html

United States

"White House Easter Egg Roll Scheduled for Monday, April 24," a White House press release available at:

http://ofcn.org/cyber.serv/teledem/pb/2000/apr/msg00122.html

"With Easter Monday You Get Egg Roll at the White House," an article by C. L. Arbelhide, posted at the National Archives and Records Administration at:

http://www.nara.gov/publications/prologue/eggroll1.html

The National Easter Seal Society web site at:

http://www.easter-seals.org/

Easter History

Crucifixion

"Crucifixion in Antiquity," an article by Joe Zias, a former curator for the state of Israel's Antiquities Authority. Posted on "The Jewish Roman World of Jesus," a web site compiled by University of North Carolina at Charlotte religious studies professor James D. Tabor:

http://www.uncc.edu/jdtabor/crucifixion.html

Holy Sites in Jerusalem

The following site, sponsored by the government of Israel's Ministry of Foreign Affairs, describes the archeology and history of the Church of the Holy Sepulchre:

http://www.israel-mfa.gov.il/mfa/go.asp?MFAH00v10

Synod of Whitby

A summary of the events leading up to and including the Synod of Whitby, by Louise Elaine Burton, posted on *Christianity Today*'s web site:

http://www.christianitytoday.com/ch/60h/60h038.html

Easter and the Calendar

Date of Easter

"When Is Easter This Year," an article by Steven L. Ware, a professor of history at Nyack College Manhattan Center. Available online at *Christianity Today*'s Christian History newsletter:

http://www.christianitytoday.com/history/newsletter/2001/mar02.html

Greek Orthodox Calendar

"The Calendar of the Orthodox Church," an article by Lewis Patsavos, Ph.D., posted on the web site of the Greek Orthodox Archdiocese of America in New York, NY:

http://www.goarch.org/access/Companion_to_Orthodox_Church/calendar.html

Spring Equinox

"From Stargazers to Starships," a web site authored by NASA employee David P. Stern, teaches basic astronomy, physics, and the history and applications of spaceflight. Also offers useful explanation of the astronomy of the seasons, solstices, and equinoxes:

http://www-spof.gsfc.nasa.gov/stargaze/Sintro.htm

Carnival

Brazil

"Carnival in Rio," pages posted by Ipanema.com, an organization dedicated to promoting tourism in Rio de Janeiro, describes Carnival in that city:

http://ipanema.com/carnival

The Brazilian newspaper *O Estado de S. Paolo* hosts the following English-language site on Carnival in Brazil:

http://www.estado.com.br/edicao/especial/carnaval/carnabre.html

England

The following site, posted by the town of Olney, England, furnishes a description and photos of its Shrove Tuesday pancake race at:

http://www.olney.co.uk/pancake99/gallery/pancake99.htm

France

Nice's Tourism Office hosts an informative web site on Carnival celebrations in that city:

http://www.carnavaldenice.net/GB/indexGB.html

Germany

"Karneval-Fastnacht-Fasching," an article on the various German Carnival celebrations that includes sub-articles "Kölner Karneval," "The Swabian-Alemannic Fasnet," and "Fasching." Available through the "German Customs, Holidays and Traditions" web site, compiled by German instructor Robert J. Shea:

http://www.serve.com/shea/germusa/karneval.htm

Greece

See "Carnival in Greece," posted by the Greek National Tourism Organization, at:

http://www.gnto.gr/1/06/0604/ea0604000.html

Italy

A history of Carnival in Venice is available through the "Guest in Venice" web site, sponsored by the Omnia Office, SAS, at:

http://www.guestinvenice.com/events/carnivalofvenice/uk/antico/storia/default.asp

Lithuania

The Lituanian Folk Culture Centre, located in Vilnius, Lithuania, has reprinted a number of excerpts from Juozas Kudrika's book, *The Lithuanians* (1991), on its web site. The following page concerns Shrove Tuesday, or Carnival, in Lithuania:

http://www.lfcc.lt/publ/thelt/node18.html#SECTION0018

Poland

This site, compiled by Dr. Ann Hetzel Gunkel, a professor of philosophy and cultural studies at Columbia College in Chicago, offers information on Polish Carnival, Lent, and Easter celebrations:

http://acweb.colum.edu/users/agunkel/homepage/easter/easter.html

Trinidad and Tobago

The "Visit Trinidad and Tobago" web site, sponsored by the Tourism and Industrial Development Company of Trinidad and Tobago, Ltd., offers a number of pages on Carnival customs and history:

http://www.visittnt.com/ToDo/Events/Carnival

United States

"Paczki Day," a brief article on Paczki Day that includes recipes, posted at the *Polish American Journal*'s web site at:

http://www.polamjournal.com/Library/Holidays/paczki/body_paczki.html

680

For the history of the Shrove Tuesday pancake race in Liberal, Kansas, see the following page, written by local resident Virginia Leete:
http://www.pancakeday.com/History.html

The following page, posted by the New Orleans's Metropolitan Convention and Visitors Bureau, gives information on Mardi Gras in New Orleans:
http://www.nawlins.com/new_site/visitor/vismardi.cfm

The Louisiana State Museum's Mardi Gras exhibit offers a range of information on and images of Mardi Gras:
http://lsm.crt.state.la.us/mgras/mardigras.htm

For more on the Mardi Gras Indians, see:
http://mardigrasneworleans.com/mardigrasindians/

Arthur Frommer's Budget Travel Online offers a useful description of Mardi Gras in New Orleans:
http://www.frommers.com/destinations/neworleans/0020010042.cfm

Folk Holidays

No Ruz

The Republic of Turkey's Ministry of Culture offers a web page describing No Ruz (Nevrus) celebrations in Turkey and Central Asia. Go to the following address, click on "Art-Culture," then click on "Folk Cultures," then click on "Nevrus":
http://www.kultur.gov.tr/english/main-e.html

"Iranian New Year No Ruz," an article by Massoume Price concerning the history and customs of this festival, posted at:
http://www.iranonline.com/festivals/Iranian-new-year/index.html

"Nowrooz Holiday Celebrates Life," a Radio Free Europe article by Abbas Djavadi and Bruce Pannier, posted at:
http://www.rferl.org/nca/features/1998/03/F.RU.980320132251.html

Walpurgis Night

The following web page, part of German instructor Robert J. Shea's site on German folk customs, offers additional Walpurgis Night folklore:
http://www.serve.com/shea/germusa/walpurgi.htm

The Catholic Encyclopedia online contains an article on St. Walburga by Gertrude Casanova:
http://www.newadvent.org/cathen/15526b.htm

Another informative page on St. Walpurga, sponsored by Catholic Community Forum:
http://www.catholic-forum.com/saints/saintw02.htm

Folk Customs, Observances, and Symbols

Easter Cards

The Greeting Card Association, an organization composed of greeting card publishers and other industry members, offers a page of facts and figures concerning greeting card sales at:
http://www.greetingcard.org

Easter Eggs

"Hungarian Decorated Easter Eggs," "Easter in Hungary," and "Handled Like a Hímestojás," three articles by Emese Kerkay, posted by the American Hungarian Educators' Association at:
http://www.magyar.org/ahfc/museum/husvet/

"Pysanky—Easter Eggs," a page sponsored by the Ukrainian Museum, New York, NY:
http://www.ukrainianmuseum.org/pysanky.html

Easter Seals

The National Easter Seal Society web site can be found at:
http://www.easter-seals.org/

Egg Roll

"White House Easter Egg Roll Scheduled for Monday, April 24," a White House press release available at:
   http://ofcn.org/cyber.serv/teledem/pb/2000/apr/msg00122.html

"With Easter Monday You Get Egg Roll at the White House," an article by C. L. Arbelhide, posted at the National Archives and Records Administration at:
   http://www.nara.gov/publications/prologue/eggroll1.html

Hot Cross Buns

"One a Penny Poker," an article on hot cross buns posted in *Devon Life Online*, an electronic magazine about life in the English county of Devon:
   http://www.devonlife.co.uk/magazine/magarticles_folder/devon_customs/onepenny/oneapenny.html

Judas Burning

"The Chasing and Burning of Judas," an article about Judas burning in the Czech Republic, written by Petr Chudoba and posted on Local Lingo's Czech Republic site:
   http://www.locallingo.com/countries/czech_republic/culture/judas.html

Passionflower

A commercial site offering botanical information and results of scientific research concerning the passionflower, print references, and further web links:
   http://rain-tree.com/maracuja.htm

Sand Dollar

Many versions of this poem can be found on the World Wide Web. One version is posted at:
   http://www.seashells.org/legendsanddollar.htm

Well Dressing

The web site maintained by Tissington Hall, in Tissington, England, describes various aspects of the local well-dressing ceremony:
  http://www.tissington-hall.com/well_dressing.htm

Religious Customs, Observances, and Related Bible Figures

General Resources

"A Holy Easter," a page of links to a wide variety of sites offering lectionary and liturgical resources, as well as information on folk customs and Easter celebrations in foreign lands. Posted by United Church of Christ minister Richard Fairchild and his wife Charlene Fairchild:
  http://www.rockies.net/~spirit/sermons/easterpage.html

Links to a variety of liturgical, Sunday school, prayer and meditation resources for Lent, Holy Week, and Easter offered by Anglicans Online, an independent organization dedicated to the collection and distribution of Anglican resources and news on the World Wide Web:
  http://anglicansonline.org/special/lent.html#holyweek

The Catholic Encyclopedia, originally published in 1913, offers a wealth of information about Roman Catholic religious customs and holidays, including Easter and its related days. As some religious practices have changed since 1913, users may wish to confirm this information with more current sources:
  http://www.newadvent.org/cathen/

The Orthodox Church in America offers a number of pages describing days of religious observance, including Lent and the individual days that fall therein, Holy Week, Easter, the Easter season, and Pentecost:
  http://www.oca.org/pages/orth_chri/orthodox-faith/worship/
  index.html

Ascension Day

This web site, maintained by Tissington Hall, in Tissington, England, describes various aspects of the local well-dressing ceremony:
   http://www.tissington-hall.com/well_dressing.htm

Dismas

Page on St. Dismas, the Good Thief, sponsored by the Catholic Forum at:
   http://www.catholic-forum.com/saints/saintd11.htm

Page on St. Dismas, the Good Thief, sponsored by Catholics Online at:
   http://saints.catholic.org/saints/dismas.html

Easter Sunday

"Pascha — Sunday of the Resurrection. Christ Is Risen! Truly He Is Risen!" a brief article on the Resurrection service posted at the Greek Orthodox Archdiocese of Australia's web site:
   http://cygnus.uwa.edu.au/~jgrapsas/pages/Pascha.htm

Eucharist

An explanation of the Orthodox understanding of the Eucharist, posted by the Orthodox Church in America web site:
   http://www.oca.org/pages/orth_chri/Orthodox-Faith/Worship/Holy-Eucharist.html

An article entitled "The Holy Eucharist," by the Rev. Thomas Fitzgerald, posted by the Greek Orthodox Archdiocese of America:
   http://www.goarch.org/access/orthodoxfaith/eucharist.html

Fasting

"Fasting," an essay by the Rev. George Mastrantonis describing Greek Orthodox fasting customs posted by the Greek Orthodox Archdiocese of America in New York, NY:
   http://www.goarch.org/access/orthodoxfaith/lent/fasting.html

The following article, from *Christianity Today's* Christian History newsletter, discusses various Lenten fasting regimens and the dishes that

Christians invented as a result of these disciplines:
   http://www.christianitytoday.com/history/newsletter/2001/mar02.
   html

Flowering of the Cross

"Easter: Promise of New Life," by Debra Illingworth Greene, pub-lished in *The Lutheran* (April 1999) and available online at:
   http://www.thelutheran.org/9904/page35.html

Good Friday

"Holy Friday," a document describing the beliefs and practices of Or-thodox Christians concerning Good Friday, posted on the Orthodox Church in America web site:
   http://www.oca.org/pages/orth_chri/orthodox-faith/worship/holy-friday.html

Holy Saturday

"Holy Saturday" a document describing the beliefs and practices of Orthodox Christians concerning Holy Saturday, posted on the Ortho-dox Church in America web site:
   http://www.oca.org/pages/orth_chri/orthodox-faith/worship/holy-saturday.html

Lent

"Great Lent," a page describing the beliefs and practices of Orthodox Christians concerning Lent, posted on the Orthodox Church in Ameri-ca web site:
   http://www.oca.org/pages/orth_chri/orthodox-faith/worship/great-lent.html

"Sundays of Lent," a document describing Orthodox Lenten services, posted on the Orthodox Church in America web site:
   http://www.oca.org/pages/orth_chri/orthodox-faith/worship/
   sundays-of-lent.html

"The Great Lent," an essay by the Rev. George Mastrantonis describ-ing the history and customs of Lent in the Greek Orthodox Church, posted on the Greek Orthodox Archdiocese of America, New York, NY, web site:

  http://www.goarch.org/access/orthodoxfaith/lent/great_lent.html

The Christian Resource Institute's page on Lenten observances and customs, written by Dennis Bratcher, a minister with a Ph.D. in biblical studies:

  http://www.cresourcei.org/cyeaster.html

Mary Magdalene

"Who Framed Mary Magdalene?," by Heidi Schlumpf, published in *U.S. Catholic* (April 2000) and available online at:

  http://www.uscatholic.org/2000/04/0004cov.htm

For an Orthodox perspective on Mary Magdalene, see the web site of *Orthodox America*, a magazine for American Orthodox Christians:

  http://www.roca.org/OA/9/9k.htm

For another Orthodox perspective on Mary Magdalene, see the page sponsored by the Greek Orthodox Archdiocese of Australia:

  http://cygnus.uwa.edu.au/~jgrapsas/pages/Magdalene.htm

Paschal Candle

"How Do We Use a Paschal Candle?" by Scott C. Weidler, posted on the Evangelical Lutheran Church of America's web site:

  http://www.elca.org/dcm/worship/qa/paschalcandle.html

Passover

For more on the rites and customs of Passover, see the following web site sponsored by the Union of Orthodox Jewish Congregations in America:

  http://www.ou.org/chagim/pesach/default.htm

Post-Easter Sundays

"Post-Easter Sundays," a document describing the beliefs and practices of Orthodox Christians concerning the Sundays between Easter and Pentecost, posted on the Orthodox Church in America web site:

http://www.oca.org/pages/orth_chri/orthodox-faith/worship/post-easter-sundays.html

Pre-Lent

"Pre-Lent," a document describing the beliefs and practice of Ortho-dox Christians concerning pre-Lent, posted on the Orthodox Church in America web site:

http://www.oca.org/pages/orth_chri/orthodox-faith/worship/pre-lent.html

Shavuot

For information on the customs and significance of Shavuot, see the following web site, sponsored by the Union of Orthodox Jewish Con-gregations of America:

http://www.ou.org/chagim/shavuot/

Stations of the Cross

Catholic Online offers a simple electronic version of the Stations of the Cross at the following address:

http://www.catholic.org/prayer/station.html

Creighton University's Online Ministries presents the Stations of the Cross as a personal meditation. Includes images, prayers, history, and an explanation of how and why to do the stations:

http://www.creighton.edu/CollaborativeMinistry/stations.html

The following site, sponsored by Christus Rex and the Franciscan Friars of the Custody of the Holy Land, takes the viewer through the Stations of the Cross with photos of the sites in Jerusalem where, according to Christian tradition, the events took place:

http://www.christusrex.org/www1/jvc/TVCmain.html

A searching, contemporary version of the stations, in which each sta-tion is identified as a site in an ordinary California town (San Mateo). Designed by United Church of Christ minister Jim Burklo:

http://www.stanford.edu/~burklo2/stations.html

Sunrise Service

"Moravian History, Terms, and Facts," a page posted by the Moravian Gift and Book Shop of Winston-Salem, North Carolina, an arm of the Board of Education of the Moravian Church:

http://www.newsalem.com/mbg/facts.htm

Index

The Index lists customs, symbols, legends, musical and literary works, historical figures and mythological characters, foods and beverages, religious groups and denominations, geographical locations, ethnic groups, keywords, and other special subjects mentioned in the text.

Index

Index

Index

Index

Index

Index

Index

Index

M

Index

O

Index

Index

T

Index

Index

Index

Holiday Titles

Encyclopedia of Christmas, 1st Edition

729 pages. Illustrated. 1999. 0-7808-0387-6. $48.

Christmas is a holiday with rich traditions and a long history, yet there is no single source in which to look up facts about its many facets. This illustrated encyclopedia provides teachers, students, and librarians with a convenient reference on virtually every aspect of Christmas, covering folk customs, religious observances, history, legends and symbols from around the world.

"Outstanding Reference Source 2000"
— *American Library Association*

The Celebrations Library: Halloween Program Sourcebook

332 pages. Illustrated. 1999. 0-7808-0388-4. $48.

The first volume in *The Celebrations Library, Halloween Program Sourcebook,* presents a selection of Halloween-related material—stories and legends, strange happenings, poems, and plays—that can be read, spoken, or performed, as well as activities and recipes to enhance its celebration. A comprehensive introduction surveys the origins, evolution, and significance of the holiday. Includes two indexes.

Holiday Symbols, 2nd Edition

694 pages. 2000. 0-7808-0423-6. $58.

This new edition describes more than 900 symbols associated with 224 popular holidays and celebrations in the United States and around the world. It describes the origins, traditions, and history of each symbol and explains its modern significance. The book also presents valuable background information about each holiday. A reading list for additional research completes each holiday entry.

"Holiday Symbols will be a working reference source for years."
— *American Reference Books Annual 1999*

Holidays & Festival Index

782 pages. 1995. 0-7808-0012-5. $84.

Provides up-to-date information on more than 3,000 observances throughout the world. It functions as a master index to the *Holidays, Festivals & Celebrations of the World Dictionary* and over twenty other standard reference works. It identifies sources on both secular and religious holidays, festivals, celebrations, commemorations, holy days, feasts and fasts, and other observances. Special features: a section on world calendars, summary tables of state and national public holidays and listing of legal holidays by country, a bibliography, and four indexes.

"A worthwhile purchase for public and university libraries."
— *Booklist,* American Library Association, Aug '95

"Highly recommended for collections supporting an interest in holidays."
— *Choice,* Association of College & Research Libraries, Oct '95

"This is a great general reference for anyone looking for bulletin board ideas and is good for curriculum support throughout the social studies, literature, foreign language, psychology, and the arts."
— *The Book Report,* May-June 1998

"Recommended for medium to large academic and public libraries."
— *Choice,* Association of College & Research Libraries, June '98

"Holiday Symbols is a required purchase for all academic, public, and school libraries. . . . This work will be in high demand."
— *RUSQ,* American Library Association, Summer '98

"The clear format, accessible language, and wide coverage should make this new title a useful addition to reference collections."
— *School Library Journal,* May '98